Photoshop® CS6
BIBLE

Photoshop® CS6
BIBLE

Lisa DaNae Dayley
Brad Dayley

WILEY

John Wiley & Sons, Inc.

Photoshop® CS6 Bible

Published by
John Wiley & Sons, Inc.
10475 Crosspoint Boulevard
Indianapolis, IN 46256
www.wiley.com

Copyright © 2012 by John Wiley & Sons, Inc., Indianapolis, Indiana

Published by John Wiley & Sons, Inc., Indianapolis, Indiana

Published simultaneously in Canada

ISBN: 978-1-118-12388-1

Manufactured in the United States of America

10 9 8 7 6 5 4 3 2 1

For general information on our other products and services or to obtain technical support, please contact our Customer Care Department within the U.S. at (877) 762-2974, outside the U.S. at (317) 572-3993 or fax (317) 572-4002.

Library of Congress Control Number: 2012936414

Brad
For D, A, & F!

DaNae
As always, to Brad, my hero, my biggest fan, my best friend.
Always and Forever.

About the Authors

Brad Dayley is a senior software engineer with almost 22 years of experience creating computer software. He has been working with Photoshop for 21 years, enjoying the transition of Photoshop from a simple image editor to the powerhouse it is today. He is the author of several books. He is an avid amateur photographer and spends most of his free time in the remote areas of the western United States with his wife DaNae and four sons (wherever a Jeep can get them).

DaNae Dayley has been working with Photoshop for 18 years and is still constantly amazed at the cool stuff it can do! With a degree in Advertising from Brigham Young University, DaNae has owned and operated a media creation business for 17 years, incorporating writing, graphic design, and video editing over the years. She also enjoys teaching Photoshop classes locally. She has co-authored several books with her husband Brad Dayley and is the author of *Photoshop CS3 Extended Video and 3D Bible* and *Roxio Easy Media Creator 8 in a Snap*. DaNae lives in Utah with her husband Brad and their four sons. When she is not at her computer, she can be found in the great outdoors (with a camera), preferably in a Jeep!

Credits

Senior Acquisitions Editor
Stephanie McComb

Project Editor
Jade L. Williams

Technical Editor
Dennis Cohen

Copy Editor
Marylouise Wiack

Editorial Director
Robyn Siesky

Business Manager
Amy Knies

Senior Marketing Manager
Sandy Smith

Vice President and Executive Group Publisher
Richard Swadley

Vice President and Executive Publisher
Barry Pruett

Project Coordinator
Patrick Redmond

Graphics and Production Specialist
Andrea Hornberger

Quality Control Technician
Melissa Cossell

Proofreading
Evelyn Wellborn

Indexing
BIM Indexing & Proofreading Services

Vertical Websites Project Manager
Richard Graves

Contents

Contents

Contents

Contents

Contents

Contents

Contents

Contents

Contents

Contents

Acknowledgments

Our sincere gratitude goes out to the following persons, without whom this book could not have happened:

Our wonderful boys who once again, sacrificed time with their mom and dad and took on extra chores so that we could have fun with our favorite hobby; playing with Photoshop and teaching others to love it as much as we do.

To our editors who made the book readable and technically accurate and kept us on track, you really rock. Thanks to Stephanie McComb for her positive attitude in keeping us on track and getting the project moving in the right direction. Thanks to Jade Williams whose tireless efforts to create a polished end product are much appreciated. Careful; one of these days we might actually get all the rules down and you might be out of a job! (Don't hurt yourself laughing; we all know it's not going to happen!) Thanks to Marylouise Wiack for keeping us "active" and cleaning up our act. We can honestly say that we loved your edits! And thanks to Dennis Cohen for using your technical expertise to watch our back and improve the quality of the book. We appreciated the fresh perspective and Mac point of view; it helped us out on many occasions. Also, thanks to the entire staff at Wiley who was very professional in helping get this project out the door.

And last, but not least, our thanks go out to the talented photographers who have so generously contributed their fantastic photos to this work: Becky Diamond for her phenomenal wedding photos; and Janece Winder of Orange Works Photography and Design, who contributed wonderful photos of all kinds.

Introduction

Welcome to the *Photoshop CS6 Bible*, the latest edition of the bestselling reference guide on Photoshop in publishing history. Now in its 18th year, the *Photoshop Bible* is the longest continuously published title on Adobe Photoshop. With numerous U.S. editions, dozens of localized translations around the globe, and hundreds of thousands of copies in print worldwide, the *Photoshop Bible* has become a must-have for Photoshop users worldwide.

We have done our very best to accurately and directly address the vast majority of functionality, features, tools, and techniques wrapped up in your Photoshop package. As you may notice throughout the book, we love Photoshop and like to tell you about the great features it has to offer. You may also notice that when something doesn't work well or is awkward, we don't hesitate to let you know. Our intent is to give you the best experience using Photoshop.

Is This Book for You?

Photoshop tends to collect users from a variety of backgrounds. From casual users just playing around to professional graphic designers creating professional materials to digital artists creating fantastic artwork to medical technicians analyzing patient images, Photoshop has something for everyone. In fact, there really isn't one specific group that you could call average Photoshop users.

Therefore, with that in mind, the *Photoshop CS6 Bible* is designed to provide enough information so experienced Photoshop users can get more out of Photoshop, but also so someone who has little or no experience with Photoshop can quickly pick up on its interface and become an expert in no time. We discuss advanced techniques and add step-by-step examples to the more complex editing concepts. Although the book is large, most sections in the book are self-contained, so experienced users can simply look up tools when they need help.

This book is really designed to be a desktop reference, but it offers more than just a quick description of the tools and features. We have incorporated examples designed to guide you through various techniques, provide our experience in tips and suggestions, and try to give you a jumpstart on how to leverage the features in Photoshop.

The specific purpose of this book is to provide you with the understanding you need to get the very best results. So sit back, load up Photoshop, and enjoy the ride!

How This Book Is Organized

This book is divided into ten parts with an accompanying website.

Part I: Getting Started with Adobe Photoshop CS6

In Part I, we introduce Photoshop and the basic workspace to familiarize you with Photoshop. We introduce you to the basics of file formats as well as opening, saving, and resizing images in Photoshop. We discuss the basics of color as it relates to images, and how to use the Photoshop tools to modify the color composition of an image. Then we show you how to use the History and Actions panels in your workflow as you begin editing images. Finally, we introduce you to Adobe Bridge, a separate application that allows you to organize and process your images.

Part II: Working with Camera Raw Images

In Part II, we discuss the basics of Camera Raw images, and how to use the Adobe Camera Raw interface to edit images before opening them in Photoshop. The purpose of this part is to familiarize you with Camera Raw image editing so you can incorporate it into your editing workflow.

Part III: Working with Selections, Layers, and Channels

In Part III, we discuss the various ways to create selections in Photoshop. We also cover the Layers panel, and how to use it for non-destructive editing. Then we cover using the Channels panel to edit and use individual color channels in an image. Selections, layers, and channels are basic functionality you need in most of your editing workflow.

Part IV: Enhancing, Correcting, and Retouching Images

In Part IV, we discuss the workflow, tools, and techniques that you can use to enhance, correct, and retouch your images. Use this part to get to know the features of Photoshop that you need to make color and lighting adjustments to photos as well as restore damaged images.

Part V: Using Paint, Paths, Shapes, and Text Tools

In Part V, we discuss the tools used to create images. Specifically, we discuss using the Paint tools to use brushstrokes to add color, textures, and adjustments to images. Then we discuss using the path tools to create vector shapes. Finally, we discuss adding textual elements to images.

Part VI: Creating Artistic Effects

In Part VI, we cover using some of tools in Photoshop to apply artistic effects to images. You can use these chapters to learn how to distort and warp parts of an image, apply a variety of filters, and combine elements from multiple images.

Part VII: Working with 3D Images

Part VII covers using the 3D capabilities in Photoshop CS6 Extended to create, modify, and enhance 3D objects.

Part VIII: Working with Video and Animation

In Part VIII, we cover using the Animation panel and several other tools and techniques to make enhancements and corrections to video with Photoshop CS6 Extended. These chapters discuss various editing concepts and techniques that allow you to make use of the Photoshop editing features when editing you videos. You will also learn how to use the Animation panel to animate images.

Part IX: Using Advanced Output Techniques

In Part IX, we cover the tools and techniques you use to output images using Photoshop, from printing and color management to preparing images for the web. We also discuss using the Photoshop batch processing and scripting capabilities to save a lot of time in your editing workflow.

Part X: Appendixes

We provide appendixes for information that doesn't fit elsewhere in the book but that we wanted to share with you. You will find tables with the most commonly used keyboard shortcuts, instructions on how to use plug-ins to add functionality to Photoshop, and a list of web resources that you can use to get more information about Photoshop and download cool stuff.

How to Use This Book

Although this book is designed for a linear, cover-to-cover read, we wanted to make it easy for you to pick and choose what areas of Photoshop you want to learn. For the most part, each chapter is self-contained. If you are new to Photoshop, take some time to look at Chapters 1 through 6 to familiarize yourself with the environment and digital editing concepts. If a chapter relies on information from another chapter, we mention that in the chapter introduction or by using a Cross-Reference note. If you want to know more about a particular workflow in Photoshop, such as color correction or adding text, use the table of contents to find the chapter, and read it thoroughly to learn all about the different tools and features you can use.

Using this book as a reference

The book is organized as a reference that you can use whenever you are having difficulties, or when you are ready to start a new topic. Each chapter covers a topic, making it easy for you to find what you are looking for in the book. We have tried to pack in as much of the Photoshop functionality and features as possible, so you can look up items in the index and read the sections in which we discuss them.

Making the most of the book's website

One of the most important aspects of digital images is color. Unfortunately, the images in this book are in grayscale except for the color insert. We have included several of the figures and projects on the website. The examples on the website enable you to see what the images look like in full color as well as practice the tasks described in the book. You should download the example projects from the book's website and use them when available.

Some of the items on the website are JPEG images, some are PSD projects, some are AVI files, and many of them have layers and objects available for you to modify. You can access this book's website at www.wiley.com/go/photoshopcs6bible.

Throughout the book, you will see the "On the Web" icon noting which figures are available on the website at www.wiley.com/go/photoshopcs6bible. Each note includes a file-name that you can use to download the item and try the concepts out for yourself.

Icons Used in This Book

This book uses icons to indicate noteworthy points. While each icon is self-explanatory, here is what each of these icons indicates:

CAUTION
The Caution icon means that you should pay special attention to the information or instructions because you could cause a problem otherwise.

The Cross-References icon refers you to a related topic elsewhere in the book. Because you may not read this book straight through from cover to cover, you can use cross-references to quickly find just the information you need.

NEW FEATURE

The New Feature icon means that a feature is new to Photoshop CS6 or has been significantly changed.

NOTE

A Note icon alerts you to some important point that requires special attention, or additional information that may be helpful.

ON THE WEB

The On the Web icon highlights references to related material on the website at www.wiley.com/go/photoshop cs6bible.

TIP

A Tip icon shows you a way to accomplish a task more efficiently or quickly.

Contacting the Authors

We would love to hear from you! Contact us at www.DayleyCreations.com.

Part I

Getting Started with Adobe Photoshop CS6

IN THIS PART

Introducing Adobe Photoshop CS6

IN THIS CHAPTER

Getting acquainted with Photoshop CS6

Benefitting from Photoshop CS6

Exploring the new features of Photoshop CS6

I f you are reading this book, you likely have access to one of the most intricate and extensive software applications available. Don't let that discourage you, though. Adobe Photoshop is also a powerful and extremely fun application to use. With throngs of fans all over the globe, over the years, Photoshop has become the pinnacle software application for image editing. In fact, if you look up Photoshop at www.wikionary.org, you will find the term *photoshop* listed as a verb meaning, "to digitally edit or alter a picture or photograph."

Photoshop draws such a big crowd because it provides amazing results when you are editing images and yet is fairly intuitive to use such that even casual users can get pretty good results without much effort. In addition, as digital imaging has advanced over the years, Photoshop has kept pace and even led the advancements in many areas.

The purpose of this chapter is to introduce Photoshop CS6, show you when to use it, and discuss the new features that have been added since version CS5. Chapter 2 dives into the details of the Photoshop application workspace.

Discovering the Versatile World of Photoshop

The simplest description of Photoshop is "a digital image-editing application." Photoshop provides the standard color- and lighting-correction capabilities historically associated with photo editing, but it also provides filtering, painting, masking, layering, and many more tools that allow you to take image editing to the next level.

Photoshop comes in two versions. The standard Photoshop edition provides all the functionality you need to create, enhance, and correct digital images. The extended edition, which costs more, provides additional functionality to work with 3D objects, video, and digital animation. The extended edition is worth the money if you are working with 3D objects or need to add color and lighting corrections and artistic effects to video. If you are not working with 3D objects or video, the standard edition is all you need.

The following sections discuss the uses of Photoshop as well as additional applications you can use with Photoshop. Their purpose is to give you a glimpse of what Photoshop is used for before showing you how to use it. Of course, the only real way to understand the capabilities of Photoshop is to delve into them as you follow along with the next 30 chapters in this book.

Knowing when to use Photoshop

Photoshop has so many tools and so much power that it can do an unlimited number of things. The following list describes the most common tasks for which Photoshop is used to help you get an idea of when you may want to use it:

- **Photo corrections.** Photoshop is able to correct digital images by restoring the original color and lighting, as well as to correct problems introduced by camera lenses. These Photoshop features are covered in Chapter 13.

- **Photo enhancements.** Photoshop also provides tools that allow you to enhance photos. For example, you can add a blur to soften a portrait or use a sharpening filter to remove camera jitter. Photoshop is also great at fixing scratches and dust marks on older images. These concepts are discussed in Chapters 14 and 15.

- **Photo compositions.** One of the strengths of Photoshop is the ability to combine multiple images to create a single image or composition. A common use of Photoshop is to take a headshot from one image and place it into another image. Photoshop also enables you to merge photos that were taken at different horizontal angles, from the same spot, and then turn them into a single panoramic image. Photo compositions are discussed in Chapter 21.

- **Artistic effects.** One of the most fun features of Photoshop is the ability to use different filters and warping tools to apply artistic effects to images. The combination of numerous tools and filters in Photoshop means that the only limitation you have when adding artistic effects is your own creativity. The tools used for artistic effects are covered in Chapters 19 and 20.

- **Painting.** Photoshop has always been a good painting application, but with the addition of the wet brush capability in CS5 as well as erodible and airbrush tips in CS6, Photoshop is now one of the best applications available to create digital paintings. What puts Photoshop ahead of the competition is that many powerful features, such as layers and masks, are also available for use with the painting tools. In addition, the painting brushes are integrated into many of the other tools in Photoshop. Chapter 16 discusses the painting tools.

- **Creating vector artwork.** Photoshop is also an excellent application to use when creating vector artwork. The path tools allow you to quickly create and manipulate vector artwork, and add vector artwork to raster images. Vector artwork, including vector text, is discussed in Chapters 17 and 18.

- **Adding text to images.** Photoshop provides tools that allow you to add text to images. The text can be resized, warped, and adjusted to create some stunning visual effects. Chapter 18 discusses adding textual elements to images.

- **Creating web images.** Another area where Photoshop excels is in preparing images for the web. Photoshop provides utilities that allow you to quickly format images with the appropriate size, file format, and colors for use in web pages. Photoshop also provides some tools you can use to slice an image into clickable sections and provides the HTML code necessary to use the slices in a web page. Outputting to the web is discussed in Chapter 30.

- **Print preparation.** Photoshop is often used to prepare images for printing by converting the color mode to CMYK, adding spot colors, and creating color separations. These topics are covered in Chapters 11 and 29.

- **Creating 3D objects.** The 3D tools in Photoshop just get better and better. Photoshop has the capability to create and manipulate 3D objects so that they can be incorporated into 2D images or video. The 3D capabilities of Photoshop are covered in Chapters 22, 23, and 24.

- **Adding textures to 3D objects.** Photoshop has a big advantage over other 3D applications when applying textures to 3D objects. With the Photoshop filter and painting capabilities, you can edit the textures of your 3D objects in ways that you may not have thought possible. Chapter 23 discusses creating and enhancing 3D textures.

- **Video corrections.** Using the color, lighting, and filter effects of Photoshop, you can quickly apply corrections to video and even add some artistic effects. Chapter 27 discusses applying corrections and effects to video files.

- **Animating images.** Another fun feature of Photoshop is the ability to add animation to your images. Animated images can give life to web pages and allow you to create short animated movies. Chapter 28 discusses animating images.

Understanding the limitations of Photoshop

Believe it or not, Photoshop is not designed to do everything. Photoshop is not designed to function as a word processor like Microsoft Word, to create charts and graphics in presentations like Microsoft PowerPoint, or to lay out brochures, magazines, or books like Adobe InDesign.

For the following tasks, you would use another application:

- **Word processing.** Most word processing applications such as Word allow you to add images to documents created with those programs, and although Photoshop supports adding text to images, it doesn't support text editing well and can't handle text flowing from one page to another. You should use Photoshop to work with the images and then import them into the word processing application.

- **Business graphics.** Photoshop doesn't do charts and presentations very well, but you can create great images in Photoshop and then use them in business applications such as Microsoft Excel or PowerPoint.

- **Page layout.** Applications such as InDesign are much more adept at laying out brochures, flyers, and documents that are mostly textual. You should create the images in Photoshop and then import them into the layout application.

- **Vector art.** Although Photoshop has a lot of capability when it comes to creating vector paths, Adobe Illustrator is a much better application for working with clipart and designing advertisements, flyers, and one-page layouts that have multiple vector objects.

Looking at What's New in Photoshop CS6

Adobe has added several great new features to Photoshop CS6 that make tools easier to use, extend capabilities, and add a lot of justification for upgrading. These new changes are discussed throughout the book. The purpose of this section is to describe the biggest changes and let you know where in the book you can find more information about the following new features:

- **Dark user interface (UI).** Arguably, the most noticeable change in Photoshop CS6 is the addition of a Dark UI. This feature is configurable in the Preferences panel and provides several different options to darken the UI components. This has been a much-requested feature that should lessen the brightness of the screen and could reduce eye fatigue when working long hours. Setting the Interface preferences is covered in Chapter 2.

- **Changes to the Crop tool.** Several new and very useful enhancements have been added to the Crop tool. The biggest is a non-destructive crop that allows you to go back and edit the crop. When you select the Crop tool again, the areas hidden by the crop are displayed so that you can easily adjust the crop to add pixels back in. The Crop tool now automatically sets the initial crop to the size of the original image so you no longer have to drag to create a crop box. When you rotate the crop in the document window, the canvas automatically expands so that you can easily preview what the final cropped canvas will look like. The changes to the Crop tool are discussed in Chapter 3.

- **Adjustments to Aspect Ratio tools.** You can now change the aspect ratio while in Crop mode. This allows you to select preset aspect ratios to flip the orientation of the crop box without exiting the tool. You can also set a custom crop size directly. The Crop tool also allows you to use constrained aspect ratio and unconstrained modes. These changes are discussed in Chapter 3.

- **Auto Curve adjustments.** The Curve adjustment feature now provides a new algorithm that analyzes an image and looks for a curve that uses all color channels that will provide the optimal brightness and contrast. The curve can be more accurately calculated by matching image characteristics to a curve database. Curve adjustments are discussed in Chapter 13.

- **Auto Level adjustments.** This is similar to the new Auto Curve adjustment feature. The Level adjustment now provides the ability to automatically calculate accurate histograms that will provide optimal brightness and contrast. Level adjustments are discussed in Chapters 12 and 13.

- **Improved lighting adjustment in Camera Raw.** Our personal favorite change in Photoshop CS6 is the new sliders in Camera Raw 7.0. The Fill Light and Recovery sliders have been replaced with new Shadows and Highlights sliders, and a new Whites slider has been added to balance the Blacks slider. The new sliders have been set to 0 and can move in either direction, allowing you to increase or decrease the brightness of each setting. Because you can deepen highlights and brighten shadows with these new sliders, you can greatly improve the look of photos that contain both shadows and highlights, bringing a better balance to their exposure. Changes made to these types of photos in Camera Raw rival HDR imagery, as demonstrated in Figure 1.1. Because this figure is in grayscale in the print version of this book, you can also find it in the center insert in full color. Making adjustments in Camera Raw is covered in Chapter 8.

- **Layer filtering.** The Layers panel has a new filtering feature that allows you to view only the layers you want to see within the panel. You can view layers based on parameters such as type, name, or effect. This feature greatly enhances the ease and capability of working with multiple layers.

- **Blur tools.** A new feature has been added to the Filter menu, implementing the Iris, Field, and Tilt-Shift blur in a completely new way. These tools now have a new panel, called the Blur Gallery that allows you to add and adjust the blur effects quickly in an image. In addition to the new panel, on-image controls are added that allow you to control size, intensity, and positioning of the blurring effect. You can also apply effects to the blur by adding a bokeh. These blur tools are discussed in Chapter 14. Figure 1.2 shows the new Blur Gallery panel along with the on-image controls that allow you to fine-tune blurring effects.

- **Wide-Angle Correction.** A Wide-Angle Correction filter has been added to Photoshop. This filter analyzes an image and makes adaptive changes that can correct perceived distortion in the image caused by wide-angle lenses. The Wide-Angle Correction filter is discussed in Chapter 14.

FIGURE 1.1

The new adjustment tools in Camera Raw 7.0 can fix problematic exposures, creating fantastic imagery.

FIGURE 1.2

The Blur Gallery provides a new panel along with on-image controls that give you direct control over the blurring effect.

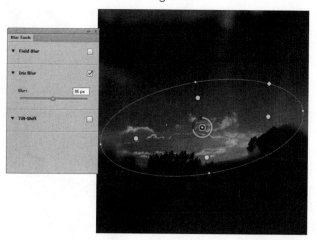

- **Content-Aware patch.** The Content-Aware patch expands the capabilities of both the Content-Aware tools that were introduced in CS5 and the Patch tool. The Patch tool works by sampling an area of an image and using it to repair another area of the image using the lighting of the repaired area and the texture of the sampled area. The new Content-Aware feature allows Photoshop to run an algorithm that looks for differences in texture and hard lines in the area that is being repaired so that the patch will be more realistic. For example, you can see in Figure 1.3 that there are two textures involved in removing the second model from the image, the cliff, and the sky. By using the Content-Aware patch tool, this is accomplished in one easy step. You can learn more about the Content-Aware patch tool in Chapter 15.

- **Erodible brush tip.** A new concept in brush tips has been added to the paint tools. The Erodible tip brush shapes provide a new drawing experience by having the shape of the brush tip change as you use it, just as a crayon or pencil would. These new tips are based on computer algorithms that calculate how to adjust the shape of the brush tip as it wears down through use. Photoshop provides several settings for the erodible tip, shown in Figure 1.4, that control how the brush tip erodes, thus changing the painting effect of the brush. The new erodible tips are discussed in Chapter 16.

FIGURE 1.3

The Content-Aware patch tool makes it easy to remove the model from an area that requires duplicating two textures.

- **Airbrush brush tips.** A new addition to the Photoshop paint tools is the airbrush brush shapes. These brush tips use computer algorithms that can mimic applying paint to the canvas in a random dispersion from multiple angl es in a 3D manner as if the brush tip was a distance away from the canvas. This simulates an airbrush or spray-painting effect. Photoshop provides several settings that control the flow and dispersion of the paint, thus changing the effect of using the brush. The new airbrush tips are discussed in Chapter 16.

- **Deco patterns.** Photoshop has enhanced its fill options with a new concept called a Deco pattern. The new Deco patterns allow you to use more than one input image patch and load new pattern scripts. Deco patterns provide much wider functionality by allowing you to offset, scale, and rotate patterns when applying a fill. Another great feature of the Deco patterns is that their transparency is persistent when applying scripting operations, making it easier to create intricate combinations by filling multiple layers with different patterns and scripts. Deco patterns are discussed in Chapter 16.

FIGURE 1.4

The brush settings allow you to control the behavior of erodible tips, enabling you to simulate crayon, pencil, or other erodible media.

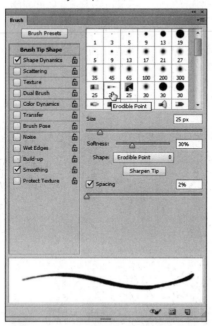

- **Vector layers.** If you use Photoshop to create and manipulate vector shapes, then you are going to be ecstatic about what has been done in CS6. Vector shapes have now been promoted to first-class citizens. The biggest change is that vector shapes can now be automatically created in their own layer. In addition, several additional tools make it much easier to apply fills and strokes to a vector shape. Chapter 17 discusses the new vector layers and the enhancements made to the shape tools.

- **Type styles.** Photoshop now applies type styles using a hierarchical model with Paragraph Styles, which control all elements of type such as justification, and Character Styles, which control the type elements such as font face, size, color, and kerning. Character Styles override Paragraph Styles, and manual settings override the Character and Paragraph Styles. The cool thing about how Photoshop is now applying type styles is that you can now create a standardized format and use that standard again and again in all of your work. Another great feature is that text created using a type style will be updated automatically later by changing the style settings. Type is covered in Chapter 18.

- **Liquify now uses the GPU.** If your video card supports it, the Liquify filter now uses the GPU. This makes the filter much faster and more efficient to use. The Mirror and Turbulence tools are still CPU-based. The Liquify filter is covered in Chapter 19.

- **Faster rendering and better placement of 3D files.** Some of the 3D changes in CS6 are behind the scenes. You'll notice right away that 3D objects are rendered using OpenGL automatically and you can render the final product using the ray tracer by clicking the Render button in the Properties panel. CS6 has also changed its coordinate system to match that of the 3D object file so that the chances of your 3D object coming in right side up are greatly increased. Neither of these modifications will change the way you work, but they will make what you do much easier. 3D editing is discussed in Chapters 22 through 24.

- **New 3D interface.** Since 3D capability was introduced in Photoshop CS3, every edition has introduced a new interface for the 3D tools and settings in an effort to make them easy to learn and use. The interface for CS6 is the best yet, using the Properties panel to display the settings for selected 3D layers and placing the 3D move tools in one location: the Options bar. The new 3D workspace opens automatically when a 3D file is opened or placed, and it is very intuitive, finally feeling like an integral part of the Photoshop repertoire, as shown in Figure 1.5. 3D editing is discussed in Chapters 22 through 24.

FIGURE 1.5

A new look for the 3D workspace is functional and user-friendly.

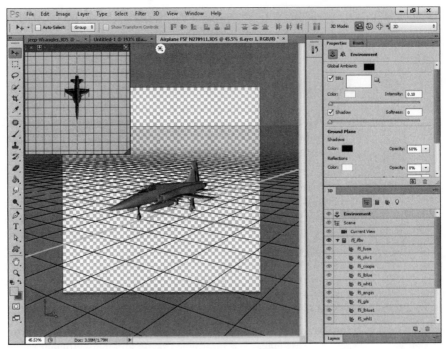

1

- **Improved look of the ground plane in a 3D scene.** The ground plane is turned on automatically when you open a 3D object, and it continues to the horizon, fading out as it goes to reduce visual clutter. (See Figure 1.5.) 3D editing is discussed in Chapters 22 through 24.

- **Picture in Picture window for 3D scenes.** The new Picture in Picture window for 3D scenes gives you a quick reference guide when manipulating 3D objects. (See Figure 1.5.) You can see your scene from two different viewpoints at the same time, and you can change the view of the Picture in Picture window for the best results. 3D editing is discussed in Chapters 22 through 24.

- **Audio has been added to the Timeline panel.** You can now listen to the audio on the video tracks that you bring into Photoshop. You can also toggle the audio on and off using the new audio button in the video Timeline. The video Timeline is discussed in Chapters 25.

- **New look and new features of the Timeline panel.** The Timeline panel has a new name, a new look, and a new menu. The capability is mostly the same with a few enhancements, such as the ability to hear and mute the audio in your video clips. The new layout, however, greatly simplifies your workflow when working with video clips. You can see the new Timeline and the new Timeline panel menu in Figure 1.6. The new features of the Timeline are covered in Chapter 25.

FIGURE 1.6

A new look for the Timeline and its menu make working with video in Photoshop easier and more efficient.

- **Video drag-and-drop transitions.** Along with the new look of the Timeline comes a new icon that allows you to drag and drop one of several basic transitions into your video clips. This allows you to create a fade between video clips, smoothly transitioning from one to the other. Learn how to use the drag-and-drop transitions in Chapter 25.

- **Animating transformations.** One of the most exciting new features of the Timeline is the Transform property. Using this property, you can animate the transform properties of the Scale and Rotate features. Learn how to animate transformations in Chapter 26.

- **Animating 3D elements.** When you have a 3D object open in Photoshop, many of the properties of that 3D object can be animated. These properties are the 3D scene position, the 3D camera position, the 3D render settings, and the 3D cross-section. You can also animate the position of the 3D lights, materials, and mesh objects in the 3D scene. You can learn how to animate these properties in Chapter 26.

Summary

This chapter introduced Photoshop CS6 by discussing the general uses of Photoshop and the new features in version CS6. Photoshop can be used for a variety of purposes, from photo editing to digital art to adding artistic effects.

In this chapter, you learned that:

- Photoshop can be used to edit, enhance, and create images in several ways.

- Photoshop CS6 includes new sliders that make Camera Raw a more powerful tool, as well as a new blur gallery that allows you to apply several new special blur effects.

- Adobe has improved the set of 3D tools that allow you to apply the editing capabilities of Photoshop to 3D objects.

Exploring the Photoshop Workspace

The Photoshop CS6 workspace has had years to develop into a fine-tuned working environment, and with bigger monitors and faster processors, working in Photoshop has only become more fun. With all the space that larger display options give you, you can easily organize the panels, documents, and tools in the workspace to provide an efficient photo-editing environment.

With all its features, Photoshop can be a bit daunting at first. The purpose of this chapter is to familiarize you with the Photoshop workspace, how to navigate, find tools, customize settings, and set the environment so it works best for you.

Touring the Workspace

At first glance, the Photoshop workspace seems a little dreary, with a lot of gray, but that is misleading. With beautiful photographs (or other colorful graphics) in the work area and fascinating tools at your fingertips, you'll soon be addicted to the Photoshop playground. In fact, you may be glad that the background not only provides a good contrast to colorful files, but also is easy on the eyes.

Therefore, without further ado, we give you the Photoshop workspace, as shown in Figure 2.1. There are four main components to the Photoshop workspace: the Photoshop menu bar, the document workspace, the Toolbox with option menus, and the panels. The following sections introduce you to each of these components, and later in this chapter, we'll explore them in more detail.

FIGURE 2.1

The Photoshop workspace features four main components.

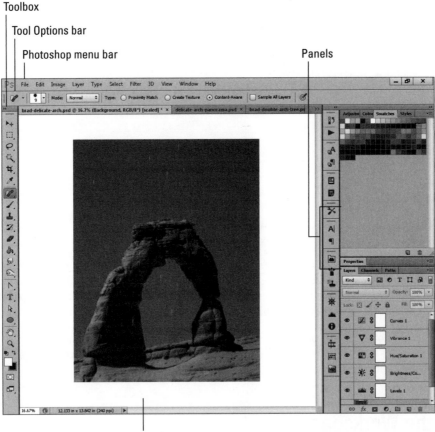

Cruising the Photoshop menu bar

The Photoshop menu bar, shown in Figure 2.2, houses sets of cascading menus that provide quick access to features, tools, and commands in Photoshop using only a few mouse clicks.

When you click a Photoshop menu bar item, a drop-down menu appears with several options. Each of these options performs different tasks such as opening dialog boxes to modify settings, performing image adjustments, or even opening additional submenus. These menus are a critical part of the Photoshop workspace because they are the only way to access certain features in Photoshop.

FIGURE 2.2

Features of the Photoshop menu bar

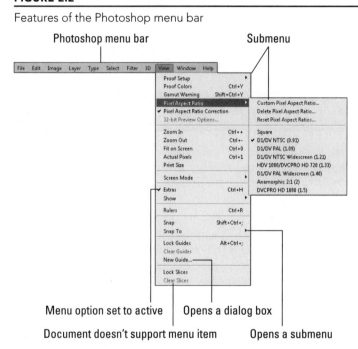

When navigating the menu bar in Photoshop, you need to understand the following basic points:

- If a menu item points to a submenu, there is an arrow to the right side, and if you hover over that item, the submenu pops up next to the open menu, as shown in Figure 2.2.

- If the menu item is only a setting, then a check mark appears when it is active, as shown in Figure 2.2. You can toggle the setting on and off by clicking the menu item.

- If the current document does not support the functionality of a menu item, then the menu item is grayed out, as shown in Figure 2.2. This means that the item is not active, and you cannot click it.

- If the menu item launches a dialog box, then an ellipsis (...) is displayed to the right, as shown in Figure 2.2.

Looking at the document workspace

The document workspace houses the documents (image files) that you are currently editing. You will use the document workspace extensively as you view and edit documents in Photoshop.

The document workspace is also home to the panels and Toolbox discussed later in this chapter. The workspace is large enough to give you the flexibility to expand your image to a larger size and keep your favorite panels open and docked as well.

> **NOTE**
>
> The screenshots in this book were taken at a screen resolution of 1024 x 768, which is a low resolution, especially if you have a larger screen. If your resolution is set higher, you have a larger work area than is shown here. If you set your resolution as high as 1920 x 1200 (which is what ours is usually set to), then you have enough space to expand your panels, tile your document windows, and generally make everything available to you at once. Of course, if your resolution is set lower than 1024 x 768, then your work area is smaller.

As you open image files, they appear in the center of the document workspace, and you have several options for viewing them. You can modify the view size and behavior, view specific information about a document, and arrange multiple documents in the view area.

Changing the view size of a document

Several ways exist to change the view size of a document in Photoshop to support the workflow that you are using. Changing the view size of a document is one of the most common tasks that you will perform in Photoshop, as you need to zoom in on an image to modify specific areas, enhance selections, and perform other tasks. You may also want to view the print size of an image, the actual screen size, or even fit the image to the screen so you can see all of it.

The View menu houses several different options to modify the view size of the document. When you click the View menu, as shown in Figure 2.3, you can choose the following options:

- **Zoom In.** Clicking this option, or press Ctrl+plus key/⌘+plus key, the image zooms up to the next zoom stop. The zoom stops are in various small increments such as .5%, .67%, 1%, 1.5% to large increments such as 100%, 200%, 300%, and so on.

- **Zoom Out.** Clicking this option, or press Ctrl+minus key/⌘+minus key, the image zooms out to the next zoom stop. The zoom stops are the same as for the Zoom In option.

- **Fit on Screen.** Clicking this option, you can see your entire image. This is your best option if you are working on your entire document (and not working with other files).

- **Actual Pixels.** Clicking this option, the pixels in the image match the pixels on the screen. Actual Pixels is the best option if you want to see the cleanest view of a specific area because no interpolation is necessary.

- **Print Size.** Clicking this option, Photoshop shows you how the document will look when printed.

- **Screen Mode.** Clicking this option, you can choose from Standard Screen mode, Full Screen mode with menu bar, and Full Screen mode.

  - **Standard Screen Mode.** This is the default mode, and it allows you to access other applications that are running.

  - **Full Screen Mode With Menu Bar.** This mode looks similar to Standard Screen mode, but you can't access other programs, for instance, through the Windows taskbar.

  - **Full Screen Mode.** This mode hides everything but the selected document so you can work without distractions. The Photoshop tools are still available to you; just hover over the tool you want to use and it appears, or press the Tab key to view all of your tools. Press Esc to return to Standard Screen mode.

FIGURE 2.3

You can change the way your image fits into the document workspace by using the View menu.

> **TIP**
>
> Don't use the zoom options in the View menu; you have several better options — the Zoom tool, the Magnify box, and the roller wheel on your mouse if you are using one — all of which are discussed later in this chapter.

In addition to the standard zoom stops, you can easily zoom in and out on the image, depending on your editing needs. Notice that at the bottom-left corner of the document window in Figure 2.4, there is a percentage representing the zoom value and the document information. You can change the size of your document by selecting the zoom value and typing a new percentage.

Another way that you can change the magnification of an image is to select the Zoom tool in the Toolbox, and then click anywhere on the image and drag the mouse to the left or right. Dragging to the left decreases the size of the image, while dragging to the right increases it.

Viewing document information

Another useful feature in the document window is the information section at the bottom. By default, the document information displays the size of your file. Keep an eye on this as you begin to add multiple layers and effects to a document; you might be surprised by how these changes can increase the size of your document.

If you click the arrow next to the document information, a pop-up list opens, as shown in Figure 2.4 that gives you several options for the information display.

FIGURE 2.4

The information section of the document window can be very useful when you are editing images. The menu allows you to display several types of information.

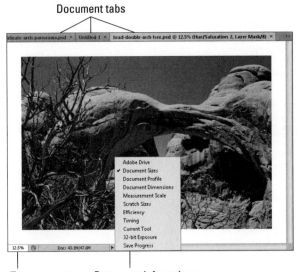

You can choose to display the following options at the bottom of the document workspace:

- **Adobe Drive.** This option shows the location of the Adobe drive used as a scratch disk.

- **Document Sizes.** This option shows the size data of the image in the format of *"print size"/"actual size."* The print size represents the size of the image if it is in a flattened state with no layers or additional channels. The actual size includes the additional space that the image takes to store the additional metadata such as channels and layers.

- **Document Profile.** This option displays the name of the color profile assigned to the document.

- **Document Dimensions.** This option displays the dimensions of the image in inches.

- **Measurement Scale.** This option shows the scale of the current zoom state of the document in pixels.

- **Scratch Sizes.** This option shows the scratch usage of the document in the format of *"memory used for this document"/"total scratch memory available."*

TIP

The scratch usage can have a major impact on how Photoshop performs. You should monitor the scratch usage when making complex adjustments to very large images.

- **Efficiency.** This option displays the percentage of time that Photoshop uses to actually perform operations instead of reading or writing to the scratch disk. If this value is below 100 percent, then Photoshop is using the scratch disk and therefore operations are slower.

- **Timing.** This option displays the amount of time Photoshop used to complete the last operation.

- **Current Tool.** This option shows the name of the currently selected tool.

- **32-bit Exposure.** This option provides a slider that allows you to easily adjust the preview image for viewing 32-bit HDR images on the monitor. The slider is only visible when you are working with a 32-bit document.

- **Save Progress.** This option opens a progress bar when you are saving an image. This is useful when you are saving large images in the background and you want to monitor the progress of the save operation.

Arranging the view of multiple documents

When multiple documents are open in the document workspace, Photoshop provides tabs for each of them. These tabs display the document name, and you can access the document for editing by clicking its tab. Using the tabs is the most economical and organized way to have multiple files open, and you probably will prefer this option most of the time.

Other View options are also available when you have multiple documents open. To change how the document windows are organized, choose Window ⇨ Arrange from the Photoshop menu bar and then choose one of the options shown in Figure 2.5.

FIGURE 2.5

Using the Window ⇨ Arrange menu, you can easily change the layout of multiple documents in the document workspace.

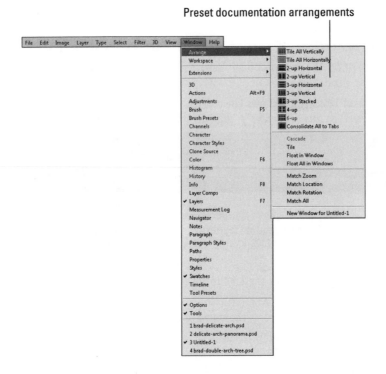

Following is a description of the multiple document arrangement:

- **Preset document arrangements.** These options automatically distribute the documents in the document work area based on a predefined arrangement of view panes. These arrangements are shown next to the menu item. Each open document takes up one pane. If there are fewer documents than panes in the arrangement, the arrangement option is inactive in the menu. If there are more documents than panes, then Photoshop places the extra documents as tabs in the top-left pane. Figure 2.6 shows the 3-up stacked arrangement. If the document is bigger than the pane, the scroll bars become active, allowing you to scroll around the image.

> **TIP**
>
> You can resize the view panes in a tiled or preset arrangement by dragging borders between the panes with the mouse. This allows you to customize your document workspace completely to support the files on which you are working.

- **Consolidate All to Tabs.** This option docks all floating windows into the document workspace. This is great when you have so many windows open that navigating them is difficult. You can also consolidate windows to the document workspace or floating group by right-clicking the tab bar at the top and selecting Consolidate All to Here.

- **Cascade.** This option cascades your documents by showing the document windows in a cascade fashion from the upper-left corner to the lower-right corner of your document workspace. Figure 2.6 shows an example of a cascading document window.

- **Tile.** This option adjusts the size of all open document windows so you can view them together in the workspace. For example, if you are working with two or more documents at the same time, cloning areas of one into another, you probably want to tile your documents in the document workspace. Figure 2.6 shows an example of tiled documents that are in a floating state.

FIGURE 2.6

Examples of some of the multi-document layouts in Photoshop

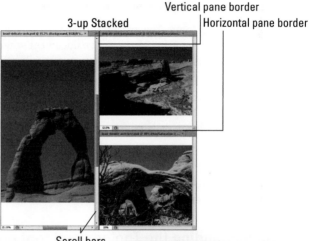

3-up Stacked

Vertical pane border

Horizontal pane border

Scroll bars

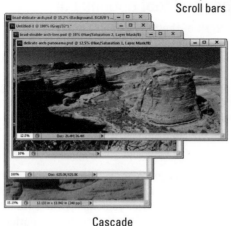

Cascade

Tile

- **Float in Window.** This option floats your documents, thereby releasing them from the document workspace or from a floating group to their own individual windows. When the document windows are floating, they are independent of the Photoshop interface, and you can use the standard operating system window controls on them. You can organize floating windows into groups by dragging one window on top of another window. When more than one document is in a floating group, their tabs are displayed at the top of the window. You can also float windows by grabbing the tab in the floating group or document workspace and dragging it out. You can add a floating document to a group or document workspace by dragging it into the tabs.

- **Float All in Windows.** This option causes all windows to float.

TIP
You can quickly cycle through open tabbed document windows by pressing the Ctrl+Tab/⌘+` hotkey sequence.

- **Match Zoom.** This option sets the zoom percentage of all open document windows to match the value of the active document window. This is useful when you are working with multiple images that eventually will be consolidated into a single document.

- **Match Location.** This option sets the center panning position of all open document windows to match the center position of the active document window. This is useful if you are working with multiple versions of the same image or a sequence of images and you want to quickly move to the same location in all windows for comparison.

- **Match Rotation.** This option sets the rotation angle of the image in all document windows to match the rotation angle of the image in the active document window.

- **Match All.** This option sets the zoom, center panning position, and rotation of all document windows to match the values of the active document window.

Understanding the Toolbox and tool options bar

The Toolbox provides easy access to all of the tools in Photoshop that require mouse or stylus interaction with the document. The Toolbox includes selection tools, painting tools, erasing tools, and much more, as shown in Figure 2.7. We discuss each of the tools available in the Toolbox later in this chapter.

The tool options bar, usually referred to as the "options bar" or the "tool menu," sits below the Photoshop menu bar. The options in the tool menu change, depending on the tool you have selected in the Toolbox. Figure 2.7 shows the different options for the Move, Brush, and Type tools.

It is always smart to keep an eye on what is going on in the options bar. When you select a tool, the options are set to default values that are commonly used, but not necessarily the values you would use in a particular situation. After you change the options for any given tool, those options stay changed, even after you use other tools. The options bar is useful and important and you'll see you'll see many examples throughout this book of different ways to set your options; and as you use Photoshop, you will soon become familiar with it.

FIGURE 2.7

The Toolbox provides access to the mouse and stylus tools. Each time you select a new tool, the tool options bar changes to reflect settings for the new tool.

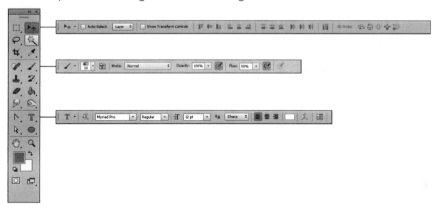

Understanding panels

The panels in Photoshop are similar to mini-applications with their own windows, controls, and menus. You will rely heavily on the Photoshop panels to do most of the editing. Photoshop has many panels, each of which provides its own set of functionality.

Panels tend to take up quite a bit of space in the work area, so Photoshop provides different display states for them. These states are expanded, collapsed into an icon, or hidden. To hide or unhide a panel, select the panel from the Window menu. Figure 2.8 shows a collapsed panel group as well as an expanded panel group. To collapse the panel group, click the Collapse button. To expand a panel in a collapsed group, click its icon.

> **NOTE**
>
> You will typically only have a small number of panels that pertain to your open workflow. This makes finding the panels you need much easier.

A panel group is one or more panels that are connected to each other. To add a panel to a group, drag the panel or icon onto the group. To remove a panel from a group, drag the panel out of the group. Organizing panel groups is no different than organizing the items on your desktop. You can decide which panels go in which groups. The bottom line is, if you know where to find a panel, you can use it much faster.

FIGURE 2.8

Panel groups can be collapsed to icons to reduce their footprint on the workspace.

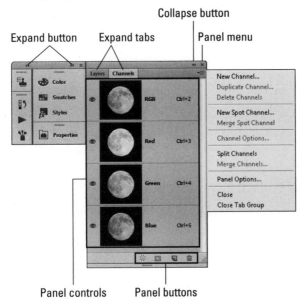

The panel groups have the following basic components, as shown in Figure 2.8:

- **Panel tabs.** These tabs are used to select which panel is visible in the group and to drag panels out of the group.

- **Collapse button.** This button collapses the panel to an icon to reduce the footprint in the work area.

- **Expand button.** This button expands a collapsed panel from an icon to provide access to the panel settings.

- **Panel controls.** This area contains the controls used by the panel to perform various tasks. Each panel has different settings.

- **Panel menu.** This menu pops out of a panel when you click the menu button in the top-right corner. The panel menus usually contain additional features that are not included in the main settings area. If you can't find something, it is probably in the panel.

- **Panel buttons.** These buttons are located at the bottom of a panel, and do things such as add or delete items or perform common tasks needed by the panel.

Another way to organize panel groups is to dock them either together or to the sides of the Photoshop workspace. You can dock panel groups by dragging the groups to the side or bottom of another group. You can dock them to the side of the workspace by dragging them until the mouse is on the workspace edge.

Using workspace presets

The workspace presets are quick ways to change the layout of the panels and tools in Photoshop, depending on the task you are performing. When you select a preset, the panel layouts are adjusted so you have easier access to the tools that are typically used for the selected task. You select a preset by choosing Window ⇨ Workspace from the Photoshop menu bar and selecting one of the options from the drop-down menu:

- **New in CS6.** This preset displays the panel icons for panels with new features in CS6, such as the new 3D tools, paintbrush, paragraph and character presets, and Mini-Bridge.

- **Essentials.** This preset gives you full access to the most commonly used panels in Photoshop, including the Navigation, Swatches, and Layers panels.

- **Design.** This preset displays the more common graphic design panels, such as the Swatches, Character, and Paragraph panels.

- **Painting.** This preset makes the paintbrush and brush presets readily available.

- **Photography.** This preset provides the Histogram and adjustment panels that make it easy to apply adjustments to photographs.

- **3D (Extended Only).** This preset displays the 3D, Mask, and Layers panels that are often used when working with 3D objects.

- **Motion (Extended Only).** This preset displays the Timeline panel and Clone Source panel, which are frequently used in animation.

- **Reset/New/Delete.** These presets take advantage of the fact that Photoshop remembers when you select a workspace preset and then adjust the panels, so you don't have to readjust them each time you start the application. The Reset option restores the currently selected workspace to the original settings, so you can start over with a fresh set of panels. The New option allows you to save the current panel layout as your own custom workspace. The new workspace then shows up in the list. The Delete option deletes the currently selected workspace preset.

Exploring the Photoshop Menu Bar

Now that you are familiar with the Photoshop workspace, you are ready to explore the Photoshop menu bar. The menus along with their keyboard shortcuts will provide you access to the majority of the features in Photoshop. Throughout the book, we will discuss most of the options contained in the Photoshop menu bar in more detail. In this section, we show you the primary purpose of each menu and highlight some of the menu options that might not be covered in other areas of the book.

Using the File menu

The File menu has many of the options that you would expect, and many of them are self-explanatory. For the most part, all the options listed are different ways to open, save, or export your documents. The first task that you will be performing in Photoshop is opening or creating a document, so you will first need to become familiar with the File menu.

The options in the File menu, shown in Figure 2.9, are covered throughout the book: opening and saving files are covered in Chapter 3, exporting to the web and mobile devices are covered in Chapter 30, and batch operations on files are covered in Chapter 31.

FIGURE 2.9

The File menu in Photoshop provides several options to open, save, and export files.

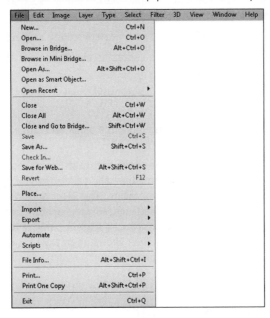

Exploring the Edit menu

The Edit menu is a familiar menu found in most applications, with many recognizable options such as cut, copy, and paste as well as additional options that are specific to Photoshop. This menu is important for modifying the document and workspace settings.

Using the Edit menu, shown in Figure 2.10, you can step backward, undoing several of the most recent changes you made. Farther down the menu, you find the transformation edits, Content-Aware Scale and Puppet Warp among them; these are covered in Chapter 19. You learn about using color in Chapter 4 and color profiles in Chapter 29. Setting preferences and using the menu and shortcut options to customize menu and shortcut behavior are covered later in this chapter.

NOTE

On Macs, the Preferences and Quit options are found under the Photoshop menu option on the left of the Photoshop menu bar.

FIGURE 2.10

The Edit menu in Photoshop provides several options to modify document and workspace settings.

Using the Image menu

The Image menu is loaded with a lot of options for changing your image. Making changes to your image is different from making changes to your file, because these options actually affect the look of your image.

Among other things, the options in your Image menu, shown in Figure 2.11, allow you to change the color mode, and resize, rotate, or duplicate your image. Neatly tucked into the Image Adjustments submenu, you find some of the most powerful tools for correcting the color and lighting of your image; these are covered in Chapter 13. The Apply Image and Calculations options blend the channels of your image and are covered in Chapter 11. Image variables and data sets allow you to create multiple images with similar components by defining and replacing layers. These options are covered in more detail in Chapter 10.

FIGURE 2.11

The Image menu in Photoshop provides several adjustment options to modify images.

The Image menu also provides an important submenu, shown in Figure 2.11, titled Analysis. The Analysis submenu is all about measuring and, of course, analyzing areas in your document. You can customize the tools found here for your own use to measure, scale, and mark your images. You can choose from six menu options. We don't list them in the order they appear in the Analysis submenu because they make more sense in the order listed here.

Ruler Tool

The Ruler tool is simply a tool that allows you to drag from one area in your image to another and measure it. The measurement information is displayed in the Info panel. By default, the measurement is displayed in pixels. The Ruler tool plays an important role in the other options found in the Analysis submenu.

Count Tool

Selecting the Count tool and clicking your document leaves a number behind, in increments of one. This allows you to count and mark multiple items in your image. If you were trying to count a flock of birds, for instance, you would click each bird until they had all been marked. The last number placed would be the number of birds in the photo.

Record Measurements

Clicking Record Measurements opens the Measurement Log panel on the bottom of your document window, as shown in Figure 2.12. As you create measurements, you click the Record Measurements button on the Measurement Log panel and the measurement details are recorded. Notice that the first measurement was taken by the Ruler tool, and the second measurement was taken by the Count tool.

You can also use the Measurement Log to export these measurements. Simply click the Export icon to export the measurements as a text file to any specified location. You can also access the Measurement Log menu by clicking the menu icon.

2

FIGURE 2.12

The Measurement Log panel allows you to record and display measurements you have taken within your document.

Export

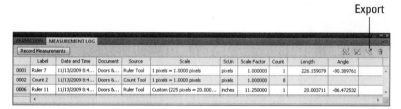

	Label	Date and Time	Document	Source	Scale	ScUn	Scale Factor	Count	Length	Angle	
0001	Ruler 7	11/13/2009 8:4...	Doors &...	Ruler Tool	1 pixels = 1.0000 pixels	pixels	1.000000	1	226.159079	-90.389761	
0002	Count 2	11/13/2009 8:4...	Doors &...	Count Tool	1 pixels = 1.0000 pixels	pixels	1.000000	8			
0006	Ruler 11	11/13/2009 8:4...	Doors &...	Ruler Tool	Custom (225 pixels = 20.000...	inches	11.250000	1	20.003711	-86.472532	

Set Measurement Scale

The measurement scale can be set to Default, which simply means that one pixel is equal to one pixel. If you choose the custom option, however, it allows you to translate a set number of pixels in your document to any other measurement you prefer.

For instance, in Figure 2.13, if you know the height of the bottom-right window pane is 20 inches, you can choose Analysis ⇨ Measurement Scale ⇨ Custom to open the Measurement Scale dialog box. The Measurement Scale dialog box automatically activates the Ruler tool so you can measure from the bottom of the window pane to the top. In the photo, this measurement is 225 pixels, shown as the pixel length in Figure 2.13. From here, you can enter any relative measurement that you choose — in this case, 20 inches. You could have just as easily entered 1 foot, 3 meters, or 7 girth units. You can save this measurement scale by clicking Save Preset and naming it.

FIGURE 2.13

Placing a scale marker in your image allows you to clearly see the scale of the image.

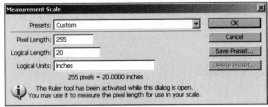

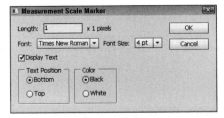

After closing the Measurement Scale dialog box, you can activate the Ruler tool and measure other areas of the photo. These measurements are recorded in the Measurement Log panel. Notice that the third measurement in Figure 2.13 was taken after the Measurement Scale was set. The scale indicates that 225 pixels = 20 inches; the scale unit is inches and the length is 20 (rounded up, of course).

Select Data Points

The Measurement Log shows data on each measurement you record. You can choose what data to keep and display by selecting specific data points. Choose Analysis ⇨ Select Data Points ⇨ Custom to display the Select Data Points dialog box. In this dialog box, you can deselect the types of information that you don't want recorded. For instance, if you don't require date and time information, you can deselect the box next to Date and Time. Every measurement you take after this point no longer displays the date and time in the Measurement Log panel.

Place Scale Marker

You can place a scale marker in your image to denote scale. To place a scale marker, choose Place Scale Marker from the Analysis submenu to open the Measurement Scale dialog box, shown in Figure 2.13. You can choose the length of the scale by selecting more than one unit of measurement.

Refer to Figure 2.13, which shows a scale marker indicating that the unit of measurement represents the 20 inches that was set for the measurement scale. If you were to change the number from 1 to 2, your scale marker would appear twice as long and would be labeled 40 inches. You can also choose to display the text and what font and size that text will be. Finally, you have the choice to display the scale marker at the top or bottom of your document and in black or white.

Understanding the Layer menu

The Layer menu is built specifically for use with the Layers panel. Layers are an important part of working efficiently and non-destructively in Photoshop, and you want to learn all you can about how they work.

Layers allow you to make modifications to a document on a separate layer from the original pixels. This allows you to easily remove the changes, turn the changes off, or even stack different adjustments and reorder them. The Layer menu, shown in Figure 2.14, allows you to manage the layers in a document. Layers and the Layer menu are covered extensively in Chapter 10.

Examining the Type menu

The Type menu is built specifically for use with the Type tools. Using the Type menu gives you quick access to options such as opening the type panels, modifying size and orientation, and extruding type to 3D.

In addition, the Type menu, shown in Figure 2.15, allows you to modify type layers by rasterizing them, to convert them to shape layers, or to warp them. You can also specify which language to use for the fonts as long as the selected fonts support that language.

FIGURE 2.14

The Layer menu in Photoshop provides several options to control the behavior of layers.

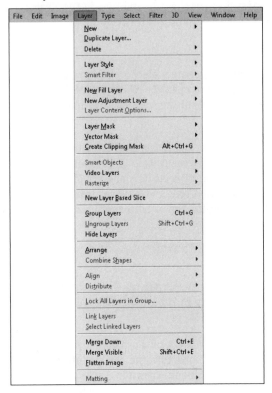

FIGURE 2.15

The Type menu in Photoshop provides several options to interact with text in your documents.

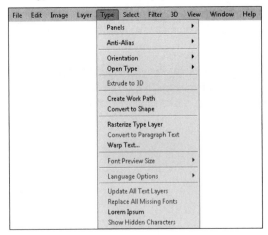

Using the Select menu

Although you might not have thought that an entire menu could be dedicated to selections, they are such an integral part of many workflows in Photoshop that a selection menu is critical. The selection tools are some of the most powerful in Photoshop. They allow you to create masks, cut precise areas out of an image, and edit only specific parts of the image.

The Select menu, shown in Figure 2.16, gives you control over the selections. For instance, you can use the Select menu to select everything or deselect everything. You can also use the selection tools to access dialog boxes to modify an existing selection. The Toolbox contains several selection tools, and they are covered, along with the Select menu, in Chapter 9.

FIGURE 2.16

The Select menu in Photoshop provides several options to manage selections.

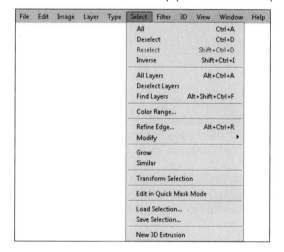

Exploring the Filter menu

Filters are placed over images to change their appearance. There are corrective filters such as Sharpen and Reduce Noise, and there are also special effects filters that can make your image look like it is being viewed through rippled glass or embossed into chrome. Filters are most definitely the fun side of Photoshop.

The Filter menu, shown in Figure 2.17, provides a list of several different filters that can be directly applied to an image. It also provides access to the Filter Gallery, which provides many more filters. You will learn more about filters and the Filter Gallery as well as how to use them and their menu options in Chapters 14 and 20.

FIGURE 2.17

The Filter menu in Photoshop provides several filtering options that can be applied to images.

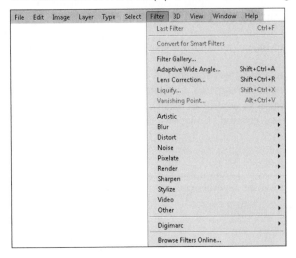

Understanding the 3D menu

The 3D menu, only available in CS6 Extended, is packed full of goodies for helping you work in the 3D environment. The 3D environment allows you to bring in 3D models and use the powerful Photoshop tools to make incredible changes to their appearance.

The 3D menu, shown in Figure 2.18, allows you to create and export 3D layers. It also provides access to several 3D utilities that allow you to perform tasks such as creating 3D extrusions and setting paint falloff. The 3D menu is covered in Chapter 22.

Using the View menu

The View menu functions as a catchall for everything that has to do with displaying documents in the Photoshop work area. Understanding this menu can be a great asset because it provides access to a plethora of tools, such as rulers and grids, that can enhance your workflow.

FIGURE 2.18

The 3D menu in Photoshop provides access to several 3D options and tools.

As shown in Figure 2.19, the View menu offers basic options for adjusting the view of your document, such as its size (fit screen, actual pixels, print size, and so on) and screen mode (full screen, full screen with menus, and standard screen) that we discussed earlier in this chapter.

Proof Options

The proof options let you soft-proof your documents before printing; these settings are covered in more detail in Chapter 29. Options for setting pixel aspect ratios are available as well; these settings are for use with video files and are covered in Chapter 25.

FIGURE 2.19

The View menu in Photoshop allows you to customize how documents are displayed in the Photoshop workspace.

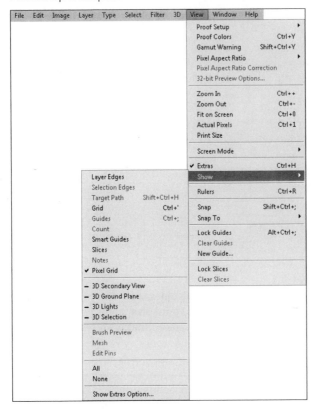

Extras and Show

You may find it interesting that the Extras option allows you to see non-printing guides such as selections, bounding boxes, and grids. If you deselect the Extras option, any of these items that are visible in your document disappear.

The Show submenu lets you customize which non-printing items are visible when Extras is selected in the View menu. The following is a list of some of the features that you can enable using the Show submenu (refer to Figure 2.19):

- **Layer Edges.** This option places a bounding box around the edge of the currently selected layer.
- **Selection Edges.** This option shows marching ants around the selection. This is on by default when you make a selection. However, you can toggle it on and off afterwards.

- **Target Path.** This option toggles displaying the target path on and off.
- **Grid.** This option places a mesh of vertical and horizontal lines, shown in Figure 2.20, that you can use to see the alignment and organization of objects more easily in your images. Photoshop also divides the grids into subdivisions of lines that are not as visible but are visible enough to be useful.

  A great feature of Photoshop is that you can force items to be snapped to grids by choosing View ⇨ Snap To ⇨ Grid from the Photoshop menu bar. This option is useful when placing images, text, and shapes in a document. You can configure the number of grid lines, colors, and styles in the Preferences dialog box, discussed later in this chapter.

FIGURE 2.20

The guides, grids, and rulers features of Photoshop allow you to better organize and align objects in your images.

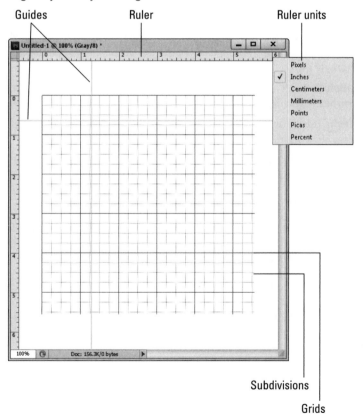

Guides   Ruler   Ruler units

Subdivisions

Grids

- **Guides.** This option helps you with object placement and organization. Guides are vertical or horizontal lines that you can add to a document by choosing View ➪ New Guide. You can force items to snap to guides by choosing View ➪ Snap To ➪ Guides from the Photoshop menu bar. The position of guides can be adjusted in the image by using the Move tool.

> **TIP**
>
> When you click and hold the mouse button on the ruler, the cursor changes to a guide adjustment cursor. You can quickly add guides to an image by clicking the ruler and dragging them into the document.

- **Smart Guides.** This option toggles the viewing of smart guides on and off.

- **Slices.** This option toggles the slice overlay on and off. Chapter 30 discusses slices in more detail as part of preparing images for the web.

- **Notes.** This option toggles the display of notes you have added to the document on and off.

- **Pixel Grid.** This option toggles the display of the pixel grid on and off.

- **3D elements.** These options toggle the display of some of the 3D elements on and off, such as cameras and lights. We discuss 3D in more detail in Chapters 22 through 24.

- **Brush Preview.** This option toggles the brush preview for the bristle and erodible tip brushes. These brush tips, as well as the preview, are discussed in Chapter 16.

- **Mesh.** This option toggles the display of the mesh on and off when using the Puppet Warp tool. We discuss the Puppet Warp tool in Chapter 19.

- **Edit Pins.** This option toggles the display of edit pins on and off when using the Puppet Warp tool. We discuss the Puppet Warp tool in Chapter 19.

Rulers

Select the Ruler option if you want rulers to appear in your document window. When rulers are enabled, a vertical ruler is displayed on the left and a horizontal ruler is displayed on the top of the document window (refer to Figure 2.20).

The rulers start at zero in the upper-left corner of your document and measure the actual print size of your document. You can change the rulers' unit of measure by right-clicking a ruler and selecting the unit from the shortcut menu. While you are moving the cursor over the documents, the exact placement of the cursor is noted in the ruler by a line that moves with the mouse.

Snap and Snap To

As you move things around in your work area, whether they are selections, panels, or objects, you can choose to have them *snap* to the guides or to other objects. For instance, as you customize your panels, they snap together so you can easily place them next to each other with no space between them and no overlaps.

The Snap To option lets you choose what elements your objects snap to: guides, grids, layers, and so on. The elements that have a check mark will draw objects you are moving like a magnet. If you want to place elements without the guides snapping them one way or the other, just deselect Snap in the View menu and you have full control.

New Guide, Lock Guides, and Clear Guides

The line under text and the bounding box around a placement in your document are guides that help you see and move these objects. You can make your own guides to help you with placement and alignment in your document. Choose View⇨New Guide, and select whether you want the guide to run vertically or horizontally and where you want it placed in your image. The New Guide dialog box asks you how many inches into your image you want the guide placed, so it's helpful to have the rulers on. You can also express the position of the guide as a percentage rather than a specific measurement.

You can lock these guides so you don't accidentally move them by choosing Lock Guides. You can also clear them out of the way entirely by choosing Clear Guides.

Lock Slices and Clear Slices

The Lock Slices option allows you to lock slices to prevent them from being altered, and the Clear Slices option allows you to clear the existing slices so you can easily clean them up. Chapter 30 discusses slices in more detail as part of preparing images for the web.

Exploring the Window menu

The Window menu is used for three main purposes in Photoshop: first, it provides access to the Arrange and Workspace submenus that we have already discussed in this chapter; second, it provides a list of the available panels that you can toggle on and off; and finally, it provides a list of open documents that you can use to select a specific document so that it becomes active.

One of the best and most common uses of the Window menu, shown in Figure 2.21, is to toggle panels on and off. The Window menu provides a comprehensive list of the panels that are available to you. From this menu, you can select the panels that you want to be visible. When a panel is visible, a check mark appears next to it. Selecting a visible panel hides the panel; selecting a hidden panel makes the panel visible. The different panels are discussed later in this chapter.

FIGURE 2.21

The Window menu in Photoshop allows you to configure the workspace by defining the arrangement of documents and specifying which panels are visible.

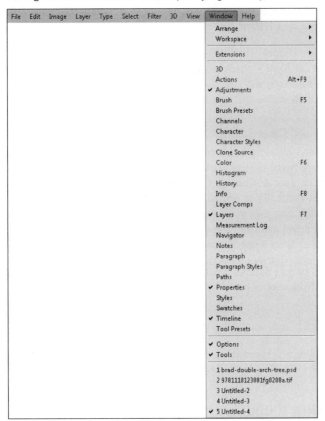

Using the Help menu

The Help menu contains information about the Photoshop version that you are currently running, as well as links to online help for Photoshop. You can also use the Help menu to see which plug-ins are installed.

> **NOTE**
>
> On a Mac, the About and Plug-in menu options are in the Photoshop menu item on the left of the Photoshop menu bar.

The Help menu, shown in Figure 2.22, contains web links to various sites that Adobe thinks might be of interest to you, such as the Photoshop Support Center and Photoshop Online. You can also use the Help menu to register, deactivate, and update your version of Photoshop. The two menu options worth noting are Photoshop Help and Deactivate.

FIGURE 2.22

The Help menu in Photoshop provides access to online help for Photoshop.

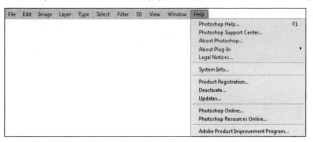

Photoshop Help

Photoshop Help is a great resource if you are stuck figuring something out. Click the Help link, and you are taken to the Photoshop Help website where you can browse through the Help contents, search the Adobe Help resources, or even view articles and threads from others who are looking for or offering help.

Deactivate

When you install Photoshop on your computer and activate it, Adobe keeps a record of it. After you have installed Photoshop twice using the single-user application, Adobe deactivates your product to prevent further use. This obviously keeps you from passing your copy of Photoshop to your friends, neighbors, and your cousin's boyfriend's sister-in-law.

The Help ➪ Deactivate option allows you to deactivate the Photoshop license on the computer from which you run it. Upon deactivating, Photoshop will not load properly; however, you can then activate the license again on another computer or even on the same computer. The Deactivation screen prompts you with these three options:

- **Suspend Activation.** This disables the license on this computer, allowing you to run Photoshop on another computer or do an uninstall and reinstall of Photoshop. The license remains on the computer.

- **Deactivate Permanently.** This permanently removes the Photoshop license from this computer. You need to completely re-enter the license to add it back to that computer. Use this option if want to permanently remove the license from the computer, for example, if you are selling it or need to do a complete system restore that would wipe out all data.

- **Cancel.** This cancels you out of deactivation without taking action. Photoshop still runs normally.

CAUTION

The Deactivate menu option is absolutely imperative for you to know if the Adobe anti-piracy policy lockout becomes a problem, or if you are restructuring your system or purchasing a new computer. In order to reinstall Photoshop on a new system, or if you need to replace the hard drive, you need to deactivate Photoshop. Go to the Help menu and choose Deactivate. Doing so allows you to activate your software the next time you install it.

Exploring Panels

The panels in Photoshop are mini-applications with their own windows, controls, and menus. You rely heavily on the Photoshop panels to do most of your editing. Photoshop has many panels, each of which provides its own set of functionality. The functionality of some panels is limited, while other panels are almost applications in their own right. We will discuss each of the panels in detail throughout the book as we cover the features that they are used for. The purpose of this section is to familiarize you with the panels that are available. Figure 2.23 shows the icons for each of the panels.

FIGURE 2.23

Photoshop provides several panels that each act as individual utilities. You can view these panels by selecting them from the Window menu or clicking their icons.

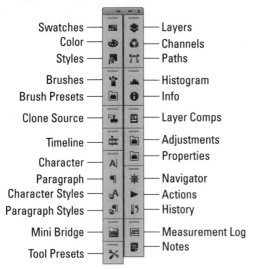

As a quick guide, the following list describes the icons for each of the panels and where they are covered in the book:

- **Swatches.** Provides a simple way to manage sets of colors that you use in different documents. See Chapter 4.

- **Color.** Allows you to quickly select any color in the possible ranges that Photoshop supports. See Chapter 4.

- **Styles.** Allows you to manage the style sets that can be applied by various tools when painting or applying filters. See Chapters 10 and 16.

- **Brushes.** Provides a robust interface that allows you to define different types of brush qualities and behaviors that are used by Brush tools. See Chapter 16.

- **Brush Presets.** Allows you to easily manage sets of brushes that can be used by the various Brush tools. See Chapter 16.

- **Clone Source.** Provides a dynamic interface to control the source used by the Clone tools to heal areas of photos and remove unwanted items. See Chapter 15.

- **Timeline (Extended only).** Provides a timeline-based utility that adds animation to images. See Chapter 26.

- **Character.** Provides options to quickly format character styles, fonts, and spacing of textual elements in images. See Chapter 18.

- **Paragraph.** Provides options to quickly format paragraph styles and spacing of textual elements in images. See Chapter 18.

- **Character Styles.** Allows you to create and save character style settings that enable you to keep text consistent between documents. See Chapter 18.

- **Paragraph Styles.** Allows you to create and save paragraph style settings that enable you to keep text consistent between documents. See Chapter 18.

- **Mini-Bridge.** Provides some of the functionality of Bridge that allows you to quickly select and organize image files. See Chapter 6.

- **Tool Presets.** Allows you to quickly view and select presets for the tool that is currently selected in the Toolbox.

- **Layers.** Allows you to select, create, edit, and manage layers. This is one of the panels you'll use most often. See Chapter 10.

- **Channels.** Allows you to view and manage each of the different color channels in an image as well as create additional channels such as alpha channels. See Chapter 11.

- **Paths.** Allows you to manage and use vector paths in images. See Chapter 17.

- **Histogram.** Provides a simple-to-understand view of the overall distribution of color and levels in an image. See Chapter 4.

- **Info.** Allows you to view color and other information about individual pixels in the image by hovering the mouse over them. See Chapter 4.

- **Layer Comps.** Allows you to easily create, manage, and view multiple versions of a layout in a single Photoshop file. See Chapter 10.

- **Adjustments.** Allows you to apply several adjustments to a layer in an image. See Chapters 10 and 13.

2

- **Properties.** Provides an additional interface with properties pertaining to other panels, such as adjustments. This has replaced the Masks panel where you create and control masks. See Chapter 10.

- **Navigator.** Provides a simple interface that allows you to quickly zoom in on areas of an image. The interface includes a slider control at the bottom that zooms in on the image. It also displays a miniature version of the image with a red rectangle that you can move to pan to a specific area of the image, as shown in Figure 2.24.

- **Actions.** Allows you to record and then reapply a series of commands that perform common tasks such as applying filter settings. See Chapter 5.

- **History.** Provides access to the history states of the document that are recorded each time you change the document. See Chapter 5.

FIGURE 2.24

The Navigator panel allows you to quickly zoom in on the image in the document window and then pan to specific locations.

- **Measurement Log.** Keeps track of measurements as discussed earlier in this chapter.

- **Notes.** Allows you to view and manage notes that you create with the Note tool. This is discussed later in this chapter.

Understanding the Tools in the Toolbox

The Toolbox provides easy access to all the tools that you use to interact directly with pixels in the document window. To enable or disable the Toolbox, choose Window⇨Tools from the Photoshop menu bar.

You can expand most of the tools in the Toolbox by pressing and holding the mouse button over them to reveal several other tools. Figure 2.25 shows the expanded menus of the Toolbox. From the expanded tool menus, you can select other tools. The icon of the currently selected tool is displayed in the Toolbox, and the cursor changes to reflect the current tool as well.

FIGURE 2.25

Photoshop provides several tool sets in the Toolbox, and you can expand the tool sets to reveal additional tools.

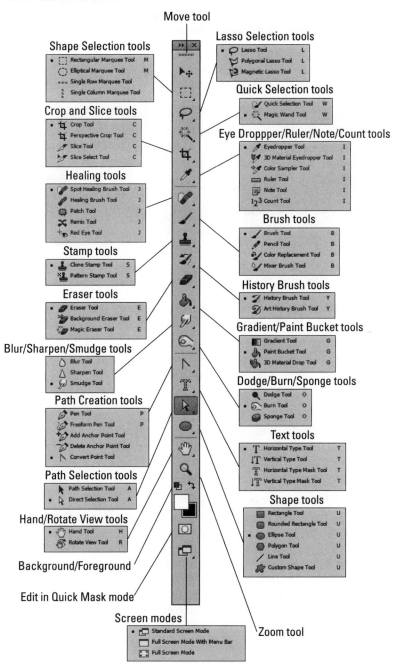

Just as with panels, the tools in the Toolbox are covered in various sections throughout the book. The purpose of this section is to familiarize you with the organization of the Toolbox and what kinds of tools you can find there.

The following list briefly describes each of the tool sets in the Toolbox, as well as where you can find more information about them in this book:

- **Move tool.** This is the only tool that allows you to move items in the document window. It allows you to move several items, including guides, objects and shapes in shape layers, and text objects.

- **Shape Selection tools.** These tools allow you to quickly select areas of the document using rectangle, ellipse, row, and column shapes. See Chapter 9.

- **Lasso Selection tools.** These tools allow you to quickly select areas of the document by using the mouse to draw a lasso around them. See Chapter 9.

- **Quick Selection tools.** These tools can intelligently select areas of the document by detecting areas that are similar to those selected by the mouse. See Chapter 9.

- **Crop and Slice tools.** The Crop tool lets you select an area of the document to keep and remove the area around it. See Chapter 3. The Slice tools are used for creating clickable hot areas for web images. See Chapter 30.

- **Eye Dropper/Ruler/Note/Count tools.** This tool set is a catchall. The Eyedropper tool is used to select foreground colors directly from pixels in the image. See Chapter 4. The Ruler tool is used to measure areas in an image. The Note tool allows you to add notes to an image that help you retain information such as to-do editing lists with the image. The Count tool allows you to count and log items in the image, which can be useful if you are working with medical images. The Ruler, Note, and Count tools were discussed earlier in the menus section of this chapter.

- **Healing tools.** These tools provide quick ways to apply brush strokes that can heal areas of an image, from removing dust and scratches to removing red eye. See Chapter 15.

- **Brush tools.** These tools allow you to apply painting techniques to repair, enhance, and create images. See Chapter 16.

- **Stamp tools.** These tools include the Clone Stamp and Pattern Stamp. The Clone Stamp tool allows you to select an area of the image and then stamp or brush that area into other parts of the image or even other documents. See Chapter 15. The Pattern Stamp tool allows you to apply a style pattern to an image using brush strokes. See Chapter 16.

- **Eraser tools.** These tools allow you to quickly remove pixel data from an image. See Chapter 16.

- **History Brush tools.** These tools are used to repair and enhance areas of an image by painting data from previous editing states of the image. For example, you could change the image to grayscale and then use brush strokes to add color to specific areas. See Chapter 5.

- **Blur/Sharpen/Smudge tools.** The Blur and Sharpen tools allow you to use brush strokes to blur or sharpen specific areas of an image. The Smudge tool allows you to use brush strokes to smudge existing pixels into each other. See Chapter 16.

- **Gradient/Paint Bucket tools.** The Gradient tool allows you to paint a gradient pattern onto an image. The Paint Bucket tool allows you to apply a paint color to sections of an image. See Chapter 16.

- **Dodge/Burn/Sponge tools.** The Dodge and Burn tools allow you to use brush strokes to lighten or darken areas of an image. The Sponge tool allows you to use brush strokes to remove or add color saturation in areas of an image. See Chapter 16.

- **Path Creation tools.** These tools allow you to create vector paths by creating lines between anchor points. See Chapter 17.

- **Path Selection tools.** These tools allow you to select and manipulate vector paths by adjusting the anchor points. See Chapter 17.

- **Text tools.** These tools allow you to add textual elements to images. See Chapter 18.

- **Shape tools.** These tools enable you to create and manipulate simple geometric vector shapes and lines as well as custom vector shapes. See Chapter 17.

- **Hand/Rotate View tools.** The Hand tool enables you to grab onto the image and pan by dragging the mouse. This feature is available only when you are zoomed in on the image, but it's very useful for navigating around your image. The Rotate View tool allows you to rotate the canvas in the document window by dragging with the mouse. If you press and hold the Shift key while rotating the canvas, the rotation occurs in 15-degree increments. Rotating the canvas can be useful if you need to align elements in the image with the vertical or horizontal axis of the display screen for editing.

- **Zoom tool.** This tool allows you to use the mouse to drag a specific rectangle to zoom in on the image. You can also zoom in at 100-percent increments by simply clicking

2

the document with the mouse. You can zoom out at 100-percent increments by pressing and holding the Shift key while clicking the document. The options bar for the Zoom tool provides several buttons to resize the document view based on actual pixels, print size, and screen size.

If you have OpenGL Drawing enabled, then you can use the Scrubby Zoom option in the Zoom tool options bar. When you enable Scrubby Zoom, you can click and drag the mouse to the left and right on the image to zoom in and out.

- **Background/Foreground.** This section of the Toolbox allows you to see and modify the current background and foreground colors. The foreground color is used by several tools to paint onto the image. The background color is used by several tools when removing pixels from the image. See Chapter 4.

> **TIP**
>
> Pressing D on the keyboard resets the foreground and background colors to black and white, respectively. Pressing X on the keyboard swaps the foreground and background colors.

The foreground is represented by the front square, and the background by the back square. The color of each is changed by clicking the square to launch a color chooser. The two colors can be switched by clicking the curved line with arrows on each end. To revert to the default colors of black and white, click the small black-and-white icon.

- **Edit in Quick Mask mode.** This option toggles between Normal and Quick Mask mode. The Edit in Quick Mask mode option allows you to tweak selections using the Brush tool to paint the exact shape. See Chapter 9.

- **Screen Mode.** This option allows you to quickly toggle between Standard, Full Screen, and Full Screen with Menu Bar modes.

> **TIP**
>
> You can activate the Quick Mask mode by pressing Q on the keyboard whenever you have an active selection in the document.

Configuring Presets

As you become more familiar with the options that are available for different tool panels in Photoshop, you realize that it takes a while to optimize some tool settings and panels for what you need them to do. If you have to do that over and over, it can become time consuming. That's where presets come into play.

A *preset* is simply a collection of saved settings that you can easily reload to make a tool behave the exact same way each time the preset is used. Presets are organized into sets that can be loaded for each tool or panel and then easily selected. You will work with presets throughout the book, but this section is designed to familiarize you with what presets are and the tools that you use to select and manage them.

Selecting tool presets

The simplest way to select tool presets is from the Preset menu option found in every tool options bar, as shown in Figure 2.26. For the Crop tool, you see presets for each of the standard photo sizes. Selecting one of the presets configures the Crop tool to crop the image to the specific size without your having to change the settings manually.

FIGURE 2.26

The Presets option in the options bar allows you to quickly configure settings for the tool by selecting a preset from a list of tool configurations.

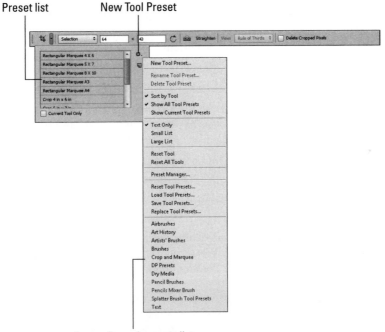

Preset list   New Tool Preset

Preconfigured presets list

From the preset menu shown in Figure 2.26, you have the following options:

- **Preset list.** Displays a list of presets. When you select an item from the list, the options in the tool are set to the values that are stored in the preset.

- **Current Tool Only.** Displays only presets that pertain to the current tool when this box is checked.

- **New Tool Preset.** Enables you to store the current tool settings as a preset when you click this button. The new preset is displayed in the preset list.

- **Rename Tool Preset.** Allows you to change the display name of a tool preset so that you can refer to it more easily. You may end up adding several new presets, so you should keep the names specific.

- **Delete Tool Preset.** Removes the selected tool preset from the list.

- **Sort by Tool.** Sorts the preset list by tool rather than alphabetically when selected.

- **Show All Tool Presets.** Displays all available tool presets in the Preset list when checked. This is useful to switch between tools without selecting them from the Toolbox.

- **Show Current Tool Presets.** Displays the tool presets for only the currently active tool when checked. If you have a lot of tool presets, then you may want to check this item so that it is easier to find them.

- **Display options.** Allow you to display the list as text only, or to include small or large tool icons.

- **Reset Tool.** Resets the settings of the current tool to the default Photoshop values.

- **Reset All Tools.** Resets all tools to the default Photoshop values.

- **Preset Manager.** Launches the Preset Manager, which we will discuss in the next section.

- **Reset Tool Presets.** Resets the current list of tool presets to the stored values. This allows you to discard any changes you have made and go back to the last time you saved them.

- **Load Tool Presets.** Loads a set of tool presets that have previously been saved.

- **Save Tool Presets.** Saves the current tool presets to disk for later retrieval.

- **Replace Tool Presets.** Replaces the current tool presets with one that has been stored on disk.

- **Preconfigured Presets list.** Lists preconfigured presets. For example, the Airbrushes presets contain several brush tip presets for airbrushing and the Crop and Marquee presets contain several presets for the Crop tool.

> **NOTE**
>
> You can select presets from the Tool Presets panel. If you deselect the Current Tool Only option, the list in the tool options bar and in the Tool Presets panel displays all currently loaded presets instead of just those for the current tool. Selecting a preset switches to that tool with the appropriate settings.

Managing presets

Presets are organized into sets, and each set is saved as a separate file on the file system. The Preset Manager allows you to create, load, and manage the sets of tool presets. To access the Preset Manager, choose Edit ⇨ Preset Manager, or click the menu icon of the Preset list shown in Figure 2.27 and choose Preset Manager from the menu.

FIGURE 2.27

The Preset Manager allows you to load, save, and manage presets for Photoshop tools as well as other types of settings such as brushes, text, and colors.

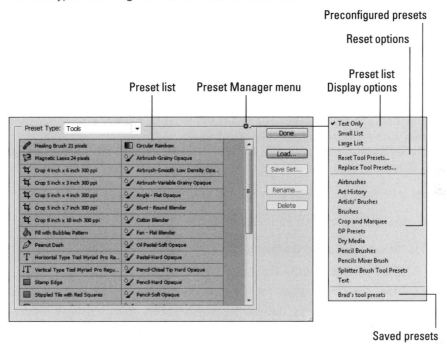

The Preset Manager provides the Preset Type option that allows you to select the preset types. In addition to tool presets, you find presets for paintbrushes, color swatches, styles, and others. When you select a different type, the list of presets changes to reflect the presets for that type.

You can use the mouse to select presets from the list, including any new ones you have created, and then use the Save Set button to save the selected presets as a new set. To load additional presets, click the Load button. When you try to load a new set, you are prompted to add the set to the current list or to append the loaded set to the existing list.

Clicking the Preset Manager Menu button loads a menu similar to the one in Figure 2.27. The menu is different for each preset type, but they are all organized into the following sections:

- **List options.** This option defines how to display the presets. You can select text only, lists with icons, and different sizes of icons, depending on the preset type.

- **Reset/Replace options.** The Reset Tool Presets option resets the preset list for the selected preset type to the Photoshop default. This is a must when you begin tweaking lists and appending sets. The Replace Tool Presets option allows you to load a preset list from a file on disk and replace the current preset list.

- **Preconfigured presets.** Photoshop provides several preconfigured presets that can be applied to the current set. The list of preconfigured presets is different for each preset type. When you select one of these sets, you are prompted to either replace the current list or append the new list to the current list.

Creating presets

When you make changes to a tool's settings in the options bar, Photoshop will remember those settings the next time you select the tool. At times, you will want to quickly toggle between different customized settings. The best way to handle this workflow is to create presets for each of the custom settings. Creating your own custom presets saves you valuable time adjusting settings that you use frequently.

Presets are created differently, depending on what type of preset you are creating.

Follow these steps to create a new tool preset:

1. **Select a tool from the Toolbox.**
2. **Adjust the settings in the options bar.**
3. **Open the Preset option for the tool (refer to Figure 2.27).**
4. **Click the New Preset button.**
5. **Enter the name that you want to use for the preset, and click OK.**

   This permanently saves the preset in the Preset Manager until you delete it.

Follow these steps to create a custom style preset:

1. **Select a layer that is not locked.**
2. **Select one of the options in the Add a Layer Style button at the bottom of the Layers panel to launch the Layer Style dialog box.**
3. **Adjust the options for each effect to be included in the preset.**
4. **Click the New Style button in the Layer Style dialog box, and name the preset.**

Follow these steps to create a custom brush or pattern preset:

1. **Select the pixels you want to use to create the brush or pattern.**

   We discuss area selections in Chapter 9.
2. **Choose Edit ⇨ Define Brush Preset or Edit ⇨ Define Pattern from the Photoshop menu bar.**
3. **Name the brush or pattern and click OK.**
4. **Select the Brush tool if you are creating a custom brush preset.**
5. **Refine the brush or pattern by adjusting the settings in the Brushes panel.**

Follow these steps to create a custom shape preset:

1. **Create a path.**
2. **Select the path in the Paths panel.**
3. **Choose Edit ➪ Define Custom Shape from the Photoshop menu bar.**
4. **Name the shape preset.**

Follow these steps to create a custom color swatch preset:

1. **Click the Foreground color in the Toolbox to launch a Color Picker.**
2. **Define the custom color.**
3. **Hover the mouse cursor over a blank area in the Swatches panel until the cursor changes to a paint bucket.**
4. **Click to add the color to the swatches.**

> **NOTE**
>
> When you save preset lists, the filename must be saved with the appropriate file extension. This actually makes the preset files easy to locate later when Photoshop searches the file system if you forget where you saved them. The default extensions are brushes (.abr), color swatches (.aco), contours (.sch), custom shapes (.csh), gradients (.grd), patterns (.pat), styles (.asl), and tools (.tpl).

Setting Preferences

Setting the preferences allows you to work in a customized environment that feels comfortable to you. Whether you like to have cursors that are more precise or you want your rulers to show centimeters instead of inches, you can make a variety of changes using the Preferences dialog box.

The preferences are under the Edit menu, so choose Edit ➪ Preferences ➪ General on Windows and Photoshop ➪ Preferences ➪ General on the Mac to open the Preferences dialog box in the General pane, as shown in Figure 2.28. All the options available in the Preferences menu are also available in the left pane of the Preferences dialog box, with the exception of the Camera Raw preferences. Simply click one to display the pane you want.

Before you get started setting preferences, though, you'll probably want to know how to restore the Adobe presets, just in case. To restore all the settings to the Adobe Photoshop defaults, press and hold the Ctrl+Alt+Shift/⌘+Option+Shift keys while you open Photoshop. You are asked if you want to delete the current settings. You have a second option if you are running Mac OS: Open the Preferences folder inside the Library folder, and drag the CS settings to the trash. The folder is automatically re-created the next time Photoshop starts.

FIGURE 2.28

The Preferences dialog box allows you to customize many of the settings in Photoshop.

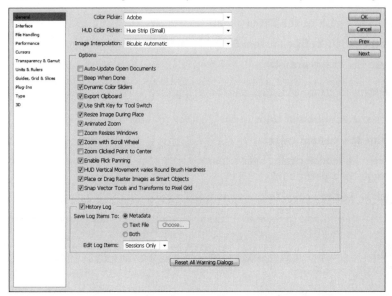

Before you get started setting preferences, though, you'll probably want to know how to restore the Adobe presets, just in case. To restore all the settings to the Adobe Photoshop defaults, press and hold the Ctrl+Alt+Shift/⌘+Option+Shift keys while you open Photoshop. You are asked if you want to delete the current settings. You have a second option if you are running Mac OS: Open the Preferences folder inside the Library folder, and drag the CS settings to the trash. The folder is automatically re-created the next time Photoshop starts.

NOTE

The Library folder in the user's home directory is hidden on the Mac, so you will need to hold down the Option key while clicking on the Go menu to have it appear in the menu.

Updating General preferences

The General preferences panel provides you with the ability to control different aspects of the Photoshop environment. This panel has several basic options that either apply to Photoshop as a whole or just don't fit well into any other menu. This is the place to start looking if you need to find a setting that doesn't directly apply to any of the other preferences panels. From the General preferences panel, you can set the following options:

■ **Color Picker.** When Photoshop operations require you to choose a color, you choose a new background or foreground color using the color picker displayed in the Toolbox. You use a color picker to choose a color. A color picker usually takes the form of a color wheel or a color palette. The Adobe color picker appears by default, and in many cases it's the best choice; it was custom designed for Photoshop, after all. You also have the option to use the standard color picker for your operating system — Mac OS or Windows. For Macs, you will be able to choose from a variety of color pickers such as a wheel and spectrum. At some point, you may install plug-ins that give you additional color picker options. They also display in the Color Picker drop-down menu.

■ **HUD Color Picker.** When you select this option, it allows you to define the style of color picker that is used by the HUD (Heads Up Display).

■ **Image Interpolation.** When images are resized, transformed, or otherwise manipulated, pixels are added or taken away to make up the difference. This is called interpolation, and the method of interpolation determines not only the quality of the resulting image, but also the speed with which the image is processed. Figure 2.29 shows examples of an image of a rose enlarged five times using each method of interpolation. We zoomed in so the difference would be much more obvious.

NOTE

You can change the image interpolation in the Image Size dialog box. A menu includes all the options available. The option you set in the preferences becomes the default option in the Image Size dialog box.

■ **Nearest Neighbor (preserves hard edges).** This option simply copies the pixels and creates identical pixels next to them. This is a much faster process, but for obvious reasons, it creates an image with jagged edges.

■ **Bi-linear.** This option takes the four surrounding pixels and averages them to create a new pixel. This creates a softer look than the Nearest Neighbor option, resulting in a smoother image but at the sacrifice of sharpness.

■ **Bicubic (best for smooth gradients).** This option goes one better than the Bi-linear option by using the eight surrounding pixels to create an average. It also creates more contrast between the pixels, restoring some sharpness to the image.

■ **Bicubic Smoother (best for enlargement).** This option is designed to create the smoothest possible transition when enlarging an image. It reduces the jagged edges and overall "filled-in" look you get when pixels are created to fill in the gaps of an image.

■ **Bicubic Sharper (best for reduction).** This option uses the Bicubic method of interpolation and adds a sharpening filter to further increase the sharpness of the pixels. This option is best for reducing the image size.

FIGURE 2.29

The image interpolation option affects the quality and look of the final image.

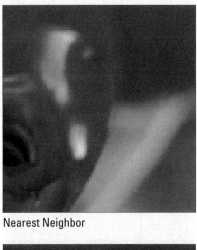
Nearest Neighbor

Bi-linear

Bicubic

Bicubic Smoother

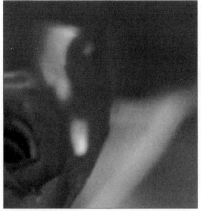
Bicubic Sharper

> **NOTE**
>
> It should be obvious from reading about image interpolation that the more you manipulate an image, the more that image deteriorates. Although some changes are usually necessary to get the results you desire, be careful how many steps you take to create those changes. If you want to make an image smaller, for instance, and you reduce it more than you anticipated, don't just make the reduced image larger. Step backward and undo the first resize and then try reducing again. You may also want to check out some of the third-party plug-ins available on the Adobe Marketplace website for enlarging images.

- **Auto-Update Open Documents.** This option tells Photoshop to automatically check the hard disk for changes made to any open file, and to update the file to reflect the saved changes. The best time to use this option is when two or more collaborators are working on the same file and you want to keep up with the changes being made by others.

- **Beep When Done.** This option causes Photoshop to beep whenever it finishes an operation. This is useful if you are making less obvious changes and want to be sure the operation is finished, or you're performing more time-consuming operations and you want to walk away from your computer while they process.

- **Dynamic Color Sliders.** When you open the Adobe color picker, you use a color slider to change the range of colors visible in the color selection box. With Dynamic Color Sliders turned on, as you move the slider, the box changes color in real time. The only reason to turn off this option is if you are using a computer that was built sometime in the last millennium and it just can't handle the real-time change without slowing you down.

- **Export Clipboard.** This option allows you to copy or cut content from Photoshop and paste it into other applications by copying the Photoshop clipboard to the operating system's Clipboard.

- **Use Shift Key for Tool Switch.** This option allows you to switch tools by pressing the Shift key and the hotkey. If this option is turned off, pressing the hotkey more than once cycles through the available tools. The Toolbox includes "tool drawers," where one or more tools hide behind the visible icons in the Toolbox. Hotkeys also provide access to these tools.

- **Resize Image During Place.** This option resizes a placed image to fit the destination document into which you are pasting it. For instance, if you are placing a very large file into an open image that is much smaller, the document resizes to fit into the smaller canvas area. If this option is not turned on, the larger document may overlap the canvas area, hiding the entire image. Keep in mind that any resizing compromises the image quality and should be kept to a minimum if possible.

- **Animated Zoom.** This option allows you to continuously zoom with the Zoom tool by pressing and holding the left mouse button. It's a great way to control how far you want to zoom in (or out), but be warned: it can be a little slow with larger files.

- **Zoom Resizes Windows.** This option works only if you are using floating windows for each of your documents. These windows are resized as your images are resized. This eliminates the white space around images that have been reduced and keeps the images that you've zoomed into in view, instead of hanging out of the edges of your window. If you use floating windows a lot, we suggest turning this option on.

- **Zoom with Scroll Wheel.** This is our personal favorite zoom preference. With this option activated, you can use the scroll wheel of your mouse, if it has one, to zoom in and out of the selected image. No looking around for the Zoom tool or trying to remember its hotkey; just use the scroll wheel, and you can take a closer look at that area of your image you are trying to get just right and then zoom right back out to fit it in the screen.

- **Zoom Point Clicked to Center.** This option extends the function of the Zoom tool. When you click an area of your image with the Zoom tool, it zooms into that area generally, but with the Zoom Point Clicked to Center option turned on, the area you click becomes the center of the zoomed image.

- **Enable Flick Panning.** This option enables you to pan smoothly around an image. You can use the Hand tool to click the document, drag quickly, and then release the mouse button, and the document continues to pan just as if you had flicked it.

- **HUD Vertical Movement varies Round Brush Hardness.** This option affects the Heads Up Display (HUD). When you select it, vertical movements in the HUD adjust the hardness of the Round Brush tip instead of the opacity.

- **Place or Drag Raster Images as Smart Objects.** This option allows you to drag and place raster images in layers. Photoshop does this by temporarily converting them to Smart Objects and then back to raster images. This option can use a lot of processing power, so you should enable it only if you are willing to sacrifice some computer speed.

- **Snap Vector Tools and Transforms to Pixel Grid.** This option automatically snaps edits done by vector tools and transforms to the pixel grid.

- **History Log.** This option lets you keep a log of what editing has been done to the file using the following settings:

  - **Save Log Items To.** This option lets you store the history as metadata inside the actual image file, as a separate text file, or both. Keeping a log as metadata makes the history data easy to transfer between systems, but it increases the size of the file, and you need to remove the history before distributing it to others.

    - **Edit Log Items.** This option allows you to specify how detailed the history is. The Sessions Only option records only the date and time you edit the file in Photoshop. The Concise option also records the text that appears in the History panel. The Detailed option also records the commands used to edit the file. Obviously, the more detailed the history, the more the file size grows.

- **Reset All Warning Dialogs.** This option enables any warning dialog boxes that have been disabled when you selected a warning dialog box's "Don't Show Again" option.

Arranging Interface preferences

The Interface preferences pane provides options for you to configure how the Photoshop workspace looks and performs. For example, you can specify colors and how panels behave. The Interface pane, shown in Figure 2.30, allows you to define the general look of the Photoshop interface, including windows, panels, and documents, using the following settings:

FIGURE 2.30

The Interface settings in the Preferences dialog box allow you to define the look and feel of the windows, documents, and panels in Photoshop.

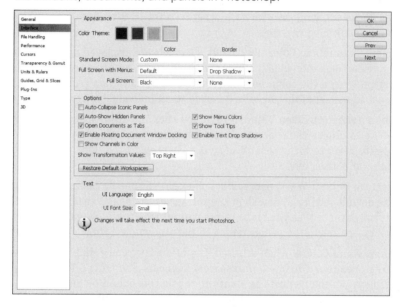

- **Appearance.** These options define the general appearance of Photoshop by setting the following options:
  - **Color Theme.** Allows you to select from four different Dark UI color themes. Each of these themes will set the menu, option bar, panel and document window background colors to different levels of darkness. This is a great feature to quickly change the appearance to be darker if you prefer to work in a darker UI.
  - **Standard Screen Mode.** Allows you to define the background color and border of windows when working in the standard screen mode.
  - **Full Screen with Menus.** Allows you to define the background color and border of windows when working in the full screen with windows mode.
  - **Full Screen.** Allows you to define the background color and border of windows when working in the full screen mode.

- **Panels & Documents.** When these options are selected, they define the behavior of panels and document windows using the following options:

  - **Auto-Collapse Iconic Panels.** When enabled, panels that are opened by clicking the panel icon close automatically when you click another panel or tool in the workspace.

  - **Auto-Show Hidden Panels.** When enabled, this reveals hidden panels on rollover.

  - **Open Documents as Tabs.** When enabled, files are opened in tabbed document windows that are docked to the document workspace. When disabled, files are opened in a floating document window.

  - **Enable Floating Document Window Docking.** When selected, you can dock floating document windows with each other to make floating document groups that can be controlled together.

  - **Show Channels in Color.** By default, channels are displayed in grayscale when you view them individually. Displaying the channels in color can give you a better perspective on the color, but it's not the best option when trying to determine tonal adjustments that need to be made to an individual channel. See Chapter 11.

  - **Show Transformation Values.** When you click the down-arrow, the list specifies where to display the contextual transformation value next to the cursor. You can specify never to turn them off or to display them at top right, top left, bottom right, or bottom left.

  - **Restore Default Workspaces.** When clicked, this button resets the workspace to the default settings. Photoshop keeps track of the panels that are opened and layout changes that you make to the current workspace. When you open the workspace again, the panels return to the way you left them.

  - **Show Menu Colors.** When selected, the colors that you define by choosing Edit ➪ Menus or Window ➪ Workspace ➪ Keyboard Shortcuts & Menus ➪ Menus are displayed in the menus. The ability to toggle this option on and off can be useful if the menu colors are distracting for some of your workflows.

  - **Show Tool Tips.** When selected, a textual description of tools, settings, windows, and panels is displayed when you hover the mouse over these items.

  - **Enable Text Drop Shadows.** When selected, text on panels has a drop shadow. This can make the interface look better.

- **User Interface Text option.** When selected, this allows you to set the language and font size used for the text in the Photoshop menus, tools, panels, and so on. You need to restart Photoshop after changing these settings.

Setting File Handling preferences

You can use the File Handling preferences to configure options for saving files, such as background saves, auto recovery, and file compatibility. The File Handling preferences pane, shown in Figure 2.31, provides the following settings to define behavior when saving files:

FIGURE 2.31

The File Handling settings in the Preferences dialog box allow you to configure options such as compatibility settings for when you save files.

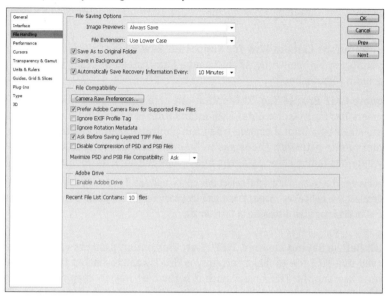

- **File Saving Options.** These options control the following behavior when saving files:

  - **Image Previews.** This option controls whether to save the preview thumbnail data to a file when you save the image. Options are Never Save, Always Save, or Ask When Saving.

  - **File Extension.** This option specifies to save the extension in uppercase or lower-case format.

  - **Save As to Original Folder.** This option causes Photoshop to default to the original folder the file was opened from when you choose File ⇨ Save As.

  - **Save in Background.** This option saves images in the background rather than asking you to wait. This can be extremely useful when you are trying to work with large images. You can save them and go back to working on them while Photoshop works on saving them.

  - **Automatically Save Recovery Information Every.** This option saves recovery information necessary to restore files in case a serious computer problem forces Photoshop to shut down. This is a great feature, but it also affects performance while the current file recovery data is being saved, especially if you have several files open. If Photoshop or your computer does crash, the files that were open will be opened again with 'recovery' in the filename, and you have the option of saving any work that was lost before the last recovery save. The default interval is 10 minutes; however, you can change this value to suit your needs.

- **File Compatibility.** These options provide the following settings for file compatibility when saving files:

  - **Camera Raw Preferences.** This button launches a dialog box where you can set Camera Raw preferences. See Chapter 7 for more information about Camera Raw settings.

  - **Prefer Adobe Camera Raw for Supported Raw Files.** This option causes Camera Raw files to be opened by Adobe Camera Raw instead of other applications, including Photoshop.

  - **Ignore EXIF Profile Tag.** This option can help you to determine whether your camera has faulty color data. EXIF information is data about a photo that is embedded by a digital camera when the photo is taken. Cameras typically embed color profile data with the image to help ensure color correctness. However, if the camera has faulty color data, the image may not look as good as it should.

 If your photos aren't looking quite right, select this option and see if they look better. If not, you may need to deselect this option for images taken with that camera. You may also try assigning a different color profile to the image, as discussed in Chapter 29.

  - **Ask Before Saving Layered TIFF Files.** This option prompts you before layers are saved in a TIFF file to make certain you don't want to flatten the file. We recommend keeping the TIFF layers since it is the best way to keep the file in a very editable state with the full range of data. However, saving layers in the TIFF file may result in a much larger file size, and some applications that support TIFFs do not support layers. Keep this setting on, just as a reminder when saving TIFF files.

  - **Disable Compression of PSD and PSB Files.** This option disables Photoshop from compressing PSD or PSB files. This increases the compatibility and slightly improves quality in certain settings; however, it also increases the size of the file on disk.

  - **Maximize PSD and PSB File Compatibility.** This option controls whether Photoshop tries to maximize the PSD compatibility between older versions of Photoshop when you save an image. Options are Never, Always, or Ask. Maximizing compatibility is good, but it comes at the cost of greater file size. This preference defaults to Ask, but if you know that you will never use an older version of Photoshop, disabling it saves you an extra mouse click.

- **Enable Adobe Drive.** This option enables Adobe Version Cue through Adobe Drive, which manages file versions when multiple people need to work on the same files. Version Cue can track changes to a file as different people work on it. This option should be enabled only if you are using Version Cue.

- **Recent File List Contains.** This option specifies the number of files to show in the File ➪ Open Recent File list. You may want to change this option based on the type of project that you are working on.

Adjusting Performance preferences

The Performance preferences pane in Photoshop provides options that allow you to configure settings that can help it perform better. Photoshop is a very memory- and disk-intensive application and as such, the better you adjust the performance, the faster it can perform complex operations such as Puppet Warp and Liquify. There are several settings that you can adjust in Photoshop, such as scratch disks, memory usage, and graphics processing, to improve its performance. The Performance preferences pane, shown in Figure 2.32, provides the following settings to improve some of the Photoshop features that are performance-intensive:

FIGURE 2.32

The Performance settings in the Preferences dialog box allow you to limit Photoshop so it does not consume resources on your system.

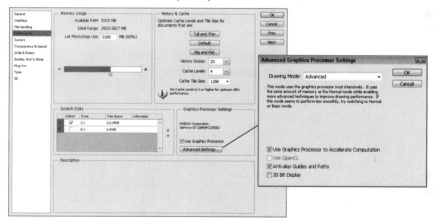

- **Memory Usage.** This section defines how much system memory Photoshop is allowed to consume. It displays the current system memory and gives a suggested range. The slider and text box define the maximum amount of RAM Photoshop is allowed to use. Processing images is very CPU- and RAM-intensive. The more RAM you allow Photoshop to consume, the faster it performs; however, less memory is available for other applications.

> **CAUTION**
>
> Allowing Photoshop to consume too much memory can lead to extremely poor system performance that affects all applications, even Photoshop. This is one case where more is not necessarily better.

- **Scratch Disks.** This section displays a list of devices that you can select for scratch disks. Photoshop uses scratch disks to cache data not currently being used when it is processing data that requires more memory than the system has available.

> **TIP**
>
> You get the best performance when working with Photoshop if you use three separate disk drives to store the Photoshop application, scratch data, and image files. This is because the disks can be seeking the three types of data at the same time. Keep in mind that putting 3 USB disks on the same hub will create a bottleneck that will actually degrade performance in some cases.

- **History & Cache.** This section defines settings for document caching and history retention that can improve how Photoshop performs. You have the following choices:

  - **Optimize buttons.** These three buttons optimize the cache for documents that are Tall and Thin, the Default size, or Big and Flat. These options take into account your computer hardware and current system settings.

  - **History States.** This option specifies the number of history states to cache. These history states are accessible from the History panel, as described in Chapter 5. A higher number gives you more states that you can use to backtrack changes but consumes more memory.

  - **Cache Levels.** This option allows you to define the behavior of the cache. Caching improves performance by storing lower-resolution versions of the image to display in the document window. This allows for much faster rendering by Photoshop. A setting of 1 essentially disables caching because the full image size is stored in the cache. This gives you a more accurate view of the image but results in slower rendering times. Increasing the cache number stores more low-resolution versions of the image, which improves performance while sacrificing rendering quality in Photoshop. You need to restart Photoshop for changes to the cache to take effect.

  - **Cache Tile Size.** This option specifies the number of bytes that Photoshop stores or processes at once. Typically, the rule is to use a larger tile size when working with larger images and a smaller tile size when working with smaller images or images with a lot of layers. You need to restart Photoshop for changes to the Cache Tile Size to take effect.

- **Graphics Processor Settings.** This section contains the Use Graphics Processor option, which allows you to enable or disable OpenGL drawing by your video adapter. OpenGL drawing uses the processor on your graphics adapter to render images. Using the video adapter to draw can significantly improve performance in many of the Photoshop features such as the Zoom, 3D, and Paint tools. Enabling OpenGL also enables several advanced features in Photoshop, such as the rotate view, bird's-eye zooming, pixel grid, and flick to scroll.

  Clicking the Advanced Settings button loads the Advanced Graphics Processor Settings dialog box, shown in Figure 2.32, that allows you to choose from the following drawing modes for OpenGL:

  - **Basic mode.** This mode uses the smallest amount of GPU memory and has the least impact on other applications running OpenGL features on the system. However, it can result in slowness in some areas of Photoshop that are GPU-intensive, such as 3D.

- **Normal mode.** This mode uses the greatest amount of GPU memory and enables additional OpenGL features, but may cause visual defects on some GPUs.

- **Advanced mode.** This mode uses the same amount of memory as Normal mode but enables even more OpenGL features that can improve performance and enhance some of the Photoshop rendering features such as zoom animation. This mode may also cause visual defects on some GPUs and interfere with other applications using the GPU.

- **Use Graphics Processor to Accelerate Computation.** This option improves the performance-heavy processing operations such as the Puppet Warp preview.

- **Use OpenCL.** This option turns on the OpenCL processing to improve performance if it is supported by the graphics adapter.

- **Anti-alias Guides and Paths.** This option causes Photoshop to anti-alias guides and paths, which makes them render more cleanly on screen. However, this also slightly impacts performance.

- **30 Bit Display.** This option increases the color fidelity on the monitor to 30 bits if it is supported.

Configuring Cursors preferences

One of the most important tools in Photoshop is the cursor. The cursor tells you where you are in the document, which in turn allows you to make precise edits and selections. The Cursor preferences allow you to configure the cursors to best fit your needs. The Cursors preferences pane, shown in Figure 2.33, provides the following settings to define the appearance and size of mouse or stylus cursors:

- **Painting Cursors.** This section defines the appearance and size of the cursor used with painting tools such as the brush. You can choose from these options:

  - **Standard.** This looks like the painting tool icon.

  - **Precise.** This displays a crosshair, which is much better for seeing the exact center of the brush stroke.

  - **Normal Brush Tip.** This creates a circle the size of the paint stroke, not taking into account any feathering caused by brush settings. This option is better for seeing the immediate area that will be affected by the brush stroke.

  - **Full Size Brush Tip.** This creates a circle that is the full pixel size of the paint stroke, including any feathered edges. This option is better for seeing the full area that will be affected by the brush stroke.

  - **Show Crosshair in Brush Tip.** This displays a crosshair in the center of the Normal and Full Size Brush tips.

  - **Show Only Crosshairs While Painting.** This changes from the Normal Brush Tip or Full Size Brush Tip to the Crosshair Tip when you are dragging the mouse. This allows you to see the size of the brush better before using the precision tip.

- **Other Cursors.** This section defines the brush tip cursor used for tools other than the painting tool.
- **Brush Preview.** This section allows you to use a color chooser to define the color that is used for the brush editing preview.

FIGURE 2.33

The Cursors settings in the Preferences dialog box allow you to set the size and appearance of cursors when working with the Photoshop tools.

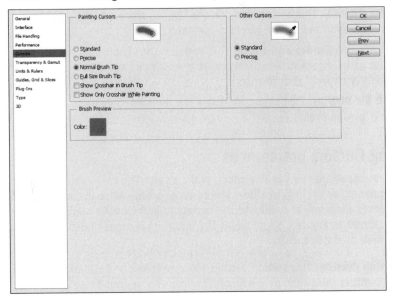

Setting Transparency & Gamut preferences

The Transparency & Gamut preferences pane is used to configure how transparent pixels appear in the document workspace. This allows you to distinguish transparent pixels from the background color. This pane, shown in Figure 2.34, provides the following settings to define the appearance of the transparency grid and gamut warning:

FIGURE 2.34

The Transparency & Gamut settings in the Preferences dialog box allow you to define the appearance of the transparency grid and gamut warning.

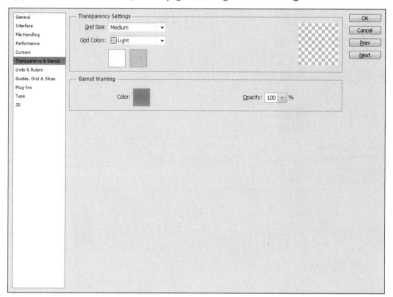

- **Transparency Settings.** This section allows you to set the size and colors of the grid used to denote transparent pixels in an image. The Grid Size options are None, Small, Medium, and Large. The Grid Colors setting provides several predefined color sets, or you can select Custom to choose your own set of colors for the grid. Typically, you have no reason to adjust the transparency colors unless you have a pattern that is similar in the image you are editing.

- **Gamut Warning.** This section allows you to specify the color used to warn you when a color is out of range for a specified color profile — for example, when you choose View ⇨ Gamut Warning or are previewing inside the Print dialog box (File ⇨ Print). The Opacity setting defines how transparent or opaque the gamut warning is when displayed. Reducing the opacity allows you to more easily see the image behind the gamut warning.

Using Units & Rulers preferences

The Units & Rulers preferences pane enables Photoshop to be versatile in representing measurements of rulers, text, and images. For example, you may want to use inches when editing one image and centimeters in another, or you may want to measure your text in millimeters instead of points. The Units & Rulers preferences pane, shown in Figure 2.35, provides the following settings to define the units, column sizes, document resolution, and point size to use in Photoshop:

FIGURE 2.35

The Units & Rulers settings in the Preferences dialog box allow you to define the units, column sizes, document resolution, and point size.

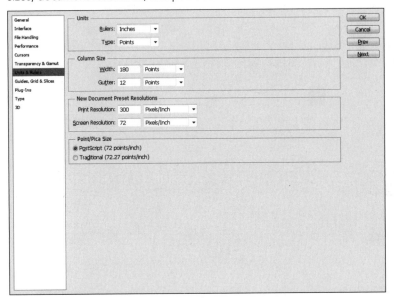

- **Units.** This section allows you to control the units used by the rulers and with type. The Rulers option specifies the units used for rulers and measurements in Photoshop. The Type option specifies the units for all the settings used by the Type tools as well as the Character and Paragraph panels.

  The options are pixels, inches, centimeters, millimeters, points, picas, and percent (where percent is in relation to the size of the image). When working in a print work-flow, using inches or picas is best. When working in a web workflow, using pixels is typically best.

- **Column Size.** This section is useful if you are preparing an image or multiple images that can be broken into columns. Several Photoshop dialog boxes use column width as a unit of measurement, including the New, Image Size, and Canvas Size dialog boxes. The columns in those dialog boxes are based on the Column Size settings.

- **New Document Preset Resolutions.** This section allows you to specify the default print and screen resolutions used when creating a new document with the File ⇨ New command from the Photoshop menu bar. Keep in mind that the screen resolution is important for images that are viewed on a computer, such as web images, but print resolution determines the print quality and size of the printed image.

- **Point/Pica Size.** This section allows you to set the number of points and picas in an inch. The PostScript method defines a pica as about 1/6 inch and a point as about 1/72 inch. Applications from years ago used a different system where there were 6.06 picas per inch and 72.27 points per inch. You should choose the Postscript setting unless you have a specific reason for using the traditional method.

Adjusting Guides, Grid, and Slices preferences

The Guides, Grid, and Slices preferences pane allows you to configure the color and look of guides, grids, and slices. Depending on the colors in the document you are working on, you may want to change the color of these lines to be more visible. Also, depending on how precise you would like to be in your image, you may want to make the grid spacing larger or smaller, especially if you are using the Snap to Grid feature. The Guides, Grid, and Slices preferences pane, shown in Figure 2.36, provides the following settings to define the color, line style, and arrangement used when displaying guides, grids, and slice bounding boxes in the document window:

FIGURE 2.36

The Guides, Grid, and Slices settings in the Preferences dialog box allow you to define the color, line style, and arrangement used to display guides, gridlines, and slice bounding boxes in document windows.

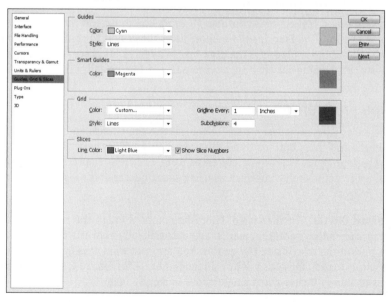

- **Guides.** This section allows you to set the color and line style for guides. You can choose any color from the menu or select Custom to launch a color chooser that lets you select any color Photoshop can display. You typically want to set the guide color to something that has a high contrast with the colors in the image so that you can see it better. You can also choose to make the guide a dashed or solid line.

- **Smart Guides.** This section allows you to set the color of the smart guides only. Smart guides are the lines that temporarily appear around the pixels on a layer when you move items. Smart guides are great at helping you align the content of one layer with the content of another layer.

- **Grid.** This section allows you to set the color and line style used when displaying the grid. You want to select a color that contrasts well with the image and also contrasts with the color of the guides so you can easily distinguish the lines from each other. You can also set the spacing between grid lines and the number of subdivisions to include between grid lines. Subdivisions show up as less apparent lines.

- **Slices.** This section allows you to specify the color of slice bounding boxes and whether to display the slice number when displaying the slice.

 For more information about slices, see Chapter 30.

Configuring Plug-ins preferences

Plug-ins are a very useful feature of Photoshop, allowing you to extend the product beyond its original programming. The Plug-ins preferences pane allows you to configure options that control the behavior of these plug-ins. The plug-ins preferences are discussed in Appendix B, along with several of the plug-ins that are available to add functionality to Photoshop.

Setting Type preferences

The Type preferences pane provides options to control the appearance and behavior of the type tools. You can use these options to do things such as enabling smart quotes that cannot be enabled in the type tools. The Type preferences pane, shown in Figure 2.37, provides the following settings to define behaviors such as using smart quotes and substituting fonts when adding text to images:

- **Use Smart Quotes.** When enabled, Photoshop scans through the text, detects the starting and ending quotation marks, and automatically converts them to quotes that curve toward the text inside the quotes. You may not want this option enabled if you are using text that contains a lot of single quotes — for example, using double quotes to signify inches and a single quote to signify feet.

 For more information about fonts, glyphs, and adding text to images, see Chapter 18.

- **Enable Missing Glyph Protection.** When enabled, Photoshop automatically makes font substitutions for any missing glyphs that appear in the text, but not in the selected font. This option can be important if you are keeping text as a vector layer and transferring the file between machines. When loaded on the second machine, if the font is not present, Photoshop automatically makes a font substitution. If this option is disabled, Photoshop prompts you first.

- **Show Font Names in English.** When enabled, the names of fonts in the font list always appear in English, even if you are working with different language fonts.

FIGURE 2.37

The Type settings in the Preferences dialog box allow you to define behaviors such as using smart quotes and substituting fonts when adding text to images.

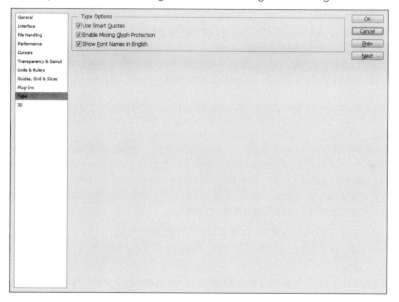

Adjusting 3D preferences

The 3D preferences pane in Photoshop Extended allows you to configure several features of the 3D tools. You can use these preference settings to enhance performance, improve object rendering, and define the look and feel of many of the 3D controls. The concepts surrounding 3D preferences are tightly coupled with the 3D chapters in this book. Therefore, we included a description of the 3D preferences in Chapter 22. Refer to that chapter for information about setting 3D preferences.

Customizing Shortcuts and Menus

Photoshop provides a tremendous amount of power by including a lot of features. Unfortunately, that means Photoshop also had to include a lot of menus. With the sheer number of menus and tools that Photoshop has to offer, you can quickly find yourself spending more time finding tools than using them. The solution to that problem is to customize your menus and to use keyboard shortcuts.

> **TIP**
>
> You can create and name several customized shortcuts or menu sets. You may want to create different sets for the type of editing you are doing and then load the set that best matches your workflow.

Customizing menus

Photoshop allows you to customize the menus in two ways: you can hide menu items that you do not intend to use, or you can color code menu items to make them easier to find. To customize the Photoshop menu bar, select Edit ➪ Menus from the Photoshop menu bar to display the Menus tab of the Keyboard Shortcuts and Menus dialog box, shown in Figure 2.38.

From the Menus tab, you can use the following options to create and manage customized menu sets:

- **Set.** This option allows you to select the default menu set or a saved menu set from the drop-down list. The Save Set icon next to the Set list allows you to save changes to the currently selected set. The New Set icon allows you to save the current menu configuration as a new set that is displayed in the Set list. The Delete Set icon removes the currently selected set from the list.

  To create a new custom menu, first make all adjustments to the menus, then click the New Set icon, and finally name the set. You can then reload that set any time you like.

- **Menu For.** This option allows you to choose whether you want to edit the application menus or the panel menus. When you change this option, either the application or panel menus are displayed, depending on which option you choose.

- **Menu list.** This list displays a selection of menus that can be adjusted. You can expand and collapse a menu in the list by clicking the triangle next to the menu name. When the menu is expanded, you can customize each menu option by doing the following:

  - **Change visibility.** You can use the mouse to toggle the eye icon to hide or show the menu item in Photoshop. Figure 2.38 shows that the Background option is hidden while the others are visible.

  - **Change color.** You can change the color used for the background of the menu item. This allows you to color code certain menu types or highlight important menu items so you can more easily find them. To change the color, select a color from the drop-down menu shown in Figure 2.38.

FIGURE 2.38

The Keyboard Shortcuts and Menus dialog box allows you to create custom menus that hide unwanted items and display important items in organized colors.

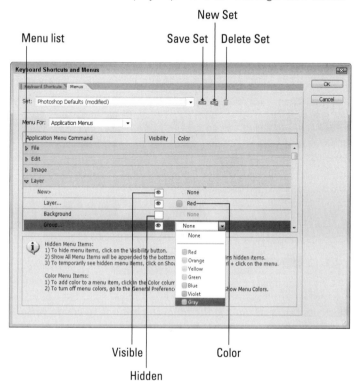

Customizing shortcuts

One of the best ways to speed up your workflow in Photoshop is by using keyboard shortcuts. Keyboard shortcuts allow you to use a key sequence to quickly perform tasks, select tools, and open panels. Throughout this book, we include the important keyboard shortcuts when describing various tools. If you take the time to learn and use these shortcuts, you will be more efficient at using Photoshop.

> **CAUTION**
>
> You should be careful not to use system wide shortcut combinations or shortcuts that are in use with other programs that you plan to use while you are using Photoshop. This can cause conflicts that result in confusion and mistakes.

Photoshop also allows you to customize the keyboard shortcuts. To customize keyboard shortcuts in Photoshop, choose Edit ➪ Keyboard Shortcuts from the Photoshop menu bar to display the Keyboard Shortcuts tab of the Keyboard Shortcuts and Menus dialog box, shown in Figure 2.39.

FIGURE 2.39

The Keyboard Shortcuts and Menus dialog box allows you to customize the keyboard shortcuts that you use to perform common tasks in Photoshop.

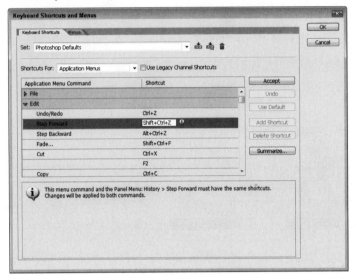

From the Keyboard Shortcuts tab, you can use the following options to create customized keyboard shortcut sets:

- **Set.** This option allows you to select the default shortcut set or a saved shortcut set from the drop-down list. As with the customizing menus, the Save Set icon next to the Set list allows you to save changes to the currently selected set. The New Set icon allows you to save the current keyboard shortcuts as a new set that is displayed in the Set list. The Delete Set icon removes the currently selected set from the list.

  To create a new custom shortcut set, make all adjustments to the shortcuts, click the New Set icon, and name the set. You can then reload that set any time you like.

- **Shortcuts For.** This option allows you to select whether to edit the shortcuts for application menus, panel menus, or tools. When you change this option, the list below changes to reflect the option you choose.

- **Use Legacy Channel Shortcuts.** This option changes the channel switching shortcuts back to the pre-CS4 form for users who are familiar with those options.

- **Item list.** This list displays a selection of shortcuts for the type selected in the Shortcuts For option. You can expand and collapse items in the list by clicking the triangle next to the item name.

To change or add a shortcut to an item, click in the Shortcut column of that item. A text box appears with a cursor. When you type a key sequence into the text box, that key sequence is added to the text box. Figure 2.39 shows an example of the text box and key sequence for the Open menu item. To apply the key sequence as a shortcut, click the Accept button. To undo the change you made, click the Undo button. To revert to the Photoshop default, click the Use Default button.

- **Add Shortcut.** This button adds an additional shortcut to the item so it has two shortcuts. This may help if you are accustomed to different shortcuts from other applications.

- **Delete Shortcut.** This button removes the selected shortcut from the item.

- **Summarize.** This button launches a dialog box that allows you to select a location to store an HTML summary of the keyboard shortcuts. After the file is saved, the summary is automatically displayed in your default web browser, as shown in Figure 2.40. This is a good way to review the settings that you made.

 Appendix A contains tables that provide a quick reference to the most commonly used keyboard shortcuts.

FIGURE 2.40

The Summarize option of the Keyboard Shortcuts and Menus dialog box generates a viewable HTML document that displays the current keyboard shortcuts.

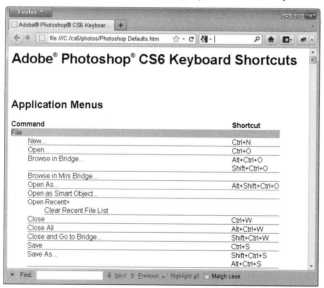

Summary

This chapter discussed the Photoshop workspace, including the document windows, menus, panels, tools, and preferences. Photoshop provides a lot of power, and if you learn how to configure and use the workspace, you can be more efficient and have much more fun.

Photoshop provides an intuitive interface in most areas and some powerful features, such as grouping document windows and customizing menus, that enable you to speed up your workflow.

In this chapter, you learned the following:

- How to organize and arrange document windows
- What's in all those menus
- How to use grids, rulers, and guidelines
- All about the tools in the Toolbox and where they are covered in this book
- How to organize panels
- How to create keyboard shortcuts to make Photoshop easier to use
- How to create and save tool presets so that you can easily configure tools for later use

Performing Image Basics

The purpose of Photoshop is to edit image files that have come from a variety of sources. Photoshop supports a large number of file formats. The different file formats can be confusing, so this chapter briefly discusses each of the different file formats to help you understand some of the benefits and drawbacks of each one.

In this chapter, you learn some important concepts about file size and resolution. Understanding the relationship between the file size, the resolution, and the ultimate destination of the file helps you to know what size and resolution to use for an image. You also learn about the different types of algorithms that Photoshop uses to resample images when changing their size. Understanding the algorithms helps you to know which ones to use to get the best results when resizing images.

This chapter also discusses how and why you should crop images. You learn how to use several tools in Photoshop to accurately crop, trim, rotate, and straighten images quickly.

Exploring File Types

If you have worked with images long enough, you have probably come across a variety of file formats. Although having just one file format would be great, the fact is that numerous file formats serve a variety of purposes. You need to understand the different types of image, video, and 3D file formats to really make the most of the features in Photoshop. Understanding the different file formats helps you make better decisions about how to save and work with files.

The following sections focus on helping you to understand the different types of file formats, where they came from, and why you should use them. After you understand these formats, you can make better decisions when importing and saving files with Photoshop.

Understanding compressed versus uncompressed

The first concept you need to understand about file formats is whether they store the file in a compressed or uncompressed form. Each format has its advantages, which is why both types exist.

An uncompressed file stores the full image, video, or 3D data in the same format in which it exists when you open the file. The size of the file on disk is the same as the size of the file in memory. A compressed file stores the data by using complex algorithms that allow you to store the file using less space on your disk. When you reopen the file, the data on disk is uncompressed using an inverse algorithm and loaded into the application in a viewable/editable form.

The advantage of using uncompressed file formats is that you always retain the data. Also, uncompressed formats are faster to load and save because the computer does not need to compress or uncompress them. The advantage of using compressed file formats is that they take up much less room on disk. With a lot of large images and especially with video, this becomes a big concern.

Two types of compression algorithms are used: lossless compression and lossy compression. The lossless compression algorithm loads the image back into memory in exactly the same state that it was before compression. However, the lossy compression algorithms "cheat" and throw away data that is not very relevant to displaying the image or video.

> **TIP**
>
> Lossy compression offers a major advantage in that you can store large images and video in a much smaller space. However, the major disadvantage is that every time you save an image using a lossy compression algorithm, you lose a bit more data. The first time you save, it probably doesn't matter much. However, after several saves, you start seeing some artifacts in the image or video. To avoid this, use a lossless or uncompressed file type when you are editing the file; when you are finished editing it, save it in the lossy format for storage. Keep a copy of the original around if you might need to edit the file again.

Using raster versus vector

Another file format concept that you need to understand is the difference between raster (or bitmap) and vector images. The data for an image is stored completely differently in these two file types. The image data is stored in raster images as a set of pixels in the image. Each pixel represents one point of light in the image. The image is constructed onscreen by simply applying the pixel data in the image to a pixel on the screen.

The data for a vector image is stored as a series of path data items instead of individual pixels. Each path data item contains the points, lines, and curves values as well as stroke and fill color that are used to render the path. These paths make up the vector image. The image is rendered constructed onscreen by using the path data to draw a series of paths.

The major advantage of using vector images is that no matter how much you increase the size of the image, the lines are always crisp because they can be redrawn each time. Another advantage of using vector images is that you can perform extremely accurate and clean adjustments to curves that are possible in raster images. The disadvantage is that you cannot make pixel-by-pixel adjustments, paint, and morph them in the same way that you can raster images.

The advantage of using raster images is that for photos and other complex images, generating enough vector lines to make the resolution good enough to view can be difficult, if not impossible. Pixels offer a much closer representation of how monitors, printers, and even the human eye work.

Most of the image file formats you use in Photoshop are raster images. Raster images are much better for storing image data and allow you to capture much more detail. You will generally use vector images when working with 3D images, text, line shapes, and paths in Photoshop.

Introducing HDR images

High Dynamic Range (HDR) images are comprised of a set of photographs taken at different exposures in a technique known as exposure bracketing. The exact same photo is taken multiple times using different ISO settings and f-stops to create a wide range of exposures for the same image. These photos can then be combined to create an HDR image with a much greater tonal range than is possible in a single photo.

Photoshop provides some tools to create and adjust HDR images. Chapter 6 discusses using the Bridge tools to create an HDR image. Chapter 13 discusses some of the tools used to adjust HDR images.

Understanding image files

Photoshop supports a variety of image file types. Most people tend to work with one or two types and leave the others alone. However, having a basic understanding of all file types helps you make better choices when you have to work with them. The following sections describe some image file types as well as their advantages and disadvantages.

Photoshop (*.PSD; *.PDD)

Photoshop natively uses its own Photoshop PSD file format. This file format contains all the information relevant to working with the image within Photoshop. For example, all the layer data you have created when working with the image is stored in the PSD file.

Use the PSD file format when working with an image in Photoshop. The work that you do in Photoshop to create adjustment layers and other changes usually represents a lot of effort. The PSD file is the only format that stores all your work so you can fine-tune your adjustments later.

The Photoshop file format maintains the full image data, so you need not worry about saving it multiple times. Photoshop PSD files can store image data in 8 bits per channel, 16 bits per channel, and 32 bits per channel. One disadvantage of the Photoshop file format is that it takes up a large amount of disk space compared with some of the other file formats.

Tagged Image File Format (*.TIF; *.TIFF)

Tagged Image File Format (TIFF) is the next best format after PSD when saving your files. You can store TIFF images in 8 bits per channel, 16 bits per channel, and 32 bits per channel. Advantages of the TIFF file format are that it stores the layers that you create in Photoshop and can store transparency in the form of an alpha channel (discussed later in this book).

TIFF images are also relatively large, so you may not want to use this file format for most images you will be working with. Another disadvantage is that TIFF images are typically not supported in web browsers, so you can't add them to web pages.

Joint Photographic Experts Group (*.JPG; *.JPEG; *.JPE)

JPEG, named after the Joint Photographic Experts Group, has become the most commonly used image format. The JPEG format provides very good image quality, supporting 16.8 million colors, combined with one of the best compression algorithms. This makes JPEG images the best quality for the file size that you can get. Consequently, most digital point-and-shoot cameras use the JPEG image format by default.

Almost every computer program can read JPEG images, and you can easily incorporate them into web pages. They also take up much less disk space than PSD and TIFF files because they are compressed.

JPEG 2000 (*.JP2; *.JPX)

The JPEG 2000 file format allows you to use either a lossless or lossy encoding and compression algorithm. The default compression format is lossy. In addition, the JPEG 2000 file format supports 16-bit color for a greater range of colors, grayscale images, and 8-bit transparency.

Although JPEG 2000 files provide a number of advancements over JPEG, they are not as widely supported and so they are still not as widely used. Adobe provides a plug-in for Photoshop that allows you to read and save files in the JPEG 2000 format.

> **CAUTION**
>
> JPEG images use a lossy compression algorithm, which means the more you change and save an image, the worse its quality becomes. You should convert your JPEG images to PSD, TIFF, or PNG-24 format to edit them and then back to JPEG format when you are finished making the changes.

CompuServ GIF (*.GIF)

The CompuServe Graphics Interchange Format (GIF) file has been used to develop web pages since the inception of the World Wide Web. The GIF format uses an 8-bit palette that is limited to 256 colors. The 8-bit palette makes the GIF images very small and easy to transfer across the Internet. This makes the GIF file format perfect for creating images such as buttons, links, and icons that are displayed on web pages.

A cool advantage of the GIF file format is that it supports animation effects within the image. This allows you to create animated controls and icons for web pages. The GIF file format is lossless, so there is no data loss when saving files.

Portable Network Graphics (*.PNG)

The Portable Network Graphics (PNG) file format was designed to replace the GIF file format for use on the Internet. The PNG file format has an advantage over GIF in that it supports 16.7 million colors as opposed to GIF supporting 256. There are two different versions of the PNG format. The PNG-8 format is an 8-bit alternative to GIF images. PNG-24 is a 24-bit lossless alternative to JPEG images.

As browsers become more adept at handling the PNG format, it will definitely replace the GIF format, but for now you should consider working with the GIF format for web images unless you need the additional colors available in PNG.

Bitmap (*.BMP; *.RLE; *.DIB)

The Bitmap (BMP) file format was developed for graphics in the Windows operating system. It is a simple format that is widely accepted by Windows applications. BMP files are not compressed, which makes their file size large. Another disadvantage is that there is not as much support outside of Windows — on Mac or Linux operating systems, for example.

RAW (*.RAW; *.CR; *.CR2; *.DNG; and several others)

The RAW image format was designed to capture the basic information collected by the CMOS sensors in digital cameras. Collecting the information directly without converting it to another file format makes the cameras work faster and results in less data loss.

> **NOTE**
> The Open File dialog box in Photoshop provides options for Camera Raw and Photoshop RAW. Photoshop RAW images are saved in the RAW file format from Photoshop. The Camera Raw options are for files that are saved in a RAW file format by the camera. There are many different file extensions for the Camera Raw option because most camera vendors have their own proprietary formats.

The biggest advantage to using the RAW file format is that you can work with the image as close as possible to the state that existed when the photo was taken. Photoshop has designed a special tool, Adobe Camera Raw (discussed in Chapter 7), specifically for editing photos in the RAW state because the results tend to be much better than in other file formats.

> **TIP**
>
> If you are taking photographs that you really want to look good, you should set your camera to the RAW setting and use the Adobe Camera Raw tools to adjust them. Afterwards, you can save them in another format, but if you think you will want to adjust them again, keep the Camera Raw files around.

One downside to the RAW file formats is that they have little support outside of image editors such as Photoshop. Another downside is that RAW is not one single format. In addition to the original .RAW file format, other vendors have added their own file formats. For example, Canon has .CR and .CR2. To address this, Adobe has .DNG (Digital Negative), which is designed to try to standardize on a single format. So far, the DNG format seems to be getting the most attention and support from hardware and software manufacturers.

Portable bitmap (*.PBM; *.PGM; *.PPM; *.PNM; *.PFM; *.PAM)

The Portable Bitmap (PBM), Portable Gray Map (PGM), and Portable Pixmap (PPM) are basic file standards. They are so basic that they serve as one of the best common denominators for transferring files between different platforms, such as going from Windows to Linux.

The other file formats tend to change files slightly when they are transferred between two different operating systems, due to differences in how the operating systems process information. Using these formats, you can overcome those problems more easily.

Another advantage of the PBM file format is that it is one of the few formats that can store image data in 8 bit-per-channel, 16 bit-per-channel, and 32 bit-per-channel formats. This is another major advantage when trying to make an image portable from one system to another.

Wireless bitmap (*.WBM; *.WBMPI)

The Wireless bitmap (WBM) file format is designed for images used on wireless devices. Wireless devices are limited in the size and number of colors that an image can contain. Using the Wireless bitmap format allows you to create images that most portable devices can display.

Encapsulated PostScript (*.EPS; *.AI3; *.AI8; *.PS; *.EPSP; *.EPSF)

The Encapsulated PostScript (EPS) file format was developed by Adobe as a means to store images in a format that PostScript printers could understand. That way, the file could be copied directly to the printer without needing to interact with the applications.

Later, Adobe realized that this was an excellent means to transfer documents between different programs. Because all Adobe programs understood how to generate and read the EPS files, it was easy for one application to read an EPS file that was generated by another program.

The greatest strength of the EPS file format is that it can contain both raster and vector images. This gives you the ability to generate a vector image in another program, such as in Adobe Illustrator, and then import it into Photoshop. Photoshop can then use the vector image, for example, as a vector path.

Another major advantage of the EPS format is that almost every desktop layout program in use can read its files. One disadvantage is that it is not truly a graphic format. The EPS format is definitely not the best format in which to store photos for later editing. Another disadvantage is that the EPS format results in a very large file size because the storage format is not efficient.

Photoshop PDF (*.PDF; *.PDP)

The PDF file format was developed by Adobe to be a standard format for files that contained both vector and raster images. It has been widely accepted as a standard file format across all operating systems.

PDF files can be read by many applications including Photoshop. When Photoshop opens a PDF file, it allows you to import the pages and images separately, as shown in Figure 3.1.

FIGURE 3.1

Choosing to import pages and images when opening a PDF file in Photoshop

The biggest advantage to the PDF file format is how widely it has been adopted. It is the *de facto* standard in publishing documents on the Internet, so it can be read everywhere. You will not use the PDF file format much in Photoshop, but it's great when you need it.

Personal Computer eXchange (*.PCX)

The Personal Computer eXchange (PCX) format was developed for use with the PC Paintbrush utility for DOS. If you don't know what DOS is, don't worry; it's best forgotten. The PCX format was widely used several years ago, but it has been replaced with the GIF, JPEG, and PNG file formats.

You probably don't need to use the PCX file format unless you are using an image that was created several years ago. Keep in mind that PCX files originally had a maximum of 256 colors, so don't expect PCX files to contain much detail.

PICT (*.PCT; *.PICT)

PICT files are like the Apple version of PCX files. The PICT file format was originally developed for use with the QuickDraw APIs used by some graphics applications. At that time, this format was one of the few that allowed a file to contain both vector and raster images. However, that functionality has been replaced by the EPS and PDF file formats.

Pixar (*.PXR)

The Pixar file format was developed in-house by the Pixar animation company. The requirements of digital animation put such a huge strain on the available applications that they had to create a custom system that included their own file format. Photoshop allows you to read images that were created using the Pixar system and to write your images out to the Pixar file format.

Flash XML Graphics (*.FXG)

Flash XML Graphics (FXG) is an XML graphics file format developed by Adobe. The specific purpose of FXG is to provide a common file format for all Adobe products. The FXG format is based on the XML language and defines a standard for raster graphics. This is still a developing file format that has a lot of potential.

Google Earth 4 (*.KMZ)

A KMZ file is a zipped archive used by the Google Earth application to display geographic data and images. A KMZ file contains one or more KML files and the supporting images. Google Earth uses the KML files similarly to how a web browser uses HTML files. Google Earth reads the KML file and interprets how to display the information and images.

Photoshop allows you to read a KMZ file and open the images it contains to edit and view. Currently, Photoshop supports KMZ files using the Google Earth 4 standard only.

Photoshop Big (*.PSB)

Many applications have a basic limit of 2GB for a file size due to the nature of the 32-bit operating system. This presents a problem for many file formats. Adobe has overcome this problem by creating a special file format called Photoshop Big (PSB).

Using the PSB file format, Photoshop can open and create files that are larger than 2GB. An advantage of the PSB file format is that it supports the 8 bit-per-channel, 16 bit-per-channel, and 32 bit-per-channel formats. However, unless you really need a file larger than 2GB, you should avoid using the PSB format. Only a few applications support it, so it is not very portable. Another disadvantage of the PSB file format is that it supports only the grayscale and RGB color models, which are discussed in Chapter 4.

OpenEXR (*.EXR)

The OpenEXR (EXR) format was developed by Industrial Light and Magic to provide a multi-resolution and arbitrary channel format for images. This can be a major advantage if you are working with complex compositing of images where you may need several different channels that do not conform to a single color mode.

Although Photoshop gives you the ability to read and even write an OpenEXR file, it does not allow you to create the additional channels. However, if you have an OpenEXR file, you can use the powerful tools in Photoshop to make adjustments to the channels.

Cineon (*.CIN)

The Cineon (CIN) file format was developed by Kodak to contain data from images scanned in from film. The Cineon format is a bit different from the standard formats such as JPEG and TIFF. Instead of RGB channels representing intensity of color, the pixel data in the Cineon format represents the printing density as seen by the print film. The purpose of using the printing density is to retain the values that originally existed on the print film.

Interchange File Format (*.IFF; *.TDI)

The Interchange File Format (IFF) was developed by Electronic Arts as a method to transfer graphic data between software. It is unlikely that you will ever need to use an IFF, but if you do, Photoshop can open it.

Scitex CT (*.SCT)

The Scitex CT (SCT) file format is used by graphics processing equipment developed by Scitex Corporation Ltd. (now Scailex Corporation Ltd.). You will generally only use this file format if you are sending print jobs to a Scitex digital printer.

Targa (*.TGA; *.VDA; *.ICB; *.VST)

The Truevision Advanced Raster Graphics Adapter (Targa) file format has been around since the birth of color displays in computers. Targa files support 8-, 16-, 24-, and 32-bit colors per pixel. Targa files support alpha channel data and are fairly transportable between systems. A common use of Targa files is to store textures used in 3D imaging such as video games or animation.

Radiance (*.HDR; *.RGBE; *.XYZE)

The Radiance format stores four bytes per pixel (red, green, blue, and an exponent byte). This allows pixels to have the extended range and precision similar to floating point values, allowing the HDR and RGBE formats to handle very bright pixels without loss of precision for darker ones. A variant of the Radiance format, XYZE, uses the XYZ color model (discussed in Chapter 29) instead of RGB.

Understanding video files

Photoshop supports a wide variety of video file formats. Each video file format is based on a digital container format. The digital container format defines how the audio and video data elements as well as metadata co-exist in the video file. The different container definitions result in different file formats.

Each of the different video file formats can be compressed using codecs, which are computer programs that encode and decode the audio/video data stream. There are several different codecs available that provide different levels of compression and quality in the file.

With the addition of the Timeline palette, Photoshop adds several video file formats to the huge list of supported file formats. Not only can you import movies with the following extensions, but you can also import image sequences with the usual image extensions that Photoshop already supports.

Photoshop allows you to import the following video file formats:

- **MOV.** The MOV file format is the native file format of QuickTime. A MOV file can contain several types of tracks — video, audio, effects, and text among them. This makes them easily editable and portable because a MOV file can be used in both the Mac and Windows platforms.

- **AVI.** AVI is one of the most popular high quality formats. AVI files usually are not compressed, although some AVI codecs compress the video file. This means that it takes up much more disk space and is difficult to share over the Internet. It has the same capability to store tracks as the MOV file format. It is the most commonly used file format in video-editing software in Windows.

- **MPG/MPEG.** MPEG (Moving Picture Experts Groups) files are based on a set of standards that define audio and video compression. There are several file formats that are based on these standards. The following are the most common standards:

  - **MPEG-2.** The MPEG-2 is the standard used by broadcast-quality television as well as DVDs. MPEG-2 files are compressed enough to be transmitted for cable/satellite television and fit onto DVD discs but retain the majority of their quality.

  - **MPEG-4.** The MPEG-4 standard utilizes additional coding complexity to achieve higher compression rates than MPEG-2. This is a much better format to be rendered on computers and the smaller file size makes it the most popular standard for use on the internet.

- **MP4.** Based on the MPEG-4 Part 14 standard. This format has overtaken MPG files in popularity on the web. MP4 is very portable and provides great compression while still maintaining high video quality.

> **NOTE**
> To play video in Photoshop, you must have QuickTime 7 installed on your computer. You can get a free QuickTime download from www.apple.com/quicktime.

Supporting 3D file formats

By adding 3D extensions, Photoshop has expanded the file formats that it supports for 3D editing. Photoshop supports these 3D file formats:

- **3ds.** The 3ds file format is used by 3D Studio Max, the most widely used 3D application. It has become such an industry standard that most 3D modeling programs export their files in this format.

- **OBJ.** The OBJ file format is also a widely used industry standard. The 3D models that come with the Photoshop bonus content are OBJ files.

- **COLLADA.** This is the file format used by the video gaming industry. It was originally developed to facilitate transporting digital content from one creation tool to another. COLLADA is also a widely supported file format with an .XML file extension.

- **U3D.** The Universal 3D file format allows users to share 3D graphics with other users who don't have the 3D modeling program used to design the image. Like JPEG or TIFF files, these files are becoming more universally available to most image viewers.

- **KMZ.** The KMZ format was discussed earlier as an image file format; however, it also provides information about the 3D geography that you see when you explore Google Earth.

Supporting the DICOM file format

A Digital Imaging and Communications in Medicine (DICOM) file is a medical image or series of images created when you have a sonogram, CT scan, MRI, or any number of procedures that take an image of the inside of your body. DICOM files are used to analyze and diagnose problems inside the body visually without doing exploratory surgery.

Photoshop gives you the ability to open and work with DICOM files. Using the powerful level and tone adjustments available in Photoshop, a trained technician can adjust images so they can more easily see problems. Photoshop also has the ability to animate a series of DICOM files by sequencing them. For example, if you have several images at timed intervals of a heart beating, Photoshop can turn the images into an animated movie.

Creating and Opening Images

When editing existing images or creating new ones, you need to know how to use Photoshop to open image files and create new ones. Creating a new image involves defining the resolution and size of a blank document and opening it in Photoshop. In this section we will give you a quick overview of how to create and open images in Photoshop. These are the very basic operations that you need to understand before you can move onto editing. The following sections give a brief overview of creating new images, opening existing images, and saving images in Photoshop.

Creating a new image

Many people only see Photoshop as a photo-editing application. However, Photoshop also allows you to create a blank image to begin editing. You can define the dimensions and resolution of the new image.

To create a new image in Photoshop, choose File⇨New to open the New dialog box, shown in Figure 3.2. When creating a new image, you need to tell Photoshop how big the image should be, how much resolution the image should have, and what color mode to use.

FIGURE 3.2

Setting the options while creating a new image in Photoshop

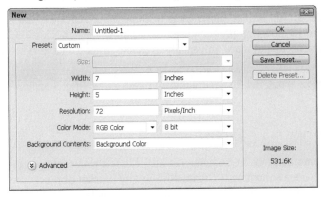

The following settings are configurable in the New dialog box when you are creating a new image in Photoshop:

- **Name.** This setting lets you specify a name for the file. Typically, you want to use a descriptive name so that later you can easily locate the document in the file system.

> **TIP**
>
> When you are copying from another document or application into a new file in Photoshop, copy the data to the clipboard first and then create the new document in Photoshop using the Clipboard preset. This creates the new document automatically to the exact size of the contents of the clipboard, avoiding the need to clip the data later.

- **Preset.** This setting provides a drop-down list of preset sizes for the image. The default is Clipboard, which creates a new image that is the same size as any image data contained inside the clipboard. You also can choose the default Photoshop size (5 x 7 inches), U.S. and international paper sizes, standard photo sizes, film and video sizes, standard web sizes, and mobile device sizes. You also can select other open images to create a new image that is the same size, which is helpful if you are using the new image to work as a composite with an existing image.

- **Size.** This setting allows you to select a size from the drop-down list based on the preset setting that you selected. For example, if you selected Photo in the Preset drop-down list, the list contains standard photo sizes such as 5 x 7 and 8 x 10. If you select the Clipboard, default Photoshop, or Custom preset, this option is not active.

- **Width.** This setting lets you specify the width of the new image. You can also select the units, which include pixels, inches, centimeters, millimeters, points, picas, and columns.

- **Height.** This setting lets you specify the height of the new image. You can also select the units, which include pixels, inches, centimeters, millimeters, points, and picas.

- **Resolution.** This setting lets you specify the resolution of the image. The available units are pixels per inch and pixels per centimeter.

- **Color Mode.** This setting lets you specify the color mode and number of channels to use when creating the image. Color mode and bit level are discussed in more detail in Chapter 4.

- **Background Contents.** This setting specifies the contents of the background of the new image. The options are White, Background Color, and Transparent. If you select Background Color, the color of the background in the Photoshop toolbox is used as the background for the image.

Opening an existing image

The first thing you typically want to do in Photoshop is open a file for editing, because Photoshop isn't worth much without an image file loaded. To open a file in Photoshop, choose File ➪ Open.

Then use the Open dialog box, shown in Figure 3.3, to navigate to where the file is located.

If you have a lot of files in the location where you are trying to open the file, it may be difficult to find the one that you want to open. You can narrow the view by selecting the file type of the image you want to open using the Files of type drop-down menu. When you select a specific file type, only files of that type are displayed.

TIP

In Figure 3.3, the thumbnails of the images are displayed to make selecting the desired file easier. You can view the thumbnails in Windows Explorer by pressing Alt+V and selecting Medium icons, Large icons, or Extra large icons from the drop-down menu.

You also can narrow the search by typing in the File name field. A drop-down list of files is displayed based on the name you are typing. As you type more characters, the list gets smaller until you can easily select the file you want. When you click the Open button, the image opens in Photoshop, ready to edit.

FIGURE 3.3

Opening an existing image in Photoshop

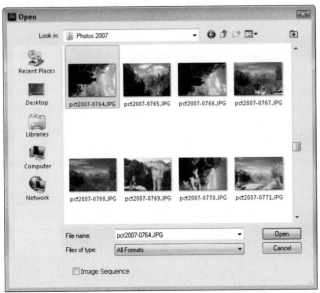

Opening an existing image as a specific file type

The first section of this chapter discussed the different types of files in Photoshop. Some are better than others, and you probably have a preference. Photoshop has a useful feature if you are opening a file in a different format that you want to use when editing. The Open As feature lets you open a file in a different format than it currently exists in on disk. This saves you the trouble of opening the file and then saving it as the format that you really want to use.

To open a file as a different format than it currently is, choose File ➪ Open As from the Photoshop menu bar to open the Open dialog box, shown in Figure 3.4. Navigate the file system to find the image, and select the file format you want to use when editing the image using the Open As drop-down menu. You cannot filter the list based on file type in the Open dialog box; however, you can still filter based on filename. When you click the Open button, the image opens in the format you specified, ready to edit.

FIGURE 3.4

Opening an existing image as a specific file format in Photoshop

Saving an image

When modifying images in Photoshop, any work you have done is lost if you do not save the changes to the file. Photoshop provides two options to save work you have done on a file: Save and Save As. The Save option simply saves the changes you have made to the file back to the original file format and filename. The Save As option allows you to save the changes to a new file format and filename.

TIP

If you are planning to use an image more than once, you should always save a copy of the original first and then work on that copy. Each time an image is edited and saved, some of the original data is changed or lost. Working on copies instead of the original ensures that each time you start again, you have the best source data in the image to work from.

For the most part, the Save option is used to save permanent changes while you are editing the document. The Save As option is used if you want to save a copy of the file to keep the original image contents, change the file format of the image, or specify additional data to preserve.

To save the changes made to an existing document in Photoshop, choose File ➪ Save. Some file formats launch a dialog box with options for that file format; however, most often, the file is saved immediately and you can continue working.

To save a copy of the file, change the file format, change the filename, or specify other options, choose File ➪ Save As to launch the Save As dialog box, shown in Figure 3.5.

3

FIGURE 3.5

Using the Save As dialog box to save changes made to an image in Photoshop

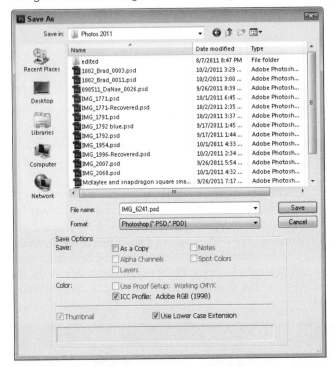

From the Save As dialog box, you can specify the following options when saving files:

- **File name.** This option lets you set the name under which the file is stored on disk. Typically, you want to specify a descriptive name that identifies the file easily.

- **Format.** This option lets you set the file format to use when saving the file to disk. This option defaults to the current format of the existing file.

- **As a Copy.** When you select this option, the filename is modified to include the word *copy* at the end.

NOTE

Normally, when you use the Save As option, the old file is closed and the newly saved file becomes the working document. However, when you select the As a Copy option, the copy is saved, but the current working document is still the original instead of the copy.

- **Alpha Channels.** When you select the Alpha Channels option, the alpha channel data is also saved in the image. This option is available only if the image contains alpha channel data and the selected file format supports alpha channel data — for example, PSD, TIFF, PDF, and GIF.

- **Layers.** When you select the Layers option, the layers data is also saved in the image. This option is available if the image contains layer data and the selected file format supports layer data — for example, PSD, TIFF, and PDF.

- **Notes.** When you select the Notes option, the notes data is also saved in the image. This option is available only if notes have been added to the image and the selected file format supports notes data.

- **Spot Colors.** When you select the Spot Colors option, the spot color data is also saved in the image. This option is available only if the image contains spot colors and the selected file format supports spot color data — for example, PSD, TIFF, PDF, and EPS (DCS 2.0).

- **Use Proof Setup.** The Use Proof Setup option is available if you configure the current view's proof setup by choosing View ⇨ Proof Setup, the View ⇨ Proof Colors option has been selected, and the selected file format supports converting to proof colors — for example, EPS files.

- **ICC Profile.** When you select this option, the configured ICC profile data is embedded in the image. This option is available only if the selected file format supports embedding ICC data.

- **Thumbnail.** This option specifies whether a thumbnail version of the image is embedded in the file's metadata. This option is available only on files that can have a thumbnail embedded.

- **Use Lower Case Extension.** This option specifies whether to use lowercase or uppercase letters for the file extension that defines the file format. Photoshop automatically appends the file extension onto the name you specify. This can be important if you are working with systems that are case sensitive. You can override this option by typing the extension manually.

Resizing Files and Adjusting Resolution

Another common operation that you will perform on files is resizing and adjusting resolution. When you resize the image you will reduce the number of overall pixels, reducing the file size. When adjusting the resolution, you will adjust the number of pixels per inch, which will increase the print quality, but also decrease the print size. After you open a file in Photoshop, you are ready to begin editing it. Some of the first edits you typically perform are resizing and resolution adjustments to make the image the size you want. This section discusses resolution and how it applies when you are resizing images.

3

Understanding resolution

Resolution is the ability to discern details in an image. In Photoshop, resolution is measured in terms of pixels per inch or pixels per centimeter. An image with more pixels per inch has more detail.

The biggest limitation of resolution is the medium on which the image is presented. For example, a typical computer monitor has a maximum resolution between 72 and 96 pixels per inch, which means that even if you have 1000 pixels per inch in an image, the detail cannot appear better than at 96 pixels per inch.

Therefore, when setting the resolution of an image, you should understand resolution capabilities of the medium from which the image will be outputted. For example, an inkjet printer may be able to print 300 to 1200 dots per inch (dpi), so a file with a resolution of 1000 dpi prints more detail than an image that contains only 96 dpi.

So why not just keep the resolution at the maximum? There are two reasons. First, the more resolution in the image, the larger the file is. If you are concerned about disk space or transmission load time on the web, then reducing the resolution helps. Second, if you are using the image in an application or function that requires a specific resolution range such as a web image, then you need to change the resolution to match those requirements.

> **TIP**
>
> It is a good practice to always maximize the resolution when editing an image until you are ready to output it. That way, all the editing is done with the maximum amount of detail. Also, if you plan to edit the image again, you should consider keeping a copy with the higher resolution.

Changing the image size and resolution

One of the most common editing functions applied to images is to change the size and resolution based on the destination of the image. For example, if you place the image on a website, the size and resolution need to be less than an image being sent to a high-resolution printer.

This section discusses the relationship between size and resolution, how Photoshop creates the resized pixels, and how to make these adjustments in Photoshop.

Understanding the resolution and size relationship

Ultimately, the digital size of an image is simply the number of pixels that it contains, and the dimensions are simply the number of pixels wide by the number of pixels high. However, when you are outputting the image, size is tied directly to the resolution capability of the output device.

For example, when you are viewing an image on a computer screen, the output dimensions of the image in inches are (the number of pixels high/72 dpi) x (the number of pixels wide/72 dpi). However, when you are printing the image to a 1200 dpi printer, the document's output dimensions are (the number of pixels high/1200 dpi) x (the number of pixels wide/1200 dpi), which is a much smaller image.

Therefore, you need to know the intended output resolution and the desired dimensions of that medium to determine the output resolution and size to set in the image. Otherwise, you may end up with an image that is too large to view on a web page or that has inadequate resolution for a printed image.

TIP

You should leave the image as large as possible when you are editing until you are ready to finally output it. The more pixels Photoshop has to deal with, the better results you see when editing. If you need to downsize the image, wait until you have finished editing it. However, if you are upsizing the image, you should change the size before you edit it.

Understanding resizing algorithms in Photoshop

An important concept that you need to understand when resizing images is what is happening with the pixels during resizing. When you reduce the size of an image by one-third, Photoshop has to take a block of 9-x-9 pixels and turn them into a block of 6-x-6 pixels while displaying the same content. When you increase the size of an image by one-half, Photoshop has to take a block of 6-x-6 pixels and turn them into a block of 9-x-9 pixels to display the same content.

The point is that when resizing an image, Photoshop has to make an intelligent determination of how to combine pixels when reducing the image and how to fill in the missing holes when increasing the size of an image. To do this, Photoshop uses complex algorithms to calculate what the resulting pixels in the new image should be. These algorithms are known as *resample methods*.

NOTE

The algorithms that Photoshop uses to resize images are available as an option at the bottom of the Image Size dialog box, which you open by choosing Image ↔ Image Size.

Photoshop provides five algorithms to resample images. Each algorithm has advantages over the others, and they all produce slightly different results. The following list describes these algorithms and when to use them:

- **Nearest Neighbor.** This method is the simplest and fastest for resizing an image. This option works by simply looking at the pixels surrounding the selection and averaging them to create the pixel in the new image. It's fast, but it produces the worst overall results, especially in images that have highly contrasting tones next to each other.

- **Bilinear.** This method uses a weighted average of the nearest pixels in the old image to determine the value of the pixel in the new image. This option is still fairly fast, but typically it provides much better results than the nearest neighbor method for both upsizing and downsizing images. The bilinear method is the best overall method to use.

3

- **Bicubic.** This method applies a convolution algorithm that uses a weighted set of numbers that are applied to the pixels in the old image to determine the value of the pixel in the new image. This option is not as fast as the nearest neighbor or bilinear methods. However, the bicubic method typically preserves finer detail. A downside of the bicubic method is that it often results in ringing artifacts (a repeating pattern around edges where there is high contrast in the image — for example, white next to black).

- **Bicubic Smoother.** This is the same as the bicubic method, except that it applies a smoothing filter to the set of pixels at the same time to help smooth abrupt edges when enlarging an image. The bicubic smoother algorithm provides the best overall results when enlarging an image.

> **NOTE**
> There are additional 3rd party plug-ins to Photoshop, available on the Photoshop Marketplace, that provide better results than even the Bicubic Smoother option.

- **Bicubic Sharper.** This is the same as the bicubic method, except that it applies a sharpening filter to the set of pixels at the same time to help keep detail when shrinking an image. The bicubic sharper algorithm provides the best overall results when shrinking an image.

Adjusting the image size and resolution

To adjust the image size and resolution in Photoshop, choose Image ➪ Image Size to open the Image Size dialog box, shown in Figure 3.6.

FIGURE 3.6

Setting options to change the image size and resolution of an image

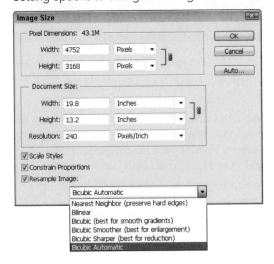

From the Image Size dialog box, you can set the following options:

- **Pixel Dimension Width.** When the Resample Image option is selected, this option allows you to change the overall width of the image in terms of pixels. You can set the units to change the dimension based on pixels or percentage. If the Constrain Proportions option is selected, when you change this value, the height dimension value also changes so that the image maintains the original proportions.

- **Pixel Dimension Height.** When the Resample Image option is selected, this option allows you to change the overall height of the image in terms of pixels. You can set the units to change the dimension based on pixels or percentage. If the Constrain Proportions option is selected, when you change this value, the width dimension value also changes so that the image maintains the original proportions.

- **Document Width.** This option allows you to change the actual document output width of the image in terms of percent, inches, centimeters, millimeters, points, picas, and columns. You can set the units used to define the new size by selecting them from the drop-down menu. If the Constrain Proportions option is selected, when you change this value, the document height value also changes so that the image maintains the original proportions.

- **Document Height.** This option allows you to change the actual document output height of the image in terms of percent, inches, centimeter, millimeter, points, and picas. You can set the units used to define the new size by selecting them from the drop-down menu. If the Constrain Proportions option is selected, when you change this value, the document width value also changes so that the image maintains the original proportions.

- **Resolution.** This option allows you to change the resolution of the image in terms of pixels per inch or pixels per centimeter. If the Resample Image option is selected, the pixel dimensions change when you adjust this value. However, if the Resample Image option is not selected, the document size changes when you adjust this value.

- **Scale Styles.** When the Scale Styles option is selected, any style effects that have been added to the image are also scaled. This is extremely useful if you want to apply effects before scaling an image.

- **Constrain Proportions.** When the Constrain Proportions option is selected, both the height and width values change when you change either of them to maintain the document's original proportions. This option applies to both the pixel dimension and document size values. When this option is unselected, you can change the height of the image without changing the width to apply distortion and elongation effects.

- **Resample Image.** When the Resample Image option is selected, Photoshop changes the actual pixels in the image to change the total image size in pixels. When this option is not selected, you are changing only the document size and resolution settings that are used when outputting the image.

- **Resampling Method.** This option provides a drop-down list of resample methods to use when changing the number of pixels in the image. This option is available only

3

when the Resample Image option is selected. You can select from the Nearest Neighbor, Bilinear, Bicubic, Bicubic Smoother, and Bicubic Sharper methods discussed earlier in this chapter.

- **Bicubic Automatic.** When this option is selected, Photoshop uses a computer algorithm to calculate the best of the above methods for resampling the image and uses that option. Typically this is sufficient, however, there are definitely times when Photoshop doesn't pick the option that gives you the results you are looking for.

> **NOTE**
> The bicubic methods are not available if you are working with a grayscale image. If you are planning to convert the final image to grayscale, you should change the size of the image first to use these options before converting the image to grayscale.

Changing the canvas size

The previous section discussed how to change the size of an image. Photoshop also allows you to change the size of the canvas that contains the image. Changing the canvas size is different than changing the image size.

Typically, the canvas size is exactly the same as the image size, so most people do not distinguish the two. Changing the canvas size allows you to either add pixels to an image or take pixels away from an image. Taking pixels away is basically the same as cropping, which is discussed in the next section.

Adding pixels to an image file is useful for a variety of purposes. The most basic purpose is simply to add a border to the image. Increasing the size of the canvas naturally creates a border of pixels around the image.

Another common reason for increasing the canvas size is to add crop marks for printing. Some printers require crop marks to crop your image precisely. Increasing the canvas size gives you the space to add crop marks to the image file.

Increasing the size of the canvas does not alter the pixels of the existing image at all. Instead, it simply adds pixels to the image file. To change the canvas size, choose Image ⇨ Canvas Size from the Photoshop menu bar to open the Canvas Size dialog box, shown in Figure 3.7.

The Canvas Size dialog box allows you to set the following options when resizing the canvas:

- **Width.** This option lets you specify the width in percent, pixels, inches, centimeters, millimeters, points, picas, and columns. If the Relative option is selected, the width is the actual border size; if the Relative option is not selected, the width is the total width of the canvas.

- **Height.** This option lets you specify the height in percent, pixels, inches, centimeters, millimeters, points, picas, and columns. If the Relative option is selected, the height is the actual border size; if the Relative option is not selected, the height is the total height of the canvas.

- **Relative.** This option lets you specify whether to set the width and height based on the total canvas or relative to the image.

- **Anchor.** This option lets you specify where to anchor the original image in the new canvas. You can select the center, top, bottom, one of the sides, or one of the corners. Typically, you want the image anchored in the center when adding a border to the document.

- **Canvas extension color.** This option lets you choose the color of the new pixels added to the canvas. This defaults to the background color; however, it has presets for foreground, white, black, and gray. You also can select Custom to open a Color Picker to specify a different color.

FIGURE 3.7

Setting options to change the canvas size of an image

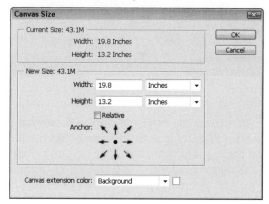

Cropping and Straightening Images

In addition to resizing images, you may want to use only a portion of an image and discard or crop the rest. Photoshop provides a great tool that allows you to quickly crop out the unwanted parts of your image. Using the same tool, you can straighten the cropping to fix problems such as a tilted camera.

This section discusses some general guidelines that help when deciding how to crop images. You also learn how to use the Crop tool and the Trim utility, included with Photoshop, to crop and straighten images.

Using general guidelines for cropping a photo

Photography is really an art form. A photo that is well composed is interesting to look at, leads the eye of the viewer to the subject, and doesn't include any distracting elements. All of these things can be improved by the right crop. Getting closer to your subject and cutting out background clutter are vital to a good crop, but knowing a few basic photography rules, such as the rule of thirds, helps you to crop your photo to the best advantage.

Getting rid of background clutter

A good reason to crop your photo is to get rid of distracting elements in the background. The subject should be the main focus of any image, and anything else in the image should complement the subject, lead your eye to the subject, and contribute to the "story" being told about the subject. Too many objects, distracting colors, or any other background that draws the eye away from the subject should be cropped out of your photo if possible.

> **NOTE**
>
> Cropping is an obvious fix for a busy background, but you have other ways to reduce the impact of a background that can't be cut out of a photo with the Crop tool. You can cut out your entire background using a Selection tool, you can blur the background, or you can convert the background grayscale.

Preserving aspect ratio

Before you pull out your Crop tool and start trimming away, you need to know what you are planning to do with your photo. If you want to print your photo in more than one size, leave yourself plenty of workable area around the edges of your photo. Don't create a custom crop size that's so tight around your subject that you'll go in later to create a 5-x-7 print and find that you can't do it without cropping out part of your subject.

Also be aware that standard print sizes such as 5 x 7 and 8 x 10 are different aspect ratios, so if you crop your photo to an 8-x-10 size, you'll have to trim the edges to make the same photo a 5-x-7 size. If you are printing the same photo in multiple sizes, save the original photo, using it to crop each size, and then save each cropped photo individually.

Applying the rule of thirds

The "rule of thirds" is a tried-and-true rule for making your photos visually pleasing, and it's very easy to follow. The essence of the rule of thirds is that the subject and the horizon in your photo should never divide your photo in half. Instead, they should divide the photo into thirds. Mentally divide your photo into thirds both horizontally and vertically. Ideally, the subject should be off-center in your photograph, directly in one of the intersections of your imaginary lines (power points), if possible. The horizon in your photo should run along the top or bottom line, rather than through the center.

In Figure 3.8, for example, you can see that the boy in this photo is almost exactly centered. To improve the composition, I want to make a crop that places him over one-third and down one-third in the shot, as you can see in Figure 3.8. I managed to crop out a distracting background as well.

FIGURE 3.8

Cropping an image using the rule of thirds to improve the look

3

Of course, just like any good rule, this one is made to be broken. If your sky is the subject of your photo and much more interesting than the ground, go ahead and place the horizon line one-sixth of the way up. You are the ultimate judge of how your photos should be composed. If you like the way a photo looks, chances are good that others will too.

Giving your subject somewhere to go

If your subject is in motion or looking off the frame of the photo, make sure to leave room in your photo for them to move (or look) into. If the viewer of your photo feels like the subject may move out of view at any moment, it leaves them with a sense of unease. Everyone wants to feel like they are in on what happens next.

I've cropped the photo in Figure 3.9 according to the rule of thirds, so it should look great, right? Not at all. In fact, aren't you just a little worried looking at the boy that he is about to lose his balance and fall down?

FIGURE 3.9

A cropped image that doesn't give the subject somewhere to go

Closing in on your subject

If you are taking portraits, a good rule of thumb is to close in as much as possible, even to the extent of trimming off the top of the head or the ears. If you want to follow the rule of thirds, use the eyes as the main subject. You can achieve a more engaging and personal photo, as you can see in Figure 3.10.

FIGURE 3.10

Cropping an image to close in on the subject

Telling a story with a photo

A picture is worth a thousand words, so when you start cropping, make sure you aren't taking out an important part of the story you want to tell. Close-ups are great, but not at the expense of an interesting environment. The cropped photo on the left of Figure 3.11 leaves the viewer wondering where these boys are and what they are doing. The wider view on the right of Figure 3.11 lets us in on the full story.

FIGURE 3.11

Cropping an image too much takes the story element out of the photo.

Cropping an image

Now that you have a good understanding about how and why to crop images, you are ready to do some cropping in Photoshop. You can crop images in Photoshop in a couple of different ways. The most common method is to use the Crop tool in the toolbox. However, you also can crop a selection, have Photoshop detect multiple scanned images, and crop them automatically.

The following sections discuss using the Crop tool to crop your images as well as cropping using the Selection tools. Automatically cropping scanned images is covered in subsequent sections.

Using the Crop tool

The Crop tool in Photoshop makes cropping your images easy and quick. To crop an image, simply select the Crop tool from the toolbox and drag the mouse across the area of the image that you want to keep to create a crop box, as shown in Figure 3.12. When you are finished selecting the area, double-click the mouse on the crop box or click the Commit button in the options bar to crop the image.

FIGURE 3.12

Cropping an image using the Crop tool in Photoshop

Crop box

Although the Crop tool is simple and quick to use, the crop box makes it very versatile. You have these options after creating the crop box:

- **Move the crop box.** You can use the mouse to adjust the position of the crop box in the image after you have created the crop box.

- **Resize the crop box.** You can adjust the size of the crop box by using the mouse to drag the corners and sides of the crop box.

- **Change the center point.** You can drag the center point icon in the middle of the crop box in Figure 3.12 to set the center position in the cropped image. However, the cropped image won't be the same size as the crop box if the center position is moved, because Photoshop must adjust the size to add enough pixels to adjust for the offset center.

> **TIP**
>
> When changing the position of the crop box, you can use the shift+arrow keys to move the box one pixel at a time. This allows you to make very small adjustments that are difficult to do with a mouse.

While working with the crop box, the following additional options are provided in the Options menu of the Crop tool (see Figure 3.13).

FIGURE 3.13

The Options menu of the Crop tool in Photoshop

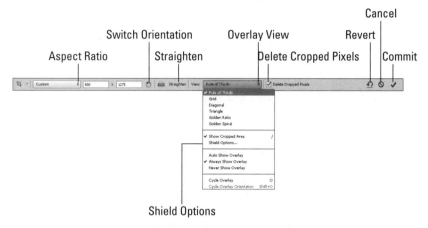

- **Aspect Ratio.** This option allows you to set the aspect ratio of the crop box based on one of the following settings:
  - **Custom.** When you select this option, you can type in specific height and width values in the two text fields provided in the option bar.
  - **Unconstrained.** If you do not have a specific aspect ratio in mind, select this option. You will be able to drag the corners and sides freely to adjust the crop box.
  - **Original Ratio.** When you select this option, as you drag the corners and sides, the image will be kept in the aspect ratio of the original image.
  - **Predefined values: 1x1, 4x5, 8x10, 8.5x11, 4x3, 5x7, 2x3, 4x6, 16x9.** This option is extremely useful when cropping images for standard print sizes. These values maintain the aspect ratio of the crop box to match the predefined values.
  - **Size and Resolution.** This option opens a dialog box that allows you to set a specific height, width, and resolution. This allows you to specify a crop box size based on a resolution other than that of the existing document. This is very useful when cropping images to be placed in other documents.
  - **Rotate Crop Box.** This option allows you to set the size of the crop box to match the available pixels as you rotate the image. When you select this option, the Rotate tool is enabled; as you drag the tool, the image rotates and the crop box is automatically adjusted to the smallest rectangle possible without overlapping the border of the image.
- **Switch Orientation.** This option allows you to switch the orientation of the crop box between landscape and portrait.

- **Straighten.** When you click the Straighten button, a ruler tool is enabled. Use the ruler tool to drag a horizontal or vertical line that matches what should be horizontal or vertical in the image. The image is automatically rotated so that the line you have drawn is true horizontal or vertical, thus straightening the image.

- **Overlay View.** This option is a very useful feature of the Crop tool, which allows you to have grid lines that help you understand the balance of the photo area that you are keeping. The View option in the Crop tool options menu, shown in Figure 3.13, allows you to select a Rule of Thirds, Grid, Diagonal, Triangle, Golden Ratio, Golden Spiral, or no overlay. The Grid overlay is useful for getting a better idea of how the uncropped area of the photo will be spaced after cropping. The Rule of Thirds overlay helps you more easily crop to match the rule of thirds guideline.

    - **Shield Options.** This option is another useful feature in the Overlay View drop-down menu of the Crop tool options in the Shield Options setting. When you select Shield Options from the Overlay View drop-down menu, a dialog box appears, allowing you to change the shield color and transparency. The crop shield covers the area of the image that is going to be cropped with a partially transparent color. This helps you visualize what is being clipped out and what is being kept. You can set the overlay color and adjust the opacity to give you the best overall view. Typically, you want enough of the background to show through so you can see what is being removed; however, the less of the background that shows through, the easier it is to see what the results of the crop will be.

- **Delete Cropped Pixels.** When you select this option, Photoshop destroys the pixels when the crop is committed. Use this option if you know you are not going to need the pixels outside the crop and want to free up memory so that Photoshop can work faster.

- **Revert Crop.** This option reverts the crop to the original settings.

- **Cancel Crop.** This option cancels the current crop operation.

- **Commit Crop.** This option commits the current crop operation.

Cropping an image to a different perspective

A great feature of Photoshop cropping is the ability to actually crop an image to a different perspective. The perspective crop box is not resized in a uniform manner; each of the corners moves independently, resulting in a skewed box. Keep in mind that the crop still results in a rectangular image. Photoshop calculates that adjusted positioning and changes the perspective of the pixels. To understand the perspective option a bit better, look at the perspective transform discussed in Chapter 19 of this book.

To crop an image to a different perspective, select the Perspective Crop tool from the toolbox. Then draw a crop box and drag the corners to create a perspective crop box as shown in Figure 3.14. When you commit the crop, the image is cropped to the new perspective, as shown in Figure 3.14.

FIGURE 3.14

When you crop an image using the Perspective Crop tool, you can completely alter the perspective of the image.

Cropping using the Selection tools

Another method of cropping images in Photoshop is to create a selection using the Selection tools and then choosing Image ⇨ Crop. This crops everything outside a rectangle around the selected area. Cropping an image using a selection has some advantages over using the Crop tool.

The Crop tool is limited in shape to a simple rectangle, whereas the Selection tools can quickly select objects of any shape. You can then crop the image to fit only the selected object. Another advantage is that you can do several different operations while a selection is highlighted that you cannot do while a crop is highlighted.

You do not have the same cropping options available when cropping using a selection. Also, even though the selection is not rectangular, the crop is. Typically, the Crop tool is the best option when you are planning to crop an area of an image. The ability to crop around a selection provides an alternative option for times when you already have an area selected that fits the area that you would like to crop.

Straightening an image

One of the most common editing tasks when working with images is straightening. Photos taken when the camera was slightly angled, or even on its side, do not look quite right.

Photoshop provides three basic methods for straightening images. One is to simply rotate the image by a specific angle, another is to rotate the image while you are cropping it, and another is to use the Crop and Straightening utility to batch-straighten scanned photos.

Rotating and flipping images

The easiest way to rotate an image in Photoshop is to choose Image ➪ Image Rotation and then select one of the following options from the drop-down menu shown in Figure 3.15:

FIGURE 3.15

Using the Image Rotation menu to rotate images in Photoshop

- **180 degrees.** This option rotates the image around the center axis 180 degrees.

- **90 degrees CW.** This option rotates the image around the center axis 90 degrees clockwise.

- **90 degrees CCW.** This option rotates the image around the center axis 90 degrees counterclockwise.

- **Arbitrary.** This option launches the Rotate Canvas dialog box, which allows you to select an angle to rotate the image as well as whether to rotate the image clockwise or counterclockwise. The image size is increased to keep the full original pixels in the rotated version, and any new space that must be added is added as the background color.

> **NOTE**
>
> When you rotate an image 180 degrees, the dimensions and pixels do not change. When you rotate an image 90 degrees, the dimensions swap places but the pixels do not change. However, when you rotate an image at an arbitrary angle, the dimensions of the image increase to retain the corners of the rotated image within the full image canvas. More importantly, the actual pixels of the original photo are altered slightly because they are no longer aligned in the same direction as they were. Therefore, some data is lost and you may end up with some residual artifacts. You should avoid rotating images several times, because each time leads to more distortion.

- **Flip Canvas Horizontal.** This option flips the entire canvas on its back in the horizontal direction. It results in a mirrored image of the original. This is similar to taking a transparent sheet and flipping it over from left to right.

- **Flip Canvas Vertical.** This option flips the entire canvas on its back in the vertical direction. This is similar to taking a transparent sheet and flipping it over from top to bottom.

Rotating while cropping

Another option is to rotate the image at the same time you are cropping it using the Crop tool. This has the advantage of not creating any additional background pixels to accommodate space that was not in the original image because the cropping will be rectangular.

As discussed earlier, you can crop an image by selecting the Crop tool from the toolbox and then selecting an area in the image to crop. In addition to the other options that were discussed, you can rotate the crop box by moving the mouse over the crop box until the rotation cursor, shown in Figure 3.16, is displayed. Then click the left mouse button and drag to rotate and straighten the image.

When you rotate the crop box, it rotates around the center point icon. You can adjust the center point to get a better angle when rotating the crop.

FIGURE 3.16

Selecting the rotation cursor around a crop box to rotate an image in Photoshop

Rotation cursor

TIP

When using the Crop tool to straighten an image, you should turn on the grid lines in the Crop Guide Overlay and use them to align the rotated crop box with an element of the image that should be either horizontal or vertical, such as a water line or a building.

Using the Crop and Straighten tool

One of the most common tasks that Photoshop is used for is retouching old photos. Often these photos are scanned in batches on a flatbed scanner. One of the biggest problems is that the photos can move around a bit and so they are not aligned very well in the final scan. Another problem is that each scanned image may contain several photos when you only want individual photos.

Photoshop provides the Crop and Straighten tool to solve both of these problems. The Crop and Straighten tool analyzes the image and looks for whitespace around the images. Then it copies the individual photos in the original image into new documents. The results are a set of new files, each containing only a single photo that is correctly rotated.

To use the Crop and Straighten tool, open the image that contains the scan of multiple photos, similar to the one in Figure 3.16. Then choose File ➪ Automate ➪ Crop and Straighten Photos from the Photoshop menu bar. You see a progress bar while Photoshop is analyzing the data in the image, and then some documents open containing the individual cropped and straightened photos from the original, as shown in Figure 3.17.

TIP

The Crop and Straighten tool can also be used even if there is only one photo in an image, as long as there is enough of a border around the photo that Photoshop can detect the edges.

Using the Ruler tool

An excellent tool for straightening images is the Ruler tool. You can use the Ruler tool to draw a line on the image and then click the Straighten button in the options menu, shown in Figure 3.18, to straighten the image based on the angle of the ruler line. The image is straightened vertically or horizontally to match the angle of the line. If the line drawn with the Ruler tool is exactly vertical or horizontal, then no change is made.

The Straighten option of the Ruler tool works best on images that have a reference plane such as the side of a building or a horizon that should be exactly vertical or horizontal. Figure 3.18 shows an example of using the ruler to straighten a seascape image. Notice that the horizon in the original is crooked, making the image look odd. A line is drawn with the Ruler tool and then when the Straighten button is clicked, the horizon matches the horizontal plane of the image.

FIGURE 3.17

Using the Crop and Straighten tool to automatically detect, crop, and straighten a series of photos contained in a single scan

FIGURE 3.18

Using the Straighten option in the Ruler tool options, you can quickly straighten an image based on the line drawn with the Ruler tool.

Trimming a border

The Trim utility provided with Photoshop allows you to quickly trim off the border around an image. This can be a useful tool when you are working with scans of older photos that contain borders, a screen shot of an image that contains a border, or a document that has empty space around the outside.

The Trim utility detects the border based on a specific color or blank pixels and then trims the edges of the document based on that color. The Trim utility allows you to specify whether to use transparent pixels, the color of the pixel in the top-left corner, or the color of the pixel in the bottom-right corner of the image to trim the edges. You also can specify which of the top, bottom, left, and right edges of the border are removed.

To use the Trim utility to trim the border around an image, choose Image ➪ Trim to launch the Trim dialog box, shown in Figure 3.19. Then specify the options and click the OK button to trim the image.

FIGURE 3.19

Using the Trim utility to trim the border of an image

Summary

This chapter discussed the basics of images and viewing files. Some file formats offer advantages over others, depending on the purpose for which you are using them. Although you will likely use the Photoshop format for most of your editing, you will probably gravitate to one of the main file types such as TIFF or JPEG for saving the edited images.

Resolution and size have a relationship based on the desired output medium of the images. Using the Canvas Size tool, you can add additional area to an image without changing any of the existing pixels in the image.

This chapter also discussed how to crop, straighten, rotate, and trim images. You can use the Crop tool to crop and straighten images. You can also straighten and rotate images using the options in the Rotate Image menu.

In this chapter, you learned the following:

- The different file formats for images, video, and 3D objects that Photoshop is capable of supporting, what they are for, and when to use them
- Opening, resizing, and adjusting the resolution of images
- Using the Image Size tool to set the size and resolution of the image to match the destination
- Guidelines to use when cropping images
- Using the Crop and Straighten utility to detect borders, crop them, and straighten photos, all at the same time

3

Understanding Colors, Histograms, Levels, and Curves

IN THIS CHAPTER

Understanding color and how Photoshop uses it

Understanding how to use histograms to analyze colors

Using the Curves tool to adjust tones

Selecting a color mode for an image

Selecting colors in Photoshop

Color is the basic element for everything that you do with images. The purpose of this chapter is to help you understand how Photoshop perceives color so you can use the tools in subsequent chapters more effectively.

Photoshop provides some very powerful tools to analyze, adjust, and select colors in your images. This chapter discusses using the histogram to understand the color composition in an image. You need to understand the histogram to make the most out of tools such as Levels and Curves.

This chapter also discusses the color modes supported in Photoshop and how to select colors based on those color modes. Understanding the color modes gives you an insight into how Photoshop perceives color and consequently how to make the most out of the editing tools provided.

Knowing Color Basics

Color is the basic element of all images. Understanding color helps you make better adjustments and corrections to your images. Photoshop gives you the option of working in several different color models, and understanding color also helps you choose the best color model.

Understanding color

The human eye can detect millions of different colors, but really, what are those colors made of? Put simply, color is made of light. Light travels in a series of waves. Visible light is made of waves traveling between a specific set of wavelengths. White light is light that contains waves of all frequencies and therefore contains all colors.

The human eye can distinguish the different wavelengths of the light waves. The wavelength of each light wave determines the color that the eye detects. For example, light waves with frequencies on the low end of the visible light spectrum are interpreted as blue, and light waves with frequencies on the high end of that spectrum are interpreted as red.

When the eye looks at an object, it is detecting the light that is reflecting off the object. Depending on the nature of the object's surface, some of the frequencies are absorbed by the surface and some are reflected into the eye, producing the colors we see.

Looking at color, intensity, and the human eye

The eye detects color in light waves through tiny receptor cells in the retina called *cones*. Light stimulates these receptor cells, and they transfer the data to the brain. There are three types of cone cells. The first type, S (short), are sensitive to the higher frequencies or shorter wavelengths of bluish light. The second type, L (long), are sensitive to the lower frequencies or long wavelengths of yellowish light. The third type, M (medium), are most sensitive to the middle frequencies or middle wavelengths of greenish light. Therefore, the color is broken down into three basic components by the eye, regardless of the complexity of the wavelength composition in the light it is receiving. This is important as you look at topics such as channels, histograms, and color management throughout this book.

Another attribute of light that affects the colors you see is the intensity. Intensity is the strength of the light reaching the eye. Basically, brighter light carries more intensity than dimmer light. Because the cones in the eye are stimulated by the light waves, less intense waves stimulate them less, resulting in a limited amount of data being collected. This limits the number of shades of a color that the eye can discern. Understanding this concept helps you when you are making adjustments and correcting photos.

The eye overcomes dim lighting by using additional receptor cells called *rods*. In bright light, the rods perform almost no function; however, in dim light, the rods transfer additional data to the brain. The data from the rods is colorless, however, which is why we don't see much color in very low lighting. This also is why indoor photos taken with a flash appear much better than those taken without a flash.

> **NOTE**
> The cones in the eye are most sensitive to colors on the upper end of the visible light spectrum. Therefore, colors such as red, green, and yellow are affected less by reducing the intensity than colors such as blue and purple. For this reason, in low lighting conditions you will lose more contrast in the purple to blue range than in the red and yellow range.

Understanding Channels and Levels

Photoshop applies the concepts of digital color in a way similar to how our eyes work. Digital color is divided into channels and levels. A channel represents a specific color, and a level represents the intensity of that color. Using combinations of different levels of channels, Photoshop can represent millions of colors.

To better illustrate this concept, you can look at how some colors are represented in Photoshop using the RGB color mode (discussed later in this chapter). Using the RGB color mode, all colors are divided into three channels — red, green, and blue, hence RGB. Each channel has an intensity level range of 0 to 255, where 0 is none of the color and 255 is full intensity of the color.

Using the RGB color model, the color red is represented as 255 in the red channel, 0 in the blue channel, and 0 in the green channel. Similarly, green is represented as 255 in the green channel and 0 in the other two channels. Yellow is represented as a combination of the red and green channels at 255 and the blue channel at 0. To get black, you set all channels to 0; to get white, you set all channels to 255. In this way, all colors can be represented as a combination of different levels of the red, green, and blue channels.

> **TIP**
>
> Often, when working with multiple images, images on multiple computers, or in different applications, you need to make certain you keep the color consistent. If you note the level value in each channel, you can easily reproduce the same color, no matter where you are working. For example, you may be working in RGB mode and need to create a specific color of blue where the red channel has a level of 26, the green channel has a level of 74, and the blue channel has a level of 158.

Each of the different color modes uses different color channels. However, all color modes use the concept of varying the levels of each channel to represent different colors or tones. Photoshop provides several tools that use the concept of channels and levels to adjust images and apply special effects. Understanding how channels and levels represent color helps you use those tools in a much broader scope.

4

Adjusting with Histograms

One of the most useful tools Photoshop provides when adjusting colors and tones in your images is the histogram. Using histograms, you can see the composition levels in one or more channels. At first, histograms may seem a bit daunting to understand; however, after you understand what they represent, your Photoshop life will never be the same. This section discusses what histograms are and how to use the histogram tools provided in several areas of Photoshop to quickly adjust the levels of channels.

Understanding histograms

The first step in adjusting images with histograms is to understand what they are. Understanding what Photoshop uses to build a histogram and what the histogram represents will help you make better adjustments.

At first glance, a histogram looks like the silhouette of a mountain range, as shown in Figure 4.1. A histogram is really just a vertical bar chart. The chart is constructed by looking at each pixel in the image and counting the number of pixels that contain a value of 0 for that channel, then the value of 1, and so forth up to the value of 255.

FIGURE 4.1

A histogram of the RGB levels of an image in Photoshop

Using the bar chart, histograms show how the levels of each channel are distributed in the image. So what does this mean? It means that you have a visual representation of the color and intensity distribution in your image.

You can interpret the visual data in the histograms in many ways to understand the composition of colors and light in an image to help you make the most out of the Photoshop adjustment tools. To illustrate this, the following sections cover how to use histograms to determine the exposure and color balance in an image.

Determining overexposure and underexposure in an image

One of the most useful features of a histogram is the ability to quickly determine how overexposed or underexposed an image is. While some photos are obviously overexposed or underexposed, the exposure of others may be difficult to determine by just looking at them. Using histograms helps you quickly tell whether an image is overexposed or underexposed.

> **TIP**
>
> When adjusting color, contrast, levels, and tone of an image, first check to see if the image is overexposed or underexposed. You want to adjust the exposure first as discussed in Chapter 13.

Images that are overexposed have mostly higher levels for all channels and almost no lower levels because more light was recorded in the image. Therefore, the histogram is skewed to the right. Figure 4.2 shows an example of an image that has been overexposed. Notice that most of the data in the image falls in the right end of the histogram.

FIGURE 4.2

A histogram of the RGB levels of an overexposed image in Photoshop

Images that are underexposed have mostly lower levels for all channels and almost no higher levels because not enough light reached the image. Therefore, the histogram is skewed to the left side instead of the right. Figure 4.3 shows an example of an image that has been underexposed. Notice that most of the data in the image falls in the left end of the histogram.

FIGURE 4.3

A histogram of the RGB levels of an underexposed image in Photoshop

Determining color balance in an image

Histograms allow you to ascertain the color balance in an image. Understanding the color balance helps when you are trying to correct color and tonal issues in images. For example, if you look at the histograms of an image that should be balanced and see that the image has a disproportionate amount of red, you can easily adjust this.

The best way to determine color balance in an image is to look at the histograms of each color channel individually. Viewing the histograms of each channel shows how much of that color is present in the image compared to the other color channels, as well as a distribution of the levels of each channel.

> **NOTE**
>
> When viewing the color channel histograms of an image, keep in mind what colors should be present. For example, if you are working with an RGB image of a boat on the ocean with a blue-sky background, you should see a lot of blue, but not much green, and almost no red. However, if the image contains people, with green trees in the background and a blue sky, then there should be a fairly even distribution of red, green, and blue.

Figure 4.4 shows the channel histograms of an RGB image. Notice that the red channel has almost no values, and the values that are present are in the lower levels. Conversely, the green channel contains a lot of data and is distributed throughout the histogram. The blue channel contains a moderate amount of data but is definitely skewed to the lower levels.

121

FIGURE 4.4

The color level histograms of an RGB image in Photoshop

Obviously, the color levels in this image are not balanced, but what does that mean? Well, if the image is of a green plant, then it just means that the image contains much more green than any other color. However, if the image is a snapshot of a person's face, then it means that their skin tone has a severe green colorcast, and you will need to add red to get the pink back in the cheeks.

Using the Histogram panel

The previous sections discussed the importance of using histograms in understanding the composition of light and color in an image. Photoshop provides a Histogram panel that helps you quickly view the important histograms of an image.

Using the Histogram panel, you can view the histograms of each of the channels, all channels together, colors, and luminosity. You also can use the histogram tool to view histograms of specific layers. In addition to the histograms, the Histogram panel can show you numerical statistics about the level composition of each histogram.

TIP

When you are making adjustments or corrections that have to do with color, hue, tone, contrast, and so on, you should display the Histogram panel for the image. Look at the overall histogram to check for over- and underexposure. Also, look at the individual channels to verify that the color balance is what you would expect for that image.

You can display the Histogram panel, shown in Figure 4.5, by choosing Window ➪ Histogram from the Photoshop menu bar. The following sections discuss how to configure and use the Histogram panel to view histograms and statistics.

FIGURE 4.5

The Histogram panel in Photoshop

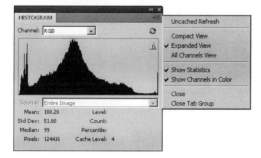

Setting Histogram panel options

The Histogram panel provides several views that you can set by selecting the menu icon shown in Figure 4.5. The following settings in the Histogram panel menu allow you to configure what information is shown in the Histogram panel:

- **Compact View.** The compact view, shown on the left in Figure 4.6, displays only the histogram image of the current channel. This view is handy if you just want to dock the histogram with several other panels to view changes as you adjust the image.

- **Expanded View.** The expanded view, shown in the center in Figure 4.6, displays the histogram image of the current channel but also provides the option to select different channels and sources for the histogram. It also displays the statistics if you have selected the Show Statistics option.

- **All Channels View.** The all channels view, shown on the right in Figure 4.6, displays the histograms of all channels in addition to everything that the expanded view shows.

- **Show Statistics.** The show statistics setting toggles the statistics on and off in the expanded and all channels views.

- **Show Channels in Color.** This option toggles the color view of channels on and off. When you select this option, the histograms of individual channels appear in the channel color. This is useful if you are viewing a specific channel, because it is easy to distinguish which channel it is.

FIGURE 4.6

The compact, expanded, and all channels views of the Histogram panel in Photoshop

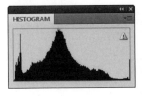
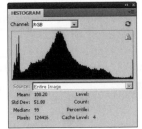
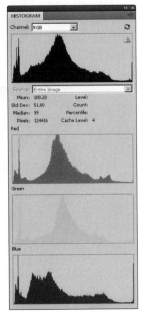

Selecting channels

The Channel menu, shown in Figure 4.7, allows you to select a specific channel to view. The channel that you select is displayed in the compact and expanded views and at the top of the all channels view. The statistics are based on the channel that you select.

FIGURE 4.7

The Channel drop-down menu in the Histogram panel of Photoshop

The following channels are available in the Histogram panel:

- **All Channels.** Selecting all the channels for the color mode option is located at the top of the Channel drop-down menu. For example, if you are using RGB, the top item is RGB and it selects all channels to use for the histogram views and statistics.

- **Single Channel.** Selecting an individual channel is also an option in the Channel drop-down menu.

- **Luminosity.** Selecting the luminosity channel calculates the histogram and statistics based on how much general light is coming from a composite of all channels. This is useful in determining the over- and underexposure.

- **Colors.** Selecting the colors channel displays a histogram that is a composite of all color channels as well as the overlapping colors they generate. This is useful for seeing the general color composition in the image.

Selecting a source

The Histogram panel allows you to select different sources from which you can calculate the histograms. Selecting one of the following options from the Source drop-down menu gives you the ability to view a histogram from any layer or adjustment layer or for the entire image:

- **Entire Image.** This option calculates the histogram based on a composite of all layers. Basically, this is the histogram of the image if you flatten out all your layers.

- **Selected Layer.** This option calculates the histogram based on the selected layer in the Layers panel. You use this option to calculate histograms on only a single layer.

- **Adjustment Composite.** This option calculates the histogram based on the adjustments made in the selected adjustment layer and all layers below it. This is useful to understand the adjustments you have made to an image in graphical form.

4

Understanding statistics

The statistics data in the Histogram panel, shown in Figure 4.8, displays the numerical values that are represented in the histogram image as well as some additional items. Most people would never need to use the statistics because image editing is really more of an art than a science. However, having specific numerical data about the histograms can be useful if you are closely comparing images.

TIP

Many of the statistics change to match the level of the pixel under the mouse cursor as you move the mouse over the image.

FIGURE 4.8

The statistics data in the Histogram panel

Mouse cursor

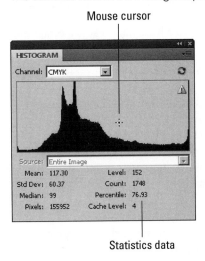

Statistics data

The following statistics are available from the statistics view in the Histogram panel:

- **Mean.** This represents the average level for the selected channel.

- **Standard Deviation.** This represents the variability of the selected channel — in other words, how varied in intensity levels the color in the selected channel is.

- **Median.** This shows the exact middle value of the intensity levels for the channel. In other words, if you took the pixels that are more intense and placed them on one side of a scale and the pixels that are less intense on the other side of the scale, they would be evenly balanced.

- **Pixels.** This shows the number of pixels in the selected channel. This can be useful to see how much data is contained in a specific layer — for example, if you create a selection mask as a layer as discussed in Chapter 10.

- **Level.** This shows the intensity level value directly under the mouse pointer when the mouse is over the histogram.

- **Count.** This shows the total number of pixels in the image that contain a level of intensity equal to the level under the mouse cursor in the histogram.

- **Percentile.** This displays the percentage of pixels in the image with intensity levels that are at or below the level under the mouse cursor in the histogram. The percentage is calculated based on a percentage of all pixels in the image, so the level to the farthest left is 0 percent and the level to the farthest right is 100 percent.

- **Cache Level.** This displays the setting for the current cache level if you select the Use Cache for Histograms option in the Preferences dialog box.

Adjusting images with the histogram tools

Some Photoshop features provide histogram tools to help you better see how to adjust and correct images. Although we cover using the tools, such as the levels adjustments, in subsequent chapters, you need to have a general knowledge of how they work.

The tools that Photoshop provides all have the same basic components. As an example, look at the Levels tool in Figure 4.9. The input levels are represented as a histogram. Below the histogram view are three triangular control handles that allow you to easily adjust the input levels of the channel in the image. To the right of the histogram are three eyedropper tools that allow you to select dark, light, and midtone points in the image to quickly adjust the input levels of the channel. The following sections briefly discuss how to use these tools. We discuss the tools in more detail in subsequent chapters as we get into correcting and adjusting images.

FIGURE 4.9

The Levels dialog box showing the histogram utility that Photoshop provides in several different tools

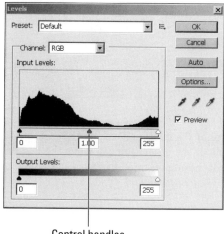

Control handles

Using the handles to adjust the histogram

The dark handle on the left controls the minimum level for the channel, the white handle on the right controls the maximum level for the channel, and the middle gray handle controls the balance of middle tones between the high and low levels.

So what do the histogram controls really do? To help clarify this, notice that most of the level values in the histogram shown in Figure 4.10 are located in the center levels. That means a relatively small number of tones are represented in the image, about 75 out of 255. The result is typically a washed-out image with very little detail.

Now move the left control over to the right until it is on the left side of the histogram mountain, and move the control on the right to the left until it is on the right side of the histogram mountain, as shown in Figure 4.10.

> ## ON THE WEB
> A file with a histogram similar to the one in Figure 4.10 can be found on this book's website as Figure 4-10.tif. You can open it in Photoshop. Try adjusting the levels and see how changing the histogram affects the image.

Notice that the values of the Histogram panel are now distributed more evenly between 0 and 255. This means a greater range of tones is represented in the image because it includes values ranging between 0 and 255 instead of just a range between about 100 and 175. The tonal range of the entire image has been extended, providing much more detail with the simple adjustment of the two sliders.

FIGURE 4.10

Adjusting the minimum and maximum levels on the Levels tool to match more closely with the actual data in the image

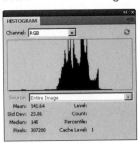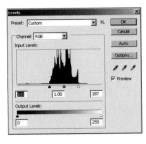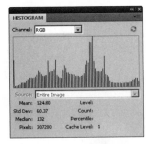

The middle handle simply adjusts the balance of the midtone levels in the histogram. When the histogram is weighted heavily to one side or the other, you can move the middle adjustment handle toward that side to balance midtones represented in the image.

For example, the Levels tool shown in Figure 4.11 is weighted heavily to the left, which means that all the data for the image is in the darker end of the levels. If you move the midtone handle to the left toward the middle of the histogram mountain, the histogram mountain moves to the right to balance on the new location of the midtone slider.

ON THE WEB

A file with a histogram similar to the one in Figure 4.11 can be found on this book's website as Figure 4-11.tif. You can open it in Photoshop. Try adjusting the levels and see how changing the histogram affects the image.

FIGURE 4.11

Adjusting the midtone levels with the Levels tool to change the midtone levels balance in an image

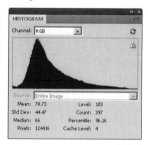 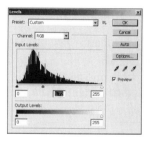 

Using the eyedroppers to adjust the histogram

The Eyedropper tools allow you to adjust the levels of a channel by selecting three points in the image. The eyedropper on the left sets the minimum level for the channel, the eyedropper on the right sets the maximum level for the channel, and the middle eyedropper controls the balance of middle tones for the channel between the high and low levels.

The eyedroppers work similarly to the control handles, except that instead of selecting a specific level for the dark, light, and midtones, you can select pixels directly in the image. To use the eyedroppers, simply click the left Eyedropper tool and select a pixel that should appear black in the image. Then click the right Eyedropper tool, and select a pixel that should appear white in the image. Finally click the middle Eyedropper tool, and select a pixel that should match the midtone for the selected color channel. In the case of all channels, select a pixel that should appear gray in the image.

TIP

The eyedroppers are fast and extremely accurate if there are items in the image that should appear black, white, and gray. If you are not certain of the colors of the pixels, use the control handles instead of the eyedroppers.

Adjusting levels with the Curves tool

Another tool that Photoshop provides to help you better see how to adjust and correct images is the Curves tool, which you access by choosing Image ⇨ Adjustments ⇨ Curves from the Photoshop menu bar. The Curves tool is one of the most difficult tools to understand, and so many Photoshop users avoid it. However, after you learn how to use it, a whole new world of color correction opens up.

While the Histogram tool allows you to change the light, dark, and midtone values for the histogram, the Curves tool allows you to apply a complex curve equation to the histogram, giving you unlimited control over the range of levels in the image. Using the Curves tool, you can completely control the tonal properties of an image.

In this section, we discuss what the curve is and how to use the Curves tool to adjust the levels in the image. Using the different Curves tools in Photoshop for specific purposes is covered in later chapters of this book.

Understanding curves

To understand how the Curves tool works, you need to understand the curve itself. The curve starts as a diagonal line with a value of 0 on the left and 255 on the right, as shown in Figure 4.12. This means that the pixels that currently have an intensity level of 0 for that channel have a value of 0 in the histogram, the pixels at level 1 have a value of 1, and so on up to 255.

> **NOTE**
>
> The grid lines in the curve window allow you to more easily tell what the values are for points on the line. The bottom-left point on the line has a value of 0, the middle point on the line has a value of 127, and the top-right point on the line has a value of 255. The point midway between the bottom-left and middle point of the line has a value of 64, and the point midway between the middle point and the top-right point has a value of 192.

FIGURE 4.12

A simple linear curve in Photoshop

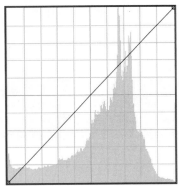

The Curve tool works by applying new level values in the histogram for each of the current levels. Think of the Selection tool as a graph with the existing level values specified along the bottom axis from 0 to 255. The new values are equal to the values of the points on the line corresponding to each of the old levels.

To help you understand the curve better, look at the following example. Figure 4.13 shows a modified curve. Notice that the points on the left (0), right (255), and middle (127) are all on the original line, which means that pixels with those level values will not change. However, the curve goes above the original line before level 127, so the pixels for each of those levels increase to match the value of the line.

Using only two points may create a bit of a problem with the tonal correction. Notice that the levels close to 0, 127, and 255 do not change as much as the levels around 64 and 192. To overcome this problem, Photoshop allows you to apply additional points to the line to further adjust the curve.

FIGURE 4.13

A curve that maps pixels with levels between 0 and 127 to higher levels, and pixels with values between 127 and 255 to lower values

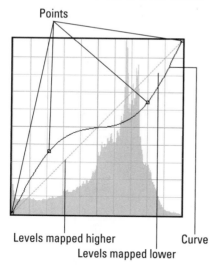

Points

Levels mapped higher   Curve

Levels mapped lower

Using the Curves tool

Now that you understand how the curve works, we discuss the features of the Curves tool that enable you to create dynamic curves that can really have an impact on the tones of your images. You can access these tools whether you are adjusting images using the Curves tool, with an adjustment layer, or in Camera Raw.

Selecting the channel

The first thing you want to do is to select the channel you want to adjust. The Channel drop-down menu, shown in Figure 4.14, allows you to select any channel or all the channels.

Adding points

You can add points to the curve by clicking the Points Curve button and then clicking the curve in the curve panel. When you select the Points Curve button, you can use the mouse to add points by clicking the curve. You can add up to 14 points to the curve, for a total of 16 points including the ends, because the end points are also adjustable. You can remove points from the line by dragging them with the mouse to the bottom-left corner or to the top-right corner of the curve panel.

TIP

The more points you add to the line, the finer your adjustments to the tonal correction are. However, adding more points makes it more difficult to make adjustments because you may need to adjust multiple points when you adjust one. To speed things up, make the bigger adjustments first, and then add more points as needed.

FIGURE 4.14

The Curves tool in Photoshop

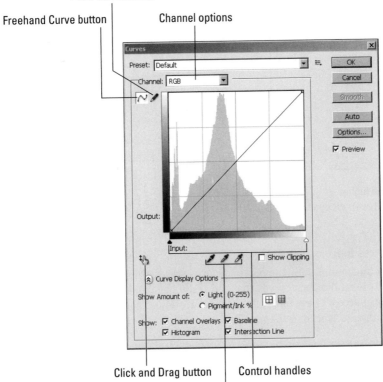

Adjusting the input levels

You can adjust the input levels using the control handles along the bottom axis of the Curves panel. This is the same thing as adjusting the minimum dark and maximum light levels in the histogram, and it limits the curved line to operate between those ranges. To adjust the input levels, simply grab one of the control handles with the mouse and drag it to the appropriate value.

TIP

You should adjust the input levels before you create your curve because adjusting the input levels afterward results in changes to the curve.

Adjusting specific levels from the image

A useful feature of the Curves tool is the ability to select a level directly from the image. This allows you to simply select a particular area of the image based on what colors or tones you see.

To adjust the levels from the image, click the Click and Drag button in the Curves tool (refer to Figure 4.14). Then use the mouse to select a pixel in the image containing the tone you want to adjust. A new point is created on the curve. While pressing and holding down the mouse button, you can move the mouse up and down to adjust the level of that point.

Creating a freehand line

If 16 points on the curve line are not enough, you can create your own line by clicking the Freehand Curve button (refer to Figure 4.14). The Freehand Curve tool allows you to create the curve by drawing a freehand line in the curve window instead of using points.

You can also use the Freehand Curve tool to make slight, non-smooth adjustments to the curve after you have created it with points. Only the areas of the curve that you draw with the Freehand tool are corrected.

TIP

You can convert a freehand line into a points curve by clicking the Points Curve button. This is helpful if you need to make some additional adjustments to the points curve after you change it using the Freehand Curve tool.

Using the eyedroppers

The eyedroppers work the same way for the Curves tool as discussed earlier in the Histogram section. Adjusting the image first with the eyedroppers sometimes gives you a better base to start from when making the tonal corrections with the curve.

Working in Different Color Modes

Photoshop provides several color modes that help you work with images. Color consists of different intensities of light at different frequencies. However, that data needs to be translated into a quantifiable form that can be understood by Photoshop, the monitor, printers, and ultimately you. This section gives you an overview of the different color modes available for use in Photoshop and why you would use them. It also helps you understand the Bits/Channel settings for the image modes.

Understanding the different color modes

A color model is simply a method to translate the light captured in an image into a digital form that the computer and other devices can understand. Each color model divides the light into one or more channels and then assigns an intensity level to each channel for each pixel in the image. Photoshop provides several color modes that match the most common color models.

Depending on what you are doing with an image, you want to use a specific color mode that provides the best management of the color. To set the color mode of an image, choose Image➪Mode and then select the mode you want to use from the Photoshop menu bar. The following sections discuss each of the color modes and what they are for.

Bitmap

The Bitmap color mode contains only one channel with only two possible levels, 0 and 255. As a result, a bitmap is a black-and-white image without color and even without shades of gray. In essence, the image becomes a series of black dots on a white background. This may not sound very useful; however, there are several good uses for these types of images.

The most common use of the Bitmap mode is outputting an image to a black-and-white laser printer. Laser printers create images as a series of black dots on the page. So working with the image as a bitmap lets you make changes to a version that appears exactly how it will when it is printed by the laser printer.

> **TIP**
> Bitmap images that are printed on low-resolution laser printers often end up darker than you would expect. Be sure to lighten the image before printing it to a low-resolution laser printer.

The Bitmap dialog box shown in Figure 4.15 lets you set the resolution and method to use when creating the bitmap from the image. You should set the resolution to the same resolution that you will be using to output the image to the printer.

You can select the following methods from the drop-down list in the dialog box:

- **50% Threshold.** This sets every pixel in the image that is more than 50-percent gray to black, and every pixel that is 50-percent gray or lighter to white. This is by far the simplest pattern; however, the result is very choppy, and the image typically doesn't look very good unless you are trying for a special effect, in which case it would be better to use the Threshold tool in the Image➪Adjustment menu.

- **Pattern Dither.** This uses a pattern to mix black and white pixels together, which results in the appearance of different shades of gray. The problem with this method is that the pattern shows up in the image, so the effect is not very smooth.

- **Diffusion Dither.** This uses an error-diffusion method of converting an image into a series of dithered pixels that are less structured than the pattern dither. The diffusion dither method produces an image similar to a mezzotint, which often is the best option for printing on low-resolution laser printers.

- **Halftone Screen.** This uses a series of dots of varying sizes and spacing that trick the eye into believing it is seeing a continuous tone. When you select the halftone screen option, an additional dialog box pops up that enables you to select the frequency, angle, and shape of the halftone dots. Typically, the best shape to use is the round shape because it is closest to what the printer generates. The frequency depends on the resolution of the printer. The higher the frequency, the better resolution you get in the image; however, if you set the frequency too high, the patterns overlap when printed and the results do not look good.

- **Custom Pattern.** This allows you to select a custom pattern, either one of those included with Photoshop or one of your own. The custom pattern creates similar results to the pattern dither. Typically, you would only use this option if you had a specific pattern that you wanted to show up in the image.

FIGURE 4.15

The options for the Bitmap mode in Photoshop

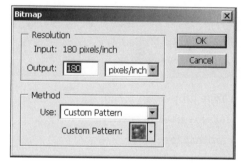

Grayscale

The Grayscale mode contains only one channel, but unlike the Bitmap mode, it can have intensity levels from 0 to 255. The Grayscale mode is useful if you are outputting the image to a black-and-white printer.

> **TIP**
>
> You can create a grayscale image from a single RGB channel by selecting that channel in the Channels panel and converting the image to grayscale. Only the selected channel is converted to grayscale. This can be useful for special effects as well as using the detail of a specific channel.

Another advantage of grayscale is that viewing and adjusting the image in grayscale reduces the overhead of dealing with three color channels. Photoshop is much faster at performing complex operations on grayscale images than on multichannel images. Having a single channel also makes it easier to make adjustments to an image because you only need to worry about adjusting that channel.

> **CAUTION**
>
> To change an image from color to grayscale, Photoshop takes a composite intensity for all three channels and reduces it to the single grayscale channel. This results in a loss of the original color channels. Therefore, make sure you have a backup copy of the file before you save it again. Also, you can often create a good grasyscale effect using other methods, such as desaturation, without losing the data in the color channels.

Duotone

The Duotone mode uses one contrasting color of ink over another to produce highlights and middle tones in a black-and-white image. Duotones typically are used to prepare images for printing. Using the Duotone Options dialog box, you can add one, two, three, or four inks to create a monotone, duotone, tritone, or quadtone image in Photoshop.

Use the following steps to configure the monotone, duotone, tritone, or quadtone options from the Duotone Options dialog box shown in Figure 4.16:

> **NOTE**
>
> The Duotone color mode option is available only for grayscale images. If you are using a color image, you need to convert it to grayscale before changing it to a duotone.

1. **Select the type of tone from the Type drop-down menu.**
2. **Click the blank swatch for each ink you need to specify.**
3. **Select the color you want to use for that tone.**

    Typically, you should use black for the first ink in the list.

4. **Click the curve for each ink you need to configure to launch the Duotone Curve tool.**
5. **Use the Duotone Curve tool to adjust the tone curve for that color of ink.**

    Typically, you do not need to adjust the curve unless you want a specific effect from that tone of ink.

6. **Click the Overprint Colors button, shown in Figure 4.16, to open the Overprint Colors dialog box.**
7. **Adjust the colors used when one ink is printed over another ink by selecting the colors for each of the overlapping options.**

FIGURE 4.16

The options for the Duotone color mode and the Overprint Colors dialog box in Photoshop

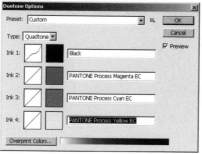 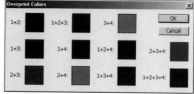

Indexed color

The Indexed Color mode contains a single channel with a single set of indexed colors. Converting an image to indexed color reduces the image to a set of the most important colors. The remaining colors are given an index between 3 and 256 in a color lookup table. Instead of using the level value of the pixel to define the intensity of the channel, it points to an index value in the lookup table for the indexed image.

To change the color mode of an image to indexed color, choose Image ⇨ Mode ⇨ Indexed Color. To view the table of indexed colors, choose Image ⇨ Mode ⇨ Color Table to open the Color Table dialog box shown in Figure 4.17. The following are settings that you can modify in the Indexed Color dialog box:

- **Palette.** This lets you select which palette to use when choosing the color to be placed in the index. You can choose a palette based on Exact, System, Web, Uniform, Local, Master, or Custom colors. The Local option selects colors local to the image. If you are working with multiple images, the Master option selects colors from a master of all images. When selecting local or master palettes, you can use a Selective, Adaptive, or Perceptual method of choosing the colors. The Selective method tries to preserve the key colors in the image. The Adaptive method simply preserves the most common colors. The Perceptual method intelligently selects colors that will provide the best transitions, rather than just the most popular ones. You also have the option to select System colors for images that will be viewed only on a computer. The Web option selects only web-safe colors for images that will be used on web pages.

- **Colors.** This specifies the number of colors to use in the color lookup table. The minimum is 3 colors and the maximum is 256.

TIP

When creating web images with file formats such as GIF and PNG-8, using fewer colors results in smaller images.

4

- **Forced.** This lets you force the conversion to keep certain colors in the image. The default option is to force only black and white to be kept. The Primaries option protects eight colors: white, black, red, green, blue, cyan, yellow, and magenta. The Web option protects the 216 colors in the web-safe colors. The Custom option allows you to preserve a specific palette of colors that you create. When you select the Custom option, a dialog box launches that allows you to specify the colors that you want to preserve.

- **Transparency.** This specifies whether to preserve the transparency in the image.

- **Matte.** This allows you to specify a matte to use when working with transparency in the image. If there is no transparency in the image, this option is inactive. If you select the Transparency option, the translucent areas in the image are filled with the matte color. If you deselect the Transparency option, the translucent and transparent areas are filled with the matte color.

- **Dither.** This specifies the method Photoshop uses to calculate replacement colors for colors being discarded from the image. The None option simply selects the closest color in the lookup table, which can sometimes result in harder edges but is typically the best option to use. The Diffusion option dithers the color randomly, creating a more natural effect. The Pattern option dithers in geometric patterns, which is usually the least desirable because the patterns show up in the image. The Noise option mixes pixels throughout the image instead of in just the areas of transition.

- **Amount.** This specifies the percentage of diffusion to use when dithering. This option is available only when you select the Diffusion dithering option. Lower values decrease the size of the file but result in harsher color transitions.

- **Preserve Exact Colors.** This turns dithering off for areas of solid color when you select the Diffusion dithering option. This option is not available unless you select the Diffusion dithering option. Using this option helps your images look better even if you have to use dithering.

FIGURE 4.17

The options for the Indexed Color mode and the Color Table dialog box in Photoshop

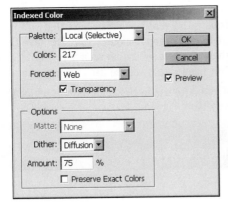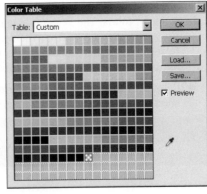

RGB color

You will likely use the RGB color model most often, as it is used by computer monitors and the human eye. Photoshop quickly processes its wide range of vivid colors.

RGB is the model that most closely matches the human eye for two reasons. First, RGB uses three colors similar to the receptors in the human eye. Second, RGB is additive, meaning that as you add more color, you get more light, in the same way that more color results in the eye seeing white.

In the RGB model, colors are divided into three channels of red, green, and blue. Each channel has an intensity level range between 0 and 255. Each color is made up of a combination of intensity levels from these three channels, resulting in the possibility of over 16.7 million different colors.

RGB provides the most vibrant use of colors of all the color models and is supported by most file formats. The one downside to RGB is that it contains more colors than can be printed, especially the brighter colors. This can result in loss of detail in some areas of your images when you print them. The solution is to use the CMYK color model if you are going to have your images professionally printed.

CMYK color

The CMYK color model is completely different from the RGB model in that it uses a subtractive method, meaning that the more color is added, the less light is seen. This is one of the reasons the CMYK model works so well for printing. Think about adding ink to a page; if you add all the colors, you get black, or rather a really deep brown.

Another difference between the CMYK model and the RGB model is that CMYK is made up of four channels: cyan, magenta, yellow, and black. The black channel is necessary because adding the ink all together makes a dark brown, not black, so if you want the printer to print true black, you must have a separate channel to specify black.

Which model should you use for general color image editing? The answer is RGB. The RGB model provides the widest range for tonal adjustment and correction. The scanner, monitor, and most other devices work in the RGB model, although the software for most printers will convert the RGB input to CMYK when sending the image to the device to be printed. Also, editing images in Photoshop in the RGB mode is much faster than in CMYK.

> **TIP**
>
> Even if you are using the RGB model, you can choose View ▷ Proof Colors to toggle the view to a simulated CMYK model. This way you can periodically check to see how the image will look when printed. Just remember to turn it off.

Lab color

The Lab color model is very different from RGB and CMYK. The Lab model does have three channels, but instead of all three being dedicated to colors, only two — a and b — are dedicated to color; the third — Lightness — is dedicated to luminosity.

The a channel maps colors ranging from deep green at level 0 to gray at level 127 to a rich pink at 255. The b channel maps colors ranging from bright blue at level 0 to gray at level 127 to a dim yellow at 255. The Luminosity channel maps the brightness of each pixel from dark at 0 to white at 255.

The Lab channel is additive like the RGB model, but it has only two channels of color mixing, and the levels of those channels are not mapping to intensity but rather tones of color. The tones add together to form brighter colors, and only the Luminosity channel provides data to darken the tone that is created by the other two channels.

You can edit images in Lab color at about the same speed as in RGB and much faster than in CMYK, so it is a fun alternative if you want to expand the way you think about mixing colors.

Multichannel

The Multichannel mode separates out the channels in the current color model into spot channels. You can use spot channels to store parts of an image that you want to print in specific inks or spot colors. For example, you can print specific inks from a Pantone library.

When you convert an image to the Multichannel model, the current channels are changed to spot channels. The channels created in Multichannel mode depend on the original color mode of the image. For example, the RGB mode is converted to cyan, magenta, and yellow spot channels, the CMYK model is converted to cyan, magenta, yellow, and black spot channels, and the Lab model is converted to three alpha channels.

> **NOTE**
> The spot channels overlap, so if you do not want ink from one channel to be printed onto ink from another channel, the data in those areas of the channel cannot overlap.

Learning about bits per channel

How many bits should you use per channel? The quick answer is 8 bits per channel, but let's look a bit closer. What does bits per channel mean? A bit is a single item of information for a computer with a value of 0 or 1. That doesn't mean much in terms of an image, but if you string millions of bits together, it can mean a lot.

Using 8 bits of information, we can define an intensity level of 0 to 255. For three channels, we can define about 16.7 million different colors for each channel. If we use 16 bits per channel, that goes up to over 281.4 trillion colors; if we go to 32 bits per channel, well, you get the idea.

So why not just use 32 bits per channel and maximize our information? The answer is disk space and speed. An image with 32 bits per channel takes up much more disk space and much more effort to edit in Photoshop. Plus, the human eye can't even detect all the colors in images containing 8 bits per channel.

And that leads to the question of why we shouldn't just use 8 bits per channel, as it is more than enough for the human eye. The answer lies in what happens during adjustments, corrections, and conversions. Each time you make a correction to an image, change the levels, add a filter, and so on, you lose a little bit of the distinguishing detail. If you perform enough corrections on an image with 8 bits per channel, you may lose noticeable detail in the image. However, if you are using an image with 16 bits per channel, the data lost is in levels that cannot be detected by the human eye, so when you convert the image back to 8 bits per channel, there is no data loss.

An image must be in the RGB or Lab color modes if you want to convert it to 16 bits per channel. To change your image to 16 bits per channel, choose Image ⇨ Mode ⇨ 16 Bits/Channel. After you have changed your image to 16 bits per channel, you can change it to 32 bits per channel by choosing Image ⇨ Mode ⇨ 32 Bits/Channel.

> **NOTE**
> An image with 32 bits per channel is considered an HDR (High Dynamic Range) image. Typically, these images are used in 3D rendering and advanced CGI animation effects.

Choosing Colors

Color is one of the most important aspects of most photos. Color changes can greatly alter the overall visual effect. You will be working with many different tools in Photoshop that require you to select colors. You need to know how to accurately set and select colors to use these tools.

Remember that even when working with 8 bits per channel, you can choose from more than 16 million colors. The following sections discuss the main methods that you will use to set and select colors.

Choosing colors with the Color Picker tool

The most common method of choosing a color is by using the Color Picker. You launch the Color Picker tool by clicking the foreground or background tool in the Photoshop toolbox.

The Color Picker tool, shown in Figure 4.18, allows you to select any color possible in Photoshop and gives you a wealth of information. The main areas of the Color Picker tool are the color chooser pane, the range slider, the new/current color view, and the color settings.

The Color Picker lets you use the mouse to select the color of any pixel displayed in the pane. The range slider lets you use the mouse to adjust the range of colors displayed in the Color Picker pane. The new/current color view simply shows the current color on the bottom and the newly selected color on top for comparison purposes.

4

FIGURE 4.18

Selecting colors using the Color Picker tool

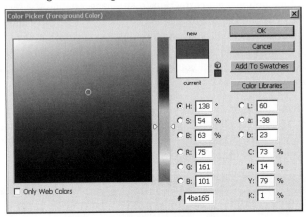

The color settings allow you to change each individual aspect of color that Photoshop uses to define a color. Selecting one of the color settings changes the types of color that can be displayed in the color chooser pane. Changing the value of one of the settings changes the selected color. This list describes the available settings in the Color Picker tool:

- **H.** Changes the hue of the color. The hue values are based on a range from 0 degrees to 360 degrees. Think of a color wheel where red is at 0/360 degrees, green is at 120 degrees, and blue is at 240 degrees. The hue setting is one of the best to use when selecting colors because it allows you to quickly move to a specific color using the range slider.

- **S.** Changes the saturation of the color. The values are based on 0% to 100%. A higher saturation means more of the color, and a lower saturation brings the color closer to gray. If you have chosen a color but you want a slightly different tone, this is the best option to select for the range view.

- **B.** Changes the brightness of the color. The values are based on 0% to 100%. Higher values mean the colors are brighter, and lower values mean they are darker. This is also useful when you have chosen a color but you want to slightly adjust the tone.

- **R.** Changes the intensity of the red channel in the color. The values are based on intensity levels of 0 to 255. Lower values mean less red, and higher values mean more intense red.

- **G.** Changes the intensity of the green channel in the color. The values are based on intensity levels of 0 to 255. Lower values mean less green, and higher values mean more intense green.

- **B.** Changes the intensity of the blue channel in the color. The values are based on intensity levels of 0 to 255. Lower values mean less blue, and higher values mean more intense blue.

- **#.** Specifies the hexadecimal code associated with the color. This is useful for colors that are specified in web pages and for specifying a particular color without having to memorize multiple values. The format of the hexadecimal code represents the level (amount) of red, green, and blue in the color. The first 2 digits represent red from 00 to FF, the middle 2 digits present green from 00 to FF, and the last 2 digits represent blue from 00 to FF.

- **L.** Changes the lightness of the color. The values are based on a luminosity of 0 to 100. Higher values approach white, lower values approach black, and middle values specify the tone of the color. This is useful when you have the color you want but want to adjust the tone just a bit.

- **a.** Changes the value of the *a* channel in the Lab color mode. The values are based on tones between −128 and 127, where −128 is green, 127 is pink, and 0 is gray.

- **b.** Changes the value of the *b* channel in the Lab color mode. The values are based on tones between −128 and 127, where −128 is blue, 127 is yellow, and 0 is gray.

- **C.** Specifies the percentage of cyan in the color. The values are based on a range from 0% to 100%, where 0% is no cyan and 100% is full intensity cyan.

- **M.** Specifies the percentage of magenta in the color. The values are based on a range from 0% to 100%, where 0% is no magenta and 100% is full intensity magenta.

- **Y.** Specifies the percentage of yellow in the color. The values are based on a range from 0% to 100%, where 0% is no yellow and 100% is full intensity yellow.

- **K.** Specifies the percentage of black in the color. The values are based on a range from 0% to 100%, where 0% is no black and 100% is full intensity black.

Another nice feature of the Color Picker tool is the ability to add the color you have chosen to the Swatches panel. This is especially nice if you have taken a long time to find just the right color. To add the color to the swatch, click the Add to Swatches button and specify the swatch name to add the color to.

The Color Picker tool also allows you to select colors from a color library such as a Pantone color. To select a color from a color library, click the Color Libraries button to open the Color Libraries dialog box shown in Figure 4.19. Select the library book from the drop-down menu, and choose the color. To change back to the Color Picker, click the Picker button.

4

FIGURE 4.19

Selecting a color from the Color Libraries tool in Photoshop

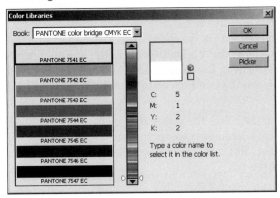

Using the Color panel

Another method of choosing a color is by using the Color panel. The Color panel provides the option of quickly selecting a color based on one of the color models or using sliders to adjust the levels of the color channels. To launch the Color panel, choose Window ⇨ Color from the Photoshop menu bar.

The working components of the Color panel, shown in Figure 4.20, are the before/after view, the Slider tools, the color ramp, and the menu. The before/after view allows you to see the original color as well as the newly selected color. The color ramp at the bottom allows you to select a color from the ramp using the Eyedropper tool that becomes visible when the mouse is over it. The Slider tools allow you to use the mouse to drag handles to quickly select the level for each available channel or to type in a specific value.

FIGURE 4.20

Selecting colors from the Color panel tool in Photoshop

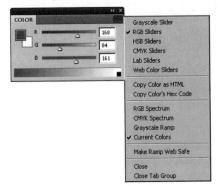

The menu of the Color panel provides the following color mode options for adjusting images:

- **Grayscale Slider.** This sets the slider control to a single slider that adjusts the level of grayscale tones. This tool is useful if you need to add gray without any other tone to the image.

- **RGB Sliders.** This sets the slider control to three sliders that allow you to adjust the intensity levels of the red, green, and blue channels.

- **HSB Sliders.** This sets the slider control to three sliders that allow you to adjust the hue, saturation, and brightness of the color.

- **CMYK Sliders.** This sets the slider control to four sliders that allow you to adjust the intensity levels of the cyan, magenta, yellow, and black channels.

- **Lab Sliders.** This sets the slider control to three sliders that allow you to adjust the values of the a, b, and luminosity levels in the Lab channels.

- **Web Color Sliders.** This sets the slider control to three sliders that allow you to adjust the hexadecimal code values of the red, green, and blue channels for web images.

- **Copy Color as HTML.** This copies the current color as the HTML code that is inserted into an HTML tag when building web pages — for example, color="#9999cc".

- **Copy Color's Hex Code.** This copies the current color as the hexadecimal code that represents the red, green, and blue values — for example, #9999cc.

- **RGB Spectrum.** This changes the color ramp to use the RGB spectrum for selecting colors using the eyedropper.

- **CMYK Spectrum.** This changes the color ramp to use the CMYK spectrum for selecting colors using the eyedropper.

- **Grayscale Ramp.** This changes the color ramp to use the grayscale ramp for selecting a shade of gray using the eyedropper.

- **Current Colors.** This changes the color ramp to use only the tonal values of the current color when selecting a color using the eyedropper.

TIP

The Current Colors ramp is useful when you have selected a color, but you want to change the tone a little bit or when you want to use multiple tones of the same color in the image.

- **Make Ramp Web Safe.** This changes the color ramp to provide only the web-safe palette for selecting colors using the eyedropper. This option is a hangover from the days when web browsers only supported a limited amount of colors in images. When selected, the color ramp changes to provide colors only within the limited color range.

Using the Swatches panel

One of the simplest ways to choose a color is by using the Swatches panel. A swatch is just a set of combined colors. The Swatches panel displays the available colors in the swatch as either thumbnails or a list. To choose a color, simply click the one you want. To launch the Swatches panel, choose Window➪Swatches from the Photoshop menu bar.

Using the Swatches panel menu shown in Figure 4.21, you can select one of the following views to display the colors available in the swatch:

- **Small Thumbnail.** This displays the colors as tiny squares in the Swatches panel. This is the most commonly used view because the colors are generally big enough to see and yet the panel doesn't take up a lot of space.

- **Large Thumbnail.** This displays the colors as larger squares in the Swatches panel. This view is useful if you have colors that are very close to each other in the swatch. Viewing larger squares makes it easier to distinguish between the colors.

- **Small List.** This displays the colors as a list with tiny squares next to the color names in the Swatches panel. You typically use this view if you want to know the name of the color when selecting it; however, it can be difficult to navigate a large swatch when in this view.

- **Large List.** This displays the colors as a list with large squares next to the color names in the Swatches panel. This view is almost never used because it is difficult to scroll through to find a color.

FIGURE 4.21

Selecting colors from the Swatches panel in Photoshop

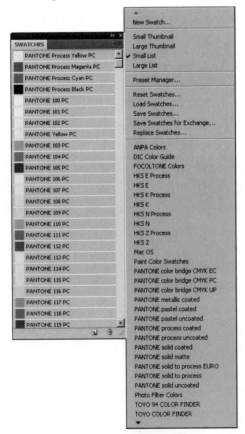

Using the menu in the Swatches panel, you also can save the colors in the current swatch as a custom swatch as well as load and replace swatches. You also can select from a list of swatches that are built into Photoshop.

> **TIP**
>
> When you open a new swatch, Photoshop allows you to append it to the existing swatch. This enables you to combine swatches that you commonly use into a single custom swatch that you can load later, allowing you to avoid constantly switching between swatches.

Selecting color from an image with the Eyedropper tool

Another way to select a color is to use the Eyedropper tool in the Toolbox. This is by far the simplest method of selecting a color. The Eyedropper tool works by selecting the color that the mouse is currently over in the image when you click the left mouse button.

The downside to using the Eyedropper tool is that the color must appear in the image. The upside to using the Eyedropper tool is that the color appears in the image. These two statements may appear to conflict; however, it depends on what you are trying to do. If the colors in the image are limited or you want to add a color that doesn't exist in the image, the Eyedropper tool will not work for you. However, if you are trying to use a color that matches the surrounding image, selecting a color from the image guarantees that it matches somewhere in the image.

When using the Eyedropper tool, the options menu shown in Figure 4.22 allows you to set the following options:

- **Sample Size.** This allows you to specify the size of the area of pixels beneath the Eyedropper tool that are sampled to determine color when you click the mouse button. The default is 11 by 11 pixels, but you can specify ranges from a single pixel to 101 by 101 pixels. The total area of pixels is sampled and the average color is selected. For images with a lot of variance, you will likely want to use a smaller sample size.

- **Sample.** This allows you to specify whether to sample pixels from all layers or only the current layer.

- **Show Sampling Ring.** When you select this option, a large ring, shown in Figure 4.22, is displayed as long as you press and hold down the mouse button. The color ring shows the current color on the bottom and the sampled color on top as you drag the mouse around the image. Notice that the current color here is black and the sample color is from the small patch of blue in the image.

> **NOTE**
>
> The Show Sampling Ring option is available only if you select Use Graphics Processor in the Performance preferences as described in Chapter 2.

FIGURE 4.22

The Sampling Ring allows you to see the previous color on top as well as the current color under the cursor on the bottom

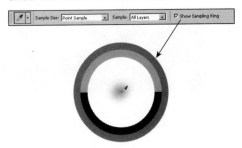

Understanding the Color Sampler tool

A subtool of the Eyedropper tool in the Photoshop Toolbox is the Color Sampler. It looks like the Eyedropper tool, but it has a crosshair in the icon. The Color Sampler tool allows you to view channel settings for up to four channels. The Color Sampler tool launches when you select a pixel.

To use the Color Sampler tool, select it from the Toolbox and use the mouse to select pixels in the image. After you select a pixel by left-clicking in the image, the Info panel appears. As the mouse moves, the data at the top of the Info panel changes, telling you the values of the RGB and CMYK channels of the pixel that the mouse is hovering over.

You can add up to four samples to the Info panel using the Color Sampler tool, shown in Figure 4.23. To delete a sample, right-click the sample using the Color Sampler tool and select Delete from the pop-up menu. To change the color mode information listed in the Info panel, right-click the sample and select the color mode.

FIGURE 4.23

Viewing color channel data in the Info panel in Photoshop

Using the HUD Color Picker

One of the best ways to quickly select a color while using another tool such as a brush is to use the HUD Color Picker. The HUD Color Picker provides a hue strip or wheel that sets the base tone for a color block. An Eyedropper cursor in the color block allows you to select a specific color from the color block or a hue from the hue strip or wheel.

> **NOTE**
>
> *HUD* stands for Heads Up Display, a term used in technology that presents controls and information to the operator without the need to look down at a control panel, for example, in military weapons systems, advanced jets, and even some games.

You launch the HUD Color Picker by pressing Alt+Shift/Option+Shift while right-clicking with the mouse. Figure 4.24 shows both the wheel and strip versions of the HUD Color Picker. Which version is displayed is defined in the General settings of the Preferences dialog box, as discussed in Chapter 2.

FIGURE 4.24

The HUD Color Picker is a very useful feature that allows you to change the color while using other tools.

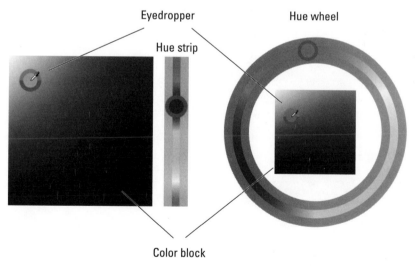

Eyedropper   Hue wheel

Hue strip

Color block

> **NOTE**
>
> The HUD Color Picker is available only if you select Use Graphics Processor in the Performance preferences as described in Chapter 2 and in 8-bit and 16-bit images.

Summary

This chapter covered everything you need to know about color to get the most out of Photoshop's tools, from how the human eye perceives it to how to select a color in Photoshop. The histogram shows you the basic composition of one or more color channels, and modifying the histogram modifies the color composition in the image.

The purpose of this chapter was to familiarize you with the relationship between light, color, the human eye, digital files, and Photoshop. You have learned the following:

- That color is simply light reflected off surfaces at different frequencies and intensities.

- How Photoshop sees colors in terms of channels and levels.

- How to understand the information contained in a histogram and how it applies to the level and channels contained in the different color modes of Photoshop.

- The purpose and how to best use each of the color modes such as RGB, CMYK, and grayscale.

- Using the color tools in Photoshop to give you the maximum information when editing your images.

Applying History and Actions

IN THIS CHAPTER

Experimenting with the non-destructive nature of Photoshop

Using the History panel to manipulate past adjustments

Creating custom actions to save time

You edit images in Photoshop by applying a series of adjustments to modify the original pixels in the image. Each adjustment builds on the others until you achieve the desired results. Photoshop provides two powerful features that allow you to be more productive by using and manipulating the sets of adjustments that you make to your images.

The history feature tracks each change you make to the individual image. This allows you to have a record of each state of the image during editing. Photoshop provides several highly useful tools that allow you to make dynamic adjustments to the image by manipulating the history states. These tools also allow you to experiment with different techniques because you can revert quickly to previous states or remove adjustments that do not work well.

The actions feature allows you to bundle a set of adjustments as an individual action. You can save actions to a file and then use them in other images. This feature saves a lot of time when you are performing similar adjustments to images.

Understanding Photoshop's Non-Destructive Features

One of the most powerful features of Photoshop is the ability to make numerous edits to images and see the effects of those edits without destroying the underlying pixel data or previous edits. Many of the edits done to images in Photoshop are the result of a series of adjustments using a variety of tools. Each adjustment builds on preceding ones until you reach the result you want. Unfortunately, it is not an exact science, and you may have to try different adjustments until you find a combination that culminates in the desired outcome.

The non-destructive features of Photoshop allow you to freely play around with the edits, tweaking them until they are just right without the fear of ruining previous edits or the original pixels in the image. In fact, you can even remove a single adjustment that you made early on without affecting the original pixels or the subsequent adjustments.

To help you understand the value of non-destructive editing, think about editing an image for hours and realizing that one of the first edits you made was a bad decision. If you could not undo that edit, the hours of work would be wasted.

The following is a list of the major non-destructive features and tools that are available in Photoshop:

- **History.** The History panel, discussed later in this chapter, provides a means of quickly viewing each of the adjustments that you have made to the image. The History panel also provides a way to create snapshots that you can easily revert to, and to remove individual edits from the history.

- **Dialog boxes.** Most of the dialog boxes in Photoshop allow you to use the key sequence Ctrl+Z/⌘+Z to undo the last adjustment you made to a field. This feature is very useful if you make a change to a value that you do not like but you cannot remember what the original value was. This feature will undo only the last change you made. To undo other changes, press and hold down the Alt/Option key and the Cancel button turns into a Reset button. When you click the Reset button, the values in all the fields in the dialog box revert to the original values from when you last opened it.

- **Layers.** Using adjustment layers, discussed in Chapter 10, you can make adjustments to the image without affecting the actual image. The adjustment layers contain adjustment data that affects how the image looks when you apply them. Layers are very useful because you can remove, reorder, and even move them from one document to another in Photoshop.

- **Layer Comps.** The Layer Comps panel is similar to the History panel, but it contains the changes made to each layer. Using the Layer Comps panel, you can easily create multiple versions of the edited image, each with its own set of changes. This makes it easy to track multiple changes to the image.

TIP

You can use the Layer Comps feature to create several versions of an image for comparison. This can be very useful if you are creating multiple versions to get approval from a client, if you are not sure what you want and want to maintain multiple "what-if" versions, or if you need different types of edits on the same image for different purposes.

- **Masks.** Masks, discussed in Chapter 10, allow you to create a protective shield over an area in a document that protects that area from any adjustments you have made. One of the major advantages to masks is that you can alter them at any time, and the alterations are automatically updated in the results because they actually sit between the adjustment layer and the layers below.

- **Alpha channel.** The alpha channel, discussed in Chapter 11, allows you to add information that you can apply to areas of the image without actually affecting the other channels. For example, you can add transparency information to an RGB image without affecting the normal pixels in the image.

- **Smart objects.** Smart objects are a useful feature of Photoshop that provide powerful, yet non-destructive adjustments to images. Using smart objects, you can combine a series of one or more layers, documents, and other components into a single combined object. Then you can apply filters and make other adjustments to the object without actually changing the contents. You can change the contents of the original object at any time, and the adjustments apply only to the updated object. This allows you to create a base source image and quickly try different edits without worrying about damaging the source image or the original pixels.

- **Crops.** Photoshop allows you to crop images in a non-destructive manner. When you start to crop an image, as discussed in Chapter 3, the Options menu displays two choices: Delete and Hide. If you select Delete, the pixels outside the crop box are thrown away and you work only with the remaining pixels. If you select Hide, the pixels outside the crop box are masked, and although you only see the pixels inside the crop box, the pixels outside the crop box are still present in the image. To restore the cropped pixels, choose Image ⇨ Reveal all. The canvas reverts to the original size, and any of the layer adjustments you have applied to the image are applied to the restored pixels.

> **NOTE**
> The Hide and Delete options in the Crop tool menu are available only if you are cropping a layer whose pixels are not locked. For more information about layers and layer locking, see Chapter 10.

- **Revert.** At any point while you are editing an image, you can revert to the original state of the file when it was opened or last saved by choosing File ⇨ Revert or pressing the F12 key. You should only use this option as a last resort, as all the changes you have made to the image are lost. However, this option saves you the time of closing the image without saving the changes and reopening it.

Using the History Panel

The History panel can be one of your best friends in Photoshop because it can save you hours of lost work. When you are editing images in Photoshop, you are really working from one change to another. These changes are tied together and build on one another.

The purpose of the History panel is to track and manage each adjustment you make to the image. The History panel is designed to give you much more flexibility and control than the traditional undo/redo functionality. Using the History panel, you can undo and even modify one, some, or all of the changes you have made to an image.

> **NOTE**
> Photoshop allows you to log some of the history information either as metadata in the file or as a separate file. You can set the history logging feature from the General panel in the Preferences dialog box, as discussed in Chapter 2.

5

The following sections discuss the History panel and how to get the most out of it. They also cover using the Eraser, History Brush, Art History Brush, and selections to roll back and modify individual edits.

Understanding the History panel

The History panel stores a list of the actions that you have performed on a document. This list provides three very useful features. First, you can see what changes you have made to the document. Second, you can undo changes that you have made to the document. And third, as we discuss later in this section, you can creatively combine items in the history to enhance your images.

You load the History panel by choosing Window ➪ History from the Photoshop menu bar. The History panel, shown in Figure 5.1, keeps track of a list of the states of the image after each edit is applied. This allows you to go back quickly in time to the state of your document after any of the edits were made. The following sections discuss configuring and using the History panel to adjust your images.

FIGURE 5.1

The History panel keeps track of the state of the image after each change is made.

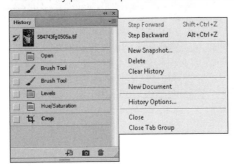

Configuring the History panel

You can configure the History panel by setting the options in the History panel menu and by setting the preferences for history in the general Photoshop Preferences. To configure options from the History panel, select History Options from the History panel menu (refer to Figure 5.1) to open the History Options dialog box, shown in Figure 5.2.

Using the History Options dialog box, you can configure the following options:

FIGURE 5.2

Setting options for the History panel

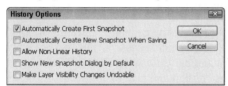

- **Automatically Create First Snapshot.** This automatically creates a snapshot of the original document when it is loaded into Photoshop. This is a useful feature that allows you to always have an original snapshot to use with the history tools; however, if you know that you do not need to use the history, then turning off this option reduces some processing overhead and memory usage.

- **Automatically Create New Snapshot when Saving.** This automatically creates a snapshot every time you save the file in Photoshop. This can be a useful feature; however, it can also be a problem if you have the tendency to save after every little change you make. You may end up with a huge list that really isn't meaningful. If you use this feature, make sure you are careful about when you save.

- **Allow Non-Linear History.** Typically, the edits to a document are built on top of each other in a linear fashion. The problem with the linear method is that if you delete one state in the history list, then all the subsequent states are also deleted. When you select the Allow Non-Linear History option, the history states become disconnected and you can delete one of the states in the middle without deleting the subsequent changes.

NOTE

Some of the changes you make to a document are very tightly connected. You should be very careful when using the Allow Non-Linear History option so you do not delete a state on which another state is depending.

- **Show New Snapshot Dialog by Default.** This specifies whether to show the New Snapshot dialog box when creating snapshots. If you disable this option, the New Snapshot dialog box is not displayed unless you select New Snapshot from the History panel menu. Disabling this option can speed up creating snapshots using the button on the History panel if you do not need to specify a name or source.

- **Make Layer Visibility Changes Undoable.** If you do not select this option, which is the default, then turning layer visibility on and off is not recorded in the history. When you select this option, turning layer visibility on or off is recorded in the history and you can undo it using the history tools.

By default, Photoshop keeps a record of, at most, 20 history states. Each history state takes up memory and requires extra computer processing by Photoshop. Generally, 20 history states is enough to work from. However, if you are working on an image that requires a single or

5

many different edits with a tool such as the painting tools and results in a separate action for each brush stroke, you may need to increase the recorded history states number, so you can revert or adjust some corrections that you are performing.

The maximum number of history states is specified in the general preferences of Photoshop. To increase the number of history states that Photoshop keeps available, choose Edit ➪ Preferences ➪ General from the Photoshop menu bar (or use the Ctrl+K/⌘+K shortcut) to open Preferences. Then select the Performance option and change the value of the History States field in the History & Cache pane.

Navigating through history states

You can navigate through the different history states either directly using the History panel or by using keyboard shortcuts. The most common method is to open the History panel, scroll through the history, and select the history state you want to view. When you select a history state, the image window changes back to that state.

A sometimes faster option is to use the Ctrl+Alt+Z/⌘+Option+Z keyboard shortcut to navigate backward through history and Ctrl+Shift+Z/⌘+Shift+Z keyboard shortcut to navigate forward through history. If you need to go back only a few adjustments to see how the image looked, then this option is by far the fastest and easiest; however, you cannot undo any of the history edits.

TIP

If you select a snapshot in the History pane, then you can use the Ctrl+Alt+Z/⌘+Option+Z keyboard shortcut to navigate backward through the snapshots and the Ctrl+Shift+Z/⌘+Shift+Z keyboard shortcut to navigate forward through the snapshots.

Using snapshots

A very useful feature of the History panel is the ability to create snapshots of the image based on a specific state. The snapshot data remains, even if the history data is deleted. This feature provides a very versatile way to make different adjustments to an image and quickly compare the adjustments.

To create a snapshot, click the Create Snapshot button at the bottom of the History panel or select New Snapshot from the History panel menu to open the New Snapshot dialog box, as shown in Figure 5.3. Name the snapshot, and select the snapshot source. The snapshot can be taken from the full document, the current layer, or all layers merged. When you click OK, the snapshot appears in the snapshots list at the top of the History panel.

You can treat the snapshots very much like the history states. You can delete them and even apply the History Brush tool to them.

FIGURE 5.3

Creating a snapshot of a history state adds a state that you can go back to at any time.

Creating documents

Another useful feature of the History panel is the ability to quickly turn a history state into a separate document. This feature is useful if you are editing an image and want to send someone multiple versions for her approval. You can make the full edit of the document and then use the History panel to create documents based on the states that you think might work.

To create a document using the History panel, select the state or snapshot to create a document from and then click the Create New Document from Current State button or select New Document from the History panel menu. A new document with the image data from the selected state or snapshot is loaded in Photoshop. The name of the new document is the name of the state or snapshot.

Deleting history

You can clear the history in a couple of ways. For example, you can select a history state and click the trash can in the History panel or select Delete from the History panel menu.

CAUTION

If the Allow Non-Linear History option is selected for the History panel, only the state that you selected is deleted. However, if the Allow Non-Linear History option is not selected, which is the default, then all subsequent history states are deleted as well. Make sure you know which option is selected before you delete a large amount of history that you need.

You can also clear out all the history in the History panel by selecting Clear History from the History panel menu. This removes all history states. The Clear History option works only on history states; snapshots remain after you clear the history.

Painting from history

A powerful feature of the History panel is the ability to select a history state and paint or erase directly from that history state or snapshot. This allows you to paint through the

5

changes that have been made until you get down to the selected history state. If you consider the number of brush styles and transparency options available when painting, then you will see that painting from history opens a variety of possibilities.

To enable painting from the History feature, you need to click the box beside the desired state or snapshot in the History panel. The box changes to the History Brush icon, as shown in Figure 5.4. Photoshop uses that state as the base level when painting from history.

FIGURE 5.4

Selecting the History Brush option for a history state enables the History Brush, the Art History Brush, and the Eraser to use the history data.

Using the Eraser tool in the History panel

One of the best features of the History panel is that it allows you to erase part of the history without having to remove all of the history. To help you understand how this works, consider the following example.

We start with the image shown on the left in Figure 5.5. Notice that the boy's shirt is very light, and the light coming through the trees is so bright that it really washes out his face in the photo. We fix this problem using a simple contrast adjustment, the History panel, and the Eraser tool, by following these steps:

1. **Choose Image ⇨ Adjustments ⇨ Brightness/Contrast.**
2. **Adjust the brightness and contrast down until you have reduced the brightness of the overall image, as shown in the middle photo in Figure 5.5.**
3. **Open the History panel by choosing Windows ⇨ History.**
4. **Click the Enable History Brush icon for the Open history state, as shown in Figure 5.6.**
5. **Select the Brightness/Contrast history state, as shown in Figure 5.6.**
6. **Select the Eraser tool from the Toolbox.**

FIGURE 5.5

Using the Erase to History option on the Eraser tool allows you to make an adjustment to an entire image and then erase a portion of that change.

FIGURE 5.6

Using the History Brush settings and configuring the Eraser tool to erase part of the history from an image

Brush style   Brush mode

Enable History Brush

7. Change the mode to Brush in the Eraser Options bar, as shown in Figure 5.6.

8. Change the brush style to a dissipating brush with a very large size, as shown in Figure 5.6.

9. Set the opacity of the brush to about 75% to allow the adjustment to be more gradual.

10. Select the Erase to History option, as shown in Figure 5.6.

11. Click the boy's face in the image several times using the Eraser tool until most of the original brightness returns to the face.

The end result is shown on the right in Figure 5.5; the face pops out a bit better than in the original.

> **TIP**
>
> Even if the Erase to History option is not checked, you can still erase the history by pressing and holding down the Alt/ Option key while using the Eraser tool.

Using the History Brush

The History Brush tool actually works in the opposite direction of the Eraser tool with the Erase to History option checked. Instead of erasing the changes made since the history state was set in the History panel, you use that history state to draw on the currently selected history state.

 Using the History Brush tool gives you a major advantage over using the Eraser tool in that you can use the brush modes to provide more effects when painting on the history. For more information about using the brush and brush modes, see Chapter 16.

Making use of the Art History Brush

The Art History Brush tool is used to erase part of the history of changes. It functions similarly to the Eraser tool with the Erase to History option checked; however, you have to think about it in reverse terms. Instead of erasing the changes made since the history state that was set in the History panel, you are using that history state to draw on the currently selected history state.

> **TIP**
>
> Using the Art History Brush tool offers a major advantage over using the History Brush tool: in addition to using the brush modes, you also can choose a style to apply to the brush, giving an impressionistic appearance. For more information about using the brush and brush modes, see Chapter 16.

Using selections when painting history

Sometimes, you want to limit the area of an image on which history is being painted. You can use selections to limit the area of the image that will be affected by the Eraser, History Brush, and Art History Brush tools. Selections are discussed in detail in Chapter 9.

Follow these steps to use a selection to limit the area painted on while using the history painting options:

1. **Click the Enable History Brush icon for the history state you want to paint from.**
2. **Select the history state you want to change.**
3. **Use the selection tools to select the area of the image you want to paint history into.**
4. **Use the Eraser, Art History Brush, or History Brush tool to paint into the image.**

   You only paint the area inside the selection.

Creating and Using Automated Actions

Photoshop does an excellent job of providing simple keyboard shortcuts (hotkeys) for most common tasks. The more you use Photoshop, the more you will rely on these shortcuts. They save a lot of time, allowing you to work at a much faster rate. However, even performing shortcuts over and over can become tedious. That is where actions come into play.

Actions are a list of operations to perform from the current window. Actions can include most of the tasks that you can perform using the shortcuts, menus, and panels in Photoshop. Actions can range from something as simple as adding a special effect to the active document to a long series of operations that include creating several new documents and layers with numerous effects, filters, and masks. There really is no limit to what you can do with custom actions.

Actions save so much time because you can perform an action, whether it involves 2 steps or 50 steps, with just the click of a button or a hotkey. Photoshop comes with several predefined action sets for various common tasks.

The predefined Photoshop action sets do everything from creating frames to applying a sepia toning effect to an image. As you work more with Photoshop, you likely will find tasks that you repeat over and over that get tedious. In these situations, you will want to create custom actions. Recording a custom action is as simple as recording the steps you take as you perform those tedious tasks.

> **NOTE**
>
> After you play an action, you can click the History tab to view the History panel and see each step that was taken by the action.

Understanding the Actions panel

The Actions panel provides a way to store and apply sets of operations to your images. One of the biggest benefits of using the Actions panel is that it enables you to store some of the tedious workflow that you consistently perform on images and apply them with a single click of the mouse.

The first step in helping you implement actions to speed up your work is to help you understand the organization of the Actions panel. You can access the Actions panel by choosing Window ⇨ Actions. By default, the Actions panel is shown with the History panel.

The Actions panel is made up of four main sections, as shown in Figure 5.7: the action list, the Actions panel menu, the toggle boxes, and the Quick Buttons.

- **Action list.** Located in the main portion of the panel, the action list is made up of three components: action sets, actions, and recorded commands.

  - **Action sets.** An action set is simply a way to file a list of actions into a category. An action set is distinguished by the folder shown next to the name of any given set. You can see two sets in Figure 5.7: Default and Video. You can load any one of seven predefined action sets from the Actions panel menu, or you can create your own. Click the triangle next to the action set name to see a list of actions contained in the set.

  - **Actions.** An action is a preset list of operations that can be performed quickly and automatically by selecting an action and clicking the Play button in the Actions panel. Click the triangle next to the action name to see a list of recorded commands contained in the action.

  - **Recorded commands.** A recorded command is a list of commands that have been recorded in a set order to perform the same series of operations every time the action is played. These commands may also contain submenus. For example, clicking the triangle next to the Stop command in Figure 5.7 shows the message displayed by the command.

- **Actions panel menu.** Available by clicking the menu button located in the upper-right corner of the panel, the Actions panel menu contains menu items that allow you to set the panel mode, add new actions, load action sets, save action sets, and set other options for the Actions panel.

- **Toggle boxes.** Located along the left side of the panel are two toggle boxes available for each action set, action, and operation in the action list. The left toggle box enables or disables the set, action, or operation. If the toggle box is not checked, the operation is not applied when you run the action. The right toggle box enables or disables any dialog boxes contained in the set, action, or operation.

  If a dialog box is displayed in the toggle box, Photoshop displays the dialog box associated with the operation when running the action. For example, if an operation adjusts the levels of an image, having the dialog box toggled on displays the Levels dialog box and waits for you to adjust the levels manually every time you run the action.

- **Quick buttons.** Located on the bottom of the panel, the Quick buttons are icons that provide quick access to the Stop, Record, Play, Create New Action Set, Create New Action, and Delete tasks for actions. These options are available in the panel menu as well.

- **Button mode.** Just when you thought you had a handle on the Actions panel, you can dramatically change the way it looks by choosing Button Mode from the Actions panel menu. Figure 5.8 shows that the actions list has converted to buttons. This allows you to simply click the action you want to perform without the dual steps of highlighting it and clicking Play. You can see that the action sets are delineated by color.

FIGURE 5.7

Using the Actions panel to manage a set of actions to perform on an image

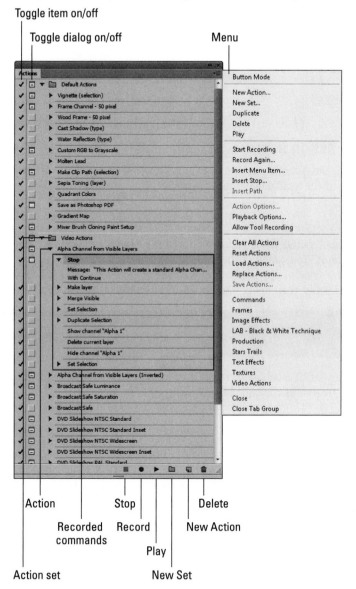

FIGURE 5.8

Using the Button mode of the Actions panel

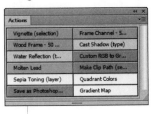

Loading existing action sets

When you initially open the Actions panel, it is populated with the default action set. At this point, you can use one of the available default actions, load an existing action set, or create a custom action set.

You can load an existing action set in one of two ways. The predefined action sets are listed at the bottom of the panel menu. These action sets are for specific purposes such as frames, image effects, and textures. You can load them simply by clicking them. You can also load action sets that you have created previously or downloaded by clicking the Load Actions option in the panel menu and then navigating to the location of the action set.

> **NOTE**
> Action sets have an .atn file extension.

When you load an action set, it is added to the action list. Photoshop automatically expands the action set to show all actions contained inside.

Creating custom actions

You can create a custom action by recording operations you want to add to the action as you apply them. After you begin recording the action, all steps that affect the current document are recorded, including creating new documents. Be prepared to perform the steps in order without any extra steps.

Follow these steps to create a custom action:

1. **Select New Set from the Actions panel menu.**

   If you want to add the action to an existing set, skip to Step 3.

2. **Type the name of the new action set, and click OK.**

3. **Select the action set you want to add a new action to, or go to Step 4 to create a new action.**

4. **Create a new action by selecting New Action from the Actions panel menu to open the New Action dialog box, as shown in Figure 5.9.**

FIGURE 5.9

Using the New Action dialog box

5. **Type the name of the new action.**

   You also can select a function key that automatically runs the action after it is recorded. And you can select a color to be used when displaying the action in Button mode.

> **NOTE**
> You will want to group like actions with like colors to make the Button mode easier to use.

6. **Start recording the action by clicking the Record button in the New Action dialog box.**

   As soon as you click Record, Photoshop begins recording operations, so be ready.

7. **Perform the desired operations in order.**

   Perform the operations as you normally would, including modifying settings in dialog boxes and so forth.

> **NOTE**
> Don't worry if you make a mistake when performing the operations. You can go back and insert forgotten operations, delete unwanted operations, and even modify operations that weren't performed correctly.

8. **Stop recording and save the action by clicking the Stop button in the Actions panel shown in Figure 5.7.**

   The new action appears in the action list.

Editing actions

You can edit an existing action in several different ways. For example, you may realize after recording an action that you need to add additional steps. You may also realize that you need to add menu items, stops, or paths to fine-tune the behavior. The following sections discuss the different ways that you can fine-tune your actions.

5

Adding a stop

A stop is an operation that pauses the running action and displays a message. The user can read the message and decide whether to continue running the action. You may want to insert a stop into actions prior to performing complex or data-changing actions. For example, if your action makes changes and then saves the document, you may want to display a message to that effect so the user can decide whether he really wants the file changed on disk.

To insert a stop into an action, select the operation that you want the stop to be inserted above and select Insert Stop from the panel menu. This opens the Record Stop dialog box, as shown in Figure 5.10. Create a warning message, and check the Allow Continue check box if you want the user to be able to continue after the stop. After you click OK, the stop is inserted before the highlighted command.

FIGURE 5.10

Using the Record Stop dialog box to insert a stop into an action

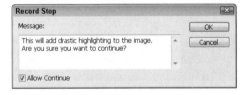

Adding operations

You may decide to add more operations to an existing action. This can be useful for a couple of purposes. For example, you may have forgotten a step when you recorded the action, or you may want to create a variation of an existing action.

To insert additional operations into an action, highlight the operation that you want to add additional operations below and click the Record button. Then perform the operations that you want to add. When you are finished recording operations, click the Stop button, and they are added to the action.

Moving operations

You can move operations from one location in the action list to another by simply dragging and dropping them in the new location. Operations can even be moved from one action set to an entirely different action set. You can select multiple operations in the same action by pressing and holding down the Ctrl/⌘ key and clicking each operation. Then you can move the selected group together.

Duplicating actions and operations

You can duplicate actions or operations by pressing and holding down the Alt/Option key while dragging and dropping them into their new location. Pressing and holding down the

Alt/Option key leaves the original operation or action in place and creates a copy of it in the new location. If you duplicate an action inside the same action set, "copy" is added to the name.

Modifying operations

Some operations can also be modified after the action is recorded. This can be extremely useful if, for example, you made a mistake or you decide later that you want the operation to use different settings. Instead of having to delete the operation and re-record it, you can just double-click the operation, and the dialog box used to create it is displayed. Change the settings that you want to modify, and click OK in the dialog box to update the action.

Inserting a menu item

To manually insert an operation into an existing action, highlight the operation right before the operation you want to insert. Then select Insert Menu Item from the Action panel menu to open the Insert Menu Item dialog box shown in Figure 5.11. You can now add an operation by clicking through the menu path of the operation. For example, if you want to zoom into your image, choose View ⇨ Zoom In. When the operation you want to insert is in the dialog box, click OK to insert the operation into the action.

Inserting a path

You can create a complex path as part of an action, but if you try to record several complex paths, each new path replaces the last one. You can create a path with a pen tool, use a path found in the Paths panel, or import a path from Illustrator. You can insert a new path into an action using the following steps:

1. **Start recording an action by clicking the Record button shown in Figure 5.9.**

2. **Select an action's name to record a path at the end of the action, select a command to record a path after the command, or select an existing path from the Paths panel.**

3. **Choose Insert Path from the Actions panel menu to add the path to the action.**

 Paths are essentially a set of points connected by lines that make up vector shapes. Paths will be covered in much more detail in Chapter 17.

FIGURE 5.11

Using the Insert Menu Item dialog box to insert an operation into an existing action

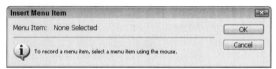

Deleting an operation

You may also want to remove operations from an existing action. To do this, you select the operations, and drag and drop them into the trash icon at the bottom of the Action panel to delete them. You can select multiple actions and delete them at the same time using the Ctrl/⌘ key.

Modifying the action name and function key

You can modify the options of an existing action, including the name, function key, and color. To open the Action Options dialog box, press and hold down the Alt/Option key and double-click the action. You can also choose Action Options from the Actions panel menu. You can then use the Action Options dialog box to modify the name, function key, and color of the action.

Saving actions

After you have created a new action or modified an existing one, you need to save the action. You do this by saving the action set, which is a document. Select the name of the action set, and choose Save Actions from the Actions panel menu. You can use the default location or browse to a location that suits you better.

Adjusting action settings temporarily by using the toggle boxes

You can temporarily adjust the actions by selectively toggling the operations in them off or on. If you click the left toggle box for an operation and deselect it, running the action skips the deselected operation. You can save a lot of time when creating new actions if you use this feature judiciously. Create an action with all the possible steps that you might want to take, and then deselect the steps that aren't necessary depending on the circumstance.

Playing actions

Now that you've learned how to create and modify actions, you can get to the fun part — using them. Playing an action is an incredibly simple process. If you are in Button mode in the Actions panel, you can simply click the button and the action is performed. If you are in List mode, select the action and click the Play button at the bottom of the Actions panel. If you've set up a hotkey for a particular action, you can use that, too.

You can also play an action starting at a particular operation in the action list by selecting that operation and then clicking the Play button.

Managing the action list

With the default action set, there are seven predefined action sets available in the Actions panel menu, and you can also create or download more. As a result, you can imagine how cluttered the Actions panel can become if it's not managed well. The following Actions panel menu options can help you keep your actions organized:

- **Clear All Actions.** The Clear All Actions option wipes the Actions panel clean of any action sets. It doesn't get much cleaner than that!

- **Reset Actions.** Choose the Reset Actions option to replace all the action sets in the Actions panel with the default set. You can also choose Append to add the default set to the actions on the panel rather than replacing them.

- **Replace Actions.** You can replace the actions in the Actions panel with an action of your choice by choosing Replace Actions from the Actions panel menu. You can browse for the action you want to add to the panel.

Summary

This chapter discussed the non-destructive features of Photoshop and how to use the history and actions features to save time and effort when editing images. Photoshop does a good job of tracking the changes that you make to images and providing tools to manipulate them.

The history tools allow you to view the set of changes you have made to the image and to manipulate them to modify the outcome of the edit. The action tools allow you to create, modify, and use actions to combine a series of changes into packages that you can quickly and easily apply to one or more images.

In this chapter, you learned the following:

- How to configure the History panel
- That creating a snapshot preserves the current state of the image to be used later
- How to use the History Brush and Eraser tools to paint a previous history state onto a later state
- How to use the Actions panel to save a lot of time when editing images
- That Photoshop provides several built-in actions
- How to create and organize custom actions

5

Using Bridge to Organize and Process Files

IN THIS CHAPTER

Creating workspaces for navigating, organizing, and processing your images

Organizing files using the Bridge application

Batch processing images using Bridge and Photoshop

Using Mini-Bridge to find and select files in Photoshop

One of the most important yet least popular tasks that is necessary when working with images is organizing and managing the image files. It is difficult to keep files organized in an effective manner, especially with the number of images that are generated by digital cameras.

Adobe has tried to solve the problem of organizing files by providing the Bridge application. Bridge is designed to simplify the process of importing, organizing, and finding files. Bridge also provides a direct interface to Photoshop, and other applications in the Creative Suite, that allows you to take advantage of their image-processing capabilities. The following sections discuss the Bridge application, how to configure it, and how to use it to quickly organize and manage your image files.

Working in the Bridge Workspaces

The Bridge utility is a versatile application that allows you to create workspaces that enable you to easily navigate, organize, and process your images. Using Bridge will help your productivity by allowing you to organize your images and quickly find them when working in Photoshop. The purpose of this section is to help you understand how the Bridge utility is organized and how to customize it to best fit your needs.

Examining the Bridge utility

The Bridge utility, shown in Figure 6.1, is divided into four main areas: the main menu bar, toolbar, window panes, and content view controls. The following sections discuss each of these parts of the Bridge utility.

FIGURE 6.1

The main areas of the Bridge utility are the main menu bar, the toolbar, the window panes, and the content view controls.

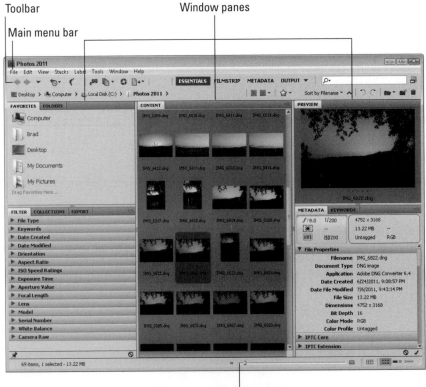

Main menu bar

The Bridge main menu bar provides access to functions of the Bridge utility that you cannot reach easily through the toolbar or the windows in the window panes area. The following is a list of the main menu bar headings with a description of the types of commands that they contain. Many of these commands are discussed later in this chapter:

- **File.** This allows you to work with the file system to create folders, move files, import files, view file information, and interact with Photoshop and other CS6 applications.

- **Edit.** This provides options that allow you to select and copy files, duplicate files, rotate files, and in Windows set preferences for the Bridge utility. The Preferences menu is under the Application menu on Macs.

- **View.** This provides settings to configure how files are viewed in the Bridge utility. You can also sort files, change to full-screen preview mode, and start a slideshow from this menu.

- **Stacks.** This provides options to create and configure stacks. Stacks are discussed later in this chapter.

- **Label.** This allows you to add, remove, and change labels and ratings files. You can use labels and ratings to filter files later.

- **Tools.** This provides options to interact with Photoshop, batch process files, manage metadata templates, and manage caches of files.

- **Window.** This allows you to control which windows are displayed in the window panes. You can also use this menu to quickly switch between workspaces in Bridge. Another option available in the Window menu is New Synchronized Window, which launches a second instance of the Bridge utility that is completely synchronized with the first, so that if you change images or windows in one, the other changes as well.

- **Help.** This provides access to the Bridge help feature and the online support for Bridge at `adobe.com`. You can also update Bridge, launch the Adobe Extension Manager, and get information about the version of Bridge from this menu.

Toolbar

The Bridge toolbar, shown in Figure 6.2, provides quick access to many of the features in Bridge without having to navigate the menus. The following list describes each of the major areas of the toolbar and what tools can be found there:

FIGURE 6.2

The toolbar in Bridge provides quick access to most of the features without having to navigate the menus.

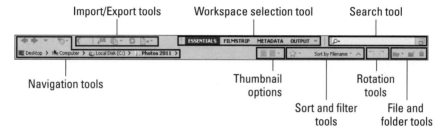

- **Navigation tools.** The navigation tools provide some shortcuts to navigating through the file system to find files. The left and right arrows allow you to navigate forward and backward through previous navigations. You can also click the down arrow to select any of the favorite locations or one of the subfolders in the current path. The Reveal Recent File or Go to Recent Folder button provides several options to navigate back to recent locations and files. The navigation bar, below the others, shows you each folder in the current path; you can select any folder to go back to that level.

> **TIP**
>
> If you click just to the right of the navigation path, a text box replaces the path display and is initially populated by the current path, where you can manually type in a file system path. This can be much faster than navigating by clicking folder icons if you know the name of the path that you want to select.

- **Import/export tools.** The import/export tools provide options to import a file from a camera, open a file in Camera Raw format, and batch rename and output files to PDF or for the web.

- **Workspace selection.** The workspace selection area allows you to quickly select the workspace option that Bridge is using. This is useful when you want to switch between options when you change from navigating the images to working with them.

- **Search.** This allows you to limit the files displayed by restricting them based on the text you type in the search field. Bridge matches the text against the filename and keywords. Only the files that contain the specified text in the filename or keywords are displayed. This is extremely useful if you are searching for a specific set of files.

- **Thumbnail options.** These allow you to quickly configure how Bridge builds thumbnails to display in the content pane. Bridge can use the thumbnails embedded in the image for faster preview; however, these thumbnails are not as high in quality as the ones that Bridge generates otherwise.

- **Sort and filter.** This area provides buttons to filter files by rating, and labels and to sort files by name or different items in the file metadata.

- **Rotation.** This allows you to quickly rotate images 90 degrees to the left or right. This is useful if you are processing images taken with a camera that was tilted on its side.

- **File and folder control.** This area allows you to quickly create folders and delete folders and files. You can also open files from the Adobe Photoshop Recent File list.

Window panes

The window panes area of the Bridge utility provides a location for window panels to dock. This area actually contains five different windows panes (refer to Figure 6.1). Each window pane can contain one or more window panels. You can access different window panels in a pane by clicking its tab at the top of the window pane.

You can drag window panels between panes by clicking the window panel tab and pressing and holding the mouse button down while moving the window panel to the new pane. Also, window panes can be resized by using the control handle in the middle of the pane bars that separate the panes.

You add and remove window panels from the window panes by selecting or deselecting them in the Window menu. The following is a list of the window panels that you can choose to view in the window panes:

- **Folders.** This displays a folder tree view in Windows and a Finder list hierarchy on Macs. Use this panel to navigate and find files in the file system.

- **Favorites.** This displays a list of favorite folders. You can drag folders from the Content panel to this panel to add them to the list. This allows you to configure a set of folders that you use often to speed up navigation.

- **Content.** This displays a list of contents of the selected folder in the Folders or Favorites panels. You can double-click folders in this panel to navigate into them to find files.

- **Preview.** This displays a preview of selected images in the Content panel. You can use the pane controls to change the size of the preview pane, which changes the size of the image displayed.

- **Metadata.** This displays the metadata information contained in the image selected in the Content panel. Each of the main metadata areas is divided into areas that you can expand and collapse. To collapse an area, click the disclosure triangle next to the area title. To expand an area, click the expansion triangle next to the area title.

- **Keywords.** This allows you to create new keywords and add keywords to the files that are currently selected in the Content panel.

- **Filter.** This allows you to quickly limit the files that are displayed in the Content panel based on ratings, keywords, creation date, and last modified date.

- **Collections.** This allows you to create and manage collections of files. A big advantage of using collections is that the files in a single collection do not need to be in the same folder on the file system.

- **Export.** You can use the Export panel to add and manage modules that allow you to export files from Bridge to other locations such as Facebook andPhotoshop.com.

Content view controls

The content view controls shown in Figure 6.3 allow you to change the view of the Content pane. These tools are useful when you need to switch between viewing a lot of images in a folder to more detailed information about a specific set of files.

FIGURE 6.3

The content view controls in Bridge allow you to quickly change how files are displayed in the Content pane.

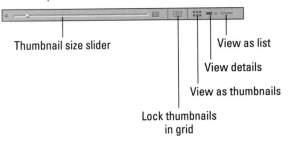

Thumbnail size slider

View as list

View details

View as thumbnails

Lock thumbnails in grid

The following list describes the different views for the Content pane:

- **Thumbnail size slider.** This allows you to quickly change the size of the thumbnails displayed in each of the content views using a slider or the smaller/larger button on the left or right side of the slider.

TIP

When working with a large number of files, use the thumbnail size slider to shrink the thumbnails so that more images are displayed in the Content pane. Then scroll down to the area where the files you want to work with are located and use the slider to increase the size of the thumbnails to more accurately select images.

- **View as thumbnails.** This shows only a thumbnail of the image and the filename.
- **Lock thumbnail grid.** This is similar to the View as thumbnails option; however, the images are locked into an evenly spaced grid. This feature is useful if you are working with images that are not the same shape.
- **View as details.** This displays the thumbnail, filename, creation date, modification date, file size, document type, and some of the metadata such as ISO, focal length, and color profile.
- **View as list.** This displays the files in a more traditional list form with columns for each of the metadata items. This view is useful because you can click the top of any column to sort the images by the values of that column.

Using the Bridge workspaces

The Bridge utility provides several different workspaces that give you a different look at the files you are working with. Each workspace automatically sets the number, size, and shape of the window panes and the window panels that are available in each pane. The different workspaces completely change the look and functionality of the Bridge utility.

> **NOTE**
> Changes you make to a workspace by adjusting window panes and window panels are persistent. The same settings are in effect the next time you switch to that workspace and when you close and reopen Bridge.

Each of these views has advantages over the others. You will likely find yourself switching between the different workspaces to accommodate your current workflow. The following are the workspaces defined in Bridge:

- **Essentials.** The Essentials workspace is the best overall workspace to navigate and find files and perform general organization. It provides a large content panel in the middle from which to select files.

- **Filmstrip.** The Filmstrip workspace is great for previewing files. It provides a large Preview panel to view the images.

- **Metadata.** The Metadata workspace is great for viewing the metadata of images. A large Content panel allows you to quickly select different files, and a Metadata panel allows you to view the metadata.

- **Output.** The Output workspace is designed to help when you want to output a series of files to a PDF file or to the web.

- **Keywords.** The Keywords workspace is designed to help you quickly add and manage keywords for images.

- **Preview.** The Preview workspace provides the largest area for previewing images. The Content panel is narrow and vertical, which is sometimes difficult to use.

- **Light Table.** The Light Table workspace displays only the Content panel. This is excellent for selecting files after you have already navigated to the files you need.

- **Folders.** The Folders workspace is designed to help you navigate the file system to find the folders and files that you need to work with.

Organizing Files in Bridge

The true value of the Bridge utility is in its ability to quickly find and organize images. Bridge provides direct access to all metadata contained in the image's file and allows you to add additional metadata in the form of keywords, labels, and ratings. Bridge also allows you to organize photos in a more usable fashion than a traditional file system by arranging them in collections and stacks. Keeping your files organized will save you time when looking for images.

Importing images from cameras and card readers

An extremely useful feature of Bridge is its ability to import files from a camera or card reader directly to your computer file system. Most cameras and card readers allow you to easily copy files to your computer, but Bridge offers many more options than just copying.

To import images from your camera or card reader to Bridge, choose File⇨Get Photos From Camera from the main menu bar or click the Get Photos from Camera button in the toolbar. The Photo Downloader dialog box appears, as shown in Figure 6.4. You can click the Advanced Dialog button to also display the images on the device, as shown in Figure 6.4. This allows you to select which images to download from the device.

Using Photo Downloader, you can specify where to download the images, what to name them, and several other options. The following sections discuss each of the options available when downloading images.

Get Photos From

The Get Photos From option provides a drop-down menu with a list of available devices. If you can plug the camera directly into the computer, it shows up in the list. Mounted memory card readers will also appear in the list.

Location

You can click the Browse button in the Location area to open a dialog box that you can use to select a destination folder for the new files. This is the location on your file system where the new image files are downloaded.

Create Subfolder(s)

You can tell Photo Downloader to create subfolders on the file system for the new files that are being imported. From the Create Subfolder(s) drop-down menu, you can select None, Custom Name, Today's date, or a variety of combinations of the shoot date with custom data, as shown in Figure 6.5. The sequence of month, day, and year used when naming the folders is noted next to each option — for example, mm, dd, and yyyy.

The Create Subfolders option can be extremely valuable if you are importing files that were taken on different dates and you want to keep them separate. Photo Downloader can automatically separate them based on the dates taken.

FIGURE 6.4

The content view controls in Bridge allow you to quickly change how files are displayed in the Content pane.

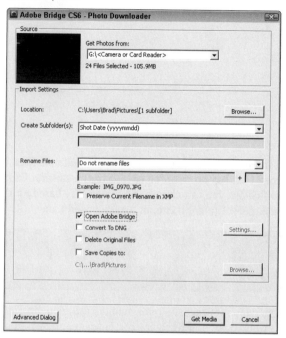

FIGURE 6.5

Selecting a subfolder creation option for a destination folder when downloading images from a camera or card reader

Rename Files

Another useful feature contained in Photo Downloader is the ability to rename files. Most cameras use a simple sequence name that has no meaning except to the camera. Using the Rename Files option in Photo Downloader, you can choose to rename files based on the current date, shoot date, custom name, parent folder name, or a customized name.

> **TIP**
> Using the parent folder name can be helpful if you are using descriptive filenames because when working with collections, you cannot easily see which folder the image resides in.

When you select the Advanced Rename option, a dialog box similar to the one in Figure 6.6 appears. The Advanced Rename option allows you to create custom filenames based on up to ten different components, including text, new extension, current filename, preserved filename, sequence number, sequence letter, date/time, and metadata.

FIGURE 6.6

Configuring custom filename options when downloading images from a camera or card reader allows you to organize files the way you want them.

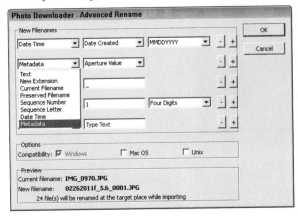

The Advanced Rename option is useful for organizing filenames based on many aspects of the image. For example, you could organize photos based on lens attribute in the metadata. Then you could easily find all the images that you took with a specific lens.

Open Adobe Bridge

The Open Adobe Bridge option is used to automatically open Bridge if it is not already open when using Photo Downloader. Because we are discussing using Photo Downloader from within Bridge, you don't need to worry about this setting.

Convert to DNG

When you select the Convert to DNG option, Photo Downloader converts the images to the DNG file format before saving them to your file system. When you enable this option, the Settings button next to it is enabled. When you click the Settings button, the DNG Conversion Settings dialog box appears, as shown in Figure 6.7.

> **TIP**
>
> You shouldn't convert files that are not in Camera Raw format, such as JPEG files, to DNG when importing them. Because they have already been converted to another format, the Camera Raw data has already been lost. Editing them will be faster by just using the current format; there is no advantage to converting them to DNG.

FIGURE 6.7

Configuring the DNG conversion settings when converting an image to DNG while downloading it

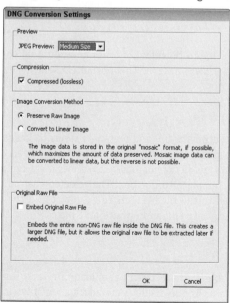

Using the DNG Conversion Settings dialog box, you can configure the following settings to be used during the conversion:

- **Preview.** This allows you to set the size of the JPEG thumbnail embedded in the DNG file to large, medium, or none. Using thumbnails can make Bridge run faster; however, they make the file size larger. If you are not sure, use the medium setting.

- **Compression.** When you check the Compressed option, the data compression used to store the DNG data is completely lossless. Unless you have a really good reason to turn this option off, you should leave it on to keep your image data intact.

- **Preserve Raw Image.** When you select Preserve Raw Image, the image data is stored in the original format if the DNG converter can read the Raw data. This is the best option because you can always convert the Raw data over to a linear form, processed into readable pixel data, but you cannot convert it back.

- **Convert to Linear Image.** This converts the image to a linear form, which stores the data more efficiently but is different from the original RAW format.

- **Embed Original Raw File.** This embeds the original RAW file inside the newly created DNG file. This option is useful for full preservation of data; however, it more than doubles the size of most files on disk.

Delete Original Files

When you select the Delete Original Files option, Photo Downloader removes the file from the camera or memory card after it has been downloaded. This option is useful in managing photos. At some point, most people end up with a memory card containing files that they are not certain have been downloaded to their computer. Using this option eliminates that problem.

Save Copies To

When you select the Save Copies To option, Photo Downloader saves an additional copy of the image file to a location specified using the Browse button. This option is useful to help you keep an automatic archive of your images.

Apply Metadata

The Apply Metadata feature allows you to automatically add metadata items to images as they are downloaded to the computer. This can save a lot of time later as you don't need to add metadata to individual files. You can select one of the custom defined metadata templates (discussed later in this chapter) using the Template to Use box. The selected custom template is applied to each image as it is downloaded to the file system. You can also add the creator and copyright metadata to the file by typing into the appropriate text boxes.

Working with image metadata

The metadata of an image is often as valuable as the pixels in the image. In fact, some files simply are not useful without their metadata. Bridge displays metadata about files in various views and even allows you to filter a list of files based on the metadata.

The metadata contained in each file can provide a lot of useful functionality. For example, the metadata of photos typically contains information about the time and date that the photo was taken, which you can use later to accurately label and organize files. Photo files also typically contain information about the camera, lens, and settings that were used for each photo. Many cameras also include GPS functionality that will include the GPS coordinates where the photo was taken. For serious photographers, this saves a lot of time recording the settings that were used for each shot. Photographers can use the settings to compare results in multiple images to get a better feel for what camera settings and lenses to use.

This section discusses the two major features of Bridge that you use when viewing and changing metadata: the Metadata panel and the File Info utility. The Metadata panel, shown in Figure 6.8, allows you to quickly view all available metadata for the image selected in the Content panel. You can access the Metadata panel by choosing Window ⇨ Metadata Panel from the main menu bar.

FIGURE 6.8

Viewing the metadata for an image file in Bridge

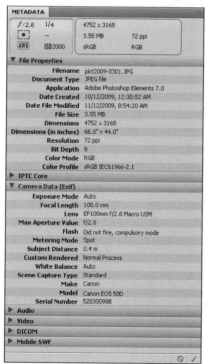

The data in the Metadata panel is organized into the following major sections (you can expand or collapse these sections by clicking the triangle next to the section title):

- **File properties.** This displays information about the image file, such as the filename, size, type, dimension, and color mode.
- **IPTC Core.** This displays the IPTC (International Press Telecommunications Council) data, including creator info, copyright description, and keywords.
- **Camera Data (Exif).** This displays information about the camera used to take the photo, including the lens, ISO setting, aperture, and so on.
- **Audio.** This displays the information about audio files, including the artist, album, song, genre, and so on.
- **Video.** This displays information about video files, such as the tape name, scene, shoot, and date.
- **DICOM.** This displays the DICOM information associated with the image, including patient name, date of birth, study information, physician, and so on.
- **Mobile SWF.** This displays information about SWF (Small Web Format) files, such as content type, persistent storage, and background alpha.

Bridge also allows you to edit the metadata associated with a file using the File Info utility shown in Figure 6.9. You can use the File Info utility to add keywords, copyright data, descriptions, and much more.

To use the File Info utility, select one or more images and then choose File ⇨ File Info from the Bridge main menu bar. After you have launched the File Info utility, select the tabs at the top to select areas of the metadata you want to alter. After you select each tab, you can add or alter certain portions of the metadata. These saved metadata changes become a permanent part of the image file so it's available later, and you can filter and search on those metadata items from within Bridge.

> **TIP**
> The File Info utility allows you to set the metadata on multiple images at the same time. When setting metadata for multiple files, select all files that have the same metadata settings and then make the changes.

Assigning ratings and labels to files

Bridge allows you to assign ratings and labels to files. Adding ratings to files helps you organize files that you like better than others. Ratings are based on values of one to five stars. This helps when you are finding files because you can filter out the ones with fewer stars.

Bridge also allows you to add labels to files to help you organize them to use later. You can label files with the Select, Second, Approved, Review, and To Do labels. To add a rating or a label to a file, choose Label from the Bridge main menu bar and then select one of the options shown in Figure 6.10.

FIGURE 6.9

Modifying the metadata for files using the File Info utility in Bridge

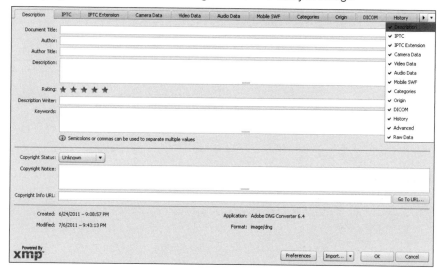

FIGURE 6.10

Adding ratings and labels to files helps you organize, prioritize, and find files more easily.

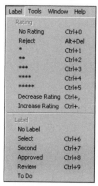

Assigning keywords to files

An extremely useful feature of file metadata is the ability to add keywords that identify or link the file with a person, event, place, or some other piece of data. Bridge makes good use of the keyword feature by allowing you to create new keywords and keyword groups and assigning them to files.

Keywords can be defined, grouped, and assigned using the Keywords panel, shown in Figure 6.11. After the keywords have been assigned to files, you can use them to find the files much more easily later.

FIGURE 6.11

Adding and managing keywords associated with files helps you organize and find files more easily.

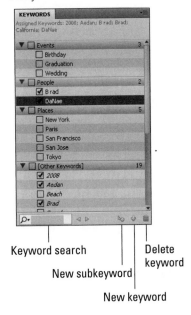

Keyword search

New subkeyword

New keyword

Delete keyword

Adding an existing keyword to a file

To add an existing keyword to one or more files in Bridge, open the Keyword panel. Then select the files in the Content panel. Finally, select the keyword you want to add to the files; the keyword is written to the metadata of the file.

Adding a new keyword

The Keywords tab displays only the basic keywords as well as keywords that exist in the selected files. If you want to add a new keyword to a file that doesn't exist already, click the New Keyword button in the Keywords panel or right-click in the Keywords panel and select New Keyword from the popup menu. A new keyword is added to the list, and you can type the name in the provided text box.

Inserting a new subkeyword

As you add more and more keywords, you realize that you need to organize them into sub-groups. Bridge allows you to add subkeywords to a keyword already in the list. If you want to add a new keyword to a file that doesn't exist already, click the New Keyword button in the Keywords panel or right-click in the Keywords panel and select New Sub Keyword from the popup menu. A new keyword is added as a sublevel to the selected keyword, and you can type the name of the new keyword in the provided text box.

> **NOTE**
>
> When you add a keyword to a file, any subkeywords under it are not added to the file. You need to add each subkeyword for them all to apply.

Finding a keyword in the list

Sometimes even having keywords divided into subgroups doesn't make it easy enough to find the keywords. You can use the search field in the Keywords panel to search for keywords. As you type into the search box, the keywords matching the search are displayed in the list. The search is not case sensitive and searches for text anywhere in the keyword name.

Renaming and deleting keywords

Bridge allows you to quickly rename and delete keywords to keep your list organized. To rename a keyword, right-click it in the list and select Rename from the popup menu. Then type the new name of the keyword. Bridge modifies the metadata in all the files containing that keyword to update the keyword name.

> **CAUTION**
>
> When renaming keywords, you should make sure that they mean the same thing in all images or you could have unexpected results. For example, if you wanted to consolidate your entire family into one keyword and replaced all the occurrences of the keyword "William" for your cousin William, and at the same time you had an image of Prince William and Kate Middleton that was tagged with the keywords "William" and "Kate," you would accidently add the royal couple to your family.

To delete a keyword, right-click it in the list and select Delete from the popup menu. The keyword is deleted from the list.

Renaming files

As discussed earlier, you can rename files as you import them from a camera or a memory card. Bridge also provides the Batch Rename utility to rename files that already exist on the file system. To rename files in Bridge, select them in the Content panel and then open the Batch Rename utility, shown in Figure 6.12, by choosing Tools ⇨ Batch Rename from the Bridge main menu bar.

FIGURE 6.12

Configuring custom filename options when renaming files in Bridge

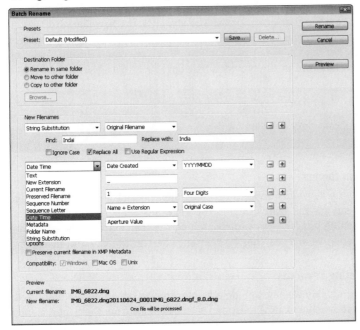

These options are available when renaming files using the Batch Rename utility:

- **Preset.** This allows you to select a default rename configuration or a configuration based on string substitution or to use one of your previous renaming configurations.

- **Destination Folder.** This allows you to specify whether you want Bridge to place the renamed files in the same folder, move them to another folder, or make a copy in another folder while keeping the original.

- **New Filenames.** This area allows you to specify custom filenames based on up to ten different components including text, new extension, current filename, preserved filename, sequence number, sequence letter, date/time, metadata, folder name, and string substitution.

- **Options.** This lets you specify whether to preserve the current file in the XMP metadata of the file. XMP (Extensible Metadata Platform) is a standard developed by Adobe for processing and storing metadata. You can also specify whether to enforce the new filename to be compatible with filename requirements on Windows, Mac, or Unix.

- **Preview.** This displays a preview of how the renamed filenames will appear.

Finding files

One of the biggest strengths of Bridge is that it can quickly find files you are looking for. Bridge provides several tools to help you do this. The following sections discuss using the Filter panel, the Find tool, and the Review mode to find files using Bridge.

Locating files using the Filter panel

Bridge enables you to quickly find files based on keywords, labels, and ratings to files and other values. To use metadata information to find files in Bridge, open the Filter panel, shown in Figure 6.13. The Filter panel keeps a list of categories of metadata that can be used to filter the list of files displayed in the Content pane. These categories can be expanded and collapsed using the triangle button next to the category title.

To filter on a specific item, expand the category and select the item. A check mark appears next to the selected item, as shown in Figure 6.13. You can select as many items as you like. Bridge displays only the items that match the criteria of the selected metadata items.

FIGURE 6.13

Filtering the list of files in the Filter panel using metadata contained in the files

Tracking files using the Find tool

Another extremely effective method of finding files in Bridge is using the Find tool, which you can access by choosing Edit ⇨ Find from the Bridge main menu bar. The Find tool, shown in Figure 6.14, allows you to quickly specify a source location and search criteria to find files. The resulting files that match the specified criteria are then placed in the Content pane.

FIGURE 6.14

Using the Find tool, you can specify a set of criteria to match in the metadata of files while searching the file system.

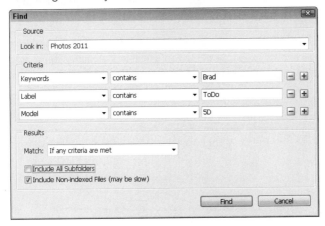

The Look in field of the Find tool allows you to specify a folder or collection to search from. You can also launch the Find tool by selecting a collection or folder in the Collections, Favorites, Folders, or Content panels and pressing Ctrl+F/⌘+F.

You can specify the search criteria on a specific metadata item or on all metadata by selecting the option from the drop-down menu. Then specify the criteria-matching option and a value. To add more criteria, click the plus button. To remove criteria, click the minus button next to the criteria. You can also specify whether to add the file if any of the criteria are met, or only if all the criteria are met. You can also tell the Find tool to include the subfolders of the selected location and non-indexed files in the search.

> **TIP**
>
> When you are creating collections, a good place to start is using the Find tool to get a list of the files that you want to place in the collection. Then select all the files in the Content panel and add them to the collection.

Viewing files using the Review Mode utility

After you have a list of files in the Content panel, one additional feature in Bridge can help you find the files you want. Typically, you view the files as thumbnails and look for specific files. Bridge provides the Review Mode utility, shown in Figure 6.15, to quickly view and locate images.

FIGURE 6.15

Using the Review Mode utility lets you scroll through a list of images in the Preview panel.

The Review Mode utility, which you access by choosing View ⇨ Review Mode from the main menu bar, displays the images in a rotating carousel view of the images in the Preview panel. This is similar to the Cover Flow view on Macs, iTunes, iPads, and iPhones. Selecting an image with the mouse brings that image to the front of the view. You can also click the left and right arrows to rotate the image to the left or to the right. Clicking the down arrow or dragging an image off the screen removes the front image from the list.

Using collections

A collection is a set of files that are grouped together in Bridge. The collection concept does not exist outside of Bridge, which offers some advantages and disadvantages. An advantage is that you can create and delete collections in Bridge without affecting the actual files on disk. You can also add files to collections, regardless of where they exist in the file system. The disadvantage is that, although you can view collections of files quickly in Bridge, you cannot view them in other applications (except Photoshop and InDesign using the mini-Bridge panel).

Using Bridge collections is useful for keeping track of files that belong together. The following sections describe creating collections of files in Bridge using the Collections panel, shown in Figure 6.16.

FIGURE 6.16

Using the Collections panel to create collections of files in Bridge

Creating collections

You create a new collection in Bridge by clicking the New Collection button in the Collections panel. A new collection appears, and you can type its name. You can rename the collection at any time by right-clicking it and selecting Rename from the popup menu. To delete a collection, right-click it and select Delete from the popup menu.

After you have created a collection, you can drag files from the Content panel onto the collection in the Collections panel. When you select a collection, all files that have been added to the collection appear in the Content panel.

Creating smart collections

Collections are great for creating one-time sets of files. A much more dynamic option is to use the smart collection feature built into Bridge. Smart collections are dynamic collections that update continually. You point them to a location, and they update every time new images are placed into that location.

A major advantage of smart collections is that they update based on a configurable filter set. The filter set is the same set that is available in the Find tool. You can specify the search criteria on a specific metadata item or on all metadata by selecting the option from the drop-down menu. For example, this allows you to add files to a smart collection only if they are taken with a certain lens or ISO setting or if they contain a specific keyword or rating.

To create a smart collection, click the New Smart Collection icon in the Collections panel to open the Smart Collection dialog box, shown in Figure 6.17. Then select the source folder to search when looking for new files. Next, set up the criteria on which to filter when adding files to the collection. You can edit the criteria at any time by clicking the Edit Smart Filter button in the Collections panel or in the Content panel when a smart collection is selected.

FIGURE 6.17

Configuring a smart collection to dynamically update the collection based on a set of criteria

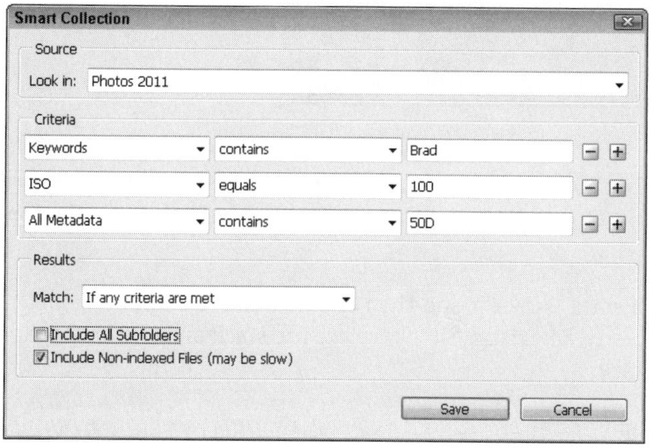

Creating stacks

The invention of the digital camera has resulted in one serious side effect: instead of just single photographs, people tend to take several. This can present a problem when organizing files in Bridge. Instead of a simple list of the photos to choose from, you end up with an extended list containing sections of nearly identical photographs that are difficult to scroll through. Bridge solves this problem with the stack feature.

The stack feature in Bridge allows you to take a group of duplicate photos and place them in a stack, just as you would on a desktop. You place the best image on top, and that is the only image you have to view when browsing in Bridge. The other images are still there and can be accessed; however, they are hidden from the general view.

> **NOTE**
>
> When you open a stack from Bridge by double-clicking it, the images open as separate files. You can also choose Tools ⇨ Photoshop ⇨ Load Files Into Photoshop Layers to load the stack into layers in the same document. This can be useful if you want to convert the layers to a smart object and then use the Layers ⇨ Smart Objects ⇨ Stack Mode options to reduce noise and enhance the images.

To create a stack from a group of images, select the images in the Content panel. Then choose Stacks ⇨ Group as Stack or press Ctrl+G/⌘+G to create the group, as shown in Figure 6.18. Instead of displaying all the images, only the top one is visible in the stack icon with a count in the top-left corner.

FIGURE 6.18

Grouping images as stacks allows you to hide duplicate images while browsing through images in Bridge.

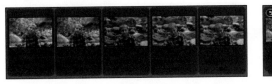

The stack can be expanded or collapsed by clicking the count icon in the top-left corner. To promote an image to the top of the stack, simply drag it to the left so it is in the top-left position in the stack.

To remove an image from a stack, select it and then choose Stack ⇨ Ungroup From Stack. To add another image or images to an existing stack, select the stack and the images and then choose Stack ⇨ Group as Stack.

All metadata operations apply to the stack, so if you add a rating, label, or keyword, it is applied to all images in the stack.

Deleting versus rejecting files

Bridge allows you to remove files from being viewed in two ways: deleting and rejecting. Deleting a file also removes it from the file system. Rejecting a file tags it so that Bridge no longer displays it normally. These options are straightforward, but you should know for sure that you want to permanently remove the file before deleting it.

To delete or reject a file in Bridge, select the file and press the Delete key. A dialog box appears that enables you to either reject or delete the file.

> **NOTE**
>
> Even if you have rejected a file in Bridge, you can still view it in the Content panel by choosing View➪ Show Rejected Files from the main menu bar.

Processing Images Using Bridge and Photoshop

Bridge is a powerful tool that allows you to organize and manage image files. In addition to organizing image files, Bridge uses an interface with Photoshop to help you process the images directly while you are organizing them. Bridge also provides a menu that directly links to Photoshop utilities allowing you to perform Photoshop image processing from the Bridge menu. The following sections discuss some of the main image-processing operations that you can perform from within Bridge.

Opening images in Photoshop

One of the most common processing tasks done in Bridge is opening images in Photoshop. Photoshop is where the images are edited. Rather than having to open Photoshop and use the standard File➪ Open dialog box, you can open images in Photoshop directly from Bridge, where you have great tools for organizing and finding them.

Bridge makes it fast and easy to open an image as its own document in Photoshop. Simply select the image (or images) that you want to open in the Content panel, and then choose File➪ Open with➪ Adobe Photoshop CS6 (default) from the Bridge main menu bar. If Photoshop is not already loaded, it loads and then the selected images are opened as separate documents in Photoshop. From there, you can edit them, as you need.

Placing images in Photoshop

Bridge also makes it possible to place images into other images in Photoshop. To place an image into another image in Photoshop, make sure the original image is active in Photoshop. Then select the image in the Content panel and choose File➪ Place➪ In Photoshop from the Bridge main menu bar. The image is placed into the original document as a smart object layer, exactly as if you had selected File➪ Place from inside Photoshop. Smart object layers are discussed in Chapter 10.

> **NOTE**
>
> When placing images from Bridge into Photoshop, you can only place a single image at a time.

Loading files as Photoshop layers

Another useful way of opening images in Photoshop from Bridge is to open them as layers in a single document. This is useful when you are working with a series of images that you need to combine into a single composition.

To open a series of images in Photoshop using the Bridge utility, select the files in the Content panel of Bridge that you want to open as layers in Photoshop. Next, choose Tools ⇨ Photoshop ⇨ Load Files into Photoshop Layers from the Bridge main menu bar. The selected images are loaded into a single new Photoshop document as individual layers, as shown in Figure 6.19.

FIGURE 6.19

Using the Photoshop interface with Bridge, you can open a series of images as individual layers in a single document in Photoshop from the Bridge interface.

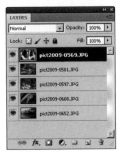

Opening in Camera Raw

When you are working with Camera Raw images, you will likely want to first open them in the Camera Raw editor, which is discussed in Chapter 7, before opening them in Photoshop. This allows you to make adjustments directly to the unprocessed Camera Raw pixel data.

Bridge allows you to open images directly into the Camera Raw editor using an underlying interface. To open images in the Camera Raw editor from Bridge, select the images in the Content panel and then choose File ⇨ Open in Camera Raw. The Camera Raw editor is launched if it is not already open, and the images are opened as individual documents.

Processing Multiple Files Using the Batch Interface

One of Photoshop's strengths is its ability to automate the processing of images. One of the utilities that Photoshop provides to automatically process images is the Batch tool. Bridge uses the Photoshop Batch tool by providing a direct link to it from the Bridge utility. This allows you to combine the strength of Bridge in organizing and finding images with the automated processing engine of Photoshop. The result is that you are more efficient in collecting files and then quickly processing them.

To use Bridge to invoke batch processing of files, select the files you want to process in the Content panel and then choose Tools ⇨ Photoshop ⇨ Batch from the Bridge main menu bar. Photoshop is launched if it is not already open, and the Batch dialog box appears, as shown in Figure 6.20.

Using the Batch utility, you can select the action set and specific action to apply to the files. Do not change the source from Bridge because it is using Bridge to get the list of files to process. However, you can modify the Destination and Errors settings. We discuss the Batch tool in much more detail in Chapter 31.

FIGURE 6.20

Using Bridge, you can select files to be processed by the Photoshop Batch process utility.

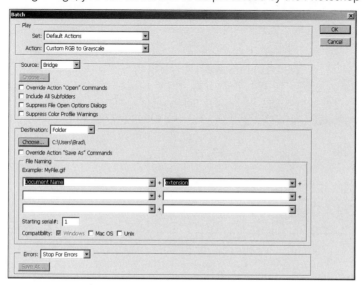

Using the Image Processor Interface

Another very useful tool that Photoshop provides when processing images is the Image Processor utility. This feature is especially useful for quickly converting a set of files to the JPEG, PSD, or TIFF formats. Bridge provides a direct interface with the Photoshop Image Processor utility, allowing you to quickly find the files using the Bridge interface and then to convert them using Image Processor.

To use Bridge, launch Image Processor, select the files that you want to process in the Content panel, and then choose Tools ⇨ Photoshop ⇨ Image Processor from the Bridge main menu bar. Photoshop is launched if it is not already running, and the Image Processor utility dialog box appears, as shown in Figure 6.21.

Using the Image Processor utility, you can set the destination of the modified images, file types to convert the images to, and actions to be performed on the files as they are converted. Photoshop provides the best conversion based on the actions specified. For more information about batch processing, see Chapter 31.

FIGURE 6.21

Using Bridge, you can select files to be processed by the Photoshop Image Processor utility.

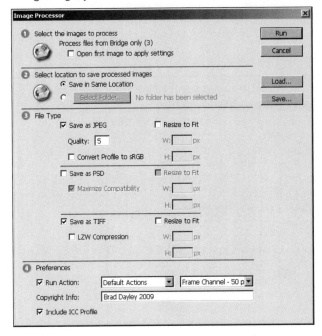

Merging photos

Merging photos was nearly impossible until the invention of digital image processing. Computers now make it possible to analyze the data in images and combine them effectively.

Two types of photo merging techniques can be applied to images. The first type is to combine a set of photos taken from the same relative position but at different points in the subject. The result is that single images, each containing part of the subject, can be combined into a larger image that contains the entire subject.

The second type of photo merge involves taking a set of images shot with the camera in the exact same location on the same subject but with different exposure settings and then combining them into an HDR (High Dynamic Range) image. An HDR image contains much more tonal depth than is traditionally possible from a single image. In fact, there is more tonal data than can be seen on a computer monitor or even when printed on high-quality photo paper.

The following sections discuss how to use Bridge to select images and then use the photo merging capabilities of Photoshop to actually merge the images.

Using Photoshop Photomerge

The Photomerge interface allows you to combine a series of photos taken at different points in a subject into a single panoramic image of the entire subject. You can select multiple images using the Bridge interface, and then launch Photomerge to combine that set of images together.

To use Bridge, launch the Photomerge utility, select the files you want to process in the Content panel, and then choose Tools ⇨ Photoshop ⇨ Photomerge from the Bridge main menu bar. Photoshop launches if it is not already running, and the Photomerge dialog box appears. You can then specify the layout and options to use to merge the images. For more information about Photomerge, see Chapter 21.

Using Photoshop Merge to HDR

Photoshop provides the Merge to HDR utility to combine a series of photos taken of the same subject, from the same position but with different exposure settings into a single combined HDR image. You can select multiple images using the Bridge interface, and then launch Merge to HDR to combine that set of images.

To use Bridge, launch the Merge to HDR utility, select the files you want to process in the Content panel, and then choose Tools ⇨ Photoshop ⇨ Merge to HDR from the Bridge main menu bar. Photoshop launches if it is not already running, a new document is created with each of the selected images as different layers, and then the Merge to HDR dialog box appears, as shown in Figure 6.22. For more information about the Merge to HDR utility, see Chapter 22.

Auto-merging images into HDR and panoramic images

The interface that connects Bridge with Photoshop also provides an Auto Collection script that automatically processes files and combines them into stacks of images that can be processed into panoramic or HDR images.

Images are collected into stacks based on capture time, exposure settings, and image alignment. The Auto Collection script analyzes each stack to determine whether the stack should be processed into an HDR image or a panorama. If the content of the images across the stack overlaps by more than 80 percent and the exposure settings vary, then the stack is interpreted to be an HDR image. However, if the content overlaps by less than 80 percent and the exposure is constant, then the stack is interpreted to be a panorama.

NOTE

Timestamps must be within 18 seconds for the Auto Collection script to process the photos.

FIGURE 6.22

Using Bridge, you can select a series of files and merge them into a single document using the Merge to HDR utility.

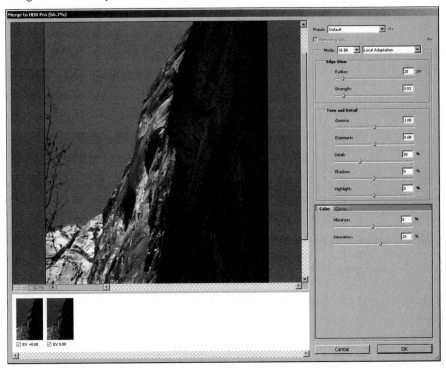

Use the following steps in Bridge to process photos into stacks of HDR and panoramic images:

1. **Choose Edit ⇨ Preferences in Windows or Adobe Bridge CS6 ⇨ Preferences on Macs to launch the Preferences dialog box.**

2. **Select the Startup Scripts panel, shown in Figure 6.23.**

3. **In the Startup Scripts panel, make certain that the Auto Collection CS6 option is selected and then click OK.**

4. **Open the Folders panel in Bridge.**

5. **Navigate to the folder with the HDR or panoramic shots.**

6. **Choose Stacks ⇨ Auto-Stack Panorama/HDR from the menu bar.**

   This creates stacks in the folder containing sets of images that can be combined into a panorama or HDR.

7. **Choose Tools ⇨ Photoshop ⇨ Process Collections in Photoshop from the Bridge main menu bar to have Photoshop automatically merge them.**

   The results appear in Bridge.

FIGURE 6.23

Enable the Auto Collection CS6 script to automatically process sets of images into panoramic or HDR images.

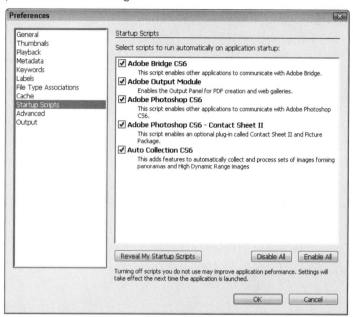

> **TIP**
>
> Running the Auto-Stack Panorama/HDR setting from Bridge is very processor-intensive on your computer, as it analyzes all the files in the selected directory. To reduce the overhead, move the files you know need to be stacked into their own directory. This reduces the amount of processing that is required.

Creating PDFs and Web Galleries

Bridge allows you to output a set of images in either a PDF or a Web Gallery. This is another useful feature of Bridge because you can use its capabilities to find the files you are looking for and then quickly output them.

Creating a PDF

To create a PDF file from a set of images, select the images in the Content panel of Bridge. Then click the Output button in the toolbar and select Output to Web or PDF to open the Output pane, shown in Figure 6.24. Click the PDF icon, set options for the PDF output, and click Save to create the PDF file.

FIGURE 6.24

Using Bridge to output a set of images to a PDF file

Here are the PDF output options:

- **Template.** The Template field allows you to select a predefined template from the drop-down menu. Several predefined templates change the settings for PDF output. You can also click the Save Template button to save changes you make to the PDF output settings as your own custom template. To delete the template, click the trash icon next to the Template field.

- **Refresh Preview.** You can click the Refresh Preview button at any time to apply the current output settings to the Output Preview window. This allows you to make changes to the settings and see how they will appear in the final PDF.

6

- **Document.** The Document panel allows you to set the page size and orientation as well as the output quality and background color. You can also add a password to the PDF file that protects it from unauthorized viewing. You can disable printing from the Document options panel as well.

- **Layout.** The Layout panel allows you to specify how images are placed on each page of the PDF file. You can set the number of columns as well as the spacing.

- **Overlays.** This panel allows you to specify whether to add the filename and extension as an overlay below the image. You also turn on and configure page numbering in this panel.

- **Header.** The Header panel allows you to enable and disable headers and define the text, font, and look of the header.

- **Footer.** The Footer panel allows you to enable and disable headers and define the text, font, and look of the footer.

- **Playback.** The Playback panel allows you to configure the behavior of the PDF file when it is played back as a presentation. You can specify to use full-screen mode, automatic advancement, and looping. You can also specify the transitions between pages.

- **Watermark.** The Watermark panel allows you to add watermarks to the created PDF file. This protects images in the file from copyright violations. You can specify to use text or an image for the watermark. You can also control the size, location, rotation, and opacity of the watermark. Using the watermark is a good idea if you are adding images to the PDF file that you want to be copy-protected.

- **View PDF After Save.** When you select this option and click Save, the saved PDF file is loaded by the default application.

Creating a Web Gallery

Using Bridge to create a Web Gallery is a great way to post images on the Internet. Bridge creates the necessary image files, web pages, and scripts to support the Web Gallery. The Web Gallery allows you to use a browser to view images in a professional interface.

To create a Web Gallery from a set of images, select the images in the Content pane of Bridge. Then click the Output button in the toolbar to open the Output dialog box, shown in Figure 6.25. Click the Web Gallery icon, and set options for the Web Gallery output. After you have the gallery the way you want it, click Save to save the gallery to the local file system, or click Upload to upload the gallery to a remote FTP server.

FIGURE 6.25

Using Bridge to output a set of images as a Web Gallery

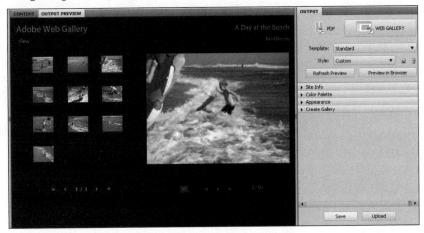

Here are the options for the Web Gallery output:

- **Template.** The Template field allows you to select a predefined template from the drop-down menu. Several predefined templates change the available styles and settings for Web Gallery output. You can also click the Save button to save changes you make to the Web Gallery output settings as your own custom template. To delete the template, click the trash icon below the Template field. Each template provides a different look and feel to the Web Gallery. Try each of them until you find a look and feel you like.

> **CAUTION**
>
> When you switch between template styles, you may lose information specified in the output settings. You should select the template style you like first before making changes to the output settings.

- **Style.** This specifies the style used in generating the gallery. Styles include Lightroom, Darkroom, Medium Thumbnails, and Small Thumbnails. The available styles may change when you change the template.

- **Refresh Preview.** You can click the Refresh Preview button at any time to apply the current output settings to the Output Preview dialog box shown in Figure 6.25. This allows you to make changes to the settings and see how they will appear in the final Web Gallery page.

- **Preview in Browser.** You can click the Preview in Browser button to view how the gallery will look in a web browser. This launches the default web browser to view the gallery contents. You can use the links in the gallery to navigate the images.

- **Site Info.** This panel allows you to specify the site information that is displayed on the Web Gallery page. You can set the gallery title, caption, contact info, and so on in this panel.

- **Color Palette.** This panel allows you to specify the background, menu, title, and thumbnail colors that are displayed on the gallery page.

- **Appearance.** This panel allows you to define the appearance and behavior of the Web Gallery. You can specify whether to display the filename, and you can specify the size and quality of the thumbnails and slideshow. You can even define the length and type of transitions to use between pictures during the slideshow. On the Airtight templates, you can specify the layout of the images, including number of columns, borders, and spacing. This panel also allows you to specify the output quality of the images being added to the image gallery.

- **Create Gallery.** This panel allows you to specify the folder on the local disk that the images and web pages will be uploaded to when you click the Save button. You can also set the FTP server address, user, password, and path to use when uploading the image gallery to a remote server. When you click the Upload button, Bridge uses a mini-FTP client to attach to the FTP server and upload the Web Gallery.

Using the Mini-Bridge Tool in Photoshop

Adobe has added a minimal version of the Bridge tool directly to the Photoshop interface, enabling you to find files without switching to another application window. This feature provides some of the useful functionality of Bridge directly from the same Photoshop interface you are using to edit images.

To launch the Mini-Bridge tool, click the Launch Mini Bridge button. The Mini-Bridge tool appears, as shown in Figure 6.26.

The Mini-Bridge tool is used similarly to the Bridge application. You should recognize most of the features that you see in Mini-Bridge from Bridge. Mini-Bridge includes only a small subset of the functionality of Bridge. However, it is a useful tool for quickly finding files from within Photoshop. This section briefly discusses the options available in Mini-Bridge when browsing for files.

> **TIP**
>
> The Mini-Bridge tool does not replace the Bridge tool for most of the things you want to do. The Mini-Bridge tool is useful when selecting files already in collections or small folders. Use Bridge for organizing your images first, and then you can use the Mini-Bridge tool to find them and open them in Photoshop. Also, for just one or two files, it is still much faster just to use the standard Open File dialog box.

FIGURE 6.26

The Mini-Bridge panel in Photoshop

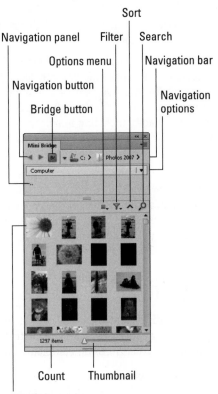

Sort

Navigation panel   Filter   Search

Options menu   Navigation bar

Navigation button

Navigation options

Bridge button

Count   Thumbnail

Content panel

The following sections discuss the panels, buttons, and menu options available when browsing in Mini-Bridge:

- **Navigation buttons.** The navigation buttons allow you to move backward and forward using the left and right arrows. The down arrow opens a popup menu that allows you to select from a list of previous folders or collections that you have visited.

- **Navigation bar.** The Navigation bars show the paths that you have navigated in the file system or in the Navigation panel. You can click any point in the path to move to that folder or collection.

- **Bridge button.** The Bridge button switches you to the Bridge application. This is a quicker way of getting to Bridge than navigating the multiple open windows on the system.

- **Navigation options.** The navigation options allow you to quickly select a point to begin navigating to images. The options are Computer, user home folder, Favorites, Recent Folders, Recent Files, and Collections. When you select an option from the Navigation Options drop-down menu, the available containers appear in the Navigation panel.

- **Navigation panel.** The Navigation panel is similar to the Favorites panels in Bridge. You can select a recent location, favorites, collections, or even `Photoshop.com` albums to browse files.

- **Content panel.** The Content panel works the same way as the Content panel in Bridge. The items in the currently selected folder or collection are displayed in the Content panel. You select items in this panel to use the Mini-Bridge tools. You can drag images out of the Content panel into Photoshop, and a new document opens for that file. If you drag an image into an existing document in Photoshop, the image being dragged is placed in that document as a smart layer.

- **Content Options button.** The Content Options button provides a drop-down menu with the option to make selections in the Content pane, start a slideshow, and switch to Full Screen or Review mode. The Content Options menu also allows you to select what information to display with the thumbnail, such as the filename, size type, date, and rating.

> **TIP**
>
> When you select recent files or folders from the Content Option menu, Photoshop provides all integrated CS components in the Navigation panel. For example, you will be able to select the recent files in Photoshop, Illustrator, Dreamweaver, and so on.

- **Filter button.** The Filter button displays a list of ways to filter items that appear in the Content panel. You can filter by ratings, labels, rejected files, and hidden files.

- **Sort button.** The Sort button displays a list of fields that can be selected to sort images in the Content panel. When you select one of the items from the Sort list, the files in the Content panel are rearranged in order, based on that selection.

- **Search.** This button launches a simple search tool to search for files. However, the Search window has a link to the advanced search in Bridge, discussed earlier in this chapter.

- **Thumbnail slider.** This slider changes the size of the thumbnail that appears in the Content panel.

Summary

This chapter discussed using the Bridge application to quickly import and organize files. Organizing files is one of the most tedious and least popular tasks that must be done when working with image files. Bridge allows you to quickly organize your files into collections. It also helps you to quickly find files by using advanced search criteria or filtering based on metadata stored in the images.

In this chapter, you learned the following:

- Importing images from cameras and memory card readers
- Using Bridge to view and modify image metadata
- Finding files quickly by searching or filtering on metadata
- Organizing images into smart collections that continually update
- Renaming multiple files at the same time
- Batch processing images using Photoshop
- Automatically merging sets of files into panoramic or HDR images
- Using the Mini-Bridge tool in Photoshop to quickly find and select images

Part II

Working with Camera Raw Images

IN THIS PART

Exploring Camera Raw Basics

While not common in point-and-shoot digital cameras, many Digital Single Lens Reflex (DSLR) cameras support a file format that is commonly called Camera Raw. If your camera supports this format and you are serious about creating great photographs, you probably want to shoot in Camera Raw.

When you capture a picture in the standard JPEG format, the camera takes the image from the image sensor and processes it before saving it to your memory card. This reduces the file size, but it discards image information that could have been used to refine your photo.

The Camera Raw format saves the unprocessed file, thereby preserving all the image data so that you can process it manually later. It's like being able to process your own negatives, tweaking them to get the color and lighting just right.

This chapter introduces you to the Camera Raw format, explaining why Camera Raw is superior to JPEG and the advantages and disadvantages of using it. We also explain what a DNG file is and introduce you to the Camera Raw workspace, explaining the tools and showing you how to set preferences.

Looking at Camera Raw Benefits

Camera Raw formats have been around for a few years now, and many photographers won't shoot in anything else. The ability to use all the image data captured by the camera's sensors, which amounts to trillions of colors, is quite exhilarating. Camera Raw files store the changes made to them as metadata, preserving all of the original information so that any editing you do is non-destructive.

Keeping original CMOS information

The sensors in your digital camera that register the light coming into the camera and convert it into a digital image are called CMOS (Complementary Metal Oxide Semiconductor) sensors. Don't worry; we're not planning to remember that either. The point is that when your camera is set to shoot JPEG images, your camera settings (such as the exposure or white balance) determine how the information is processed, and everything that is considered extra data is discarded. After the image is processed, it is compressed, further reducing the quality and size, to create a JPEG file. When you download that JPEG file onto your computer and make changes to it in Photoshop, every recompression performed when saving the collected changes further reduces the quality.

Perhaps an example will help to illustrate the data that is lost with a JPEG image. If you have set the white balance on your camera to capture a photo in fluorescent lighting and you forget to change that setting to capture photos outside, those photos will have an unsightly blue-green colorcast. Because the images have been processed by your camera with the fluorescent setting, the information that would correct the white balance has been discarded, making it next to impossible to adequately correct the color of those images.

A Camera Raw file, on the other hand, does not discard any of the information gathered by the CMOS sensors. Instead, it processes it according to your camera's settings, saves those settings as the default settings in the metadata, and then saves all the information gathered by the CMOS sensors as the image file.

This can happen because cameras can capture as many as 14 bits per color channel, but JPEGs can store only 8 bits per channel. Camera Raw files, on the other hand, can store up to 16 bits per channel.

With 8 bits per channel, each color channel can have 256 distinct tones. Using 8 bits per channel allows an image file to contain over 16 million different colors. With 16 bits per channel, each color channel can have 65,536 distinct tones. Using 16 bits per channel allows an image file to contain trillions of different colors.

You may be asking yourself whether you really need that many different colors, especially since the human eye can detect only about 7 million colors at best. But you'd be surprised at the difference using 16 bits per channel can have when adjusting levels on problem images. The more tones per channel, the more options Photoshop has when adjusting the levels in an image. For example, an image that is almost completely bleached out by overexposure or completely black from underexposure can be salvaged into a printable form using 16 bits per channel.

This means that more information is available to draw from than you can see in your image. For instance, consider the first example shown in Figure 7.1. This photo is seriously overexposed. At first glance, you might think that the photo doesn't have enough pixel information to save it. If it were a JPEG image, you'd be right; those pixels would be gone, or at least very faded.

Lucky for us, this photo was taken in Camera Raw. The pixel information isn't missing; the camera was just set to a higher exposure than it should have been. With a few tweaks in Adobe Camera Raw, you can readjust the exposure settings, in effect reinterpreting the information captured by the CMOS sensors and recovering most of the color information, as you can see in the second photo in Figure 7.1. A definite advantage!

7

FIGURE 7.1

Camera Raw files contain so much more information than JPEGs that this photo was saved.

ON THE WEB
Open Figure 7-1.dng from the book's website. Can you recover the highlights?

Editing non-destructively

Changes made in the Camera Raw format are saved as metadata. All photo files have *metadata* — embedded information that tags along with the file. Even scanned photo files have at least the date they were created and their size embedded as information that your computer can access and display, even if your photo isn't open in a photo-editing application. Photos taken with a digital camera have a good deal more information. You'll find almost everything you want to know about an individual photo file: the date and time it was taken; what camera was used; whether the flash was used, suppressed, or not needed; focal length; white balance setting; and the list goes on. Figure 7.2 is just a sample of the metadata that is available for an image.

FIGURE 7.2

This is some of the metadata that is available for a Camera Raw image.

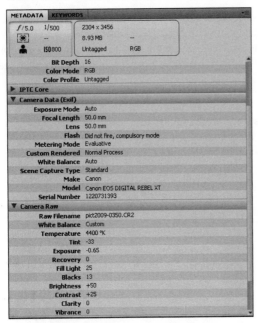

 Bridge displays metadata in its own panel. You can find more information about metadata in Chapter 6.

In a Camera Raw file, there is even more information; even Camera Raw files are processed by your camera. The difference is that the processing information is saved, not as the actual image file, as it is with a JPEG, but as metadata that is stored with the file.

When you open a file in a Camera Raw format, it opens in the Camera Raw application that ships with Photoshop. The version that comes with Photoshop CS6 is Camera Raw 7. This application allows you to make changes to your image, but unlike changes made to a JPEG image, these changes are not permanent, nor do they erode the quality of the pixels. That's because the changes you make are also saved as metadata.

If you've used Photoshop or another digital photo-editing application to change the exposure or color of your JPEG or TIFF photos in the past, you are going to be impressed by how clean and easy it is to change a Camera Raw image. When you change the color or lighting of a JPEG image in a standard editor, what you see in the photo is what you get. In other words, the visible pixels are all you have to work with, and when you change settings such as the brightness or saturation, you actually alter the existing pixels in the photo file. If you adjust the exposure a little too high, leaving areas of your photo completely white (specular highlights), that color information is irretrievable after you've saved the photo. Other changes to your photo can leave "bruises," eroding the quality as well as the believability of your photo.

Changing the settings of a Camera Raw image is very different. You aren't actually changing the pixels in the photo; you are simply changing the way the pixel information is interpreted by changing the metadata. Because there is so much more of that information than there is in a JPEG file, you have much greater latitude for interpreting the information. You never lose color information in a Camera Raw file because if you set the exposure too high, it is always retrievable just by readjusting the settings.

> **NOTE**
>
> Non-destructive editing holds true as long as you are processing your photo in Camera Raw. After you open it in Photoshop and make changes to it, you are required to save it in a standard image format. The RAW file isn't overwritten; you simply create a new JPEG, TIFF, or PSD file in addition to the RAW file.

So mess with your Camera Raw files as much as you want. If you go overboard with the settings, no worries; you can just click the default button and everything goes back to the way it started. You can do this even after the file has been closed and reopened, or even if you are in a completely different Camera Raw editor. You can also save your own settings as well as the default settings so they are retrievable even after you've made other changes to them.

Saving time

Processing your photos in Camera Raw can actually save you time over processing JPEGs in Photoshop. Consider the following:

- The Camera Raw files are already processed according to your camera settings and look just like the same shot taken with a JPEG setting. If your camera settings were right on, then great! You don't even need to open your photos in Camera Raw.

- When you do open your photos in Camera Raw, processing them is much simpler than using adjustments in Photoshop to clean your image. With all the extra color information at your fingertips, finding the right settings is simple.

- Camera Raw handles these files really well. The changes you make to your photos in Camera Raw happen in real time. Processing in Camera Raw, especially after you are familiar with the application, doesn't need to take more than a few seconds.

- You can batch process your RAW images. If you have taken several photos in the same lighting conditions, for instance, you can adjust the white balance on all of the photos at the same time.

- If you aren't using your photos in a composite or adding special effects to them, there's no need to open them in Photoshop. You can even save a JPEG copy (or one of several other file formats) right from Camera Raw.

Understanding Camera Raw File Types

You've probably noticed that we've referred to Camera Raw formats in the plural sense. That's because it's not a universal format — there are at least as many Camera Raw formats as there are brands of cameras that capture it. It seems everyone wants to implement Camera Raw in their own way. Because so many formats are constantly being added, it's hard to find applications that read them. Windows can't even preview or display Camera Raw files without a plug-in, and eBay certainly doesn't recognize any of them.

It's conceivable that some of these formats won't stand the test of time and that 10 or 15 years from now, you won't be able to open your Camera Raw files. If you own laser discs, you know that this is reality! The difference is that instead of just having to spend more money on the same movie, you are losing your irreplaceable photographs.

However, there is good news. Even as more Camera Raw formats become available, the Adobe Camera Raw editor continues to be updated so it can read those formats. At least for now, you are probably covered.

Some of the more notable Camera Raw file types are the Canon formats (CR2, CRW), the Nikon formats (NEF, NRW), and the Sony formats (ARW, SRF, SR2). Your camera has its own format, and you should get to know that particular format because no two are exactly alike. If you have a newer or less common format, make sure you can open your files in Camera Raw. You could look for supported formats, but the easiest way is to simply open a photo in Camera Raw. If it works, you're good to go.

> **NOTE**
> Adobe is constantly updating the supported RAW formats. If your files don't open on the first try in Camera Raw, make sure you've installed the latest updates.

Creating an XMP sidebar file

When you change a supported file format using Camera Raw, those changes are saved as metadata so your settings are permanent unless you want to change them. The caveat is that even though Adobe can access many Camera Raw file formats, they are still proprietary, so Adobe can't change those files. Adobe gets around this by creating a second sidecar file that contains the new metadata. It is called a *sidecar* file because it's connected to the Camera Raw file that it interprets and moves right along with it if you save it in a different location. A sidecar file has the extension .xmp (eXtensible Metadata Platform) When you start to see these files floating around in your photograph folders, you'll know what they are.

Converting RAW formats to DNG files

No matter what RAW format your camera supports, if Adobe supports it, you can convert your files to DNG files. The .dng file extension stands for Digital Negative, and it is the Adobe

Camera Raw format. Many proponents are fighting for it to become an industry standard. This would alleviate the fear of losing your valuable image data in the future as Camera Raw formats are dropped and no support is available for them in new software applications.

You can convert your Camera Raw files into DNG files by downloading the DNG converter from the Adobe website (www.adobe.com). It's free and simple to use. However, it takes a bit of time to run, so plan on walking away from your computer while it processes your files.

TIP

Bridge also converts your RAW files to DNG files while they are being imported from your camera or card reader. Choose Bridge as the method of importing these files and check the Convert to DNG option in the dialog box.

There are two excellent reasons to convert your Camera Raw files into DNGs, and we highly recommend that you convert them even if you save a copy of your files in the original format.

The first reason is that DNG is becoming a popular and accepted file format. A few cameras out there even capture in DNG, including Leica, Samsung, Casio, and Hasselblad. You can easily convert your Camera Raw files into DNG files using the converter and open it in several applications that support it. The chance of it becoming obsolete is small, and its popularity precludes it from doing so without plenty of warning.

The second reason is getting rid of the XMP files. Because DNG is the native Camera Raw format from Adobe, Camera Raw has the power to embed the metadata inside the file, eliminating the need to add the XMP sidecar file. This means less clutter and less chance of your settings getting lost in the shuffle.

Opening Images in Camera Raw

Opening Camera Raw files isn't any different from opening any other type of file; you find your file or files in Bridge and double-click them to open them. Photoshop launches if it's not already open, but Camera Raw also launches, allowing you to process your image before opening it in Photoshop for the more traditional editing process. If you are just cleaning up an image, Camera Raw can do all the editing required for most photos.

NOTE

Although you can open several files in Camera Raw at once, you need to do this all at the same time. If you try to open an additional file while Camera Raw is already launched with a file open, your new file won't open until you've exited the current instance of Camera Raw.

You can also open JPEG and TIFF files in Camera Raw. This gives you a quick editor for adjusting color and light in these file types. To open a file in Camera Raw, right-click the thumbnail in Bridge and select Open in Camera Raw. You can also set the preferences in Camera Raw to automatically open when these files are opened in Photoshop. You can learn more about how to do this in the discussion of preferences later in this chapter.

NOTE

When you use the Open in Camera Raw option after right-clicking an image, Camera Raw opens in Bridge instead of Photoshop.

The Camera Raw dialog box opens every time you open a Camera Raw file, even if it's a file that you've already processed. Don't worry; the settings are just as you left them. You can either readjust them or click Open Image to access Photoshop.

TIP

You really don't need to open Camera Raw every time you want to work with a RAW image in Photoshop. If you've already processed your photo and like your settings, or you're just satisfied with the way the photo looks, press the Shift key as you double-click to open it; it opens directly into Photoshop, bypassing Camera Raw.

Getting to Know the Camera Raw Workspace

The Camera Raw workspace is very different from working in Photoshop. The different corrections are made primarily through the use of a few key tools and sliders, making the workspace efficient and incredibly easy to use. The main features of the Camera Raw workspace are shown in Figure 7.3.

Following are the main features of the Camera Raw workspace:

- **Document Window.** The Document window displays the document that is currently selected in the filmstrip. At the bottom, you see the Zoom Level drop-down menu. From this menu, you can select a zoom percentage or the fit-to-screen option. Next to the Zoom Level, the document name is displayed. In the bottom-right corner of the document window are arrows that let you toggle through the documents in the filmstrip.

- **Filmstrip.** The filmstrip shows all the documents that are currently open in Camera Raw. You can select more than one by pressing the Shift or Ctrl (⌘) keys while you select, or by clicking the Select All option. Select more than one file to make the same changes to all of them at once, such as setting the white balance on several photographs taken at the same time. You probably want to select all the files you want opened in Photoshop before you close Camera Raw.

- **Camera Raw tools.** These are the tools that help you make adjustments in Camera Raw. They do everything from setting the white balance to correcting red eye.

- **Histogram.** The histogram is a very important feature for correctly setting the levels of color and brightness values in your image. Understanding the histogram helps you make better adjustments. If you are unsure what the histogram represents and how to use it, see Chapter 4.

- **Image adjustment tabs.** You can adjust a Camera Raw image in several ways, from color settings to lens adjustments. These adjustments are all represented in the image adjustment tabs, which you will learn more about in this and the next chapter.

- **Image adjustment panel.** The Image adjustment panel changes based on the Image adjustment tab that you have selected. Each panel has several different adjustment settings that modify the way your image is interpreted.

FIGURE 7.3

The Camera Raw workspace is a simple but extremely powerful utility.

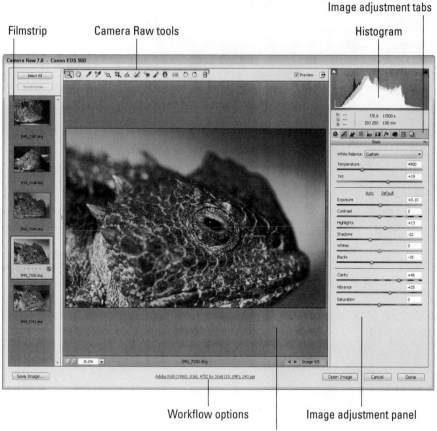

Filmstrip   Camera Raw tools   Image adjustment tabs   Histogram

Workflow options   Image adjustment panel

Document window

Changing Your Workflow Options

The Workflow options in Camera Raw allow you to change the color profile and bit depth of the image you are working on. Understanding these options and how they affect your editing will give you the power to make the most of your RAW files.

At the bottom of the Camera Raw workspace is a blue link that tells you the workflow options that you are currently working with. Clicking this link, as shown in Figure 7.4, opens the Workflow Options dialog box, as shown in Figure 7.5.

FIGURE 7.4

This is not only important information, but also a link to the Workflow Options dialog box.

Click to adjust Workflow options

FIGURE 7.5

The Workflow Options dialog box allows you to reset important features of your images in Camera Raw.

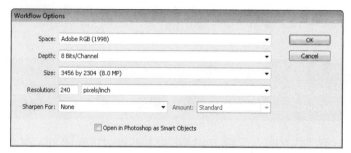

Setting the color space

Space is the first setting in the Workflow options. Space enables you to set the color space in which you want to work. You can choose from four color profiles and two grayscale profiles (if you have changed your RAW file to grayscale), as shown in Figure 7.6. If you don't see the profile you want, choose ProPhoto RGB and convert to your desired color space after opening your image in Photoshop.

FIGURE 7.6

You can choose from four color profiles and two grayscale profiles in the Space drop-down menu.

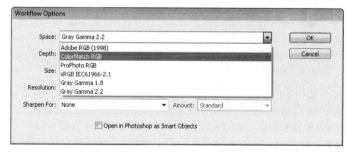

Choosing a bit depth

The Depth setting allows you to choose to work with either 8 bits per channel or 16 bits per channel. Remember that the bits-per-channel setting determines how many tones your color channels can contain. At 8 bits per channel, you have access to over 16 million colors, but 16 bits per channel gives you trillions of colors. The more colors you have access to, the easier and better your corrections are in Camera Raw. It stands to reason that you want to work with 16 bits per channel as often as possible.

So why is it that when you open Camera Raw for the first time, it is set at 8 bits per channel? Well, although technology is getting better all the time, there are still a limited number of file types and applications that can support 16 bit-per-channel images. For example, when you change the setting in Camera Raw to 16 bits per channel and open your image in Photoshop, a few options — such as the Filter Gallery — are grayed out because they don't support 16 bits per channel.

> **CAUTION**
>
> 16-bit images are also memory-intensive, so the computer you are using will be a factor in whether or not you want to process in 16-bit. You'll need a current computer with plenty of RAM.

The bottom line? You probably want to work with images that are set at 16 bits per channel to make any adjustments necessary in Camera Raw. If you want to make changes to your image that require an 8 bit-per-channel setting, you can change your Image mode to 8 bits per channel in Photoshop by choosing Image ⇨ Mode ⇨ 8 Bits/Channel.

> **NOTE**
>
> We're pretty sure that Adobe sets your images to 8 bits per channel in the Camera Raw workspace as a default because they don't want you to pull your hair out over not having access to the Filter Gallery in Photoshop later on. When you set your images to 16 bits per channel, that setting stays set until you change it, so the next photo you open in Camera Raw is also set to 16 bits per channel. Remember this small detail so you won't pull your hair out over options you think you should have in the Photoshop workspace. Take a deep breath, and remember to convert your image back to 8 bits per channel.

Adjusting image size

You can adjust the size of your image in Camera Raw by resampling it, just as you would in Photoshop. This is one change in Camera Raw that is destructive. Whenever you resample an image, you trust an algorithm to selectively add or destroy pixels to make your image larger or smaller. Although resizing is often necessary, resizing an image over and over is unwise.

You can make your image smaller by choosing a megapixel size with a minus sign next to it, or make it larger by choosing a megapixel size with a plus sign next to it, as shown in Figure 7.7. You can return to the original size by choosing the megapixel size in the middle. The one benefit of a Camera Raw file here is that returning to this original size restores your original settings. (If you did this in Photoshop with a JPEG, it would just resample to the original size.)

Notice that these sizes don't show your image dimensions. The dimensions of your image are based not only on the number of pixels, but also on the resolution. Changing the resolution does not change the number of pixels used in your image, however.

FIGURE 7.7

Make your image smaller by selecting a megapixel setting with a minus sign, or larger by selecting one with a plus sign.

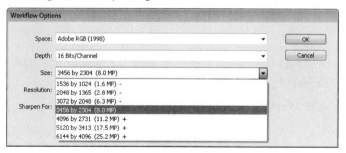

Setting the resolution

Setting the resolution of your photo changes the print size and quality. It takes the available pixels and determines how many of them to pack into a linear inch. Your computer screen displays at 72 to 133 ppi (pixels per inch) and many digital cameras shoot at the smaller resolution of 72 ppi, leaving you with a photo that has huge dimensions. When you take your photo in to be printed, the photo processor resizes your photos to the appropriate size and resolution, starting with the resolution. As a result, a photo printed at 72 dpi looks extremely pixelated, giving it a jagged look. Increasing the resolution to at least 200 dpi gives you a much better result.

Increasing the resolution automatically reduces the size of your image without resampling it. Instead of spreading 72 pixels per inch over 30 inches of photo, you can use the same pixels to pack 300 pixels per 7 inches of photo, giving you not only a better print resolution, but also a more reasonable print size.

Applying output sharpening

The Sharpen For/Amount option enables you to apply output sharpening for screen, glossy paper, or matte paper. This option is best for when you are planning to use your image straight from Camera Raw without opening it in Photoshop. Sharpening an image is usually the last step you take before output because sharpening not only loses its effectiveness as other adjustments and filters are placed over it, but it is also one of the more destructive edits, making visible changes to the pixels of your photo.

After you have chosen an output to Sharpen For, you can choose to sharpen a high, standard, or low amount.

Opening images as Smart Objects

Opening your RAW image as a Smart Object makes it a little more complicated to work with in Photoshop, but it protects it from the Photoshop edits and allows you to open it back up in Camera Raw and make additional changes to it. Smart Objects operate very differently from image files. You can't make adjustments directly to them, thus limiting changes to the layer adjustments. The filters added to a Smart Object are also added as separate sublayers. After you've learned more about Smart Objects and how they work, the benefits and drawbacks of this option will be clearer to you.

 You can learn more about Smart Object layers in Chapter 10.

Now that you've seen the Workflow options, the blue readout at the bottom of Camera Raw should make sense to you. You can glance down at any time to check your Workflow option settings and click to make changes if they are not set correctly for the image you are working on.

> **NOTE**
>
> The Workflow Options settings stay the same as the last time you set them, even if you are working on a new image in Camera Raw. Even if you resize an image, the next image is set to the same resize option. This is convenient if you want your color workspace to always be set to ColorMatch RGB, but it's something to be aware of when working with different sizes of documents that you may or may not want sharpened.

Setting Preferences

Camera Raw Preferences allow you to make changes to the way the image file is handled in Camera Raw. You can access the Camera Raw preferences by clicking the Open Preferences icon in the tool menu, as shown in Figure 7.8. You find options in the Preferences dialog box that enable you to adjust sharpness, create a cache, process various file formats, and save images.

Saving images

The General preferences allow you to change the way your images are saved. You can choose to save your changes to a RAW file as a DNG file or an XMP file and choose where to store that XMP file. You can also change your sharpness settings to apply sharpness to the saved file or just to the preview.

FIGURE 7.8

The Camera Raw Preferences dialog box offers a variety of setting.

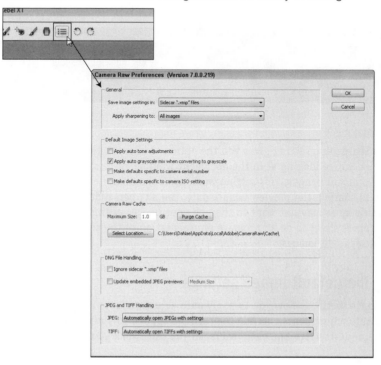

Changing image settings

Changes made to Camera Raw images are not actually stored in the RAW image file. Instead, these changes are stored in a separate location. These settings can be stored in one of three ways:

- A sidecar file with a filename ending in .xmp
- A Camera Raw database that Photoshop provides on the local computer
- A part of a Digital Negative (DNG) file.

The sidecar XMP files are files with the same name as the Camera Raw image file, except they end in .xmp. These files have the advantage of being able to transfer from one computer to another along with the Camera Raw image.

The Camera Raw database is a simple database that is part of the Photoshop application on the computer. Using the Camera Raw database means that you do not need to worry about any secondary files; however, the database is not available if you open the image on other computers.

If you choose to save your Camera Raw files in the DNG format, the settings you make in Camera Raw are embedded in the file, eliminating the need for a sidecar XMP file and making the settings portable.

NOTE

The default preferences you configure are applied only to Camera Raw images that have not been opened in Camera Raw. Camera Raw images that have been opened before use their previous settings. This is an excellent reason to review and set your preferences long before you open more than one file in Camera Raw.

Applying Sharpening

The Applying Sharpening setting gives you the option to sharpen the image preview only, which is the one you're looking at in the document window, or to sharpen the image output as well by selecting all images. This setting works with the Sharpness slider in the Detail tab. If you choose to sharpen the preview images only, the Sharpen slider does not affect the output image. You may or may not want to sharpen your images at this stage, but you probably want the Sharpness slider to be an accurate representation of the sharpness applied, so this setting is best set to all images.

Changing the default image settings

The default image settings allow you to apply auto adjustments to images that are opened in Camera Raw. Auto adjustments override the settings applied to your image by your camera, but they are non-destructive and changeable, so you can tweak your images on a case-by-case basis.

You can also make your preferences specific to the camera or ISO setting in this area of the Camera Raw Preferences. That means the preference settings will only be applied if you are using the specified camera or ISO setting.

You can change the following default settings:

- **Apply auto tone adjustments.** When you open an image in Camera Raw, it reads the settings made by the camera to the metadata of your image and previews your image with those settings. If you check Apply auto tone adjustments, Camera Raw reads all the metadata and tries to apply its own settings for the best image. You can also apply auto settings by clicking the Auto link in the Basic panel, so we recommend you leave this option unchecked and try the auto settings on a photo-by-photo basis.

- **Apply auto grayscale mix when converting to grayscale.** When you create a grayscale image from a RAW image by selecting the Convert to grayscale option in the HSL/Grayscale panel, you are presented with a color mixer that allows you to set the grayscale tones of the various color information in your image. By default, Camera Raw sets those tones to an auto balance, hoping for the best mix to begin with. This is a good place to start, so we recommend leaving this setting checked.

- **Make defaults specific to camera serial number.** If you shoot with multiple cameras that use different initial settings, then select the Make defaults specific to camera serial number option. When you are adjusting an image and save the default settings, the settings are applied only to images taken by the same camera.

- **Make defaults specific to camera ISO setting.** If you are shooting at different ISO settings that require their own auto adjustments, select the Make defaults specific to camera ISO setting option.

Modifying the Camera Raw cache

The Camera Raw cache specifies the amount of space allotted to Camera Raw for processing information. The higher the memory, the more temporary information Camera Raw can store on your computer. This memory on your computer is always allocated to Camera Raw, making it useless for anything else. The default is set to 1GB. If you increase the size, it can reduce processing time in Camera Raw. You can choose to create this cache on any drive connected to your computer.

Handling DNG files

The DNG File Handling options allow you to specify how DNG files will be created from other files, including Camera Raw formats, JPEGs, and TIFFs. You can choose to use the XMP files or embed a JPEG preview in your DNGs for easier handling.

When using DNG files, you can choose from these two options:

- **Ignore sidecar ".xmp" files.** If you have decided to work using the DNG file format, selecting the Ignore sidecar ".xmp" files option stores your settings embedded in your DNG file, and an XMP file is not created.

- **Update embedded JPEG previews.** If you are working with DNG files, you can select the Update embedded JPEG previews option so other applications can preview the image without having to read the Camera Raw data. You can choose to set the preview file size to either medium or full size.

Handling JPEG and TIFF file formats

When you open JPEG or TIFF files in Camera Raw, you can use the tools found in the workspace, but without the benefit of the increased color depth found in RAW images. You can choose to open these files automatically in Camera Raw, or never.

Choose these options for either JPEG or TIFF files:

- **Disable JPEG/TIFF support.** This prevents JPEGs or TIFFs from being opened in Camera Raw.

- **Automatically open JPEGs/TIFFs with settings.** You can specify whether to open a JPEG or TIFF in Camera Raw. To open one of these file types in Camera Raw, right-click the image preview in Bridge and choose Open in Camera Raw.

- **Automatically open all supported JPEGs/TIFFs.** This automatically opens supported JPEGs and TIFFs in Camera Raw before opening them in Photoshop. You can make tonal and color changes more quickly in Camera Raw than in Photoshop, but you don't have the tonal range that you do with a RAW image. These changes are permanent and destructive to a JPEG or TIFF file.

Using the Camera Raw Panel Menu

The Camera Raw panel menu is very useful for creating different settings in the same image. You can choose to use the Camera Raw defaults (the settings your camera processed your image with), use the custom settings, or switch back to the previous settings. You can save as many different settings as you like and access them using this menu. You can access the Camera Raw panel menu by clicking the Panel menu icon under the Image Adjustment tabs, as shown in Figure 7.9.

FIGURE 7.9

The Camera Raw panel menu gives you many options for saving and retrieving your settings.

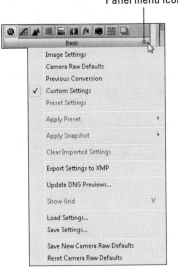

Panel menu icon

In this menu, you have the following options:

- **Image Settings.** This option applies to images that you have previously opened and changed in Camera Raw. A check mark next to it indicates previous settings. After making additional changes, you can select this option to return to those settings.

- **Camera Raw Defaults.** If your image is newly opened in Camera Raw, this option is selected. You can click it at any time to return to the original Camera Raw settings.

- **Previous Conversion.** This option applies the settings used for the last image open in Camera Raw to the current image. This is handy if you have photos that were taken at the same time with the same camera in the same lighting conditions.

- **Custom Settings.** After you make changes to an open image, the Custom Settings option is checked. This allows you to preview the original image by selecting Camera Raw defaults or Image Settings and then returning to the changed image by clicking Custom Settings.

- **Preset Settings.** This option displays any presets you have applied to your image.

- **Apply Preset.** This option displays a preset menu that allows you to apply presets to your image. If you apply more than one preset, it is added to the previous preset(s) unless it falls into the same category. For instance, applying Clarity +15 to Exposure +25 sets both Clarity and Exposure to those values. Applying Clarity +15 to Clarity +25 simply reduces the clarity from +25 to +15.

- **Apply Snapshot.** This option allows you to load any snapshots you have taken in the Snapshot panel. We show you how to do this later in this chapter.

- **Clear Imported Settings.** This option allows other applications that use Camera Raw, such as Photoshop Elements, to clear the settings created using Photoshop. Because fewer options are available to users of Photoshop Elements, this clears settings that these users have no access to and can't modify.

- **Export Settings to XMP.** You can export the current settings to the XMP file by clicking this option. This is only a temporary save, however. When you click Done or Open Image, these settings are overwritten by the current settings. You can click Cancel, however, and these settings become the saved default.

- **Update DNG Previews.** This option allows you to update the JPEG previews in your DNG file. You can also set the size of these previews. If you've set your preferences to update these previews, they are updated when you close or export your image.

- **Show Grid.** This option places a grid over your image.

- **Load Settings.** This option allows you to load a saved setting.

- **Save Settings.** This option allows you to save your settings as a preset. A dialog box opens that gives you the option to select or deselect each setting individually to save in your preset. The preset is saved as an XMP file in the location of your choice. The Preset panel allows you to save and load your setting easily. You will learn more about presets later in this chapter.

- **Save New Camera Raw Defaults.** Choose this option to save your current settings as the Camera Raw defaults. This gives you the power to change default settings that you may not like, such as automatic sharpening.

- **Reset Camera Raw Defaults.** This option resets the defaults to the original Camera Raw settings.

7

Creating Snapshots

As you make changes to your images in Camera Raw, you may want to save several versions of those changes. For instance, you may want to save the original image and the special effect you created with it. Using the Snapshots panel, you can create and save different versions of your image that are saved as metadata and are always accessible. To open the Snapshots panel, click the Snapshots Image adjustment tab, as shown in Figure 7.10. There's not much here, just an empty panel with a New Snapshot and Delete icon at the bottom.

FIGURE 7.10

The Snapshots panel isn't much until you add to it.

Snapshot icon

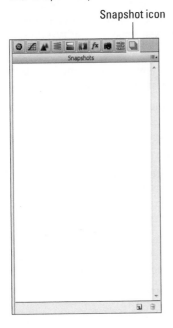

To create a snapshot, click the New Snapshot icon at the bottom of the Snapshots panel. A dialog box opens allowing you to name the snapshot you've just created. After you name it and click OK, the dialog box closes and the Snapshot name appears in the Snapshots panel, as shown in Figure 7.11. As you adjust your image, you can continue to create as many snapshots as you need.

ON THE WEB
You can access Figure 7.11 with the saved snapshots on the book's website as Figure 7-11.jpg.

FIGURE 7.11

After you've added one or more snapshots, you can return to their settings by selecting them in the Snapshots panel.

New Snapshot

You can access these snapshots at any time by simply clicking the name in the Snapshots panel. When you are finished in Camera Raw, the snapshot that is selected is the exported image.

Saving Presets

As you adjust the settings in Camera Raw, keep in mind that you can use the settings on more than just the image you are adjusting. You can save them as presets and use Bridge to apply them to other images. You can also apply them to other images within Camera Raw.

Open the Preset panel by clicking the Preset tab. Just like the Snapshots panel, the Preset panel is pretty bare until you add your own presets to it. Click the Add New Preset icon on the bottom of the Preset panel. The dialog box shown in Figure 7.12 opens, giving you the option to choose which settings will be saved in the new preset. You can also name your preset to help you find it more easily.

FIGURE 7.12

You can choose which settings will be changed to create a preset.

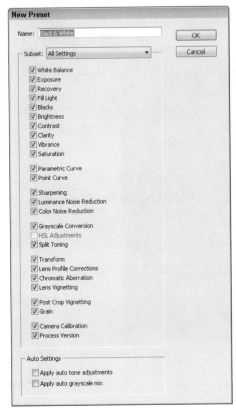

After you have created a preset, you can change your settings to match it by highlighting it in the Preset panel. You can also access the settings in Bridge by choosing Edit ➪ Develop Settings and selecting a preset. The setting is adjusted for all selected images.

Exporting Camera Raw Files

When you are finished with your image in Camera Raw, you have several options for exporting it. You can open your file in Photoshop, close it out, or save it using a different filename or format. Using the buttons at the bottom of the screen, as shown in Figure 7.13, you can open your image in Photoshop, cancel your changes, and close your image, or click Done to close your image with the new settings saved.

NOTE

If you have selected "Open in Photoshop as Smart Objects" in your Workflow Options, the Open button reads "Open Object(s)" rather than "Open Image(s)."

FIGURE 7.13

Export your document using one of these three buttons or the Save Image button.

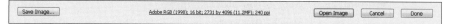

Camera Raw formats are large, unwieldy, and generally not accepted for printing or sharing on the web. In order to make your Camera Raw files share-friendly, you need to save them in a more accepted file format, generally JPEG. You can also convert your files to DNGs, TIFFs, or PSDs. To explore your options, click the Save Image button (refer to Figure 7.13) to open the Save Options dialog box, as shown in Figure 7.14.

FIGURE 7.14

The Save Options dialog box allows you to change the name or file format of your Camera Raw file.

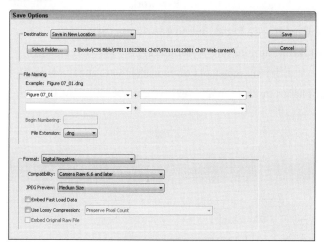

The options available in the Save Options dialog box are as follows:

- **Destination.** You can choose to save your files in the same location, or a new location.
- **File Naming.** You have several options for naming a file or multiple files: the batch saving options and the File Extension option.
  - **Batch saving options.** If you have several photos open in Camera Raw, you can change their filenames and save them in sequence using these options.
  - **File Extension.** Using the File Extension drop-down menu, you can save your file as a DNG, JPEG, TIFF, or PSD file.
- **Format.** A format is automatically chosen when you choose your file extension, or vice versa. The option you choose in this section changes the dialog box to display the options for each file format.

After you are finished setting your options, click Save and your file is saved according to your settings. This does not replace your original Camera Raw file, of course; it creates a new file.

Summary

By this time, you should have a good idea of why Camera Raw formats have become so popular and why it is important to have a non-proprietary format to save these files in. In addition, you should know quite a bit about the Camera Raw workspace including the following:

- Where the tools and menus are found and how to access them
- How to set your workflow options and preferences
- How to create several different snapshots of your image settings
- How to open your images in Photoshop or export them as different file types

Processing Photos with Camera Raw

IN THIS CHAPTER

Exploring Camera Raw tools

Correcting several photos simultaneously

Fine-tuning the white balance

Adjusting light settings

Correcting color

Making targeted adjustments

Creating fun effects

Tweaking camera quirks

Adding the finishing touches

N ow that you are familiar with the Camera Raw workspace and the preferences and menus, it's time to jump in and start adjusting your RAW images. In some cases, you will find the tools and controls so easy to use that you may start opening your JPEGs and TIFFs in Camera Raw in order to quickly make basic adjustments. In other cases, if you are familiar with Photoshop, you will be frustrated that the tools are so completely foreign and so limited compared to what is available to you in Photoshop.

Getting to Know the Camera Raw Tools

Before you can make adjustments in Camera Raw, you need to become familiar with the tools and how they work. The tools are found at the top of the Camera Raw interface, as shown in Figure 8.1. Some of the tools are fairly basic, and you are probably already familiar with how they work, such as the Zoom and Hand tools. Other tools have specialized functions, such as the Targeted Adjustment tool and the Graduated Filter.

FIGURE 8.1

Taking a closer look at the Camera Raw tools

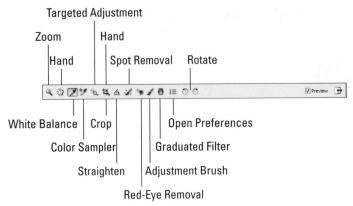

We cover these tools in depth later in this chapter, but for now, we'll provide you with a quick reference list.

- **Zoom tool.** Use this tool to get a closer look at an area of your photo. The photo zooms to the point where you click the Zoom tool. To zoom back out, just press and hold the Alt/Option key to change the plus sign in the magnifying glass to a minus sign before you click. You can also use the Zoom menu at the bottom of the document window to choose a setting.

- **Hand tool.** Use this tool when your image is bigger than the document window; you can grab the image with the Hand tool and move it around in your window to look at other areas of your photo.

- **White Balance tool.** Use this tool to select an area of your photo that is white or neutral gray and change the white balance of your photo based on that selection.

- **Color Sampler.** Use this tool to find the RGB values of areas in your image. These values change as you correct the tone and color of your photo, giving you a numerical representation of the changes taking place in your image. Simply click a color in your photo to place a marker and display the RGB settings above the image, as shown in Figure 8.2. You can place up to ten color samples. To clear the color samples, click Clear Samplers.

- **Targeted Adjustment tool.** Use this tool to choose one pixel in your image and change its value in the histogram, which changes the values of the other colors in the histogram as well. Click the area of your photo that you want to adjust and hold down the left mouse button while you drag side to side or up and down. This changes the value of the pixel you click, altering the relative values in the histogram. If you click a darker pixel, the darker areas of your photo change dramatically while the lighter areas do not change as much. This holds true if you click a midtone or a light area of your photo as well; those areas are affected more than others are.

FIGURE 8.2

The Color Sample RGB information corresponds to the numbered color sample areas displayed in the photo.

Color Sample RGB values

 Again — and we promise it will happen often throughout the book — knowing how the histogram works and how colors relate is important to understanding how the Color Sampler and the Targeted Adjustment tools work. Both color and histograms are discussed in depth in Chapter 4.

- **Crop tool.** Select the Crop tool, then click and drag around the area you want to crop. If you want to straighten the image as well, just use the rotating arrow that appears when you hover over one of the corners, and rotate the cropped area. Double-click to finish. One difference you'll notice about cropping in Camera Raw is that even cropping is a non-destructive edit. Even after opening and closing the image and creating numerous other settings, you can click the Crop tool to display the entire image and reset the crop boundaries, as shown in Figure 8.3.

- **Straighten tool.** Use this tool to straighten a photo. Drag it in what should be a straight horizontal line in your photo, and your image rotates to compensate. This tool is also non-destructive; you can correct the results at any time.

FIGURE 8.3

Even though this image was cropped the last time it was opened, you can change the crop by clicking the Crop tool and displaying the entire image.

  Except for being non-destructive, cropping and straightening work in Camera Raw very similarly to the way they work in Photoshop. That's why they get just a measly little bullet point here. If you want to read more about cropping or straightening, see Chapter 3.

- **Spot Removal tool.** Use this tool to correct areas in your photo that need touchups. This tool is covered in greater detail later in this chapter.

- **Red-Eye Removal tool.** Use this tool to correct red-eye. This is covered later in this chapter.

- **Adjustment Brush.** Use this tool to make adjustments to just one area of your photo in Camera Raw. Although this sounds straightforward, it is actually more complicated than it sounds, so we take you through it step by step later in this chapter.

- **Graduated Filter.** Use this tool to make gradual changes to areas of your photo. For instance, you may have a darker foreground coupled with an overexposed sky. Use this tool to correct one or the other gradually for realistic results. This tool is covered later in this chapter.

- **Open Preferences.** Click this icon to open the Preferences dialog box where you can adjust several of your Camera Raw preferences. These were covered in Chapter 7.

- **Rotate.** Use these buttons to rotate your image 90 degrees clockwise or counter-clockwise.

- **Toggle Full Screen Mode.** Use this button to fill your screen with the Camera Raw utility or to reduce it to a floating box within Photoshop.

Synchronizing Adjustments in Multiple RAW Images

You can correct several photos at once using the Camera Raw interface. This is a real time-saver if your photos have been taken in similar lighting conditions. For example, you might have several outdoor shots of the same wedding. When you make changes to the photo that is displayed in Camera Raw, those changes are also applied to any selected photo in the film-strip. Using the Synchronize option, you can choose which changes apply to selected photos and which ones do not apply to other selected photos in the filmstrip.

To make changes to multiple photos, they must first be open in Camera Raw. Select multiple images in Bridge, and double-click to open them in Camera Raw. You see them displayed in the filmstrip in Camera Raw, as shown in Figure 8.4.

FIGURE 8.4

When you open multiple photos in Camera Raw, they appear in the filmstrip.

You can select more than one image at once by using the Shift key to select images in sequence or the Ctrl/⌘ key to select images one at a time. You can also click Select All to select all the images in the filmstrip.

To synchronize which changes are made to all the selected images, click Synchronize. This opens the Synchronize dialog box, shown in Figure 8.5. Use the drop-down list or select individual check boxes to specify which options change across all the selected photos in Camera Raw.

FIGURE 8.5

Use the Synchronize drop-down list to choose which changes will be made to all the selected photos.

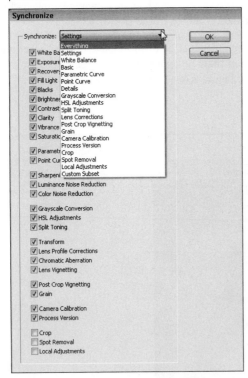

After you are finished making batch changes, you can select your photos one at a time to preview the changes and tweak them individually, but the bulk of the adjustments are already made, saving you a lot of time in processing your files.

Adjusting the White Balance

Your camera has a White Balance setting that tells it what lighting is being used when a photo is captured. For example, a fluorescent light leaves a greenish-yellow cast on your photos, giving your whites a greenish-yellow tinge. Your camera can compensate by adjusting the color information to filter out the colorcast. But just like any automatic process, the camera compensation is not ideal for all images.

If your photo is a RAW image, you don't have to worry if the White Balance setting on your camera is correct or if it compensated correctly for a particular lighting situation. You can adjust the white balance after the photo has been shot using Camera Raw. Not that you want to shoot all your images in tungsten mode, but you could.

Getting the white balance correct is the single most important thing you can do to improve the colors in your photo. Even photos that look good can be improved with a simple white balance adjustment, and photos taken in horrible lighting situations can be improved dramatically. The before photo in Figure 8.6 shows an image taken under indoor lighting without a flash. It's hard to tell in the grayscale version printed here, but if you look at the color version in the center insert, you'll see that it has a very yellow colorcast. The after photo shows the same image after a simple White Balance adjustment. The colorcast is gone, and the boys look much better.

FIGURE 8.6

With a click of the White Balance tool, this photo goes from scary yellow to beautiful color.

Before   After

8

241

In Camera Raw, you can reset the white balance correctly in three different ways:

- Use the White Balance tool
- Change the lighting settings
- Use the Temperature and Tint sliders

Using the White Balance tool

The White Balance tool can be an effective way to quickly correct the colors in your photo, or it can be an exercise in frustration. It all depends on the photo you are trying to correct and the area on which you use the tool. The White Balance tool can be found in the tool menu at the top of the Camera Raw interface.

To use the White Balance tool, select it and click an area of your photo that should be white or a neutral gray, as shown in Figure 8.7. Camera Raw automatically adjusts the colors in your photo to correct the white balance based on your selection. Picking just the right color in your photo can be challenging. It's not always easy to determine an area that is white or neutral gray. If you're not satisfied with the results, just continue to click different areas and the white balance is set anew each time.

FIGURE 8.7

Use the White Balance tool to select a white or neutral gray area of your photo.

If you choose an area that is too bright for the White Balance tool to sample, you hear an alert and no change takes place. If you do it a second time, a dialog box pops up, letting you know that the area you are selecting is too bright to be sampled.

Changing the lighting settings

You can use the White Balance menu shown in Figure 8.8 to change the lighting settings based on the lighting where your photo was taken. If you took a photo on a cloudy day and it turned out too cool, you can choose Cloudy to warm it up. If you took a photo under fluorescent lighting and your photo has that nasty yellow cast, you can choose Fluorescent to filter it out. You get the idea. Of course, you may find that selecting a setting from the menu based on the light in which you took the photo may not always give you the best result. You should preview and experiment with the different options before you decide on one.

FIGURE 8.8

You can use the White Balance menu to choose a lighting setting similar to the White Balance setting on your camera.

You can also choose the best option from the drop-down list and then use the Temperature and Tint sliders to tweak the colors until they are just right.

NOTE

It's not hard to change the white balance settings so you like the colors in your image. If you ever want to start over from the camera settings, however, choose As Shot from the lighting settings menu.

Using the Temperature and Tint sliders

If you prefer to "eyeball" the changes to your white balance, you can adjust the Temperature and Tint sliders in the Basic panel, as shown in Figure 8.9. The Temperature slider adjusts the levels of yellow and blue in your photo, and the Tint slider adjusts the levels of red and green. A good rule of thumb is to find an object in your photo that you want to be a certain color (skin tones or whites are fairly easy to determine) and tweak the sliders until you have just the color you want.

FIGURE 8.9

Use the Temperature and Tint sliders to eyeball the white balance of your image.

The Temperature and Tint sliders are also ideal for tweaking your image after you've made a white balance adjustment using the White Balance tool or the White Balance menu. We usually try the tool first and then tweak the results using the sliders.

> **TIP**
>
> Add a neutral color card to your shot, and you can set your white balance easily by clicking the card in your photo after bringing it into the Camera Raw interface. A light-gray piece of paper works really well. After you've used it to set your white balance, simply crop it out of the photo. If you are taking several photos in the same lighting conditions, you can remove the card after the first shot and set the white balance for all the photos at once.

Adjusting Lighting

The next six settings in the Basic panel adjust the exposure and lighting of your photo in different ways. This is where you'll really see a difference in the quality of a Camera Raw image over a JPEG. Look at Figure 8.10, for example. The before photo is a shot of balloons taken in the early morning light, creating a dark image where the balloons are just silhouettes on the background of the eastern sky. If this image were a JPEG, making the image lighter would result in a grainy photo with a lot of color noise. The after image in Figure 8.10 shows that fixing this image in Camera Raw turned out a better result; some noise was created, but not nearly as much as if this image had been a JPEG.

> **ON THE WEB**
>
> You'll find the before image saved as Figure 8-10 on the website. Can you fix the exposure?

FIGURE 8.10

Changing the exposure on a dark Camera Raw image created much less noise than if the image had been a JPEG.

> **NOTE**
>
> Two highlighted buttons at the top of the light and color adjustments found in the Basic panel are labeled Auto and Default. To see the settings that Camera Raw thinks are best for your image, click Auto and the settings are adjusted to a mathematical interpretation of where the colors and tonal ranges really belong in your image. Because the Auto setting is formulaic, you will probably want to do some tweaking. The Default link resets your image to the settings that it opened with, whether these are the original Camera Raw settings created by your camera or settings that you created on a previous occasion when you opened your image.

As you change the light settings of your image, keep an eye on your specular highlights and deep shadows. As you increase and decrease your exposure, you run the risk of creating areas where the pixel information is lost because they are too light or too dark. Be sure to keep these areas manageable. Click the Highlight clipping warning and Shadow clipping warning icons in the Histogram, shown in Figure 8.11, to show clipped highlights in red and clipped shadows in blue.

> **TIP**
>
> Holding down the Alt/Option key while adjusting the Exposure and Recovery settings shows you clipped highlights in your image. White areas have no color detail, and red and yellow areas are clipped in one or two channels. Holding down the Alt/Option key while adjusting the Blacks shows clipped shadows in black.

You also create some noise as you use these sliders. The noise becomes more visible the more you adjust the sliders. You can reduce some noise in the Detail tab, but noise reduction is never an ideal fix; if possible, try to prevent noise in the first place.

FIGURE 8.11

Use the clipping warnings to show you areas that have lost all color information.

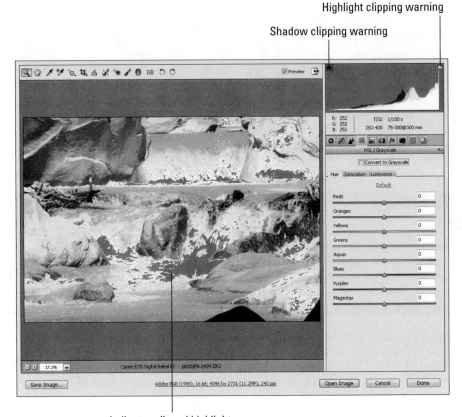

Highlight clipping warning

Shadow clipping warning

Indicates clipped highlights

Change the lighting of your image by using the following sliders in the Camera Raw interface:

- **Exposure.** This slider adjusts the lightness or darkness of your image. The results are similar to changing the aperture setting on your camera. In fact, the numbers on the Exposure slider are in increments that correlate to f-stops: 1.0 is similar to widening your aperture by one f-stop and so on.

- **Contrast.** This slider adjusts the contrast between the midtones in your image, creating (or reducing) contrast without significantly changing the highlights or the shadows.

- **Highlights.** This slider attempts to recover detail from highlights, or brighter areas of your photo. Rather than targeting the entire image, this slider looks for color detail in the extreme highlights of your image and makes them darker in an effort to recover any blown-out areas of your image. You will often want to use Highlights in conjunction with other settings, such as Exposure and Shadows, so you can achieve a good balance of lighting in your photo.

- **Shadows.** This option does the opposite of Highlights, adjusting and targeting the shadows in the photo. The Shadows slider is a real miracle worker when either the foreground or the background of your photo is much darker than the other. Consider Figure 8.12, where the background has been seriously overexposed. Adjusting the exposure and highlights until the background is visible and then using the Shadows slider to bring the exposure of the boy back to an optimal setting improves this photo dramatically.

FIGURE 8.12

Adjusting the highlights and shadows brings the exposure of the entire photo into balance.

ON THE WEB

You'll find the before image saved as Figure 8-12 on the website. Can you adjust the exposure so that both the foreground and background look good?

- **Whites.** This setting determines how white your whites will be in the photo; you can brighten them by moving the slider to the right, or deepen them by moving the slider to the left. This increases or reduces contrast in your image.

- **Blacks.** This setting is the opposite of the Whites setting, of course. You can brighten or deepen the blacks in your image by moving this slider one way or the other.

An advantage to using Camera Raw to adjust your exposure is that you can create two amazing images with the same shot. Consider the balloons again. By reducing the exposure and fill light and increasing the blacks, I can change the focus of the image from the balloons to the sky, as shown in Figure 8.13.

FIGURE 8.13

You can adjust Camera Raw files to create different looks with the same photo.

> **NOTE**
>
> If you are familiar with Camera Raw 6.0 or earlier, you'll notice that the settings have changed significantly. We love the changes. With the ability to increase or decrease both shadows and highlights, we've been able to make some incredible improvements to our images, getting exposure settings that look like HDR images (see Chapter 13). If you've opened a Camera Raw file and adjusted it in a previous version of Camera Raw, you'll notice that the adjustment sliders from the previous version will appear in Camera Raw 7.0. To use the new and improved sliders, click the exclamation point that appears at the bottom of the Camera Raw document window.

Adjusting Color and Clarity

You can adjust the color of a RAW image in the Basic panel for a general fix, the Tone Curve panel for a targeted fix, and the HSL panel for a highly precise adjustment that allows you to make custom decisions about your color in eight different color ranges. Don't be overwhelmed with all these options for changing and adjusting the color of your images. As with most situations (in life as well as in Photoshop), it's best to start with the basics and work up, depending on how much control you want to have over the color.

Working in Photoshop is an art form, not a science — even when it comes to correcting color. Although the basic tools are fairly simple and straightforward, adjusting tonal curves takes a little practice and effort before you can do it well without thought, and adjusting color levels in the HSL panel can very quickly get out of hand! The best way to become proficient is to jump in and work with these tools until you feel comfortable using them to adjust the photos that really matter.

Tweaking clarity, vibrance, and saturation

Clarity, vibrance, and saturation can be adjusted in the Basic panel of Camera Raw. These adjustments are so useful and popular that the default panel is the best place for them. They are also the easiest of the color adjustments to use and to get right.

As well as improving the overall color and clarity of your images, these settings can compensate for loss of color and clarity due to the tonal adjustments. This is a great way to create stunningly colorful images, similar to taking pictures with a high-saturation film.

You can adjust the clarity and saturation of your image by adjusting these sliders:

- **Clarity.** This adjustment clarifies the edges in the image, restoring definition and sharpness by increasing the contrast of the midtone pixels. This works like magic to reduce hazy or dull images that are a result of poor shooting conditions or using other settings that reduce contrast, such as the Highlights and Shadows sliders.

  For example, look at the difference between the before and after images in Figure 8.14. While the first image is very hazy and flat, the second image takes advantage of the Clarity adjustment to make a dramatic difference in its clarity and crispness.

ON THE WEB

Try your hand at adjusting the clarity of the before image, which is saved as Figure 8-14 on the website.

- **Vibrance.** This adjustment saturates only the areas of the image that are of a lower saturation without affecting the areas that are already highly saturated. It also leaves skin tones unaffected, making it ideal for saturating images with human subjects.

- **Saturation.** This adjustment saturates the image uniformly, giving you the ability to reduce the colors in your image to grayscale or to increase the color of your image to as much as double the saturation. Colorful photos, such as flowers or balloons, are especially fun to over-saturate in order to create a color statement.

FIGURE 8.14

Using just the Clarity adjustment made a big difference in this image.

Adjusting the Tone Curve

Discussing the Tone Curve in the section on adjusting color may seem odd, because it adjusts the lightness of your image as much as the color. The Tone Curve gives you more control over which areas of your photo are brightened or darkened, as well as which colors pop and which ones fade. It takes practice to get a feel for exactly how the curve works, however, so you might find yourself inadvertently making drastic and unwanted changes. You can easily restore the default settings and start over, though, so don't despair.

We'll do our best to demystify the Tone Curve so your practice has purpose. The Tone Curve panel has two tabs: the Parametric tab, which allows you to make limited changes to the Tone Curve using sliders, and the Point tab, which allows you to make changes to the Tone Curve using points on the actual curve.

The Parametric panel

It's harder to take your changes too far with the Parametric tab because it limits the changes you can make to the sliders. It's quicker, easier, and generally more user-friendly than the Point tab. However, it doesn't give you nearly as much latitude for making changes as the Point tab.

The first thing you should notice in the Parametric tab, shown in Figure 8.15, is the histogram that represents the tonal layout of your image. In the image, most of the pixels are in the midtone range or higher, as you can see by the high peaks in the middle and to the right. As a general rule, you would look at this histogram and know immediately that the photo it represents is low in contrast. That isn't a bad thing for some images, but this one is hazy and unclear, and it has enough shadow that there should be plenty of pixels in the lower end of the histogram. This is a photo that will definitely benefit from a tonal curve correction.

> **NOTE**
>
> It's important to look at images in conjunction with their histograms to decide whether the histogram represents areas that need to be corrected. A picture taken on a snowy day might resemble the histogram in Figure 8.15 and look bright and clear. The histogram by itself is not an indicator of whether an image is a good one or in need of improvement. Instead, it is a guide to help you make the right changes to improve your image.

FIGURE 8.15

In the Parametric Tone Curve, the histogram represents the tonal layout of this image.

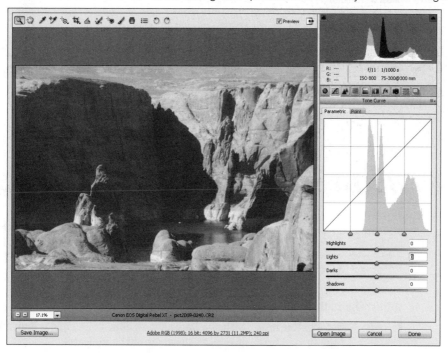

> **ON THE WEB**
>
> Figure 8.15 needs a lot of work. Fortunately, you can improve it dramatically using the Parametric Tone Curve. Give it a try by downloading Figure 8-15 from the website and following the steps for changing the tonal curve.

Fix the photo shown in Figure 8.15 by following these steps:

1. **Adjust the indicators directly under the histogram so they represent a more balanced tonal range, as shown in Figure 8.16.**

   This doesn't change your image, but it affects how the tonal sliders underneath affect your image. The Shadows slider adjusts the pixels to the left of the first indicator, the Darks slider adjusts everything between that indicator and the next, and so on.

2. **Adjust the Shadows slider.**

   In this image, the dark and shadow pixels need the most work, so it's best to start there. Move the slider to the left to darken the shadow in the image. Click the shadow clipping warning in the main histogram to preview any shadows that are being clipped. (You won't find any in this photo, but it's a good habit to get into.) Stop when you are satisfied with the result.

3. **Adjust the Darks slider.**

   With the balanced histogram shown in Figure 8.16, this slider is really touchy and creates an image that is too dark with very little adjustment.

FIGURE 8.16

Adjusting the indicators determines how the sliders affect the image.

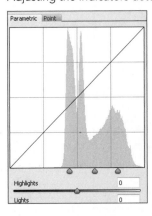

4. **Adjust the indicators under the histogram again.**

   In order to get a better result with the Darks slider, adjust the middle indicator farther left, so the second pixel spike is to the right of the indicator.

5. **Adjust the Darks again.**

   Now, as you move the Darks slider, you get a better range to play with. Again, stop when you see that you've found a good balance.

6. **Adjust the Lights slider.**

   This slider also needs to move left, but not much.

7. **Adjust the Highlights slider.**

   Moving this slider to the right adds contrast to the image. Again, you should take advantage of the highlight clipping warning in the main histogram. You can find clipped highlights in this image.

You can continue to tweak the indicators and the sliders to get a feel for the changes they are making and to get the best final result. When you are finished, you should have a result similar to Figure 8.17. Add Clarity and Contrast to this photo, and you have a finished product that is practically a miracle considering what you began with.

FIGURE 8.17

With these final settings, you can already see a marked improvement in the photo.

The Point tab

The Point tab gives you much more latitude for changing your image, but it is also more difficult to use than the Parametric tab. In the following steps, we'll show you how to correct the same image used in Figure 8.15 by using the Point panel instead of the Parametric panel:

1. **Click the Panel menu, and choose Camera Raw Defaults to reset the image.**

   If you used the Parametric tab to change the curves, you want to start over from the original image settings. You should have the image and settings shown in Figure 8.18.

FIGURE 8.18

The Points Tone Curve gives you very precise results.

2. **Use the drop-down list to choose an appropriate setting.**

   I changed the image in this example to the Strong Contrast Preset. This improves the image, but not enough. You can continue to customize the settings to get a better result.

3. **Tweak the points on the curve, if necessary.**

   Adjusting these points on the curve performs a similar function to the indicators in the Parametric histogram. By changing their location on the diagonal, you can change which pixels are affected as you use them to bend and stretch the curve. Change these points closer to the histogram so more tones are affected by each point, as shown in Figure 8.19. Note that as soon as you do this, the name in the Curve drop-down list changes to Custom.

TIP

You can add points to the curve by clicking the curve where you want to add them. You can remove a point by dragging it quickly off the curve.

FIGURE 8.19

Move the points on the histogram so more tones are affected by their adjustment later.

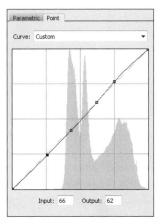

4. **Adjust the area where you want the biggest change first.**

   In this example, the biggest change you want to make to the photo is to increase the dark areas for more contrast, so start with the lower-left point first. Move the point *slowly* down. You can drag it up and down the curve line as you do this to further customize your adjustment.

TIP

For more controlled adjustments, use the arrow keys to move the selected point by increments of one. The up and down arrow keys adjust the curve, and the left and right arrow keys adjust the point placement on the curve.

5. **Click to add another point on the curve, if necessary.**

   The shadows in this photo appear too washed out. Adding another point lower on the curve gives you more control over them.

6. **Continue to move the points on the curve, adding more when necessary.**

   This is where practice and experience comes in. Each photo reacts differently, and you've probably noticed that even a small change can really mess up your image. Just keep working with it until you get the result you want.

It doesn't take long to adjust the point curve before you can see that it is indeed more versatile, but also much more difficult to control. Because we could add points to the curve, the end result was better than what we achieved with the Parametric adjustment, as you can see in Figure 8.20. Notice that the background above the cliffs is much clearer because we added another point to the highlights.

FIGURE 8.20

The Points adjustment is more precise, bringing out more detail.

Adjusting hue, saturation, and luminance

Figure 8.21 shows the HSL/Grayscale panel. HSL stands for Hue, Saturation, and Luminance. Each setting has a subpanel, and the color sliders in each subpanel allow you to make changes to the color in these precise color ranges.

FIGURE 8.21

The HSL/Grayscale panel allows you to adjust individual colors in your photo.

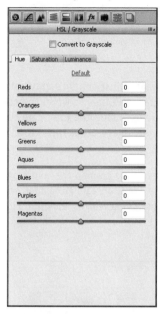

Hue adjustments

In this tab, you can literally change the color in your images. Using the Reds slider, you can change the reds in your image to bright pink or warm orange, for instance. Each pixel in your image is assigned to one of the color ranges represented by the sliders. The brighter the colors are in your image, the more visible these changes are.

You can use the hue adjustments to give a photo a warmer or cooler feel, or just to enhance or change specific colors in your image. Have fun playing with the colors, but watch your skin tones; they can be negatively affected.

TIP

Use the Default link found in each panel to reset the sliders to zero for that panel.

Saturation adjustments

The Saturation tab has the same color sliders as the Hue panel, and not surprisingly, they allow you to add to or reduce the saturation of the targeted color. You can use this feature to make more selective color enhancements than the Vibrance slider can give you, or you can even create specialized images where only one or two selected colors are saturated and the rest are in grayscale.

Luminance adjustments

The Luminance tab sets the tint or shade of the selected color, adding black or white to it in order to adjust the brightness of that color. Use these sliders to get your colors just right or to add contrast to your image.

Creating a grayscale photo

The color sliders are not just for color fixes; they make great adjustments to grayscale brightness values as well. Most color images don't make great grayscale images when they are simply converted, brightness value for brightness value. However, using the Grayscale Mix sliders, you can change the brightness values that the colors in your image are mapped to in order to create a fantastic grayscale image.

The first thing to do is to click the Convert to Grayscale check box to map the colors in your image to the corresponding grayscale values. This brings up the Grayscale Mix panel, with the same color sliders that are present in each of the HSL/Grayscale panels, as shown in Figure 8.22.

FIGURE 8.22

A grayscale photo with the Auto settings applied

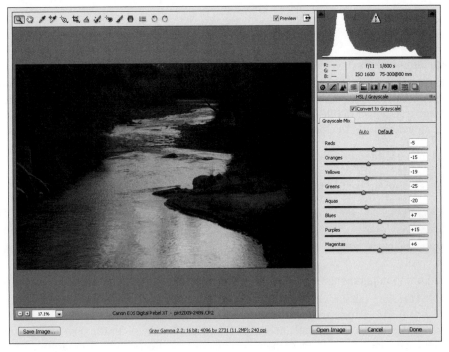

When you convert your image to grayscale, the Auto setting is applied, which is the Camera Raw interpretation of what's best. You can click Default to see what the straight conversion would look like, but it's not usually as good as the Auto setting. Or you can tweak the color sliders to map the brightness values of the selected color to different brightness values in your grayscale image, changing the brightness and contrast of selected areas of your photo. Figure 8.23 shows what a big difference changing the grayscale mix can make.

FIGURE 8.23

After tweaking the grayscale mix, the sparkle is enhanced in the water.

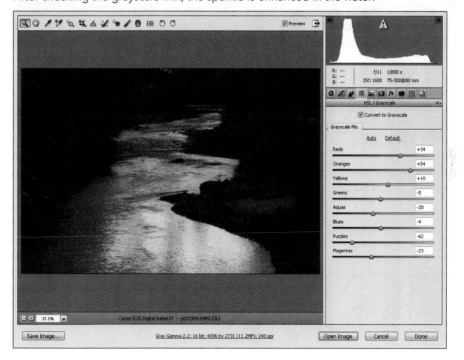

Using Split Toning

The Split Toning panel is used to create a color-mapping overlay over the shadows and/or highlights of an image. This can have the same effect as placing a warming or cooling filter over a color image. Using the Split Toning panel has the added benefit of applying different filters to the highlights than to the shadows. This allows you to cool down highlights while warming up shadows, for instance, to reduce the effect of heavy shadows.

When you apply the Split Toning effect to a grayscale image, it adds a color tone (or two) to the image. You can create sepia tones or other color effects over your black-and-white photo.

In the Split Toning panel shown in Figure 8.24, you can see the separate Hue and Saturation sliders for the highlights and shadows (thus the name, Split Toning). The middle slider sets the balance between the highlights and the shadows. As you move it to the right, more pixels are considered highlights; as you move it to the left, more pixels are considered shadows.

You can use the Hue sliders to choose a color to add to your highlights or shadows, move the Saturation sliders to the right to determine how much color to add, and set the Balance slider to determine which color to add where.

TIP

To apply a single color tone to any image, set the Balance slider all the way to the right or left.

FIGURE 8.24

The Split Toning panel maps color to your image.

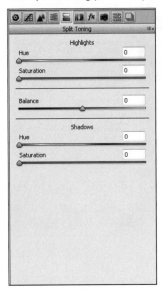

Correcting and Retouching

After you've made general corrections to the light and color of your photo, it's time to make on-the-spot corrections. You can remove flaws or red-eye in your photo, use the adjustment brush to make color or lighting corrections to selected areas of your photo, or create a graduated filter to apply a color or lighting effect gradually. Although all these changes have the potential to bruise your image or create noise, they are considered non-destructive edits because you can always return to the original Camera Raw settings.

Cloning and spot removal

The Spot Removal tool allows you to make localized spot correction and cloning fixes to anything from lens spots to blemishes. In Camera Raw, this tool is limited compared to the tools you find in Photoshop for cloning and healing. For basic fixes, however, it works just fine.

> **TIP**
>
> If you have a lens or sensor spot that appears in multiple photos and can be fixed adequately in Camera Raw, be sure to take advantage of the fact that you can fix multiple photos at once. You can open them all at once in Camera Raw or use the batch editing capabilities of Bridge, which you can read about in Chapter 6.

To use the Spot Removal tool, follow these steps:

> **ON THE WEB**
>
> You can download Figure 8-25.dng from the website and follow the steps to learn how to use the Spot Removal tool.

1. **Open a file containing a spot or blemish you want to fix.**

   This example uses Figure 8-25 from the website.

2. **Click the Spot Removal tool.**

   This changes your cursor to a crosshair and opens the Spot Removal panel, as shown in Figure 8.25.

3. **Select an option from the Type drop-down list.**

   This example uses the Heal option, which takes the texture, lighting, and shading from the sampled areas and places them over the blemish. The Clone brush simply makes a copy of the sampled area and places it over the blemish, feathering the edges so they blend in.

4. **Select the spot you want to fix.**

   In this example, drag to create a circle that is just larger than the blemish, and release the mouse button. A red circle indicating the area to correct is created over the blemish, and a second, green, circle is also created, indicating the area that is being used to create the patch.

FIGURE 8.25

Is this a beauty mark or a blemish? Either way, the Spot Removal tool gets rid of it.

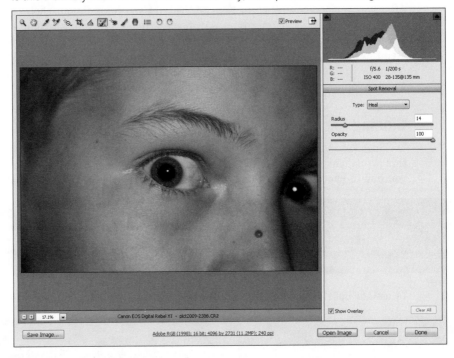

5. **Move either circle, if needed.**

   Camera Raw makes a guess at which area is the best to take a patch from when it places the green circle. This guess is frequently wrong. Move either circle by hovering over the center of it until the arrow and plus sign appear, as shown in Figure 8.26, and then grabbing and moving it to a better location.

6. **Resize the circles, if needed.**

   You can also resize both circles by using the Radius slider or by hovering over the edge of either circle until the two-directional arrow appears, and then dragging them to the right size.

7. **Deselect the Show Overlay option to remove the circles from view and make sure everything looks good.**

FIGURE 8.26

Wait until the cursor changes to an arrow and plus sign before you move one of the circles.

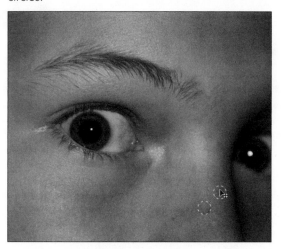

8. **Repeat Steps 3 to 7 to make any additional healing or cloning changes.**

   As you click to create new circles, the old red circles turn purple, indicating that they are not active, and the old green circles disappear.

NOTE

To start over, click Clear All to remove all sampled and fixed areas.

9. **Select any other tool to exit the Spot Removal panel.**

You can use the Opacity slider to reduce the effect of the spot removal, either before or after you have created the healing circles. The Opacity (as well as the Radius) works only on the active circles.

Removing red-eye

You can make quick red-eye fixes in Camera Raw from the Red Eye Removal panel, which you access by clicking the Red Eye Removal tool. Use the tool to drag a marquee around each red eye, making the marquee a little larger than the actual eye, as shown in Figure 8.27. Deselect the Show Overlay check box so you can see how well your fix worked. Use the Pupil Size and Darken sliders to tweak the fix and get it perfect.

FIGURE 8.27

Red-eye removal takes seconds with the Red Eye Removal tool in Camera Raw.

Using the Adjustment Brush

The Adjustment Brush provides the ability to make targeted adjustments to only the areas in your image that need them. Camera Raw does this by creating a mask over everything but the selected areas and making adjustments over that mask, similar to the way adjustment layers work in Photoshop.

Selecting the Adjustment Brush opens the Adjustment Brush panel and sets the Mask option to New, as shown in Figure 8.28. The Adjustment Brush works differently from any other tool in Photoshop, using pins instead of layers to mark each adjustment. The number of adjustments made depends entirely on how you use the Mask options.

FIGURE 8.28

The Adjustment Brush panel provides a limited number of adjustments that you can make to targeted areas of your image.

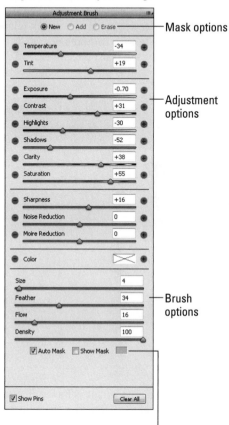

Mask options — Adjustment options — Brush options — Mask overlay color

Setting the Mask options

The Mask options include New, Add, and Erase. Whenever you select New, a brush stroke over your image creates a new mask with new settings, and places a new pin. After the first brush stroke, the Mask option automatically changes to Add. When you select Add, the brush strokes you make are added to the currently selected mask. You can also select Erase, which allows you to use the brush to erase areas in the currently selected mask.

NOTE

Don't be confused by all this talk of brushing on a mask. You are probably wondering how an adjustment can be applied through a mask. Actually, each new mask is applied to the entire image and the Adjustment Brush erases portions of it so the adjustment can filter through.

Using the pins

The pins that are placed every time you create a mask with the adjustment brush are only general indicators of the area where the adjustment is taking place. A pin is placed at the beginning of the first stroke you make when creating a new mask. To see the areas that are being affected by your adjustment, hover over the center of a placed pin, and the mask temporarily appears over the adjusted areas. Figure 8.29 shows an image with two pins placed. The pin placed over the cliff is outlined in green (as you can see by the black circle inside of it), indicating that it is selected. Adding or erasing affects the mask this pin is associated with.

FIGURE 8.29

Create a new mask that places a new pin whenever you want to make a separate adjustment.

The second pin is placed towards the bottom of the photo. The cursor is hovering over it, and the mask appears green, indicating that the waterfall is being affected by the adjustment. We have purposely changed the color of the mask, which would normally appear white, to contrast with the already white water. You can toggle off the visibility of the pins by clicking the Show Pins check box or pressing the V key.

Setting the Brush options

The Brush options are similar to brush options that you find throughout Photoshop. They determine what each of your brush strokes looks like. You can change the following options to customize your brush:

- **Size.** This option sets the size of the brush. The brush appears over your image as a solid circle surrounded by a dotted circle with a crosshair in the center. You can change the brush size by moving the slider or pressing the bracket keys.

- **Feather.** This option makes the edges of your Adjustment Brush gradually transparent so that the adjustments blend better with your image. The solid circle inside the brush indicates where the feathering begins, and the dotted circle around the outside of the brush indicates the amount of feathering being applied.

- **Flow.** This option changes the flow amount to control how quickly the adjustment is applied.
- **Density.** This option, similar to opacity, determines how translucent the adjustment is.
- **Auto Mask.** This option confines the edges of your brush strokes to areas that are a similar color to the center of your brush strokes.
- **Show Mask.** This option enables you to keep the mask on while you work. You can change the color of the mask by double-clicking the mask color and selecting any color you like.

Setting the Adjustment options

You can set the Adjustment options either before or after you create a mask. As you brush to create the mask on your image, the adjustments are applied as you set them. After you have finished applying the mask, you can make changes to the adjustments as long as the pin for that mask is selected. The adjustments you can make should be familiar to you by now:

- **Temperature.** This adds a warmer or cooler colorcast to the selected areas of your photo.
- **Tint.** This corrects the color for greens and reds.
- **Exposure.** This adjusts the amount of light in the area you have selected. This is a uniform adjustment and can create clipped highlights and shadows, so be aware of these areas as you tweak your exposure.
- **Contrast.** This adjusts contrast mostly in the midtone ranges of the selected area.
- **Highlights.** This brightens or deepens the appearance of the highlights in the selected area.
- **Shadows.** This brightens or deepens the appearance of the shadows in the selected area.
- **Clarity.** This adjusts local contrast to add depth to the selected area.
- **Saturation.** This adjusts the amount of color in the selected area.
- **Sharpness.** This adjusts the contrast between edges in the selected area.
- **Noise Reduction.** This reduces the graininess of the selected area.
- **Moiré Reduction.** This reduces the random patterns that can appear when two grids overlap. A pixelated photo of a striped shirt will sometimes create a moiré pattern, for instance.
- **Color.** This adds a color to the selected area.

Now that we have introduced you to the options in the Adjustment Brush panel, we will show you how to make targeted adjustments step by step, so you can see how it is done. Figure 8.30 is a photo of a waterfall. We would like to make targeted adjustments to the water so that it appears crisp in this photo without creating the hard, contrasty effect that excessive sharpening would create on the surrounding cliff and bushes. We can also make targeted adjustments to the cliff face, increasing the saturation and clarity.

FIGURE 8.30

You can use the Adjustment Brush to enhance the detail of this image.

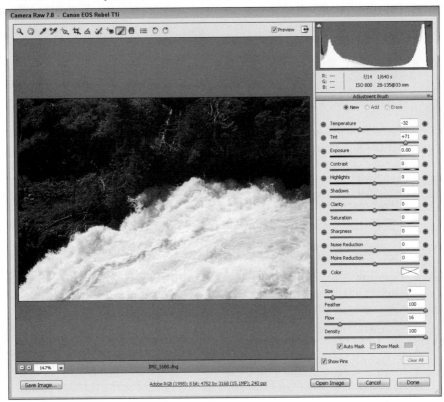

Make targeted adjustments to the photo of the waterfall by following these steps:

ON THE WEB
You can download Figure 8-30 from the website and follow the steps to learn how to use the Adjustment Brush.

1. **Open the image you want to adjust.**

   In this example, we opened Figure 8-30 in Camera Raw.

2. **Click the Adjustment Brush tool to open the Adjustment Brush panel, as shown in Figure 8.30.**

3. **Click the Show Mask option to display your brush strokes.**

4. **Set your Brush options.**

   Resize the brush so the solid inner circle is a reasonable size to quickly and accurately select the waterfall. Set the Feather option low so that the selection you make will be precise, about 20. Set the Flow to 50 and the Density to 100. Double-click the mask overlay color to set it to any bright color, except white.

5. **Specify a type and amount for the adjustment you want to make.**

   Increase the Sharpness level to 100. The adjustment brush won't work until you are brushing on at least one change. You can make further changes after you have created your mask.

6. **Brush a mask over the area you want to affect.**

   This example is changing the waterfall. Pay particular attention to the areas where the waterfall meets the cliff so that you can get a precise selection.

7. **Deselect the Show Mask check box so you can view the changes you make with the Adjustment options.**

8. **Set your Adjustment options.**

   Raise the Clarity all the way to 100. This, along with the adjustment you made to the sharpness, gives the waterfall a crisp, frozen look. You should also reduce the highlights and exposure and increase the contrast, so that the water appears green with white caps, rather than just white.

> **NOTE**
>
> Alternately, you can make the water look softer and smoother by reducing the Sharpness and Clarity to –100.

8

9. **Select New to create a new adjustment mask.**

   Click the Show Mask check box again.

10. **Drag your brush across the areas you want to affect to create a mask over them.**

    Brush over the cliff and bushes.

11. **Deselect the Show Mask check box.**

12. **Reset your adjustment options.**

    The cliff face doesn't need as much adjustment as the water. Warm it up, brighten it, and give it a little more saturation.

Your final image should look similar to Figure 8.31. Despite the number of steps in this exercise, the adjustments to this image were made in a relatively short amount of time.

FIGURE 8.31

With targeted adjustments, you can make the water look crisp and colorful.

Creating a Graduated Filter

Another way to create an adjustment over just part of your image is to use the Graduated Filter. The Graduated Filter does just what you might think it does: it creates a gradual adjustment over a targeted area of your image. Except for the selection process, it works very similarly to the Adjustment Brush.

The image in Figure 8.32 has good color and exposure — except for the sky, which is overexposed. Using the Graduated Filter, the overexposure can be improved.

ON THE WEB

You can download Figure 8-32 from the website and follow the steps to learn how to use the Graduated Filter.

Follow these steps to learn how to use a Graduated Filter:

1. **Select the Graduated Filter to open the Graduated Filter panel, as shown in Figure 8.32.**

   It should look familiar to you; the options are identical to those used in the Adjustment Brush panel.

2. **Set the adjustment option that you want to apply to the image.**

   You need to decrease the exposure of this image, so set this option first by moving the Exposure slider to the left. You can only select an area with the Graduated Filter after at least one option has been changed.

270

FIGURE 8.32

The sky in this image is washed out and overexposed, but the Graduated Filter can improve that.

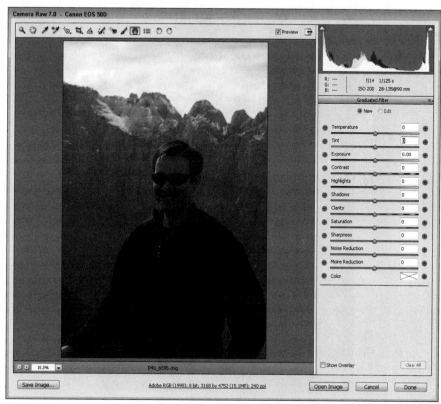

3. **Add a Graduated Filter by dragging to select the area you want to affect.**

   Starting in the center of the sky, drag the filter straight down until you can see the detail in the clouds all the way down to the tops of the cliffs, as shown in Figure 8.33. The green line (which is the top line in this figure) indicates the area where the Graduated Filter is applied most heavily. It is applied on both sides of the green line. The red line (the bottom line) indicates the outermost edge of the feathering that makes up the Graduated Filter. No adjustments are made to the outside of the red line.

FIGURE 8.33

The Graduated Filter indicators show you where the filter is being applied.

4. **Adjust your selection, if necessary.**

   You can expand, rotate, or move the Graduated Filter indicator using the icons that appear as you hover over it. Tweak it until you think you've got the best results.

5. **Edit the Adjustment settings.**

   Tweak the adjustments until you get the best results. You may want to try Steps 4 and 5 interchangeably a few times until you get the hang of how the Graduated Filter works.

   When you are finished, the exposure in your image should be greatly improved, as shown in Figure 8.34.

FIGURE 8.34

Color and depth are added to the sky by using the Graduated Filter.

Creating Artistic Effects

You can't create many artistic effects in Camera Raw just yet, but you can add grain or a vignette to your image using the Effects panel. Both effects can add depth and interest to a photo, and as always in Camera Raw, these edits are completely reversible.

Open the Effects panel by clicking the Effects tab in the Adjustment tabs, as shown in Figure 8.35. This panel provides sliders to add and customize grain or a vignette to your image.

8

FIGURE 8.35

The Effects panel allows you to add grain or a vignette to your image.

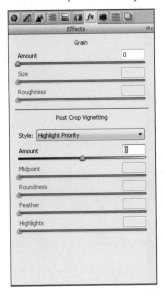

Adding grain to your image

When you add grain to your image in Camera Raw, it is added to areas that are out of focus more heavily than it is added to areas that are in focus. This adds depth and interest to the softness created by a short focal length. Use the following sliders to add and fine-tune grain in your image:

- **Amount.** Adjust the Amount slider to the right to add grain to your image.

- **Size.** This determines the size of the grain added to your image.

- **Roughness.** This adds contrast between the grains to enhance the roughness of the texture.

You can see the effect of adding grain to an image in Figure 8.36.

Adding a vignette

A vignette is a soft, circular border around an image that highlights an area of the image, as shown in Figure 8.37. In Camera Raw, a vignette is created uniformly around the edges of your image, targeting the center by default. When cropping an image, take care that the focal point of your photo is close to the center.

To create a vignette, change the following options:

- **Style.** Choose Highlight or Color priority from the Style drop-down list. The Highlight Priority option adds black or white pixels to create the vignette. Color Priority either lightens or darkens the existing colors in the image to create the vignette.

- **Amount.** Adjusting this slider above 0 creates a lighter vignette; the higher the value, the more opaque the vignette is. Going lower creates a darker vignette.
- **Midpoint.** This slider adjusts the size of the vignette.
- **Roundness.** Moving this slider to the right creates a rounder vignette, while moving it to the left causes it to conform to the shape of the image.
- **Feather.** This slider sets the softness of the vignette edges.
- **Highlights.** This slider pulls highlights out of the image in the darker areas to create depth. It is available only if you have created a dark vignette.

FIGURE 8.36

Adding grain to this photo gave the soft background a grittier, more interesting texture.

FIGURE 8.37

Adding a vignette highlights the focal point of an image.

Correcting Camera Quirks

The lens of your camera can introduce distortion and color abnormalities to your image. Sometimes a vignette will be created. These distortions prevent your photo from looking its best. The Lens Corrections and Camera Calibration tabs have options that can help you correct these anomalies.

Making lens corrections

The lens of your camera can introduce flaws to your photo such as distortion, chromatic aberration, and vignetting. Camera Raw can work to fix these flaws with the adjustments available in the Lens Corrections tab in the Image Adjustment panel. In order to make these adjustments, you need to know what these flaws are and how they are created.

Lens distortions are introduced when you stand too close to a subject or when you use a special lens such as a wide-angle or fish-eye lens. These lenses will bubble or pinch the center of your image so that it appears distorted. You can correct these distortions by using the Distortion sliders in the Lens Corrections tab.

If you zoom in to an image until you can distinguish the pixels, you'll probably notice a color fringe around some of them, especially highlights. This is called *chromatic aberration,* and it's caused either by the inability of the camera lens to focus all the colors onto the sensor at once or by those colors being focused but slightly different sizes, producing color fringes. Camera Raw can correct the second type of chromatic aberration by defringing the pixels.

We just showed you how to create a vignette as an artistic effect, but what if your lens has created the vignette and you don't want it? You can remove it by using the Lens Vignetting sliders to adjust for it, almost the exact opposite of creating one in the Effects tab.

The Lens Corrections tab has two sub-tabs — Profile and Manual — as shown in Figure 8.38. The Profile tab creates an automatic adjustment based on the lens stored in your metadata, and the Manual tab allows you to make custom changes on your own.

Camera Raw has several built-in lens profiles. If you used a digital SLR camera to capture your image, chances are Camera Raw can make adjustments specific to the lens that you used to create your photo. In the Profile tab, click Enable Lens Profile Corrections to see if your lens is recognized. If it is, corrections will automatically be made based on the profile of your lens. You can then make custom adjustments using the three sliders at the bottom of the panel. If your lens is not recognized, you will want to use the Manual tab.

The Manual tab gives you more latitude in making the correctional adjustments, but you'll need to know which adjustments are necessary. It's helpful if you know which lens was used, even if Camera Raw doesn't recognize it; then you will know which Distortion slider to use.

To correct chromatic aberration, Click the Defringe down arrow and select Highlight Edges or All Edges from the menu. This will remove the fringes of color from all the pixels in your image, or just the pixels that are considered highlights.

FIGURE 8.38

The Lens Corrections tab has options for fixing distortion and color fringes introduced by your camera's lens.

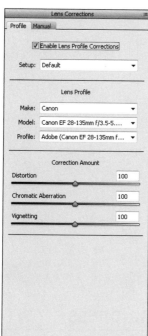 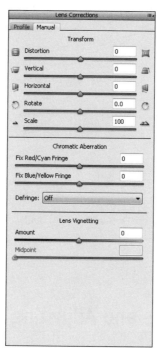

Setting camera calibration

Cameras all come with their own way of defining and interpreting color, and these color profiles are part of what is saved to the metadata of your image files. When you bring an image into Camera Raw, it has its own methods of interpreting color and chooses profiles that are the best for your particular camera make and model.

After you click the Camera Calibration tab to open the Camera Calibration panel, you can choose which profile to use from the Name drop-down list in the Camera Profile panel, as shown in Figure 8.39. You can see a significant difference in the color of your image by clicking through these profiles. After choosing a profile for your image, you can tweak it by using the color sliders to adjust individual colors and saturation.

FIGURE 8.39

The camera profiles in your Camera Calibration tab may be different than the ones shown here.

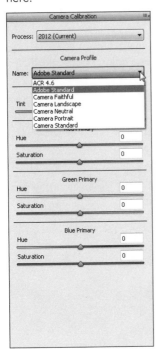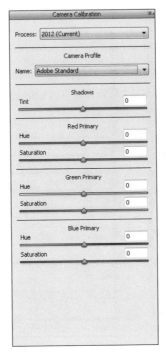

Reducing Noise and Adjusting Sharpness

When you have completed all the other changes to your image in Camera Raw, you are ready to open the Detail tab shown in Figure 8.40, where you can adjust the sharpness and reduce noise in your image. The "noise" in a photo is the random speckles in an image that detract from its uniformity, reducing the noise makes your image cleaner. It can also add a blurred look to your image, so it is best to reduce noise before sharpening your image. Adding sharpness to your image can add crispness and clarity to it, reducing blurriness and enhancing edges. You make these adjustments last because their effectiveness is reduced when other adjustments are added to them.

Reducing noise

Noise is defined as random pixels throughout your image that give it a messy look. Noise is introduced in several ways. For example, the higher the ISO setting on your camera, the more noise is created in your image. Lightening, as well as other adjustments, also creates noise.

FIGURE 8.40

The Detail tab allows you to make the final adjustments to your image.

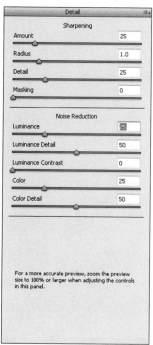

You can reduce the noise in your image by adjusting the following settings:

- **Luminance.** This reduces the amount of grayscale noise.
- **Luminance Detail.** This preserves the detail of the edges, counteracting the blurring effect created by increasing the luminance.
- **Luminance Contrast.** This counteracts the blurring created by increasing the luminance, but to a smaller degree than the Luminance Detail slider. It increases the contrast between the bits of grayscale noise.
- **Color.** This reduces the amount of color noise.
- **Color Detail.** This allows you to preserve the detail in the edges of your photo, counteracting the blurring effect created when the color noise is reduced.

> **NOTE**
>
> Keep in mind that Photoshop reduces noise by blurring your image and decreasing contrast of individual pixels. Sharpening also affects your image at the single-pixel level. It is important to preview your image zoomed in at least 100 percent in order to see and fine-tune the effects of both noise and sharpening on your image.

Sharpening

Sharpening works by increasing the contrast around the edges of your image to bring it more into focus, adding detail to your image. Camera Raw sets the default sharpening at 25 for RAW images. This is not a huge amount; in fact, it is comparable to the sharpness your camera automatically applies to a processed image. A lot of experts will tell you, though, that adding any sharpening by default is a bad idea, so if you want to change the default setting to 0, reset the slider and choose Set New Camera Raw Defaults from the Adjustment Tabs menu.

Sharpen your photo by using the following adjustments:

- **Amount.** This sets the amount of sharpening applied to your image. The amount you choose is directly tied to your Radius and Detail settings.
- **Radius.** This setting enables you to choose your radius based on the size of the detail in your image. An image with very small detail should have a small Radius setting. Images with larger details can get away with a larger Radius setting, but keep an eye on that preview; a large Radius setting can introduce an unnatural amount of contrast to your image.
- **Detail.** This setting heightens the detail of your image as you raise it by applying the sharpness to higher-frequency areas of your photo. A very high detail setting gives your image an almost textured look.
- **Masking.** This setting, if raised, applies more of the sharpening effect to the edges of your image and less to the overall image.

> **TIP**
>
> If you hold down the Alt/Option key while you adjust the Sharpening sliders, you see a preview of what the control is doing to your image. This is a great way to become more familiar with the Sharpening controls and to find the optimal setting for your image.

Summary

This chapter really went into the fundamentals of using Camera Raw. You learned about color and light and how they can be adjusted using the tools and panels in Camera Raw. Specifically, you learned how to do the following:

- Change the light settings to improve the exposure and contrast in an image
- Make color corrections to an image or individual colors in that image
- Make targeted adjustments to only selected portions of your image
- Create artistic effects with your images
- Apply the finishing touches by correcting camera aberrations, sharpening, and reducing noise in your image

Part III

Working with Selections, Layers, and Channels

IN THIS PART

Creating Selections

Eventually, you'll want to make changes to just a part of your photo. Whitening teeth, swapping backgrounds, or targeting areas of a photo to leave in color even as you turn the rest to black and white are just a few examples of things you can do when specific areas of a photo are selected. Knowing the different selection tools that are available to you in Photoshop and how and when to use each one is integral to effectively make these types of changes.

When you create a selection in a photo, you can change the area inside the selection without affecting any other part of the photo. You'll sometimes hear selections called selection masks, because they effectively mask the unselected portions of a photo from the changes being made. You can also use selections to create masks and paths, enhancing your selective creativity even more.

When you have created a selection, you can select any layer in your Layers panel and have the selection apply to that layer. This is handy when you are creating masks or cutouts, because you can create a selection from one image layer and apply to another.

Before we show you how each selection tool works, we cover the basics, including the Select menu and the options that are available. After we show you the ins and outs of all the selection tools, we show you how to put the finishing touches on your selection and finally how to output your selections as masks.

Getting Familiar with the Select Menu

The Select menu, shown in Figure 9.1, has options that help you to create and use a selection. Some of these options are holdovers from before the powerful selection tools such as the Quick Selection tool and the Refine Edge dialog box were available. Some options you will use occasionally, and other options you will find indispensable. Being familiar with these options can empower you in the way you create selections.

FIGURE 9.1

The Select menu provides you with options to customize your selection process.

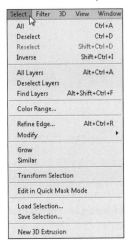

The following options appear in the Select menu:

- **All.** This option enables you to select your entire image, or select around everything in a selected layer.

- **Deselect.** This option deselects everything.

- **Reselect.** This option re-selects your selection. Although you can use the Undo option to immediately bring your selection back, you can use the Reselect option even after you've made other changes to your image in the interim.

- **Inverse.** This option reverses the areas that are selected in your image.

- **All Layers.** This option enables you to select all layers simultaneously when you have two or more layers in the Layers panel.

- **Deselect Layers.** This option deselects any layers that are selected.

- **Find Layers.** This option changes the Layer filtering mode in the Layers panel to Name, so you can enter search criteria and find a particular layer. For more information on layer filtering (see Chapter 10).

- **Color Range.** This option allows you to create a selection in your image based on one or more colors.

- **Refine Edge/Refine Mask.** This option allows you to refine the edges of a selection or mask.

- **Modify.** This option pre-dates the Refine Edge dialog box, and therefore contains many of the same options that allow you to refine the edge of your selection or mask:

  - **Border.** This is the only Modify option that isn't found in the Refine Edge dialog box. It allows you to select just the border of an object, as opposed to the entire object. After making a selection, choose Select ⇨ Modify ⇨ Border, and the Border Selection dialog box appears, as shown in Figure 9.2. You can type the width of the border in pixels, ranging from 1 to 200, and the border is created, centered on the original selection. The border selection is soft-edged, feathering out from the original selection, as you can see in the effect created using the Border Selection tool in Figure 9.2.

FIGURE 9.2

You can use a border selection to create special effects.

ON THE WEB

You can access the JPEG of the moon as well as the final PSD file used in Figure 9-2 by downloading both versions from the website.

9

- **Smooth.** This option reduces the "hills and valleys" in your selection by smoothing the edges of the selection based on the pixel value you enter.

- **Expand.** This option increases the overall size of the selection by expanding it by the number of pixels indicated.

- **Contract.** This option decreases the overall size of the selection by contracting it by the number of pixels indicated.

- **Feather.** This option makes the specified pixels on both the inside and outside edges of the selection gradually transparent. This allows changes you make to the selection to blend with the surrounding areas, whether you apply an adjustment to the selection or create a mask with the selection.

- **Grow.** This option expands your selection based on color. The areas that are adjacent to the selection that fall within the tolerance range specified in the Magic Wand tool (covered later in this chapter) are also selected.

- **Similar.** This option expands your selection based on color, but using the entire image rather than just the adjacent areas.

- **Transform Selection.** This option allows you to scale and rotate your selection.

- **Edit in Quick Mask Mode.** This option creates an overlay or mask over the areas of your image that are not selected. This mask can be changed using the Paintbrush or Eraser tools to make precise refinements to your selection. If you prefer, you can access it more quickly from the Toolbox. The Quick Mask is covered in greater detail later in this chapter.

- **Load Selection.** This option allows you to reload any saved selections.

- **Save Selection.** This option allows you to save the current selection and retrieve it at any time, even after the file is closed and reopened, as long as you save the file with a .psd extension.

Using the Selection Tools

In Photoshop, you will find there are as many shapes and sizes of potential selections as there are images. To make the process of selecting as simple and efficient as possible, Photoshop provides tools that you can use to make specific types of selections, as shown in Figure 9.3. You can use these tools in conjunction with each other for more versatility. With the advancements made to the tools, options, and refinements over the last few versions of Photoshop, selection has gone from a tedious process to an enjoyable one.

 Some selections are easier to make using a specific color channel rather than the full image. For more information on color channels, see Chapter 11.

Exploring the Marquee tools

The Rectangular and Elliptical Marquee tools allow you to select areas in your photo that are roughly rectangular or elliptical shapes. For example, you can select a building with the Rectangular Marquee and a ball with the Elliptical Marquee. The Row and Column Marquee tools select a one-pixel row the width or height of your image. Because these tools are simple and precise, they make these selections very quickly.

FIGURE 9.3

The Toolbox contains many tools that enable you to create selections.

You can find the Marquee tools in the drawer of the Toolbox, as shown in Figure 9.4. Click and hold the triangle at the bottom of the Rectangular Marquee tool to choose between the tools, or press Shift+M to toggle between them.

FIGURE 9.4

The Marquee tools are grouped together in the Toolbox.

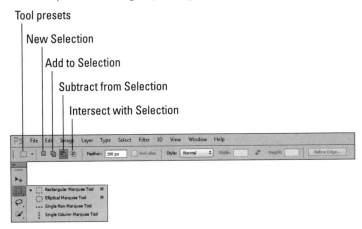

When you select a tool from the Toolbox, the Options bar enables you to change the way each tool functions through a wide range of selections. Located under the Menu bar, the Options bar changes as you select different tool sets. To show or hide the Options bar, choose Windows ⇨ Options from the main menu bar.

The Marquee tool options, shown in Figure 9.4, are as follows:

- **Tool presets.** You can save and retrieve your favorite tool settings using the Tool presets drop-down list. Click the little black arrow to see a menu of available options.

- **New Selection.** When you select this option, every time you drag the selection brush, you create a new selection and the old selection disappears.

- **Add to Selection.** When you select this option, everything you select is added to the current selection. This makes it easy to do the detail work after the initial selection is made.

- **Subtract from Selection.** When you select this option, you can subtract areas from the current selection.

- **Intersect with Selection.** This option selects only those areas that were in the first selection you made as well as the second, and deselects anything that was selected only once.

> **NOTE**
>
> When adding to a selection, subtracting from a selection, or creating an intersection, you can use the tools interchangeably. For example, you can add an ellipse to a rectangle or add a rectangle to a selection made with the Quick Selection tool.

- **Feather.** This option makes the specified pixels on both sides of the edges of the selection gradually transparent. This allows changes you make to the selection to blend with the surrounding areas, whether you apply an adjustment to the selection or create a mask with the selection. This option is not available with the Row and Column Marquee tools because you can't feather a single pixel line.

- **Anti-alias.** This option creates a smoother-edged selection. It is available only for the Elliptical Marquee tool because the other tools have straight-lined selection borders and don't require smoothing.

- **Style.** This drop-down list allows you to choose Normal to create a freehand selection, Fixed Ratio to create a freehand selection that is constrained to a certain ratio, or Fixed Size to type in exact values for your selection.

- **Width and Height.** Whether you want to set a ratio or an actual dimension, you can type the width and height in these boxes. You don't have to use pixels (px); you can also type in inches (in) or centimeters (cm).

- **Refine Edge.** This option enables you to perfect and finish your work by refining the edge of a selection. Refine Edge is covered later in this chapter.

Using the Rectangular Marquee tool

You can use the Rectangular Marquee tool to easily select rectangular objects in your image. Of course, it's not very often that you want to select something that's a perfect rectangle in a two-dimensional image; even buildings usually have a skewed shape due to perspective. A more realistic use for the tool is to create a new document from a selected portion of your photo without overwriting the original photo or to select an area of your photo that you want framed.

To create a rectangular selection, check your options on the Options bar. Do you want the edges of your selection feathered? Perhaps you are creating different print sizes of the same document, so you need to set the width and height for a 5 x 7 or 8 x 10 ratio setting. After you have double-checked all your options, click the Rectangular Marquee tool in the Toolbox and drag diagonally across the area of your image that you want to select. Figure 9.5 shows a rectangular selection that was created with a 90-pixel feather. The edges are rounded because of the feather. The Quick Mask is turned on, so you can see the effects of the feathered edges.

Using the Elliptical Marquee tool

You can use the Elliptical Marquee tool to select round or elliptical objects in your image, to copy rounded areas of your image into other documents, or to create a vignette. We often use it when correcting a tough case of red-eye. It's a little trickier to use than the Rectangular Marquee tool, because you have to imagine a box around the oval you want to draw and start at the top corner of that box to get the selection placed just right. It's mostly a matter of trial and error. The good news is that if you get the right size, you can always pick the selection up and move it to the right position.

9

FIGURE 9.5

Using the Quick Mask makes it easy to see how feathering the edges of a selection softens it.

TIP

You can also press and hold the Alt/Opt key as you drag with the Elliptical Marquee tool to start the selection from the center.

TIP

Holding down the Shift key while you use either the Rectangular or the Elliptical Marquee tool results in a perfect square or a perfect circle, depending on the tool, of course.

Looking at the Lasso tools

The Lasso Selection tools have been in Photoshop for much longer than the Quick Selection tools and in many ways have been superseded by them. Before the Quick Selection tool, the Magnetic Lasso was the best tool in the arsenal for selecting irregular edges that blended into the background; now ours is a bit dusty. However, the Lasso and the Polygonal Lasso tools can still be very useful.

The options for the Lasso and the Polygonal Lasso tools are identical. They are also very similar to the Marquee tool options. The Magnetic Lasso tool has the most involved option menu of all the selections tools, so we will cover these additional options in the Magnetic Lasso tool section.

You can find the Lasso tools in the drawer of the Toolbox, as shown in Figure 9.6. Click and hold the triangle at the bottom of the Lasso tool to choose between the tools, or press Shift+L to toggle between the tools.

FIGURE 9.6

The Lasso and Polygonal Lasso tools Options bar is very basic.

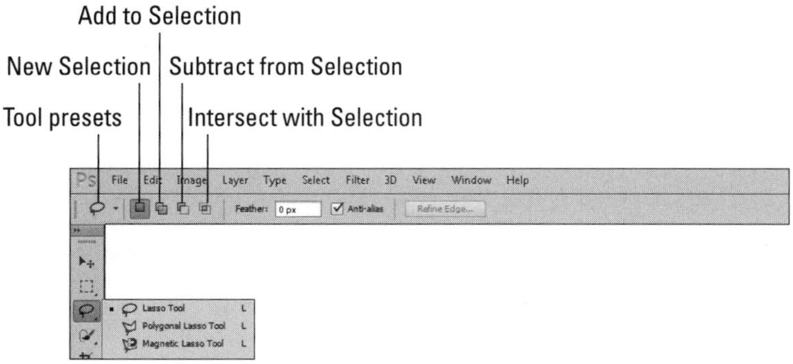

When you select a tool from the Toolbox, the Options bar enables you to change the way each tool functions through a wide range of selections. The Options bar, located under the Menu bar, changes as you select different tool sets. To show or hide the Options bar, choose Windows ⇨ Options from the main menu bar.

The Lasso and Polygonal tool options, shown in Figure 9.6, are as follows:

- **Tool presets.** You can save and retrieve your favorite tool settings using this drop-down list. Click the little black arrow to see a menu of available options.

- **New Selection.** When you select this option, every time you use the Lasso tool, you create a new selection and the old selection disappears.

- **Add to Selection.** When you select this option, everything you select is added to the current selection. This makes it easy to do the detail work after the initial selection is made.

- **Subtract from Selection.** When you select this option, you can subtract areas from the current selection.

- **Intersect with Selection.** This option selects only those areas that were in the first selection you made as well as the second, and deselects anything that was selected only once.

- **Feather.** This option makes the specified pixels on both the inside and outside edges of the selection gradually transparent. This allows changes you make to the selection to blend with the surrounding areas, whether you apply an adjustment to the selection or create a mask with the selection.

- **Anti-alias.** This option creates a smoother-edged selection.

- **Refine Edge.** This option enables you to perfect and finish your work by refining the edge of a selection. Refine Edge is covered later in this chapter.

9

Using the Lasso tool

The Lasso is a selection tool that is easy to understand. You use it to create a selection by drawing a freehand border around the area you want to select, as shown in Figure 9.7. It can be useful for selecting areas that are easy to freehand or selecting a general area to start from before using more precise selection techniques, such as the Color Range dialog box. You can also use it to touch up other selections.

FIGURE 9.7

The Lasso tool creates versatile selections by simply following wherever you draw.

> **CAUTION**
>
> As you use the Lasso Selection tool, be sure to close your selection by finishing relatively close to where you started. Photoshop automatically draws a straight line between the beginning point and the end point, and if that line intersects other areas of the selection, you may end up with quite a different selection than you were envisioning.

Using the Polygonal Lasso tool

The Polygonal Lasso tool is useful for selecting areas in your photo that are angular but not rectangular and hard to select with the Quick Selection tool, because the colors and textures in the photo are very similar. Even rectangular objects are usually skewed in photographs, making the Polygonal Lasso tool a better choice than the Rectangular Marquee tool for selecting them.

The building pictured in Figure 9.8 has simple angles, but they are not easy to select with the Rectangular Marquee. The Quick Selection tool would be tricky to use, because of the similarities in color and texture throughout the photo, making the Polygonal Lasso tool the best choice.

Use the Polygonal Lasso tool to make a selection by following these steps:

1. **Choose the Polygonal Lasso tool by clicking and holding the triangle on the Lasso tool icon in the Toolbox and selecting the Polygonal Lasso tool.**

   You can access the current Lasso tool by pressing the L key.

2. **Click the corners of the object you want to select, and the Polygonal Lasso tool locks the selection to each corner you click and selects a straight line between each one, as shown in Figure 9.8.**

FIGURE 9.8

Click each corner of your selection to anchor the Polygonal Lasso tool.

3. **Close the selection by clicking the corner where you started or by double-clicking to release the Polygonal Lasso Tool.**

   Your selection is created, as shown in Figure 9.9.

FIGURE 9.9

The Polygonal Lasso tool helps you make angular selections.

Using the Magnetic Lasso tool

The Magnetic Lasso tool is a precursor to the Quick Selection tool, and it works similarly by looking for edges close to the area where you are dragging the cursor and sticking to them. This makes your selection more precise than a freehand selection, but using the Magnetic Lasso tool is not as efficient as using the Quick Selection tool.

In addition to the standard Lasso tool options, the Magnetic Lasso tool has additional options, as shown in Figure 9.10:

FIGURE 9.10

The Magnetic Lasso tool has additional options that allow you to customize it for the best selection.

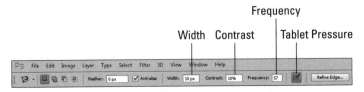

- **Width.** This field specifies how many pixels from the pointer the Magnetic Lasso tool searches for edges. This can be a benefit over the Quick Selection tool because the Quick Selection tool samples the entire document looking for similarities in what you are selecting and can sometimes select more than you were anticipating.

- **Contrast.** This field allows you to adjust the level of contrast needed for the Magnetic Lasso tool to determine an edge. If the area you are selecting blends into the background, you want to set your contrast low.
- **Frequency.** This field sets the frequency of the anchor points that are used.
- **Tablet Pressure.** Use this option with a stylus tablet. When you select this option, you can increase the width of your pen by increasing the pressure on your tablet.

You can use the Magnetic Lasso tool by clicking and dragging your beginning point as close as possible to the border of the area you want to select. The Magnetic Lasso looks within a certain radius (set by the Width option) for edges or contrasting pixels, and places anchor points along your selection. As you drag, anchor points are set down to show where the edges of your selection will appear, as shown in Figure 9.11.

As long as you are making your selection, you can change the anchor points in one of two ways. If an anchor point isn't set automatically in a place where you need one, click to add an anchor point. If anchor points are set in areas where you don't want them, you can use the Delete key to back up your anchor line one point at a time.

FIGURE 9.11

You see a line of anchors following your selection with the Magnetic Lasso tool.

> **CAUTION**
> As you work with the anchors in the Magnetic Lasso tool, remember that the tool is still carrying a selection line that leaves a wake of anchors no matter where you take it. If you are not careful, you'll create a selection mess reminiscent of trying to work with hot glue.

Your selection is open and changeable until you close it by either returning to the beginning and clicking the first anchor point or double-clicking to release the selection. After you've done that, the anchor points disappear and your selection is created.

Examining the Quick Selection tools

The Quick Selection and Magic Wand tools work by using the colors in your image to define a selection. The Magic Wand tool allows you to pinpoint a color and select areas in the document that are the same color. The Quick Selection tool takes you one step further by using color as well as edges in your photo to aid you in dragging a precise selection around different kinds of elements in your image.

You can find the Quick Selection and Magic Wand tools in the drawer of the Toolbox. Click and hold the triangle at the bottom of the Quick Selection tool to choose between the tools, or press Shift+W to toggle between them.

When you select a tool from the Toolbox, the Options bar enables you to change the way each tool functions through a wide range of selections. The Options bar, located under the Menu bar, changes as you select different tool sets. To show or hide the Options bar, choose Windows ⇨ Options from the main menu bar.

Looking at the Quick Selection tool

The Quick Selection tool is the best selection tool in the Photoshop Toolbox. The Quick Selection tool works by selecting adjacent areas that are similar in color and texture to the area over which you are dragging. It works well for almost anything, because you drag the selection roughly around the edges of the area that you want to select. The tool automatically finds the edges of your selection and creates a more precise selection than you could make freehand. The Quick Selection tool fine-tunes selections made by the other selection tools as well.

Before using the Quick Selection tool, familiarize yourself with the following options and their functions in Figure 9.12 to get the most from this tool's capability:

FIGURE 9.12

The Quick Selection tool is considered the best selection tool.

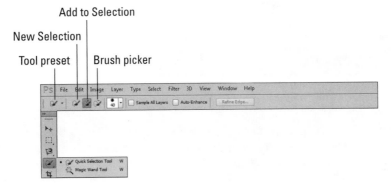

- **Tool presets.** You can save and retrieve your favorite tool settings using the Tool presets drop-down list. Click the little black arrow to see a menu of available options.

- **New Selection.** When you select this option, every time you drag the selection brush, you create a new selection. As you use the Quick Selection tool, it begins with the New selection option and automatically changes to the Add to selection option after your first selection.

- **Add to Selection.** When you select this option, everything you select is added to the current selection. This makes it easy to zoom in and do the detail work after the initial selection is made.

- **Subtract from Selection.** When you select this option, you can subtract areas from the current selection.

- **Brush picker.** This drop-down list enables you to set the size and style of your selection brush. When using the selection tools, size can make a difference in your selection. For example, a larger brush has a larger tolerance and is less likely to find the more detailed edges.

- **Sample All Layers.** When you select this option, the Quick Selection tool uses color and textures from all available layers to determine the edges of your selection.

- **Auto-Enhance.** This option smoothes out the edges and reduces the blockiness of your selection, automatically performing some of the refinements so you don't have to, using the Refine Edge dialog box. Auto-Enhance is time-consuming and doesn't give you any control, however, so it isn't usually the best option.

- **Refine Edge.** When you select this option, refining the edge of a selection is the finish work that perfects your selection.

Working with the Quick Selection tool

The Quick Selection tool enables you to select the background of a photo and add a little blur to it, so that the object in the foreground is the clear subject of the photo. In the following example, the contrast between the subject and the background makes this an easy task with the Quick Selection tool.

You can select an area in your photo by following these steps:

1. **Click the Quick Selection tool in the Toolbox, or press W.**

2. **Click the Brush picker and then select a size and brush style from the Quick Selection options menu at the top of the preview window, as shown in Figure 9.13.**

   The size and softness of the brush determine the detail of the edge selection. For large, hard edges, use a large brush for a faster selection. To fine-tune smaller areas, use a smaller brush size.

9

FIGURE 9.13

The Brush picker option for the Quick Selection tool allows you to modify the size and hardness of the Quick Selection tool.

Brush picker

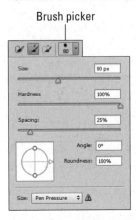

TIP

Use the bracket keys, [and], to quickly reduce and expand your brush size.

3. **Drag a rough outline around the area you want to select.**

As we dragged around the boy in Figure 9.14, the selection outline adhered to the edges of his body. You don't need to make this selection continuously; you can add to and subtract from it as you go.

FIGURE 9.14

The Quick Selection tool uses color and texture to define a selection.

ON THE WEB

You can try your hand at creating this selection by downloading Figure 9-14 from the website.

4. **Use the Add to Selection and Subtract from Selection options to fine-tune your selection.**

Zoom in on hard-to-define areas and reduce your brush size to make the smaller selections. If you select too much, use the Subtract from Selection tool to take the extra area out.

This is a simple example of how to create a selection with the Quick Selection tool. From beginning to end, it took less than five minutes to select the boy off the background of the sample image. Later in this chapter, we will show you how you can further refine any selection to achieve superior results.

Looking at the Magic Wand tool

Nested with the Quick Selection tool is the Magic Wand tool. The Magic Wand tool enables you to create a selection by targeting areas that are the same or a similar color. This tool works best if the areas that you do not want to select are a contrasting color.

Before using the Magic Wand tool, familiarize yourself with the following options and their functions, shown in Figure 9.15, to get the most out of this tool:

FIGURE 9.15

The Magic Wand tool options allow you to customize how the tool works.

- **Tool presets.** You can save and retrieve your favorite tool settings using this drop-down list. Click the little black arrow to see a menu of available options.

- **New Selection.** When you select this option, every time you drag the selection brush, you create a new selection and the old selection disappears.

- **Add to Selection.** When you select this option, everything you select is added to the current selection. This makes it easy to do the detail work after the initial selection is made.

- **Subtract from Selection.** When you select this option, you can subtract areas from the current selection.

- **Intersect with Selection.** This option selects only those areas that were in the first selection you made, as well as the second, and deselects anything that was selected only once.

- **Sample Size.** This drop-down list allows you to determine the size of the color sample taken by the Magic Wand tool. For instance, a point sample only uses the color of the single pixel chosen by the Magic Wand. If you choose 3 x 3 average, Photoshop averages the color of a 3 x 3 pixel radius around the pixel that you choose.

- **Tolerance.** The tolerance level determines how many shades of the color you choose with the Magic Wand are selected. A higher tolerance selects more shades; a lower tolerance selects fewer shades. The level you set depends entirely on your photo.

- **Anti-alias.** Selecting this option creates a smoother-edged selection.

- **Contiguous.** When you select this option, only the appropriate colors that are contiguous in the area where you click the Magic Wand are selected. If this option is off, all the colors in the document within the specified tolerance range are selected.

- **Sample All Layers.** When you select this option, the Magic Wand tool uses color and textures from all available layers to determine the edges of your selection.

- **Refine Edge.** When you select this option, refining the edge of a selection is the finish work that perfects your selection. Refine Edge is covered later in this chapter.

Working with the Magic Wand tool

The Magic Wand tool enables you to select adjacent pixels within a color range in an image by selecting that specific color range. In the following example, we want to select the pistils to create a stylistic photo where the pistils are the only element of the lily in color. (We know, none of it is in color, but work with us here.)

Using the Magic Wand tool is as easy as following these steps:

1. **Choose the Magic Wand tool from the Toolbox, or press Shift+W.**

   The Magic Wand tool is nested behind the Quick Selection tool.

> **TIP**
>
> When the Magic Wand tool is hidden behind the Quick Selection tool, pressing W activates the Quick Selection tool. Simply press Shift+W to toggle to the Magic Wand tool. You can also change your preferences so that you don't need to use the Shift key. Choose Edit ➪ Preferences ➪ General (Photoshop ➪ Preferences ➪ General on the Mac) and deselect Use Shift Key for Tool Switch. After you've done this, you can toggle through every tool using the single hot key assigned to the tool without having to use the Shift key at all.

2. **Change the tolerance level.**

   Because we want to select different shades of orange in your photo and the surrounding area is cream, we use a high tolerance of 75.

3. **Uncheck Contiguous.**

   We are choosing several unconnected areas that are all the same color, so we want to sample the entire document.

4. **Click the color in your photo that you want to select.**

   The Magic Wand tool is different from every other selection tool in that it doesn't require you to click and drag, just click a color. If you want to select different shades, choose an area that is midrange between the lightest and darkest shades you want to select. Photoshop selects everything in your photo that is the color you click and uses the tolerance setting to determine the range of other colors that are selected. By choosing a midrange pixel to sample and with a high tolerance on a contrasting background, we got a nearly perfect selection in Figure 9.16.

FIGURE 9.16

The Magic Wand tool easily selected the bright orange pistils (along with the freckles) on the cream-colored lily.

ON THE WEB

You can try your hand at creating this selection by downloading Figure 9-16 from the website.

5. **Use the Add to Selection or Subtract from Selection options to add or subtract areas from your selection.**

   You can choose an entirely different color to add to the selected area than the color you used for the first selection.

Refining Your Selection

After you have created your selection, you may need to add or subtract areas to and from your selection that were not correct the first time, or smooth out edges by taking out fringe colors. Adding the final changes through adjusting selections and refining edges will produce professional results.

Adjusting a selection

After you have made your initial selection, there are several ways that you can add final changes to complete your selection, such as using the selection tools, transforming a selection, creating and adjusting a path, or using the Quick Mask mode to paint areas in or out of your selection. These adjustments can help make your selection perfect so that your changes blend smoothly.

Using the selection tools

All selection tools have the option to either add to or subtract from the selection. It doesn't matter what tool you used to create the original selection, you can use any other selection tool to add to or subtract from that selection. This makes the selection tools very versatile to work with.

For instance, in Figure 9.17, the Magic Wand did a great job of selecting an almost perfect outline of the snapdragon. Of course, a few spots here and there need to be added to or subtracted from this selection. Adjusting the tolerance levels or trying to add or subtract using the Magic Wand tool can be an effort in frustration — remember that the Magic Wand tool samples colors every time you use it, and so you could click to add or subtract areas you don't want and end up with even more areas that are wrong.

FIGURE 9.17

With one click, the Magic Wand tool can create a nearly perfect selection, but the best way to clean up the selection is to use a different selection tool.

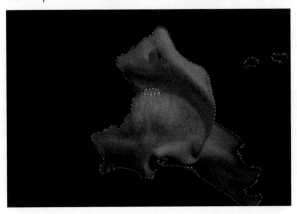

The better option is to use the Quick Selection tool, or even the Lasso tool, to clean up this selection . Just click the tool of choice, make sure the Add to or Subtract from option is selected, and you have more control to clean up your selection.

Transforming a selection

You can also change a selection by transforming it. This option is best when you have a selection that is almost the right shape, but just needs a little nudge here and there so that it fits.

For instance, in Figure 9.18, we use an Elliptical Marquee to select the iris of the eye, but because of the perspective of the shot, the eye isn't an exact symmetrical ellipse. This is a good time for a transformation.

To transform a selection, choose Select ➪ Transform Selection, and your selection is bounded by a transformation box. Use the handles to nudge the edges of your selection until it's where you want it to be.

FIGURE 9.18

The Transformation option can change the shape of your selection.

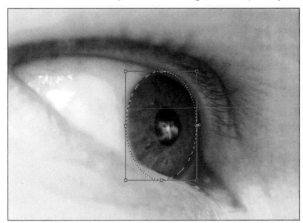

Now that you have the transformation box activated, you can use the Transform tools in the Edit menu to skew, warp, or otherwise distort your selection in any way you want to. Choose Edit ➪ Transform, and choose from one of several options on the Transform submenu.

CAUTION

Typically when you want to use the Transform option, you can use the hot-key combination Ctrl+T/⌘+T to create a transformation box; however, don't use the hot key here! If you do, you will be transforming the area that has been selected rather than the actual selection. Stick with the Select menu for choosing this option.

If using the Transform tools in the Edit menu seems too advanced right now, don't worry; you can get a full run-down in Chapter 19.

Using paths

The most frustrating thing to us about the Magnetic Lasso tool is all those handles, or anchor points, that disappear the minute the selection is completed. Wouldn't it be much more convenient if they stuck around so you could go back and adjust your selection? Fortunately, you *can* adjust your selection using handles by turning it into a path.

After you've created a selection, turn it into a path and correct it by following these steps:

1. **Choose Window ⇨ Paths from the main menu bar.**

   This opens the Paths panel, shown in Figure 9.19.

FIGURE 9.19

The Paths panel is empty until a path is made.

Load Path as Selection

2. **Click the Make work path from selection icon at the bottom of the Paths panel, as shown in Figure 9.19.**

   This changes your selection into a path.

3. **Select the Direct Selection tool from the Toolbox, as shown in Figure 9.20.**

FIGURE 9.20

The Direct Selection tool allows you to select one anchor point at a time.

4. **Use the Direct Selection tool to click an area of the path that needs adjusting.**

   Anchor points appear, and you can adjust the anchor points as needed to correct your selection, as shown in Figure 9.21.

FIGURE 9.21

With the Direct Selection tool, you can drag anchor points and change the path.

5. **(Optional) If you need to add anchor points to your path, select Add Anchor Point Tool from the Toolbox, as shown in Figure 9.22, and click the path to add an anchor point.**

6. **After you complete your adjustments, click the Load path as a selection icon in the bottom of the Paths panel (refer to Figure 9.19) to turn your path back into a selection.**

 To learn about paths and how and why you should create them, see Chapter 17.

FIGURE 9.22

To add anchor points to your path, you need the Add Anchor Point tool.

It was unfair to drop you into this exercise before explaining paths a little better, but it's good to know at this point that selections can become paths, and vice versa. You'll probably use this option to create paths from selections more often than using a path to create or adjust a selection because this method of adjusting your selection is time-consuming, and in most cases it isn't the most efficient option. It can be very precise, however, and it's good to know that it is a possibility.

Using Quick Mask mode

We are big fans of the Quick Selection tool. Even if we don't make an initial selection with it, we often use it to make any needed adjustments afterwards. Sometimes even the Quick Selection tool fails us, however, and we need a more precise method of adjusting our selection.

The Quick Mask allows you to apply freehand adjustments to your selection by painting a mask over the areas that you don't want selected and erasing the mask out of areas that you do, or vice versa.

> **TIP**
>
> The Quick Mask is not only a good way to touch up your selection; it's also a good idea to turn it on even if you think your selection is perfect. Many times, you'll see areas of your selection that you missed with the marching ants but are much easier to see with the color overlay.

The Quick Mask icon is found at the very bottom of the Toolbox, as shown in Figure 9.23. It's not really a tool; it's just a shortcut to using the Quick Mask. Click it or press Q to turn on Quick Mask mode.

FIGURE 9.23

The Quick Mask icon is at the bottom of the Toolbox.

Quick Mask icon

When you've activated Quick Mask mode, your image looks like Figure 9.24, with a red color overlay (called a rubylith) covering the areas of your image that are unselected. This indicates that those areas are protected from any changes you make to the image, much like a stencil. Notice how easy it is to see that we've missed an important area of the background under the boy's arm.

FIGURE 9.24

It's hard to tell with this grayscale image, but the Quick Mask overlays the entire background of this image with a rubylith.

You can make a few changes to the Quick Mask. Double-click the Quick Mask icon to open the Quick Mask Options dialog box, as shown in Figure 9.25. From here, you can double-click the color field to open the Color Picker and choose an alternative color, change the opacity of the mask, or invert the mask so it covers the selected area rather than the rest of the image.

FIGURE 9.25

The Quick Mask Options dialog box allows you to change the color and opacity of the mask or to invert it.

In Figure 9.24, the swimsuit is red, so we will change the overlay to a different color to see the border of the Quick Mask more clearly. A bright green works really well, because there is no other area of green in the photo.

To add to the selected area, you need to erase the Quick Mask; follow these steps:

1. **Click the Eraser tool in the Toolbox, as shown in Figure 9.26.**

FIGURE 9.26

The Eraser tool allows you to erase portions of the masked area.

Eraser tool

2. **Set the brush size in the Options bar.**

    You want your eraser slightly smaller than the area you are painting. (Press the bracket keys, [and], to quickly change the size of your eraser or brush.)

3. **Set Opacity to 100% in the Options bar.**

    You can feather the edges of your selection later.

4. **Erase the Quick Mask from areas that you want to be selected by dragging the Eraser tool over those areas, as shown in Figure 9.27.**

FIGURE 9.27

By erasing the Quick Mask, we are adding to the selected area.

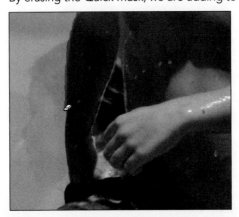

For subtracting areas from the selection, you can use the Brush tool to paint in the Quick Mask:

1. **Click the Brush tool in the Toolbox, as shown in Figure 9.28.**

FIGURE 9.28

The Brush tool allows you to add to the masked area.

Brush tool

2. **Set the brush size in the Options bar.**

   You want your brush slightly smaller than the area you are painting.

3. **Set Opacity to 100% in the Options bar.**

4. **Apply the Quick Mask to areas that you don't want selected by dragging the Brush tool over those areas, as shown in Figure 9.29.**

FIGURE 9.29

By using the Brush tool to add to the Quick Mask, we are subtracting from the selected area.

9

309

Refining the edges

After you've made your selection as perfect as you can, it's time to put the finishing touches on it by refining the edges. The Refine Edge dialog box includes features such as the Edge Detection tool, which ensures your selection is spot-on; smoothing and feathering options that soften the edges; and output settings that allow you to create layers, masks, and a new document with your selection.

You can access the Refine Edge dialog box, shown in Figure 9.30, by clicking Refine Edge in the Options bar.

FIGURE 9.30

The Refine Edge dialog box provides options for perfecting a selection.

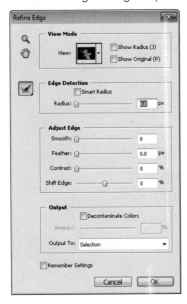

Changing your View Mode

By using View Mode, you can determine how your selection is previewed, while working in the Refine Edge dialog box. The View Mode section includes the following options:

- **Hand tool.** This tool works the same here as it does in the Toolbox; you can use it to move your document around in the document window so you can see the desired area.

- **Zoom tool.** This tool works just like the Zoom tool in the Toolbox; you can use it to zoom into areas that you are previewing or adjusting. Getting a closer look at the edges as you make changes to them is never a bad idea.

- **View.** This drop-down menu, shown in Figure 9.31, gives you different ways to view your selection. You can keep the marching ants, use a color overlay, or use different ways of alternating black, white, and transparency. How you decide to view your selection is determined in part by your personal preference, but it is mostly a matter of what works best with your particular image. Take note of the hot keys that allow you to change views quickly. Changing views as you work and double-checking your edges helps you finish with a more accurate result.

FIGURE 9.31

The Refine Edge dialog box gives you many different options for viewing your selection.

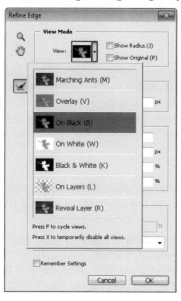

- **Show Radius.** This view option works with the Edge Detection options to show your chosen radius. Figure 9.32 shows the On Black view with the radius highlighted.

- **Show Original.** You can see the original document without any selection indicated by checking the Show Original option. This comes in handy when the selection borders get in the way of determining where an edge should be. Simply click Show Original, and you can take a look without the hindrance of a selection border.

FIGURE 9.32

A view of the radius set around the edges of our selection. To make it more visible, we set the radius extremely high at 50.

Using the Edge Detection options

The Edge Detection options can help to make those detailed refinements that are nearly impossible any other way. Wispy hair, for instance, is notoriously hard to select. The Edge Detection tools allow you to more easily make these types of selections. They work by searching the edges of a selection in a specified radius for edges that are more defined and probably (but not always) more accurate for your selection.

The options for edge detection are as follows:

- **Smart Radius.** The Smart Radius option automatically sets a radius for edge detection based on the tonal irregularities around the edges of the original selection. You can use this option for a quick, automatic edge-detection solution.

- **Radius.** This slider allows you to set your own radius for edge detection. If your selection is accurate to begin with, you want to use a low setting. Photoshop searches within the radius you set for a better edge for your selection. If it finds a better edge, it moves the edge of the selection. You can preview the area that is being searched by activating the Show Radius option in View Mode (refer to Figure 9.30). Be sure to get a close-up of your edges as you make changes so you can be sure they are accurate.

- **Refine Radius tool.** After you have set your radius to a good overall setting for your selection, you might discover spots where the radius is too big or too small to find the correct edge. You can fix these individual areas one at a time by using the Refine Radius tool. The Refine Radius tool works like a paintbrush to brush in a larger radius or erase areas of a radius. Click the little black triangle in the lower-right corner of the icon to display both tools, as shown in Figure 9.33, and choose the tool you need. Display the radius by clicking the Show Radius option, and use the Refine Radius tool to make your desired changes.

FIGURE 9.33

You can manually add to or subtract from the set radius by using the Refine Radius tool.

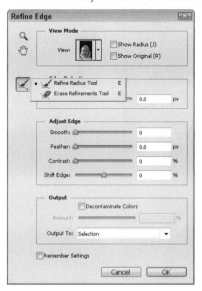

You can give the Edge Detection options a try by following these steps:

On the Web

Try using the Edge Detection options on this example by downloading Figure 9-34 from the website.

1. **Open a file that has edges that are difficult or nearly impossible to select.**

   This example involves a subject with delicate curls.

2. **Using any combination of selection tools, create the best selection you can.**

   Don't worry about being too precise in the areas on which you plan to use Edge Detection. Aim for the best selection that you can, as shown in Figure 9.34.

3. **Click the Refine Selection button in the Options bar.**

   This button is available, regardless of which selection tool you have chosen. Click it to open the Refine Edge dialog box (refer to Figure 9.30).

4. **Click the Refine Radius tool.**

   Because you are selecting a diverse area when detecting hair, the Refine Radius tool is usually the best option.

FIGURE 9.34

Making selections around hair is a difficult process; however, you can leave the areas around the hair loosely selected.

5. **Brush the areas where you want the Edge Detection to occur.**

   The Edge Detection tool looks for contrast in these areas and tries to determine the best edge for your selection. You will notice that there are semi-transparent areas. These areas are feathered edges and will help your selection blend when you make changes to it.

6. **Click Show Radius in the View Mode section of the Refine Edge dialog box.**

   This allows you to see the areas that are affected.

7. **Click the black triangle next to the Refine Radius Tool button and choose Erase Refinements Tool.**

   Use the Erase Refinements tool to erase areas you have selected.

8. **Repeat Steps 5 to 7 as needed.**

   Every time you make a pass with the Refine Radius tool, the edges are recalculated, so keep trying if you don't get the result you want the first time.

9. **When you have the best result possible, exit the Refine Edge dialog box.**

   You can see the result we got in Figure 9.35. You can output your selection in different ways. If you didn't get the exact result for which you were looking, click OK to exit the dialog box and make your own changes to the selection.

FIGURE 9.35

In the photo showing the result, the hair was selected more precisely by using the Edge Detection tool.

Adjusting edges

The Adjust Edge section of the Refine Edge dialog box gives you control over the hardness, smoothness, and placement of your selection edge and includes these settings:

- **Smooth.** Increasing the smoothness of your selection reduces jagged edges and softens corners. If your selection is mostly rounded edges, increasing the smoothness probably improves it by reducing areas of pixelation. If your selection has sharp corners, however, increasing the smoothness rounds and softens the corners, so go easy and keep an eye on your corners.

- **Feather.** Feathering the edges of your selection makes them gradually transparent, so that the selection blends better with whatever changes you make to it. It's better to feather your edges here, in the Refine Edge dialog box, than by using the Feather option found in many of the selection tools. Here you can preview the feathered edges in real time if you have any of the overlay views selected.

- **Contrast.** Increasing the contrast sharpens the edges of your selection and reduces the noise around the selection.

- **Shift Edge.** The Shift Edge option replaces the Contract/Expand option found in earlier versions of Photoshop. Moving the slider to the left expands your selection, and moving it to the right contracts your selection. The slider works with the radius that you specified in the Edge Detection settings to determine how far to move the selection. For example, if you shift your edge by 30 percent, you are shifting it by 30 percent of the radius setting, which means that if your radius is set at 10 pixels, you are shifting the selection by 3 pixels.

Choosing Output settings

The Output settings determine the outcome of your selection. Here are the options you have:

- **Decontaminate Colors.** When you cut a selection out of one image to place into another image or document, the selection often displays a halo or color fringe that is either a reflection of the color around the selection or simply a bleeding of that color. With this simple option, Photoshop has supplied you with a powerful tool to reduce or even eliminate such halos. Select the Decontaminate Colors check box, and Photoshop samples the edges of your selection for color values that are different from the actual selection and reduces those colors. When you select this option, your output choices become limited.

- **Amount.** This slider allows you to adjust how much color is reduced by the Decontaminate Colors option.

- **Output.** The Refine Edge dialog box allows you to output your selection in different formats as you exit, saving you several steps in the process. These are the options for saving your selection:

  - **Selection.** This option returns you to the marching ants and lets you decide on your own changes from there.

  - **Layer Mask.** This option creates a layer mask over the layer you are currently working with. Your deselected areas become transparent.

  - **New Layer.** This option pastes your selection into its own layer and turns off the visibility of the original layer, so the unselected areas of your image still appear transparent, but your entire image remains available in the original layer.

  - **New Layer with Layer Mask.** This option creates a new layer containing the entire image with a layer mask placed over the deselected areas, and turns off the visibility of the original layer, as shown in Figure 9.36. This has the same visual effect on the image as the previous two options.

  - **New Document.** This option creates a new document and places the selection in it, leaving the original document unaltered.

  - **New Document with Layer Mask.** This option creates a new document with the entire image from the original document, but places a layer mask over it so only the selected areas are visible.

FIGURE 9.36

The Layers panel showing a new layer with a layer mask created from a selection

 Masks are an extension of selections and are really the same concept taken one step further. To understand masks, however, it is important that you understand layers. Layers are covered in Chapter 10.

> **CAUTION**
>
> Your edge refinement is applied when you close the Refine Edge dialog box. If you decide later to change the settings, you need to undo the previous edge refinement, or you will just be adding the new settings to the first edge refinement.

Using the Color Range Selector

The Color Range selector is not a tool in the Toolbox, but rather a dialog box that you can launch from the Select menu. It works similarly to the Magic Wand, because it makes selections primarily based on color. However, it gives you a little more control over what is selected by letting you customize the settings and preview the results before making the selection.

A unique feature of the Color Range dialog box is that it works within a selection as well as the entire image, so you can make a general selection around the area that you would like to ultimately select color from, and only that area is used in the dialog box, as shown in Figure 9.37. After your selection is made, and you click OK in the Color Range dialog box, the original general selection disappears and the selection made by the Color Range dialog box takes its place.

When using the Color Range dialog box, don't forget to use the features shown on the Options bar in Figure 9.37. You can select the sample size, choosing to take the exact color of the pixel sampled or averaging several surrounding pixels together. There are also a variety of options for choosing which layers you would like to sample from.

FIGURE 9.37

The Color Range dialog box is versatile when it comes to selecting color or tonal ranges.

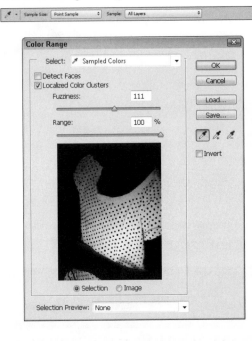

ON THE WEB

Use the Color Range dialog box to select the pink shirt in this photo by downloading Figure 9-37 from the website.

The Color Range dialog box has the following options:

- **Select.** This drop-down list gives you the option to use a sample from the image as a basis for your selection, or you can choose to use a specific color, tonal ranges, or out-of-gamut colors.

- **Detect Faces.** This option becomes available when you select the Localized Color Clusters option. It allows Photoshop to detect and select skin tones more precisely.

- **Localized Color Clusters.** Select this option if you are choosing more than one color and you want to restrict the selection to the same general area.

- **Fuzziness.** This slider works much like the tolerance levels of the Magic Wand. The higher the fuzziness, the more varied the colors in your selection are. The best thing about it is that you can preview the selected areas as you move the slider, allowing you to set a precise fuzziness level before creating your selection.

- **Range.** This slider works with the Fuzziness slider to determine how large an area in your image to select from. Again, having the preview is priceless.

- **Selection/Image.** With these options, you can preview either the selection or the image. The Selection preview is shown as a mask where the selected areas are anything in the upper half of the brightness scale. In Figure 9.37, the shirt is the only item in the image that is selected when the Color Range dialog box is closed. The Image preview is shown just as you see it in your document window, with no indication of what has been selected. This option is handy if you are using the Selection Preview option described next.

- **Selection Preview.** This drop-down list changes the image in your document window to reflect the areas that are selected. You can choose to display it in several ways: grayscale (which mimics the selection window), black matte, white matte, and quick mask. The option that works best depends entirely on the colors in your image and the colors you are selecting.

- **Save.** This option allows you to save your Color Range settings for later use.

- **Load.** This option allows you to load saved Color Range settings.

- **Eyedropper.** This tool is used to select the color: you place the tip over the color that you want to select and click the mouse. Every time you do, a new selection is made.

- **Add to Sample.** If you would like to select additional areas after creating an initial selection, you need to use this tool. It adds to your selection rather than replacing it.

- **Subtract from Sample.** This tool subtracts areas from your selection.

- **Invert.** This option is used to create a selection around everything in your image except for the colors that you choose.

> **NOTE**
> You can use the Refine Edge dialog box on any selection, even one made by the Color Range dialog box. Click Select ⬧ Refine Edges to open the Refine Edge dialog box.

Summary

Selections highlight areas of an image that can be modified while leaving the rest of the image untouched. In this chapter, you learned that selections come in many different shapes and sizes, and many selection tools make creating those selections a fun and simple process. After a selection is made, many other tools allow you to change and refine those selections so they can be perfect.

After reading this chapter, you should have the skills to do the following:

- Understand the selection menu and use it to optimize your use of the selection tools

- Use the Quick Selection tool to make fast selections based on the edges of your image

- Use both the Magic Wand and the Color Range dialog box to make selections based on color

- Use selection marquees to make selections based on shape
- Create different Lasso selections
- Use the Options bar to optimize your selection
- Add to or subtract from a selection
- Refine the edges of your selection based on different parameters

Learning All About Layers

IN THIS CHAPTER

Presenting layers

Looking at the Layer menus

Exploring the Layers panel

Using non-destructive Fill and Adjustment layers

Adding layer effects

Working with Smart Objects

Protecting areas with a layer mask

Saving multiple layouts using Layer Comps

Finalizing your graphics by merging layers

When you open an image in Photoshop for the first time, that image is one layer, just as if you'd laid a photo out on a table. When you add elements to that image such as text or another image, think of it as putting a transparency containing those items over the original image. Rather than destroying the integrity of the image, you are simply adding layers to it to change the way it looks. That's exactly how the Layers panel works. You can keep stacking up the layers to change the way your image looks, and those layers don't have to contain objects; they can be composed of a filter or style. Meanwhile, your original image is still available to you in its original, unaltered state.

That's the basic idea, anyway. Of course, because this is the digital world of Photoshop, a great idea has become so much better over time. Everything from changing the settings of filters that were added months ago to animating is all part of the Layers panel in Photoshop CS6, and having a good, solid understanding of how it all works is essential to your Photoshop success.

A basic understanding of the Layers panel, including the icons and menu options, is a good place to start. Then we show you the different kinds of layers you can add. We end the chapter by showing you everything you need to know about layer masks. After you've been introduced to the Layers panel, you'll be ready to get into the substance of what Photoshop is all about — image correction and special effects, where the Layers panel is used constantly.

Introducing Layers

You'll soon discover that layers are your best friends when working in Photoshop. They provide you with an easy and versatile way to make changes to a project, because each element of your project is self-contained and very editable. This means that as long as you keep layers in your document, your Text can always be moved and changed, your adjustments can be reset, duplicated, or moved and if you use the Layers panel correctly, even changes such as cloning and healing are easy to edit and change.

Although we are going to show you the ins and outs of the Layers panel and how to add special effects and adjustment layers later in this chapter, we want to start by diving right in and showing you what your document looks like with multiple layers and how to work with those layers. This will provide you with a basic understanding of how layers look and how they work so that you can move forward with confidence.

Understanding multiple layers

Figure 10.1 shows a type layer on top of an image layer. This is about as basic as two layers get. As you can see in the photo, the type layer is opaque so the image can't be seen through it.

FIGURE 10.1

Two different layers in the Layers panel

Look at the Layer menu. Each layer is represented by a thumbnail and a row in the Layers panel. The layer at the bottom of the list — the image, in this case — is the layer that is on the bottom of the "transparencies." All the layers placed above it cover it in some way, and the hierarchy goes from there.

The image in Figure 10.1 is a background layer. When you open a new image in Photoshop, it automatically becomes the background layer. A background layer is locked, so you can't make changes to the layer such as transforming it or adding effects to it, and it can't be moved; it is always the bottom layer. You can make the background layer into a regular layer by double-clicking it and giving it a name. You can also create a background layer from a regular layer by choosing Layer ⇨ New ⇨ Background from Layer in the main menu bar.

TIP

Although you can find options for working with layers in both the Layer menu and the Layers panel menu, we like to take a shortcut by right-clicking individual layers. A menu pops up with more specific options for that particular layer. For instance, a type layer pops up a menu that includes all the type options and none of the Smart Object options.

The text is a type layer, as indicated by the T in the layer thumbnail. In order to make changes to the layer, you must select it by clicking the thumbnail and highlighting it in the Layers panel. Then you can use the tools or Layer menu options to make changes.

NOTE

Probably the most frustrating aspect of layers for the new user, and even admittedly for those of us who have been around the block a time or two, is that you can't make any changes to a layer unless it is selected in the Layers panel. We've done it many times — tried to move or make changes to a layer and nothing happens or the wrong layer is affected. Keep this rule in the back of your mind, and it soon becomes a habit to check the Layers panel to make sure the correct layer is selected before trying any changes.

After you've turned your background layer into a standard layer, you can swap layers by dragging and dropping them above or below one another, as shown in Figure 10.2. Of course, in this example, with the text layer on the bottom, it is no longer visible in the image.

FIGURE 10.2

You can move layers around by dragging and dropping them in the Layers panel.

Speaking of visibility, the "eye" icons next to the layers indicate that they are visible. Click the eye next to either layer, and the visibility is turned off as if the layer never existed. It can't be seen or changed until you turn the visibility back on.

Adding new layers

Layers can be created in many different ways; adding additional images to your document, turning selections into layers, and adding text or shapes to your document are only a few of these ways. As you add each new layer, it is placed above your currently selected layer. You can, of course, move it from there.

We show you how to add layers that modify your image, such as adjustment layers or layer styles, later in this chapter. Smart Objects are another area of layers that require their own section. In this section, we show you the basics of adding new elements to your document as separate layers. These new elements can be another image, text or shape layers, or a selection.

Adding another document as a new layer

If you are combining two or more documents into one image either by merging them or by creating a photo collage, adding additional documents as new layers to your original document couldn't be easier. Here are four easy ways of doing so:

- **Use the Place command.** Choose File ⇨ Place to open the Place dialog box with the original document open. Browse to locate the file that you want to add as an additional layer, and open it. The file appears in your original document as a new layer. You have the option of resizing or rotating it before accepting the placement.

- **Use Mini-Bridge.** Use the Mini-Bridge panel to find the image that you want to bring in as a new layer and drag it from Mini-Bridge into your document. The new image is placed as a new layer into your original document, and you have the option of resizing or rotating it before accepting placement. You can place images in the same way using the full Bridge application as well.

- **Copy and paste.** Copy and paste your documents into one another as additional layers. Open the document with which you want to make a second layer. Press Ctrl+A/⌘+A to select all. Press Ctrl+C/⌘+C to copy your selection. Open the document into which you want to paste the selection. Press Ctrl+V/⌘+V to paste the previous document into the new one. This method has a drawback from the previous two placement methods because your new layer is imported into your document at its original size. In order to resize it, you need to choose Edit ⇨ Free Transform.

- **Move layers between documents.** Choose Window ⇨ Arrange ⇨ Float in Window to float your selected document in a separate window. Click the image layer of the document you want to move, and drag it to the original document, as shown in Figure 10.3. The layer is copied from the first document into the second one. This option is especially beneficial if you want to move more than one layer, because all the selected layers can be moved at the same time. These layers are placed at their original size.

FIGURE 10.3

You can drag and drop a layer, or even multiple layers, between documents.

Adding text or shapes as a new layer

Adding text or shapes as layers in your document is a no-brainer, because when you use the Text or Shape tools, a new layer is automatically created with these elements on it. These layers are identified by Photoshop as either a text or a shape layer, giving them a unique look, as well as their own menu options. Text and shapes are covered in Chapters 17 and 18.

> **NOTE**
>
> You can add a new shape to an existing shape layer, in which case a new layer is not created. In the Options bar, click Path Operations and choose any option except New Layer to add a shape to a highlighted shape layer in the Layers panel.

Creating selections to make a new layer

Selections can be made in the document you are working on, or in other documents to be copied and pasted into the original. In Chapter 9, we show you how to export selections as new layers using the Refine Edge dialog box. If you have a layer containing a selection in one document that you want to place into another document, you can move just that layer into your destination document by dragging and dropping it. You can also use the Copy and Paste commands to copy a selection and paste it as a new layer into the same document or a different one. You don't need a special Paste command; using the Paste command automatically creates a new layer.

Using the Layer Menus

When it comes to layers, two menus do all the work: the Layer menu, located in the menu bar at the top of the screen, and a compact version in the Layers panel menu, located in the

10

top-right corner of the Layers panel. These menus have some identical options, but some options are found in one menu and not the other.

As with any panel, tool, or dialog box in Photoshop, knowing the menu options that are available while working with layers is what gives you the power and versatility to make the Photoshop creations you've envisioned. We've listed the menus here as a reference; they'll be much easier for you to understand after you've read this chapter and worked a little bit with layers, but be sure to come back to this list, because we guarantee you'll find options you forgot about.

We start with the Layer menu, because it has the most options, and then move on to the options that are found only on the Layers panel menu.

Getting to know the Layer menu

The Layer menu has many options that help you use the layers in your Layers panel to their full capacity, as shown in Figure 10.4. Some of these options are available for all layers and some of them are only available for certain types of layers such as vector layers or Smart Layers.

FIGURE 10.4

The Layer menu gives you many options for working with layers.

The Layer menu has the following options for working with layers:

- **New.** Enables you to create a variety of new layers by using the following options:
  - **Layer.** Creates a new blank layer in the Layers panel.
  - **Background from layer.** Turns the current layer into a locked background layer and places it at the bottom of the layer stack.
  - **Group.** Creates a group in the Layers panel. Layer groups are covered later in this chapter.
  - **Group from Layers.** Creates a group in the Layers panel and adds all selected layers to that group.
  - **Layer via Copy.** Creates a new layer containing the last item copied into the clipboard.
  - **Layer via Cut.** Creates a new layer containing the last item cut.
- **Duplicate Layer.** Creates an exact copy of the layer that is selected.
- **Delete.** Enables you to delete layers by using the following options:
  - **Layer.** Deletes the currently selected layer.
  - **Hidden Layers.** Deletes any layers that have the visibility icon turned off.
- **Layer Style.** Adds a new layer style to the currently selected layer. Layer styles include several different effects such as drop shadows and inner glows. They are covered later in this chapter; we also discuss several of the Photoshop effects throughout the book.
- **Smart Filter.** Allows you to make changes to any Smart Filters attached to the selected layer. Smart Filters are covered later in this chapter and used throughout the book.
- **New Fill Layer.** Adds a new layer to the Layers panel that contains a fill. This fill can be a color, gradient, or pattern.
- **New Adjustment Layer.** Adds an adjustment layer. This is an image enhancement that is placed as a non-destructive layer over your image. These adjustments range from levels to hue and saturation adjustments. Fill and adjustment layers are covered in more depth later in this chapter.
- **Layer Content Options.** Opens the settings of a selected Smart Filter, fill layer, or adjustment layer so you can change them.
- **Layer Mask.** Creates a new pixel mask on the selected layer.
- **Vector Mask.** Creates a new vector mask on the selected layer.
- **Create Clipping Mask.** Creates a clipping mask using the layer below the selected one. Masks are covered in greater detail later in this chapter.
- **Smart Objects.** Provides options for creating and using Smart Objects. These enable you to perform nondestructive edits to layers in several ways. Smart Objects are discussed in detail later in this chapter.

10

- **Video Layers.** Provides options for working with video layers. These are covered when we discuss working with video in Chapter 26.

- **Rasterize.** Creates a raster image from the vector objects listed in the Rasterize submenu. As discussed in Chapter 3, a vector object is based on a set of values that describe lines, while a raster image is one that is made up of pixels.

- **New Layer Based Slice.** Creates a slice that conforms to the proportions of the selected layer. Slices are used when creating files for the web. This is covered in Chapter 30.

- **Group Layers.** Groups the selected layers.

- **Ungroup Layers.** Ungroups the selected layers.

- **Hide Layers.** Turns off the visibility of selected layers.

- **Arrange.** Changes the position of the selected layer or layers in the Layers panel relative to the option chosen. For instance, you can bring a selected layer to the front, which places it at the top of the Layers panel.

- **Combine Shapes.** Allows you to combine two or more shape layers in several different ways, including by combining them, subtracting the overlap, subtracting anything that doesn't overlap, and cutting one shape out of the other.

- **Align.** Aligns the objects on the selected layers based on the parameters found in the Align submenu. For instance, you can center all the selected layers with each other so that they are symmetrical. We might use this option to center text inside an image or border.

- **Distribute.** Moves each layer the exact same distance from one another based on the parameters in the Distribute submenu. To use this option, at least three layers must be selected and none of the layers can be locked.

- **Lock All Layers in Group.** Locks all the layers in the group with the selected layer.

- **Link Layers.** Links two or more selected layers. When layers are linked, moving, resizing, or otherwise transforming one layer also affects any linked layers, just as if you had all the linked layers selected in the Layers panel.

- **Select Linked Layers.** Selects all the layers that are linked.

- **Merge Down.** Merges the selected layer or layers with the layer directly beneath them.

- **Merge Visible.** Merges all layers with the visibility icon turned on. (This option also appears as Merge Layers if more than one layer is selected.)

- **Flatten Image.** Merges all the layers into a single background layer.

- **Matting.** Enables you to remove halos by using the following options:

  - **Color Decontaminate.** Reduces a color fringe or halo around the edges of a selection by reducing the saturation of any color on the edges that isn't found in other areas of the selection.

- **Defringe.** Removes halos from selections by replacing aberrant color with pixels farther into the selection.
- **Remove Black or White Matte.** Removes halos around images whose edges have been anti-aliased and that have been cut out of a black or white background. The anti-aliasing caused the edges of these images to blend with the background, creating a halo.

Getting to know the Layers panel menu

The Layers panel menu, shown in Figure 10.5, displays the options that are used most often on the Layer menu. A few of the options do basically the same thing as options found in the Layer menu but go under a different name. Some of the options have to do strictly with the Layers panel, so they are found only in the Layers panel menu.

FIGURE 10.5

The Layers panel menu has several options that apply only to the Layers panel.

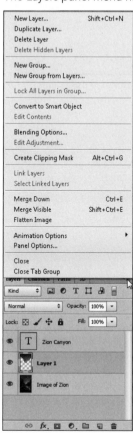

The following additional options are found in the Layers panel menu:

- **Convert to Smart Object.** This option converts the selected layer into a Smart Object for use with Smart Filters. This option is found in the Layer menu under the Smart Objects option. It is discussed later in this chapter, as well as in areas of the book where filters are discussed.

- **Edit Contents.** This option allows you to make changes to the contents of a Smart Object, which are kept in a different file to protect them from changes.

- **Blending Options.** This option opens the Layer Style menu where you can create a Blending option for the selected layer. This is not as easy or straightforward as simply using the Blending options menu found on the Layers panel. Blending options are covered later in this chapter.

- **Animation Options.** These additional options for the Layers panel deal with animation. These options can be shown automatically when an animation is being created, or they can be turned on or off. Animation options are discussed in Chapter 26.

- **Panel Options.** This option opens the Layers Panel Options dialog box shown in Figure 10.6, which allows you to change how your Layers panel appears and how layers are shown.

FIGURE 10.6

Use the Layers Panel Options dialog box to change the way the Layers panel looks and displays layers and effects.

- **Close.** This option closes the Layer panel.
- **Close Tab Group.** This option reduces the entire tab group containing the Layers panel to an icon.

Looking at the Layers Panel

The Layers panel is arguably the most used panel in Photoshop. It is so popular that it appears in every panel preset. Whether you are using Photoshop to enhance your photographs or working with 3D objects, the Layers panel is a vital part of your workflow.

The panel is found in the lower-right corner of the Photoshop workspace, but as you learned in Chapter 2, you can move it to any position you would like. It works out well at the bottom, though, because the Layers panel has a tendency to grow. You'll see what we mean very soon.

A quick look at the Layers panel, shown in Figure 10.7, shows several icons, settings, and drop-down lists. These elements are covered throughout this chapter.

FIGURE 10.7

The Layers panel is the most used panel in Photoshop.

Filtering layers

The top area of the Layers panel is new with the release of Photoshop CS6, and it allows you to filter your layers based on layer type. When you have a document that is heavy on layers, as shown in Figure 10.8, it is useful to be able to sort those layers in several ways so that only the layers that you specify are visible in the Layers panel. Figure 10.9 shows the filtering menu as well as the icons that you can use to filter your layers.

10

FIGURE 10.8

It is useful to filter layers when you are working with a document that is layer heavy.

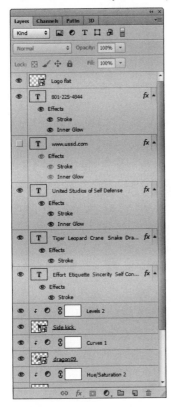

FIGURE 10.9

Several ways to filter your layers.

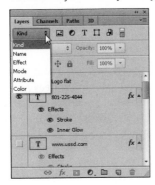

Filter your layers by clicking on the layer-filtering menu and choosing a filter. Each filter has several options that are displayed in icon form, as a menu, or as a text box.

These are the options you have for filtering your layers:

- **Kind.** Allows you to filter your layers by what kind of layers they are. The icons shown in Figure 10.9 appear in the Layers panel when Kind is selected. You can choose from the following kinds of layers by clicking the appropriate icon:

  - **Pixel.** Pixel layers are generally image layers, or photographs composed of pixels.

  - **Adjustment.** Adjustment layers are layers placed over other layers to apply a lighting or color adjustment over them.

  - **Type.** A Type layer is a layer containing text.

  - **Shape.** A Shape layer is any vector layer that is not considered text, such as created shapes or clipart.

  - **Smart Objects.** A Smart Object layer is really a pointer to another document that can be composed of an image, vector art, or even 3D art. The Smart Layer document can be composed of several layers itself.

- **Name.** Allows you to filter your layers by typing a name in the given field. This is one of many great reasons to give your layers descriptive names.

- **Effect.** Enables you to filter your layers by the effect that you've applied to them. When you select this option, a menu appears, allowing you to choose from the effects available in Photoshop.

- **Mode.** Allows you to filter by the blending modes used on your layers. Use the menu that appears to choose a blending mode.

- **Attribute.** Enables you to choose from several different options, such as whether you want locked layers, visible layers, or layers to which effects have been applied.

- **Color.** Allows you to assign a color to any layer when it is created or by right-clicking it and selecting a color from the pop-up menu. When you choose the color filter, you can filter your layers by the colors you have assigned them.

To toggle quickly between filtered layers and a view of all layers, use the Turn layer filtering on/off icon to the right of the filter options in the Layers panel.

Changing the Opacity and Fill settings

The Opacity and Fill settings both allow you to change the opacity of a selected layer, but in different ways. The Opacity setting is just that, a representation of the opacity of the selected layer. The higher the percent that is displayed, the more opaque the selected layer is. As the percentage goes down, the layer becomes more transparent.

The Fill setting also adjusts opacity, but only the opacity of the fill. A normal image layer disappears just as easily with a Fill adjustment as an Opacity adjustment, but a shape or text layer reacts very differently. Adjusting the fill opacity on a shape layer reduces just the fill,

10

while the outline (or stroke) remains, along with any styles that have been applied. You can also add a Layer style to any type of layer and reduce the fill opacity to reduce the visibility of the layer, leaving only the Layer style visible. This is a handy way of creating shadows, glows, and other effects without the original layer showing.

You can adjust both the Opacity and the Fill settings in three ways:

- **Type a new percentage.** Highlight the percentage that is shown and type a new percentage. If you know exactly what percentage to use, this is probably the fastest method.
- **Use the drop-down slider.** Click the down arrow to display the drop-down slider and use it to adjust the setting.
- **Use the scrubber.** Click and drag over the setting name (Opacity or Fill), and a two-sided arrow appears. Drag left to decrease the setting and right to increase it. The scrubber is by far the easiest method.

Changing the lock settings

The Layers panel has four different lock settings, as shown in Figure 10.10. Locking different aspects of your layers means that those aspects can't be changed. Each lock works on a different aspect of your layer, giving you a wide range of versatility. Select the layer you want to lock, and then decide which lock you want to use.

FIGURE 10.10

The Layers panel has different types of lock settings that allow you to protect your layers.

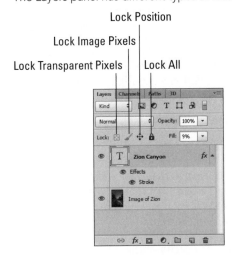

Here are the four different options for locking your layers:

- **Lock Transparent Pixels.** This option locks all the transparent pixels in your image with a single click. You can add fills, make color corrections, or add styles or filters to the rest of the image, but the transparent pixels remain pristine.

- **Lock Image Pixels.** This option protects the image pixels from the paint tools.

- **Lock Position.** This option locks the position of the objects in the layer, so that you can't move them. You can still change other things about the layer, adjusting the color or adding a filter, for instance. A background layer is automatically position locked.

- **Lock All.** This option keeps your layer visible, but protects it from any accidental changes.

Blending modes

Blending modes create amazing special effects by changing the way layers affect each other. At the beginning of this chapter, we asked you to imagine that layers were like transparencies stacked on top of one another. Using blending modes is an example of how using digital technology has taken this idea one step further. Imagine that your transparencies are made of gel rather than plastic, and that rather than sitting on top of one another, they can blend with each other. Then imagine that you can determine which areas of the images on your transparencies would blend and how. Last but not least, imagine that you finish blending them, and you hate the result, but you find that you can pull them apart and start all over with your original images.

Blending modes do more than blend two images together. They can be used on any layer that is added to your Layers panel. You can use them to change the way a layer style is applied, to blend a pattern into an image, or even to change an adjustment layer into a special effect.

The menu at the top of the Layers panel shown in Figure 10.11 displays the different blending modes you can use to choose how the selected layer affects the layers under it. The blending modes are difficult to explain and much easier to see. To differentiate between them, the explanations below are pretty technical, so we strongly advise you use a Photoshop document with two different layers to try them out as you read about them, giving you a more hands-on tutorial. When we refer to the layer value, we are speaking of the layer that is selected when the blend mode is applied. The base value is the layer that is under the selected layer, or the layer that is blending with the selected layer. The blending modes are divided into six general categories, as explained in the following sections.

Choosing Normal and Dissolve blending modes

The Normal blending mode is the default setting in the Layers panel, and when it is used, layers act as you would expect. When the opacity of a layer is set to 100 percent, any pixels in that layer completely cover the layers below. As you reduce the opacity of a Normal layer, it becomes universally more transparent. If you choose the Dissolve blending mode, it looks the same at 100 percent opacity as the Normal mode, but as you reduce the opacity, the selected layer disintegrates or dissolves, losing pixels rather than opacity.

10

FIGURE 10.11

The Blending modes menu allows you to blend your layers together.

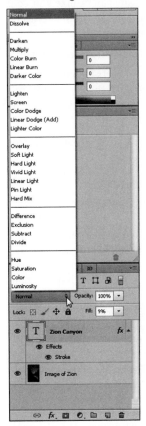

The Normal/Dissolve blending modes are as follows:

- **Normal.** This is the default option. The blend is applied uniformly by painting each pixel based on the layer value and opacity setting to make it the resulting pixel.

- **Dissolve.** This blend is applied by randomly replacing the pixels with either the base value or the layer value, depending on the pixel location and the opacity setting. Using this option allows you to dissipate the effect of the layer more than just changing the opacity.

Using darkening blending modes

The next group within the Blending modes menu contains darkening effects. Each of these five blending filters leaves the darker areas of the selected layer opaque and creates translucency in the lighter areas of the image.

The darkening effects are as follows:

- **Darken.** The blend is applied by replacing the pixels with the darker of the base value or the layer value. In other words, the layer is applied only to pixels in the underlying image that are lighter than the value of the layer pixel. This has the effect of darkening the image and can be extremely useful if applying filters to overexposed images.

- **Multiply.** The blend is applied by multiplying the base value of each pixel by the layer pixel value. Multiplying a pixel by black always produces black, and multiplying a pixel by white leaves the pixel value unchanged. This mode has the overall effect of darkening the image. Multiply is great for creating shadows or to generally darken your image.

- **Color Burn.** The blend is applied by darkening the base channel based on the blended color by increasing the contrast between the two colors. This has the effect of darkening the image as well as increasing color contrasts.

- **Linear Burn.** The blend is applied by decreasing the brightness of the bottom layer based on the value of the top layer pixel, darkening the image.

- **Darker Color.** The blend is applied by replacing each channel of a pixel with the darker between the base pixel channel and the layer pixel channel. This option works a bit better than using the Darken mode because it uses the darkest values from each channel to create the resulting color.

Using lightening blending modes

The lightening blending modes work opposite to the darkening blending modes. Instead of leaving the dark areas opaque, the lighter areas of the selected layer remain opaque and the dark areas are translucent.

The lightening blending effects are as follows:

- **Lighten.** The blend is applied by replacing the pixels with the lighter of the base value or the layer value. This has the effect of lightening the image and can be extremely useful if applying filters to underexposed images.

- **Screen.** The blend is applied by multiplying the inverse of the channel values of the layer and base pixels. This results in a lighter color than either the layer value or the base value. This has the same effect as projecting multiple photographic slides on top of each other.

- **Color Dodge.** This applies the blend by decreasing the contrast between the color of the channels in the layer pixel and the base pixels. This lightens the base pixels using the layer pixel values.

- **Linear Dodge (Add).** This applies the blend by increasing the brightness based on the layer value of each channel, lightening the image.

- **Lighter Color.** This applies the blend by replacing each channel of a pixel with the lighter between the base pixel channel and the layer pixel channel. This option works a bit better than using the Lighten mode because it uses the lightest values from each channel to create the resulting color.

10

Adding contrast blending modes

These blending modes create contrast between the selected layers and the layers under them, making the lighter areas lighter and the darker areas darker.

The contrast blending modes are as follows:

- **Overlay.** This applies the blend by mixing the layer values with the base pixels while preserving the shadows and highlights. This reduces the effect of extreme layer adjustments that dramatically reduce the detail in the original image.

- **Soft Light.** This applies the blend based on the gray value of the filtered pixel. If the value of the layer pixel is darker than 50-percent gray, then the base pixel is darkened using a multiplying method. If the value of the layer pixel is lighter than 50-percent gray, then the base pixel is lightened using a dodging method. This has a similar effect to shining a diffused spotlight on the image.

- **Hard Light.** This applies the blend based on the gray value of the layer pixel. If the value of the layer pixel is darker than 50-percent gray, then the base pixel is darkened using a multiplying method. If the value of the layer pixel is lighter than 50-percent gray, then the base pixel is lightened using a screening method. This has a similar effect to shining a harsh spotlight on the image. This option is great for adding shadows while applying the filter.

- **Vivid Light.** This applies the blend based on the gray value of the layer pixel. If the value of the layer pixel is darker than 50-percent gray, then the base pixel is darkened by increasing the contrast. If the value of the filtered pixel is lighter than 50-percent gray, then the base pixel is lightened by decreasing the contrast.

- **Linear Light.** This applies the blend as a combination of Linear Burn, Linear Dodge, and Vivid Light. The lighter colors brighten, but not as much as using Linear Dodge; and the darker colors darken, but not as much as using Linear Burn.

- **Pin Light.** This applies the blend based on the gray value of the layer pixel. If the value of the layer pixel is darker than 50-percent gray, then the darker of the layer pixel and base pixel is used. If the value of the layer pixel is lighter than 50-percent gray, then the lighter of the layer pixel and base pixel is used.

- **Hard Mix.** This applies the blend by adding the value of each RGB channel in the layer pixel to the corresponding RGB channel in the base pixel. The values above 255 and below 0 are clipped, so this can result in a large loss of detail.

Using difference blending modes

These blending modes blend the layers based on the difference between the two layers. The following blending modes look for variations in the layers to create special effects:

- **Difference.** This applies the blend by setting the resulting pixel to the value of the difference between the layer pixel and the base pixel. Blending white inverts the pixel value, and blending black results in no change.

- **Exclusion.** This applies the blend similarly to the Difference blend mode, but has less contrast.

- **Subtract.** This applies the blend by subtracting the brightness value of the pixels in the base value from the corresponding pixels in the layer value. The result is divided by a scale factor and then added to the offset value. The brighter the source, the more the blending mode subtracts.

- **Divide.** This applies the blend by dividing the brightness value of the pixels in the base value from the corresponding pixels in the layer value. This option has a much larger variance than the Subtract blending mode.

Looking at the color blending modes

The final group of blending modes gives the selected layer a color influence over the layers under it. The color blending effects are as follows:

- **Hue.** This applies the blend by creating the resulting pixel using the luminance and saturation of the base value but the hue of the layer value. This reduces the blend to affect only the hue of the base value.

- **Saturation.** This applies the blend by creating the resulting pixel using the luminance and hue of the base value but the saturation of the layer value. This reduces the blend to affect only the saturation of the base value.

- **Color.** This applies the blend by creating the resulting pixel using the luminance of the base value but the hue and saturation of the layer value. This limits the blend so that it does not affect the brightness of the base value.

- **Luminosity.** This applies the blend by creating the resulting pixel using the hue and saturation of the base value but the luminance of the layer value. This limits the blend so that it affects only the brightness of the base value.

Blending images using blending modes

As you can see, it's actually hard to describe the effects that blending modes can have on your image. The layers you are working with really make a difference in how the blending modes look, so the best way to get a feel for them is to jump in and play with them using your own images.

Here is an example of how to blend two images together using blending modes:

ON THE WEB

You can create this effect yourself or look at the finished PSD file by downloading Figures 10-12a, 10-12b, and 10-12c from the website.

1. **Open an image in Photoshop to be your base image.**

   For the effect we are going to use in this example, a darker image would be best, such as the first photo shown in Figure 10.12.

2. **Add a second image as a layer on top of the first image.**

   This image should have highly contrasting light and dark areas, such as the second photo in Figure 10.12.

10

3. **From the Blending modes menu, choose the Linear Dodge (Add) blending mode.**

   Make sure your top layer is selected. The Linear Dodge (Add) blending mode is a lightening blending mode, which means that only the lighter areas of the image are visible. The photo of the fireworks is ideal because only the fireworks themselves are now visible, as shown in the last image in Figure 10.12.

FIGURE 10.12

Using the Linear Dodge (Add) blending mode makes the lighter pixels in the fireworks image visible and the darker pixels transparent, leaving a great view of the image underneath.

Here is another example of using blending modes. In this example, we are going to add a colorcast to a photo. This is a good way to create sepia-toned images, but you can use any color you want:

ON THE WEB

You can see the final image in color or try adding a colorcast yourself by downloading Figures 10-13a and 10-13b from the website.

1. **Open an image to which you want to add a colorcast.**

2. **Choose Solid Color from the New Adjustment Layer menu in the Layers panel.**

   The Color Picker dialog box opens.

3. **Choose a color to tint your photo.**

   A dark brown creates a beautiful sepia-tone, but you can choose any color you want. (The dark browns can be found in the orange/reds at the bottom of the color spectrum.)

4. **Click OK.**

   The color fill is added as a new layer, leaving your image looking like a rectangle of solid color.

5. **Choose Color from the Blending modes menu in the Layers panel.**

   Be sure the color layer is selected when you do this. Now the color fill affects the image by using the brightness values of the image to map the color fill onto the image, as shown in Figure 10.13.

FIGURE 10.13

Although you can't actually see the colorcast, you can see by the Layers panel that the blending mode has been applied.

This exercise created a solid colorcast. The best thing about using blending modes is that the effects are only as limited as your creativity. You can change the look of this effect by reducing the opacity of the color fill layer, or better yet, changing your image into a black-and-white photo before doing so.

TIP

When creating your own colorcasts, create a Levels adjustment layer over your image *after* the colorcast has been created. Adjusting the levels can increase the contrast of your image and give the colorcast more "pop."

Linking layers

On the bottom of the Layers panel is a set of icons for working with layers. The left icon, shown in Figure 10.14, is the Link layers icon. Layers that are linked move together and are resized together, and creating a selection on one also creates a selection on all of them.

To link layers, select two or more layers by pressing and holding down the Shift key to select contiguous layers, or pressing and holding down the Ctrl/⌘ key to select layers that are not contiguous in the Layers panel. When you have two or more layers selected, the Link layers icon becomes active. Click it to link the selected layers. The linked layers display a link icon, as shown in Figure 10.14.

10

FIGURE 10.14

The most powerful tools in the Layers panel have deceivingly simple icons.

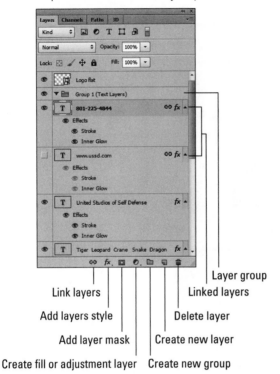

Link layers
Add layers style
Add layer mask
Create fill or adjustment layer

Layer group
Linked layers
Delete layer
Create new layer
Create new group

Creating layer styles, layer masks, and fill and adjustment layers

The most versatile icons in the Layers panel are the Add layer style, Add layer mask, and Create fill or adjustment layer icons, as shown in Figure 10.14. Along with Smart Objects, these are the most powerful, non-destructive tools in the layers repertoire. Because the options related to these icons are extensive, each is covered later in this chapter under its own heading.

Grouping layers

Just as you create folders on your computer's hard drive to organize your files, you can create groups in the Layers panel to organize your layers. Click the Create new group icon in the Layers panel, and a new group appears, as shown in Figure 10.14. You can rename the group by double-clicking the name in the Layers panel or by right-clicking it and selecting Group Properties from the pop-up menu.

To add layers to a group, simply drag and drop them onto the group. These layers still behave in the layer hierarchy just as they are placed, but now you can toggle the group closed by clicking the little black triangle in the group layer, hiding the layers inside the group. If you are working with many different layers, this is extremely useful.

Creating a blank layer

In order to take full advantage of layers in Photoshop, you need to be able to create a blank layer for your own use. This is handy when you want to make changes to your image that you want to be able to edit at any time. When painting, for example, creating a blank layer to paint the changes on leaves the pixels in the original layer undamaged. To create a blank layer, click the Create new layer icon on the Layers panel and a new transparent layer is created directly above whichever layer you have selected.

Throwing layers away

At the bottom-right corner of the Layers panel is a trash can icon. You can delete layers by selecting them and clicking the trash can. If your layer has a mask, you can delete the mask by selecting just the mask. Do this by clicking directly on the mask. You see a highlight appear around it, showing that it is selected. Click the trash can, and the mask is deleted. If you have the layer thumbnail selected, the entire layer disappears, including any masks or filters. You can also delete layer styles or sublayers added to a smart object by dragging them to the trash icon.

Applying Worry-Free Fill and Adjustment Layers

A fill or adjustment layer can adjust the color, levels, or brightness and contrast of your image. These changes are added as a separate layer placed in the layer hierarchy directly over the selected layer. They are portable and editable, and you can create layer masks for each one. You can use blending modes to change the way they affect other layers, and because they are full layers, you can turn them into Smart Objects.

The best thing about a fill or adjustment layer is that it does not change the pixels of your original image; this is the best part of non-destructive editing. All the options available for fill or adjustment layers can be applied directly to an image file by choosing Image ⇨ Adjustments. These adjustments are made directly to the image, however, and are destructive.

NOTE

Vector layers, such as text, shapes, or 3D files cannot be adjusted by using the Image ⇨ Adjustments menu. The only way you can apply these adjustments to vector layers is by placing a fill or adjustment layer over them in the Layers panel.

10

Choosing a fill or adjustment layer

You can place a fill or adjustment layer into your file by clicking the Create fill or adjustment layer icon in the bottom of the Layers panel. This icon looks like a half-black, half-white circle. Clicking this icon opens the Fill or Adjustment layer menu, which includes 18 options, as shown in Figure 10.15. Clicking the option you want opens a dialog box on the Adjustments panel, which allows you to adjust the settings for that option. These options and settings are covered in the next few sections.

FIGURE 10.15

Choosing a fill or adjustment layer

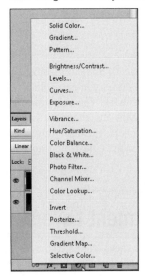

Learning the basics of fill layers

A fill layer is a Color Fill, Gradient, or Pattern that is added as its own layer in the Layers panel. After you have added one, it fills the entire canvas. It may seem ridiculous at first to fill the canvas with a color or pattern, completely covering your original file, especially because the Fill dialog box doesn't have many options. Remember that you are working with a separate layer, however. After you have added a fill, you can reduce the opacity or use a blending mode to create a colorcast, use masks to create a background, or use a clipping mask to cut custom shapes from the fill layer. In Figure 10.16, you can see an example of how we used a pattern fill to create a custom border for a photo.

 Clipping masks are covered in chapter 17.

FIGURE 10.16

Creating a pattern fill was an important step to creating this custom border.

ON THE WEB
You can see the layers used to create this effect by downloading Figure 10-16 from the website.

To create any one of these layers, choose the Create fill or adjustment layer icon in the Layers panel and select Solid Color, Gradient, or Pattern from the pop-up menu. Each option opens a dialog box.

 Although these dialog boxes are fairly straightforward, they are covered in greater detail in Chapter 16.

Learning the basics of adjustment layers

Adjustment layers change the lightness or color of your image. When you add an adjustment layer to your image, you don't see a dialog box; you use the Properties panel, shown in Figure 10.17, where you can make changes to the adjustment layer. This is handy, because you can go back to this panel at any time to edit your adjustment layers.

Adding adjustment layers goes beyond using a non-destructive layer to improve the look of your photo. Using layers gives you the option to create masks that allow you to apply adjustments to selected areas of your image, providing the ability to change the mask as well as the adjustment at a later time, if needed.

10

FIGURE 10.17

The Properties panel lets you make changes to adjustment layers in your Layers panel.

For instance, the Exposure option is meant to correct exposure problems in your image. This is a handy adjustment to use in conjunction with a mask that can cover correctly exposed portions of your photo as you adjust areas that are too light or too dark. Figure 10.18 is an example of using a selection to isolate the boy and lighten the exposure on him to create a dramatic improvement in the photo.

FIGURE 10.18

Using the exposure adjustment selectively makes the boy a stronger focal point in this image.

You can also use layers in conjunction with adjustments to create two different versions of your image. For instance, if you want to create a black-and-white version of a color photo, but keep the color photo available, you can use a Black and White adjustment layer and toggle the visibility to see it in black and white or in color.

Another reason to use the Black and White adjustment layer is that most color photos do not convert well to black-and-white images, because they are usually lacking in contrast. In Figure 10.19, the first image was converted to black and white by changing the color mode to grayscale. You can see that the result is bland and not very engaging. The second image has a Black and White adjustment layer placed over it. The ability to adjust the levels of color in the image gives you the power to make the reds darker (the pistils and freckles) and the yellows brighter (the flower), increasing the contrast of the image and making it a much better image overall.

FIGURE 10.19

Creating a successful black-and-white photo from a color photo takes more than just removing the color information.

 The actual adjustments are covered in detail in Chapters 12 and 13, because you need to do much more to them than just add another layer to the Layers panel.

10

Editing the properties of a fill or adjustment layer

After you have created a fill or adjustment layer, you can go back at any time to edit the properties of the effect created with the layer. Simply select the layer and the Properties panel displays the fill or adjustment settings. You can make any changes you desire.

Creating Layer Style Special Effects

A layer style is any one of several effects including Drop Shadow and Inner Glow. Each layer style is contained in its own sublayer and can be edited, turned off, or discarded. These sublayers can even be turned into their own full layers and can be moved, filtered, color corrected, and edited just like any other layer in Photoshop.

The Layer Style menu icon (*fx*) is located at the bottom of the Layers panel. You can add a layer style to your file by clicking the *fx* icon to open the Layer Style menu and choose a layer style. When you have added a new style, it is displayed as a new sublayer under the object layer, as shown in Figure 10.20.

FIGURE 10.20

A layer style is added to the Layers panel as a sublayer of the selected layer rather than an independent layer.

NOTE

You can also open the Layer Style dialog box by Choosing Layer ⟳ Layer Style and choosing a layer style from the submenu.

The Layer Style dialog box is very versatile. After you have opened it, you can choose one or more styles to add to your object by clicking the box next to the style name to add a check mark to it. Highlight the style name by clicking it, and the dialog box changes to give you the settings for that style. In Figure 10.21, you can see the Layer Style dialog box with three different layer styles selected.

FIGURE 10.21

You can add more than one layer style at a time using the Layer Style dialog box.

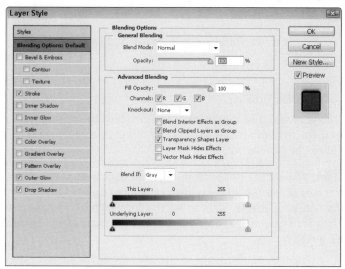

Choosing a layer style

Several layer styles are available, all with very different effects. Here is a list of what they are and what they do:

- **Drop Shadow.** This option creates a shadow behind your image or selection. You can set options such as the shadow size and distance.

- **Inner Shadow.** This option casts a shadow over your image. You can set options such as the opacity and choke.

- **Outer Glow.** This option allows you to add a glow around your image. You can set options such as the color of the light and the size of the glow.

- **Inner Glow.** This option is like the Outer Glow, but it creates a glow inside your image. You can change options such as the opacity and technique.

- **Bevel & Emboss.** This option creates edge effects that give a 3D look to images or objects in your file. We applied a bevel to the frame in Figure 10.16 to make it pop up.

- **Satin.** This option creates a gradient wave across your object that mimics the look of satin. You can set options such as distance and size.

- **Color Overlay.** This option adds a color over your object. You can change the color or the opacity to get a solid color or a mixture of colors.

- **Gradient Overlay.** This option changes the shadow and color of your object. You can choose from several preset gradients or create one of your own.

10

- **Pattern Overlay.** This option sets a pattern over your 3D object like the Color and Gradient Overlay. You can set the opacity to completely cover your object or to mix with the object's color. You can also set the scale of the pattern to be larger or smaller.

- **Stroke.** This option creates an outline of your object. You can change the color, width, and position.

Adjusting layer style options

As you highlight each style available in the Layer Style dialog box, the settings for that style are displayed. Some of these settings are self-explanatory; others are not. Here is a list of the settings that you might not be familiar with:

- **Use Global Light.** This setting makes all the light settings in the layer styles universal. That means that if you add an inner glow and a drop shadow, the angle of the light is the same for both effects. You can set the light angle and height of the global light in any layer style option that uses lighting and the changes will be made to all selected lighting styles.

- **Contour.** This setting controls the shape of the layer style. The shape of the contour represents the color fade from a set opacity to transparent. For example, the default contour is a diagonal line. When creating a bevel, the diagonal line will create that bevel on just one side of the selected layer at a 45 degree angle (based on your light settings). If you were to choose a stepped contour, all of the edges of the selected layer would be affected, creating an outline. You can use preset contours or create one of your own.

- **Anti-Aliased.** This setting gives the contour softer edges.

- **Layer Knocks out Drop Shadow.** This setting simply keeps the drop shadow from being seen through a transparent layer.

- **Jitter.** This setting is available when you are creating a gradient glow. It randomizes the colors used for the glow.

Whether you create one layer style at a time or use the dialog box to create several at once, each style shows up as its own sublayer of the selected layer. Notice in Figure 10.20 how the layer style is grouped under an Effects heading. You can turn off the layer styles collectively by clicking the eye next to the Effects heading, or you can do this individually by clicking the eye next to the style you want to hide.

You can make changes to the layer styles at any time by opening the Layer Style dialog box. Rather than duplicating a layer style, the changes you make are reflected on the styles already shown in the Layers panel.

> **TIP**
> You can add styles you've created to the Styles panel by dragging and dropping them there. You can also use any of the styles on the Styles panel by clicking them.

Creating a separate layer from a layer style

The way a layer style is created in the Layers panel is neat and efficient, and it locks the layer style to the object that it was created for. Occasionally, though, you will want to create an independent layer from a layer style so you can edit the layer style separately from the image layer.

For instance, you may want to create an outline of an object and just use the outline in a composite. Also, you may want to create a shadow and separate it from the object, giving it greater distance than you can create through the layer style settings.

You can create a drop shadow and make a separate layer out of it by following these steps:

ON THE WEB
You can follow along with this exercise by downloading Figure 10-22 from the website and looking at the layers.

1. **Open or create a document with at least two separate layers.**

   At least one layer should be an object that doesn't fill the entire canvas, such as the photo cutout shown in Figure 10.22, or a text or shape layer.

2. **Select the cutout layer by clicking it.**

   The layer appears in highlight, indicating that it is selected.

3. **Click the icon labeled "Add layer style" at the bottom of the Layers panel.**

   This opens the Layer Style dialog box (refer to Figure 10.21).

4. **Select the Drop Shadow layer style.**

   A drop shadow appears on the layer you selected. Do not worry about changing the settings at this point.

5. **Click OK to close the Layer Style dialog box.**

6. **Right-click the Drop Shadow sublayer and select Create Layer from the pop-up menu.**

   The effect changes to a regular layer on your Layers panel, as shown in Figure 10.22.

7. **Select the Drop Shadow layer.**

   Now you can make changes directly to the drop shadow.

8. **Choose Edit ⇨ Transform from the menu to resize, skew, and distort your shadow, so that it flows away from its original layer.**

   Once you're finished transforming the shadow, accept the transformations.

9. **From the Blending modes menu, select the Soft Light blending mode.**

   The shadow appears with a softer look, allowing it to blend better with the background.

10

10. **Double-click the thumbnail of the Drop Shadow layer to open the Drop Shadow dialog box.**

    Now you can make any changes needed to give the shadow a more realistic appearance. For this example, you can see our final result in Figure 10.22.

FIGURE 10.22

A layer style can become its own editable layer.

Creating Smart Objects

You can apply another type of change to your image by using the Filter menu. The Filter menu has always been the fun menu in Photoshop, where you could change your photos into stained-glass windows or liquid metal. Additional filters are available, including those that perform noise reduction and sharpen your images.

Adding filters to a file has always been a tricky trial-and-error process that can be time-consuming and frustrating. Even if it's something you do on a frequent basis, every new file means adding different filters in a different order for different reasons. Smart Filters take a time-consuming process that almost seems like work and turns it into play.

A Smart Filter is added to your image on a separate sublayer much like the layer styles. This gives you the capability to edit it, move it, or discard it at will without having to go back in your step history or change any of the other filters or effects you may have added to your object.

Because Smart Filters are sublayers, they are non-destructive to your image. You can view the image with the filter or turn off the view of the filter, so you can see the image without the effect. This is especially helpful when you add more than one filter because you can see exactly how the filters affect each other. You can even swap the filters around, changing the order in which they are applied to your image.

Because each filter is contained in its own sublayer, you can also make adjustments to the filter after the fact. By clicking the icon shown on the right side of the filter sublayer, you can adjust the blend mode. You can also right-click the filter sublayer and choose Edit the Filter to adjust the original settings of the applied filter.

Unlike the fill and adjustment layers or the layer styles, Smart Filters do not have their own icon on the Layers panel. In fact, before you can add Smart Filters to any layer, you need to turn that layer into a Smart Object. Turning a layer into a Smart Object actually saves that layer as a separate file so it is protected. We go into that in more detail later in this chapter.

Converting a layer to a Smart Object

You can convert any pixel or vector layer to a Smart Object. To convert a layer to a Smart Object and add Smart Filters, select that layer and choose Filter➪Convert for Smart Filters. The following warning appears: "To enable re-editable smart filters, the selected layer will be converted into a smart object." After you've clicked OK to accept this, the layer thumbnail changes to a Smart Object thumbnail, as shown in Figure 10.23.

FIGURE 10.23

A Smart Object thumbnail includes the Smart Object icon in the lower-right corner.

Smart Object icon

The primary characteristic of a Smart Object in Photoshop is that the layer is saved as a separate embedded document in the original file. This allows the layer to maintain its image quality no matter how many edits or filters are used and reversed. Double-click the Smart Object and a dialog box appears letting you know that after any changes are made to the original layer, you can save those changes and they will be updated in the Smart Object. Once you click OK, *a new document opens* containing the original layer before it was turned into a Smart Object. Make the changes you want and then save and close this document to return to your original document containing the Smart Object.

10

> **NOTE**
> You can't change any of the pixel data in a Smart Object. This is because a Smart Object is an aggregate, not composed of distinct pixels. In order to change pixels, the file needs to be a raster file. Changing a Smart Object into a regular layer will rasterize it.

Adding Smart Filters

Now that you've changed your layer into a Smart Object in Photoshop, you can click the Filter menu and most of the options are highlighted for use as Smart Filters.

> **NOTE**
> Certain filters, such as Liquify and Vanishing Point, are not available as Smart Filters.

From here, you can choose a filter or open the Filter Gallery to add a filter to your Smart Object. Choose Filter ⇨ Filter Gallery from the menu. In the Filter Gallery that appears, you can apply more than one filter before exiting by adding subsequent filter layers. You can click each layer to change the properties of that filter, or you can drag them up and down to change the order in which they are applied.

 The Filter Gallery is a great place to play. You can learn all about filters and how to use the Filter Gallery in Chapter 20.

After you've exited the Filter Gallery, you see that the filter you applied has been added as a Smart Filter sublayer in the Layers panel. The Smart Layer is labeled "Filter Gallery" because the Filter Gallery was used to create the filter.

You can also choose individual filters from the Filter menu. For instance, choose Filter ⇨ Artistic ⇨ Colored Pencil to apply that particular filter. When you choose a filter from the Filter menu without using the Filter Gallery, the layer is named with the filter applied, as shown in Figure 10.24.

The image in Figure 10.24 has three filters applied: To see the image without the wave effect, you can simply click the eye on the filter layer. When the eye disappears, so do the effects applied by the Filter Gallery.

Making changes to Smart Filters

You can adjust the settings of any layer by double-clicking that layer. The Filter Settings dialog box opens and allows you to make changes to the original filter settings.

FIGURE 10.24

The Smart Filter layers are labeled with the filter applied.

You can also change the look of the filter layer by changing the blend mode of the layer. Double-click the Filter Blending Option icon that appears on the right side of the filter layer. This opens the Blending Options dialog box, where you can choose from a list of several modes that change the way the filter is applied, as shown in Figure 10.25.

You can also rearrange the order in which the filters are applied to the Smart Object by simply dragging and dropping them into a different order. This can change the look of your image because each filter affects the filters that were added before it but not after it. For instance, if you placed the Oil Paint filter above the Filter Gallery filter in Figure 10.26, you would get a better result than if these filters were placed in the opposite order.

You can also create masks so that filters are applied only to a selected portion of your image. We discuss how to do this in the next section.

10

FIGURE 10.25

You can change the blending options for each filter to change the way it affects the image.

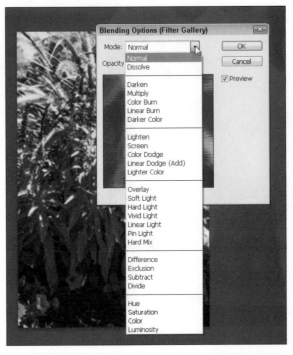

Filter Blending Option icon

FIGURE 10.26

Adding the Oil Paint filter last gives you a better result.

Manipulating Layer Masks

Think of a mask as a stencil. If you place a stencil over an area that you are painting, it protects the areas that are covered and creates a painted design at the same time. Masks in Photoshop work the same way, but you can do so much more with an image than just paint over it. Every enhancement or filter available in Photoshop can be applied to just a portion of your image while leaving the rest of your image untouched using masks.

A layer mask is what most people think of when you mention masks in Photoshop. Figure 10.27 shows a layer mask. Just like a stencil, the black parts cover areas of the image that will be unaffected by any changes made to this layer. It also makes those areas transparent so that any layers underneath will be visible.

FIGURE 10.27

Placing a mask in a layer protects portions of it from edits.

The white areas of the mask are areas that will be affected by any changes made to the layer. These areas behave just as if they were all the image pixels contained in this layer. One of the best aspects of using digital "stencils" is that it is incredibly easy to create semi-permeable areas of a mask with grayscale tones. The lighter a grayscale area is, the more any changes you make to your image affect those areas.

Creating masks

You can create layer masks in several ways. In most cases, you begin by creating a selection. After you've created a selection, turning it into a mask is fairly simple. After you've created a mask, you can move it between layers to facilitate image composites and special effects.

Using the Add layer mask icon

The fastest way to create a mask is to click one of the Add layer mask icons in the Layers panel or in the Masks panel, as shown in Figure 10.28. If you have an area in your image selected, a mask is created from that selection. You can also create a mask from a path. If no selection or path is active, the mask is blank.

10

FIGURE 10.28

Click the Add layer mask icon to quickly add a mask to a selected layer.

Two different types of masks can be created using these icons: a pixel mask and a vector mask. The type of mask you create depends on whether you create the mask from a selection or a path.

- **Pixel masks.** Pixel masks are rasterized masks and behave just like raster images, as discussed in Chapter 3. They are built from pixels and lose quality if you resize them. If you create a mask from a selection, it is a pixel mask, whether you use the Add layer mask icon in the Layers panel or the Add pixel mask icon in the Masks panel. If you click the Add vector mask icon in the Masks panel, the selection is not used to create a vector mask on the selected layer.

- **Vector masks.** Vector masks are built mathematically and are recomputed as they are resized so they don't lose quality. You can create a vector mask from a path either by creating a path or turning a selection into a path. These masks can be edited using only vector tools, such as the pen tools or the shape tools. Just as you can't use a selection to create a vector mask, you can't use a path to create a pixel mask.

Using the Refine Edge dialog box

We showed you the ins and outs of the Refine Edge dialog box in Chapter 9. You can use this dialog box to export your selection as a mask over your current layer, a mask over a new layer, or a mask over a new layer in a new document. Regardless of which option you choose, your selection is changed into a mask with properties identical to the mask shown in Figure 10.27. Using the Feather option in the Refine Edge dialog box adds an increasingly transparent edge to your mask, which is indicated by levels of grayscale.

Creating type masks

You can create type masks over your image by using the type mask tools found in the Toolbox, as shown in Figure 10.29. These tools work like the type tools, but rather than creating solid text on a separate layer, the type mask tools create a selection that surrounds the type on the selected layer. After you've created a selection using type, you can create a mask from that selection using the Refine Edge dialog box or the Add layer mask icons.

FIGURE 10.29

The type mask tools can create masks in your image using type.

 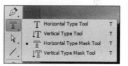

Looking at clipping masks

Clipping masks are not created using a selection, nor do they look like a traditional mask in your Layers panel. A clipping mask is created by taking the shape of one layer and cutting that shape out of the layer above it.

You can create a clipping mask by following these steps:

ON THE WEB
Try it yourself by downloading Figures 10-30a and 10-30b from the website.

1. **Open an image you want to clip.**

   This can be any image you want. We've chosen the Halloween photo shown in Figure 10.30.

2. **Double-click the background layer to turn it into a regular layer.**

   You can name the layer if you want to.

3. **Create a layer with a cut-out to clip from.**

   This can be a shape layer, a text layer, or a selection from another image. We chose the shape of a maple leaf that we copied and pasted into its own layer, as shown in Figure 10.30.

FIGURE 10.30

We combined these two images with a clipping mask.

4. **Place the layer with the cut-out underneath the image layer.**

   If you've created a new layer in your document, it was automatically placed above your image layer. Click and drag it underneath your image layer.

5. **Select the image layer.**

   This is the layer that you want to be visible in the end. Our selected layer is the one with the jack-o'-lanterns.

6. **Right-click the image layer, and select Create Clipping Mask from the pop-up menu.**

   This uses the bottom layer as a template to cut the top layer, as shown in Figure 10.31. The bottom layer becomes a silhouette for the top layer.

> **TIP**
>
> A quick way to create a clipping mask without using the menu is to press the alt/option key and hover over the dividing line between the two layers until the clipping icon appears and click, instantly creating clipping mask. The clipping icon looks like an emptly layer thumbnail with an arrow pointing down.

FIGURE 10.31

The clipping mask used the leaf as a template to cut out the jack-o'-lantern image for a fun fall effect.

ON THE WEB

Check out the final product by downloading Figure 10-31 from the website and looking at the layers.

Creating a clipping mask changed the way the layers look in the Layers panel, but not by placing a mask thumbnail in the selected layer. Instead, the layer containing the jack-o'-lantern image has an arrow pointing down to indicate that this layer is being affected by the layer underneath.

You can release the clipping mask by right-clicking the top layer again and choosing Release Clipping Mask from the pop-up menu.

Editing masks

After a mask thumbnail has been placed in your Layers panel, you can edit it using the image, the channels, or the Masks panel. This allows you to make changes to which areas of your image are being affected.

Making changes to a mask by painting on the image

To edit a mask using an image, you must have the mask selected in the layer. Make sure the mask thumbnail has a white highlight around it, rather than the image thumbnail, shown in Figure 10.32. This is sometimes hard to see, so click back and forth a couple of times to see the difference.

10

After you have selected the mask, you can use the Brush and Eraser tools to add to or subtract from the masked area. Using the Brush tool adds to the mask and using the Eraser tool subtracts from it. Use these tools directly on your image. The only difference you see is a change in the mask's effects. Depending on what those changes are, this might not be the ideal way to edit your mask, because it is hard to be precise if the effects of the mask aren't obvious.

FIGURE 10.32

The white outline showing that the mask is selected means we are making changes to the mask with the brush, rather than the image.

The mask is highlighted

 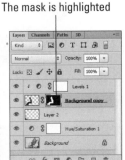

> **NOTE**
> Reducing the opacity on either the Brush or Eraser tool paints levels of grayscale, creating a semi-permeable area of your mask.

Editing masks using the Channels panel

A better option for editing this mask is to use the Channels panel. With the mask selected in the Layers panel, open the Channels panel, as shown in Figure 10.33. The Channels panel contains the color channels found in your image, but it also contains any masks placed in your image. When you open the Channels panel, the mask channels are not visible. If you turn the visibility icon on, a rubylith appears in your image, reminiscent of the Quick Mask discussed in Chapter 9. Now as you make changes to the mask, you can see them clearly.

If you would like to make changes to the mask all by itself, without a view of the image, you can deselect the visibility icon in the full color channel (RGB in this example) and only the mask is visible in your document window, as shown in Figure 10.33.

FIGURE 10.33

You can edit the mask by itself by turning off the visibility of the color channels in the Channels panel.

Editing masks using the Properties panel

The Properties panel offers the most comprehensive way to edit masks, not only giving you the option to add to or subtract from them, but also allowing you to refine the edges, choose a color range, or invert it. You can also change your mask into a selection.

Figure 10.34 shows the Properties panel with a mask selected. The following options are available:

FIGURE 10.34

When a mask is selected, the Properties panel displays the mask properties.

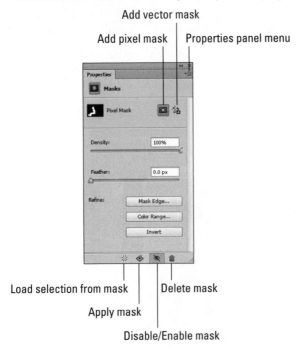

- **Mask thumbnail.** The mask thumbnail shows you the currently selected mask as well as whether the mask is a pixel mask or a vector mask.

- **Add pixel mask.** This button adds a pixel mask to the selected layer. If that layer contains an active selection, it is converted to the mask.

- **Add vector mask.** This button adds a vector mask to the selected layer. If that layer contains an active path, the path is converted to the mask.

- **Density.** This slider adjusts the density or translucency of the mask.

- **Feather.** This slider adjusts the gradual translucency of the edges of the mask, creating a feathering effect.

- **Refine.** This menu item contains the following options:

  - **Mask Edge.** This button opens the Refine Edge dialog box (covered in Chapter 9) and allows you to make refinements to the edge of your mask.

  - **Color Range.** This button opens the Color Range dialog box allowing you to add specific colors to your mask, similar to the Color Range dialog box discussed in Chapter 9.

- **Invert.** This button inverts the mask, selecting areas that were not previously selected and deselecting areas that were. Areas that are semitransparent also are inverted.

- **Load selection from mask.** This option does not disable the mask, but allows you to make changes to it as if it were a selection. The marching ants appear on your image, and you can use selection tools to add to or subtract from the mask. You can also use the Quick Mask to paint in changes to the mask.

- **Apply mask.** This option combines a selected mask with the image by clicking it, turning all masked areas into transparent pixels and deleting the mask.

- **Enable/Disable mask.** This "eye" icon allows you to see the image as if no mask were applied. When the eye has a red line through it, the mask effects are not visible in the image.

- **Delete mask. This icon deletes the selected mask when clicked.**

- **The Masks panel menu.** The Masks panel menu has options that allow you to add or subtract selections to or from your mask. You can also see the mask properties that allow you to change the color of the overlay and give names to your masks.

Unlinking and moving masks

To unlink a mask from its layer, simply click the link icon between the layer thumbnail and the mask thumbnail in the layer. When the mask is unlinked, it is no longer transformed with the image when you resize or move it.

You can also move masks from one layer to a different layer. You would probably do this if you wanted to create a selection in one layer, but use the mask in an entirely different layer. The following example shows you what we mean.

The first image in Figure 10.35 is a photo of some boys gathered around a table at the zoo. The second image is a cold baby giraffe that just wants a bit of hot chocolate. In order to create the photo composite you see in the last image in Figure 10.35, we had to create a mask on the layer containing the image of the boys and move it to the layer containing the image of the giraffe.

ON THE WEB

Give this effect a try, or see our final results, by downloading Figures 10-35a, 10-35b, and 10-35c from the website.

We selected the grouchy boy in the foreground using the Quick Selection tool and then inverted the selection so the grouchy boy was the only thing that was deselected. After refining the edges, we exported this selection as a new layer with a mask. Now we could make changes to everything in this image except the grouchy boy. The problem was that we didn't actually want to make changes to this image; we just wanted to insert the giraffe in between the two boys on the left. The best way to do this was to place the mask we had just created on the *giraffe,* so the outline of the boy was cut out of the giraffe.

10

FIGURE 10.35

This baby giraffe just wants to join in the fun. Moving masks from one layer to another made this final image possible.

First, we placed the giraffe in the photo just where we wanted it, as shown in Figure 10.36. It was fairly obvious that it didn't belong to this image; we could fix that, though. By clicking and holding the mask thumbnail, we dragged it to the layer containing the giraffe, also shown in Figure 10.36, effectively masking the portion of the giraffe that we wanted to appear behind the boy, creating the effect that the giraffe was part of the picture.

FIGURE 10.36

Masks can be moved from one layer to another by clicking and dragging them.

Creating Layer Comps

Layer comps enable you to create, view, and then display multiple versions of a design within one file by recording layers. The Layer Comps panel is a way to take pictures of three different layer arrangements within the same document: the layer visibility, position, and appearance. For instance, if you were creating a brochure and a flyer that had the same images and text but different layouts, you could make a layer comp for each one in the same document.

To create layer comps, follow these steps:

1. **Create a layout in Photoshop.**

   This layout is completely up to you. You can see an example of a flyer in Figure 10.37.

2. **Open the Layer Comps panel.**

   Choose Window⇨Layer Comps from the main menu bar. The panel is very simple and has few options.

ON THE WEB

You can see how layer comps work by downloading Figure 10-37 from the website.

3. **Click the Create new layer comp icon to create a new layer comp.**

   You can give it a custom name if you like. Layer properties such as position, visibility, and appearance are saved in this layer comp.

10

FIGURE 10.37

The Layer Comps panel shows a layer comp for each of our designs.

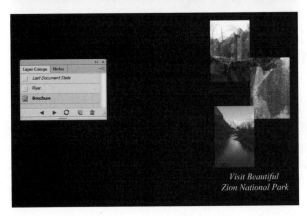

4. **Make changes to the position, transparency, or appearance of your layers.**

   These are the only changes that can be preserved in your layer comp, so resizing or deleting your layers is out of the question.

5. **Click the Create new layer comp icon again, and save your new layer comp.**

   You should have two layer comps in the dialog box, as shown in Figure 10.37. You can toggle back and forth between them by selecting the icon next to them to make them visible.

Merging Layers

When you have made your changes and you are sure that you don't need separate layers any longer, you can merge them. Not only does this clean up your Layers panel, but it also reduces the size of your file. Each layer you add makes the file bigger, as shown in Figure 10.38. The two different file sizes listed in the document window are the document size and the document size with layers, respectively.

FIGURE 10.38

The document window shows the size of the original document followed by the size of the document with layers.

You can merge your layers in several ways. Choose one of the following options from the Layers panel menu:

- **Merge Down.** This option merges the selected layers with the layer immediately below them.
- **Merge Layers.** This option merges the selected layers. Use it when you want to merge some, but not all, of your layers.

- **Merge Visible.** This option merges the layers that are visible, leaving any layers that have the Show/Hide layer icon (the eye) turned off.
- **Flatten Image.** This option flattens all the layers, leaving you with a background layer that contains the visible information of all the layers. After you've flattened your image, you can't make changes to the individual elements that were contained in the layers; they are now part of the background layer.

Summary

Knowing how to use layers is an important part of effectively using Photoshop. This chapter covered everything you need to know about the Layer menus, the Layers panel, and layers themselves. Although you may have some questions about the effects that can be added to the Layers panel, you should be able to add them, move them, and edit their settings. You have the skills to perform the following tasks:

- Adding layers to your document in several different ways
- Moving and editing those layers in your document as well as the Layers panel
- Using blending modes to effectively combine layers
- Creating effects layers such as adjustment layers, layer styles, and smart object layers and understanding how they work
- Creating layer masks to perform several different functions
- Saving multiple layouts using Layer comps
- Merging layers to reduce clutter and file size

Exploring Channels

Color channels are a core component of both color and grayscale images. Color images are composed of separate color channels that, when combined, make up the colors in the image. Understanding the color channels and the tools that Photoshop provides will help you make better use of the color data in your images.

Photoshop provides two main tools to help you manipulate and manage the color channels in images: the Channel Mixer and the Channels panel. Using these tools, you can see, manipulate, and even create channels in your image to increase your options when making selections and adjustments.

This chapter discusses using the Channel Mixer to mix, swap, and combine the color data in your images and using the Channels panel to manage channels, create and use alpha channels, and create spot color channels.

Understanding Color Channels

In Chapter 4, we discussed how the images that we see are just light emitted from a computer screen or reflecting off a photo. We also discussed that the colors we see can be divided into the levels of three frequency ranges of light-stimulating receptors in the eye. Photoshop uses this same concept to represent digital images. Each pixel in a color digital image contains a series of values that define the actual color of the pixel. For example, each pixel in an RGB image contains a value describing the level of red, a value describing the level of green, and a value describing the level of blue.

A channel is the series of values that represents the specific level of a single color, opacity, hue, saturation or brightness for each pixel in the entire image. For the red channel, each pixel contains only one value describing the level of red. Splitting the image into individual color channels allows Photoshop to provide some very powerful tools when editing images and creating special effects.

Photoshop provides tools to adjust channels based on the color mode of the image. For example, if the color mode is RGB, Photoshop provides red, green, and blue tools; if the color mode is CMYK, Photoshop provides cyan, magenta, yellow, and black tools.

Photoshop treats individual channels as grayscale images because color is based on the mix of the channels; with only one channel, Photoshop cannot determine color. That is why when you view a single channel of an image, it is displayed in grayscale.

An advantage to breaking color into channels is that each color channel contains part of the detail of the image. Notice the three channels shown in Figure 11.1. Each channel contains different parts of the detail that make up the entire image. Breaking the image up into detail gives you greater options when trying to work with the detail in the image.

FIGURE 11.1

The red, green, and blue color channels of an image each contain part of the full detail in the image.

Original

Red channel

Green channel

Blue channel

On the Web

You can find the image shown in Figure 11.1 on this book's website as Figure 11-1.jpg. You can open it in Photoshop and view each of the color channels.

Using the Channel Mixer

One of the most powerful, yet least used, tools in Photoshop is the Channel Mixer. The Channel Mixer allows you to fine-tune the level of each color channel in the image separately. To reach the Channel Mixer, shown in Figure 11.2, choose Image⇨Adjustments⇨Channel Mixer from the main menu bar. The Channel Mixer provides a simple interface to mix values between the different channels in the image.

You may wonder whether mixing channels is the same thing as adjusting the colors in the image using one of the other adjustment tools. The answer is no. When you mix two or more channels, you are not mixing the colors of the channels so much as you are mixing the detail provided in the channels. Mixing the channels allows you to change the detail levels in each channel, which provides a different result when you later make other adjustments such as changing the hue or tone in the image.

Note

The Channel Mixer is available only when you are using the RGB and CMYK color modes. If you need to eventually work in the lab, grayscale, or other color modes, you want to do the channel mixing before changing the color mode from RGB or CMYK.

FIGURE 11.2

The Channel Mixer allows you to mix the channels to create new channel data.

The Channel Mixer provides these options when mixing the channels in an image:

- **Preset.** This allows you to select from a previously saved mix of channels. Photoshop provides several black-and-white preset settings that apply different color filters, including infrared. This is useful if you need to make the same mix to more than one photo or if you want to save a certain mix and then try others. To save the current Channel Mixer settings, select Save Preset using the drop-down menu button next the Preset drop-down menu.

- **Output Channel.** This allows you to select the output channel that receives the mix of data from the set of source channels.

> **CAUTION**
> The current data in the output channel is overwritten by the values specified in the set of source channels.

- **Red.** This specifies the percent of the red channel levels to mix into the output channel. You can use the slider or type in the value directly.

- **Green.** This specifies the percent of the green channel levels to mix into the output channel. You can use the slider or type in the value directly.

- **Blue.** This specifies the percent of the blue channel levels to mix into the output channel. You can use the slider or type in the value directly.

- **Constant.** This specifies the grayscale value of the output channel. When you specify negative values, more black is added to the output channel. When you specify positive values, more white is added.

- **Monochrome.** When you select this option, the output channel is changed to gray and the preview of the image is in grayscale. This is the perfect option to use when you want to adjust a color image before converting it to grayscale.

There are three basic reasons to mix the color channels in an image. The most common is to selectively control how color channels are mixed to create a grayscale image. A second reason is to mix channels with more detail to enhance channels with less detail. The third reason is to completely swap channels to create special effects without altering the other channels.

Mixing colors with the Channel Mixer

Using the Channel Mixer, you can specify the amount of level data, or detail, from each of the three channels to mix into one single channel. This allows you to change the actual color channel composition of the image.

Color mixing is done by selecting an output channel in the Channel Mixer and then setting the percentages of each color channel that you will use to form the new channel. For example, consider a single RGB pixel. If you use the Channel Mixer to change the red channel to be a composite of 0 percent red, 50 percent green, and 50 percent blue, then the red value for each pixel would be changed to 0 percent of the red value plus 50 percent of the green value plus 50 percent of the blue value. The percentage values are based on what is already there, for example if the pixel contained level values of 100 for red, 50 for blue and 200 for green, then the level of the output channel pixel would contain 0 from red plus 50 from blue plus 100 from green or 150.

Color mixing is useful when you have a channel in an image that contains very little detail because it was taken in colored lighting or some other situation that alters the color tone in the image. Using a mix of the other two channels, you can add more detail to channels that are lacking.

The Channel Mixer allows you to enter negative % values. Negative values have the opposite effect of positive values. They take the percentage of the value of the channel and subtract that from the overall level in the output channel.

> **CAUTION**
>
> The Channel Mixer allows you to use any combination percentage values of –200 percent to 200 percent for each source channel. That means you can end up with a total percentage that is not 100 percent. If you change the values such that the total does not equal 100 percent, the overall tonal content of the image is altered. This typically is not a desired result.

Swapping colors

A great way to apply a special effect in an image is to completely swap color channels. This has the effect of changing the look of the entire image without altering the actual detail in the image. The effect changes, depending on the color channels that you swap and the content of the channels in the image.

To swap colors in an image, follow these steps:

1. **Choose Image ⇨ Adjustments ⇨ Channel Mixer from the main menu bar to launch the Color Mixer, shown in Figure 11.3.**
2. **Set the Output Channel to Red.**
3. **Change the value of the Red channel to 0%.**
4. **Change the value of the Blue channel to 100%.**
5. **Set the Output Channel to Blue.**
6. **Change the value of the Red channel to 100%.**
7. **Change the value of the Blue channel to 0%.**
8. **Click OK.**

   The Red and Blue color channels are swapped in the image. The result is that the red tones are changed to blue, and vice versa, as shown in Figure 11.4. Although you cannot see the full effect on the image in Figure 11.4, you can go to this book's website and follow these steps to see the full effect.

FIGURE 11.3

Changing the Red channel to 100 percent blue and the Blue channel to 100 percent red

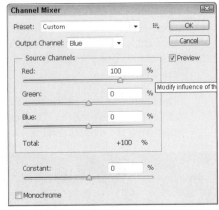

FIGURE 11.4

Swapping the Red and Blue channels results in a complete change to the color tones in an image, which can create some fantastic effects.

ON THE WEB

You can find the image shown in Figure 11.4 on this book's website as Figure 11-4.jpg. You can open it in Photoshop and use the steps in this section to see the changes when you swap the blue and red color channels. As another experiment, you could try to swap the green and red color channels.

Converting color to grayscale

The most common use of the Channel Mixer is to prepare images to be converted to grayscale. When you convert an image to grayscale, Photoshop uses 40 percent of the red and green channels and 20 percent of the blue channel. For general purposes, those values have produced the best results.

The Channel Mixer gives you complete control over how much of each channel is applied to the output when converting a color image into grayscale. Use these steps to convert an image to grayscale using the Channel Mixer:

1. **Open the image in Photoshop, as shown in Figure 11.5.**
2. **Choose Image ⇨ Adjustments ⇨ Channel Mixer from the main menu bar to launch the Channel Mixer.**

FIGURE 11.5

Color image to be converted to grayscale using the Channel Mixer

ON THE WEB

You can find the image shown in Figure 11.5 on this book's website as Figure 11-5.jpg. You can open it in Photoshop and use the steps in this section to see the effects of mixing the channels to create a better grayscale image.

3. **Check the Monochrome check box.**

   This changes the output channel to Gray. The Red and Green source channels are set to 40% and the Blue channel is set to 20%, as shown in Figure 11.6. The image will be converted to a monochrome grayscale. The image results of the default values are not very appealing, as shown in Figure 11.6.

4. **Adjust the Red slider, which has the effect of adjusting the red levels in the image.**

   In this example, the value is changed to 0%, as shown in Figure 11.7.

5. **Adjust the Green slider, which also has the effect of adjusting the image, but in this case, it reveals a different set of detail in the green levels.**

   In this example, the value is changed to 110%, as shown in Figure 11.7.

6. **Adjust the Blue slider, which has the effect of adjusting the blue levels in the image, bringing back some of the detail lost from increasing the red and green channels.**

   In this example, the value is left at 20%, as shown in Figure 11.7.

FIGURE 11.6

The initial results of selecting the Monochrome check box are somewhat disappointing.

7. **Click OK to apply the Channel Mixer settings to the image, as shown in Figure 11.7.**

   The results are much better contrast and tone than was achieved with the default values in Figure 11.6. Setting the values in the Channel Mixer varies greatly between different images. You will want to play with the sliders trying different values while previewing the results in the images.

8. **After you have applied the Channel Mixer settings, choose Image ⇨ Mode ⇨ Grayscale to convert the color model of the image to Grayscale.**

NOTE

When you choose Image ⇨ Mode ⇨ Grayscale from the menu, although Photoshop suggests using Image ⇨ Adjustments ⇨ Black & White adjustment to convert the image to grayscale. You do not need to use the Black and White adjustment tool because the channels have already been adjusted. The Black and White adjustment tool is discussed in Chapter 12 and is a bit simpler than using the Channel Mixer, but you may get better results using the Channel Mixer method.

FIGURE 11.7

The results of using custom values in the Channel Mixer to create the Grayscale channel are much better than those with the default settings.

Using the Channels Panel

The Channels panel provides access to all the channels contained in an image. It allows you to look at each color channel in the image separately. Using the Channels panel, you can also create spot channels as well as split, duplicate, and merge color channels.

To open the Channels panel, shown in Figure 11.8, choose Window ➪ Channels from the main menu bar or use the F7 shortcut key and select the Channels tab.

NOTE

When working with RGB and CMYK images, the top entry in the Channels panel is a composite channel of the RGB or CMYK channels. When you select the composite channel, all the component channels are selected.

Using the Channels panel, you can view and select individual channels, remove channels, and create new channels. The following sections discuss using the Channels panel to work with the color channels in an image.

FIGURE 11.8

The Channels panel allows you to manage individual color channels in images.

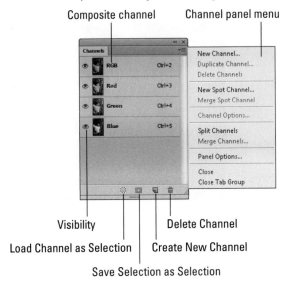

Composite channel   Channel panel menu

Visibility   Delete Channel

Load Channel as Selection   Create New Channel

Save Selection as Selection

Selecting channels

A useful feature of the Channels panel is the ability to select one or more of the channels individually. When you only select one channel, changes that you make by drawing, erasing, and applying filters are made to that channel only. This allows you to create special effects on specific channels or fine-tune adjustments to a single channel.

You can select channels in the Channels panel by clicking them with the mouse or by pressing the Ctrl+#/⌘+# key sequence listed next to the channel name. When you select the composite channel (RGB or CMYK), the image display shows the results of all three channels. When you select an individual channel, the image display shows a grayscale rendition of the levels of the selected channel. To select multiple channels, use the Ctrl/⌘ or Shift keys. When you select multiple channels, the image display shows the results of the combined channels.

You can also specify whether a channel is visible by clicking the Visibility button next to the channel in the Channels panel. When the eye icon is displayed in the box, the channel is visible in the image display. When the eye icon is not displayed in the box, the channel data is not used to render the image display.

Deleting channels

You can delete a channel from an image by selecting the channel in the Channels panel and then clicking the trash icon (refer to Figure 11.8). When you delete a channel, the level data contained in that channel is removed from the image.

When you delete one of the component channels from an RGB or CMYK image, the composite channel is also removed and the color mode of the image changes to Multichannel. Typically, you only delete channels that you add to an image, such as an alpha channel or a spot channel.

Duplicating channels

A useful feature of the Channels panel is the ability to quickly duplicate one of the existing channels. This allows a lot of flexibility when editing channels. After you duplicate the channel, you can make adjustments to the duplicate channel and simply change the visibility between the duplicate and the original to see the different effects. You can also use this feature to save a channel as another document.

To create a duplicate of an existing channel, right-click the channel in the Channels panel and select Duplicate Channel from the drop-down list. A dialog box similar to the one in Figure 11.9 appears. You can specify the following settings when duplicating a channel:

- **As.** This is the name of the channel.
- **Document.** This selects the document where the duplicate channel will be added. Document defaults to the current image file; however, you can select any open document or a new file.
- **Name.** This specifies the name of the new file if Document is set to new.
- **Invert.** This creates a completely inverted copy of the original channel. The lighter areas of the copy are dark, and vice versa.

FIGURE 11.9

Creating a duplicate channel in Photoshop

Splitting and merging channels

Photoshop also provides the ability to split the channels contained in an image into separate document files. This is useful when you want to apply a lot of adjustments to the individual channels and then merge them later.

To split the channels of an existing image into multiple documents, select Split Channels from the Channels panel menu (refer to Figure 11.8). The current document is replaced by a set of documents representing each channel in the image, as shown in Figure 11.10. You can then edit and save each channel separately.

To merge the channels back into a color image, select Merge Channels from the Channels panel menu. A Merge Channels dialog box similar to the one shown in Figure 11.11 appears, allowing you to specify the color mode and number of channels to be included in the new color image. Click OK to open the Merge *Mode* dialog box (where *Mode* is the color mode you are creating), also shown in Figure 11.11. This dialog box allows you to specify which files to use for each channel of the specified color mode when creating the color image.

> **NOTE**
> The images that you want to merge into a color image must be monotone images. They must also be open in Photoshop for the Merge Channels option to be active.

Sharing channels between images

Photoshop makes it extremely easy to share channels between images. This is useful when you need to move channel data between documents.

To move a channel between two documents, simply select the channel in the Channels panel and drag it to another image, as shown in Figure 11.12. A new alpha channel is created in the second image. The contents of the alpha channel are the levels from the selected channel in the original image.

FIGURE 11.10

Splitting color channels of an image results in a new set of grayscale documents being created, each containing the data from a separate channel. The filenames are the same as the original with an additional letter denoting the channel.

Red

Blue

Green

FIGURE 11.11

Merging multiple grayscale images back into a color image using the Merge Channels feature

FIGURE 11.12

Channels can be shared between documents in Photoshop by selecting a channel from the Channels panel and then dragging it into another image document.

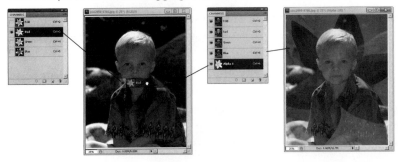

Making Channel Selections

One of the major advantages of having access to the separate channels in Photoshop is the enhanced ability to make selections. Because each channel provides a different aspect into the detail of the image, each has different contrast in relation to each part of the image.

Because you can select each channel individually, you can use individual channels to make different selections in the image. For example, when you want to select a specific item in the image, you would use the color channel that provides the greatest contrast around the edges of that item.

This example illustrates how to use channels to make better selections:

1. **Open the image in Photoshop, as shown in Figure 11.13.**

2. **Choose Window ⇨ Channels to open the Channels panel.**

3. **After the Channels panel is open, view each channel individually.**

FIGURE 11.13

Selecting the rock and the sky in this image will be easy using the Channels panel.

4. **Select the channel that provides the best contrast for the selection you want to make.**

   In this example, the first selection you want to make is that of the rock the boys are standing on. Notice from Figure 11.14 that the red channel provides the best contrast between the rock and the rest of the image.

FIGURE 11.14

Each channel has different contrast levels, allowing some to be better for selecting certain objects than others.

Red channel   Blue channel   Green channel

5. **Use a selection tool to create the selection.**

   In this example, you use the Quick selection tool, discussed in Chapter 9, to draw across the center of the rock, so it is selected as shown in Figure 11.15.

6. **Click the Save Selection as Channel button to save the selection as an alpha channel, also shown in Figure 11.15.**

FIGURE 11.15

Selecting the rock in the red channel is easy with the Quick selection tool because of the higher contrast.

 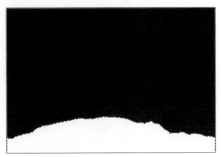

Next you want to select the sky in the background. Notice from Figure 11.14 that the blue channel provides the best contrast around the edges of the sky. So you want to select the blue channel this time.

7. **Use the selection tool to create another selection.**

   In this example, you use the Quick selection tool to draw across the sky and pick up the edges around the boys to create the selection shown in Figure 11.16.

8. **Again click the Save Selection as Channel button to save the selection as an alpha channel.**

FIGURE 11.16

Selecting the sky in the blue channel is easy with the Quick selection tool because of the higher contrast.

Using the channel method, you create the two selections more easily than if you were using the composite RGB channel. The resulting selections are now channels that you can use as needed for further editing, as shown in the Channels panel in Figure 11.17.

FIGURE 11.17

The selections created have been added as alpha channels in the Channels panel.

ON THE WEB

You can find the project file used in this example on this book's website as Figure 11-13.psd. You can open it in Photoshop and play around creating selections using different color channels.

Understanding the Alpha Channel

You can store a selection in an additional channel called an alpha channel. The alpha channel describes additional information used when processing the actual pixel data. The alpha channel does not provide any data about the color content of a pixel, but rather how to process the data.

The main purpose of the alpha channel is to provide transparency information that can be applied to an image. As with the other channels, each pixel in the alpha channel can have a value from 0 to 255 where 0 represents that the pixel is 100-percent transparent and 255 represents that the pixel is 100-percent opaque.

Another useful feature of alpha channels is that you can use them to store and retrieve selections for later use. The alpha channels allows quick access to previous selections, and you can even share alpha channels between documents by dragging them from one document to another.

Creating alpha channels

Alpha channels are created from selections. The simplest way to create an alpha channel is to make a selection and then save the selection as an alpha channel using these steps:

1. **Open an image in Photoshop.**
2. **Choose Window⇨Channels from the main menu bar to open the Channels panel.**

3. Select an area of the photo that you want to use for alpha channel data, as shown in Figure 11.18.

4. Click the Save Selection as Alpha Channel button in the Channels panel, to convert the selection to an alpha channel.

5. An alpha channel is created containing the current selection.

FIGURE 11.18

Selecting the sky in an image and converting it to an alpha channel

Create Channel from Selection button

ON THE WEB

You can find the project file used in this example on this book's website as Figure 11-13.psd. You can open it in Photoshop and play around with the alpha channels using different color channels.

Loading selections from alpha channels

One of the best features of alpha channels is the ability to retrieve the selection information used to create them. This allows you to work with several selections in one or multiple files without having to constantly save and reload them.

You can retrieve selection data from an alpha channel by selecting the channel in the Channels panel and clicking the Load Channel as Selection button at the bottom of the panel. This clears the current selection if there is one and creates a new one from the selection data in the selected alpha channel.

Modifying alpha channels

A great thing about alpha channels is that they are actually channels with real data that can be adjusted using filters and painting tools. This allows you to modify the alpha channel in a variety of ways. One of the easiest ways is to simply use a paint tool to paint directly on the channel.

The following example uses the paint tool to quickly modify the existing alpha channel created in the preceding section:

1. **Select the alpha channel in the Channels panel.**

   The image display shows the alpha channel, as shown in Figure 11.19.

2. **Select the Brush tool from the Toolbox.**

3. **Change the foreground color to white.**

4. **Use the Brush tool to paint white over any pixels that you would like to include in the selection.**

   In the example in Figure 11.19, the boy on the right is removed.

FIGURE 11.19

Modifying the content of an alpha channel is as simple as painting away the areas of the channel that you want to exclude or painting in the areas that you want to include.

Understanding alpha channels versus layer masks

A layer mask is similar to an alpha channel; in fact, when you link a layer mask to a layer, the layer mask appears in the Channels panel. However, a layer mask applies to a specific layer and not the entire image. The alpha channel applies as a separate channel to the entire image.

The difference between alpha channels and layer masks is most apparent when you are viewing the image in Photoshop. When you create an alpha channel, the view doesn't change, as you can see in Figure 11.20. However, when you create a layer mask using the same selection, the pixels in the layer mask are masked from the layer and from the image view, as shown in Figure 11.20.

FIGURE 11.20

When you add a layer mask to a document, the representation of the pixels in the layer is altered, but when you add an alpha channel to a document, the pixels in the other channels are not altered.

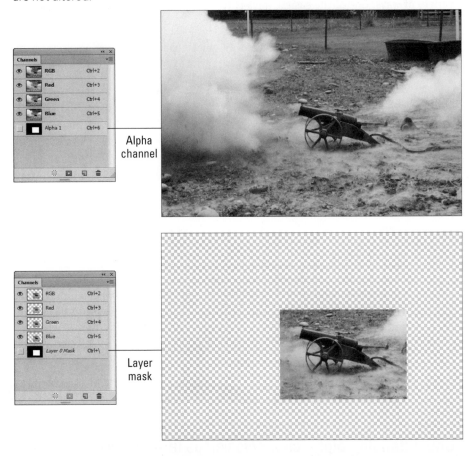

NOTE

When you save a file in a format that supports the alpha channel, the alpha channel data is stored as a separate channel and does not affect the pixel values in the rest of the channels. When you save a file with layer masks, the layer mask is flattened and the pixels in the channels of the image are altered.

Changing the channel options for alpha channels

You can change what the data contained in the alpha channel means by setting the channel options. You can name the channel, specify the display color and opacity, as well as what the color indicates.

The channel options are set by selecting Channel Options from the Channels panel menu to display the Channel Options dialog box, shown in Figure 11.21. From the Channel Options dialog box, you can set the following channel options:

- **Name.** This allows you to select a name that appears in the Channels panel for this channel. It's useful if you are working with several alpha channels.

- **Masked Areas.** When you select this option, the masked areas are highlighted by the overlay color selected in the Color field. This helps when determining the nature of the selection. Use this option when you want to see the actual pixels of the data that is not being affected by the alpha channel.

- **Selected Areas.** When you select this option, the selected areas are highlighted by the overlay color selected in the Color field. Use this option when you want to display a color field over the pixels of the data that is being affected by the alpha channel.

- **Spot Color.** When you select this option, the alpha channel is converted into a spot color channel and the Opacity option changes to a Solidity option. Spot colors are discussed in the next section.

- **Color.** This specifies the color of the channel overlay. The overlay appears in the document window when the alpha channel visibility is on in the Channels panel. This allows you to more easily view the alpha channel selection because either the selection or the mask is overlaid with the specified color. When you click the color, a color chooser window appears, allowing you to specify the color.

- **Opacity.** This specifies the opacity of the overlay channel. Turning up the opacity allows you to better see the pixels behind the overlay. You may need to play around with this setting to see enough of the background image to determine the exact selection.

- **Solidity.** This specifies the Solidity of the spot color channel. Turning up the solidity adjusts how much tint of the spot color is applied to the image or other channels when merged with the spot color channel.

FIGURE 11.21

Setting the alpha channel options allows you to specify the color of the overlay and whether the selection or the mask is overlaid with color when the alpha channel is visible.

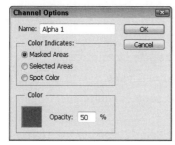

Using Spot Color Channels

Spot colors are used for offset printing. A spot color is simply a single color that is impressed on the paper in a single pass through the printer. Offset printing is the process of printing in multiple passes using one spot color per pass.

You use spot colors when printing images for two main reasons. First, it is much less expensive to use spot colors when printing than mixing the standard CMYK inks to create the colors needed. Second, you may want to add a color to your image that cannot be created using a mix of the CMYK inks.

Creating a spot color channel

The process of creating a spot color channel is similar to that of creating an alpha channel with a few extra steps. The following steps take you through an example of creating a spot channel:

1. **Open the image in Photoshop as shown in Figure 11.22.**

FIGURE 11.22

A selection in an image in Photoshop can be used to create a spot channel.

2. **Use the Magic Wand tool to select the area of the image that you want to turn into a spot channel.** In the case of Figure 11.22, you would want to select the outside of the martial artist.

3. **Press Ctrl+C/⌘+C to copy the contents of the selection into the clipboard.**

4. **Choose Window ⇨ Channels to open the Channels panel.**

5. **Select New Spot Channel from the Channels panel menu to open the New Spot Channel dialog box, as shown in Figure 11.23.**

6. **Click the Color field to open the Select Spot Color dialog box.**

   Choose the color you want to use for the spot color. In this case, Pantone 2717 EC is chosen.

7. **Set the Solidity of the spot color.**

   This example uses 50%.

   FIGURE 11.23

   When creating a spot channel, you need to specify the color and solidity to use for the ink tone.

8. **Click OK to create the spot color channel.**

   The new channel appears in the Channels panel, as shown in Figure 11.24.

   FIGURE 11.24

   The spot channel is created from the selection; however, it is a solid spot channel with no detail.

9. **Select the new spot channel in the Channels panel.**

10. **Click the Load Channel as Selection button in the Channels panel to load the selection used to create the spot channel.**

11. **Press Ctrl+V/⌘+V to paste the contents saved to the clipboard into the spot channel.**

    The spot channel becomes a tonal spot channel, shown in Figure 11.25, instead of a solid. When printed, the spot color selected in Step 6 is used to print the pixels in that area of the image.

FIGURE 11.25

Pasting the contents of the original selection into the spot channel selection creates a tonal spot channel that can print the detail in a single ink color.

Merging spot color channels

The spot channel can be merged into the rest of the image. The solidity value of the spot channel determines how much of the spot channel ink is applied to the pixels in the image. To merge the spot channel with the background data in the image, select Merge Spot Channel from the Channels panel menu.

> **Caution**
>
> Merging the spot channel flattens the spot channel layer into the rest of the image. The spot channel no longer exists, so you cannot get the selection back or alter the color.

Removing ink overlap using spot color channels

When printing spot colors, you need to be careful that ink from the image content does not overlap the ink from the spot colors. Overlapping image content and spot colors results in ink mixing, which typically is not a desired result.

To prevent the colors from overlapping, you need to create *knockout,* a transparent area of artwork revealing the contents from other layers. You can achieve this by setting the background color to white and deleting all pixels in the image content under the spot color so the spot color ink is the only ink printed on that portion of the paper.

Creating a knockout can create another problem. Because there is no ink beneath the knockout, a white border may appear around the spot color if the ink doesn't print perfectly. To solve this problem, you can create a trap between the spot color and the image content, shrinking the selection of the spot color by 1 pixel. This allows each of the spot colors to bleed into the image content a bit and eliminate the white border.

Even a photo that looks as if it's beyond saving can be fixed quickly by using the White Balance tool in Camera Raw. With a single click, this photo changed from an image with a horrible colorcast to an image where the colors were true.

Usually it is very difficult to get a single exposure of a sunset photo to have the range of color that can be seen by the human eye. Either the sky is washed out, as seen in the before image in this example, or the foreground is too dark to make out much detail. Using the Shadow and Highlight sliders in Camera Raw helped to create a more balanced exposure and adding Vibrance and Clarity brought out the amazing colors found in southern Utah's Zion National Park. Camera Raw adjustments are covered in Chapters 7 and 8.

High Dynamic Range (HDR) images are created using a bracketed set of photos containing under and over-exposed shots. Using the Merge to HDR Pro utility (discussed in Chapter 13), you can import a set of bracketed images into Photoshop. The Merge to HDR Pro utility provides powerful tools that can give you amazing results as you bring your photos to life with a full range of colors.

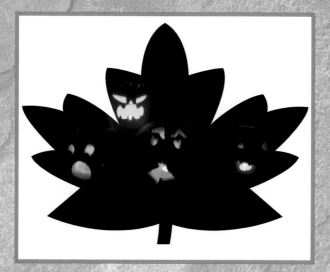

Using a clipping mask, we created a fun Halloween image using a photo of jack-o'-lanterns and a leaf shape. Learn how to use a clipping mask in Chapter 10.

Adding a color fill layer and changing the blending mode to color, we created a colorized version of this nostalgic photo. Fill and adjustment layers as well as blending modes are covered in Chapter 10.

Creating composites involves more than just adding layers on top of one another. Reducing the opacity of the layer containing the tropical fish adds the color and texture of the river to the fish, making it blend in much better with the photo. You can see this effect demonstrated in Chapter 21.

Layers, selections, and masks were instrumental in creating this image. Creating a selection around the building in the foreground and then creating a mask placed the boy behind the building and in front of the rest of the city. The Clone Stamp tool was used to place a building in his hand. You can create this composite for yourself using the steps in Chapter 21.

The Curves Adjustment tool (see Chapter 13) is a powerful feature that provides the ability to restore colors lost through age, poor exposure, and poor lighting. This figure shows how adjusting the color curves for the red, green, and blue channels can restore the color to a washed-out photo.

An Exposure adjustment (see Chapter 13) allows you to simulate an increase or reduction in the exposure of a photo after it has already been taken. In this image, adjusting the exposure settings allowed us to create a great exposure effect that accentuated the highlights in the sun's rays and water.

Using a Hue/Saturation adjustment on the background image of the flowers made the flowers match the model so that this image didn't clash. The resulting photo is well composed and pleasing to the eye. You can learn how to create hue and saturation adjustments in Chapter 13.

Using the Magic Wand tool to select the orange elements and mask them before applying a Black and White adjustment to this photo created a stunning selective color effect.

Using the Smart Sharpen tool gives you an incredible amount of control when sharpening images. In this image, we were able to not only control the sharpening amount and radius, but also fine-tune the amount of sharpening applied to the shadows and highlights.

The Photoshop Blur Gallery allows you to create some stunning visual effects. In this image, we used the Iris Blur tool to blur the area around the hummingbird. Then we applied a Bokeh enhancement to generate the highlighting effect in the background.

Using the Healing Brush and Clone Stamp tools, we were able to remove the distracting elements from in front of this turkey. These tools are covered in Chapter 15.

The Clone Stamp tool can be used on video files, such as this 3D video file. In order to change the image in the photo frame, we resized and rotated the image using the Clone Source panel. It was simple to change the image in each frame of the video by using the Timeline panel to move one frame at a time and change the rotation of the image each time, cloning it in to each frame.

Although perfect results are rare when using the Remix tool, it can aid you in making changes to the composition of an image, as shown in this photo. With a few more adjustments, you would never know that the boy was not originally placed there.

The Clone Stamp tool can be used for special effects as well as fixing images. This composite was created in part by using the Clone Stamp tool to create a profusion of flowers around the fairy.

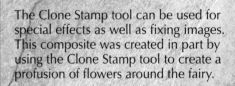

The Content-Aware feature in Photoshop allows you to quickly remove unwanted elements from a photograph. In this example, we used the Spot Healing brush (see Chapter 15) to remove some unwanted tourists from a photograph of Delicate Arch.

In this image, we used a series of paths (see Chapter 17) to create a yin yang image then applied it as a vector mask to a photograph. This image incorporates textual elements (see Chapter 18) in English and Chinese. In all, we used eight separate layers (see Chapter 10) to create the final results.

This figure takes a simple piece of text and uses some special effects to add a visual element to the word in order to accentuate the meaning of "speed." To create the effect, we duplicated the text layer (see Chapter 18), and then we applied a wind filter (see Chapter 20), followed by a series of hue and saturation changes to generate the yellow and red tones. Then we applied a layer style to the top layer to make the word pop out of the image.

This figure shows some of the painting capabilities of Photoshop. By using several different layers, you can easily construct a painting without the risk of ruining your previous work. We created the sky layer by adding a gradient fill. We then added the ground by painting an earth tone. We generated the grass by using the Grass Brush tool with a scattering effect. We added the clouds on a separate layer using a soft brush tip and a blending effect. We painted the bison using the new Mixer Brush tool. These painting techniques are all discussed in Chapter 16.

Ice

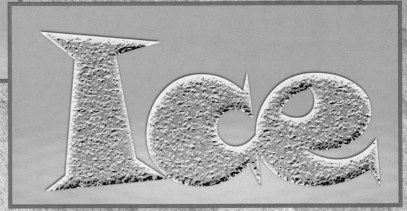

This example shows a simple effect that can easily be added to a block of text to create an icy appearance. The effect was generated by adding a layer style (see Chapter 10) to a text layer and applying a bevel, inner glow, and drop shadow.

Chrome

Chrome

Chrome

In this image, we created a rectangle (see Chapter 17) and then applied a gradient and pattern fill (see Chapter 16). Then we added a textual element (see Chapter 18) and applied a layer style to both the rectangle and text to create a chrome appearance similar to what you would see on older cars.

REFLECT

REFLECT

In this image, we added a textual element (see Chapter 18) and applied a layer style (see Chapter 10) to give it a nice look. Then we duplicated the layer and flipped it vertically. We converted the new layer to a smart object (see Chapter 10) and applied a perspective transformation to it (see Chapter 19) to generate the reflection. The final touch was to add a gradient mask so that the reflection dissipated as it moved away from the original text.

The Content-Aware Scale feature can completely change the composition of an image. You can see that the entire palace is present in both images, but its shape has significantly changed. You can learn how to use the Content-Aware Scale feature in Chapter 19.

Using the Puppet Warp transformation is like turning your image into clay; suddenly you can bend and manipulate a layer to reposition and reshape it. We used the Puppet Warp tool on this spider to create the illusion of movement. You can learn about the Puppet Warp tool in Chapter 19.

The skew and warp transformations were an integral part of creating the effect that you see in this image where the lower part of the model has been placed along a different plane than the upper part of the model. You can learn more about the transformation tools in Chapter 19.

Chrome

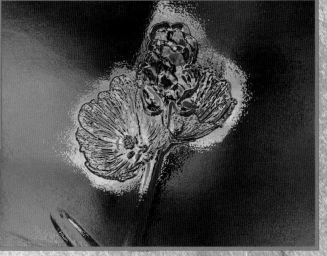

With filters, you can create many different effects, some to correct, some to change the lighting, and some to add an artistic flair to your images. These are just a few examples of the many things you can do.

Stained Glass

Watercolor

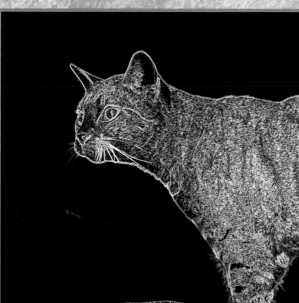

Glowing Edges

Oil Paint

Although this is obviously not a real image, creating a drop shadow and then separating it from the elephant allowed us to distort it to look like a real shadow, thus increasing the realism.

Using layer styles along with this 3D animation of a ball bouncing around a lighted lamp allowed us to simulate the lamp being broken. You can learn how to create layer styles such as drop shadows and separate them into their own layers in Chapter 10.

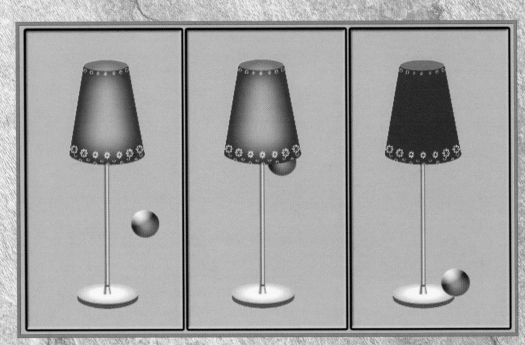

11

> **NOTE**
>
> Trapping is a prepress technique that involves creating small overlaps between adjacent colors in an image. Trapping allows the colors to bleed together to avoid white outlines that can occur because of misalignment when printing.

Follow these steps to create a knockout and trap to prevent spot colors from overlapping:

1. **Create the spot channel as described earlier in this chapter.**
2. **Select a spot channel in the Channels panel.**
3. **Click the Load Channel as Selection button to create the selection of the channel.**
4. **Click the composite channel for the image in the Channels panel.**

   The selection is now visible in the composite channel of the image.

5. **Set the background color to white.**

   White means that no ink will be printed on that portion of the paper.

6. **Create the trap by choosing Select ➪ Modify ➪ Contract to open the Contract Selection dialog box.**
7. **Set the Contract By option to 1 pixel.**

   This allows the spot channel to overlap onto the image content so the inks overlap, eliminating the possible white border between the two.

8. **Create the knockout by pressing the Delete key to delete the image content beneath the spot color.**

   If the Fill dialog box appears instead of just deleting the pixels, select white and click OK.

Summary

This chapter discussed using the Channel Mixer to have direct access to mixing, swapping, and combining the color data in your images. Using the Channel Mixer allows you to change the color composition without changing the original detail in the image.

This chapter also discussed how to use the Channels panel to view and manage channels including alpha channels and spot color channels. Alpha channels are not color channels; instead, they contain information such as transparency about certain areas of an image. Spot colors are used when printing specific colors in passes rather than a mix using the standard CMYK inks.

In this chapter, you learned the following:

- How to mix the color channels to create a better grayscale conversion
- That swapping two color channels can drastically change the look of an image without affecting the detail
- That you can split channels into multiple monotone documents, edit them, and then merge them back into a single color image
- How to share channels between multiple images
- That alpha channels can be created from a selection
- How to use alpha channels to store and retrieve selection data
- How to effectively create spot color channels that can be used in offset printing

Part IV

Enhancing, Correcting, and Retouching Images

IN THIS PART

Optimizing Adjustment Workflow

IN THIS CHAPTER

Optimizing adjustment workflow

Making quick-fixes with auto adjustments

Creating non-destructive and easy-to-edit adjustment layers

Using the Properties panel to make adjustments

E very edit you make to your photo alters the pixels, reducing the quality and increasing the possibility of *bruising* — visible areas of pixel distortion. Even if you make your edits using non-destructive layers, the visible end result is the same. Some adjustments are more destructive than others are, so creating a workflow that takes you from the least destructive to the most destructive is a very important step in achieving the best results possible.

As you add adjustments to your image, the fastest and most efficient way to do so is by using the Fill and Adjustment menu on the Layers panel. This creates a new layer for each adjustment, making them non-destructive. After you have created an adjustment layer, you can modify it by using the Properties panel.

This chapter explains the importance of workflow and introduces you to the adjustment layers and the Properties panel.

Understanding Workflow

Using an organized workflow to edit your images is the best way to make non-destructive edits. It is a good organizational habit to get into, so you aren't inadvertently skipping important steps when correcting your photos.

Not all images need the same amount of editing, but you'll want to follow the same order for each one, skipping steps when they aren't required. Here's a good workflow to follow:

1. **Correct your photos in Camera Raw.**

   Whether your photos are RAW images, TIFFs, or JPEGs, you can open them in Camera Raw, make relatively quick, non-destructive changes to them, and then save them or open them in Photoshop. Follow the same workflow in Camera Raw as in Photoshop to create your edits.

   > **NOTE**
   > If you open a JPEG in Camera Raw and make changes to it, you must save it as a TIFF, PSD, or DNG file to preserve the metadata and keep the edits non-destructive. After you save your changes to a JPEG file, they become part of the image and you cannot reverse them.

2. **Open your image in Photoshop.**

   Whether you are coming from Bridge, Camera Raw, or another program, the following steps require you to edit your image in Photoshop.

3. **Crop, straighten, and resize your photo.**

   Unless you want several different aspect ratios (such as 4x6 and 8x10), you should crop your photo strictly to the area you want.

4. **Correct overall lighting.**

   Correcting the lighting in your image is usually instrumental in correcting the color, so you should always do this first.

5. **Correct the overall color.**

   If you correct the lighting and there is still a colorcast to your image, now is the time to correct it. This is also the time to make overall color changes, such as transforming your photo to black and white or adding a lens filter to warm or cool your photo. After you've corrected both lighting and color in your image, it should look pretty good, with lighting and color at the best settings and evenly distributed across your image. Now you are ready to make targeted adjustments.

6. **Clean the unwanted elements out of your photo using the Clone Stamp and Healing Brushes.**

   While your lighting and color are still uniform, you want to clean up scratches, lens spots, blemishes, or stray elements in your photo that distract from the subject. These tools in Photoshop are fantastic and create realistic results, although they can still cause visible areas of pixel distortion.

7. **Combine images.**

   If you are combining two or more images to create a collage or special effect, now is the time to do it. If you are using the Clone Stamp tool to create head swaps or otherwise add elements from one photo to another, you want to make sure the lighting and color are as uniform between the two images as possible before you begin. This makes the next step much easier.

8. **Make targeted lighting adjustments.**

   When your image is uniformly correct, you can start correcting areas in the image that are still not ideal, such as an overexposed sky. You can make these adjustments by creating a selection or mask so the adjustments are applied only to the targeted area. This is where you need to be careful with how the adjustments are applied by watching edges for halos, hardness, or aberrations that prevent your changes from looking natural.

9. **Make targeted color adjustments.**

   As with lighting, some areas of your image may need a targeted color correction. You may also want to create a color effect, such as oversaturating areas of your photo or creating a black-and-white photo with color accents.

10. **Add filters or layer styles to create artistic effects.**

    Now that your image is put together and the lighting and color are just right, you can add layer styles and filters to create amazing images to your heart's content. You can add these effects to your entire image or to targeted areas. These changes dramatically alter the pixels in an image or selected areas, so again watch your edges.

11. **Reduce noise and sharpen your image.**

    Because each previous change can create noise and distort sharpness to further decrease image quality, these changes should be the last you make.

12. **Prepare your image for output.**

    Whether you are preparing your image to be printed or exported to the web, you want to adjust your color settings accordingly and save it in the correct format.

Making Auto Adjustments

Before you start making your own adjustments, you should know that Photoshop could make several adjustments for you. These adjustments are great for quick fixes on photos that you don't want to spend a lot of time on. If you are new to Photoshop, they are a great way to get started on your own adjustments. Three auto adjustments are available in the Image menu: Auto Tone, Auto Contrast, and Auto Color. Auto buttons are also available in the Levels, Curves, and Black and White dialog boxes.

An *auto adjustment* is an algorithm that uses the brightness values in an image to take a best guess at the adjustment you are applying. Although auto adjustments are frequently better than the original image, they are rarely the best possible settings to use.

You can customize the way that the auto color corrections are applied to your image for the best results. Choose Image ⇨ Levels or Curves. In either of these dialog boxes, click the Options button. This opens the Auto Color Correction Options dialog box, as shown in Figure 12.1.

FIGURE 12.1

The Auto Color Correction Options dialog box

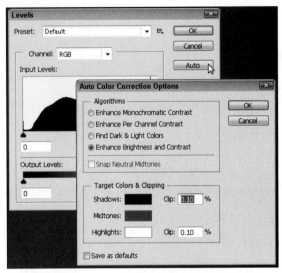

Photoshop can use four algorithms when making auto adjustments. The Levels and Curves adjustment can use any one of the four, and you specify which one in this dialog box. You can choose from the following options:

- **Enhance Monochromatic Contrast.** This is the algorithm used to set the Auto Contrast. It enhances shadows and highlights by increasing the contrast in the midtones of an image, clipping the color channels uniformly. This preserves the color integrity, but although it doesn't introduce a colorcast, it doesn't remove one either; an important element of both the Levels and Curves adjustments.

- **Enhance Per Channel Contrast.** This algorithm is used by the Auto Tone adjustment. It finds the lightest and darkest areas of each color channel and adjusts them individually to create the most contrast of the three algorithms. Although this adjustment may introduce colorcasts or even fringing, this is a good setting in most cases for Levels or Curves because it adjusts the lighting balance of each color channel.

- **Find Dark & Light Colors.** This algorithm is used by the Auto Color adjustment that uses an average of the darkest and lightest pixels in your image to create contrast with the least amount of clipping. The Auto Color adjustment uses the Snap Neutral Midtones option to find colors that are close to neutral, and changes their values so they are indeed neutral, shifting the values in the entire image to match.

- **Enhance Brightness and Contrast.** New in CS6, this option is also the new default setting. This auto adjustment searches a database for a curve that will create the optimal brightness and contrast across all channels — a definite improvement to the Levels and Curves auto adjustments.

12

NOTE

A neutral color is easy to find or create with RGB values; each of the three values is identical.

You can also set the target colors that determine what colors are considered highlights, mid-tones, and shadows. The defaults here of .1 percent are on the high side if you are working with images that have been scanned or taken at high resolution with modern equipment. As a result, you might want to change these settings to a lower number if you are working primarily with these types of images and want to use the Auto adjustments; .05 percent or even lower will give you less dramatic results.

The bottom line is that you can use the Auto adjustments for a quick fix that might actually work if you take the time to figure out which setting is best with each individual image. Does this sound like too much work for something that was supposed to be easy? We think so, too. Stick to custom adjustments; you'll have less to remember, and your images will look better in the long run.

 There are ways to create "custom" Auto adjustments from the Curves and Levels adjustment panels as well. You can read more about this in Chapter 13.

Creating Adjustment Layers

In addition to using the menu to add an adjustment to your project, you can create adjustment layers that are non-destructive and easy to edit. These adjustments appear as separate layers in the Layers panel and you can adjust them easily using the Properties panel.

To create a new adjustment layer, click the Create new fill or adjustment layer icon at the bottom of the Layers panel to open the fill or adjustment layer popup menu, as shown in Figure 12.2.

Here is a quick list of the adjustment layers that are available to you:

- **Brightness/Contrast.** This option gives you two basic sliders. The first slider adjusts the brightness of the image, unilaterally enhancing or reducing the brightness of the pixels. The second slider adjusts the contrast, changing the value of the midtones in the image by making the tones on the dark side 50-percent darker and the tones on the light side lighter.

- **Levels.** You can adjust the levels of the brightness values in your file by adding a Levels layer to it. As you choose the Levels option, you see a histogram that represents the brightness values found in your file. By adjusting the sliders, you can increase (or decrease) the darkness of your darkest pixels or increase (or decrease) the brightness of your brightest pixels. You can do this in all the color channels together or in each one individually.

- **Curves.** The Curves option allows you to add up to 14 points along the tonal range from shadows to highlights. The dialog box also includes a preset menu to give you a jumping-off point.

- **Exposure.** The Exposure option is meant to correct exposure problems in your image. Change the Exposure, Offset, and Gamma Correction to give your file highlights or dark tones similar to overexposing or underexposing a picture.

- **Vibrance.** This option works selectively to saturate areas of your image that have less color while leaving already saturated areas alone.

- **Hue/Saturation.** This option allows you to change the hue, saturation, or lightness of the different color channels contained in your file or all of them at once. You can use a drop-down menu to choose a color range or use the eyedropper to customize the color you change.

- **Color Balance.** The Color Balance panel gets right to the point. You can change the levels of the color channels in your file using the Highlights, Midtones, or Shadows. This is the easiest way to affect individual colors directly in your file.

- **Black & White.** This option gives you the most power in creating a black-and-white image from a color photo. The Black & White adjustment includes options that let you set the levels of the colors in your image so that they are mapped to the grayscale values that you choose.

- **Photo Filter.** Using a Photo Filter on your image mimics using the same filter on your camera. You can use one of 20 preset filters or change the color of the filter using the Select Filter Color dialog box.

- **Channel Mixer.** The Channel Mixer lets you adjust the color levels in each channel separately. A drop-down menu gives you several preset options. Learn more about the Channel Mixer in Chapter 11.

- **Color Lookup.** The Color Lookup option allows you to create a selection, turn it into a mask, and modify that mask in different ways by changing the transparency, feathering the edges, or creating a color range selection.

- **Invert.** The Invert option changes all the colors in your file to their exact opposite, creating a negative image. The Invert adjustment doesn't have any panel controls; it simply changes every color to 255 minus its original value.

- **Posterize.** Using the Posterize option on your image allows you to change the color brightness range from 2 to the full 255. When you set the levels at a low range, you reduce the number of colors used in the image, giving the colors a banded look.

- **Threshold.** Using the Threshold option changes your file into a true black-and-white image — not grayscale. The dialog box contains a slider that allows you to set the Threshold level. Every color above that brightness level is changed to white, and every color below that level becomes black. Although it doesn't make your image look very good, it is ideal for finding the brightest and darkest values of your image. This helps you choose settings for many of the other adjustments.

- **Gradient Map.** A Gradient Map takes a gradient and uses the lowest tones of the gradient to replace the darkest tones of your file and the highest tones to replace the lightest tones and the mid-tones of the gradient to replace everything in between.

- **Selective Color.** This option allows you to change the level of colors individually. Choose from nine color options in the drop-down menu, and change the CMYK sliders to adjust that color.

FIGURE 12.2

Creating an adjustment layer

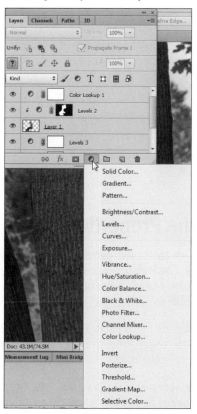

When you click any one of these Adjustment menu options, an adjustment layer is created above the selected layer in your Layers panel, and the Properties panel changes to display the settings for that adjustment, as shown in Figure 12.3. To edit any one of your adjustment layers, select it in the Layers panel and the settings reappear in the Properties panel, allowing you to adjust them.

FIGURE 12.3

Choosing Levels from the fill and adjustment layer popup menu creates a Levels adjustment layer and opens the Levels settings in the Properties panel.

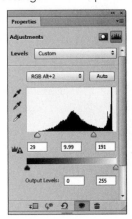

Making Adjustments Using the Properties Panel

By default, the Properties panel is docked just above the Layers panel in the Photoshop workspace. When you select a layer in the Layers panel, the Properties panel changes to reflect the properties of that layer. For example, when you have a Levels adjustment layer selected, the Properties panel displays the Levels adjustment options.

When an adjustment is displayed in the Properties panel, new icons appear on the bottom of the panel, as shown in Figure 12.4. You can reset the adjustment to the default settings, toggle the visibility, or return the adjustment to the previous state.

You can also choose to clip the adjustment to the layer below it. Generally, when you add a layer to the Layers panel, it affects all the layers below it, but if you want your adjustment to affect only one layer below, you can click the Clip adjustment to next layer icon. You know that your adjustment layers are clipped to the layer below them because they look like the layers in Figure 12.5, with an arrow added to the adjustment layer pointing to the layer below. The layer that is being affected by the adjustment has an underlined name.

FIGURE 12.4

New icons appear in the Properties panel when an adjustment layer is highlighted.

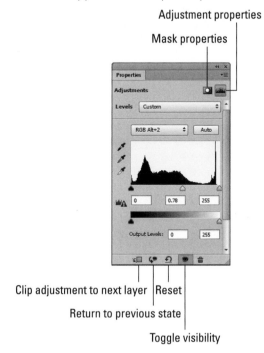

FIGURE 12.5

An adjustment layer that has been clipped to the layer below it does not affect any other layer.

Summary

This chapter introduced you to the workflow you should use when applying adjustments, corrections, and artistic effects to your images. It also introduced you to the auto adjustments and changing adjustments in the Properties panel, so you will know how these elements work as you use them in the following chapters.

In this chapter, you learned about:

- Workflow organization
- Making auto adjustments
- Using the Properties panel

Lighting and Color Adjustments

IN THIS CHAPTER

Adjusting lighting and exposure

Changing color balance

Adjusting levels in images to restore detail

Using the Curves tool

Making specific color and tone adjustments to images

Creating HDR images

The most common edit that you will perform on photos is correcting the lighting and color. Photoshop provides a number of tools that adjust the color and lighting in different ways. As you become more familiar with these tools, you can adjust problems in images such as overexposure, underexposure, and colorcasts. You can also make minute adjustments to images that make a big difference in their overall appearance.

This chapter discusses most of the tools available in the Image ⇨ Adjustments menu and the Adjustments panel. Many of these tools have overlapping functionality, so you are not locked into one specific tool to adjust an image. Try all the tools we discuss in this chapter, and then use the tools that work best for you.

> **NOTE**
>
> Remember that most of the techniques you learn in this chapter can be applied as an adjustment layer. That means you can use a selection to create the adjustment layer and then apply the color adjustments only to that specific area of the image. This allows you to be much more aggressive with the changes you make because you aren't modifying the rest of the image.

Applying Quick Adjustments to Light and Color

Photoshop provides several tools that allow you to make quick adjustments to the lighting and color in images. In the background, these tools are simply adjusting the level values in the color channels of the image. However, these tools provide a nice interface where you can adjust them in specific ways. We like to think of the adjustment tools as "canned" solutions to simple color and lighting issues.

The following sections discuss using the Photoshop adjustment tools to fix lighting and color problems, and making subtle adjustments that enhance the appearance of photos. These tools work well for most of the problems you will encounter in images. Later in this chapter, we discuss using the Levels and Curves tools to make adjustments that are more complex.

Adjusting brightness and contrast versus exposure

One of the most common problems you may encounter with photos is that they are either too dark or too light due to lighting or exposure problems. Photoshop provides two tools to fix lighting problems quickly in your images: the Brightness/Contrast tool and the Exposure tool.

To understand how these tools work, you must first look at the reason why a photo is too dark or too light. Photos are too dark because not enough light was received by the camera, because either the aperture was too small or the exposure time was too short. The end result is that too many pixels are in the low levels of all color channels, making the image dark with limited details. The opposite is true for photos that are too light.

You can use both the Brightness/Contrast tool and the Exposure tool to correct photos that have been overexposed or underexposed. However, they work a bit differently and produce different results.

The biggest difference between the two tools is that the Brightness/Contrast tool works with the color space that exists in the image and the Exposure tool works with a linear color space called gamma 1.0. Because the Exposure tool is not limited to the current color space, it can make more dramatic lighting corrections. The downside of the Exposure tool is that when working outside the color space in the image, some data loss occurs in the form of more abrupt changes between tones.

> **TIP**
>
> The Exposure tool was designed to be used in HDR images with much greater tonal ranges, even though it does work with 8-bit and 16-bit images. A good rule to follow is to use the Brightness/Contrast tool when working with 8-bit images and the Exposure tool when working with HDR images. Then, if you can't get the lighting correction you need with the Brightness/Contrast tool, you can use the Exposure tool to get a better result.

Using the Brightness/Contrast tool to adjust lighting

The Brightness/Contrast tool allows you to adjust both the brightness and contrast levels in an image. The Brightness/Contrast tool options are as following:

- **Brightness.** Adjusting the Brightness slider to the right increases the level values of all color channels in an image, making the image lighter. Adjusting the slider to the left decreases the level values of all color channels in an image, making the image darker.

- **Contrast.** Adjusting the Contrast slider to the right spreads the level values out, which generates more in the image. Adjusting the slider to the left contracts the level values more tightly, giving less contrast.

Typically, to correct an image that is underexposed, you need to increase the brightness first and then increase the contrast to bring back some of the detail lost by increasing the brightness. To correct an image that is overexposed, you need to decrease the brightness and then increase the contrast to bring back the detail.

Figure 13.1 shows the effects of adjusting the brightness and contrast on a photo that was underexposed. Notice that by increasing the brightness and contrast, you can see more detail in the photo.

ON THE WEB

You can find the image shown in Figure 13.1 on this book's website as Figure 13-1.psd. Open it in Photoshop and try adjusting the brightness and contrast.

Using the Exposure tool to adjust lighting

The Exposure tool allows you to adjust the exposure values of the image, increasing or decreasing the lighting and contrast. The Exposure tool allows you to set the following values:

- **Preset.** This menu allows you to select from a list of predefined Exposure tool settings.

- **Exposure.** This slider adjusts the highlight end of the tonal scale. Adjusting the exposure to the right lightens the lighter pixels. Adjusting the exposure to the left darkens the lighter pixels. This setting has only a minimal effect on the darkest pixels of the image.

- **Offset.** This slider adjusts the darker and middle end of the tonal scale. Adjusting the offset to the right lightens the darker pixels. Adjusting the offset to the left darkens the midtone and darker pixels. This setting has only a minimal effect on the lightest pixels of the image.

- **Gamma Correction.** This slider applies gamma correction to the image. Adjusting the gamma value to the left (between 1 and 0) darkens the image. Adjusting the gamma value to the right (between 1 and 10) lightens the image.

- **Black eyedropper.** When you use the black eyedropper to select a pixel in the image, the Offset value is adjusted by setting the selected pixel to zero.

- **White eyedropper.** When you use the white eyedropper to select a pixel in the image, the Exposure value is adjusted by setting the selected pixel to white. White is 1.0 for HDR images and 0.0 for non-HDR images.

- **Midtone eyedropper.** When you use the midtone eyedropper to select a pixel in the image, the Exposure value is adjusted by setting the selected pixel to midtone gray.

13

FIGURE 13.1

Increasing the brightness and contrast on an underexposed image reveals more of the detail.

Follow these steps to use the Exposure tool to adjust the lighting and contrast of an image in Photoshop:

1. **Choose Window ⇨ Adjustments from the main menu bar to load the Adjustments panel shown in Figure 13.2.**

2. **Click the Exposure button (see to Figure 13.2) to add an Exposure adjustment layer to the image.**

FIGURE 13.2

Click the Exposure button in the Adjustment panel home pane.

The Properties dialog box opens, allowing you to adjust the exposure settings.

3. **Try to use the eyedroppers to set a baseline for setting the exposure.**

   Use the black eyedropper to select an item in the image that should be black, the white eyedropper to select a white pixel, and the midtone eyedropper to select a gray pixel. On many photos, the eyedroppers simply don't work. If they don't work, just move to the next step.

4. **Adjust the Exposure to get the overall light pixels in the image to show as much detail as possible.**

   Don't worry if the image looks a bit faded at this point.

5. **Adjust the Offset, typically in the opposite direction than you adjusted the Exposure, until the image is less faded.**

6. **Adjust the Gamma Correction until the image looks better.**

7. **Tweak the Exposure, Offset, and Gamma Correction settings until you get the best overall lighting and contrast in the image.**

Figure 13.3 shows the effects of adjusting the Exposure, Offset, and Gamma Correction settings on a photo that was severely underexposed. Notice that increasing the Exposure allows you to see more details in the image. However, the image is now a bit grainy because we adjusted the values outside the tonal range of the image.

FIGURE 13.3

Increasing the Exposure and decreasing the Offset on an underexposed image in the Exposure tool interface reveals much more of the detail in the image.

Exposer drop-down menu

White eyedropper

Midtone eyedropper

Black eyedropper

Changing the color balance

The Color Balance adjustment tool allows you to adjust the balance between each color in the color channels with its complementary color. Changing the color balance adjusts the overall hue of the color channel. This allows you to quickly fix a single color that is out of place or adjust all the colors in the image. The Color Balance Properties are as follows:

TIP

The Color Balance tool is extremely useful when you are trying to add color to a black-and-white image. You can select specific areas of the image and adjust the color balance to those areas to create color tones.

- **Tone.** A nice feature of the Color Balance adjustment tool is the ability to specify whether you want to adjust the color balance for the pixels in the highlights, mid-tones, or shadows range. Separating the color balance into tonal ranges allows you to focus on one specific tonal range, fixing the color for that range before moving on.

- **Color sliders.** To adjust the color balance, simply drag the color sliders to the left or right to adjust the balance between each color and its complementary color. Adjusting the balance shifts the hue of the color, for example, from red to cyan or blue to yellow.

- **Preserve Luminosity.** You can specify whether to preserve the luminosity, which typically is the best option. Preserving the luminosity forces the color balance adjustments to change so that the luminosity stays the same. This keeps the color balance adjustments from washing out the image.

The following example demonstrates how to use the Color Balance adjustment tool to fix the colors in an image that has been overloaded with a single tone:

1. **Open the image in Photoshop shown in Figure 13.4.**

    The orange leaves of the background have really added a yellow hue to the entire image, and none of the colors pop.

2. **Choose Window ⇨ Adjustments to load the Adjustments panel shown in Figure 13.5.**

3. **Click the Color Balance button shown in Figure 13.5 to add a Color Balance adjustment layer to the image.**

FIGURE 13.4

This image has such intense orange in the leaves that it dominates the other tones in the image.

FIGURE 13.5

Adding a Color Balance adjustment layer to an image in Photoshop

The Properties dialog box opens, allowing you to adjust the color balance settings.

4. **Select the Highlights tone, adjust the Blue color to the right +10, and then adjust the Red and Green colors to the left −5 to compensate.**

This brings more blue into the lighter pixels.

5. **Select the Shadows tone, adjust the Blue color to the right +20, and then adjust the Red and Green colors to the left –5.**

   This time we don't compensate in the Red and Green channels as much because we want the shadows to pop more with less yellow in them.

6. **Select the Midtones tone, adjust the Blue color to the right +10, and then adjust the Green color to the left –10 to give the midtones a bit less green.**

   The Red color stays the same for the Midtones because we don't want to adjust the skin tone.

7. **View the resulting image shown in Figure 13.6.**

   Notice that the colors have much more depth and the tree and the boy really stand out much better.

FIGURE 13.6

Adjusting the color balance allows other colors to pop out of an image that is over-dominated by a specific tone.

13

ON THE WEB

You can find the image shown in Figure 13.6 on this book's website as Figure 13-6.psd. Open it in Photoshop and see how the adjustment makes the colors pop better.

Making selective color adjustments

One advantage and disadvantage of the Color Balance tool is that it adjusts all the colors for the selected tonal range. This is an advantage when you want to adjust all the pixels in a tonal range uniformly. However, this presents a problem if you want to, say, adjust only the blues in the sky without adjusting the rest of the image.

The Selective Color adjustment tool allows you to adjust only the tones of a specific color instead of a tonal range. This allows you to focus on adjusting the blues or greens or other colors individually using the following options:

- **Colors.** This list allows you to select the red, blue, green, cyan, magenta, yellow, white, black, or neutral color tones to be adjusted. Only the color tones that fall into the selected color are adjusted.

- **Color sliders.** These sliders adjust the percentage of cyan, magenta, yellow, or black used for each color. Drag the slider or type the percentage in the text box.

- **Relative.** This option tells Photoshop to use the amount of cyan, magenta, yellow, or black based on its percentage of the total. For example, if the total of all sliders is only 50 percent and cyan is set to 20 percent, the actual value used for cyan is 40 percent.

- **Absolute.** This option tells Photoshop to use the amount of cyan, magenta, yellow, or black based on its absolute setting regardless of the total. For example, if the total of all sliders is only 50 percent and cyan is set to 20 percent, the actual value used for cyan is only 20 percent.

The following example demonstrates how to use the Selective Color adjustment tool to enhance specific color tones in a photo:

1. **Open the image in Photoshop shown in Figure 13.7.**

   The colors in this photo were really toned down due to the haze and the lack of a good filter on the camera.

2. **Choose Window ⇨ Adjustments to load the Adjustments panel shown in Figure 13.8.**

3. **Click the Selective Color button shown in Figure 13.8 to add a Selective Color adjustment layer to the image.**

   The Properties dialog box opens, allowing you to adjust the individual colors.

4. **Select the Relative option shown in Figure 13.8.**

   This allows you to make changes that are more dramatic to the colors.

5. **Select Reds in the Colors list, and adjust the Cyan slider to the left as much as possible and the Magenta slider to the right +35% to make the red in the rocks come out.**

   Notice that the change doesn't at all affect the colors in the sky.

FIGURE 13.7

The colors in this image are really toned down.

6. **Adjust the Black slider to the right 50% to bring out more detail in the red rocks.**

7. **Select Blues in the Colors list, and adjust the Cyan, Magenta, and Black sliders to the right +100 to give the sky a deep blue.**

   Notice that the change doesn't at all affect the colors in the rocks.

FIGURE 13.8

The Selective Color adjustments in Photoshop

8. **View the resulting image shown in Figure 13.9.**

   Notice that the colors have much more depth. The blues and reds now stand out much more without adding a colorcast to the other tones.

FIGURE 13.9

Adding a Selective Color adjustment layer to the image and adjusting the reds and blues allows you to restore color to a washed-out image.

ON THE WEB

You can find the image shown in Figure 13.9 on this book's website as Figure13-9.psd. Because the book is in black and white, you can't really see the results of the image adjustments in the book. Open the file in Photoshop and see how the Selective Color adjustment restores the reds and blues without affecting the other colors.

Applying Photo Filter to images

Photoshop provides the Photo Filter adjustment tool to simulate using various color lens filters on photos. Photographers use color lens filters to correct lighting problems or to adjust the color temperature of photos. Using color filters can fix photos that otherwise would have a colorcast. Using warming and cooling filters can enhance the tones in a photo.

Using lens filters creates a couple of problems, though. One is that because the light must pass through another medium, there is a reduction in the light reaching the camera. The second problem is that the data in the photo is permanently altered by the adjustment made by the lens filter.

The Photo Filter adjustment tool allows you to make image adjustments that simulate what the image would have looked like if a color filter had been used when the photo was taken. The advantage of using Photoshop to apply the color adjustment is that the original photo data can remain intact in the original layer. You can also tweak the density of the filter adjustments and try several different ones until you get it right. You don't get a second chance using lens filters in the field. To use the Photo Filter adjustment tool, choose Image ⇨ Adjustments ⇨ Photo Filter to open the Photo Filter dialog box shown in Figure 13.10.

FIGURE 13.10

Using the Photo Filter adjustment tool, you can simulate the effect that using a color lens filter would have had when the photo was taken. You can also tweak the density and color of the filter.

13

NOTE

Using the Photo Filter tool gives you many more options and is easier than using actual lens filters. However, there is no real substitute for using the appropriate lens filter on your camera. If you know you really need to use a lens filter to correct a lighting problem and are confident in the results, use an actual filter to get a better effect than Photoshop can provide.

Using the Photo Filter dialog box, you can make the following adjustments:

- **Filter.** This menu allows you to select from the predefined filters, including Warming Filter (85), Warming Filter (LBA), Warming Filter (81), Cooling Filter (80), Cooling Filter (LBB), Cooling Filter (82), Red, Orange, Yellow, Green, Cyan, Blue, Violet, Magenta, Sepia, Deep Red, Deep Blue, Deep Emerald, Deep Yellow, and Underwater.

- **Color.** This option allows you to select a specific color instead of a predefined filter. Clicking the Color box allows you to use a color selector to select any of the colors that Photoshop can produce to use as a color filter.

- **Density.** This slider allows you to set the density of the color filter. A lower density has less effect on the image, but if you use too high a density, you begin to lose detail.

- **Preserve Luminosity.** This option specifies whether to preserve the luminosity, which typically is the best idea. Preserving the luminosity forces the filter adjustments to change such that the luminosity stays the same.

Replacing specific colors

Photoshop allows you to replace an individual color selectively in an image with another color using the Replace Color adjustment tool. This allows you to adjust the tone of a specific color range or even replace it with another set of colors. For example, you can replace a dull blue with a brighter blue or even bright yellow without changing the other colors in the image.

To use the Replace Color adjustment tool, choose Image ⇨ Adjustments ⇨ Replace Color to open the Replace Color dialog box. The Replace Color dialog box, shown in Figure 13.11, allows you to select a specific color and the tones around it and then select a replacement color. The replacement color is applied to the image, replacing the original color tones without affecting any other colors.

The Replace Color adjustment tool allows you to adjust the following settings:

- **Localized Color Clusters.** This option specifies whether to select only color clusters that are contiguous to each other. Using this option makes color selection a bit more accurate when the color is localized to one area of the image. However, if the color is spread throughout the image, do not use this option.

- **Eyedroppers.** This option allows you to select colors from the image. The plus dropper adds to the selection, while the minus dropper removes the color from the selection. The adjusted selection is displayed in the Selection view below the eyedroppers.

- **Color.** This option opens a color chooser dialog box that allows you to choose any available color in Photoshop to replace in the image.

- **Fuzziness.** This slider specifies the range of tones to include in the selection color. Low fuzziness means that only tones close to the selected color are chosen. High fuzziness means that a broader range of tones is included.

- **Selection view.** This shows the selection as white with non-selected areas of the image as black, so you can see what areas of the image will be affected by the color replacement.

- **Selection/Image.** These options allow you to toggle the selection view between the selection and the actual image. This helps you see how the color selection relates to the image.

- **Hue.** This slider adjusts the hue of the color that will replace the existing color in the image.

- **Saturation.** This slider adjusts the saturation of the replacement color. Adjusting the saturation to the right deepens the change; adjusting the saturation to the left tones down the replacement color.

- **Lightness.** This slider adjusts the lightness of the color that will replace the existing color in the image.

- **Result.** This color swatch displays the resulting color from the Hue, Saturation, and Lightness adjustments. You can also click the color swatch to launch a color chooser and use it to specify a color.

FIGURE 13.11

Using the Replace Color adjustment tool, you can replace specific colors in an image.

Selection view

Eyedroppers

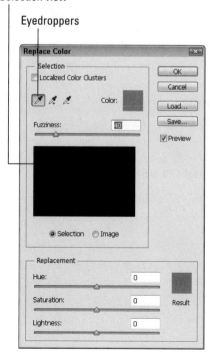

The following steps take you through an example of using the Replace Color adjustment tool to replace the color in an image:

1. **Open the image in Photoshop shown in Figure 13.12.**

FIGURE 13.12

The red color of the rose is about to change in the following steps.

2. **Choose Image ⇨ Adjustment ⇨ Replace Color to load the Replace Color dialog box.**

3. **Use the eyedropper to select a color in the image.**

    In this case, select one of the petals of the rose. Notice how those color tones have been added to the selection view in Figure 13.13, but that much of the rose remains unselected.

4. **Adjust the Fuzziness slider left or right to adjust the selection.**

    In this case, the rose is the only red element in the image, so we adjust the fuzziness all the way to the right and most of the remainder the rose is added to the selection, as shown in Figure 13.13.

5. **Use the plus and minus eyedroppers to fine-tune the selection.**

   In this example, we used the plus eyedropper to add some of the missing parts of the selection while leaving only the darkest and lightest tones in the rose, as shown in Figure 13.13. You may also need to make additional adjustments to the Fuzziness as you adjust with the eyedroppers.

FIGURE 13.13

Using the eyedropper to select a color creates a small selection; increasing the fuzziness increases the selection to include more of the similar tones; finally, using the plus eyedropper, we selected the rest of the rose.

  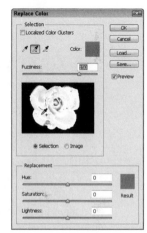

6. **After you have the selection finalized, adjust the hue to the replacement color.**

   You can also click the Color box to open a color chooser to select the color. In this example, we changed the red in the rose to a blue, as shown in Figure 13.14.

7. **Adjust the saturation and lightness to get the best effect in the image.**

   In this example, we increased the saturation by 6 to deepen the blue a bit and then decreased the brightness by 11 to compensate. The results are shown in Figure 13.14, where the rose is now blue, but the green background remains unchanged.

ON THE WEB

You can find the image shown in Figure 13.14 on this book's website as Figure13-14.psd. The adjustment was made to a duplicate layer so you can see both images.

FIGURE 13.14

Adjusting the hue, saturation, and lightness of the selected color changes the rose from red to blue.

Using the Variations tool

The Variations adjustment tool in Photoshop allows you to easily make the most of the general color correction changes that Photoshop has to offer from a single interface. This tool is extremely useful if you are editing images and you're not quite sure what color correction needs to be made.

The biggest strength of the Variations adjustment tool is that you can preview all possible changes as thumbnails in the same view before you make them. You can also adjust only the highlights, midtones, shadows, or saturation and specify the coarseness of the changes.

To use the Variations adjustment tool, choose Image ➪ Adjustment ➪ Variation in Photoshop to open the Variations dialog box, as shown in Figure 13.15. From the Variations dialog box, you can view and make the following adjustments:

- **Original/Current Pick.** This section displays the original and current images side by side so you can always see the differences that the change has made.

- **Shadows.** This option allows you to make adjustments only to the shadows in the image. Using this option allows you to make both color and lighting corrections to the darker areas of the image.

- **Midtones.** This option allows you to make adjustments only to the midtones in the image. Using this option allows you to make both color and lighting corrections to the midtones.

- **Highlights.** This option allows you to make adjustments only to the highlights in the image. Using this option allows you to make both color and lighting corrections to the lighter areas.

- **Saturation.** This option allows you to make adjustments only to the saturation of pixels in the image.

- **Fine/Coarse.** This slider adjusts how coarse the adjustments should be. Adjusting the slider left to Fine makes subtle changes, and adjusting it right to Coarse makes much more dramatic adjustments.

- **Show Clipping.** This option allows you to show the clipping that occurs when you adjust pixels in the images such that their level value goes out of range (below 0 or above 255); the pixel data is lost because the values out of range are clipped back into range.

- **Color adjustments.** This section allows you to add more of any color hue to the image by clicking More color thumbnails (refer to Figure 13.15). This option is available for adjusting the shadows, midtones, or highlights in the image.

NOTE

Adding colors is not an additive, for example, if you click More Yellow twice and then More Cyan twice, the pixels in the Current Pick view return to the original state.

- **Lightness adjustments.** This section allows you to increase or decrease the lightness levels to the shadows, midtones, or highlights in the image.

- **Saturation adjustments.** When you select the Saturation option, you can use these adjustments to add and remove saturation from the image.

13

FIGURE 13.15

Using the Variations adjustment tool, you can quickly see possible color, lighting, and satura- tion adjustments in thumbnails and then apply the changes by clicking the thumbnails.

Changing the shadows and highlights in images

Adjusting shadows and highlights is a great way to correct or enhance photos to give them additional depth and detail. Many lighting and color adjustments tend to focus on the entire tonal range, but adjusting shadows and highlights allows you to add detail that is lost in the upper and lower ranges without affecting the midrange colors that make up most of an image.

Photoshop provides the Shadows/Highlights adjustment tool, so that you can work with only the upper or lower tonal ranges in an image. Using the Shadows/Highlights adjustment tool, you can focus on specific problems where areas of an image are too bright or too dark, causing limited detail. You can also use the Shadows/Highlights adjustment tool to make subtle corrections to images to increase the detail and contrast. To use this tool, choose Image ⇨ Adjustments ⇨ Shadows/Highlights in Photoshop.

Fixing shadows

The Shadows section of the tool allows you to bring back some of the detail that is lost in areas of the image that are too dark due to problems such as backlighting issues. To fix the shadows in an image, use the following adjustments in the Shadows/Highlights adjustment tool:

- **Amount.** This slider specifies how much correction to make to the shadows in the image. By increasing this value, it results in a more dramatic correction. However, if you increase the value too much, the corrected values may cross over and become brighter than the highlights in the image.

- **Tonal Width.** This slider sets the range of tones that are involved in the correction. By increasing this value, it results in more of an effect on the midtones and highlights in the image. By decreasing this value, it results in only the affected shadows. When you are trying to correct only a dark area of the image, you should decrease the tonal width to close to zero.

- **Radius.** This slider specifies how many surrounding pixels to use to determine whether an area falls in the Shadows tonal range. A smaller radius value means that fewer pixels are used and the shadow correction will be more precise. However, if the radius is too small, some areas of the image may not be corrected properly. You need to play around with the radius until the adjustment provides the best outcome.

> **TIP**
> Set the Radius amount to roughly the size of the subjects of interest in the image. This ensures that those subjects are most accurately corrected.

Fixing highlights

The Highlights options of the Shadows/Highlights adjustment tool allow you to focus on areas of the image that are too bright. For example, you can correct overexposed areas in the image due to a flash or direct sunlight. To fix the highlights in an image, use the following adjustments in the Highlights section:

- **Amount.** This slider specifies how much correction to make to the highlights in the image. Increasing this value results in a more dramatic lighting correction. However, if you increase the value too much, the corrected values may cross over and become darker than the shadows in the image.

- **Tonal Width.** This slider sets the range of tones that are involved in the correction. Increasing this value results in a greater effect on the midtones and shadows in the image, while decreasing this value results in only the affected highlights. When you are trying to correct only a dark area of the image, you should decrease the tonal width to close to zero.

- **Radius.** This slider specifies how many surrounding pixels to use to determine whether an area falls in the Highlights tonal range. A smaller radius value means that fewer pixels are used and the highlights correction will be more precise.

Adjusting after shadows or highlights are corrected

After you have adjusted the shadows or highlights, you may need to adjust the color and contrast in the full image to make the image look more natural. To adjust the color and contrast of the image after fixing highlights and shadows, use the following adjustments in the Shadows/Highlights adjustment tool:

- **Color Correction.** This slider adjusts the saturation of the colors in the areas of the image that have been corrected by the shadows and highlights adjustments. This option is available only in color images. Increasing this value adds more color, and decreasing it reduces the amount of color. Typically, you want to add more color to areas of the image that were too dark or too light because those areas tend to have less color detail than the rest of the image and will look a bit odd.

- **Brightness.** Available only for grayscale images, this slider adjusts the brightness of an entire grayscale image. Increasing this value increases the brightness, and decreasing it reduces the brightness.

- **Midtone Contrast.** This slider adjusts the contrast in the midtone pixels of the image. You can use this option to help the midtones match the adjusted shadows and highlights. Increasing this value increases the contrast in the midtone pixels only.

- **Black Clip.** This field specifies how much the shadows are clipped to level 0 when you adjust them. Increasing this value provides greater contrast; however, too much of this value results in loss of detail.

- **White Clip.** This field specifies how much the highlights are clipped to level 255 when you adjust them. Increasing this value provides greater contrast; however, too high a value results in loss of detail.

Figure 13.16 illustrates the effects of using the Shadows/Highlights adjustment tool to correct an image that has been negatively affected by lighting conditions. Notice that the original image has dark and light areas with not much detail because too much light is reflecting off the lake. After adjusting the shadows, highlights, and midtones, the darker areas include more detail and the brightness of the lake is toned down.

13

FIGURE 13.16

Using the Shadows/Highlights adjustment tool, you can quickly adjust problems with areas of an image being too light or too dark.

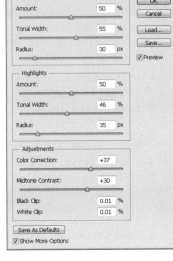

ON THE WEB

You can find the image shown in Figure 13.16 on this book's website as Figure13-16.jpg. Open the file in Photoshop and make the changes shown in this example to restore the detail and tone down the brightness.

Creating customized black-and-white photos

When you convert a color image into a black-and-white photo, you are really combining three channels (red, green, and blue) of data into only one grayscale channel. Although this can be done in any number of ways, we will talk about the three most common methods.

One way to convert a color image to grayscale is to use only one of the three channels, for example, only the red channel. The problem with this method is that it gives you only the red data in the image, leaving out all of the other data. This works well for some effects, but you likely want more detail in your image.

A second way is to use a combination of the three channels. For example, you could create grayscale data by taking 40 percent of the red value, 40 percent of the green value, and 20 percent of the blue value and adding them together to get the value for each grayscale pixel. By using the best combination of the three channels, you can get the most detail from the image. This works very well, as you learned in the Channel Mixer section of Chapter 11. In fact, this is the default method that Photoshop uses to convert color images to grayscale and is generally the recommended method of conversion.

A slightly more complex way to generate the grayscale data from the color channels is to focus on percentages of each color tone. This allows you to maximize the amount of detail, create the best contrast, and optimize the overall appearance of the resulting black-and-white photo. The drawback to this method is that it requires some guesswork and a bit of trial and error to get the best effect.

The Black and White adjustment tool allows you to use combinations of reds, greens, and blues, as well as cyans, magentas, and yellows to generate the grayscale data in the black-and-white image. By specifying percentages of these color tones, you can customize the resulting levels that go into the grayscale channel of the black-and-white photo.

To use the Black and White adjustment tool to create a customized black-and-white photo, choose Image ⇨ Adjustments ⇨ Black & White in Photoshop to open the Black and White dialog box, as shown in Figure 13.17. Then use the adjustment sliders to set the amount of each color to include when creating the grayscale channel.

13

FIGURE 13.17

Using the Black and White adjustment tool, you can create customized black-and-white photos using combinations of the red, yellow, green, cyan, blue, and magenta colors in a color image.

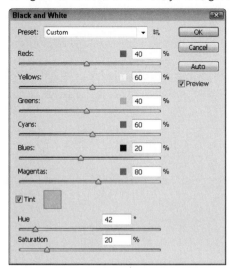

> **TIP**
>
> When you use the Black and White adjustment tool to create black-and-white photos, keep in mind that increasing the percentage of a color lightens those pixels in the resulting image, while decreasing the percentage of a color darkens those pixels. For example, if you wanted to darken the sky in the black-and-white photo, you would decrease the percentage of blue that is included in the resulting image.

> **NOTE**
>
> The percentages of all colors in the adjustment tool do not need to equal 100 percent. In fact, if they do, the image likely will be too dark. Because the cyan, magenta, and yellow channels are combinations of the red, green, and blue channels, and vice versa, there is a lot of overlap. Just keep in mind that as you increase or decrease the total percentage, the overall brightness of the black-and-white photo is also increased or decreased.

A nice feature of the Black and White adjustment tool is the ability to add a tint to the resulting image. This is a great way to create a sepia effect in the image because the tint takes into account the current color values along with the adjusted percentages when creating the overlaying tint.

To add a tint to the resulting black-and-white image, select the Tint option. Then adjust the Hue setting until you have the correct color in the tint, and adjust the Saturation setting to set the appropriate density of the tint. After adjusting the saturation of the tint, you may need to tweak the hue a bit to adjust for the change in tone.

Fine-Tuning Hue and Saturation

Hue and saturation are by far the most important properties that define the color in an image. Hue refers to how the actual color tone of the pixel in the image appears to the eye. Hue is measured in degrees around the color wheel, where 0 degrees and 360 degrees are red, 120 degrees is green, and 240 degrees is blue.

Saturation refers to the difference of the color against its own brightness — in other words, how brilliant the pixel appears to the eye. Low saturation means almost gray, and high saturation is the fully brilliant color.

You adjust the hue and saturation of images for two main reasons. One is to change the color tones that were affected by adverse lighting, such as a yellow cast caused by fluorescent lights. The second reason is to bring back the intensity of colors that is lost due to the use of filters, haze, and limited lighting, as well as other adjustments made in Photoshop. This section discusses using the Hue/Saturation adjustment tool to fix the color tones in images.

Using the Hue/Saturation tool

The most important tool you can use to adjust the color in images is the Hue/Saturation adjustment tool. Changing the hue of an image can drastically alter the overall effect of the image. For example, by changing the hue more towards red warms up the image, and more towards blue cools off the image. Changing the saturation affects the overall brilliance of the colors.

Using the Hue/Saturation adjustment tool, you can change the hue, saturation, and lightness of all colors in the image, or you can adjust specific colors. You can access the Hue/Saturation tool by choosing Image ⇨ Adjustments ⇨ Hue and Saturation or by adding an adjustment layer to the image, as shown in Figure 13.18.

FIGURE 13.18

Using the Hue/Saturation adjustment tool, you can make both specific and general adjustments to the colors in an image.

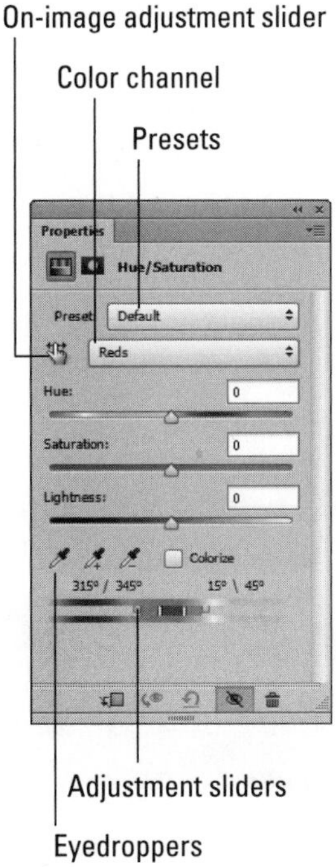

On-image adjustment slider

Color channel

Presets

Adjustment sliders

Eyedroppers

From the Hue/Saturation settings, you can set the following options:

- **Presets.** This list allows you to select one of the predefined Photoshop presets or one of your own saved presets. You can save the settings you make in the Hue/Saturation tool as a preset by selecting Save Hue and Saturation Presets from the Adjustments panel menu. Photoshop provides the following presets to adjust the hue and saturation of your images quickly:

  - **Default.** This option uses the middle values for hue, saturation, and lightness.

  - **Cyanotype.** This option applies a blue monotone effect to the entire image.

  - **Increase Saturation.** This option increases the saturation of all colors by +10, giving a slight saturation boost to make the colors stand out.

  - **Increase Saturation More.** This option increases the saturation of all colors by +30, giving a larger saturation boost to make the colors stand out more.

  - **Old Style.** This option decreases the saturation by −40 to reduce the amount of color in the image. Lightness is also increased by +5 to compensate for the lost color.

  - **Red Boost.** This option decreases the hue by −5 and increases the saturation by +20 to make the reds pop more.

  - **Sepia.** This option makes the image a monotone by selecting Colorize and adjusting the hue to red and the saturation down to only 25 to give the image a sepia look.

  - **Strong Saturation.** This option increases the saturation of all colors by +50 to make the colors really stand out.

  - **Yellow Boost.** This option increases the hue by +5 and increases the saturation by +20 to make the yellow colors pop a bit.

  - **Custom.** This option allows you to make your own changes to the hue, saturation, and lightness in the image.

  - **Color channel.** This option allows you to select the master color channel to change all colors or select the red, yellow, green, cyan, blue, or magenta color tones.

> **NOTE**
>
> If you move the adjustment color outside of the tonal range of a color into another color's tonal range, the color channel name changes to the new color tone. For example, if you select the red color channel and adjust it to green, the Adjustment color list displays Green 2 instead of Red for the color channel.

- **Hue.** This slider adjusts the hue of the selected color channel based on the location of the slider or the value in the text box.

- **Saturation.** This slider adjusts the saturation of the selected color channel based on the location of the slider or the value in the text box. Increasing the saturation makes the colors brighter, and decreasing the saturation dims the colors toward gray.

- **Lightness.** This slider adjusts the lightness of the selected color channel based on the location of the slider or the value in the text box.

- **On-image adjustment tool.** This tool is a great way to adjust the hue or saturation of a specific color in the image. When you select the On-image adjustment tool option, the mouse cursor changes to an eyedropper. Simply select the color you want to change in the image, and drag the mouse to adjust the saturation. The color channel changes to match the color of the selected pixel. As you drag the mouse to the left, the saturation decreases, and as you drag the mouse to the right, the saturation increases. To adjust the hue, press and hold the Ctrl/⌘ key when you select and drag the image. The color channel changes to match the color of the selected pixel. As you drag the mouse to the left, the hue moves toward the yellow side of red, and as you drag the mouse to the right, the hue moves toward the magenta side of red.

- **Eyedroppers.** The eyedroppers allow you to define the hue of color channels by clicking specific pixels in the image. This allows you to use real pixels in the image to define colors. The eyedroppers are not available when the Master color channel is selected. The regular eyedropper sets the middle of the color channel to the value of the pixel selected in the image. When you use the plus eyedropper, the color of the selected pixel is added to the color channel, increasing the tonal range. When you use the minus eyedropper, the color of the selected pixel is removed from the color channel, decreasing the tonal range.

- **Colorize.** This option is used either to add color to a grayscale image or to create a monotone image from a color image. The color channels are flattened, and the hue, saturation, and lightness values apply to the entire image. The only color in the image is the color range of the current hue value.

- **Adjustment sliders.** The Adjustment sliders are the most powerful feature of the Hue/Saturation tool. The Adjustment sliders allow you to specifically define the range of the colors being affected by the hue, saturation, and lighting. You can also define how the color boundaries are feathered out into other colors. You can use the mouse to adjust the sliders in the following areas, as shown in Figure 13.19.

  - **Left Falloff Handle.** This handle adjusts the area of the left falloff used to feather the color correction into other colors. By increasing the falloff area, it results in more feathering of the color changes into the adjacent colors. Adjusting this handle does not affect the hue range at all.

  - **Left Falloff Area.** Moving the left fallout area doesn't affect its size; however, the hue range area is increased or decreased.

  - **Left Range Handle.** Moving this handle adjusts both the hue range area and the left fallout area. As the hue range area increases, the left fallout area decreases, and vice versa.

  - **Hue Range Area.** Moving this area moves the entire set of handles without changing their respective sizes. The hue range area specifies the colors that are directly affected by the hue, saturation, and lightness changes. Increasing the hue range area includes more of the adjacent tones in the correction, just as decreasing the hue range area focuses on a specific color. You may have to vary this setting for specific needs. For example, if you want to correct a specific color, then you need the range to be as small as possible.

13

- **Right Range Handle.** Moving this handle adjusts both the hue range area and the right fallout area. As the hue range increases, the right fallout area decreases, and vice versa.

- **Right Falloff Area.** Moving the right fallout area doesn't affect its size; however, the hue range area is increased or decreased.

- **Right Falloff Handle.** This handle adjusts the area of the right falloff used to feather the color correction into other colors. By increasing the falloff area, it results in more feathering of the color changes into the adjacent colors. Adjusting this handle does not affect the hue range at all.

FIGURE 13.19

Using the Adjustment sliders of the Hue/Saturation adjustment tool, you can specify both the specific color range and the surrounding fallout ranges that are used to feather adjustments.

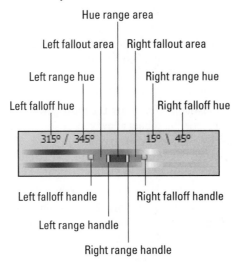

Adjusting the hue and saturation to make colors pop

The biggest strength of the Hue/Saturation adjustment tool is its ability to make hue, saturation, and lighting changes to specific color ranges. This allows you to fix certain colors in an image without affecting other colors.

The following example demonstrates how to use the Hue/Saturation adjustment tool to enhance the colors in an image:

1. **Open the image in Photoshop shown in Figure 13.20.**

   The colors in this image are really dulled by the haze that was present the day the photo was taken.

FIGURE 13.20

The colors in this image are very dull and a bit washed out by the haze present when the photo was taken.

2. **Choose Window ⇨ Adjustments in Photoshop to open the Adjustments panel shown in Figure 13.21.**

3. **Select the Hue/Saturation adjustment tool, as shown in Figure 13.21, to add a Hue and Saturation adjustment layer to the image and open the Hue/Saturation Properties panel.**

13

FIGURE 13.21

Selecting the Hue/Saturation option from the Adjustments panel in Photoshop adds an adjustment layer to the image and opens the Hue/Saturation Properties panel.

4. **Select the Reds color channel, as shown in Figure 13.22, and increase the saturation of red to +50.**

   This makes the red colors in the leaves pop.

5. **Select the Yellows color channel, and increase the saturation of yellow to +50, as shown in Figure 13.22.**

   This brings out the yellow and orange in the leaves.

6. **Select the Blues color channel, and adjust the range for the blue color adjustment.**

   The blue colors present a problem. We wanted to correct the blue in the sky and the water, but not affect the other colors as much, so we narrowed the range, as shown in Figure 13.22. We also increased the size of the right fallout area to allow the blue changes to feather over a bit into the magentas and reds.

7. **Adjust the saturation and hue.**

   Increase the Saturation to +50 to bring out the blue in the sky and water, and increase the Hue to +25 to create a richer tone of blue in the sky and water.

FIGURE 13.22

Adjusting the saturation of reds and yellows in the image makes the color of the leaves stand out much more. Using the adjustment sliders to change the range of blues allows you to focus on the sky without affecting the other colors.

8. **View the results shown in Figure 13.23.**

FIGURE 13.23

Using the Hue/Saturation tool, we made the red and yellow leaves pop out and changed the color and intensity of the sky and water to give the photo a brilliant color tone.

ON THE WEB

You can find the image shown in Figure 13.23 on this book's website as Figure13-23.psd. Because the book is in black and white, you cannot really see the adjustments in the image. Open the file in Photoshop and make your own changes to the Hue/Saturation adjustment layer to see the effect in action.

Adjusting Levels

The most basic adjustment you can make to the color and lighting in an image is to change the level composition of the color channels. Adjusting the level composition can restore detail to an image and fix a variety of lighting problems.

Photoshop allows the Levels adjustment tool to give you direct access to the levels of the color channels. You can access the Levels adjustment tool by choosing Image ⇨ Adjustments ⇨ Levels or by selecting a Levels adjustment in the Adjustments panel.

This section discusses how to configure and use the auto levels adjustment as well as how to make custom levels adjustments to your images.

 The concept of color channel levels was introduced in Chapter 4. You should read that chapter before reading this section because you need to understand how color channel levels work to get the most out of using the Levels tool.

Using the Levels adjustment tool

The best way to use the Levels adjustment tool is to add a Levels adjustment layer. The Levels adjustment layer allows you to adjust the tonal levels in an image without actually adjusting the background image. Adjusting the levels allows you to brighten and darken tones and colors in the image, restoring detail that might have been lost due to improper lighting or exposure.

To add a Levels adjustment layer to the image, select the Levels icon in the Adjustments panel. This loads the Levels Adjustment Layer options in the Properties panel, shown in Figure 13.24.

FIGURE 13.24

Using the Levels adjustment tool, you can adjust the levels of color channels to change the color composition and bring detail back into an image.

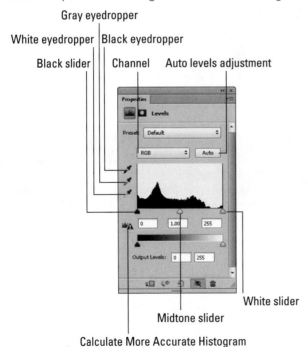

The Levels adjustment tool allows you to adjust the composite channel or any single color channel using the following controls:

- **Preset.** This drop-down list allows you to select a default Photoshop preset or one of your own saved ones. You can save the settings you make in the Levels tool as a preset by selecting Save Levels Preset from the Adjustments panel menu. Photoshop provides the following predefined adjustments to quickly adjust the levels in an image: Default, Darker, Increase the Contrast 1, Increase the Contrast 2, Increase the Contrast 3, Lighten Shadows, Lighter, Midtones Brighter, Midtones Darker, and Custom.

- **Channel.** This drop-down list allows you to select the composite channel or one of the individual color channels. Making levels adjustments to the composite channel changes the entire image. Making changes to an individual color channel allows you to fix level problems associated with a specific color without affecting other colors.

CAUTION

Adjusting the levels of color channels separately changes the color composition in the image. If the general color tones match up well, you should not change the levels of the color channels separately because you may end up with some colors that do not match the rest of the colors in the image.

- **Black slider.** This slider sets the level value in the image that equates to the desired lowest level in the color channel (essentially black). All values lower than the value of the black slider is clipped to 0. Typically, you want to set the black slider to the left edge of the histogram mountain and ignore the few pixels that are scattered to the left.

- **White slider.** This slider sets the level value in the image that equates to the desired highest level in the color channel (essentially white). All values higher than the value of the white slider are clipped to 255. Typically, you want to set the white slider to the right edge of the histogram mountain and ignore the few pixels that are scattered to the right.

TIP

If you press and hold the Alt/Option key while adjusting the Black and White sliders, the areas of the image that are being clipped are displayed in the document window, as shown in Figure 13-25. This is extremely useful for helping you to understand what detail will be lost when the clipping occurs. You can also turn this feature on permanently by selecting Show Clipping for Black/White Points in the Adjustment panel menu.

- **Midtone slider.** The levels of the pixels between the black and white sliders are distributed to fill the entire 0–255 range. The midtone slider sets the balance point used for distributing the pixels. The pixels below the value of the midtone slider are distributed between 0 and 127, and the pixels greater than the value of the midtone slider are distributed between 128 and 255. Typically, you want the pixels to be evenly distributed, so you want to move the midtone slider toward the area of the histogram that has the largest number of pixels.

13

FIGURE 13.25

Pressing and holding down the Alt/Option key while adjusting the Black and White sliders displays the clipping in the document window.

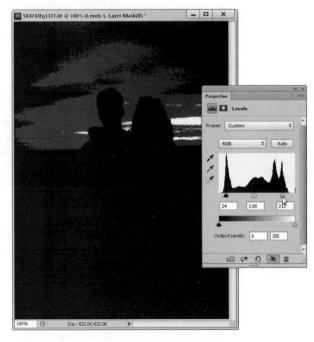

- **Output Levels.** The Output Levels sliders allow you to set the minimum and maximum values for the distribution of levels in the results from the level adjustments. For example, if you set the black slider to 50 and the white slider to 200, the output is distributed between 50 and 200 instead of 0 and 255, which limits the detail by 100 level values. Typically, you want to change this option only if you are planning to combine an image with another image that provides the detail in the omitted level values.

- **Black eyedropper.** This tool allows you to sample the value to be used for black pixels directly from the image. Using the black eyedropper tool sets the value of the black slider to the level of the selected pixel. If you press and hold the Alt/Option key while using the Eyedropper tool, the image document shows the clipped portions of the image, as shown in Figure 13.25.

- **White eyedropper.** This tool allows you to sample the value to be used for white pixels directly from the image. Using the white eyedropper tool sets the value of the white slider to the level of the selected pixel. If you press and hold the Alt/Option key while using the Eyedropper tool, the image document shows the clipped portions of the image, as shown in Figure 13.25.

- **Gray eyedropper.** This tool allows you to sample the value of a gray pixel directly from the image. The value of the gray pixel is used to calculate the balance of the color channels because a gray pixel of any level should have an equal amount of red, green, and blue.

- **Calculate more accurate histogram.** Occasionally Photoshop will detect that a more accurate histogram can be calculated using a computer algorithm. When this occurs, an icon is displayed in the Levels tool (refer to Figure 13.24). When you click this icon, Photoshop calculates a new histogram. There are trade-offs though. To calculate the more accurate histogram, Photoshop has to make assumptions. If those assumptions are wrong, you can lose a slight amount of the detail in the image.

- **Auto.** Clicking the Auto button applies the Auto Levels adjustment to the image. The next section discusses setting the options for the Auto Levels adjustment.

13

> **NOTE**
>
> Photoshop calculates the histogram based on the frequency of levels in the image. However, with some images and layer adjustments, the normal method for calculating histograms can be inaccurate. For those images, Photoshop displays an additional Calculate a more accurate histogram button with a triangle-warning icon that allows you to use a more accurate, if less consistent, method for calculating the histogram. Sometimes this option produces better results, but not always, especially if the histogram is evenly distributed.

Configuring the Auto Levels adjustment

For many images, the Auto Levels adjustment in Photoshop is sufficient to correct problems with levels. To use the Auto Levels adjustment option, you click the Auto button on the Levels adjustment tool. Because adjusting levels is complex, Photoshop allows you to configure the following options by selecting Auto options from the Adjustments panel menu; pressing and holding the Alt/Option key (which changes the Auto button to Options) and then clicking the Options button; or clicking the Auto options button in the Non-layer adjustment tool to display the Auto Color Correction Options dialog box shown in Figure 13.26.

FIGURE 13.26

Using the Auto Color Correction Options dialog box, you can adjust the algorithms and settings that Photoshop uses when performing an Auto Levels adjustment.

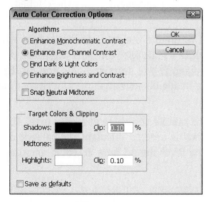

The Auto Color Correction Options dialog box options are as following:

- **Enhance Monochromatic Contrast.** When you select this option, all channels are clipped identically, which preserves the overall color relationship while making highlights appear lighter and shadows appear darker. This option is available by choosing the Image ➪ Auto Contrast command.

- **Enhance Per Channel Contrast.** When you select this option, Photoshop tries to maximize the tonal range in each channel. This results in a much more dramatic correction and provides the greatest amount of detail. However, you run the risk of introducing a colorcast. This option is available by choosing the Image ➪ Auto Tone command.

- **Find Dark & Light Colors.** When you select this option, Photoshop finds the average lightest and darkest pixel in the image and uses those pixels to maximize the contrast while still preserving as much detail through minimal clipping. This option is available by choosing the Image ➪ Auto Color command.

- **Enhance Brightness and Contrast.** When you select this option, Photoshop tries to optimize the color correction based on enhancing the brightness and contrast in the image. This option can have a dramatic impact on photos that have reduced color due to poor lighting conditions.

- **Snap Neutral Midtones.** When you select this option, Photoshop finds the most neutral color in the image and adjusts the midtone values to make that color neutral.

- **Shadows.** This option allows you to set the color used for the darkest shadows when performing the Auto Levels adjustment. You can also specify the amount of clipping that can occur in the shadows during the Auto Levels adjustment.

- **Midtones.** This option allows you to set the color used for the midtone balance when performing the Auto Levels adjustment.

- **Highlights.** This option allows you to set the color used for the lightest highlights when performing the Auto Levels adjustment. You can also specify the amount of clipping that can occur in the highlights during the Auto Levels adjustment.

- **Save as defaults.** When you select this option, the values you specify are used as the defaults when you use the Auto Levels adjustment. These values are preserved even if Photoshop is closed and opened again.

Adjusting levels to increase detail in images

Adjusting the levels in an image can help lighten dark areas, reduce the brightness of highlighted areas, restore detail to images, and remove colorcasts. The following example takes you through the process of using the Levels adjustment tool to adjust the levels in a photo:

1. **Open the image in Photoshop shown in Figure 13.27.**

   The photo is dim due to poor lighting when it was taken.

2. **Choose Window ➪ Adjustments in Photoshop to open the Adjustments panel, shown in Figure 13.28.**

3. **Select the Levels adjustment to add a Levels adjustment layer to the image.**

   The Properties dialog box opens, allowing you to adjust the levels.

13

FIGURE 13.27

The lighting in this image is poor because it was taken so close to sundown, so it's lacking contrast and detail.

FIGURE 13.28

Selecting the Levels tool from the Adjustments panel in Photoshop adds an adjustment layer to the image and launches the Levels adjustment tool.

4. **Select the Red channel, and adjust the black and white sliders.**

   Move the black slider to the left edge of the histogram mountain and the white slider to the right edge of the histogram mountain, as shown in Figure 13.29, to drop the lower levels that are not needed.

5. **Select the Blue channel, and adjust the black and white sliders.**

   Move the black slider to the left edge of the histogram mountain and the white slider to the right edge of the histogram mountain, as shown in Figure 13.29, to drop the lower levels that are not needed.

6. **Select the Green channel, and adjust the black and white sliders.**

   Move the black slider to the left edge of the histogram mountain and the white slider to the right edge of the histogram mountain, as shown in Figure 13.29, to drop the lower levels that are not needed.

7. **Adjust the midtone level.**

   Move the midtone level to 1.17, as shown in Figure 13.29, to get rid of the green cast that exists in the image due to the color of the sky and ocean.

FIGURE 13.29

Adjusting the black and white sliders in each of the color channels drops pixel values that are not really needed and creates room in those levels for additional detail. Adjusting the midtone range of the green channel removes the green colorcast in the image.

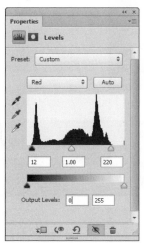
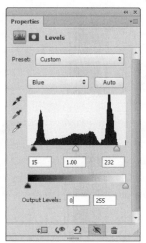
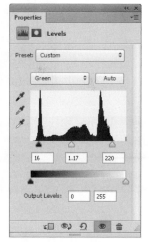

8. **View the results shown in Figure 13.30.**

FIGURE 13.30

Using the Levels adjustment tool restored a lot of the detail and contrast in the image and removed the green colorcast.

ON THE WEB

You can find the image shown in Figure 13.30 on this book's website as Figure 13-30.psd. Check out the file to see the resulting color and lighting changes. You can use the Levels adjustment layer to play around with the level values and see how different settings affect the image.

Making Adjustments with Curves

The most powerful tool Photoshop has for adjusting color and lighting is the Curves adjustment tool. The Curves adjustment tool provides a dynamic and flexible interface that allows you to make dramatic changes to the lighting and color in images. Although it takes a bit of practice and patience to learn the Curves adjustment tool, after you are familiar with it, you can make changes in images that you may not have thought possible.

You can access the Curves adjustment tool by choosing Image ⇨ Adjustments ⇨ Curves or by selecting a Curves adjustment in the Adjustments panel. This section discusses how to configure and use the Curves adjustment tool to make changes to the color, lighting, and contrast in your images, as well as how to configure and use the Auto Curves adjustment.

The concept of using curves to adjust color channel levels was introduced in Chapter 4. You should read that chapter before reading this section because you need to understand how color channels work to get the most out of using the Curves tool.

Using the Curves tool

The Curves tool provides a dynamic way to adjust the tone and color levels in an image. With the Curves tool, you can use the mouse to alter a line graphically that maps the input tones to the output tones. This gives you much more control over the changes to the tonal levels in the image.

The best way to use the Curves tool is to add a Curves layer to the image by selecting the Curves tool in the Adjustments panel. This loads the Curves tool shown in Figure 13.31.

FIGURE 13.31

Using the Curves tool, you can adjust the levels of color channels to change the color composition and bring detail back to an image.

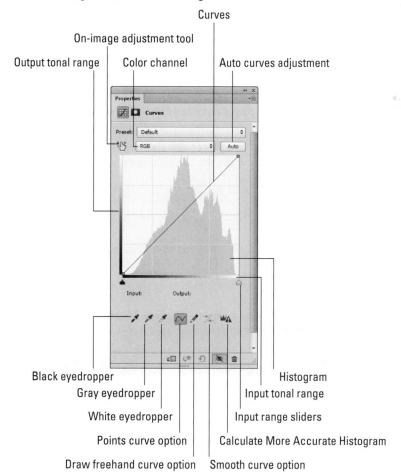

13

The Curves adjustment tool allows you to adjust the composite channel or any single color channel using the following controls:

- **Preset.** This list allows you to select one of the predefined Photoshop presets or one of your own saved presets. You can save the settings you make in the Curves tool as a preset by selecting Save Curves Preset from the Adjustments panel menu. Photoshop provides the following predefined adjustments to adjust the levels of images quickly: Default, Color Negative, Cross Process, Darker, Increase Contrast, Lighter, Linear Contrast, Medium Contrast, Negative, Strong Contrast, and Custom.

- **Color channel.** This list allows you to select the composite channel or one of the individual color channels. Making curves adjustments to the composite channel changes the entire image. Making changes to an individual color channel allows you to fix level problems associated with a specific color without affecting other colors.

CAUTION

Adjusting the curves of color channels separately changes the color composition in the image. If the general color tones match up well, you should not change the levels of the color channels separately because you may end up with a colorcast or some colors that do not match the rest of the colors in the image.

- **Black eyedropper.** This tool allows you to sample the value to be used for black pixels directly from the image. Using the black eyedropper tool sets the value of the black slider to the level of the selected pixel.

- **Gray eyedropper.** This tool allows you to sample the value of a gray pixel directly from the image. The value of the gray pixel is used to calculate the balance of the color channels because a gray pixel of any level should have an equal amount of red, green, and blue.

- **White eyedropper.** This tool allows you to sample the value to be used for white pixels directly from the image. Using the white eyedropper tool sets the value of the white slider to the level of the selected pixel.

- **Auto.** Clicking the Auto button applies the Auto Curves adjustment to the image. You will learn more about setting the options for the Auto Curves adjustment later in this chapter.

- **Output Tonal Range.** This displays the output levels range used by the vertical values of the curve.

- **Input Tonal Range.** This displays the input levels range used by the horizontal values of the curve.

NOTE

The Input and Output Tonal Ranges for CMYK are the opposite of those for RGB — in other words, light to dark instead of dark to light. This is because the CMYK color model is subtractive instead of additive.

- **Input Range sliders.** These sliders allow you to set the minimum and maximum input values for distribution of curves in the results from the curves adjustments. Adjusting the sliders limits the input range of the curve.

- **Points Curve option.** When you select this option, the curve is adjusted using control points. You can add points by clicking the curve. To change the curve, drag one of the points on the curve, as shown in Figure 13.32. You can add as many as 14 points to the curve to make very specific tonal adjustments to the image.

FIGURE 13.32

Using the Points Curve option, you can add points to the histogram curve by clicking the curve, and then adjust the curve by dragging the points.

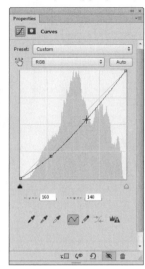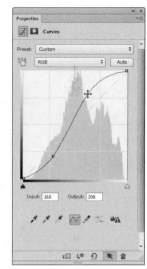

- **On-image adjustment tool.** When you select this option, the mouse cursor changes to an eyedropper. As you move the mouse over the image, a circle icon hovers over the curve at the level value of the pixel under the mouse. When you select a pixel in the image, a point is added to the curve at the level value of the selected pixel. You can then change the Output value of the curve at that point by dragging the mouse up and down. This option is available only when you have selected the Points Curve option.

- **Draw Freehand Curve option.** When you select this option, you can change the curve by drawing freehand on the image (see Figure 13.33). The areas of the curve corresponding to the line drawn by the Freehand tool are removed from the curve line, and the Freehand Output values are used. By drawing freehand, you can more accurately change the Output values of specific Input values. This gives the Curves tool a lot of power, just as the freehand lines in Figure 13.33 specifically alter the output values for the input ranges they are drawn over.

- **Smooth Curve option.** Each time you click the Smooth Curve option, the curve is smoothed a bit until it eventually becomes the original diagonal linear curve. This allows you to reduce the variation between the levels. This option is extremely useful in joining areas of the curve that are not connected after you use the Draw Freehand Curve tool, as shown in Figure 13.34. This option is available only when you have selected the Draw Freehand Curve option.

451

FIGURE 13.33

Using the Draw Freehand Curve option, you can draw directly on the Curves tool to set the Output values for specific Input values.

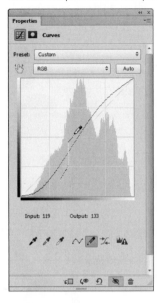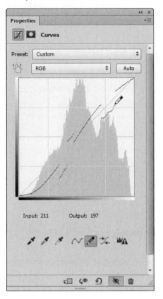

FIGURE 13.34

Using the Smooth Curve option connects areas of the curve that are not connected when you use the Freehand tool. It smoothes the curve out, reducing the variation in Output levels.

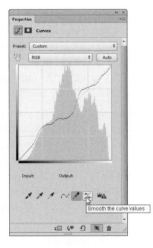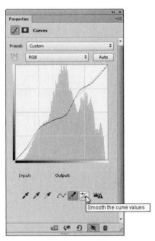

Configuring the Curves tool

A great feature of the Curves tool is its ability to change its look and feel to better fit your editing style or project needs. You can configure several options that change the appearance of the Curves tool, such as grid size and channel overlays.

To configure the display options for the Curves tool, click the Curves Display Options icon at the bottom of the Non-adjustment Layer tool, or in the Adjustments panel menu to launch the Curves Display Options dialog box, as shown in Figure 13.35.

FIGURE 13.35

Adjusting the display options for the Curves adjustment tool in Photoshop

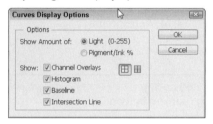

In the Curves Display Options dialog box, you can set the following options:

- **Light.** When you select this option, the histogram shown in the Curves tool is based on the light levels.

- **Pigment/Ink %.** When you select this option, the histogram shown in the Curves tool is based on the actual pigment used to generate the output image.

- **Channel Overlays.** When you select this option, the curves for all individual channels are displayed in their respective colors. This option is very useful if you are making curves adjustments to more than one color channel.

- **Histogram.** When you select this option, the histogram of the selected channel is displayed in the background of the Curves view. You likely want to keep this option selected so you can see the distribution of levels as you adjust the curve.

- **Baseline.** When you select this option, the baseline curve (diagonal line) is displayed so you can gauge the size of the deviation you are making with the Curves adjustment.

- **Intersection Line.** When you select this option, intersecting lines are displayed so you can make adjustments that are more precise.

- **Grid size.** The two grid size buttons allow you to switch between large and small grids. Smaller grids make the view a bit more confusing but allow you to be more precise.

Configuring the Auto Curves tool

For many images, the Auto Curves tool in Photoshop is sufficient to correct the levels problems in your images. To use the Auto Curves tool option, click the Auto button on the Curves tool. The Auto Curves tool uses the same options as the Auto Levels adjustment discussed earlier in this chapter.

Adjusting the curve to correct color and contrast in images

Adjusting the curves in an image can help fix severe contrast problems, restore detail, and remove color problems. The following example takes you through the process of using the Curves tool to adjust the color levels in a photo:

1. **Open the image in Photoshop shown in Figure 13.36.**

   The photo is completely washed out because of overexposure.

FIGURE 13.36

The detail in this image is extremely limited because it was overexposed, and the huge shadow on the rock presents a big problem for contrast.

2. **Choose Window ⇨ Adjustments in Photoshop to open the Adjustments panel shown in Figure 13.37.**
3. **Select the Curves adjustment and then open the Curves tool, as shown in Figure 13.37, to add a Curves adjustment layer to the image.**

FIGURE 13.37

Selecting the Curves tool from the Adjustments panel in Photoshop adds an adjustment layer to the image and launches the Curves tool.

4. **Select the RGB channel, and adjust the sliders.**

   Move the black slider to the left edge of the histogram mountain and the white slider to the right edge of the histogram mountain, as shown in Figure 13.38, to drop the lower level values that are not contributing to the image anyway.

   Notice how the image immediately reveals additional detail.

FIGURE 13.38

Adjusting the white slider to the edge of the histogram immediately gives you additional detail in the image.

5. **Add a point to the curve in the lower levels.**

   Add the point, as described in Chapter 4, and adjust it down slightly to bring back some of the detail in the darker areas of the image.

   Notice that the image darkens slightly, and you actually lose some detail in the upper levels, as shown in Figure 13.39.

FIGURE 13.39

Adding a point to the curve lets you adjust the levels down slightly to retrieve some detail in the lower levels, but you lose detail in the upper levels.

6. **Add another point to the curve in the middle levels.**

   Adjust this point down slightly to get some of the detail back in the midtones.

   This keeps the detail in the lower levels, but it still adds some detail back in the middle levels, as shown in Figure 13.40.

FIGURE 13.40

Adding another point to the curve lets you adjust the middle levels down a bit to gain some detail, but you still lack detail in the upper levels.

7. **Add another point to the curve in the upper levels.**

Adjust this point up slightly to restore some of the detail in the upper levels.

This keeps most of the detail in the lower and middle levels, but it restores some detail in the upper levels, especially in the clouds, as shown in Figure 13.41.

FIGURE 13.41

Adding another point to the curve lets you lower the upper levels slightly to gain some detail in the upper levels without affecting the lower levels.

8. **Adjust the points to achieve the best overall color and lighting in the image.**

Notice that adjusting the three points slightly adds some detail in certain areas, as shown in Figure 13.42. You may need to add more points to fix specific level ranges. The more you play with the points in the curve, the better you'll understand the curve adjustment. You can always remove points from the curve by dragging them out of the curve window.

ON THE WEB

You can find the image shown in Figure 13.42 on this book's website as Figure13-42.psd. Check out the file to see the resulting color and lighting changes. You can use the Curves adjustment layer to play around with the Curves tool and see the effect of adding and adjusting points.

FIGURE 13.42

Adjusting the points adds even more detail to the image.

Using the Match Color Tool to Change Colors

The Match Color tool can use the color composition of one image to adjust the color composition automatically of another image. This helps the images match more closely when placed side by side.

When you need to correct color in several photos from the same shoot, the Match Color tool is your best option (see Figure 13.43). For example, when you are color correcting a set of photos that are slightly washed out from UV interference, you see a large change when you adjust the hue and saturation to bring back the color. As you work with more images, your eyes adjust to the color-corrected images and you tend to overcorrect. The result is that the final images don't match the initial images.

FIGURE 13.43

The Match Color tool provides several options to control how colors are adjusted in a target image by using the colors in a source image.

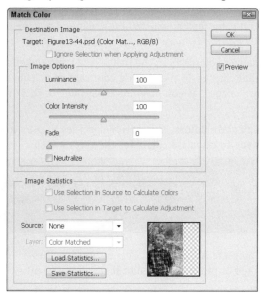

Open the Match Color tool by choosing Image ➪ Adjustments ➪ Color Match. When applying a color match to an image, you can use the following options to control the color matching process:

- **Target.** This shows the image and layer that will be affected by the color match. This option also shows the color mode of the target image.

NOTE

Only the selected layer in the destination file is affected by the color match.

- **Ignore Selection when Applying Adjustment.** When you select this option, the color match applies to the entire image instead of just a selection.

NOTE

A great feature of the Match Color tool is that you can apply the color matching change to a selection rather than the entire image. For example, you may want to change the background colors without changing the subject's skin tones.

- **Luminance.** This slider adjusts the brightness of the color match adjustment.

- **Color Intensity.** This slider adjusts the color saturation applied by the color match. Increasing this value makes the colors pop more; decreasing it makes the color change more subtle.

- **Fade.** This slider adjusts the percentage of color match adjustment to apply to the image. A value of 0 means a full color match adjustment; a value of 100 means no color match adjustment.

- **Neutralize.** This option neutralizes colorcasts in the image, reducing the effects of the color match adjustment that can result in a general colorcast. It is a good idea to try this option when correcting images, as you may not always notice that the color match has resulted in a colorcast.

- **Use Selection in Source to Calculate Colors.** This option specifies to use only the selected area in the source image to calculate colors for the color match.

TIP

It is usually best to use selected areas of known colors to apply the color adjustment to images. This can reduce colorcasts and result in adjustments that are more accurate. For example, you may want to select a person's face in both the source and target images to make sure skin tones match.

- **Use Selection in Target to Calculate Adjustment.** This option specifies to use only the selection in the target image to calculate the color match adjustment.

- **Source.** This menu specifies the source image. All open documents in Photoshop appear in the list.

- **Layer.** This menu specifies the layer to use in the source file.

- **Load Statistics.** This option allows you to load a previously saved set of color statistics and use those instead of a source image.

- **Save Statistics.** This option allows you to save the statistics from the layer of an image specified by the Source and Layer options. This allows you to store a specific set of colors that you can use later to adjust other images.

- **Source view.** This field displays the image specified by the Source and Layer options so you can verify that you have the correct image selected.

Figure 13.44 shows an example of using the color in one image to adjust the colors in another image. The colors in the source image have already been adjusted to a desired level. The Match Color tool takes the color composition from the source image and applies it to the target image, resulting in a much better color match.

ON THE WEB

You can find the image shown in Figure 13.44 on this book's website as Figure13-44.psd. This file contains both the original layer and the color-matched layer so you can see the results of applying the color match.

FIGURE 13.44

The Match Color tool adjusts the colors in a target image by using the colors in a different source image.

Working with HDR Images

High dynamic range images (HDR) are created from a set of bracketed photos at varying exposures. This allows you to include more tonal ranges in the images than you can store in a single digital photo. This results in images that reflect more of the colors and intensity levels found in the real world, such as nature scenes. HDR images are either 16-bit or 32-bit images allowing you to have more detail than the original images and lose less detail when making adjustments. Bracketed photos can be imported into Photoshop using the Merge to HDR Pro utility.

Creating HDR images

One of the most difficult challenges in photography is capturing a large tonal range with the limited capabilities of the equipment. To solve that problem, you can use a bracketed set of photographs and the Merge to HDR Pro utility in Photoshop to create a 32-bit HDR image. Bracketed photos consist of three or more images where one photo is at the correct exposure and the rest are either overexposed or underexposed.

The Merge to HDR Pro utility allows you to select the bracketed photos and then apply a series of adjustments to them to collect a full 32-bit tonal range. From the Merge to HDR Pro utility, you can make the following lighting and color adjustments:

- **Preset.** This list allows you to select one of the predefined HDR tonal adjustments supplied with Photoshop or to specify Custom to create your own.

- **Remove ghosts.** When you select this option, Photoshop removes ghosts that are created because the bracketed photos are not perfectly aligned.

- **Mode.** This list allows you to set the image output mode to 8-bit, 16-bit, or 32-bit.

- **Method.** This list allows you to specify one of the following methods used by the Toning tool to adjust the lighting and color:

  - **Exposure and Gamma.** This option allows you to manually adjust the brightness and contrast of the HDR image. Only those two settings will be available in the HDR Toning tool.

  - **Highlight Compression.** This option automatically compresses highlight values in the HDR image so that they match the range of luminance values that 8-bit-per-channel images support. None of the following options will be available.

  - **Equalize Histogram.** This option automatically compresses the dynamic range of the HDR image while trying to preserve some contrast. None of the following options will be available.

  - **Local Adaptation.** This option allows you to adjust the following options in the HDR image. The HDR Toning utility uses the values to calculate the amount of correction necessary for local brightness regions throughout the image.

- **Radius.** This slider specifies the area size used to define local brightness.

- **Strength.** This slider specifies how far apart the level values for two pixels must be before they are no longer part of the same brightness region.

- **Edge Smoothness.** When you select this option, Photoshop tries to preserve smoothness around edges while increasing detail.

- **Gamma.** This slider allows you to make a gamma correction to the tones in the image.

- **Exposure.** This slider allows you to adjust the exposure up or down. Remember that the dynamic range of the HDR images contains multiple levels of exposure.

- **Detail.** This slider specifies a percentage amount of detail to preserve when making the other adjustments.

- **Shadow.** This slider allows you to adjust only the levels of the shadow (darker) tones up and down.

- **Highlights.** This slider allows you to adjust only the levels of the highlight (lighter) tones up and down.

- **Vibrance.** This slider adjusts the intensity of colors in the image.

- **Saturation.** This slider adjusts the saturation of color in the image while trying to minimize the amount of clipping that result.

- **Curve.** When you select this tab, you can use a Curve tool to adjust the tones in the image.

The following example takes you through the process of creating an HDR image from a set of bracketed photos.

1. **To access the Merge to HDR Pro utility, choose File ⇨ Automate ⇨ Merge to HDR Pro in Photoshop.**

   This launches the Merge to HDR Pro file selector, as shown in Figure 13.45.

FIGURE 13.45

The Merge to HDR Pro file selector allows you to select bracketed images to be merged into an HDR image.

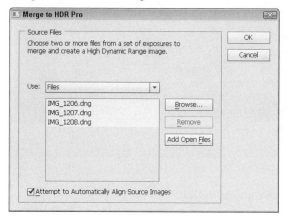

2. **Select the bracketed files that you want to merge into an HDR image.**

   From the Merge to HDR Pro file selector, you can select Files or Folder from the Use list. If you select File, then all of the files you select will be combined to form the HDR image. If you select Folder, then all of the files located in the folder you select will be combined to form the HDR image. You can also select files by clicking the Add Open Files button, which selects all files currently open in Photoshop. The Remove button allows you to remove files from the list.

3. **Select the Attempt to Automatically Align Source Images option.**

TIP

If you select the Attempt to Automatically Align Source Images option, then Photoshop tries to align the images. Photoshop usually gets the alignment right if you select this option; however, sometimes it gets it wrong. Try creating the HDR image with this option both on and off, and choose the one you like best.

4. **Click OK to launch the Merge to HDR Pro utility shown in Figure 13.46.**

FIGURE 13.46

The Merge to HDR Pro utility allows you to quickly adjust the lighting and color of HDR images.

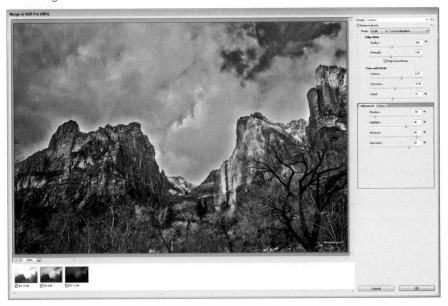

5. **Select the Remove ghosts option.**

You should remove ghost edges before trying to adjust the rest of the image so that they do not interfere with interpreting your other changes.

6. **Adjust the gamma to get the overall tones in the image correct.**

   In this image, we adjusted the gamma up to 0.75.

7. **Adjust the exposure to get the optimal detail back in the image.**

   In this case, we decreased the exposure by .35. You may need to go back and adjust the gamma again after adjusting the exposure.

8. **Adjust the detail to get the look you want for the image.**

   If you increase the Detail setting, then the image gets harder; reducing the Detail setting makes the image a bit softer. In this case, we reduced the detail to 70% to create a slightly surreal effect in the image.

9. **Set the radius and strength of the Edge Glow.**

   In this case, we set the radius up to 200px and the strength up to 1.6 to bring out the edges of the mountains against the clouds and add to the slightly surreal scene.

10. **Select the Edge Smoothness option.**

11. **Adjust the Shadow and Highlight options.**

    In this case, we decreased the shadows to add more depth to the clouds and lower areas of the image, and increased the highlights to brighten the highlights on the cliffs.

12. **Adjust the vibrance to increase the color brilliance.**

    For this HDR image, we increased the vibrance all the way up to 80% because we were looking for a slightly surreal effect.

13. **Adjust the saturation to bring out more color.**

    In this image, we increased the saturation by 50% to add more color to the cliffs and the blue sky.

14. **Click the Curve tab and use the curve to fine-tune the image adjustments.**

    The results are shown in Figure 13.47.

ON THE WEB

You can find the image shown in Figure 13.47 on this book's website as Figure13-47.psd. This file contains the HDR image.

FIGURE 13.47

Using the Merge to HDR Pro utility, you can combine a set of bracketed photos into a 32-bit HDR image with much greater tonal range.

Bracketed Photos

Merged HDR Image

Converting HDR images to 8 bits per channel

You will need to convert the HDR image to 8-bits per channel before you can use it outside of Photoshop. The HDR Toning tool provides an incredible amount of control when adjusting the color and tone of 32-bit-per-channel HDR images to convert them to 8-bit-per-channel images.

> **TIP**
>
> Although the HDR Toning tool is designed to convert HDR images to 8-bit-per-channel images, it can also be applied to non-HDR images. We've found that you can sometimes get better results using the HDR Toning tool than with a simple levels adjustment. After applying the adjustment, you still get the message saying that the image is converted to an 8-bit-per-channel image, but because it was already an 8-bit-per-channel image, it won't matter.

To access the HDR Toning tool, shown in Figure 13.48, choose Image ➪ Adjustments ➪ HDR Toning from the main menu, or choose Image ➪ Mode ➪ 8-Bits/Channel from the main menu.

FIGURE 13.48

The HDR Toning tool allows you to quickly adjust the lighting and color of HDR images.

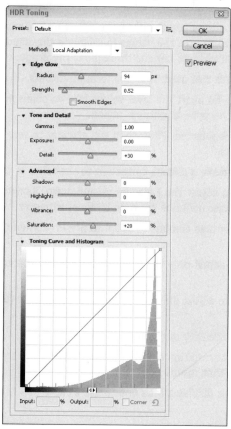

From the HDR Toning tool, you can make the following lighting and color adjustments:

- **Preset.** This list allows you to select one of the predefined HDR tonal adjustments supplied with Photoshop, or to specify Custom to create your own. The button next to the Preset drop-down list allows you to save the current settings to a file as well as load previously saved presets.

- **Method.** This list allows you to specify one of the following methods used by the HDR Toning tool to adjust the lighting and color:

  - **Exposure and Gamma.** This option allows you to manually adjust the brightness and contrast of the HDR image. Only those two settings are available in the HDR Toning tool.

  - **Highlight Compression.** This option automatically compresses highlight values in the HDR image so they match the range of luminance values that 8-bit-per-channel images support. None of the following options is available.

13

- **Equalize Histogram.** This option automatically compresses the dynamic range of the HDR image while trying to preserve some contrast. None of the following options is available.

- **Local Adaptation.** This option allows you to adjust the following options in the HDR image. The HDR Toning utility uses the values to calculate the amount of correction necessary for local brightness regions throughout the image.

- **Radius.** This slider specifies the area size used to define local brightness.

- **Strength.** This slider specifies how far apart the level values for two pixels must be before they are no longer part of the same brightness region.

- **Smooth Edges.** When this option is selected, Photoshop will attempt to smooth sharp edges created by other adjustments.

- **Gamma.** This slider allows you to make a gamma correction to the tones of the image.

- **Exposure.** This slider allows you to adjust the exposure up and down. Remember that the dynamic range of the HDR images contains multiple levels of exposure.

- **Detail.** This slider specifies a percentage amount of detail to preserve when making the other adjustments.

- **Shadow.** This slider allows you to adjust only the levels of the shadow (darker) tones up and down.

- **Highlight.** This slider allows you to adjust only the levels of the highlight (lighter) tones up and down.

- **Vibrance.** This slider adjusts the intensity of colors in the image.

- **Saturation.** This slider adjusts the saturation of colors in the image while trying to minimize the amount of clippings that result.

- **Toning Curve and Histogram.** This display allows you to use a curve tool to adjust the tones in the image.

Summary

This chapter discussed most of the tools available in Photoshop that adjust the color and lighting in images. Although color and lighting changes all just involve adjusting the values of color channels in the images, several tools make it easy to focus on specific adjustments in images.

In this chapter, you learned the following:

- How to use the Exposure tool to fix lighting problems in images.

- How to use the Shadows/Highlights tool to adjust the upper and lower color levels quickly in an image.

- How Photoshop can simulate the effect of using a lens filter on a photo that was taken without one.

- How to replace one color with another to change the look of a photo completely.

- How to create black-and-white photos from color images.

- How to adjust individual color channels to make some colors pop while not affecting the other colors.

- How to use the powerful and flexible Curves tool to restore detail to images with severe lighting problems.

- Using the Merge to HDR Pro and HDR Toning utilities, you can create HDR images.

13

Applying Sharpness, Blur, and Noise Adjustments

IN THIS CHAPTER

Using sharpening filters to sharpen an image

Applying blurring filters to soften the background in an image

Reducing noise and removing dust and scratches in an image

A common problem when working with photos is blurriness and noise. To overcome these problems, Photoshop provides three classes of filters: sharpen, blur, and noise. It is important to remember that when you apply filters to an image, you are altering the pixels based on computer algorithms and not optical data. Therefore, the adjustments that Photoshop can make are limited in their effectiveness.

This chapter discusses using the sharpening filters to enhance blurry images and make edges stand out, using blur filters to apply softening effects to images, and using noise reduction filters to remove noise and unwanted artifacts from images.

 Sharpening, blurring, and noise reduction filters are discussed in greater detail in Chapter 20. Before getting too far in this chapter, you should review the section in Chapter 20 that discusses creating and using non-destructive Smart Filters.

 When you apply the sharpening, blurring, and noise reduction filters in this chapter as Smart Filters, you can use blend modes to significantly change how the filters are applied. Before reading this chapter, you should look at the section in Chapter 10, which discusses blend modes in detail. This will help you to understand additional options available when blending rather than applying filters normally.

Using Sharpening Filters to Sharpen Images

The best way to get a sharp photo is to shoot a sharp photo in the first place. Nothing can take the place of an optically sharp image. Unfortunately, you don't always shoot perfectly sharp photos. And even if you do, you may lose some sharpness when making adjustments to the photo in Photoshop.

For these reasons, Photoshop includes some powerful sharpening filters that make your images look better. To sharpen a photo, Photoshop uses some algorithms that analyze the image, find edges of objects, and then adjust the pixels in the image to maximize the contrast between the edges with minimal impact on the overall appearance of the photo.

> **TIP**
>
> The best way to apply sharpening filters is to create a duplicate layer of the background and then turn that layer into a Smart Object. Then apply the filter to the Smart Object so you can add several filters, turn them on and off, and try different settings.

Keep in mind that the more sharpening you do in your images, the more anomalies you introduce, such as false edges and ringing artifacts. The amount of sharpening you can do is limited by the amount of detail in your image as well as the size of the image; when it comes to sharpening, bigger is better.

> **NOTE**
>
> Ringing artifacts can appear in images when you sharpen areas with abrupt transitions. They show up as "echoes" radiating away from the transition, almost like ripples in a pond.

The following section discusses the basic sharpening tools in Photoshop as well as some of the more advanced ones.

> **NOTE**
>
> The sharpening filters significantly alter the pixels in the image. You should always apply the sharpening filters after you have made all other adjustments to avoid spreading some of the anomalies caused by sharpening the image.

Understanding basic sharpening filters

The simplest way to sharpen images is to use one of the three basic filters supplied by Photoshop. These basic filters apply slightly different techniques to sharpen images. They perform a predefined amount of sharpening to an image and do not provide an interface to customize the amount of sharpening that takes place.

The following list describes the basic sharpening filters that are available when you choose Filter ⇨ Sharpen in Photoshop:

- **Sharpen.** This filter performs a simple sharpening on an image. The filter scans the pixels in the image looking for boundaries denoted by a pixel not matching adjacent pixels in one direction or another. The filter then changes the value around the boundaries to increase the contrast and make the edge more definable.

- **Sharpen More.** This filter works the same way as the Sharpen filter except that the Sharpen More filter is more aggressive about finding edges and how much to increase the contrast. This increases the sharpness around the edges, but it can introduce a considerable amount of noise in images.

- **Sharpen Edges.** This filter works similarly to the Sharpen and Sharpen More filters except that the Sharpen Edges filter is more aggressive when it finds areas of higher contrast, sharpening those areas more than the Sharpen More filter. This filter is great if you have items in the image that have edges that contrast highly against the surrounding background.

- **Smart Sharpen.** This filter gives you more control over the sharpening effect by allowing you to set the sharpening amount, method, radius, and angle.

- **Unsharp Mask.** This filter uses a different method of sharpening by finding pixels that are different from the surrounding pixels and then increasing the contrast in the surrounding pixels. The Unsharp Mask filter is discussed in the next section.

The following example takes you through the process of using the basic sharpening filters to sharpen an image:

1. **Open the image in Photoshop, as shown in Figure 14.1.**

    Notice that the image is blurry.

FIGURE 14.1

A very blurry image opened in Photoshop

14

2. **Right-click the background layer in the Layers panel, and select Duplicate Layer from the menu, as shown in Figure 14.2.**

    This displays the Duplicate Layer dialog box.

3. **Name the duplicate layer in the Duplicate Layer dialog box, shown in Figure 14.2, and click OK to create the layer.**

    The new layer is added to the Layers panel.

FIGURE 14.2

Duplicating the background allows you to create a copy of the image to work with without damaging the original pixels.

4. **Right-click the new layer, and select Convert to Smart Object from the menu, as shown in Figure 14.3.**

FIGURE 14.3

Making the duplicate layer a Smart Object allows you to apply the filters as Smart Filters.

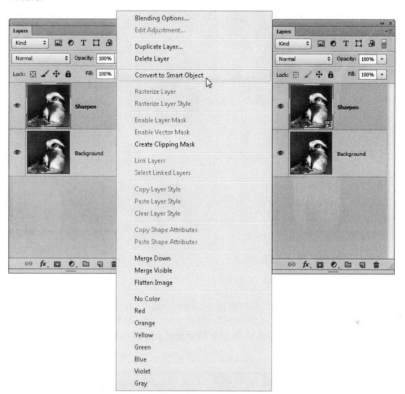

5. **Choose Filter ⇨ Sharpen ⇨ Sharpen to apply the Sharpen filter to the Smart Object.**

6. **Choose Filter ⇨ Sharpen ⇨ Sharpen More to apply the Sharpen More filter to the Smart Object.**

7. **Choose Filter ⇨ Sharpen ⇨ Sharpen Edges to apply the Sharpen Edges filter to the Smart Object.**

    The Sharpen, Sharpen More, and Sharpen Edges filters are applied as Smart Filters to the Smart Object, as shown in Figure 14.4.

FIGURE 14.4

Applying the Sharpen, Sharpen More, and Sharpen Edges filters as Smart Filters to the blurry image.

The results of applying the Sharpen, Sharpen More, and Sharpen Edges filters are shown in Figure 14.5. Notice that the Sharpen filter does not have as drastic an effect on the image as the Sharpen More filter, and that the Sharpen Edges filter applies more sharpness to the image.

ON THE WEB

You can find the file used to create the image shown in Figure 14.5 on this book's website as Figure 14-5.psd. Open it in Photoshop and see the effects of the Sharpen, Sharpen More, and Sharpen Edges filters. The sharpen filters are applied as a separate layer, so you can delete that layer or hide it and try to make your own adjustments as you follow along with the exercises.

Using the Unsharp Mask filter

The Unsharp Mask filter uses a more advanced method of sharpening images than the basic sharpening filters. Instead of detecting the edges in the image, the Unsharp Mask filter finds pixels that are different from the surrounding pixels by a specified threshold. Then it increases the contrast in a specified set of surrounding pixels called a neighborhood. In other words, if a pixel is darker than the surrounding neighborhood, then the neighborhood is lightened.

FIGURE 14.5

Notice the results of the Sharpen, Sharpen More, and Sharpen Edges filters on the image. Sharpen More makes a bigger difference than Sharpen, and Sharpen Edges applies changes mostly around the edges of the wing and body.

Original   Sharpen filter

Sharpen More filter   Sharpen Edges filter

Figure 14.6 shows the Unsharp Mask dialog box that appears when you choose Filter ➪ Sharpen ➪ Unsharp Mask. Using the Unsharp Mask dialog box, you can set the following values to use when sharpening an image:

- **Preview size.** The minus and plus buttons adjust the size of the image in the preview window of the Unsharp Mask dialog box. You can drag the image inside the preview window to adjust the position of the preview or simply click the preview image.

- **Amount.** This slider specifies the amount used to increase the contrast of the pixels in the neighborhood when sharpening. A greater value here creates a more dramatic sharpening effect in the image.

14

- **Radius.** This slider specifies the size of the neighborhood to use when calculating whether a pixel doesn't match the surrounding pixels. A greater radius means that a larger area of the image is affected by the sharpening, so the edge transitions are more gradual. A smaller radius means that a smaller number of pixels are affected, so the edge transitions are more abrupt.

- **Threshold.** This slider specifies the threshold used to calculate whether a pixel matches the surrounding neighborhood. A larger value here means that only significant differences between a pixel and its neighbors are sharpened. Typically, you want to use a threshold value between 4 and 20 pixels.

Use the following steps to apply an Unsharp Mask filter to an image in Photoshop:

1. **Open the image in Photoshop.**

2. **Right-click the background layer and select Duplicate Layer from the menu to display the Duplicate Layer dialog box.**

3. **Name the duplicate layer in the Duplicate Layer dialog box, and click OK to create the layer.**

   The new layer is added to the Layers panel.

4. **Right-click the new layer, and select Convert to Smart Object from the menu (refer to Figure 14.3).**

5. **Choose Filter ⇨ Sharpen ⇨ Unsharp Mask to apply the Unsharp Mask filter to the Smart Object.**

   The Unsharp Mask dialog box appears, as shown in Figure 14.6.

6. **Adjust the size of the preview by clicking the plus and minus buttons, and drag the image until you have a preview area that includes the part of the image you are most interested in sharpening.**

   In Figure 14.6, we adjusted the size and dragged the image so that the tiger's face was visible in the preview area.

7. **Adjust the Amount value to set the amount of sharpening to take place.**

   In this example, we set the value to 100% to make a large change.

8. **Adjust the Radius value to include enough of the surrounding pixels to detect the change and provide a smooth transition along the edges.**

   In this example, we set the radius to 9 pixels so we could get enough of the surrounding pixels.

9. **Adjust the Threshold value until only the areas you want sharpened are being sharpened by the filter.**

   You may need to go back and adjust the Amount and Radius values if you don't get a threshold setting that you like.

10. **Click OK to apply the Unsharp Mask filter as a Smart Filter to the layer.**

FIGURE 14.6

The Unsharp Mask filter allows you to set the amount of sharpening, the radius of the neighborhood to sharpen, and the threshold to use to determine pixels that need sharpening.

The results of applying the Unsharp Mask filter are shown in Figure 14.7.

ON THE WEB

The fine tune adjustments of the Unsharp Mask filter will be much more apparent in Photoshop than a printed book, so we strongly suggest that you try it out for yourself. You can find the file used to create the image shown in Figure 14.7 on this book's website as Figure 14-7.psd. Open it in Photoshop to see the effects of the Unsharp Mask filter and try making your own adjustments.

FIGURE 14.7

Notice the results of the Unsharp Mask filter on the image. The grass and the stripes on the tiger have been sharpened by the filter.

| Original | Unsharp Mask filter |

Applying Smart Sharpen

The most powerful tool that Photoshop has to sharpen images is the Smart Sharpen filter. The Smart Sharpen filter uses the same algorithm as the Unsharp Mask filter. However, the Smart Sharpen filter also includes the ability to fine-tune the amount of sharpening that takes place in the highlights and shadow areas of the image. The Smart Sharpen filter also allows you to specify the type of blur you want to remove from the image. Figure 14.8 shows the Smart Sharpen dialog box that is displayed when you choose Filter ⇨ Sharpen ⇨ Smart Sharpen.

FIGURE 14.8

The Smart Sharpen filter allows you to set the amount of sharpening, the radius of the neighborhood to sharpen, and the type of blur to be corrected by the sharpening filter.

Using the Smart Sharpen dialog box, you can set the following values when sharpening the image:

- **Preview size.** The minus and plus buttons adjust the size of the image in the preview window of the Smart Sharpen dialog box. You can drag the image inside the preview window to adjust the position of the preview or simply click the preview image.

- **Settings.** This menu allows you to save the current settings as a preset filter and select it later. This allows you to apply the same filter settings to several images to correct similar blurring caused by lens or camera issues. You can also delete a preset filter by clicking the trash can icon.

- **Amount.** This slider specifies the amount used to increase the contrast of the pixels in the neighborhood when sharpening. A greater value here creates a more dramatic sharpening effect in the image.

- **Radius.** This slider specifies the size of the neighborhood to use when Photoshop calculates whether a pixel matches the surrounding pixels. This value is also used to determine the size of the area affected by the Smart Sharpen filter. A greater radius means that a larger area of the image is affected by the sharpening, so the edge transitions are more gradual. A smaller radius means that fewer pixels are affected, so the edge transitions are more abrupt.

- **Remove.** This list specifies the type of blur you are trying to remove from the image. You can specify Gaussian, Lens, or Motion. Gaussian blurs are introduced into images when you make image adjustments such as noise reduction or image resizing. Lens blurs are introduced into the image due to focus problems. Motion blurs are introduced into images by either camera or subject motion.

- **Angle.** This field allows you to select the angle of motion when you select the Motion option in the Remove drop-down list. This gives Photoshop an idea of the motion of the target in the image and allows the algorithms to be much more aggressive when fixing motion blur.

- **More Accurate.** When you select this option, Photoshop takes much more time processing the Smart Sharpen filter, but it gives you a much better sharpening effect.

To fine-tune the sharpening that takes place in the shadows of the image, select the Advanced option in the Smart Sharpen dialog box, and then click the Shadow tab to set the following options, shown in Figure 14.9:

- **Fade Amount.** This slider specifies the amount used to increase the contrast in neighboring pixels when sharpening pixels in the shadows range.

- **Tonal Width.** This slider adjusts the range of tones that are included in the shadows range. Moving the slider to the left decreases the maximum value that is considered to be in the shadows.

- **Radius.** This slider specifies the size of the neighborhood to use when calculating whether a pixel belongs to the shadows range.

FIGURE 14.9

You can fine-tune the Smart Sharpen filter to set the amount of sharpening that takes place in the shadows range.

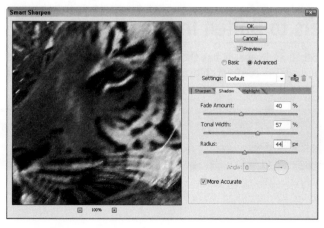

To fine-tune the sharpening that takes place in the highlights of the image, select the Advanced option in the Smart Sharpen dialog box and then click the Highlight tab to set the following options, shown in Figure 14.10:

- **Fade Amount.** This slider specifies the amount used to increase the contrast in neighboring pixels when sharpening pixels in the highlights range.
- **Tonal Width.** This slider adjusts the range of tones that are included in the highlights range. Moving the slider to the left decreases the maximum value that is considered to be in the highlights.
- **Radius.** This slider specifies the size of the neighborhood to use when calculating whether a pixel belongs to the highlights range.

FIGURE 14.10

You can fine-tune the Smart Sharpen filter by setting the amount of sharpening that takes place in the highlights range.

Using Blur Filters to Soften Images

When you apply a blur filter to an image, it has the opposite effect of a sharpening filter. Instead of finding edges and adding contrast, blurring reduces the contrast, making edges softer. Photoshop has 11 blur filters.

> **CAUTION**
>
> Photoshop blurs images by smoothing out some of the details. However, the detail is permanently lost, so you likely want to apply the blurring filters on a separate duplicate layer to avoid losing your original data.

Each blur filter reduces the contrast at different levels and in different ways. If you choose a Gaussian Blur, for example, each pixel is compared to pixels around it in an even radius, and pixels that are closer count more when calculating the blur value than pixels that are farther away. Choosing a blur filter softens the edges in your image by blurring only those pixels that are in high-contrast areas. If you choose a Box Blur, each pixel is compared to pixels around it in a box shape, giving the end result an edgier appearance. If you really want an interesting result, choose a Shape Blur, where you can choose from dozens of shapes to use for the pixel comparison.

Understanding the automatic blur filters

The first three blur filters on the Filter ⇨ Blur menu are automatic blur filters, meaning that they don't require any input from the user. These filters are Average, Blur, and Blur More.

- **Average.** This filter takes the average color of the frame (or selected area) and fills the entire frame with that color. It's not a great photo enhancer, but it can be useful for creating matching backgrounds when placing odd-sized photos in a video file.

- **Blur.** This filter automatically smoothes the color transitions in an image to soften the edges.

- **Blur More.** This filter works the same as the Blur filter by smoothing the color transitions in an image to soften the edges. The Blur More filter is several times stronger than the Blur filter, although it is still very subtle.

Using the Gaussian, Box, and Shape Blur filters

The Gaussian Blur, Box Blur, and Shape Blur filters blur all the pixels throughout an image or selection rather than selected pixels in high-contrast areas, as the Blur and Blur More filters do. The pixels are blurred by reducing the contrast between each pixel and the surrounding pixels. The surrounding pixels are determined by which one of these filters you use and the Radius setting.

Gaussian Blur

The Gaussian Blur compares the pixels in an even radius around each pixel and applies a weighted average to each pixel to reduce its contrast to the surrounding pixels. This results in a general softening of the image. You can apply a Gaussian Blur filter by choosing Filter ⇨ Blur ⇨ Gaussian Blur to open a dialog box that allows you to set the radius of the blur. The radius, of course, is the number of pixels around each pixel that this pixel is compared to. Figure 14.11 shows the effect of creating a selection around the subject and then applying a Gaussian Blur filter. Notice that the Gaussian Blur is very smooth.

FIGURE 14.11

A Gaussian Blur has been liberally applied to the background to clearly demonstrate the effect.

Box Blur

A Box Blur compares the pixels in a box shape rather than the feathering-out comparison of the Gaussian Blur. The result is a blur with edges. You can apply the Box Blur by choosing Filter ⇨ Blur ⇨ Box Blur. This filter has the same dialog box as the Gaussian Blur, consisting of a preview window and a Radius setting, as shown in Figure 14.12. With the Radius setting turned up to 80, you can clearly see the difference in the blur filters. Figure 14.12 also illustrates one of the down sides to the Box Blur. Notice that the area around the boy, and in particular between the boy's arm and his body, is not very blurred. This is because of the radius setting. The larger the radius setting, the less blurring occurs around the edges of the selection or mask.

FIGURE 14.12

The Box Blur gives the background an edgy look.

Shape Blur

As if having a soft blur or an edgy blur weren't enough, Photoshop gives you the choice of literally dozens of shapes to use when comparing pixels. The Shape Blur works in the same way as the Gaussian Blur and Box Blur, except the pixels are compared to one another in the shape you choose. Maybe someone at Adobe had too much time on his hands, but the result can create some very interesting blur effects.

Open the Shape Blur dialog box by choosing Filter ⇨ Blur ⇨ Shape Blur. You can see in Figure 14.13 that the dialog box is full of all sorts of fun shapes that you can use in the Blur filter. Click the menu button next to the list of shapes to add additional sets of shapes to the selectable list. Of course, the preview window and the Radius setting are part of the dialog box as well. The higher you set the Radius setting, the more likely you are to see a real difference in the effects created by each shape. Figure 14.13 shows an example of what the star shape does for this blur effect.

FIGURE 14.13

The Shape Blur has a completely different look than either the Gaussian Blur or the Box Blur, despite having the same radius of 200 pixels.

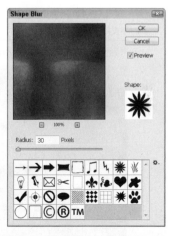

ON THE WEB

You can find the file used to create the image shown in Figures 14.11, 14.12, and 14.13 on this book's website as Figure 14-11.psd. Open it in Photoshop to see the effects of the blur filters. Each of the Gaussian, Box, and Shape filters is in its own Smart Object layer, so you can turn the blurs on and off to see the different effects.

14

Creating a direction blur

The Motion Blur and Radial Blur filters create the illusion of motion in your image. These filters are very useful in adding a motion effect to either the entire image or a specific selection. A Motion Blur adds a directional blur that moves across the 2D plane of the image. A Radial Blur adds blurring that radiates outward from a central point in the image.

Adding a Motion Blur to an image

The Motion Blur simulates movement in a straight path, which you determine by setting the angle in the dialog box. The following example takes you through the process of adding a Motion Blur to an image:

1. **Open the image in Photoshop.**
2. **Select the area of the image where you want to add the Motion Blur, and press Ctrl+C/⌘+C to copy the selection to the clipboard.**
3. **Add a new layer to the image using the Layers menu.**
4. **Paste the contents of the clipboard into the newly created layer, as shown in Figure 14.14.**

FIGURE 14.14

Paste the clipboard contents into the new layer.

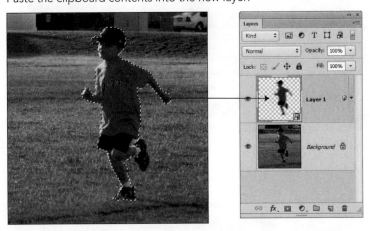

5. **Right-click the new layer, and select Convert to Smart Object.**

6. **Choose Filter ⇨ Blur ⇨ Motion Blur to apply a Motion Blur filter to the Smart Object.**

   The Motion Blur dialog box appears, as shown in Figure 14.15.

   FIGURE 14.15

   The Motion Blur filter allows you to set the angle and direction of the blur that is applied to the image.

   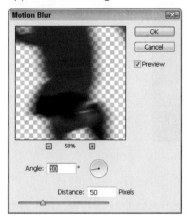

7. **Adjust the Angle to match the relative direction of the motion you want in the image.**

   In the example, we adjusted the angle to 10 degrees to match the slope of the field.

8. **Adjust the Distance to the desired number of pixels.**

   A small number of pixels blurs the image only slightly. Increasing the Distance increases the amount of movement in the subject and makes the image blurrier. In this example, we increased the distance to 50 to make the runner look like he was moving faster.

9. **Click the OK button to apply the Motion Blur filter to the image.**

   In the final image in Figure 14.16, notice that the runner now looks like he's moving quickly while the background remains stationary.

ON THE WEB

You can find the file used to create the image shown in Figure 14.16 on this book's website as Figure 14-16.psd. Open it in Photoshop to see the effects of the Motion Blur filter.

14

FIGURE 14.16

Adding a Motion Blur filter to an image can give the appearance that an object is in motion or, in this case, in faster motion than the original image.

Radial Blur

The Radial Blur filter allows you to add blurs that radiate outward from a central point. To apply a Radial Blur, choose Filter ⇨ Blur ⇨ Radial Blur and set the following options, as shown in Figure 14.17:

- **Amount.** This slider specifies the amount of blur to apply to the layer.

- **Spin.** This option gives the image the illusion that it is spinning in a circular motion.

- **Zoom.** This option blurs the edges of the image more than the center, creating the illusion that the image is moving rapidly toward or away from the viewer.

- **Quality.** This section allows you to specify Draft, Good, or Best. The better the quality, the better the results look; however, the Radial Blur filter takes a lot of processing power, so you should try it out in Draft mode first and then increase the quality after you get the desired results.

- **Blur Center.** This pane allows you to drag the center of the blur to any location in the image. The lines show the amount of blurring that will take place.

ON THE WEB

You can find the file used to create the image shown in Figure 14.17 on this book's website as Figure 14-17.psd. Open it in Photoshop to see the effects of the Radial Blur filter and play around with the direction and amount of the blur.

FIGURE 14.17

The Radial Blur offers Spin and Zoom options.

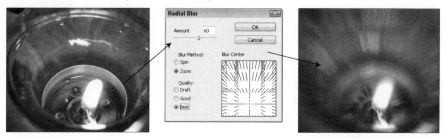

Adding a Surface Blur

The Surface Blur filter is the opposite of the Blur and Blur More filters. Rather than softening the edges, the Surface Blur works by softening the midtones, leaving the edges sharp and crisp. This is perfect for smoothing out slight imperfections or noise in an image without losing crisp detail.

Applying a Smart Blur

The Smart Blur allows you to blur with more precision by using radius and threshold settings that allow you to specify the number of pixels involved and what the difference in the pixels should be before the filter is applied to them. The Smart Blur is a great option if you are not sure exactly what blur effect you would like to add to an image.

To apply a Smart Blur, select Filter➪Blur➪Smart Blur from the main menu bar and set the following options, as shown in Figure 14.18:

- **Radius.** This slider specifies the area of pixels that are searched to determine whether a pixel is dissimilar to its neighbors and should be blurred.

- **Threshold.** This slider specifies the amount of dissimilarity a pixel must have with its neighbors before the filter is applied to it.

- **Quality.** This list allows you to specify a Low, Medium, or High quality. The better the quality, the better the results look; however, the Smart Blur filter takes a lot of processing power, so you should try it out in Low mode first and then increase the quality after you get the desired results.

- **Mode.** This list allows you to specify a Normal, Edge Only, or Overlay Edge blur. The Normal setting gives you basic blurring results. The Edge Only setting turns the image entirely black and creates white edges. The Overlay Edge setting overlays the edges in the image with white.

FIGURE 14.18

The Smart Blur allows you to specify the area of pixels and threshold to use when blurring the image.

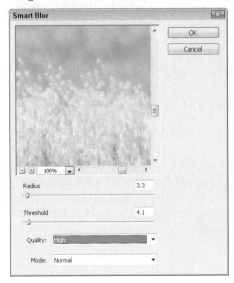

Faking Lens Blur

The Lens Blur is by far the most advanced blur filter available. It presents a very involved dialog box that allows you to change the field of depth to the specular highlights of your image. The whole point of the Lens Blur is to allow you to blur parts of your image while leaving other areas in sharp focus.

The Lens Blur dialog box shows a full preview of your image by default. Because the changes you make probably affect different areas of your image differently, you can see the effects your changes have on your full image. Because the precise changes made by the Lens Blur can take time, you have the option of choosing between a faster or more accurate preview. The following sections discuss the adjustments that you can make in the Lens Blur dialog box, shown in Figure 14.19.

Preview

The preview pane for the lens blur is very big and can be slow when rendering large images. To let you choose between speed and accuracy, Photoshop provides the Faster and More Accurate options. The faster preview renders more quickly but is less like the actual filter than the more accurate setting. Which option you use depends on whether you have time to wait.

FIGURE 14.19

The Lens Blur dialog box is loaded with options for creating a custom blur.

Depth Map

An image or video file in Photoshop is just a pixel map. Photoshop can't determine which areas of an image should be in focus and which shouldn't be. Setting the Depth Map tells Photoshop which pixels to keep sharp and which ones to blur. You can create a Depth Map in several ways. Selecting None from the Source drop-down menu blurs the pixels in your image indiscriminately. Choosing Transparency blurs the pixels based on their Transparency values. If you select Layer Mask, the blurring is based on the grayscale values in the layer mask. For example, if you create a gradient layer mask, the lighter areas of the gradient are less blurry than the darker areas.

The best way to create a Depth Map is to create and load an alpha channel. (See Chapter 11 for more information on creating an alpha channel.) The dark areas of the alpha channel are treated as the foreground of the image, and the light areas are treated as the background. Figure 14.20 shows an alpha channel that matches the shape of the bison in the Lens Blur dialog box (refer to Figure 14.19). When you've created an alpha channel, it appears in the Source drop-down list, and you can use it to determine which pixels are blurred. Click anywhere on your image to choose the pixel brightness that determines which areas of your picture stay in focus.

FIGURE 14.20

The Channels panel contains an alpha channel created with a selection.

If you select a source other than None, you can choose the focal distance of the blur by adjusting the slider. As the focal distance changes, the area inside the alpha channel becomes sharper and the area outside the alpha channel becomes more blurred. You can also invert the effects on the respective parts of the alpha channel by selecting the Invert option.

Iris

You can specify the size and shape of the aperture of a camera using the Iris settings in the Lens Blur dialog box. These settings allow you to simulate the different types of irises found in different cameras. The Iris settings allow you to change the following options:

- **Shape.** This list allows you to specify the shape of the iris in terms of the number of blades, from 3 to 8.
- **Radius.** This slider determines the number of pixels sampled to create the blur effect.
- **Blade Curvature.** This slider specifies the curvature of the blade in a range between 0 and 100. The curvature of the blade affects the amount of blurring around the edges in the image.
- **Rotation.** This slider specifies the rotation of the iris in degrees. This allows you to apply the filter at different rotations that affect the results of the blur.

Specular Highlights

When you blur a photograph using a mathematical formula, your whitest whites tend to dissipate and be replaced with duller tones. This would never happen in a real photo, no matter how blurry it became. You can readjust the whites in your image by using the following settings to add specular highlights:

- **Brightness.** This slider specifies the value by which you want to increase the whites to bring back the brilliance.
- **Threshold.** This slider specifies the levels affected by the Brightness setting. The default is 255, meaning only pure white. As you move the slider to the left, darker pixels are included.

Noise

All photographs contain noise, even blurry ones. To create a more realistic blur, you can add noise to your image using the following settings:

- **Amount.** This slider specifies the amount of noise to add when blurring.

- **Uniform.** This option adds noise uniformly to the image in a linear fashion, so the effect is consistent.

- **Gaussian.** This option adds noise based on the amount of sharpening or blurring that occurs in the pixels. The Gaussian effect appears more natural but does occasionally create some artifacts in the image.

- **Monochromatic.** This option adds noise as gray instead of based on the color of the surrounding pixels. This can appear more natural, but this option typically worsens the overall effect.

Introducing the Blur Gallery

In version CS6, Photoshop introduces the Blur Gallery. The Blur Gallery is different from other blurring filters in that it launches multiple panels that you can use to make changes by clicking the OK button and applying the changes to the images when you are finished. The Blur Gallery consists of two panels: an options bar and several on-image controls. You can access the Blur Gallery by choosing Filter ⇨ Blur ⇨ Field Blur, Iris Blur, or Tilt-Shift Blur in Photoshop.

Using the Blur Gallery tools allows you to soften your images with extreme dexterity and flexibility. The Blur Gallery Options bar provides functionality to control some of the external factors of the blur operation such as selection bleeding and focus. The Blur Tools panel contains controls that allow you to add up to three different types of blur filters to the image: the Field Blur, Iris Blur, and Tilt-Shift Blur. The Blur Effects panel provides controls to add lighting and color effects, such as a bokeh, to the blur filter. The on-image controls allow you to pinpoint specific areas of an image to blur and control the blurring behavior.

Using the Blur Gallery Options bar

The Blur Gallery Options bar allows you to control how the filters in the Blur Gallery are applied, as well as the output from the Blur Gallery, as shown in Figure 14.21.

FIGURE 14.21

The Blur Gallery Options bar allows you to control the behavior and quality of the Blur Gallery filter.

Remove All Pins

The following list describes the options that are available in the Blur Gallery Options bar:

- **Selection Bleed.** This list becomes available when you are adding a blur to a selected area of the image. This option determines how much the selected areas will blend and bleed with the unselected areas. This option is very important to use if you want the blur effect in the selection to blend well with the surrounding pixels.

- **Focus.** This drop-down list specifies the amount of the non-blurred area of a specific pin that will be preserved when you place multiple pins. You can set a specific focus for each pin by selecting the pin and adjusting this setting.

- **Save Mask to Channels.** This is a great option for adding additional effects to your blur later. Each pin you place generates a blur field. When you select this option, the blur fields generated by the pins are merged and the results of the intensity of the blur are translated into an alpha channel in the Channels panel, as shown in Figure 14.22. In Figure 14.22, we have added several blur pins; for the ones directly on the flowers, we set the blur to 0, and on the others, we set the blur to 25px. These blur pins result in the individual flowers being in focus, and the elements around them being out of focus. You can apply any of the alpha channel techniques to the image using the newly created channel.

FIGURE 14.22

Selecting the Save Mask to Channels option in the Blur Gallery creates a new alpha channel in the Channels panel when you apply the blur.

- **High Quality.** When you select this option, the bokeh highlighting is more accurate. Keep in mind that this option results in more processing time for complex filters and large images.

- **Preview.** When you select this option, you can see a preview of the blur effects in the image.

- **Remove All Pins.** When you click this button, all blur pins are removed and you can begin again with a fresh image.

Using the on-image controls

When you are applying blur tools, each tool provides a set of on-image controls that you can use to fine-tune the size, location, and effect of the blur. You will want to become familiar with these controls, so you can easily adjust the blur to provide the exact effect for which you are a looking.

Field Blur tools

The Field Blur tools allow you to quickly add and position blurring field to different areas of your images to obscure some aspects or enhance the focus of other areas. Figure 14.23 shows the Field Blur panel as well as the on-image tools for Field Blur. These tools appear when you choose Filter⇨Blur⇨Field Blur from the main menu bar. The following list describes each of the available options in the Field Blur panel and on-image tools:

- **Blur.** This slider in the Field Blur panel adjusts the blur amount of the selected pin up and down.

- **Blur pin cursor.** The blur pin cursor is the mouse cursor that is provided when you open up the Blur Gallery. When this cursor is active, Photoshop places a blur pin on the image when you click the right mouse button.

- **Blur pins.** Blur pins show the center of the blur fields that have been placed on the image. The blur fields radiate out from the blur pin.

- **Active blur ring.** When you select a blur pin with the mouse, the blur ring becomes active. Notice that part of the ring is white and part is black. The part that is white denotes the amount of blur that is being applied to that field. Each blur pin can have different settings for the blur amount.

TIP

You can drag the ring around with the mouse to increase and decrease the blur amount. You can also drag a blur pin around with the mouse to reposition it on the image.

14

FIGURE 14.23

The on-image controls for the Field Blur allow you to adjust the blur amount as well as the location of the blur fields.

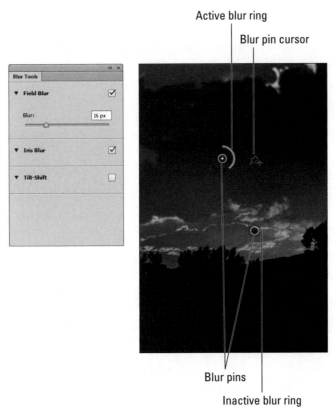

Active blur ring

Blur pin cursor

Blur pins

Inactive blur ring

Iris Blur on-image tools

The Iris Blur tools allow you to quickly add and position a graduated blurring field to different areas of your image. The graduated blurring field gets gradually sharper as you move toward the center. Figure 14.24 shows the Iris Blur panel as well as the on-image tools for Iris Blur. These tools appear when you choose Filter ➪ Blur ➪ Iris Blur from the main menu bar. The following list describes each of the available options in the Iris Blur panel and on-image tools:

- **Blur.** This slider increases and decreases the blur amount of the selected pin.

- **Blur pin cursor.** This is the mouse cursor that is provided when you open the Blur Gallery. When this cursor is active, Photoshop places a blur pin on the image when you click the right mouse button.

- **Blur pins.** Blur pins show the center of the blur fields that have been placed on the image. The blur fields radiate from the blur pin until they run into the edge of the image, or the blur field from another pin.

- **Active blur ring.** When you select a blur pin with the mouse, the blur ring becomes active. Notice that part of the ring is white and part is black. The part that is white denotes the amount of blur that is being applied to that field. Each blur pin can have different settings for the blur amount.

- **Ellipse.** This shows the general edge of the blur effect. The parts of the image that are inside the ellipse are not blurred, while the parts outside the ellipse are blurred.

- **Ellipse handles.** These handles allow you to use the mouse to resize the ellipse. Just drag a handle to change the size.

- **Roundness knob.** Dragging the roundness knob with the mouse allows you to adjust the ellipse to be more or less rectangular.

- **Feather handle.** There are four feather handles in an ellipse. As you adjust them, you adjust the amount of feathering that occurs around the edge of the ellipse. The closer to the ellipse they are, the less feathering takes place, making the blur edge more distinctive.

FIGURE 14.24

The on-image controls for the Iris Blur allow you to adjust the blur amount as well as the location, shape, and feathering of the blur fields.

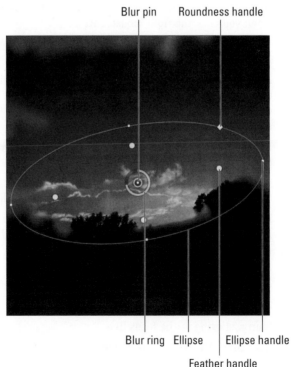

Blur pin   Roundness handle

Blur ring   Ellipse   Ellipse handle

Feather handle

Tilt-Shift Blur on-image tools

The Tilt-Shift Blur tools allow you to quickly add and position horizontal or vertical burring effects to an image, which can give your images better depth. Figure 14.25 shows the Tilt-Shift Blur panel as well as the on-image tools for the Tilt-Shift Blur. These tools appear when you choose Filter➪Blur➪Tilt-Shift from the main menu bar. The following list describes each of the available options in the Tilt-Shift Blur panel and on-image tools:

- **Blur.** This slider in the Tilt-Shift panel increases and decreases the blur amount of the selected pin.

- **Distortion.** This slider allows you to adjust the amount of distortion created in the lower blur zone. The distortion radiates from the blur pin. For example, if you slide the blur pin to the right, then the lower blur zone is distorted to the right.

> **Tip**
> No matter how much you rotate the Tilt-Shift focus zone, Photoshop will remember which blur zone was the original lower zone and will therefore keep the distortion in that zone.

The distortion created by this slider radiates from the blur ring. Move the blur ring parallel to the focus lines within the focus zone to see the difference.

- **Blur pin cursor.** The blur pin cursor is the mouse cursor that appears when you open the Blur Gallery. When this cursor is active, Photoshop places a blur pin on the image when you click the right mouse button.

- **Blur pins.** These pins show the center of the blur fields that have been placed on the image. The blur fields radiate from the blur pin.

- **Active blur ring.** When you select a blur pin with the mouse, the blur ring becomes active. Notice that part of the ring is white and part is black. The part that is white denotes the amount of blur that is being applied to that field. Each blur pin can have different settings for the blur amount.

- **Rotate handle.** This handle allows you to rotate or tilt the direction of the blur. Simply click the handle and drag the mouse to the left or to the right.

- **Tilt Angle.** This indicator displays the angle of the rotation. This is useful if you want to create a blur effect to match a specific angle in the image.

- **Focus lines.** The area between these lines remains in focus. You can drag each of the focus lines to change that area of the image that will remain in focus.

- **Feather lines.** The area between these lines and the focus lines are feathered to provide a smooth transition to the blur zone.

- **Focus zone.** This area remains in focus.

- **Transition zone.** The part of the image in this area is feathered from focused to blurry, starting at the focus line.

- **Blur zone.** The part of the image in this area is uniformly blurred.

FIGURE 14.25

The on-image controls for the Tilt-Shift Blur allow you to adjust the blur amount as well as the angle, location, and feathering of the blur fields.

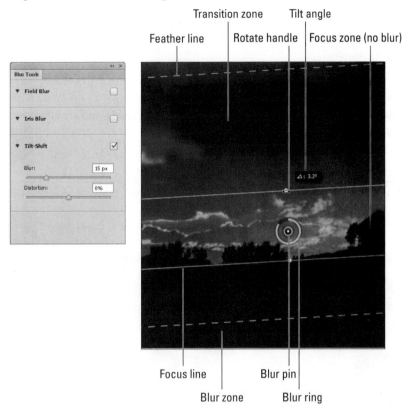

Applying a Field Blur

The most dynamic of the Blur Gallery tools is the Field Blur. By changing the amount of the blur and the location of the blur pins, you can create some fantastic blur effects with the Field Blur. You can create extremely intricate blur designs by adding more blur pins.

In the following example, you will add front and rear blur fields to this image of flowers, giving it a depth of field:

1. **Open the image in Photoshop.**

2. **Choose Filter ⇨ Blur ⇨ Field Blur.**

   This opens the Blur Gallery.

3. **Move the blur pin to the area of the image you want to remain in focus, as shown in Figure 14.26.**

4. **Set the blur value of that blur pin to 0.**

   This creates a field that will protect that part of the image.

5. **Add a blur pin above the area that you want to remain in focus, as shown in Figure 14.26.**

6. **Set the value of that blur pin to 25.**

   This blurs everything above the center blur field.

7. **Add a blur pin below the area that you want to remain in focus, as shown in Figure 14.26.**

FIGURE 14.26

Adding three Field Blur pins using the Blur Gallery, you can quickly add depth of field to a flat image.

8. **Set the value of that blur pin to 20.**

   This blurs everything below the center blur field.

9. **Click the OK button.**

   Notice that the center of the image remains in focus but the areas above and below are blurred, giving the image a depth of field just as if the photo was shot with a wide aperture.

Applying an Iris Blur

The simplest way to accentuate a subject in a photo is to blur around the edges of the photo. The Iris Blur is perfect for softening the edges of an image similar to a vignette effect. By changing the amount of the blur and the shape of the ellipse, you can create some very professional blur effects with the Iris Blur.

In the following example, you will add a soft feathering effect to the edges of a photograph to accentuate the subjects in the foreground:

1. **Open the image in Photoshop.**

2. **Choose Filter ⇨ Blur ⇨ Iris Blur.**

   This opens the Blur Gallery.

3. **Move the blur pin to the center of the area of the image that you want to remain in focus, as shown in Figure 14.27.**

4. **Drag the roundness knob to adjust the ellipse to be more rectangular, as shown in Figure 14.27.**

5. **Drag the ellipse handles to resize the ellipse to exclude only the area that you want to be totally blurry, as shown in Figure 14.27.**

6. **Set the value of that blur pin to 25.**

   This blurs everything outside the ellipse.

7. **Adjust the feather handles until you get just the right amount of feathering around the edges.**

8. **Make any other minor adjustments to the ellipse, feather handles, or blur amount until the image looks the way you want.**

9. **Click the OK button.**

   Notice that the center of the image remains in focus, but there is a nice softening effect around the edges.

14

FIGURE 14.27

Adding an Iris Blur using the Blur Gallery, you can quickly add a soft edging effect to an image.

Applying a Tilt-Shift Blur

The Tilt-Shift Blur allows you to apply blurring effects along straight lines in your images, which is great for landscapes and perspective views. Changing the amount of the blur, the angle, and feathering, you can create some very dramatic blur effects with the Tilt-Shift Blur.

In the following example, you will use the Tilt-Shift Blur tool to soften the ridgeline and enhance the cloud formations in a sunset image:

1. **Open the image in Photoshop.**

2. **Choose Filter ⇨ Blur ⇨ Tilt-Shift.**

   This launches the Blur Gallery.

3. **Move the blur pin to the center of the area of the image that you want to remain in focus, as shown in Figure 14.28.**

4. **Drag the rotate handle to match the tilt in the focus line to that of the skyline, as shown in Figure 14.28.**

   In this example, we rotated the focus line more than 180 degrees so that we could distort the clouds in the sky above the sunset.

5. **Adjust the focus lines so that they only include the area that you want to remain in focus.**

6. **Adjust the feather lines to exclude only the area that you want to be totally blurry, as shown in Figure 14.28.**

7. **Set the value of that blur pin to 25.**

   This blurs everything outside the focus lines.

8. **Adjust the position of the blur pin to the right or to the left to add distortion to the lower blur zone.**

9. **Adjust the distortion setting in the Tilt-Shift pane until you get the right amount of distortion in the lower blur zone.**

10. **Make any other minor adjustments to the tilt, transition zones, focus zones, blur pin, blur amount, and distortion settings until the image looks the way you want.**

11. **Click the OK button.**

    We now have a nice softness to the skyline, almost making it look like an evening mist, and the upper clouds more dramatic.

14

FIGURE 14.28

By applying a Shift-Tilt Blur using the Blur Gallery, you can add a dramatic effect to a sunset image.

 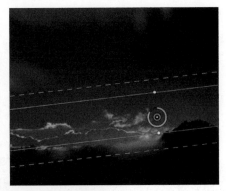

Adding blur effects in the Blur Gallery

A great feature of the Blur Gallery is the ability to add effects to the blurred section of an image. These effects can enhance the overall effect of the blur.

The Blur Effects panel, shown in Figure 14.29, is launched when you select any of the Blur Gallery filters. Using the Blur Effects panel, you can adjust the following options when adding a bokeh effect:

- **Light Bokeh.** This slider allows you to specify the intensity of the bokeh. The greater the value, the larger the image enhancement.

- **Bokeh Color.** This slider specifies the amount of color to include in the bokeh. A value of 0% is neutral, and 100% is full color.

- **Light Range.** This slider allows you to set the upper and lower brightness values that will be impacted by the Light Bokeh effect. Typically, you want to keep the difference between the light and dark at around 5.

FIGURE 14.29

Applying a bokeh effect can add some nice aesthetic qualities to the blurred areas of the image.

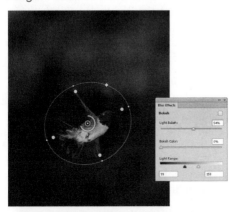

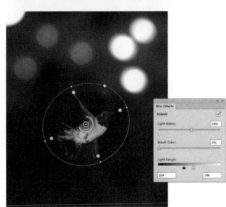

Light Bokeh at 60%

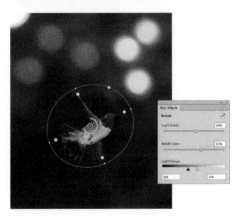

Color Bokeh at 75%

Reducing Noise in an Image

Noise results from pixels that don't belong in an image. Some types of noise include excessive grain, pixelation, and half-toning. Excessive grain can be caused by low lighting, high ISO settings, and even by adjustments in Photoshop. Pixelation occurs when artifacts are left over after an image is resampled to a higher resolution, rotated, or transformed in other ways. Half-toning and Moiré patterns are some examples of artifacts that can be introduced during a scan of a printed image.

The two types of noise are color (chroma) noise and luminance noise. *Color noise* manifests itself as colored artifacts that don't match the image and they become more apparent the more you zoom in on the image. Typically, color noise is more visible in one color channel than the others. *Luminance noise* manifests as bright-gray pixels in grainy images or halos.

Reducing noise and removing dust and scratches can improve the look of images. This section discusses some of the methods of reducing noise in images using the noise filters found in the Filter ⇨ Noise menu.

Using the Despeckle filter

The Despeckle filter is much like the Surface Blur filter. It detects the edges in your image by finding high-contrast areas and blurring the areas in between the edges, reducing the overall noise in the image. You apply the Despeckle filter to the image or layer by choosing Filter ⇨ Noise ⇨ Despeckle.

The Despeckle filter has no dialog box to control the amount of blurring that takes place, so it is limited in what it can do. However, you can apply the Despeckle filter as many times as you want to the image. Each time you apply the Despeckle filter, more smoothing occurs.

Applying a Median filter

The Median filter removes noise from an image by searching each pixel to find pixels that are of similar brightness. If it finds pixels that are different from their surrounding pixels, it replaces them with a pixel value that is determined by the median brightness value of the surrounding pixels. Pixels that vary too much from the neighboring pixels are ignored when calculating the median, so they don't skew the median value.

The Median filter allows you to specify the radius of the area to use when calculating the median value. The best value of the radius varies, depending on the variance of pixels in the image. You can use a higher radius value for images that contain little variance.

To apply a Median filter to an image, you choose Filter ⇨ Noise ⇨ Median. Figure 14.30 shows an example of using the Median filter on an image. Notice that when you zoom in on the hawk's tail, the sky and even the feathers show some noise. When you use a Median filter with a radius of 2, the noise is cleaned up. Some detail is lost due to blurring, but it is still acceptable. However, when you use a Median filter with a radius of 5, you lose a great deal of detail. You need to play around with the filter to figure out the best radius value to remove the noise while minimizing detail loss.

FIGURE 14.30

The Median filter allows you to configure a radius setting that controls the area affected by the filter. Too small a radius does not clean up the noise, but too large a radius removes too much detail.

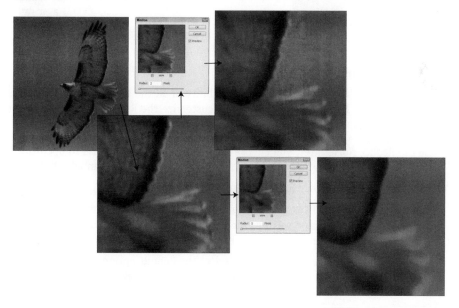

Reducing dust and scratches

You can reduce the imperfections in your image by choosing Filter ⇨ Noise ⇨ Dust and Scratches. The key to success with this filter is to find a good balance between the Radius and Threshold settings.

Turning up the Radius while leaving the Threshold at 0 quickly reduces the dust in your image but also adds a blur to it. By increasing the Threshold, you can keep most of the sharpness in the image and still reduce the imperfections, as shown in Figure 14.31.

 Using the Clone and Healing tools is usually a better method of removing dust and scratches from images. We discuss the Clone and Healing tools in more detail in Chapter 15.

FIGURE 14.31

Getting a good result from the Dust & Scratches filter is a balancing act between adjusting the Radius and Threshold settings.

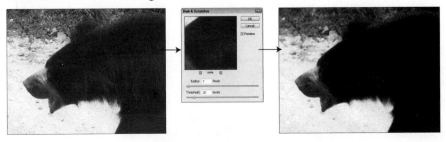

Reducing noise

The Reduce Noise filter provides the most flexibility of all the Noise filters. The different settings in the Reduce Noise dialog box help you customize the Reduce Noise filter to best match the needs of each specific image.

To use the Reduce Noise filter, you choose Filter ⇨ Noise ⇨ Reduce Noise to open the Reduce Noise dialog box, shown in Figure 14.32. From this dialog box, you can adjust the following settings:

- **Basic/Advanced.** This option toggles between Basic and Advanced modes. In Basic mode, you change the settings for all channels at once. In Advanced mode, you adjust settings to reduce noise in each channel individually.

- **Settings.** This menu allows you to select the default option or one of the previously saved presets. You can save a preset by clicking the Save button and delete it by clicking the trash can icon.

- **Strength.** This slider specifies the amount to reduce the luminance noise in the image when the filter is applied, by increasing or decreasing the intensity of the overall noise reduction.

- **Preserve Details.** This slider specifies the percentage of detail that must be preserved. To reduce noise, you must sacrifice some detail. Use this setting to make certain you maintain at least a minimum amount of detail in the image. Typically, you should set this option at 60% or higher.

- **Reduce Color Noise.** This slider specifies the percentage of color noise to remove from the image. If you set this value too high, Photoshop has difficulty distinguishing between color noise artifacts and simple variations in the image. This option is necessary only if color noise exists in the image.

- **Sharpen Details.** A great feature in the Reduce Noise tool, this slider specifies the percentage of detail to try to gain during the filter process. Noise reduction is done by blurring and results in lost detail. This option allows you to specify how much sharpening is applied after the blurring to get regain some of that lost detail. Be careful not to set this value too high, or you will introduce new noise into the image.

- **Remove JPEG Artifact.** When you select this option, the Reduce Noise filter minimizes the blocky image artifacts and halos that can be created when a JPEG file is resampled and then saved again.

- **Per Channel.** This panel allows you to select specific color channels so you can individually customize the Strength and Preserve Details options differently for each color channel.

FIGURE 14.32

The Reduce Noise dialog box allows you to balance the strength of the noise reduction with preserving detail. You can also fine-tune the noise reduction based on individual color channels.

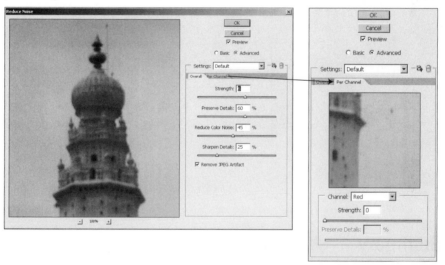

> **TIP**
>
> Removing the noise blurs your picture. Photoshop includes the Sharpen Details setting with this feature to counteract that blurring. You can use this setting or use a more powerful sharpening filter after you have reduced the noise.

Adding noise

In addition to removing noise, Photoshop also allows you to introduce noise into an image. Adding noise to an image adds graininess to it that can simulate film grain, add a texture effect, or camouflage areas that have been corrected.

To add noise to an image, you choose Filter⇨Noise⇨Add Noise to open the Add Noise dialog box, shown in Figure 14.33. You can add noise using the Uniform setting, which randomizes the values used to create the noise pattern, or using the Gaussian setting, which uses the bell curve to create the values. When you add noise to an image, it can appear in varied colors, which can change the color integrity of your file. To avoid this, choose the Monochromatic option to create noise as shades of gray.

FIGURE 14.33

The Add Noise dialog box allows you to introduce noise into an image to simulate film grain, add a texture effect, or camouflage areas that have been corrected.

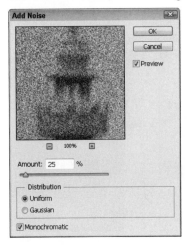

Summary

Using the Photoshop filters allows you to correct blurriness or noise problems in images and make adjustments to soften harsh areas of a photo. This chapter discussed using the sharpening filters to fix blurry images and enhance edges, blurring filters to apply softening effects, and noise reduction filters to remove noise and unwanted artifacts from images.

In this chapter, you learned the following:

- The Smart Sharpen filter allows you to fine-tune the sharpening effect to match the type of blurring problems that occur in a photo

- Using an Unsharp Mask filter can restore missing detail to an image

- Applying a blurring filter to the background of a photo softens the overall appearance of the image

- Using the Field, Iris, and Tilt-Shift filters in the Blur Gallery allows you to quickly add dramatic blurring effects to your images

- Using Motion Blur can make an object in a photo appear to be moving

- Applying a noise reduction filter removes unwanted noise from an image

- You can remove dust and scratches from damaged images

- You can remove JPEG artifacts caused by the compression algorithm used when saving JPEG images multiple times

14

Cleaning Up Digital Images with Cloning and Healing Tools

IN THIS CHAPTER

Removing blemishes with the Healing Brush tools

Reconstructing images using the Clone Stamp

Combining Cloning and Healing techniques for best results

E ven the best photos can have problems that keep them from being perfect: dust and scratches, unsightly backgrounds, or just the presence of an ex-boyfriend. Even the most beautiful photo models can have blemishes, bulges, or cellulite. Family pictures are only as good as the family member who has her mouth open or the person with his eyes closed. The Healing Brush tools and the Clone Stamp are designed to correct these problems and make bad photos good and good photos great.

You can use these tools to create artistic effects as well, adding elements to your photos that wouldn't normally be there and blending images together seamlessly. We'll show you how these tools work in depth, and before you know it, your ex will be history.

Using the Healing Brush Tools

We wish we had a Healing Brush that worked in real life. From acne to carpet stains, our lives would certainly be much easier. The idea behind the Healing Brushes is to take a flaw — such as acne, lens spots, or even unknown people — and remove it by covering it with a patch made by subtly copying and blending the surrounding areas of the image. The Healing Brushes blend the pixel information of the sampled area with the lighting, texture, and transparency information of the target area, so the finished product is an area that blends better than a straight clone. This is especially useful for areas that are similar but consist of many different tones, such as a face.

The Spot Healing Brush works automatically, choosing which areas to blend. The Healing Brush tool allows you to choose which area is used to create the overlay, and you can use the Patch tool to create a selection around the targeted area and preview the resulting fix. The Remix tool is new in

Photoshop CS6 and allows you to expand or contract objects or to move objects from one area of your photo to another. The Red Eye tool doesn't really fit with the description of the Healing Brushes, because the patch it creates is just composed of dark pixels, but it is a fast fix for a common photographic problem, so it is grouped in the Toolbox with the Healing Brushes.

You access the Healing Brushes, the Patch tool, the Remix tool, and the Red Eye tool by clicking and holding the triangle at the bottom of the Toolbox icon, as shown in Figure 15.1, or by pressing J (Shift+J to toggle through the tools).

FIGURE 15.1

The Spot Healing Brush, Healing Brush, Patch, Remix, and Red Eye tools are all found together in the Toolbox.

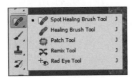

Using the Spot Healing Brush

Sometimes we wonder if Adobe didn't feel like they acted too soon when they named the Magic Wand. The Quick Selection tool is definitely more magical, and the Spot Healing Brush makes things disappear faster than you can say "abracadabra!"

The Spot Healing Brush is primarily used for targeting small blemishes or spots that are surrounded by areas free of defect. Because it doesn't allow you to manually set a sample area, it's a hit-and-miss tool. When it works, it's a one-click-wonder, and when it doesn't, the results are usually extremely bruised and smudged pixels. Thank goodness for the Undo option and the History panel!

You can change options to determine how the Spot Healing Brush works by selecting a brush type in the Options bar, as shown in Figure 15.2. The options are Proximity Match, Create Texture, and Content-Aware.

FIGURE 15.2

The Options bar for the Spot Healing Brush

Proximity Match

When you set the Spot Healing Brush to its default option of Proximity Match, it uses the areas in or around the targeted area to replace the targeted area. If these areas aren't consistent with what you want your end result to be, you can end up with a very interesting patch.

To show you what we mean, look at Figure 15.3. Cleaning the spots off this girl's cheek by just clicking them with the Spot Healing Brush is easy, and presto — they disappear! Try that with the spots around her mouth and nose, however, and you can see in the second photo that she starts to acquire an extra body part.

Create Texture

In targeted areas that are surrounded by variance, such as under the child's nose in Figure 15.3, you can use the pixels inside the targeted area by choosing the Create Texture option. This creates the patch with the pixels inside the targeted area instead of outside the targeted area. The third photo in Figure 15.3 shows the end result using this option, and it looks much better.

FIGURE 15.3

Using the Proximity Match option works great in areas that are consistent, but the Create Texture option is better in areas of variance.

| A face in need of serious clean-up | Using the Proximity Match option can duplicate body parts | Using the create texture option |

Content-Aware

The Content-Aware option actually samples multiple areas to create a patch that matches a background with distinctly different areas. Although it doesn't work with body parts very well, it seems to do a fair job with rough borders, such as the one created by the surf in Figure 15.4. You can see that the ocean and the sand were not only cloned to create the new patch, but cloned in a way that they lined up with the rest of the photo.

FIGURE 15.4

The Content-Aware option makes easy work of taking objects out of a variegated background.

Using the Spot Healing Brush is as simple as using the cursor to paint over the area you want to remove from your image. Photoshop then creates a blended patch based on the options you select to cover the targeted blemish.

ON THE WEB

You can find the photos shown throughout this section saved as Figures 15-3, 15-4, and 15-5 on the website. Use Figure 15-5 to follow along with the exercise.

Follow these steps to use the Spot Healing Brush to correct a spot or blemish in an image:

1. **Open an image that has one or more spots that need correcting.**

   Figure 15.5 is a great photo, but there is a fly in the boy's hair. Zoom closer to the blemish if you want a better view.

FIGURE 15.5

There's a fly in this boy's hair that distracts from an otherwise great photo.

2. **Click the Spot Healing Brush to select it.**

3. **Change the brush size to slightly larger than the area you want healed.**

> **NOTE**
>
> If your blemished area is elongated, you can use a smaller brush size, but you must cover the blemish in one stroke by clicking and dragging the left mouse button to mark the entire blemish before releasing it so the blemish outside the stroke isn't used to heal the area inside the stroke.

4. **Choose a healing mode from the Mode drop-down menu in the Options bar.**

    The Normal healing mode creates the blended patch that we described to you. The Replace mode works like the Clone Stamp to actually replace the selected area by copying and pasting the source exactly how it appears, not blending the pixels at all. This option is rarely a good idea with the Spot Healing Brush because you don't get to pick the replacement pixels. The other modes correspond to the blending modes and create lighter or darker versions of the patch.

15

5. **Choose a type of correction from the Options bar.**

   For the photo in Figure 15.5, we selected Proximity Match because we wanted the color and texture of the surrounding hair to become the patch.

6. **Choose Sample All Layers in the Options bar if you are using a second, empty layer, as shown in Figure 15.6, to make the healing changes.**

FIGURE 15.6

Don't forget to choose Sample All Layers if you are making non-destructive edits to a second, blank layer.

TIP

Using a second layer on which you will apply changes is always an excellent idea. It gives you a canvas to work with and erase changes from, as well as leaving your original image unchanged.

---

7. **Click the blemish with the Spot Healing Brush, as shown in Figure 15.7.**

   You can click and drag if needed to cover the entire blemish.

   Photoshop processes the patch and places it. If you used the Content-Aware option, this might take some time. Your results may or may not be satisfactory. Continue with the following steps to see how the Spot Healing Brush works differently each time you use it.

FIGURE 15.7

When using the Spot Healing Brush, be sure to cover the entire blemish with one pass.

8. **Undo and then use the Spot Healing Brush repeatedly to see several different results.**

   You probably see a different result every time. In other words, if at first you don't succeed....

9. **Make a second pass, and even more, if necessary.**

   Sometimes making two or three passes cleans up edges left by the initial pass. If the Spot Healing Brush works, you should get results similar to Figure 15.8.

15

FIGURE 15.8

When the Spot Healing Brush works, it's almost impossible to tell that your image ever had a blemish.

If you don't get the results that you want, you can move on to the more advanced tools.

Using the Healing Brush

The Healing Brush tool works similarly to the Spot Healing Brush tool, with the added advantage that you get to set the sample point so that you can choose the area where the fix comes from. For instance, Figure 15.9 is a photo of a wild turkey that would look much better if there wasn't vegetation marring the image, particularly the branch in the foreground that is so out of focus that it is very distracting. Using the Spot Healing brush, even multiple times, results in severely bruised and unnatural pixels due to the large size of the blemish. The Healing Brush works much better in situations like this.

FIGURE 15.9

Because the blurred branch is such a large blemish on a variegated background, the Healing Brush is the best tool to fix it.

Follow these steps to use the Healing Brush to correct this image:

ON THE WEB

Use Figure 15-9 from the book's website to follow along with this exercise.

1. **Open an image in need of the Healing Brush tool to correct it.**

   If necessary, change the background to a layer by double-clicking and renaming it.

2. **Select the Healing Brush from the Toolbox, or press J (Shift+J to toggle to it if it is nested behind another tool).**

3. **Select a brush size from the Options bar.**

   Or use the brackets for a quick brush size change.

4. **Alt-click/Option-click to set the sample point.**

   In Figure 15.10, the crosshair shows that we have chosen the feathers that have not been marred by the blurry branch. You can reset the sample point as many times as you need to throughout the healing process by repeating this step. For instance, you will want to select an area of grass to fix the bottom portion of the branch.

15

5. **Drag over areas that you want to be healed, as shown in Figure 15.10.**

   Unlike the Spot Healing Brush, you can make several passes to completely cover an area if you need to. As you drag, notice that the sample point moves along with your cursor, sampling areas in line with what you need to heal. If you have the Aligned option deselected, releasing the mouse returns the sample point to the original starting point. If Aligned is selected, the sample point remains the exact same distance from your Healing Brush tool, no matter how many times you release your mouse.

FIGURE 15.10

Set the sample point by Alt-clicking/Option-clicking. The sample point follows your cursor as you drag the Healing Brush.

6. **Make as many passes as necessary to clean up any branches or other elements in front of the turkey.**

   When you are finished, your photo should look like Figure 15.11.

Instead of using a sampled area, you can use a pattern with the Healing Brush tool. This fix takes the texture of the pattern you choose and adds it to the color of the area you pass the Healing Brush over. To use a pattern, choose Create Texture from the Healing Brush Options bar. In Figure 15.12, we used the Healing Brush to give the background of this photo dimension.

FIGURE 15.11

Without the branches in front, this photo is more engaging.

FIGURE 15.12

The Healing Brush can create textures.

15

Another benefit of the Healing Brush is that you can use the Clone Source panel to create multiple samples, sample from different files, and modify the size and rotation of the source. The Clone Source panel is an important tool in creating the best fixes with both the Healing Brush and Clone Stamp, but it is an integral part of the Clone Stamp and is covered in detail in that section of this chapter.

> **TIP**
>
> Both the Spot Healing Brush and the Healing Brush frequently leave a blurry smudge instead of a clean fix. This is a good time to try again, because this result rarely happens every time you try to heal your photos.

Fixing larger blemishes with the Patch tool

The Patch tool allows you to heal larger areas easily and preview the target area being used. It also uses the source more thoroughly to completely cover the area that needs fixing, so color is not left behind as frequently as it is with the Healing and Spot Healing Brushes.

The Patch tool has a new option in Photoshop CS6 that enables you to use the Content-Aware engine to match the background as closely as possible. You can choose the Normal setting or the Content-Aware setting from the Options bar, as shown in Figure 15.13. You want to use the Normal setting to blend the area to be fixed with the area that you are using to create the patch. For instance, skin tones or areas with similar backgrounds are blended much better to create more realistic shading. The Content-Aware option uses the color and texture information from the background areas around your selection, creating a complete cover-up rather than a blend.

FIGURE 15.13

The Options bar for the Patch tool allows you to choose from a normal patch fix or a content-aware patch fix.

The boy in Figure 15.14 has a skinned area on his forehead that needs to be fixed. However, when applied to such a big area, the Healing and Spot Healing Brushes leave smudges with pink highlights. In this situation, the Patch tool is ideal.

FIGURE 15.14

The skinned area on this boy's forehead is easily fixed with the Patch tool.

The Patch tool is extremely easy to use; follow these steps to get the best results:

ON THE WEB

Use Figure 15-14 from the book's website to follow along with this exercise.

1. **Open an image that needs to be patched.**
2. **Select the Patch tool from the Healing Brush tools flyout in the Toolbox.**
3. **Select a Patch option from the Options bar.**

   For a normal patch fix, select Normal. If you want to make a selection around the area that needs correcting, select Source. If you want to make a selection around the area you are using to correct the image, select Destination. For this example, we selected Source.

NOTE

If you choose Transparent in the Patch options, the patch has a transparent background and simply creates an overlay on the patched area.

4. **Draw around the area that you want to heal.**

   The Patch tool creates a selection much like the Lasso Selection tool. Draw around the area you want to select, and close the selection. You can use the Selection options in the Options bar to add to or subtract from the selection, but it doesn't have to be exact.

15

5. **Click and drag the selection over the area that you want to use to fix the patch.**

   The selection itself won't move, as you can see in Figure 15.15, but an identical selection shows the area you are using. Additionally, the pixels inside your original selection change to preview the fix. This preview is not the final result; after you release the mouse button, the two areas are blended to create a seamless patch.

FIGURE 15.15

Simply drag the selection to an area that can be used to fix the blemish and release the mouse button for a fantastic fix.

6. **Press Ctrl+D/⌘+D to deselect the selected areas and see your final results.**

You can make a content-aware fix using the same steps outlined for the normal fix; the difference occurs in how you apply the patch. In Figure 15.16, for instance, the normal patch blended in a lot of color from the source and left a blotchy residue. By using the content-aware fix, we got a much better result.

Using the Content-Aware fill

The Content-Aware fill isn't found with the Healing tools, but it takes unwanted elements seamlessly out of an image. The Content-Aware feature uses an algorithm that seamlessly fills in a selected area of a photo in a short amount of time. The Content-Aware fill and the Content-Aware patch work similarly, but the Content-Aware patch allows you to choose the area you would like to mimic.

FIGURE 15.16

The content-aware patch fix is very effective.

Normal patch

Content-aware patch

Because the Content-Aware tool works with the Selection tools, it is possible to make precise selections. For instance, the second boy in Figure 15.17 doesn't look like he wants to be in this photo. Using the Quick Selection tool, you can select areas that need to be precise, such as those bordering the first boy. We left the other areas with a rough selection on purpose so the Content-Aware fill didn't take on the look of a silhouette.

ON THE WEB

You can try using the Content-Aware fill on this image. Download Figure 15-17 from the website.

15

FIGURE 15.17

Using the Selection tools allows you to target precise areas on which to use the Content-Aware fill.

After you've made a selection in an image, choose Edit ⇨ Fill to open the Fill dialog box, as shown in Figure 15.18. Choose Content-Aware from the Use menu. After you click OK, the Content-Aware algorithm takes over, searching your photo for appropriate areas to use in replacing the area that was selected. This can be a memory-intensive process, but when it is finished, your image should look close to realistic. You can see in Figure 15.19 that our image is certainly not perfect, but it takes relatively little cleanup to make it look good.

NOTE

The Content-Aware algorithm is memory intensive, and large files can take several minutes and use a considerable amount of RAM. Be sure to make allowances for this.

TIP

The Content-Aware tool, much like the Healing Brushes, doesn't return the same results every time you use it. If you're not happy with the first results you get, try again.

FIGURE 15.18

Choosing the Content-Aware option in the Fill dialog box

FIGURE 15.19

The Content-Aware algorithm makes short work of removing even large elements from images.

Using the Remix tool

New to Photoshop CS6, the Remix tool allows you to make things bigger or smaller, or to move them around in your photo. It does this by using the Content-Aware algorithm to copy areas and put them in the right places in your image. It's much easier to show you what we mean than to explain it.

15

You can try out the Remix tool by following these simple steps:

1. **Open an image that you would like to extend.**

   We chose the building shown in Figure 15.20.

2. **Select the area of your image that you want to extend.**

   You can use any selection tool you want. The Remix tool allows you to create a free-hand selection, but it is difficult to be precise. The more precise your selection, the better the Remix tool works.

3. **Select the Remix tool from the Healing Brush tools flyout in the Toolbox.**

4. **Set the Remix options in the Options bar.**

   To expand the object, select Expand from the Remix pop-up menu. Selecting Very Strict from the Adaptation menu works best with items that have hard lines, such as the building. For items that are less precise, choose a less strict option.

5. **Drag the selection in the direction that you want the object to expand.**

   We've noticed that smaller movements net better results, so the building in Figure 15.20 became incrementally taller, but not a lot taller.

FIGURE 15.20

The Remix tool allowed us to make this building taller.

Another use for the Remix tool is moving objects around in a variegated background. For instance, toys scattered on a carpet can be moved around almost seamlessly. We'll show you how it works.

You can move objects around in a photo with the Remix tool by following these steps:

1. **Open an image containing an item or items with a variegated background.**

   We chose to move the boy in Figure 15.21.

2. **Select the area of your image that you want to move.**

   You can use any selection tool you want. The Remix tool allows you to create a free-hand selection, but it is difficult to be precise. The more precise your selection, the better the Remix tool works.

3. **Select the Remix tool from the Healing Brush tools flyout in the Toolbox.**

4. **Set the Remix options in the Options bar.**

   To move the object, select Move from the Remix pop-up menu. Because our photo does not have hard lines, we selected Very Loose from the Adaptation menu. For items with hard lines, choose a more strict option.

5. **Drag the selection to the area of the photo where you would like to place it.**

   It didn't matter that we had some overlap in the boy; the Remix tool was still able to move him with a minimal amount of bruising, as you can see in Figure 15.21.

Remember that just like any of the healing or content-aware tools, the Remix tool works differently every time you use it, so if you don't like the results you get the first time, try again.

FIGURE 15.21

The Remix tool moved the boy from one side of the photo to the other.

15

Fixing red-eye

The Red Eye tool is easy to use. Click and hold the arrow on the Healing Brush icon in the Toolbox to open the other choices, and click the Red Eye tool; your cursor turns into a cross-hair. You can adjust the pupil size and darken amounts in the Options bar. Center the cursor on the eye, and click. Photoshop takes it from there, darkening the red in the targeted area.

> **NOTE**
>
> Sometimes a subject's red eyes are so washed out that it is difficult to get a good fix with the Red Eye tool. When that happens, the next step is to select the red eye using the Elliptical Marquee. Using a Hue and Saturation adjustment, target the red in the eye and desaturate it. If that doesn't work, the last resort is to actually paint (or clone) new pixels into the eye area.

Using the Clone Stamp Tool

The Clone Stamp tool is the miracle worker that takes off ten pounds, performs head swaps, and adds improbable elements (like giant spiders) to ordinary photos. Knowing how to use this tool effectively gives you the power to create great images from photos that were originally so-so.

The Clone Stamp tool looks like a rubber stamp in the Toolbox, as you can see in Figure 15.22. It is nested with the Pattern Stamp tool, which allows you to brush patterns into your image and is covered in Chapter 16. Clicking the Clone Stamp icon also opens the Clone Source panel.

FIGURE 15.22

The Clone Stamp tool looks just like a rubber stamp.

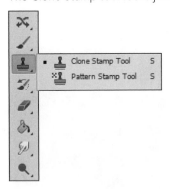

Cloning involves copying an area from an image and then painting it in the same image or a different one. This is useful for removing unwanted elements from an image or adding elements to an image. When you use the Healing Brushes to fix an image, they can leave smudgy-looking areas due to over-blending. The Clone Stamp tool doesn't blend at all (except around the edges, if you choose a soft brush). Because of this, it is more precise than the Healing Brushes, but it can leave obvious edges. It is a powerful tool that takes practice and a measure of creativity to use properly.

In the following section, we show you how to use the Clone Stamp tool and the Clone Source panel, and we provide several examples that demonstrate different ways of using the Clone Stamp as well as tips and tricks for creating a fantastic end result.

Looking over the Clone Stamp options

The Clone Stamp tool has options that make it very versatile so that you can use it in any given situation. You can create seamless fixes or create an effect using blending modes or a change in opacity. You can work with just one layer or you can sample multiple layers. Just like every tool in the Toolbox, when you select the Clone Stamp, the Options bar changes to display the options that are specific to the Clone Stamp. As you can see in Figure 15.23, they are similar to the options for the Healing Brushes, with a few options added.

FIGURE 15.23

The Clone Stamp Options bar provides several options for customizing the Clone Stamp tool to fit your needs.

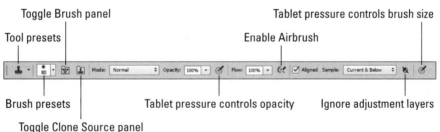

Here are the options and what they do:

- **Tool presets.** This creates a tool preset for the Clone Stamp or loads a preset you have already created.
- **Brush presets.** This displays a list of Photoshop presets for the brush that will be used with the Clone Stamp. Use one of these presets or create your own.

15

- **Toggle Brush panel.** Click this button to open or close the Brush panel.

- **Toggle Clone Source panel.** Click this button to open or close the Clone Source panel.

- **Mode.** This drop-down menu sets the blending mode for the new pixels that are added to your image. Using a blending mode other than Normal can create some great artistic effects.

- **Opacity.** This drop-down list controls the opacity of the pixels that are added to your image.

- **Tablet pressure controls opacity.** If you are using a tablet rather than a mouse, you can change the opacity based on the pressure you exert. This option overrides the Opacity setting.

- **Flow.** This drop-down list controls the rate at which new pixels are applied.

- **Enable Airbrush.** When you enable this option, pixels continue to appear around the brush as long as you hold down the left mouse button, creating a pooling effect.

- **Aligned.** When you select this option, the clone source is locked with the very first brush stroke and doesn't move even when you release the mouse. This is ideal when you are cloning very specific areas, such as a face or other object that you don't want to move. If you are cloning a fix, however, and you want to reset the Clone tool every time you release the mouse button, deselect this option.

- **Sample.** This drop-down menu lets you choose which layers to sample while cloning.

- **Ignore adjustment layers.** If you've already applied adjustment layers to your image and you don't want to add them to the cloning mix, select this option.

- **Tablet pressure controls brush size.** If you use a tablet, you can choose this option to let the pressure determine the brush size. This option overrides the size in your brush presets.

Learning the basics of cloning

Before we show you the more advanced cloning techniques, let's start with an exercise that demonstrates the basic use of the Clone Stamp. The candid shot of a boy climbing a tree in Figure 15.24 captures a moment of childhood, but is marred by the branch in the foreground. Removing the branch in front of him makes the boy the focus of the photo without any distractions.

ON THE WEB

Can you clone out the branch? Follow along by downloading Figure 15-24 from the book's website.

FIGURE 15.24

An almost-perfect image

You can use the Clone tool to erase an object from an image by following these steps:

1. **Open an image with an area that you want to change.**

2. **Click the Clone Stamp tool in the Toolbox.**

3. **Select a brush from the Options bar.**

   A soft brush usually works best for blending in edges.

4. **Place the cursor over an area that you want to clone.**

   It's usually better to choose an area that's as close as possible to the area being fixed so that lighting, color, and texture will be as even as possible.

5. **Press and hold the Alt/Option key as you click the image.**

   This sets the clone source of the image.

6. **Drag over the area where you want to apply the clone.**

   The clone source is copied to that area. The crosshair shows the area that is currently being cloned, as you can see in Figure 15.25.

15

FIGURE 15.25

Dragging over your image with the Clone Stamp copies precisely the area the cross-hair is over.

7. **Reset the clone source as needed by pressing and holding the Alt/Option key and clicking your image.**

8. **Repeat Steps 4 through 7 until the object is gone from your image.**

    When you get to areas that have hard lines, such as the seam on the boy's sleeve, make sure to clone the seam just above or below so that you can line up the seam perfectly. If you take your time and are careful, you will never know there was more to your image, as shown in Figure 15.26.

> **NOTE**
> Although we can use the Clone Stamp by itself to fix the photo of the boy, the Healing Brushes work better in some areas. For instance, the part of the branch in front of the trunk of the tree is fixed much faster and better with the Spot Healing Brush.

FIGURE 15.26

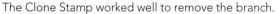

The Clone Stamp worked well to remove the branch.

That's it for the basics of using the Clone Stamp. Are you ready to make it a lot more fun? The Clone Source panel gives you the capability to use a different image, resize your clone source, or even tilt the clone source.

Utilizing the Clone Source panel

The Clone Source panel expands the use of the Clone Stamp tool by providing five different clone sources that can be saved and re-used as well as letting you resize, rotate, and flip your clone source. Using the options found on this panel, you can transfer portions of one photo into another, resize it to fit, and tilt or flip it so that it blends just right.

You can open the Clone Source panel in three ways: clicking the toggle button for the Clone Source panel in the Options bar, clicking the Clone Source icon in the panel, or choosing Window ⇨ Clone Source. Any one of these methods opens the Clone Source panel, shown in Figure 15.27, and with it a whole new world of possibilities.

FIGURE 15.27

The Clone Source panel options

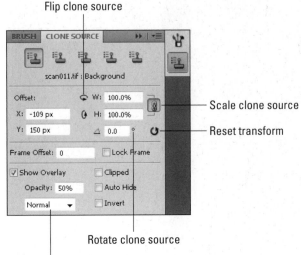

Flip clone source

Scale clone source

Reset transform

Rotate clone source

Overlay blending mode

We introduce you to the options in the Clone Source panel and then show you how they work by taking you through an exercise that uses many of the options.

You will find these options in the Clone Source panel:

- **Clone samples.** The Clone Source panel includes five Clone Sample icons, which enable you to set and store five different clone sources. You can create and use these sources in any document.

- **Offset.** The offset values indicate how far you've moved the clone source from its original position.

- **Flip clone source.** You can flip the clone source vertically or horizontally using the rotating arrows next to the Width and Height percentage fields.

- **Scale clone source.** This option is incredibly useful, especially when you are cloning specific objects from one file into another. Often the clone source needs to be resized to fit into the new document. Type a percentage or use the slider that appears when you hover over the W or H icons. If you want, you can select the link icon to maintain the aspect ratio.

- **Rotate clone source.** Type a rotation degree in this field or use the slider to rotate your source.

- **Reset Transform.** Click this button to change the settings of the Clone Source panel back to the defaults.

- **Frame Offset.** When you are cloning from one frame to another frame using a video file, the frame offset indicates how many frames you are from the clone source.

- **Lock Frame.** Selecting this option locks the clone source in a video file to the original frame it was created on. With this option deselected, as you move from frame to frame cloning a video, your clone source also moves the same number of frames, so the frame offset is consistent. If you want to use the original frame, even while you move through different frames, select Lock Frame.

- **Show Overlay.** This option creates an overlay with the clone source so you can preview the changes you are making with the Clone Stamp.

- **Opacity.** This drop-down list sets the opacity of the overlay. The default setting of 50 percent allows you to clearly see the background at the same time as the clone source and in most cases determine where to place your first stroke.

- **Overlay blending mode.** If you find it hard to distinguish between the overlay and the original image, you can set the blending mode of the overlay to lighten or darken it so it is more easily distinguishable.

- **Clipped.** By default, the clone source overlay is clipped to the area indicated by your Brush tool. This is great for fix-ups where you aren't cloning specific items, but you'll find yourself toggling this option on and off frequently as you work with specific objects.

- **Auto Hide.** Selecting this option shows the overlay when you release your mouse button and hides the overlay as you paint in cloned areas.

- **Invert.** Selecting this option inverts the overlay so it is easier to distinguish from the background image.

> **TIP**
>
> If you are planning to use the Clone Source panel frequently, or at least for an extended period of time, you might want to dock it with the main panels to keep it out of your work area. Drag it into place and drop it when you see a blue highlight indicating it is linked to the other panels in the main area.

Now that you've had an overview of what these options are, we will show you a real-world example that demonstrates the usefulness and scope of the Clone Source tools. In this example, we use a video file instead of an image, not because it's necessary, but simply to demonstrate that image files are not the only files that can be changed with the powerful Photoshop tools.

Figure 15.28 is a frame of a 3D video we created years ago. The photo in the file is outdated, and we want to replace it with a newer one. The Clone Stamp is just the tool we need.

15

FIGURE 15.28

We used the options in the Clone Source panel to change the photo in this video frame.

ON THE WEB

The video for this exercise is available on the website as Figure 15-28.avi, but if you prefer to do this exercise with an image file, the JPEG of this frame is available as Figure 15-28.jpg. You can also find the clone source file saved as Figure 15-29. This file has a skew transformation to make it proportional to the falling frame and a bevel and emboss effect added to give it dimension inside the frame. These changes weren't strictly necessary, but they make the switch more realistic. You can learn how to make these changes in Part VI.

Follow these steps to use the options found in the Clone Source panel:

1. **Open the image you are using for a clone source.**

   The image in this example is shown in Figure 15.29.

2. **Select the Clone Stamp tool from the Toolbox.**

3. **Open the Clone Source panel, and select the first Clone Source icon.**

4. **Alt-click/Option-click inside the clone source file to set your clone source.**

5. **Open the file you want to clone into.**

   In this example, we used the video file in Figure 15.28. If you want to use the video file, use frame 0;00;07;08.

FIGURE 15.29

We used this photo to replace the photo in the video.

> **NOTE**
>
> If you use the video file, Photoshop asks you if you want to correct the aspect ratio when you open it. Click Yes. You are informed that the aspect correction is for preview purposes only. Click OK.

6. **Deselect the Clipped option in the Clone Source panel to reveal the full overlay, as shown in Figure 15.30.**

   If the opacity of your overlay is too high, reduce it so that you can see through to the underlying image. Wow! The image is much larger than the video file.

7. **Resize the clone source so it fits where you want it.**

   It took us a bit of trial and error to get the source photo just the right size, but we'll clue you in: we set our Width and Height at 2.8 percent.

8. **Rotate the clone source so it lines up where you want it.**

   To get our image to line up with the photo frame, we set our angle at −22.2 degrees.

9. **Select the Invert option.**

   Now that the photo file lines up so well with the original and they are both a bit pixilated, it is harder to see the overlay. Selecting the Invert option makes it easier to line them up.

10. **Clone in the new image.**

    After you've lined them up, click to anchor the clone source and make as many passes as needed to clone in what you want. In this case, we cloned the entire source image, so we cheated and made our clone brush huge so we could apply the clone with just one click, as you can see in Figure 15.31. With other images, you may have to be much more precise. Our next exercise demonstrates that.

15

FIGURE 15.30

Resizing this image is definitely a must!

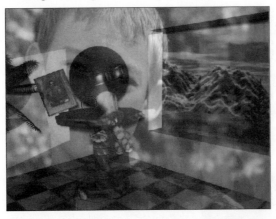

> **NOTE**
>
> You need to deselect the Invert option to see your results.

FIGURE 15.31

Using the Clone Source panel made this clone not only possible but also a very simple process.

Using the Clone and Healing Brushes Together for Optimal Effect

Now that you have a feel for how the Clone Stamp and Healing Brushes work, we will show you a couple of examples of advanced techniques that are frequently used, so you can see not only the steps that make up the process, but also how using the Clone Stamp and Healing Brush tools together creates the best end result.

We start with an old photograph that has missing areas and scratches and move on to arguably the hardest cloning technique, head swapping.

Fixing damaged photos

Most of us treasure old photos of long-gone loved ones. Being able to scan them and preserve them digitally is wonderful; being able to correct them digitally is even better. Figure 15.32 shows an old photo with a scratch and a discolored area that need to be repaired.

FIGURE 15.32

Old photos are a good test of the power of the Clone Stamp and Healing Brush tools.

15

We wanted to try out the Content-Aware fill and see how well it fixes the problem areas. We were surprised because it did a decent job and certainly looks much better than the original. Let's see if we can do a better job with the Clone Stamp and Healing Brush tools.

ON THE WEB
Can you fix the worn and torn areas of this photo? Follow along by downloading Figure 15-32 from the book's website.

Follow these steps to repair this old photo:

1. **Open the image from the website.**

2. **Zoom into the scratch over the window.**

    It's hard to make precise changes unless you can see what you're doing.

3. **Click the Clone Stamp tool to select it.**

4. **Choose a soft brush so the edges of your fix blend well.**

    Size it so it covers just one seam of the curtain because you want to maintain control of individual areas.

5. **Click the Airbrush in the Options bar to activate it.**

    This allows you to hold down the mouse button long enough to fill in the pixels that will start out soft because of the soft brush.

6. **Select the Clipped option in the Clone Source panel.**

    Because you are cloning small areas, this should be adequate to see what you are doing without being distracting.

7. **Alt-click/Option-click one of the seams created by the curtains.**

    Because the area has so many seams, cloning takes several steps. The best areas to clone are either directly over or under the scratch.

8. **Drag slowly over the scratch, being careful to keep the seams in line, so that the curtain runs continuously.**

    Pause long enough in each area to fill in the pixels fully, as shown in Figure 15.33.

9. **Repeat Steps 7 and 8 until you've filled in the area damaged by the scratch.**

    Be sure to use a seam whenever possible so the lines stay consistent. Work until your result looks like Figure 15.34.

10. **Zoom back out, and then zoom in on the discolored area by the boys' legs.**

11. **Repeat Steps 7 and 8 for this area as well.**

    It doesn't have as many seams, but making sure they line up makes your results look all the better.

FIGURE 15.33

Cloning in the seams makes the clone look realistic.

FIGURE 15.34

The window area is repaired.

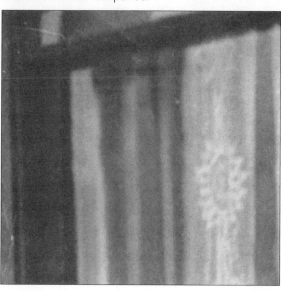

12. **When you are finished with these two areas, use the Spot Healing Brush to target white flecks and other areas of the photo that need a little cleanup.**

    You may need to use the Clone Stamp in one or two areas that have seams, such as the siding. When you are finished, you should have a result similar to Figure 15.35.

FIGURE 15.35

The Content-Aware fill worked much faster and did a fair job, but it couldn't compete with the human touch!

Using the Content-Aware fill   Using the Clone Stamp and Healing tools

Swapping faces with multiple images

With four boys, being able to swap faces is the only way we ever get a decent family picture. These days, face swapping is often used to get the perfect shot. Some face swaps are easier than others. If the shots are nearly identical and the background is just right, it may just be a matter of replacing the expression on one face for another. But even when the circumstances seem ideal, as you see in this next exercise, it's the little things like posture and the tilt of the head that can make this technique complicated.

Figure 15.36 shows two photos that were taken in the same photo shoot of the same kids with the same lighting and background. In this exercise, we are replacing the head of the boy in the second photo with his head in the first.

FIGURE 15.36

Ready for a head swap? Let's take the head of the boy in the first image and clone it into the second image.

ON THE WEB

Follow along by opening Figures 15-36a and 15-36b from the website.

Follow these steps to create the perfect head swap:

1. **Open Figure 15-36a from the website.**
2. **Choose the Clone Stamp from the Toolbox.**
3. **Choose a soft brush and set it to a size you are comfortable with.**
4. **Select the First Clone Source icon in the Clone Source panel.**
5. **Alt-click/Option-click directly above the boy's nose.**
6. **Open Figure 15.36b from the website.**
7. **Create a new layer by clicking the New Layer icon in the Layers panel.**

   Use this layer to clone into.

8. **Deselect Clipped in the Clone Source panel.**

   This displays the entire image as an overlay. Right away, you can see that the source is too big to paint into the second image. If the opacity of your overlay is too high, reduce it so that you can see through to the underlying image.

9. **Reset the scale of the clone source to 89 percent.**
10. **Line up the ears of the overlay with the ears of the original image.**

    Click once to lock the clone in place.

11. **Select Clipped in the Clone Source panel.**

    This allows you to clearly see the areas that have been changed and the areas that still need work.

15

12. **Drag over the boy's face to change it.**

    Be sure there are no soft areas where the pixels aren't filled in completely. Do the best you can with the edges so the two photos blend seamlessly wherever possible. Don't worry; your results right now will be far from perfect, as demonstrated in Figure 15.37.

    FIGURE 15.37

    The first pass with the Clone Stamp leaves several areas that need to be changed back.

13. **Use either the History Brush or the Eraser tool to change any areas back to the original photo that you shouldn't have cloned over.**

    In Figure 15.37, the dog's ear is starting to look transparent, and the boy seems to have two collars on the other side.

> **NOTE**
> The History Brush can be softened so the changes blend in. This isn't always the best option; the dog's ear, for instance, needs to have a hard line drawn back in, but as you change areas with the wall as the background, a soft brush works best. The Eraser works only if you are using a second layer.

14. **Repeat Steps 12 and 13, paying attention to each area to note any aberrations.**

    You probably won't end up with a perfect result, as you can see in Figure 15.38. There is no easy way to get rid of the two collars or line up the shirt so that it matches.

FIGURE 15.38

Even finding the right balance between the images leaves areas that need detail work.

15. **Click the second Clone Source icon in the Clone Source panel.**

    You want to keep the original clone in place so you can use it for repairs.

> **CAUTION**
>
> It is very easy to forget to change between the two clone sources. If you accidentally reset the first clone source, you can't recover it; you have to reset it as closely as possible to use it again to make changes, so be cautious.

16. **Use the second clone source to make small repairs.**

    Alt-click/Option-click the shoulder line on the right side and clone it over the second collar. Also be sure to fix the inside of the shirt, blending the collar and shirt line so it looks natural. Use all the tricks we've shown you so far. Double-check and triple-check areas you have cloned for seams that are out of place, smudges, or unnatural areas. When you are finished, your results should resemble Figure 15.39.

> **TIP**
>
> To create a clean seam for the shoulder, we cloned the boy's arm and rotated the source to replace the seam in the shoulder area.

15

FIGURE 15.39

The powerful Clone Stamp worked its magic, and it's hard to tell that this isn't the original image.

Summary

In this chapter, you learned how to use the Healing Brushes and Clone Stamp to correct and modify your images. You also read about the Content-Aware tools. Using the Clone Source panel, you should be able to make adjustments that help your clone source fit the image you are working with.

At this point, you should be familiar with these tools:

- The Spot Healing Brush
- The Healing Brush
- The Patch tool
- The Content-Aware fill
- The Remix tool
- The Red Eye tool
- The Clone Stamp

Part V

Using Paint, Paths, Shapes, and Text Tools

Editing with Paintbrush Tools

IN THIS CHAPTER

Using paint-brushing techniques

Using brush-style editing tools to edit photos

Customizing paintbrush settings

Painting with brush and non-brush tools

Applying painting and tracing techniques

Although Photoshop is typically thought of as a photo-editing package, it also includes an arsenal of tools that makes it one of the premier painting applications. In fact, the word "painting" in Photoshop means much more than it does in most other painting applications.

What makes painting so effective in Photoshop is that Adobe combined the powerful photo-editing tools with the paintbrush tools so that you can use paintbrush strokes to apply localized photo editing and you can apply photo-editing techniques to your painting.

This chapter discusses the Brush tools available in Photoshop for both editing and painting purposes. It also covers how to configure custom brushes to increase the capability of those tools. Before you begin painting in Photoshop, you likely want to switch to the Painting workspace by choosing Window ➪ Workspaces ➪ Painting from the main menu bar. This configures the workspace specifically to support the painting tools.

Painting in Photoshop

Painting in Photoshop means much more than just painting colors onto a blank document with a brush. Painting means using brushing techniques to apply effects to fix problem areas of photographs, retrace history, blend layers, and apply and mix colors.

In this chapter, we discuss the tools and techniques that you can use to apply some specific changes to images, create artwork, and create dramatic artistic effects. Before we start, though, you should know a few things about painting:

- Brushing techniques are applied by selecting the tool, setting the brush and tool options, and then dragging the cursor on a specific area of the document using a mouse or stylus pen.

- Painting is applied to the currently selected layer in the Layers panel, although some of the tools sample from all the layers to apply the painting effect.

- When you have a selection active, the painting effect applies only inside the selection. This allows you to use the powerful Selection tools to fine-tune your painting.

- Painting is a destructive task that alters pixels. It is a good idea to paint from a copy of the background layer if you are altering a photo and then to apply the change only when you feel that the painting is finished.

- You can paint on vector layers, but you need to convert them to Smart Object layers first.

- Painting is not an exact science. You may need to try different brush styles, sizes, settings, and strokes to achieve the results you are looking for.

Understanding the Painting Tools

The best way to understand painting in Photoshop is to look at the brush-based tools that Photoshop provides. Understanding how these painting tools work can make you more effective at both editing photos and applying artistic effects. This section discusses the painting tools and how to use them.

You use three types of paintbrush style tools to paint in Photoshop: editing, painting, and mixing. Editing tools paint by adjusting the pixels directly beneath the tool. Painting tools paint by applying color to the pixels directly beneath the tool. Mixing tools paint by mixing color with the pixels directly beneath the tool.

TIP

When you are using any of the painting tools, keep in mind that pressing and holding the Shift key while dragging the cursor results in applying the stroke in a straight horizontal, vertical, or diagonal line. You can also press and hold the Shift key as you click the painting tool in two different locations in the image to create a straight paint stroke between the two points.

Many of the painting tools in Photoshop are designed to take advantage of the benefits of using tablet devices. Tablet devices provide a stylus and pad that work in tandem to simulate the experience of drawing with a pencil or other medium. The tablet is able to sense the direction, speed, pressure, tilt, and so on of the stylus. This information is transferred to the Photoshop tools where they are able to apply that information as intelligent brush strokes. The results can be amazing when compared with simply using a mouse. If you are planning to use the painting tools, you should seriously consider adding a tablet to your equipment.

Working with painting tools in blending modes

Many of the painting tools provide blending modes that define the behavior and look of the effect, and how it blends to the pixels beneath. Blending modes are computer algorithms that define methods to combine two pixels into one pixel. The idea is that instead of using one pixel or the other, you can define several ways to combine the two pixels to create a different outcome.

As you begin using the painting tools, you'll notice that many of the tools offer a blending mode setting of some sort. The painting tools use blending modes for a variety of purposes. For example, the Brush tool allows you to set a blending mode that defines how the paint from the brush interacts and blends with the pixels below. And when adding a texture to a brush, a blending mode is used to define how the pixels from the pattern blend with the paint in the brush to create the texture.

The following sections describe the different blending modes and how they relate to the painting tools. For the sake of the descriptions, we refer to the pixels below the brush as the base pixels.

Choosing a basic blending mode option

In Photoshop, there are four basic blending modes that enable you to edit or paint a graphic:

- **Normal.** This is the default option for most of the Brush tools. No blending is applied; instead, the value of the new pixels is the value created by the paintbrush. When painting tools use the Normal mode, the foreground color that is applied is based on the opacity, flow, and airbrush settings. When editing tools use the Normal mode, the tool manipulation is applied using the normal editing algorithm.

- **Dissolve.** The blend is applied by randomly replacing the pixels with either the paintbrush value or the pixels beneath, depending on the pixel location and the opacity setting. Using this option allows you to dissipate the effect of the painting effect, more than just changing the opacity.

- **Behind.** The painting effect is applied only on the transparent areas of the layer. This mode works only when you deselect the Lock Transparency option for the layer.

- **Clear.** This applies the painting effect as transparency. It's similar to the Eraser tool, but it works with the Shape, Paint Bucket, Brush, and Pencil tools to apply the transparency. This mode works only when you deselect the Lock Transparency option for the layer.

> **NOTE**
> The Behind and Clear blending modes are not available if the selected layer in the Layers panel is locked.

Applying a darkening blending mode

The blending modes menu contains darkening effects. These five blending filters reduce the painting effect in the darker areas and apply more paint to the lighter pixels below. The result is that the effects tend to darken the overall image:

- **Darken.** The blend is applied by replacing the pixels with the darker of the base value or the paintbrush value. In other words, the painting effect is only applied to the underlying pixels that are lighter than the value of the brush pixel. This has the effect of darkening the image.

- **Multiply.** The blend is applied by multiplying the base value of each pixel by the paintbrush pixel value. Multiplying a pixel by black always produces black, and multiplying a pixel by white leaves the pixel value unchanged. This mode has the overall effect of darkening the image.

- **Color Burn.** The blend is applied by darkening the base channel; based on the brush color, Photoshop increases the contrast between the two. This has the effect of darkening the image as well as increasing color contrasts.

- **Linear Burn.** This darkens the image as it applies the blend by decreasing the brightness based on the value of the paintbrush pixel.

- **Darker Color.** The blend is applied by replacing each of the channels of a pixel with whichever is darker: the base pixel channel or the paintbrush pixel channel. This option works a bit better than using the Darken mode because it uses the darkest values from each of the channels to create the resulting color. For example, this mode may use red and green from the base pixel and blue from the paintbrush pixel.

Selecting a lightening blending mode

The lightening blending modes have the opposite effect of the darkening blending modes. As you apply the painting effect, the results tend to lighten darker areas of the image while not significantly impacting the lighter areas of the image:

- **Lighten.** The blend is applied by replacing the pixels with the lighter of the base value or the paintbrush value. This has the effect of lightening the image and can be extremely useful if applying filters to underexposed images.

- **Screen.** The blend is applied by multiplying the inverse of the channel values of the paintbrush and base pixels. This results in a lighter color than either the paintbrush value or the base value. This has the same effect as projecting multiple photographic slides on top of each other.

- **Color Dodge.** This applies the blend by decreasing the contrast between the color of the channels in the paintbrush pixel and the base pixels. This lightens the base pixels using the paintbrush pixel values.

- **Linear Dodge (Add).** This lightens the image as it applies the blend by increasing the brightness based on the paintbrush pixel value of each channel.

■ **Lighter Color.** The blend is applied by replacing each channel of a pixel with whichever is lighter: the base pixel channel or the paintbrush pixel channel. This option works a bit better than using the Lighten mode because it uses the lightest values from each channel to create the resulting color.

Adding contrast blending modes

These blending modes create contrast between the paintbrush effect and the base pixels, making the lighter areas lighter and the darker areas darker:

■ **Overlay.** This applies the blend by mixing the paintbrush values with the base pixels while preserving the shadows and highlights. This reduces the effect of extreme layer adjustments that dramatically reduce the detail in the original image.

■ **Soft Light.** This applies the blend based on the gray value of the paintbrush pixel. If the value of the paintbrush pixel is darker than 50-percent gray, the base pixel is darkened using a multiplying method. If the value of the paintbrush pixel is lighter than 50-percent gray, the base pixel is lightened using a dodging method. This has a similar effect to shining a diffused spotlight on the image.

■ **Hard Light.** This applies the blend based on the gray value of the paintbrush pixel. If the value of the paintbrush pixel is darker than 50-percent gray, the base pixel is darkened using a multiplying method. If the value of the paintbrush pixel is lighter than 50-percent gray, the base pixel is lightened using a screening method. This has a similar effect to shining a harsh spotlight on the image. This option is great for adding shadows while applying the filter.

■ **Vivid Light.** This applies the blend based on the gray value of the paintbrush pixel. If the value of the paintbrush pixel is darker than 50-percent gray, the base pixel is darkened by increasing the contrast. If the value of the paintbrush pixel is lighter than 50-percent gray, the base pixel is lightened by decreasing the contrast.

■ **Linear Light.** This acts as a combination of the linear dodge and linear. If a paintbrush pixel is darker than 50-percent gray, then the pixels in the image are darkened by the brush stroke. If a paintbrush pixel is lighter than 50-percent gray, then the pixel in the image is lightened by the brush stroke.

■ **Pin Light.** This applies the filter based on the gray value of the paintbrush pixel. If the value of the paintbrush pixel is darker than 50-percent gray, the darker of the paintbrush pixel and base pixel is used. If the value of the layer pixel is lighter than 50-percent gray, the lighter of the paintbrush pixel and base pixel is used.

■ **Hard Mix.** This adds the value of each RGB channel in the paintbrush pixel to the corresponding RGB channel in the base pixel. The values above 255 and below 0 are clipped, which can result in a large loss of detail.

Blending two layers

The Difference, Exclusion, Subtract, and Divide blending modes blend two layers based on the difference between the layers:

- **Difference.** This applies the blend by setting the resulting pixel to the value of the difference between the paintbrush pixel and the base pixel. Blending white inverts the pixel value, and blending black results in no change.

- **Exclusion.** This works similar to the Difference blend mode, but generates less contrast providing better effectiveness when aligning images.

- **Subtract.** This applies the blend by subtracting the pixel value in the paintbrush from the corresponding pixel in the image. The resulting pixel value is divided by a scale factor and then added to an offset to make certain it still falls in the 0–255 range. As a result, the darker the paintbrush pixel is, the less effect it has on the image pixel.

- **Divide.** This works the same way that the Subtract blend mode does, but the image pixel is divided by the paintbrush pixel. This increases the range of variance in changes in the image pixels.

Finishing with a color blending mode

The final group of blending modes gives the selected layer a color influence over the layers under it:

- **Hue.** This applies the blend by creating the resulting pixel using the luminance and saturation of the base pixel but the hue of the paintbrush pixel. This reduces the blend to affect only the hue of the base pixels.

- **Saturation.** This applies the blend by creating the resulting pixel using the luminance and hue of the base pixel but the saturation of the paintbrush pixel. This reduces the blend to affect only the saturation of the base pixels.

- **Color.** This applies the blend by creating the resulting pixel using the luminance of the base pixel but the hue and saturation of the paintbrush pixel. This limits the blend so it doesn't affect the brightness of the base pixels.

- **Luminosity.** This applies the blend by creating the resulting pixel using the hue and saturation of the base pixel but the luminance of the paintbrush pixel. This allows you to apply it so it affects only the brightness of the base pixels.

Applying color with painting tools

Painting tools enable you to apply new color and modify existing color to the pixels in a specific region under the tool. This is a basic concept that has been around for decades. Photoshop enhances the paint technique by allowing you to select specific brush styles, sizes, and settings that control how pixels are painted in almost unlimited ways. The painting tools can be found in the Toolbox as shown in Figure 16.1. This allows you to quickly switch between painting and other operations in Photoshop.

TIP

You can select the painting tools using the B hotkey, and you can toggle through the Brush, Pencil, Color Replacement, and Mixer Brush tools by using the Shift+B hotkey sequence.

FIGURE 16.1

The painting tools allow you to apply color to images using a variety of brush and pencil strokes.

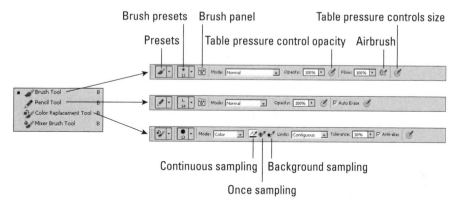

The following list describes the painting tools that you use to add color to your images:

- **Brush and Pencil tools.** The Brush and Pencil tools work basically the same way with one distinct difference. Brush tool strokes have a soft edge that is created by anti-aliasing the edges of the stroke so the edge blends slightly with the surrounding image. Pencil tool strokes have a crisp, hard edge that is not blended with the surrounding image. Figure 16.2 shows an example of the Brush and Pencil tool strokes applied with the same brush style.

FIGURE 16.2

The Brush tool applies the stroke with soft edges, and the Pencil tool applies the stroke with hard edges.

Brush tool stroke

Pencil tool stroke

Even though the concept is simple, the Brush and Pencil tools provide an incredible range of results. Using the Brush and Pencil tools, you can configure the following settings in the tool menus that control how the brush and pencil strokes are applied to the image:

- **Presets.** As with all presets in Photoshop, the Presets option allows you to quickly save the tool settings and then load and select them later.

- **Brush Preset.** The Brush Preset drop-down menu allows you to select the style of brush to use for the tool. You can also set the size and hardness of the brush.

  The size of the brush determines the area of pixels that are affected by the brush stroke, and the hardness of the brush determines the intensity of the stroke. When painting, harder brushes mean more color is added; when editing, harder brushes mean that a more dramatic effect is applied.

> **NOTE**
>
> The settings that you apply using the Brush panel add to or override the settings you specify in the Brush Preset Picker drop-down menu. You will probably want to select a brush using a combination of the Brush Preset Picker option, the Brush panel, and the Brush Presets panel.

Using the Brush Preset Picker pop-up menu, you can manage the set of listed brushes. You can rename and remove brushes, load different sets of brushes, and even manage the appearance of the lists, as shown in Figure 16.3.

- **Brush panel.** Selecting the Brush Panel option displays the Brush panel, which allows you to control a variety of options for every aspect of the brush behavior. The Brush panel is covered in more detail later in this chapter.

- **Mode.** This drop-down menu specifies the blending mode used to apply the brush stroke to the pixels below. The blending mode can have a major impact on how the brush strokes look. Instead of just applying the brush stroke to the pixels below, Photoshop blends the pixel data in the brush stroke with the pixel data in the selected layer, based on the blend mode algorithm. Blend modes are covered in more detail later in this chapter.

- **Opacity.** This drop-down menu allows you to specify the opacity of the painting tool. A larger amount of opacity means that the underlying pixels are affected more by the painting stroke. A value of 100% means that all pixels are affected; 0% means that none of the pixels are affected.

- **Tablet Pressure Controls Opacity.** When you choose this option, the pressure on the stylus tip defines the percentage of opacity involved when painting. This is a great option to fine-tune your strokes using a more realistic effect, if you have a stylus pen.

- **Flow.** The Flow drop-down menu controls the rate at which the tool effect is applied to the pixels below. A value of 100% means that the pixels are affected immediately. Adjusting the flow lower applies the effect more slowly, allowing you to move the brush before the full effect of the tool is applied to the underlying pixels. Using this option, you can give your stroke effect a more realistic look just as if you were painting at different speeds with a real brush.

- **Airbrush.** When you select this option, the stroke is applied in gradual tones to the image. This option typically works better when used in conjunction with a reduced flow setting.

- **Auto Erase.** This option allows you to use the Pencil tool to paint over areas containing the foreground color using the selected background color. When you select this option and the cursor is over the foreground color when you begin dragging, the area is painted with the background color. When you select this option and the cursor is not over the foreground color when you begin dragging, the area is painted with the foreground color. In other words, this doesn't erase, but simply replaces any pixels with the foreground or background color depending on the color underneath the mouse when dragging was initiated.

- **Tablet Pressure Controls Size.** When you select this option, the stylus pressure overrides the brush or pencil size when painting.

FIGURE 16.3

The Brush Preset Picker pop-up menu options allow you to quickly select a brush and set the size and hardness. You can also manage the list of brush styles that are displayed.

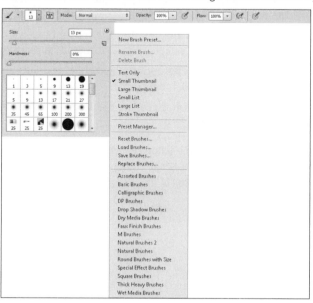

- **Color Replacement Tool.** The Color Replacement tool works similarly to the Brush tool except that it applies the paint, specified by the foreground color in the Toolbox, only to a specified color. This is a great way to replace one color in the image with another without affecting the surrounding pixels. A sample color is selected, and as you apply the Color Replacement tool, Photoshop analyzes the pixels below the tool, determines which pixels match the sample color, and paints only those pixels. Only the pixels that match the sampled color are replaced, as shown in Figure 16.4.

  Using the Color Replacement tool, you can configure the following settings in the Tool Options bar, shown in Figure 16.1, that control how the Color Replacement strokes are applied to the image:

  - **Continuous Sampling.** When you select this option, the Color Replacement tool continuously samples the pixel directly beneath it to determine what color pixels to paint. When this option is set, it behaves similarly to the Brush tool, depending on the other settings.

  - **Once Sampling.** When you select this option, the color to replace is determined by the pixel directly below the tool when you first click and begin to drag the mouse. This option is great for quickly selecting the color to replace directly from the image.

  - **Background Sampling.** When you select this option, the color to paint is determined by the background color in the Toolbox.

  - **Limits.** This drop-down menu allows you to set the limit of erasing to Discontiguous, Contiguous, or Find Edges. Discontiguous replaces the pixels wherever they occur. Contiguous replaces only the pixels that are immediately adjacent to the changeable pixels. Find Edges replaces pixels while trying to keep the edges in the image distinct.

  - **Tolerance.** This drop-down menu specifies the tolerance to use when determining whether a pixel matches the sample color and should be replaced.

  - **Anti-alias.** When you select this option, Photoshop uses anti-aliasing to soften the edges around the pixels being replaced.

- **Mixer Brush tool.** The Mixer Brush tool is a bit different from the painting tools and is covered later in this chapter.

Figure 16.4 shows an example of using the Color Replacement tool to paint a different color onto a flower. Notice that only the petals of the flower are affected. We used the Sampling options to sample a petal, so only the pixels that are similar to the color of the petals are altered, leaving the others alone.

FIGURE 16.4

The Color Replacement tool allows you to use brush strokes to paint over a specific color while leaving the other colors alone.

Painting with editing tools

Editing tools enable you to paint by using different algorithms to manipulate the pixels in a specific region under the tool instead of laying down a new color. These tools allow you to control the shape and the size of the area of pixels affected by the tool. You manipulate the pixels by dragging the mouse or using a stylus pen.

The editing tools allow you to fix or enhance problem spots in images. For example, you can use the Spot Healing Brush tool to remove blemishes, or the Sharpen tool to enhance the sharpness of a specific area of a photo. The following sections discuss the editing tools that you use to paint edits on photos in Photoshop.

Making quick fixes with the healing tools

The healing tools shown in Figure 16.5 allow you to quickly fix problem areas of photos, such as scratches, red-eye, or even the removal of unwanted objects.

 For a more detailed explanation of how to use the healing tools to edit photos, see Chapter 15.

FIGURE 16.5

The healing tools allow you to use brush strokes to quickly fix and remove problem areas in photographs.

Choosing a Stamp tool to replace pixels

The Clone Stamp tool shown in Figure 16.6 allows you to quickly fix problem areas of photos, such as scratches and unwanted objects, by using other areas of the photo as a source to replace pixels using a Stamp brush.

 For a more detailed explanation of how to use the Clone Stamp tool to edit photos, see the section on cloning in Chapter 15.

The Pattern Stamp tool works similarly to the brush tool except that it paints a pattern instead of a color. The options for the Pattern Stamp tool include the following:

- **Pattern Picker.** This option allows you to select a pattern to paint from the drop-down menu.
- **Aligned.** When you enable this option, the pattern in each new brush stroke is aligned with the previous brushstroke. This allows you to keep the pattern aligned as you paint multiple strokes.
- **Impressionist.** Selecting this option softens the pattern to give it an artistic effect rather than a crisp pattern.

FIGURE 16.6

The Clone Stamp tool allows you to use a stamp effect to quickly fix or remove problem areas in photographs.

Pattern Picker

Using history tools

The history tools shown in Figure 16.7 allow you to use brush effects to paint previous edit states of the document onto the current state. These tools allow you to use a painting effect to reveal effects from previous edit states.

 For a more detailed explanation of how to use the history tools to revive effects from previous states, see Chapter 5.

FIGURE 16.7

The history tools allow you to use a paintbrush to paint data from a previous edit state of the document onto the current state, thus restoring effects to specific areas of the image.

Choosing an eraser tool

The eraser tools, shown in Figure 16.8, are designed to erase pixels from the image. However, the eraser tools provide several settings that offer you a lot of flexibility when removing pixels. Eraser tools apply to the selected layer in the Layers panel, so you can restrict the erasing to a specific layer.

> **TIP**
>
> You can select the Eraser tools feature using the E hotkey, and you can toggle through the eraser tools by using the Shift+E hotkey sequence.

FIGURE 16.8

The eraser tools allow you to remove pixels from a layer in the image and replace them with transparency or background color.

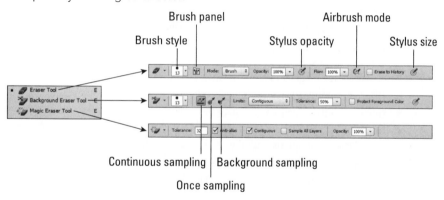

You can use three types of eraser tools, as shown in Figure 16.8:

- **Eraser.** The Eraser tool is designed to remove pixels from the current layer and replace them with transparency or the background color using the following options:

  - **Mode.** This drop-down menu allows you to erase using a Brush, Pencil, or Block tool. The Block mode is simply a square tool that's useful in hard-to-erase corners. The Pencil mode allows you to select the pencil tip, but the edges are hard for crisp erasing. The Brush mode enables you to erase using all the functionality of brush strokes, so you can smooth the edges of the area being erased.

  - **Opacity.** This drop-down menu allows you to specify the opacity of the Eraser tool. The higher the opacity, the more the underlying pixels are removed as you paint on them.

  - **Stylus Opacity.** When you select this option, the pressure on the stylus tip defines the amount of opacity that is applied when erasing.

- **Erase to History.** When you select this option, instead of erasing to transparent or background pixels, the Eraser tool erases to a previous history state, as described in Chapter 5.

- **Flow.** The Flow drop-down menu controls the rate at which the erase effect is applied to the pixels below. A value of 100% means the pixels are erased immediately. Reducing the flow amount applies the erasure more slowly, allowing you to move the brush before fully erasing the underlying pixels.

- **Airbrush Mode.** When you select this option, the erasure is applied gradually to the image to soften the edges of the area being erased. This option typically works better when used in conjunction with a reduced flow setting.

- **Stylus Size.** When you select this option, the stylus pressure overrides the brush or pencil size when erasing.

- **Background Eraser tool.** The Background Eraser tool is designed to erase a specific color from the layer instead of just erasing everything. This is an extremely useful tool to remove monotone elements from images or to clean up a specific color from a layer. The Background Eraser tool provides the following options:

  - **Continuous Sampling.** When you select this option, the Background Eraser tool continuously samples the pixel directly beneath it to determine what color of pixels to erase. When you set this option, it behaves similarly to the regular Eraser tool, depending on the other settings.

  - **Once Sampling.** When you select this option, the color to erase is determined by the pixel directly below the tool when you first click and begin to drag the mouse. This option is great for quickly selecting the color to erase from the image.

  - **Background Sampling.** When you select this option, the color to erase is determined by the background color in the Toolbox.

  - **Limits.** This drop-down menu allows you to set the limit of erasing to Discontiguous, Contiguous, or Find Edges. Discontiguous erases the pixels wherever they occur. Contiguous erases only the pixels that are immediately adjacent to the first selected pixel. Find Edges erases pixels while trying to keep distinct edges in the image.

  - **Tolerance.** This drop-down menu specifies the tolerance to use when determining whether a pixel matches the sample color and should be erased.

  - **Protect Foreground Color.** When you select this option, the color in the foreground of the Toolbox is protected from erasure. This option is typically used to erase everything but one color, as shown in Figure 16.9.

FIGURE 16.9

The Eraser tool erases all pixels, whereas the Background Eraser tool can be used to erase or preserve specific colors, and the Magic Eraser tool finds and erases pixels with similar colors.

16

Original

Background Eraser tool

Eraser tool

Magic Eraser tool

- **Magic Eraser tool.** The Magic Eraser tool offers a fast way to erase similar pixels throughout your image. Simply click a pixel in the image, and Photoshop scans the rest of the image and automatically removes all pixels that are similar using the following options:

  - **Tolerance.** This drop-down menu allows you to set the tolerance that Photoshop uses when determining whether the pixel matches the selected pixel and should be erased.

  - **Anti-alias.** When you select this option, Photoshop uses anti-aliasing to smooth the edges between the pixels being erased and the pixels remaining.

  - **Contiguous.** When you select this option, only pixels that are contiguous in similar color to the selected pixel are erased.

  - **Sample All Layers.** When you select this option, pixels in all layers are sampled to determine the color to be used when erasing pixels. When this option is not selected, the Magic Eraser tool samples only from the selected layer. This can be useful in removing pixels from one layer that match the pixels in another layer without affecting the other layer.

Figure 16.9 shows an example of how each eraser tool works. Notice that the Eraser tool erases all the pixels, but because we have set the foreground color to the color of the flowers, the Background Eraser tool does not erase the flowers. Also notice that the Magic Eraser tool erases most of the color of the flowers from the image.

Selecting the right Sharpen, Blur, or Smudge tool

The Sharpen and Blur tools, shown in Figure 16.10, allow you to use Brush tools to apply sharpening and blurring techniques to specific areas of an image. The Smudge tool samples the pixels in the image below the tool and applies those pixels as you drag the mouse or stylus across the image. The result is that the pixels in the image are combined with the sampled pixels, producing a smudging effect.

 For a more detailed explanation of sharpening and blurring images, see Chapter 14.

FIGURE 16.10

The Sharpen and Blur tools allow you to use brushing techniques to apply sharpening and blurring to specific areas of an image. The Smudge tool allows you to use brush techniques to smudge areas of an image.

The following list describes some of the specific options available in the tool menu for the Blur, Sharpen, and Smudge tools:

- **Mode.** This drop-down menu allows you to set the blending mode to use when applying the blur, sharpen, or smudge effect. The options are Normal, Darken, Lighten, Hue, Saturation, Color, and Luminosity.

- **Strength.** This drop-down menu allows you to set the strength of the effect from 0 to 100 percent. Applying a higher strength makes the blur, sharpen, or smudge effect more dramatic.

- **Sample All Layers.** When you select this option, Photoshop uses all layers to calculate the effect that is applied to the current layer. Keep in mind, though, that only the current layer is affected.

- **Protect Detail.** When you select this option, the Sharpen filter tries to protect the detail in the image.

- **Finger Painting.** When you select this option, instead of sampling the image to fill the Smudge tool, Photoshop uses the foreground color. The effect is similar to dipping your finger in paint and then dragging it across a wet image.

Figure 16.11 shows an example of how the Blur, Sharpen, and Smudge tools work. Notice that the Blur tool can blur out the center of the image without affecting the detail in the rest of the image, just as the Sharpen tool can sharpen just the center. The Smudge tool has a completely different effect in that it smudges the pixels in the center just as if they were wet paint on a canvas.

Choosing a Dodge, Burn, or Sponge tool

The Dodge, Burn, and Sponge tools, shown in Figure 16.12, allow you to use brush techniques to apply lightening, darkening, and saturation adjustments to specific areas of an image. The Dodge tool applies a lightening effect to the pixels as you drag the mouse or stylus across the image. The Burn tool applies a darkening effect to the pixels as you drag the mouse or stylus across the image. The Sponge tool either saturates or desaturates the pixels as you drag the mouse or stylus across the image.

> **TIP**
> You can select the Dodge, Burn, and Sponge tools using the O hotkey, and you can toggle through them by using the Shift+O hotkey sequence.

 Lighting and saturation corrections are discussed in more detail in Chapter 13.

FIGURE 16.11

The Blur, Sharpen, and Smudge tools apply blurring, sharpening, and smudging to specific areas of the image using paint strokes.

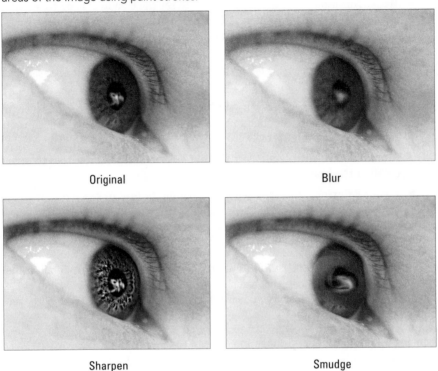

Original   Blur

Sharpen   Smudge

FIGURE 16.12

The Dodge, Burn, and Sponge tools allow you to use brush techniques to apply lightening, darkening, and saturation adjustments to specific areas of an image.

The following list describes some of the specific options available in the tool menu for the Dodge, Burn, and Sponge tools:

- **Range.** This drop-down menu specifies the tonal range to which you want to apply the Dodge or Burn effect. The available tonal ranges are Shadows, Midtones, and Highlights.

- **Exposure.** This drop-down menu allows you to set the amount of exposure applied with the Dodge or Burn tool. A larger percentage in the Exposure setting results in a more dramatic effect.

- **Protect Tones.** When you select this option, Photoshop limits the amount of adjustment in the Dodge and Burn tools so that they have a minimal effect on the color tones.

- **Mode.** This drop-down menu allows you to specify whether to apply a color saturation or desaturation effect with the Sponge tool.

- **Flow.** The Flow drop-down menu controls the rate at which the saturation or desaturation effect is applied to the pixels below. A value of 100% means the pixels are affected immediately. Adjusting the flow lower applies the affect more slowly.

- **Vibrance.** When you select this option, the effect of the Sponge tool is limited to keep as much of the vibrance of tones as possible.

Figure 16.13 shows an example of applying the Dodge and Burn tools to help the look of a photo that was taken at the wrong angle during a sunny day. Notice in the original that the hair shines too brightly and a bad shadow appears on the other side of the face. Using the Dodge tool, we lightened the face a bit to restore some of the detail, and using the Burn tool, we darkened the highlight in the hair.

FIGURE 16.13

Using the Dodge and Burn tools, you can apply brushing techniques to darken highlights and brighten shadows.

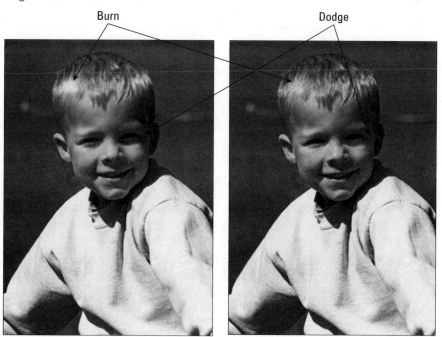

Burn   Dodge

Painting with mixing tools

The Mixer Brush tool is designed to mix the paint in the brush with the pixels below to produce the effect of using real paint. The Mixer Brush tool is extremely dynamic and versatile in how it mixes the paint with the pixels below.

The Mixer Brush tool lets you use the color palette to mix paint into the image, use a dry brush to mix the paint on the image, set how much paint is applied to the brush, and apply other changes to create an effect similar to painting with actual wet paint on a physical medium.

The Mixer Brush tool is available in the painting tools set in the Toolbox and you can select it by pressing Shift+B to toggle through the painting tools. The following list describes some of the options in the Tool Options menu, shown in Figure 16.14, when you select the Mixer Brush tool (for descriptions of the other options that are not listed, see the painting tools section earlier in this chapter):

FIGURE 16.14

Options for the Mixer Brush tool allow you to set the color and control the paint mix, color, and cleaning of the brush.

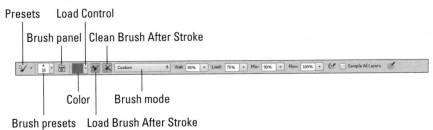

- **Color.** This field displays the current paint that's loaded in the brush. This feature is critical when you are painting with wet paint so you can see what colors of paint will be applied with the brush strokes. The area in the center is the area of the brush at the tips that most affects the pixels. The area to the outside corresponds to the area of the bristles farthest from the tips and does not affect the pixels as much.

  When the brush is clean, this displays a transparent pattern. When the brush is full of a single color, this displays a solid color. When the brush is mixed, it displays the mix of colors as shown in Figure 16.15. When the outside area is transparent, only the tip of the brush is wet. When you click the Color field, it launches a color chooser that allows you to set the color of paint that is applied using the brush strokes.

- **Load Control.** This drop-down menu allows you to quickly load or clean the brush. You also have the option of setting the Load Solid Colors only. This loads the brush with a solid color only. If you use this option with the Clean Brush After Stroke option, the brush is loaded with a single color only.

FIGURE 16.15

The Color field displays the paint that is currently loaded in the brush. An empty brush is transparent, and a mixed brush shows all mixed colors.

Empty   Single color   Mixed

- **Load Brush After Stroke.** When you select this option, the brush is reloaded with the foreground color after each stroke. This is a great way to paint a large area, but it can result in more paint being added to the canvas than you may expect, because the paint in the brush is constantly being replenished.

- **Clean Brush After Stroke.** When you select this option, the brush is cleaned after each stroke. If you use this option with the Load Brush After Stroke option, the brush is always loaded with the foreground color only.

- **Brush Mode.** This drop-down menu allows you to quickly set the wetness, load, and mix of the brush stroke to preset values. Essentially, it's the same thing as defining how thin the paint is and the heaviness of the mixture of paints as the stroke is applied to the canvas. You can specify wetness levels between dry and very wet, where dry means a solid stroke and very wet means the paint is very thinly applied to the pixels. You can specify mixture levels of light or heavy. You also have the option of selecting custom values and setting specific values. Figure 16.16 shows an example of some of these settings.

FIGURE 16.16

Using different wetness, load, and mixture levels changes the way that paint is applied to the pixels below.

Dry, light load

Dry, heavy load

Wet, light mix

Wet, heavy mix

- **Wet.** This drop-down menu specifies the exact percentage to use for the wetness of the paint on the brush. The wetter the paint, the thinner the amount of paint that is applied.

- **Load.** This drop-down menu specifies the percentage of paint to place into the brush each time the brush is loaded.

- **Mix.** This drop-down menu specifies the percentage of mixing that occurs between the paint in the brush and the pixels below when you apply the brush stroke to the image.

- **Sample All Layers.** When you select this option, the Mixer Brush tool samples all the layers in the document when applying paint. Keep in mind that the resulting painting effect is applied only to the selected layer.

> **TIP**
>
> Using the Sample All Layers option, you can create a blank layer to paint on that makes the painting effect non-destructive. You can even paint on multiple new layers, so that you can try different techniques until you find one you like.

Using the Brush Panel

The Brush panel is by far the most complex and capable tool in defining how painting strokes are applied to an image. The Brush panel has two purposes: to select the type of brush and to define the behavior of the brush when applying brush strokes.

Using the options available in the Brush panel, you can define the shape, bristle length, stiffness, texture, and many more features of the brush used to apply the painting effects to the image. At any time, you can reset the settings used in a brush by selecting Reset Brush Controls from the Brush panel menu.

You can open the Brush panel by pressing F5 on the keyboard, selecting the Brush panel option from one of the painting tools, or choosing Window ➪ Brush from the main menu bar. The following sections discuss how you can control the different brush settings.

Selecting the brush tip shape

The shape of the brush tip controls the actual pixels that are changed during each movement of the brush stroke. Different brush shapes can result in very different effects. You may need to play around with a few of the shapes until you are familiar with the different shape effects.

The brush tips are displayed and selected when you click the Brush Tip Shape button, as shown in Figure 16.17. The brush tips available are based on the currently selected set from the Brush Presets panel, which is discussed later in this chapter. To change the set of brushes displayed in the Brush Tip Shape list, click the Brush Presets button and select a different list from the panel.

You can select from two types of brush tips: flat and bristle. Flat brush shapes are the traditional shapes that Photoshop has had for years. Flat brushes define a set of pixels that are affected. Bristle brushes are simple shapes with bristling behavior that provide an experience much closer to using a physical brush. The following sections describe these brush tips in more detail.

Selecting flat brush shapes

Flat brush shapes are based on rasterized shapes, as you can see in Figure 16.17. The solid pixels in the shape are used to sample and apply the painting effect during each movement of the mouse. Many different tip shapes can be applied to your images, and the more you play with them, the better you understand how they can be applied.

FIGURE 16.17

Setting the shape of a flat brush

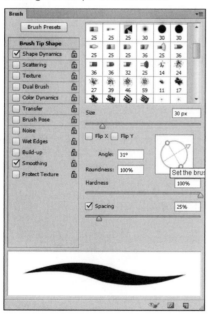

In addition to selecting the brush tip shape, you can also configure some additional properties of the brush tip shape:

- **Shape.** This scroll box allows you to select one of the brush shapes from the current list selected in the Brush Presets panel.

- **Size.** This slider adjusts the size of the brush.

- **Flip X/Flip Y.** These check boxes allow you to flip the brush tip shape along the X or Y axis. This allows you to create mirror images of the brush either vertically or horizontally. Using mirrored brush techniques can help if you are using very large brush strokes to create symbols or characters.

- **Angle.** This field sets the angle of the brush from 0 to 360 degrees. Tilting the angle of the brush affects how the stroke looks, especially at the beginning and end.

- **Roundness.** This field sets how round the brush is. Round brushes paint much more evenly than thin brushes. However, thin brushes can paint into corners and generate angled effects that round brushes cannot.

- **Hardness.** This slider sets the hardness of the brush. Hard brushes are much more dramatic in the painting effect than soft brushes. When working with wet paint, high hardness can result in the skipping effect where the bristles skip instead of smoothly flowing.

- **Spacing.** This slider specifies the spacing of the brush stroke from 1 percent to 1000 percent. Using a spacing of 1 percent makes the stroke flow smoothly. Using a high spacing value results in the stroke being applied at intervals. Typically, you want to set this option very low unless you are trying to scatter the effect of the brush stroke.

Choosing bristle brush shapes

Bristle brush shapes are based on computer algorithms that calculate how to apply the paint based on a set of digital bristles. Using the Brush Tip Shape settings shown in Figure 16.18, you define the shape and nature of the bristles. When you use the bristle brush to apply the painting strokes, Photoshop uses the bristle brush settings to determine how the painting effect is calculated during each movement of the mouse.

FIGURE 16.18

Setting the shape of a bristle brush

Brush preview

The available bristle brush shapes are shown at the top of the list in Figure 16.18. In addition to selecting the brush tip shape, you can configure some the following settings to define the nature of the bristle brush:

- **Shape.** This drop-down menu specifies the shape of the bristle brush tip. You can select Blunt, Curve, Angle, Fan, or Point. You can also select round or flat versions of these brush tips.

- **Bristles.** This slider specifies the amount of bristles present in the brush tip. More bristles give you a smoother effect, and fewer bristles give you more textured strokes.

- **Length.** This slider specifies the length of the bristles from 1 percent to 500 percent. The longer the bristles, the more paint the brush holds and the more sweeping the strokes are.

- **Thickness.** This slider specifies the thickness of the bristles. A higher thickness value results in a more textured effect because the bristles show up better, whereas thinner bristles result in smoother effects.

- **Stiffness.** This slider specifies how flexible each bristle is. More flexible bristles allow for more sweeping strokes, a softer look, and more sensitive effects. Stiffer bristles provide more dramatic effects and add a greater amount of texture to the stroke.

- **Angle.** This slider allows you to set the angle of the brush as you apply the stroke. Adjusting the angle changes the shape of the brush stroke, especially at the end.

Photoshop provides a Bristle Brush preview that allows you to see the shape of the bristle brushes. You can toggle the Bristle Brush preview on and off by clicking the button on the bottom of the Brush panel (see Figure 16.18). Figure 16.19 shows some of the sizes and shapes that are available using different settings for the bristle brush.

> **NOTE**
> You must select the Enable OpenGL Drawing option in the Performance tab of the Preferences panel for the Bristle Brush preview to be enabled. To open the Preferences panel, press Ctrl+K/⌘+K.

FIGURE 16.19

Photoshop provides a Bristle Brush preview window that allows you to see the shape of the bristle brush based on the settings you apply in the Brush panel.

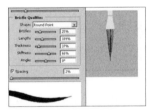
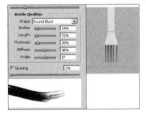
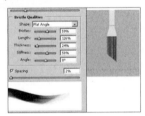

One of the most useful features of the Bristle Brush preview is that it allows you to see the behavior of the painting stroke through a simple animation. As you paint, the brush comes down to the bottom of the preview pane. The dashed line close to the bottom represents the paper, and you can see the bristles bending as the brush stroke is applied. This feature is most useful if you are using a stylus pen, because it also shows you the pressure and angle of the brush, as shown in Figure 16.20.

> **NOTE**
> The preview window shows two different views of the brush: the top and side views. To toggle between the two views, click the preview window.

FIGURE 16.20

The Bristle Brush preview window animates the movement of the brush and bristles when you are applying paint strokes. You can see the curvature of the bristles caused by the pressure and angle of the stylus pen.

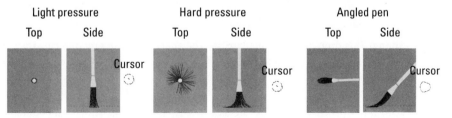

Selecting erodible tip brush shapes

Erodible tip brush shapes are based on computer algorithms that calculate how to adjust the shape of the brush tip as it wears down with use. Using the Brush Tip Shape settings shown in Figure 16.21, you define the shape and nature of the erodible tip. When you use the erodible tip brush to apply the painting strokes, Photoshop uses the brush settings to determine how the brush tip erodes, thus changing the painting effect of using the brush.

FIGURE 16.21

Setting the shape of an erodible tip brush

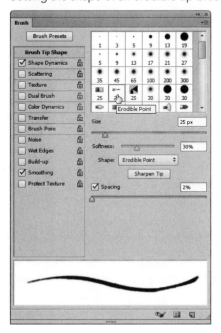

You can configure some the following settings to define the nature of the erodible tip brush:

- **Size.** This slider specifies the size of the erodible tip. The larger the tip, the more paint is applied, and the larger the effect that erosion will have on the brush.

- **Softness.** This slider specifies how fast the erodible tip will erode. The higher you set the softness, the faster the tip will erode.

- **Shape.** This drop-down menu specifies the shape that the erodible tip starts out as. You can specify a tip shape of point, flat, square, round, and triangle. The shape of the tip greatly affects how erosion changes the flow of paint onto the canvas. For example, a pointed tip erodes faster and changes more rapidly than a flat tip.

- **Sharpen Tip.** When you click the Sharpen Tip button, the tip is reset to its original state. You may find yourself sharpening the tip often to maintain the specific effect that you want from the erodible tip.

- **Spacing.** This option specifies the spacing between applications of paint from the erodible brush. A setting of 0% means that the brush continually paints onto the canvas, while a setting of 100% means that the paint is applied once for each size value of the brush. For example, if you set your brush to 25 pixels, then the paint is applied from the brush once every 25 pixels as you paint.

Photoshop provides an Erodible Tip Brush preview that allows you to see the shape of the erodible brushes. You can toggle the Brush preview on and off by clicking the button on the bottom of the Brush panel (see Figure 16.21). Figure 16.22 shows some of the sizes and shapes that are available using different settings for the erodible brush.

FIGURE 16.22

Photoshop provides an Erodible Brush preview window that allows you to see the shape of the erodible brush based on the settings you apply in the Brush panel.

Photoshop provides the same type of preview as with the Bristle Brush preview, which enables you to see the behavior of the painting stroke through a simple animation. As you paint, the brush comes down to the bottom of the preview window. The dashed line close to the bottom represents the paper, and you can see the erodible tip wearing away as you apply the brush stroke. This feature is most useful if you are using a stylus pen, because it also shows you the pressure and angle of the brush.

Selecting airbrush shapes

Airbrush shapes are based on computer algorithms that calculate how to apply paint to the canvas in a 3D style as if the brush tip was a distance away from the canvas and was spraying paint. Using the Brush Tip Shape settings shown in Figure 16.23, you define the shape and nature of the airbrush tip. When you use the airbrush to apply the painting strokes, Photoshop uses the brush settings to determine how to apply the airbrush effect on the canvas.

FIGURE 16.23

Setting the shape of an airbrush

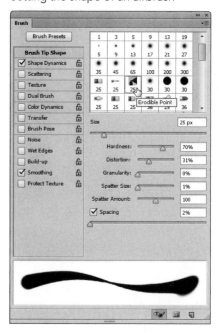

You can configure some the following settings to define the nature of the airbrush:

- **Size.** This slider specifies the size of the erodible tip. The larger the tip, the more paint is applied, and the larger the effect that erosion has on the brush.

- **Hardness.** This slider specifies how cleanly the paint is applied to the canvas. The higher the setting, the less diffused the paint becomes as you apply it to the canvas. As a result, the edges are much crisper. Reducing the hardness setting results in softer edges around the painted area.

- **Distortion.** This slider specifies the amount of distortion to apply to the paint spray. This can help provide a more realistic look if you are going for a graffiti effect.

- **Granularity.** This slider specifies the size of each individual spray particle. Increasing this value allows you to more readily show the actual spray droplets.

- **Splatter Size.** This slider specifies the size of the splatter droplets that are a trademark of spraying paint. This adds an interesting effect, although for general airbrushing, you want to set this size to 0%.

- **Splatter Amount.** This slider specifies how many splatter droplets are painted on to the canvas.

- **Spacing.** This option specifies the spacing between applications of paint from the airbrush. A setting of 0% means that the brush continually paints onto the canvas, while a setting of 100% means that the paint is applied once for each size value of the brush. For example, if you set the brush to 25 pixels, then paint is applied from the brush once every 25 pixels as you paint.

Photoshop provides an Airbrush preview that allows you to see the shape, angle and splatter effect of the airbrush. You can toggle the Brush preview on and off by clicking the button on the bottom of the Brush panel (see Figure 16.23). Figure 16.24 shows some of the sizes and shapes that are available using different settings for the airbrush.

FIGURE 16.24

Photoshop provides an Airbrush preview window that allows you to see the shape of the airbrush based on the settings you apply in the Brush panel.

Photoshop provides the same type of preview as the Bristle Brush preview, which enables you to see the behavior of the painting stroke through a simple animation. As you paint, the shape of the airbrush stream is rendered in the preview pane. This feature is most useful if you are using a stylus pen, because it also shows you the pressure and angle of the brush.

Setting the brush behavior

In addition to setting the brush shape and attributes, Photoshop provides many additional options that define the behavior of the brush as you apply painting strokes. You can select these options in the Settings menu below the Brush Tip Shape setting. These settings can be toggled on and off by selecting or deselecting the check box next to them.

You can also lock and unlock the settings by clicking the lock icon next to the name. Locking the setting keeps the values static, even as you toggle between other brushes and change other settings. Settings that are not locked can be reset to the default values by selecting Reset All Locked Settings from the Brush panel options menu. This feature is great if you need to reset the behavior of the brush and start over.

The following is a list of the simple behavior settings in the Brush panel that do not have additional dialog box options:

- **Noise.** This adds noise along with the paint as you apply the stroke. This has the effect of adding extra texture to the paint stroke and minimizing harsh changes made by editing paint tools.

- **Wet Edges.** This option adds an appearance of wetness to the edges of the paint strokes, which can help soften the edges of the strokes. This option is neither needed nor available when you are using the Mixer Brush tool.

- **Airbrush.** When you select this option, the stroke is applied in gradual tones to the image. This is a great way to soften the effect made by editing paint tools.

- **Smoothing.** When you select this option, the brush stroke produces smoother curves. This option is most effective when you are using quick paint strokes with a stylus. This is a nice option, but it may produce a slight lag time when rendering the stroke.

- **Protect Texture.** When you select this option, the same pattern and scale are applied to all brush presets that have a texture to help simulate a consistent canvas texture when painting with multiple, textured brush tips.

The following sections cover the more advanced behavior settings in the Brush panel that contain extra dialog box options.

Configuring the Shape Dynamics settings

The Shape Dynamics settings, shown in Figure 16.25, are designed to help you control the size, angle, and shape of the brush when you apply the actual painting stroke.

FIGURE 16.25

Setting the shape dynamics of the brush tip

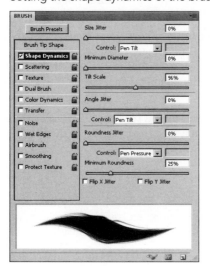

Here are the settings you can configure to control the Shape Dynamics effect:

- **Control.** The Control setting defines what input is used in determining the variance applied by the jitter settings. Setting the Control to Fade allows you to specify the number of steps over which the jitter adjustment is applied. The other settings allow you to use the pen pressure, tilt, and stylus wheel values to control the variance that's applied. The Size Jitter, Angle Jitter, and Roundness Jitter settings all have Control settings that allow you to define how the value of each is controlled.

- **Size Jitter.** The Size Jitter settings control the variation in the brush tip's size as you create the stroke by dragging the cursor. A Size Jitter setting of 0 percent means that the brush tip size doesn't change at all during the stroke. The higher the percentage, the more the size dynamically changes as you make the stroke. The Minimum Diameter setting specifies the minimum size that the jitter can reduce the brush as you are applying the stroke.

  Using the Pen Tilt setting to control the size jitter gives you the most control. If you are using the Pen Tilt option in the Control setting, you can use the Tilt Scale option to define the amount of variance in the Size Jitter. The larger the Tilt Scale setting, the more variance you see in the size of the brush.

- **Angle Jitter.** The Angle Jitter setting allows you to vary the angle of the brush based on different Control options. In addition to the regular Control options, if you have a stylus tablet that Photoshop recognizes attached to your system, you have the option to use the following:

  - **Rotation.** This varies the angle of the brush based on the rotation of the stylus pen.

  - **Initial Direction.** This varies the angle based on the initial direction of the brush stroke. This is similar to holding the brush at a specific angle throughout the stroke and is a great option if you are using the brush to add calligraphic text.

  - **Direction.** This varies the angle based on the current direction of the brush stroke. This reduces the impact that flat brushes have when changing angles.

- **Roundness Jitter.** The Roundness Jitter setting allows you to vary the roundness of the brush as you are creating the stroke. The rounder the brush, the more consistent the brush stroke is. Reducing the roundness allows for more dramatic brush strokes to appear in the image. You can specify a Minimum Roundness value that keeps the brush from varying too much.

- **Flip X Jitter/Flip Y Jitter.** The Flip X Jitter option flips the jitter across the X axis of the painting stroke. The Flip Y Jitter option flips the jitter across the Y axis of the painting stroke.

Creating a scattering effect

The Scattering settings, shown in Figure 16.26, are designed to help you apply a scattering effect as you apply the brush stroke. The Scattering option creates the effect of scattering the brush tip in a random displacement along the path of the stroke, as shown in Figure 16.27.

FIGURE 16.26

Setting the Scattering options of the brush tip

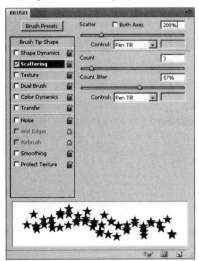

Here are the settings that you can configure to control the Scattering effect:

- **Control.** The Control setting defines what input is used in determining the variance of paint splatters size and distribution applied by the scattering settings. Setting the Control to Fade option allows you to specify the number of steps over which the scattering adjustment is applied. The other settings allow you to use the pen pressure, tilt, rotation, or stylus wheel values to control the variance that is applied.

- **Scatter.** The Scatter settings control the variation in the scattering of the brush as you apply the stroke. The variance of the scattering is controlled by the method specified in the Control setting.

- **Both Axes.** When you select this option, the brush tip is scattered both horizontally and vertically. When this option is not selected, the brush tip is scattered only horizontally or vertically in a direction perpendicular to the movement of the stroke.

- **Count.** This slider specifies the number of brush tips to include in the scattering.

- **Count Jitter.** This slider specifies the amount by which to vary the scattering and how to control the variance of the count based on the Control setting.

Applying a texture effect

The Texture settings, shown in Figure 16.28, are designed to help you apply a texture effect to the brush strokes. Using the texture effect, you can simulate textures such as an oil paint canvas or wall that show up in the brush strokes.

FIGURE 16.27

The effect of using the scattering option. One of the lines is drawn without scattering, and the other with scattering.

Without scatter

With scatter

FIGURE 16.28

Setting the texture options of the brush tip

Here are the settings that you can configure to control the Texture effect:

- **Texture.** You can click this drop-down menu to select a texture from the patterns list that is currently selected in the Presets Manager. When you display the list, you can click the triangle button to display a list of preset lists and options to load and save presets.

- **Invert.** This option inverts the pattern used to apply a texture to the brush stroke.

- **Scale.** This slider sets the size of the pattern applied to the brush stroke. Setting this value too high makes the pattern very apparent in the brush strokes. Setting it too low makes the pattern too small to see.

- **Brightness.** This slider controls the brightness of the texture.

- **Contrast.** This slider controls the contrast between brightness and darkness in the texture.

- **Texture Each Tip.** When you select this option, the texture is applied individually to each brush mark in the brush stroke rather than to the entire stroke when it is finished. Although invoking this option is very CPU-intensive, it is required for the depth variance option to have an effect.

- **Mode.** This drop-down menu specifies the blending mode to use when applying the texture pattern to the brush stroke (before it is applied to the pixels below). This setting does not override the blend mode setting in the Brush tool options.

- **Depth.** This slider specifies how deeply the paint penetrates into the texture. A value of 0 percent means that no pattern shows through.

- **Minimum Depth.** This slider specifies the minimum penetration depth that is applied to a stroke, even if the variance control reduces penetration below that level.

- **Depth Jitter.** This slider allows you to vary the depth that is applied to the texture as the brush stroke is being created. Increasing this value can give the texture a more dramatic appearance.

- **Control.** This drop-down menu defines what input is used in determining the variance applied by the depth texture setting. Setting the Control to Fade allows you to specify the number of steps over which the depth texture variance is applied. The other settings allow you to use the pen pressure, tilt, rotation, or stylus wheel values to control the depth variance that is applied.

Applying the dual brush strokes

The Dual Brush option allows you to use two brushes at the same time to apply each stroke. Using the Dual Brush option can add a whole new level of dynamics to your brushing techniques. When you select the Dual Brush option, the Brush panel dialog box changes to allow you to select the second brush. You can also select the blending mode used to combine the two brush strokes before they are applied together to the image. You can also set the size, spacing, scatter, and count to use in the second brush.

Painting with multiple colors simultaneously

The Color Dynamics option, shown in Figure 16.29, provides a dynamic coloring effect by changing the brush stroke from the foreground to the background color as you apply the stroke. Using the Color Dynamics option allows you to essentially paint with two colors at the same time.

The Foreground/Background Jitter slider controls the jitter between the foreground and background colors. A value of 0 percent applies only the foreground color. A larger value means more jitter between the two colors.

You can adjust the variance between the foreground and background colors using the Control setting. The Control setting defines what input is used in determining the variance between the foreground and background colors. Setting the Control to Fade allows you to specify the number of steps over which the color variance is applied. The other settings allow you to use the pen pressure, tilt, rotation, or stylus wheel values to control the color variance that is applied.

You can also vary the hue, saturation, brightness, and purity in the colors by adjusting the sliders in Figure 16.29.

FIGURE 16.29

Setting the color dynamics options of the brush tip

Controlling the brush stroke with the Transfer option

The Transfer option, shown in Figure 16.30, gives you an additional level of control over how the brush stroke is applied to the pixels below by varying settings such as wetness, flow, and opacity. The Transfer option really has two modes: one for painting and editing brushes, and one for the Mixer Brush tool.

When you have a painting or editing brush selected, you can use the Transfer option to set an amount of Opacity Jitter and Flow Jitter that occurs when applying the brush strokes. Increasing the Opacity Jitter and Flow Jitter varies the intensity of the brush stroke and thus varies the effect of the painting tool in a dynamic way.

You can adjust the variance in all the Transfer controls using the Control setting. The Control setting defines what input is used in determining the variance in each transfer setting. Setting the Control to Fade allows you to specify the number of steps over which the variance is applied. The other settings allow you to use the pen pressure, tilt, rotation, or stylus wheel values to control how the variance is applied.

FIGURE 16.30

Setting the transfer options of the brush tip

Using the Brush Presets panel

The options for configuring the shape and behavior of brushes are limitless. This makes the ability to save brush settings a critical part of using the painting features in Photoshop.

The Brush Presets panel, shown in Figure 16.31, displays a list of the preset brushes with their corresponding brush stroke preview. The Brush panel menu also allows you to set the preview mode to text only; small, medium, or large thumbnails; and small or large thumbnail lists. You can also select one of the many sets of preset brush lists from the panel menu. Brush presets can be added, renamed, and removed from the current list using the buttons at the bottom of the panel menu.

The panel menu provides the following options to manage the brushes that are available in the presets list:

- **Reset Brushes.** This option resets the preview list to the Photoshop default.
- **Load Brushes.** This option launches a dialog box to load a saved set of brushes from a file. The new set is added to the existing set.
- **Save Brushes.** This option launches a dialog box to save the current set of brushes as a new preset file. This is the best way to permanently organize the brushes you are using.
- **Replace Brushes.** This option launches a dialog box to load a saved set of brushes from a file. The new set replaces the existing set.

FIGURE 16.31

Managing the preset brush list

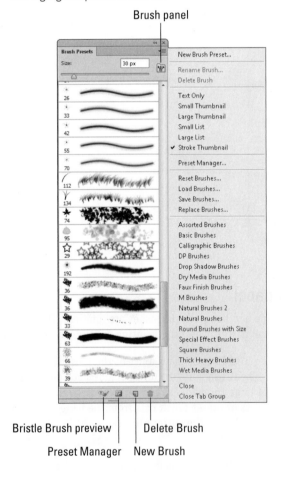

Painting with Non-Brush Painting Tools

In addition to the brush style painting tools listed earlier, Photoshop provides the Paint Bucket and Gradient tools, which allow you to paint large areas of an image with a color, gradient fill, or pattern. These tools apply paint using a general filling method rather than individual brush strokes. Painting with the Paint Bucket and Gradient Fill tools provide an effective means to quickly add background color and depth to an image.

The Paint Bucket and Gradient tools can be found in the Toolbox as shown in Figure 16.32. This allows you to switch between these tools and other tools quickly when you're trying to add color while painting in Photoshop.

FIGURE 16.32

The Paint Bucket and Gradient tools allow you to add paint to an image by filling an area rather than using individual brush strokes.

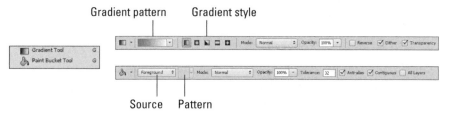

Gradient pattern   Gradient style

Source   Pattern

Applying paint to layers

The Paint Bucket tool applies paint to a layer when you click a pixel. All pixels that match the pixel directly below the cursor are replaced by the foreground color or a pattern. The Paint Bucket tool paints only to the layer currently selected in the Layers panel. Also, if a selection exists, the Paint Bucket tool paints inside that selection only.

You can set the following options when using the Paint Bucket tool:

- **Source.** This allows you to select either the foreground layer or pattern.
- **Pattern.** You can use this option to select a pattern to fill the image from the drop-down menu shown in Figure 16.33. You can also select from several pattern sets using the pop-up menu next to the pattern list, also shown in Figure 16.33. Using this menu, you can load and save the preset lists, open the Preset Manager, and add new patterns.

FIGURE 16.33

The Paint Bucket tool allows you to fill an area using a pattern from a list. The pop-up menu next to the patterns list allows you to load different sets of patterns, load and save pattern presets, and even create new patterns.

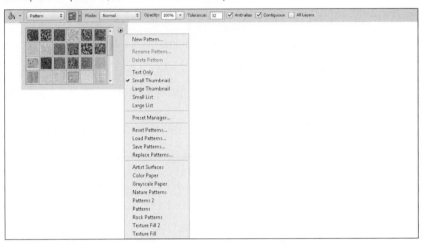

- **Mode.** This drop-down menu allows you to select the blending mode to use when applying the paint to the image.
- **Opacity.** This box sets the opacity of the filling paint.
- **Tolerance.** This box sets the tolerance to use in determining whether a pixel matches the color of the selected pixel.
- **Anti-alias.** This option allows you to toggle anti-alias smoothing around the edges of the paint fill. When you select this option, the edges blend more with the surrounding pixels.
- **Contiguous.** When you select this option, the fill occurs only in pixels of the same color that are also contiguous to the selected pixel. When this option is disabled, all the pixels in the image that match the selected pixel are painted.
- **All Layers.** When you select this option, Photoshop uses all layers to sample the selected pixel instead of just the selected layer. This helps if you want to paint in a layer based on a pixel color that exists in a different layer.

Figure 16.34 shows some examples of applying paint with the Paint Bucket tool. The first fill is a solid foreground color. Notice that only the black portion of the image is painted. The second fill is a pattern fill with the Contiguous option selected. Notice that only the white pixels contiguous to the cursor are filled in.

FIGURE 16.34

Using the Paint Bucket tool, you can quickly paint over a color in the image with another color or pattern.

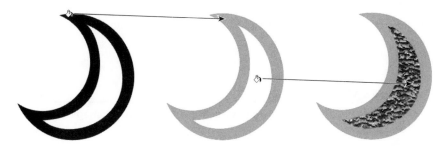

Filling a selection with a color or pattern

The Fill tool allows you to fill in the current selection of the canvas with either a solid color or a pattern. This can sometimes be easier to use than the Paint Bucket tool. You can control which pattern is used as well as the blending mode and opacity to use for the fill.

To fill the current selection, choose Edit ➪ Fill from the main menu bar to open the Fill dialog box shown in Figure 16.35. Then set the following options:

- **Use.** This drop-down menu allows you to select one of the following options to use as a fill source:
  - **Foreground Color.** This option fills with the currently selected foreground color.
  - **Background Color.** This option fills with the currently selected background color.
  - **Black.** This option fills with black.
  - **White.** This option fills with white.
  - **Gray.** This option fills with a gray that is 50% white and 50% black.
  - **Content Aware.** This option is available when you have an active selection in the document. Photoshop will analyze the pixels around the outside of the selection and use them to apply a content aware fill inside of the selection. This is one of the easiest ways to remove unwanted objects from an image. Simply select the item you want to remove and then apply a content-aware fill.
  - **Pattern.** This option enables the Custom Pattern selector and will fill with the currently selected custom pattern.
  - **History.** This option fills with the currently selected foreground color.
- **Custom Pattern.** This drop-down menu allows you to specify a custom pattern.
- **Mode.** This drop-down menu allows you to specify which blending mode to use when applying the fill.
- **Opacity.** This field specifies how opaque the fill will be as it is applied to the canvas.

- **Preserve Transparency.** When you select this option, the fill will not be applied to transparent pixels in the image.
- **Scripted Patterns.** This option applies the pattern using a scripted method rather than the standard tiling.
- **Script.** This drop-down menu specifies which script to run when applying the custom pattern to the canvas.

FIGURE 16.35

Using the Fill tool, you can quickly paint over a color in the image with another color or pattern.

In addition to the standard patterns, Photoshop also allows you to fill using a scripted pattern. Typically when you apply a pattern fill, the pattern is tiled together to fill the area. A scripted pattern is applied to the image based on a predefined set of operations.

To apply a scripted pattern fill, choose Edit ➪ Fill from the main menu bar and then select the Scripted Patterns option, as shown in Figure 16.36. You can then select one of the following predefined scripts:

- **Deco Brick fill.** This pattern script offsets every second row by half of the pattern width. The color of the input pattern is randomly varied to increase realism.
- **Deco Cross Weave fill.** This pattern script rotates the pattern by 90 degrees and offsets it a bit to create small gaps. Once again, the color and input pattern is randomly varied to increase realism.
- **Deco Random fill.** This pattern script takes the pattern and places it on the canvas in random sizes and locations.
- **Deco Spiral fill.** This pattern script begins at the center and spirals the pattern outward, regardless of the shape of the paintable area.
- **Deco Symmetry fill.** This pattern script places the input pattern into different plane tilings. You should use thinner patterns with transparency to get the best effects from this script.

Figure 16.36 shows an example of using a scripted pattern. In this case, we simply selected a zebra striped pattern and then applied the Deco Cross Weave pattern to it. Notice that each tile is rotated 90 degrees.

FIGURE 16.36

Applying the Deco Cross Weave scripted pattern to a custom pattern easily provides a very cool patterned background.

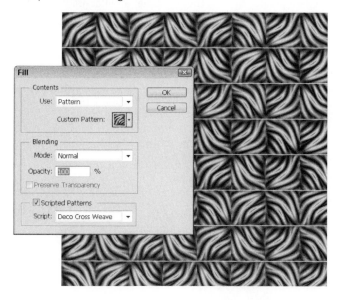

Applying a gradient fill

The Gradient tool applies a gradient fill by selecting start and end points in the image. The Gradient tool paints only on the layer currently selected in the Layers panel. Also, if a selection exists, the Gradient tool paints only inside that selection.

You can set the following options when using the Gradient tool:

- **Gradient pattern.** This option allows you to select a gradient pattern or launch the Gradient Editor. The Gradient Editor is discussed in the next section.
- **Gradient style.** This option allows you to set the gradient style. You can select from the linear, radial, angled, reflected, and diamond styles.
- **Mode.** This drop-down menu allows you to select the blending mode to use when applying the gradient fill to the image.
- **Opacity.** This field sets the opacity of the filling paint.
- **Reverse.** This option reverses the direction of the gradient fill.

- **Dither.** This option adds a dithering effect as the gradient is applied that makes the transitions appear smoother.
- **Transparency.** When you select this option, the transparency in the gradient allows the pixels below to show through. When this option is not selected, the gradient has no transparency.

Figure 16.37 shows some examples of applying paint with the Gradient tool. In one example, a linear gradient is used to paint inside a rectangle. Notice that the angle of the gradient follows the angle between the two points. In the other example, a radial gradient is used to fill in a circle. Notice that with the radial setting, the gradient flows in all directions from the first selected point.

FIGURE 16.37

Using the Gradient tool, you can add a linear gradient at an angle or a radial gradient that radiates out from the first selected point.

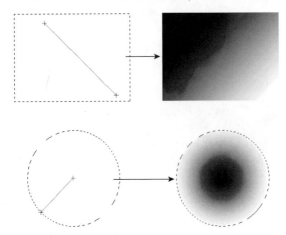

Creating custom gradients

The Gradient Editor allows you to define your own custom gradients. The Gradient tool is so dynamic and powerful that there are limitless types and styles of gradient fills that you can create for your images.

To define a new custom gradient, click the gradient pattern in the Gradient tool options menu to open the dialog box shown in Figure 16.38, and set the following options:

- **Name.** This field specifies the name of the gradient. This name appears in the gradient lists and when you hover the mouse above the icon.

- **Gradient Type.** You can choose from two types of gradients: Solid and Noise. The Solid gradient is created from solid color points that blend into each other. The Noise gradients are created by setting specific color channel settings and then generating a gradient based on noise (randomly selected colors) in those channels.

- **Smoothness.** This field defines how smooth the transition between two colors appears.

- **Transparency stops.** You can use these sliders to set the transparency value for a specific spot in the gradient. For each transparency stop, you can set the opacity and a location value. The location value corresponds to the midpoint diamond shown between two stops. The closer the location is to the transparency stop, the less effect the stop value has in that direction.

- **Color stops.** These sliders allow you to set the color value for a specific spot in the gradient. For each color stop, you can set the color and a location value. The location value corresponds to the midpoint diamond shown between two stops. The closer the location is to the color stop, the less effect the color stop value has in that direction.

FIGURE 16.38

Using the Gradient Editor, you can create custom gradients that involve several colors and transparency levels.

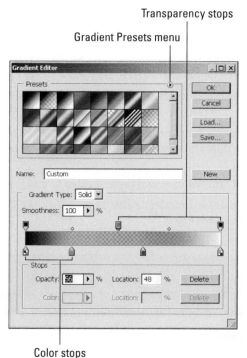

Transparency stops

Gradient Presets menu

Color stops

Clicking the Gradient Presets menu button shown in Figure 16.38 displays a menu that allows you to select, load, and save sets from the preset lists.

Applying Painting Techniques

The tools discussed so far in this chapter provide an incredible arsenal for creative minds. They can be applied in limitless ways. So far, we have discussed only the basic behavior of the tools. In this section, we show some examples and techniques to use the tools to paint creatively. These techniques are only a few of many that can help you get the most from the painting tools in Photoshop.

 One technique not listed here is to add a stroke to a shape or path. Using paths to create shapes and then adding a fill and stroke to them is a great way to paint specific objects. To learn more about paths and shapes, see Chapter 17.

Painting from a blank canvas

The most basic form of painting is to use a blank canvas and use painting tools to paint onto the canvas. You can paint onto a blank canvas using countless methods, and this example simply gives you a few steps to try out some different techniques:

1. **Open the blank image using the default Photoshop size of 7 by 5 inches.**

2. **Select the Gradient tool, and set the foreground color to a blue sky color and the background color to white.**

3. **Use the Gradient tool to create a linear gradient from the top of the canvas down.**

   You can use the Shift key to help you draw the gradient in a perfect vertical line. The gradient shown in Figure 16.39 is drawn by dragging from the top of the image down to the center of the image.

4. **Select the Rectangle Shape tool, and set the background color to a soft brown.**

5. **Use the Rectangle Shape tool to draw a rectangle that is brown on the bottom of the canvas, as shown in Figure 16.39.**

   You now have a skyline.

> **NOTE**
> If you create the rectangle as a shape layer, you need to set the Style option to the default of None so that a gradient style is not applied to the gradient.

6. **(Optional) Create and select a new layer.**

   Although this step is optional, it is a good idea and shows how you can add to a painting on a separate layer without affecting the bottom.

FIGURE 16.39

Adding a gradient fill and a solid rectangle quickly creates the appearance of a skyline.

7. **Select the Brush tool, and from the Brush Presets list, select the grass brush, shown in Figure 16.40. Launch the Brush panel to configure a new brush.**

8. **Set the size of the brush to 134, enable the Shape Dynamics, Scattering, Color Dynamics, and Smoothing options.**

   Set the Scattering to 33 percent, the Count to 2, and the Count Jitter to 100 percent, as shown in Figure 16.40. This creates a brush that scatters the grass as you paint the strokes onto the canvas.

FIGURE 16.40

Selecting a grass brush style and adding a scattering effect as well as shape and color dynamics helps create a brush that quickly applies a grass technique to the image.

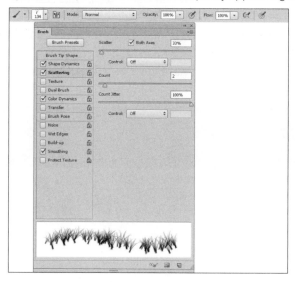

9. **Set the foreground color to a soft gold, and paint the grass onto the new layer, as shown in Figure 16.41.**

   Notice how the brush technique scatters the grass.

FIGURE 16.41

Applying the grass brush over the soft brown gives the appearance of a grassy field.

10. **Create and select a new layer.**

11. **From the brush styles list, select the soft brush, shown in Figure 16.42, and launch the Brush panel to configure a new brush.**

12. **Set the size of the brush to 223, and enable the Shape Dynamics, Scattering, and Smoothing options.**

    This time, on the Shape Dynamics, increase the Size Jitter to 100 percent and set the Minimum Diameter to 100, as shown in Figure 16.42. This creates a brush that varies the size of the soft brush and helps create a soft cloud effect.

13. **Set the foreground color to white, and paint the clouds onto the new layer, as shown in Figure 16.43.**

    Notice how the brush technique varies the size of the stroke and helps create the variance in the clouds.

ON THE WEB

The project used to create the image in Figure 16.43 is available on this book's website as Figure 16-43.psd. You can see the different layers and the final image.

FIGURE 16.42

Selecting a soft brush style and adding a jitter to the size as well as a scattering effect helps create a brush that quickly applies a cloud effect to the image.

FIGURE 16.43

Applying the soft brush over the gradient sky gives the appearance of soft clouds.

Tracing edges from an existing image

A common technique that artists use is sketching the subject area prior to painting it. Photoshop provides a great method for sketching general shapes: you simply create a new layer and then use the Pencil tool to draw the edges. Remember that when you press and hold the Shift key, you can draw straight vertical or horizontal strokes, and when you press and hold the Shift key and click in two different locations, you draw a straight stroke between them.

When you are tracing the image, it is a good idea to create three extra layers. The topmost layer is the layer you draw on. The next layer should be a simple white canvas that you can turn off when you are tracing and turn on to see what the tracing looks like, as shown in Figure 16.44. The next layer down sits above the image as an adjustment layer; its purpose is to lighten the image to make it easier to see your tracing lines while you are tracing but still see the image behind.

Figure 16.44 shows an example of loading an image, creating a new layer, and then using the Pencil tool to trace some general shapes. Notice that the finished product automatically provides a good perspective in the sketch.

> **ON THE WEB**
>
> The project used to create the image in Figure 16.44 is available on this book's website as Figure 16-44.psd. You can see the different layers used to create the sketch.

Using wet paint on an existing image

One of the biggest advancements in Photoshop in the past few years is the addition of the Mixer Brush tool. The Mixer Brush tool allows you to treat pixels already existing in an image as wet paint. You can use the Mixer Brush tool to brush around the paint that already exists, which can fix small portions of images or apply an effect to larger areas. You can use all the power of the Brush panel to create special brushes and then use them as wet paint on the image.

> **TIP**
>
> You could also start by choosing Filter ⇨ Artistic ⇨ Dry Brush filter to simulate brush strokes in the image before applying your own wet paint technique. The Dry Brush filter applies a similar technique, but it's very limited, whereas you have limitless possibilities when using your own hand and the plethora of brush styles Photoshop has to offer.

FIGURE 16.44

Using a new layer and the Pencil tool, you can quickly trace shapes in the image below to create a quick sketch to paint from.

Figure 16.45 shows an example of using a simple fan brush with the Mixer Brush tool to create brush strokes on an image to simulate the appearance of an oil painting. The cool thing about this effect is that it was applied in only a few minutes. If you spend longer, you can really fine-tune the brush strokes and create some nice artwork.

In Figure 16.45, we disabled the Load Brush After Stroke option so no new paint would be added. We also enabled the Clean Brush After Stroke option so the brush would be clean before touching the image again. This allowed us to keep the paint from mixing too much.

FIGURE 16.45

Using the Mixer Brush tool, you can easily apply a painting stroke technique to a photo.

Summary

Photoshop merges its world-class photo-editing tools with its paintbrush tools to provide the best of both worlds. This chapter discussed the Brush tools available for editing, such as the Dodge and Burn tools, as well as the tools Photoshop provides for painting, such as the Paint and Mixer Brushes. You can use these tools to edit photos, paint new images, and even combine painting with photo editing.

The Brush panel enables you to create custom brushes that extend your capability in editing and painting images. You can also use Photoshop blending modes to apply the effects from the Brush tools in a variety of ways.

In this chapter, you learned about the following:

- Customizing the Brush tool settings using the Brush panel
- Using some Brush tools for editing localized areas of images and some for painting pixels
- Adjusting the blending mode to completely change how brush stroke effects are applied to the pixels below
- Erasing specific pixels in the image
- Tracing techniques to quickly give you a basis and perspective for painting images
- Using the wet paint capabilities of Photoshop to create a painting from an existing image

Working with Paths and Vector Shapes

Vector data is completely foreign to most of the other functions in Photoshop that deal with pixel manipulation. Vector paths and shapes are derived from a series of mathematical functions rather than specific values for individual pixels. This chapter focuses on helping you understand how vector paths are created and manipulated as well as how to use them to create selections, masks, and shapes that can be applied to images.

Understanding Paths

You must understand the nature of paths in order to use them when working in Photoshop. Basically, a path is a series of lines called vectors. Each vector is made up of a coordinate in the image, a value that defines the direction, a value that defines the length, and parabolic parameters that define the contours. Instead of storing an image as a series of pixel values, the path data is stored as a series of mathematical functions that define the vector lines that make up the image.

Paths offer some definite advantages over simple pixel data:

- The vector data is common to many different computer graphics applications, so you can save a vector image in one application and then use it and even manipulate it in another application without losing any data integrity. For example, you could create a path shape in Photoshop and then open it in Illustrator and still be able to manipulate it.

- Paths can be resized to a much larger size without losing their sharpness. For instance, most fonts are based on vector paths, and that is why you can increase the size of the font and still keep the crisp edges.

- Vector paths can be manipulated several times without generating pixelation.

The following sections discuss the types of paths that you can create in Photoshop as well as the components that make up the paths.

Building path components

Two basic components are involved in creating a path: the line segments and the anchor points. The anchor points fix the end points of each line segment to the canvas below. Each line segment in the path requires one anchor point at each end. However, you can add several anchor points to a path, and a line segment is generated between them using a mathematical function.

The basic purpose of anchor points in a path is to provide a fixed point that allows a change of direction or curve in the lines. For example, Figure 17.1 displays a simple path with several anchor points. Notice that at each anchor point, the path changes direction.

FIGURE 17.1

A path is made up of a series of anchor points connected by line segments. The anchor points allow the path to change direction.

Line segments

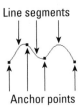

Anchor points

The shape of the curve in each line segment is controlled by direction points attached to the anchor points of the line segment, as shown in Figure 17.2. The direction points control the angle at which the line segment leaves the anchor. Between the anchor and the direction point is another line called the direction line, also shown in Figure 17.2.

The length of the direction line denotes how far the line segment moves away from the anchor point before being pulled back into the next anchor point. The longer the direction line, the farther away from the anchor point the line segment moves in that direction before curving back toward the next anchor point, as shown in Figure 17.2.

There are two types of anchor points: corner points and smooth points. Corner points can produce sharp transitions in direction between line segments, while smooth points always produce a smooth transition in direction between line segments.

FIGURE 17.2

The direction point and line indicate the direction and how far the line segment moves away from the anchor point before moving back toward the next anchor point.

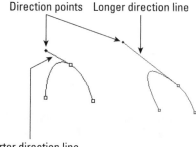

The direction points in a smooth anchor move simultaneously, so the line segments on both sides of the anchor point are adjusted at the same time. The direction points on a corner anchor move independently, so only one segment attached to the anchor moves at a time. This allows you to create a sharp corner, as shown in Figure 17.3.

FIGURE 17.3

The direction points attached to a smooth anchor point both move simultaneously, resulting in a smooth curve. The direction points attached to a corner anchor point move independently, allowing for a sharp angle.

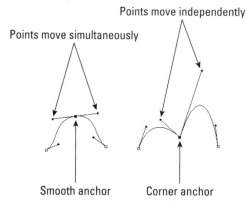

Defining types of paths

You will work with several different types of paths in Photoshop. Paths are built from a series of points that connect lines. To create complex vector shapes requires combinations of straight or linear paths, curved paths, open paths, which have endpoints that don't connect to other points, and closed paths where all points connect to each other. We will discuss paths later in this chapter, so you need to understand the different path types in the following list:

- **Linear.** A linear path is a simple, straight line that moves directly from one point to another, as shown in Figure 17.4.

- **Curved.** A curved path is a line that does not move in a straight line from one point to another, but instead follows a parabolic curve, as shown in Figure 17.4.

- **Open.** An open path is a set of one or more lines that has both a starting point and an ending point, as shown in Figure 17.4.

> **NOTE**
> You can convert an open path into a closed path by dragging one of the open anchors over the top of the other one. The mouse icon changes to indicate that the two anchors will be linked. When you release the mouse button, the two anchors are converted into a single corner anchor.

- **Closed.** A closed path is a set of one or more lines that do not have a starting point or an ending point, as shown in Figure 17.4. You create a closed path by placing the end point of the last line in the exact coordinates of the starting point of the first line, creating an entirely closed area. Closed paths are called path components, path shapes, or path layers.

FIGURE 17.4

Photoshop has several different types of paths, including linear, curved, open, and closed.

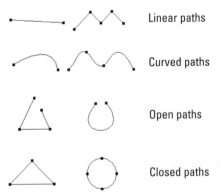

Linear paths

Curved paths

Open paths

Closed paths

- **Working.** The working path is the current set of paths that you are actively working on that have not yet been saved. You can have only one working path active at a time, so you need to save the path using the Paths panel (discussed later in this chapter) when you are finished with it before you can open another working path.

- **Clipping.** A clipping path is a special type of path used to control what areas of the image are visible when viewed in a page layout or illustration application. This allows you to hide parts of the image in the final layout without actually deleting those areas of the image.

 Paths can also be applied as vector masks. This allows you to create complex paths using the tools described in this chapter and apply them as vector masks to images. See Chapter 10 for information about how masks are used.

Exploring the Vector Path

When working with vector paths, you use several different tools and panels to create, manipulate, and use the paths. The Pen tools allow you to create paths, add points, modify points, and delete points from paths. The Path Selection tools allow you to move entire paths as well as individual points on a path. You use the Paths panel to manage and use paths in your documents. This section discusses these tools; in the following section, you learn how to use them to create and manipulate vector paths.

Using the Pen tools

The most fundamental vector path tools are the Pen tools. You use the Pen tools to create path anchor points when you create your custom paths. You also use the Pen tools to delete or add anchor points to existing paths and convert anchor points.

There are several Pen tools, as shown in Figure 17.5. The point-to-point and Freeform Pen tools allow you to create paths. The other Pen tools also allow you to manipulate a path by adding or removing individual points from it.

Pen tools

The keyboard shortcut P selects the Pen tools, and Shift+P toggles between the Pen tool and Freeform Pen tool. The following list describes what each of the Pen tools does:

- **Pen tool.** Using this tool, each time you click the document, an anchor point is added and a straight line segment is added between the previous anchor point and the newly created anchor point. You can use the Pen tool to add direction points as you are adding anchor points in a couple of different ways.

  You can add points to the path as smooth anchors. When you press and hold the mouse button and drag as you add an anchor point, the anchor point is added as a smooth anchor, a set of direction points/lines follows the movement of the mouse, and the new line segment curves according to the direction and length of the direction lines, as shown in Figure 17.6.

17

FIGURE 17.5

Using the Pen tools, you create paths, add points, modify points, and delete points from paths.

FIGURE 17.6

Using the Pen tool, you can add simple anchors by clicking the mouse button, add curved anchors by clicking and dragging the mouse, and add corner anchors by dragging an existing anchor to add a single direction point/line.

Adding a smooth anchor

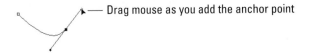

— Drag mouse as you add the anchor point

Adding a direction point to an anchor

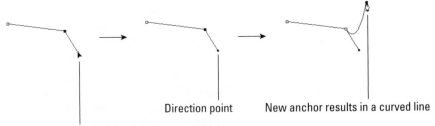

Direction point   New anchor results in a curved line

Select the existing anchor and drag the mouse

> **TIP**
>
> If you press and hold down the Shift key when you are using the Pen tool, the next anchor is snapped to 45-degree-angle increments. This is useful if you need to keep your path symmetrical or add straight horizontal or straight vertical lines to your path.

You can also add a direction point to an anchor after you have already added the anchor. When you click an existing anchor (at either end of the path) using the Pen tool, a direction point/line follows the mouse. When you release the mouse, a direction point/line is added to the anchor and the anchor becomes a corner anchor. When you add the next point, the line segment between the two points adheres to the previously added anchor point, as shown in Figure 17.6.

> **TIP**
>
> For faster manipulation of paths, use the Auto Add/Delete option in the Pen tool. When you hover over an existing path with the Pen tool, the Pen tool toggles between the Add Anchor Pen tool and the Delete Anchor Pen tool. This allows you to use a single tool to add and remove points from the existing path.

- **Freeform Pen tool.** Using this tool, you can draw a freehand line on the document by clicking and dragging the mouse. As long as you are dragging the mouse, a line is drawn. When you release the mouse, the line is converted to a path with the necessary anchor points, as shown in Figure 17.7.

FIGURE 17.7

Using the Freeform Pen tool, you can draw a line on the document and Photoshop converts it to a path with the necessary points.

- **Magnetic.** Selecting the Freeform Pen tool gives you the Magnetic option in the Options bar. When you select the Magnetic option, the line you draw with the Freeform Pen tool tries to follow the boundaries of edges. This is a great option when you are trying to use the Freeform Pen tool to trace around an object in the background image.
- **Add Anchor Point tool.** Using this tool, you can add an anchor to an existing path. Simply select the Add Anchor Point tool, and click the path to add the anchor.

- **Delete Anchor Point tool.** Using this tool, you can remove anchors from the path by clicking them with the mouse. The line segments on either side of the anchor are combined into a single line segment. Be careful when removing anchors from the path because it may drastically alter the appearance of the path.

- **Convert Point tool.** Using this tool, you can convert corner anchor points to smooth anchor points and smooth anchor points to corner anchor points.

  Smooth anchor points are converted to corner anchor points when you select them with the Convert Point tool. Photoshop displays the direction points and lines that normally move simultaneously. Then you use the Convert Point tool to drag one of the direction points to change the curve across the sharp point to an angle, as shown in Figure 17.8.

  Corner anchor points are converted to smooth anchor points when you click them with the Convert Point tool and drag the mouse to add and adjust the direction points and lines that define the curve across the anchor point, as shown in Figure 17.8.

FIGURE 17.8

Using the Convert Point tool, you can toggle anchor points between smooth anchors and corner anchors.

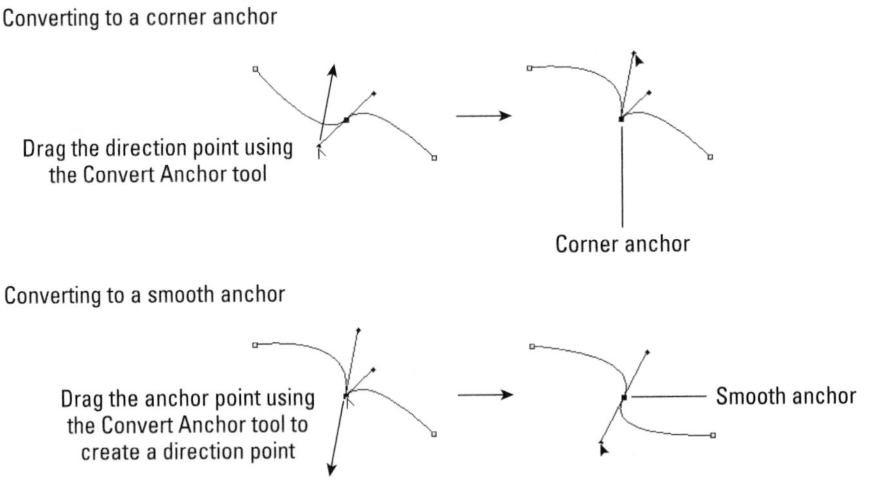

Converting to a corner anchor

Drag the direction point using the Convert Anchor tool

Corner anchor

Converting to a smooth anchor

Drag the anchor point using the Convert Anchor tool to create a direction point

Smooth anchor

Pen tool options

When you select the Pen tool, several useful options become available in the Options bar. The Pen tool allows you to use specific drawing modes. Depending on which drawing mode you select, you will have slightly different options in the Options bar, shown in Figure 17.9. The Pen tool options allow you to toggle among Pen, Freeform Pen, and Shape tools; toggle among the Shape, Path, and Fill modes; and define how the path area is generated.

FIGURE 17.9

Using the Pen tool options, you can set the Pen type and mode and define the path area.

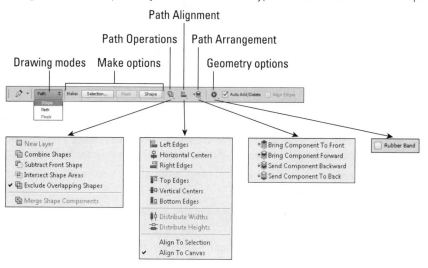

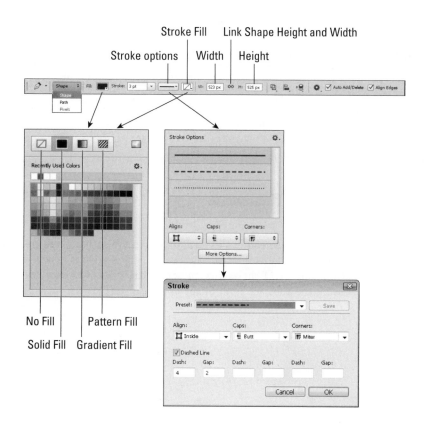

The following list describes the options that are available for the Pen tool:

- **Drawing modes.** Clicking this menu allows you to toggle among the Shape, Path, and Pixels modes. When you select Shape, you are drawing to a new vector layer. When you select Path, you are drawing to the currently selected path in the Paths panel. When you select Pixels, you are drawing raster pixels directly to the currently selected layer; however, the Pixels option is not available in the Pen tool.

- **Make options.** Clicking these buttons allows you to make a selection, vector mask, or shape from the currently selected path geometry.

- **Add to Path Area.** Selecting this option adds the path you are creating to the current working path; any overlapping areas are still in the path. Figure 17.10 shows how an open path is added to the current circle path using the Add to Path Area option.

- **Path Operations.** Clicking this drop-down menu allows you to choose an option for the currently selected paths:

  - **New Layer.** Selecting this option creates a new vector layer from the path.

  - **Combine Shapes.** Selecting this option adds the path you are creating to the current working path; any overlapping areas are still in the path. Figure 17.10 shows how an open path is added to the current circle path using the Combine Shapes option.

FIGURE 17.10

When using the Combine Shapes option, the area inside the new path is added to the existing working path.

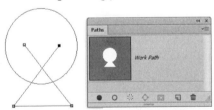

- **Subtract Front Shape.** Selecting this option deletes the path you are creating from the current working path — in other words, any overlap is removed from the working path. Figure 17.11 shows how an open path is removed from the current circle path using the Subtract Front Shape option.

FIGURE 17.11

When using the Subtract Front Shape option, the area inside of the new path is removed from the existing working path.

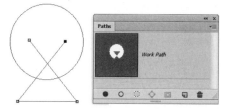

- **Intersect Shape Areas.** Selecting this option alters the current working path to include only those areas where the original current working path and the newly created path overlap each other. Figure 17.12 shows how an open path is intersected to the current circle path using the Intersect Shape Areas option.

FIGURE 17.12

When using the Intersect Shape Areas option, the working path is altered to include only the area of overlap between the older working path and the newly created path.

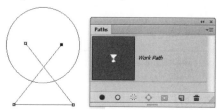

- **Exclude Overlapping Shapes.** Selecting this option alters the current working path to include only those areas where the original current working path and the newly created path do NOT overlap each other. This can be a bit tricky until you figure out that all paths including the working path must overlap. Figure 17.13 shows how the exclusion path is created when an open path is intersected by the current circle path using the Exclude Overlapping Shapes option.
- **Merge Shape Components.** Selecting this option merges the currently selected shape components into a single shape component based on the operation you selected in the Path Operations menu.

FIGURE 17.13

When using the Exclude Overlapping Shapes option, the working path is altered to include only the area where the older working path and the newly created path do not overlap.

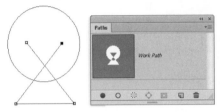

- **Path Alignment.** Clicking this button displays a menu that provides options to align and distribute the currently selected paths based on their edges, centers, width, and height. The Path Alignment menu is separated into the following sections:

  - **Alignment tools.** The Alignment tools allow you to align two or more selected paths to the top, right, vertical center, left, right, and horizontal center. These options are useful to arrange paths in exact lines and position them accurately. For example, Figure 17.14 shows two items centered vertically with each other using the Alignment tools.

FIGURE 17.14

Selecting multiple paths and clicking the Align Vertical Center option aligns the centers of the paths with each other.

  - **Distribution tools.** The Distribution tools allow you to distribute three or more selected paths evenly to the top, right, vertical center, left, bottom, and horizontal center. These options are useful to evenly arrange paths in exact lines and position them accurately. For example, Figure 17.15 shows an example of using the Distribute Horizontal Center option to evenly distribute a set of four paths.

  - **Align To options.** The alignment takes into account the relative placement of the currently selected paths when you select the Align To Selection option. The alignment uses the canvas position to align the paths when you select the Align To Canvas option.

- **Path Arrangement.** Clicking this button displays a menu that provides options to arrange the z-position of the path relative to the other paths in the layer. For example, you can send the currently selected path to the back if you want it to appear behind the other paths in the layer.

FIGURE 17.15

Selecting multiple paths and clicking the Distribute Horizontal Center option aligns the centers of the paths with each other.

- **Geometry options.** Selecting the Rubber Band option causes the segment line to be drawn and updated while you are adding anchor points. This is an extremely useful feature, but it does use up extra processing power and might be a bit sluggish on slower computers.

- **Auto Add/Delete.** Selecting this option and hovering over an existing path with the Pen tool, toggles the Pen tool between the Add Anchor Pen tool and the Delete Anchor Pen tool. This allows you to use a single tool to add and remove points from the existing path.

- **Align Edges.** Selecting this option aligns pixel shapes to the edges of the pixel grid.

- **Fill.** Clicking this field allows you to specify a fill for the selected path. When you click Fill, the Fill dialog box appears (refer to Figure 17.9). You can choose to fill the selected path with nothing, a solid color fill, a gradient fill, or a pattern, as shown in Figure 17.16. Without a fill or stroke, the path contains no actual pixel data that will render when printed.

FIGURE 17.16

Using the Options bar, you can easily set the fill style for the current path.

No Fill   Solid Fill   Gradient Fill   Pattern Fill

- **Stroke.** Clicking this button displays a list where you can select a size of stroke that will be applied along the path or type in a specific size.

- **Stroke options.** Clicking this button opens the Stroke Options panel (refer to Figure 17.9). From this panel, you can set the following options that define the attributes of the stroke:

  - **Stroke.** Allows you to select from solid, dashed, or dotted lines.

  - **Align.** Allows you to specify whether to align the stroke to the inside, outside, or center of the path line.

  - **Caps.** Allows you to specify how the end caps of lines will look. You can select butt, rounded, or square caps. This option also affects the dashed lines.

  - **Corners.** Allows you to specify how the corners of the stroke are applied. They can be mitered, round, or beveled.

  - **More options.** Opens the Stroke dialog box (refer to Figure 17.9). From this dialog box, you can also specify the size of the dashes and gaps as well as up to three different dashes in a sequence.

- **Stroke Fill.** Clicking this button opens the Fill dialog box (see Figure 17.9), where you can specify the fill to use for the stroke.

- **Width.** Typing a number in this field allows you to set the exact width of the path.

- **Link Shape Height and Width.** Clicking this button constrains the width and height of the shape as you change either amount so that the proportions remain the same.

- **Height.** Typing a number in this field allows you to directly set the height of the path.

Using the Path Selection tools

Once you have created a path, you can adjust it using the Path Selection tools. These tools allow you to move the path as well as manipulate the location and behavior of individual anchor points.

By using the Path Selection tools, shown in Figure 17.17, you can easily manipulate the size, shape, location, and look of the path. You also use these options to combine paths into shapes.

FIGURE 17.17

Using the Path Selection tools, you can select, move, and scale one or more paths, as well as edit individual anchor and direction points on a path.

Path Selection tools

The keyboard shortcut A selects the Path Selection tools, and Shift+A toggles between the Path Selection tool and the Direct Selection tool. The following list describes the purpose of each Path Selection tool:

- **Path Selection tool.** Use this tool to select, move, or scale a single path or a group of paths. You select multiple paths by pressing the Shift key.

> **TIP**
>
> If you press and hold down the Alt/Option key while dragging a path with the Path Selection tool, a duplicate of the path is created and you drag the duplicate instead of the original path. This is a great way to create multiple copies of the same path.

- **Direct Selection tool.** Use this tool to select one or more individual anchor points on a path. You can use the Direct Selection tool to drag and reposition the anchor points. You can also use the Direct Selection tool to adjust the direction points of the selected anchor to change the curve of the line. You can select and manipulate multiple points on the path by pressing and holding down the Shift key as you select the anchor points.

> **TIP**
>
> You can change the Path Selection tool into the Direct Selection tool on the fly by pressing and holding down the Ctrl/⌘ key. This saves you time if you need to toggle back and forth.

> **TIP**
>
> When you select a path using the Path Selection tool, you can fine-tune its position by using the arrow keys on the keyboard. When you select one or more anchor points using the Direct Selection tool, you can fine-tune the position of the anchor point or points by using the arrow keys.

Path Selection tool options

When you select the Path Selection tool, several useful options become available in the Options bar, as shown in Figure 17.18. The Path Selection tool options are very similar to those in the Options bar for the Pen tool. The menus behave the same, depending on whether you are selecting a path in a vector layer or a path in a normal layer.

FIGURE 17.18

Using the Path Selection tool options, you can define how paths combine, as well as align multiple paths.

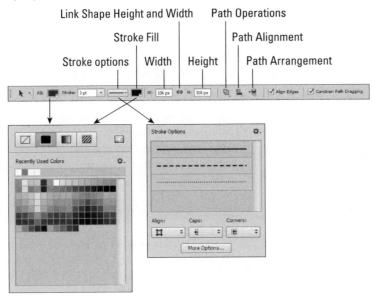

Understanding the Paths panel

A very useful feature for working with vector paths is the Paths panel. The Paths panel gives you a visual perspective of the current paths. It also allows you to manage and modify multiple paths in a single document.

The Paths panel, shown in Figure 17.19, provides buttons and a menu that allow you to manage the current paths in your document. From the Paths panel, you can select paths, convert paths to selections, and vice versa, as well as create new paths.

FIGURE 17.19

The Paths panel allows you to create, adjust, and manage the paths in your images.

From the Paths panel, you can use the following options:

- **Fill path with foreground color/Fill Path.** This option fills the currently selected path with the current foreground color. The path does not need to be closed, but it does need at least two line segments that do not form a straight line.

- **Stroke path with brush/Stroke Path.** This option applies a bitmapped brushstroke to the path. The currently selected brush style and size are used to trace the lines in the path on the image. Even though the path is visible on the screen, it isn't visible in the saved image or in the printed image unless a fill or brushstroke is applied. For example, Figure 17.20 shows the effect on an image when a brushstroke is applied to a path.

FIGURE 17.20

Applying a brushstroke to a path makes it visible in the actual image. The currently selected brush style and size, as well as the current foreground color, are used.

- **Load path as a selection/Make Selection.** This option creates a new selection using the line segments of the currently selected path in the Paths panel. Creating selections from a path is extremely useful for three purposes: to use the capabilities of paths to create and manipulate line segments using the anchors; to apply a path to an image; or to alter the pixels below the path before applying it to the image.

- **Make working path from selection/Make Work Path.** This option converts the current selection in the image to a path. This is a great way to create complex paths from existing images. For example, it was easy to select the darker areas of the image of the moon in Figure 17.21 and create a path from them.

FIGURE 17.21

You can use the Make working path from selection option to quickly create complex paths using areas of existing images that are easy to select.

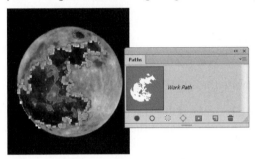

- **Create a path/New Path.** This option adds a new path to the Paths panel, and you can begin to add path components to it.

- **Delete current path.** This option removes the currently selected path from the document.

- **Duplicate Path.** This option creates a copy of the currently selected path and adds it to the Paths panel as a new path.

- **Clipping Path.** This option creates a clipping path in the image. The dialog box allows you to set the flatness of the clipping path in terms of device pixels. Printers use the value specified in the flatness field to determine the granularity to use when applying the clipping path. The lower the flatness field, the crisper the clipping looks. You can also select which path to use for the clipping path.

- **Panel options.** These options, found in the Paths panel menu, display a dialog box, allowing you to set the size of the thumbnail that is used to view the path in the Paths panel list.

TIP

You share paths between documents by selecting them in the Paths panel of one document and then dragging and dropping them into another document window in Photoshop.

Free transforming paths

One of the coolest features of vector paths in Photoshop is the free transform functionality. The Free Transform option allows you to quickly size, rotate, skew, and warp paths using a few simple mouse strokes.

To access the Free Transform tools, right-click the path using the Path Selection tool, and then from the pop-up menu, select Free Transform Path. A bounding box appears around the path and a new Options bar appears, as shown in Figure 17.22.

FIGURE 17.22

Using the Free Transform tool Options bar, you can quickly set the size, angle, and skew of the path.

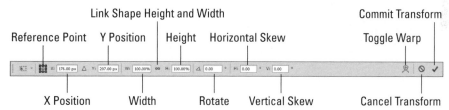

Using the Options bar, you can set precise values for the following Free Transform options:

- **Reference Point Location.** This option specifies the pivot point for resizing, rotating, and skewing the path.

- **X Position.** This field specifies the x-coordinate of the pivot point of the path. This is a quick way to place the path exactly where you need it horizontally.

- **Y Position.** This field specifies the y-coordinate of the pivot point of the path. This is a quick way to place the path exactly where you need it vertically.

- **Width.** This field allows you to set the exact width of the path.

- **Link Shape Height and Width.** This option constrains the width and height of the shape as you change either one so that the proportions remain the same.

- **Height.** This field allows you to set the height of the path.

- **Rotate.** This field specifies the rotation angle used to rotate the path. You can use this option to rotate the path by an exact number of degrees.

- **Horizontal Skew.** This field specifies the number of degrees to skew the path horizontally.

- **Vertical Skew.** This field specifies the number of degrees to skew the path vertically.

- **Toggle Warp.** This option allows you to toggle between the warp transform and the normal bounding box transforms.

- **Cancel Transform.** This option cancels the current transform and exits out of Free Transform mode.
- **Commit Transform.** This option commits the current transform of the path and exits out of Free Transform mode. You can also press the Enter key on the keyboard to commit the transform.

In addition to setting precise values, in Free Transform mode you have a new set of menu options when you right-click the bounding box of the path, as shown in Figure 17.23. These menu options make it very simple to make some quick transformations to a path using your mouse. You can easily apply one or more of the transformations to a path.

FIGURE 17.23

Using the Free Transform menu, you can quickly scale, skew, rotate, and warp a path.

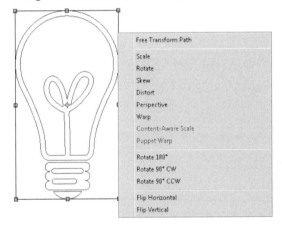

Using the Free Transform menu, you can make the following transformations to the path:

- **Scale.** This option allows you to adjust the size of the path by dragging on the control handles of the bounding box.
- **Rotate.** This option allows you to rotate the path by dragging the corner of the bounding box. Figure 17.24 shows an example of using the rotate handle to rotate a vector path. Notice the rotation icon showing the angle of rotation.
- **Skew.** This option allows you to adjust the skew of the path by dragging the control handles of the bounding box. Figure 17.25 shows an example of dragging the bottom-right corner of a vector path to skew the right side. Notice that the skew angle is displayed in the skew icon.

FIGURE 17.24

Using the Free Transform rotate tool to rotate a path

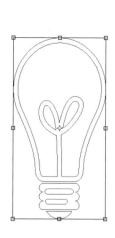
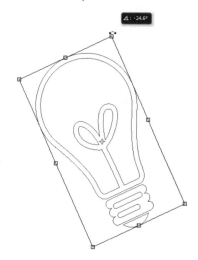

FIGURE 17.25

Using the Free Transform skew tool, you can skew a path by dragging a corner of the bounding box with the mouse.

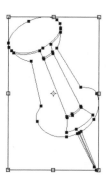
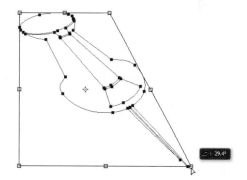

- **Distort.** This option allows you to distort the path along a corner by dragging a control handle of the bounding box.

- **Perspective.** This option uses the Perspective tool in Photoshop to adjust the perspective of the path. The Perspective tool is a great feature if you need to adjust a path to fit the perspective of an image you are working on. Figure 17.26 shows an example of using the Perspective tool to make a vector path representing an envelope appear to be heading away from the screen.

FIGURE 17.26

Using the Free Transform perspective tool can quickly change the look of a vector.

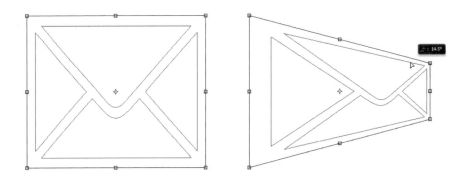

- **Warp.** This option adds a warp mesh to the bounding box. The Warp tool is by far the most dynamic and capable of all of the Path Transform tools. You can grab any point in the mesh and warp the path however you like. Figure 17.27 shows the use of the Warp tool to totally transform the look of a vector path.

FIGURE 17.27

Using the Free Transform warp tool, you can manipulate the path from any location on the grid to completely change the dynamics of the path.

  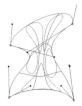

- **Rotate 180°.** This option rotates the path 180 degrees.
- **Rotate 90° CW.** This option rotates the path 90 degrees clockwise.
- **Rotate 90° CCW.** This option rotates the path 90 degrees counter-clockwise.
- **Flip Horizontal.** This option flips the path along a vertical axis.
- **Flip Vertical.** This option flips the path along a horizontal axis.

> **NOTE**
>
> The reference point location that you set in the Options bar of the Free Transform tool is used for all of the Path Transform tools. Make sure you set this option correctly before you begin transforming a path.

Exploring Paths

Understanding paths can help you in many aspects of Photoshop from creating vector art to creating highly accurate masks. In the previous sections, we discussed path components, the vector tools used to create paths, and the Paths panel, which is used to manage paths. In this section, we apply that knowledge to some of the common tasks that you can perform when working with paths. The following sections take you through some examples of creating and using paths.

Creating a path

There are many reasons to create paths in Photoshop. You can use paths to generate highly accurate masks, create vector art, or use them to define the flow of text. The first example we look at is creating a basic path using the following steps:

1. **Select the Ellipse tool.**
2. **Set the mode to Path in the Options bar of the Ellipse tool.**
3. **Draw two circles by pressing and holding down the Shift key, as shown in Figure 17.28.**

FIGURE 17.28

Selecting the Ellipse tool from the Toolbox with the mode set to Paths allows you to add circles to the current path.

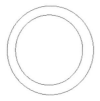

4. **Use the Path Selection tool to select both circles, and then click the Exclude overlapping shapes option in the Path Operations menu of the Options bar of the Path Selection tool to remove the center of the inner circle from the path area.**

5. **Click Merge Shape Components in the Path Operations menu of the Options bar of the Path Selection tool to combine the paths, as shown in Figure 17.29.**

FIGURE 17.29

Using the Exclude overlapping shapes option on the two paths removes the inner area from the path shape area.

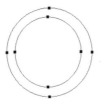

6. **Use the Pen tool to add the points shown in Figure 17.30.**

FIGURE 17.30

Using the Pen tool, you can create a simple handle by adding four path points.

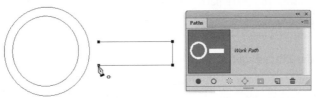

7. **Use the Path Selection tool to move the new path so it touches the existing circles.**

8. **Use the Convert Point tool to adjust the corners for the handle so they are round by dragging the direction points, as shown in Figure 17.31.**

   Click each corner to convert the corner to a smooth anchor, and then drag away from the corner to add and shape the curves.

FIGURE 17.31

Using the Convert Point tool converts the corners to smooth anchors and allows the line segments in the handle to become curves.

9. **Select both the handle and the circles, and then select Merge Shape Components in the Path Operations menu of the Options bar of the Path Selection tool to combine the paths, as shown in Figure 17.32.**

FIGURE 17.32

Using the Merge Shape Components option creates a single path from the two selected paths, completing the magnifying glass shape.

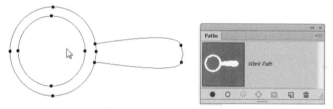

Creating vector shapes from paths

Using paths to create vector shapes allows you to add elements to an image that can be resized and shaped and still maintain perfectly crisp edge. In this example, we convert the path from the previous example into a vector shape using the following steps:

1. **Select the path using the Path Selection tool.**

2. **Right-click the selected path to open the menu shown in Figure 17.33.**

3. **Select Define Custom Shape from the menu to open the Shape Name dialog box shown in Figure 17.33.**

4. **Name the shape, and click OK to add the new shape to the Custom Vector Shapes menu, as shown in Figure 17.33.**

   You can view the Custom Vector Shapes menu by choosing Edit ⇨ Preset Manager and then selecting Custom Shapes in the Preset Type drop-down menu.

FIGURE 17.33

Converting a shape to a path is as simple as right-clicking it and selecting Define Custom Shape from the shortcut menu. The new shape is added to the Custom Vector Shapes list.

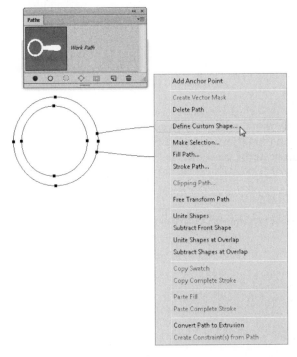

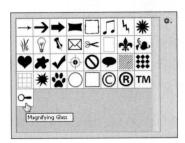

Creating a clipping mask

Using a path to create a clipping mask will allow you to create a highly accurate clipping mask that can be an easily fine-tuned clip out a specific area of an image. In this example, we create a clipping mask that you can save with the file to mask any area outside of a specific object when the file is printed:

1. **Open an image in Photoshop.**

2. **Use the Pen tool to create a path around an object in the image, as shown in Figure 17.34.**

   You need to adjust the curved anchor points so the line segments follow the perimeter of the object.

FIGURE 17.34

Use the Pen tool to create a path around an object in the picture. The object is the only thing included when the clipping mask is applied.

3. **Select the working path in the Paths panel.**

4. **Select Save Path from the Paths panel menu.**

   Photoshop doesn't allow you to make a clipping path until you have saved the path with a new name. In this case, we named the path Salt Shaker, as shown in Figure 17.35.

FIGURE 17.35

Use the Save Path dialog box to give the path a meaningful name. The working path is changed to the saved path name in the Paths panel.

5. **Select Clipping Path from the Paths panel menu to launch the Clipping Path dialog box, shown in Figure 17.36.**

6. **Select the saved path, and set the flatness.**

   In this case, we set the flatness to 5 device pixels to maintain adequate sharpness while still supporting most printers. Flatness determines the number of lines used to draw the curve. A lower flatness value results in a greater number of straight lines used to draw the curve and consequently a more accurate curve. Flatness values can range from 0.2 to 100.

FIGURE 17.36

Select the path and flatness when creating the clipping path.

7. **Click OK to make the path a clipping path.**

8. **Save the file as a format that supports clipping masks, typically EPS or TIFF.**

   The file is created with the clipping path data.

Creating vector masks

Using a path to create a vector mask will allow you to create a mask that can be easily fine-tuned to fit a specific area of an image. You can also resize the path to create additional clipping masks that maintain crisp edges. In this example, we use the following steps to create a vector mask that will be added to a layer to mask part of the image:

1. **Open an image in Photoshop.**

2. **Use the vector tools to create a path around an object in the image, as shown in Figure 17.37.**

   In this case, the path is a simple ellipse around the dog's face.

3. **Select the working path in the Paths panel.**

4. **Select Save Path from the Paths panel menu.**

   Photoshop doesn't allow you to make a vector mask from the path until you have saved the path, as shown in Figure 17.37.

FIGURE 17.37

Create a path around the area of the image that you want to include in the vector mask.

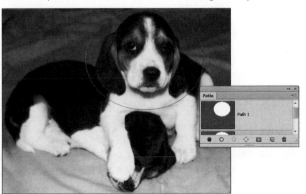

5. **If you are using a background layer, convert the background to an unlocked layer by double-clicking it, and then select it in the Layers panel, as shown in Figure 17.38.**

6. **Select the saved path in the Paths panel so Photoshop uses the selected path to create the vector mask.**

7. **Open the Properties panel if it is not already open.**

8. **Click the Add Mask icon in the Paths panel.**

   A mask is added to the Properties panel, as shown in Figure 17.38.

9. **Select the Add a vector mask option in the Masks panel to add the vector mask to the image, as shown in Figure 17.38.**

    The layer mask is added to the layer, and a copy of the layer vector mask is added to the Paths panel.

FIGURE 17.38

Using the selected path to create a vector mask on a layer in the image

ON THE WEB
You can find the image shown in Figure 17.38 on this book's website as Figure 17-38.psd. It contains a good shape to practice using vector paths to create masks.

Using Vector Shape Tools

The easiest way to describe a vector shape is as a vector path applied as a mask to a fill layer. Unlike paths, vector shapes apply pixel data to a document. Vector shapes can be applied to a document either by directly painting the shape pixels onto a layer or as their own layer, which is called a vector shape layer.

When you use the Pixels option to apply vector shapes to documents, the vector shapes you apply are immediately rasterized and painted onto the pixels in the selected layer in the Layers palette. This replaces the pixel data below them.

When you use the Shape option to apply vector shapes to documents, the vector shapes are added as vector shape layers. You can edit the vector shape layers later.

When you use the Path option, vector shapes will be applied to the current layer as a vector path. You can use all of the features we have already discussed in this chapter to work with the new vector path.

This section discusses the vector shape layers, although most of the tools work the same with the Shape, Path, or Pixels option selected.

Working with vector shape tools

Creating vector shapes is almost identical to creating vector paths, with the exception that a color can be used to fill in the contents of the vector shape and a stroke can be used to represent the vector lines. You use paths when you want to use a vector without actually adding pixel data to the output image, and you use shapes when you want the vector to actually be represented in the image.

You can add vector shapes to a layer either by selecting the Pen tool from the options menu or by selecting one of the vector shapes from the Shape tools in the Toolbox, shown in Figure 17.39.

The keyboard shortcut U selects the Shape tools, and Shift+U toggles between the Shape tools. When you select a vector shape, a Shape tool Options bar appears, similar to the one in Figure 17.40. Choose the Shape mode to add the vector shapes as shape layers.

> **NOTE**
>
> The principles you learn in this section for using the Shape mode apply the same way to the Fill Pixels mode. The only difference is that in the Fill Pixels mode, you are directly writing to the background or layer instead of as a shape layer.

FIGURE 17.39

Using the Shape tools, you can add vector shapes to images.

FIGURE 17.40

The Shape tool Options bar is identical to the Pen tool Options bar. However, when you select the Shape Layers option, additional options become available.

Notice that the Shape tool Options bar is identical to the Pen tool Options bar when you are in Paths mode. This is a major advancement in Photoshop CS6 because it makes it much easier to deal with vector paths and layers. For instance, you can add a stroke or fill to a path now, just as you can a vector layer. You can also adjust the alignment and arrangement of both vector objects and vector paths. For a more detailed explanation of each of the menu items, refer to the vector paths sections earlier in this chapter.

The only difference between the options menus for vector paths and vector shapes is in the Geometry options menu. The geometry options are different for each type of vector shape. The following sections describe each of the shape tools and the options available in the Geometry Options menu for each of the Shape tools.

Rectangle tool

The Rectangle tool creates a rectangle when you drag the mouse between two diagonal corners. Using the Shift key while dragging the mouse creates a square. The Rectangle tool provides many options in a drop-down list, as shown in Figure 17.41.

FIGURE 17.41

Additional options for the Rectangle tool

Click the down arrow next to the custom shape button to view the following option:

- **Unconstrained.** This option allows you to create a rectangle at any size.
- **Square.** This option forces you to create a square rectangle.
- **Fixed Size.** This option allows you to set the height and width of the rectangle.
- **Proportional.** This option forces the rectangle to match the proportions of the height and width that you specify.
- **From Center.** This option allows you to select the first location to be the center of the rectangle and then to select one of the corners to create the rectangle, instead of dragging from corner to corner.
- **Align Edges.** This option snaps the corners to the pixel grid.

Rounded Rectangle tool

The Rounded Rectangle tool allows you to create a rectangle with rounded corners by dragging the mouse between two diagonal corners. Using the Shift key while dragging the mouse creates a square. When you select this option, a Radius option becomes available in the Options bar that allows you to set the radius of the corners of the rectangle. The Rounded Rectangle tool provides the same additional choices in the options drop-down menu as the Rectangle tool.

Ellipse tool

The Ellipse tool allows you to create an ellipse by dragging the mouse between two diagonal corners. Using the Shift key while dragging the mouse creates a circle. The Ellipse tool provides the same additional choices in the options drop-down list as the Rectangle tool, with the exception that the Square option is a Circle option and there is no Snap to Pixels option.

Polygon tool

The Polygon tool creates a polygon with the number of sides specified by the additional Sides option shown in Figure 17.42. You create the polygon by dragging the mouse between two diagonal corners. You can use the Shift key while dragging the mouse to force the polygon into a 45-degree angle.

FIGURE 17.42

Additional options for the Polygon tool

The Polygon tool provides the following choices from the options drop-down list:

- **Radius.** This option allows you to set the radius of the polygon in inches.
- **Smooth Corners.** This option makes the corners of the polygon smooth anchors instead of corner anchors.
- **Star.** This option indents the line segments between the corner anchors of the polygon toward the center by the amount you specify in the Indent Sides By field.
- **Smooth Indents.** This option makes the corners of the indents smooth anchors instead of corner anchors.
- **Line tool.** The Line tool allows you to create a line with the thickness that you specify in the Weight field. You create a line by dragging the mouse between two points. You can use the Shift key while dragging the mouse to force the line into a 45-degree angle. The Line tool provides the following arrowhead options from the options drop-down list, shown in Figure 17.43:

FIGURE 17.43

Additional options for the Line tool

- **Start.** This option adds an arrowhead to the first point selected.
- **End.** This option adds an arrowhead to the last point selected.
- **Width.** This field specifies the width of the arrowhead relative to the weight of the line.

- **Length.** This field specifies the length of the arrowhead relative to the weight of the line.

- **Concavity.** This field specifies how concave to make the arrowhead relative to the weight of the line.

Custom Shape tool

The Custom Shape tool creates a custom shape that you select from the additional Shape menu, shown in Figure 17.44. You add the custom shape to the image by selecting a shape from the list and then dragging the mouse between two diagonal corners. You can use the Shift key while dragging the mouse to create the shape in even proportions.

FIGURE 17.44

Additional options for the Custom Shape tool

Adding vector shape layers

Adding vector shapes as their own layer allows you modify the shape without affecting other layers, hide the vector shape, drag and drop the layer into other documents, and several other benefits. Now that you have a good understanding of the available vector shape tools, you should try adding a few shapes to a document to get the hang of it. The following examples take you quickly through the steps to apply the vector tools in a few different ways.

The first example we look at creates a simple square by keeping the Rectangle tool in proportion using the Shift key. The technique here is similar for creating all the vector shapes in proportion. Use the following steps:

1. **Select the Rectangle tool from the Toolbox.**
2. **Click the Shape option in the Options bar to create a new layer with the shape.**
3. **Press and hold down the Shift key and drag diagonally across the screen to create the square, as shown in Figure 17.45.**

   Notice that the shape is forced into a square and that a new shape layer is added to the Layers panel.

FIGURE 17.45

Using the Shift key to create a square shape layer

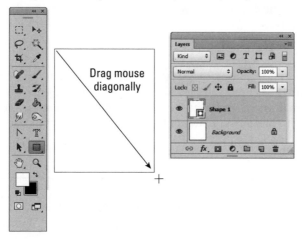

In the next example, we use the Polygon tool to add an eight-sided star with an overspray technique to give it more depth. Use the following steps:

1. **Select the Polygon tool from the Toolbox.**

2. **Click the Shape option in the Options bar to create a new layer with the shape.**

3. **Select the Smooth Corners, Star, and Smooth Indents options from the Polygon tool options, as shown in Figure 17.46.**

   Also set the Indent Sides By option to 50%. This makes the polygon a star with smooth corners and indents.

4. **Type 8 in the Sides field in the Options bar to create an eight-sided polygon.**

5. **Position the mouse in the center location for the polygon, and click and drag the mouse out to create the polygon vector layer shown in Figure 17.46.**

6. **Click the *fx* button in the Layers panel and add a Bevel & Emboss effect to the newly created vector layer.**

   Notice that the polygon Shape layer has the Bevel & Emboss and Satin effects applied to create the overspray effect.

FIGURE 17.46

Selecting the Smooth Corners, Star, and Smooth Indents options for a polygon creates a star shape. Selecting the Overspray Text option in the Style options applies a bevel effect.

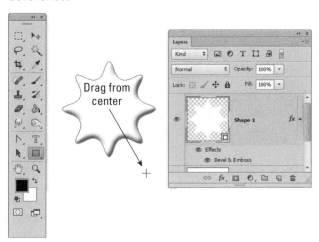

The final example we show uses the Exclude Overlapping Shape Areas option to combine the polygon created in the previous example with a circle to create a completely different shape. Use the following steps after completing the steps from the previous example:

1. **Select the Ellipse tool from the Shape tool menu.**

2. **Select the From Center option from the Ellipse tool options drop-down menu.**

   This allows you to use the center of the polygon as the starting point, which is much easier than trying to figure out where to draw the corner of the ellipse creation box.

3. **Select the Exclude Overlapping Shape Areas option from the Options bar so only the areas of the circle that are outside the polygon are included in the new shape area.**

4. **Position the mouse in the center of the polygon, press and hold down the Shift key, and drag outward to create the circle, as shown in Figure 17.47.**

   Notice that only the area outside of the polygon is included in the shape area shown in the Layers panel.

5. **Use the Path Selection tool to select the circle, and then use the keyboard arrow keys to reposition the circle so it is exactly around the perimeter of the polygon.**

6. **Select Merge Shape Components from the Path Operations menu to combine the vector shapes into a new shape area, as shown in Figure 17.47.**

FIGURE 17.47

FIGURE 17.47

Using the Exclude Overlapping Shape Areas option creates a shape that includes only the area of the circle that is outside the polygon.

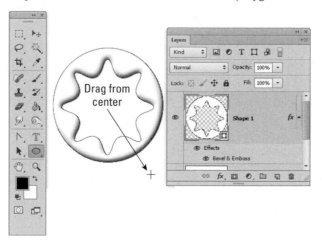

Adding custom vector shapes

Adding custom vector shapes works the same way as adding normal vector shapes, with the exception that you have some additional options for managing the custom shapes from the Shape Selection options in the Shape options menu.

The Shape Options bar, shown in Figure 17.48, is displayed when you select one of the Shape tools from the Toolbox. When you select the drop-down arrow, the Shapes list appears, as shown in Figure 17.48. You can select any shape, and when you click and drag the mouse on the document, the shape is added just as in the previous examples.

The Shapes list provides an options menu that includes the following options:

- **Rename Shape.** This option opens a dialog box where you can change the name of the selected shape. The name appears when you hover over the shape in the tool and in some of the other panels in Photoshop.

- **Delete Shape.** This option deletes the currently selected shape from the Shapes list.

- **View options.** These options allow you to set the mode for viewing shapes. You can select Text Only, which displays only the shape names, two sizes of thumbnails, or two sizes of list views. The list views include a thumbnail as well as the shape name.

- **Preset Manager.** This option launches the Preset Manager dialog box with the Custom Shapes option selected, where you can create and manage presets for the Custom Shapes list.

- **Reset Shapes.** This option replaces the current list of shapes with the default list.

- **Load Shapes.** This option allows you to load a set of shapes from a previously saved file. The new shapes are added to the current list of shapes.

- **Save Shapes.** This option allows you to save the current set of shapes as a file. This is useful if you are creating your own custom shapes so you have them available later and can distribute them to others.

- **Replace Shapes.** This option allows you to load a set of shapes from a previously saved file. The current list of shapes is replaced by the new list.

- **Preset lists.** This section provides several preset lists of shapes that make it easier to find shapes you want. You can select any of them from the list, and the current Shapes list is replaced by the selected preset list.

FIGURE 17.48

When using the Custom Shape tool, you can select custom shapes from a drop-down list. You can also manage the Custom Shapes lists by saving and loading list files and by selecting preset lists.

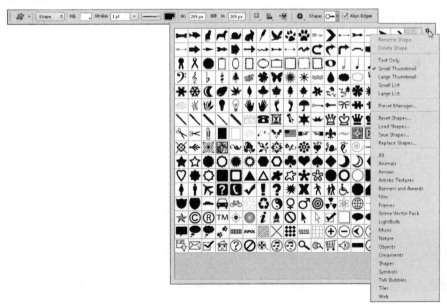

643

Editing a vector shape

A great feature of vector shapes is that they include the anchor and line information from the vector paths that created them. This allows you to edit the vector shapes after you have added them to your document. The following example takes you through adding a custom shape to a document and then editing it with the vector tools:

1. **Select the Custom Shape tool from the main menu bar.**

2. **Click the Shape Layers option in the Options bar to create a new layer when the shape is added.**

3. **Select the Heart Card shape from the Shapes list in the Options bar.**

   The Heart Card shape is in the Shapes preset list in the Preset Manager.

4. **Drag the mouse diagonally to add the heart to the document.**

5. **Select the Direct Selection tool from the Toolbox, and click the heart to expose the anchors, as shown in Figure 17.49.**

FIGURE 17.49

Shapes contain the vector anchor and line information of the vector paths used to create them so you can edit a vector shape at any time using the vector path tools.

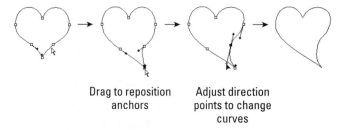

Drag to reposition anchors   Adjust direction points to change curves

6. **Select the Direct Selection tool from the Toolbox and drag the bottom anchor points of the heart, as shown in Figure 17.49.**

7. **Select the Direct Selection tool from the Toolbox and drag the direction points of the curve, as shown in Figure 17.49, to give the heart a new look.**

> **NOTE**
> You cannot edit vector shapes that are applied to a document using the Fill Pixels option in the Shape tool Options bar because the vector shape is rasterized into pixel data and painted onto the layer.

Summary

This chapter discussed how to create and manipulate vector paths and shapes. Vector paths provide a distinct advantage over pixel data because you can resize them without losing any of the image crispness. That makes them useful for creating shapes, masks, and selections that you can resize without losing the sharpness in the edges. Vector shape layers are vector shapes applied as masks to a fill layer.

In this chapter, you learned these concepts:

- How to create a vector path using the vector path tools
- How to manipulate individual anchor points on a path to define the position of line end points and the curvature of the line
- How to create a clipping mask
- How to create a vector mask that provides a mask which can be manipulated using the vector path tools while maintaining its crisp edges
- How to add a stroke and fill to a vector path to make the path visible in an image
- How to create a vector shape from a vector path
- How to edit vector shapes after they have been added to an image

17

Summary

Working with Text

Text can be an extremely important element to images, not only to add information but also to contribute to the overall appearance. Photoshop provides the ability to add text to images as vector objects. This chapter discusses the tools used to add and edit text, as well as applying textual elements to images in creative ways. The tools in Photoshop allow you to configure and control the format and flow of the text, and provide a way to edit the text right down to the character shapes.

Learning a Little Bit about Text

Before jumping into adding text to images, let's look at what text really means inside Photoshop. When you initially consider text, you probably think about letters, words, and paragraphs. Then as you apply the term *text* to a computer application, you start to include the concept of fonts or typefaces. Although the terms *font* and *typeface* are used synonymously, they are actually bit different. A *font* consists of a set of letters, numbers, and symbols that have the same weight and style. A *typeface* is a collection or family of fonts that have the same overall appearance but different weights or styles. For example, many typefaces include regular, bold, and italic font versions.

The following is a list of the different font types that you can work with in Photoshop:

- **PostScript.** PostScript or Type 1 fonts were designed long ago by Adobe to be used with PostScript printers. These fonts have mostly been replaced by OpenType fonts, but you may run into them if you need to use an older font to match older material.

- **TrueType.** TrueType fonts were developed by Apple to compete with PostScript fonts. TrueType fonts are actually made up of vector paths and allow the text to appear crisp, even when it is resized. These fonts also allow special characters or symbols to be included with the font as "glyphs." Although TrueType fonts are still widely used, they are being replaced by OpenType fonts.

- **OpenType.** OpenType fonts were developed by Adobe to replace both PostScript and TrueType fonts by embedding the PostScript information in with the TrueType packaging. OpenType fonts are also made up of vector paths and allow some additional glyph capability, including glyphs that are created by applying two letters together (such as ff), fractions, and superscripting suffixes, like the *st* in 1st.

When working in Photoshop, you should adjust your thinking about text. In reality, Photoshop treats text as a group of vector shapes that represent letters, words, and paragraphs. Selecting a font simply means that you are changing the set of shapes that are used to represent the letters. Thinking about text in this way helps as you start to use some of the more advanced features and apply artistic effects with text.

Using the Text Tools to Add Text to Images

Photoshop provides several tools that give you a lot of flexibility and control when adding text to images. Text can be added to images to provide information or as a visual element. The Text tools in Photoshop provide dynamic ways of adding both. This section discusses setting up preferences for these tools and using them to add and edit text in your images.

Setting type preferences

Before you start working with text, you may want to set the type preferences in Photoshop. Setting the type preferences allows you to define how the text and paragraph tools behave and what features are available in the panels. To set the type preferences, press Ctrl+K/⌘+K to open the Preferences dialog box and select the Type option, as shown in Figure 18.1.

Use the dialog box to set the following options:

- **Use Smart Quotes.** When you select this option, Photoshop detects the open and close quote characters in the text and treats them differently so they point in the direction that they apply.

- **Enable Missing Glyph Protection.** If you open a file in Photoshop that contains a font that is not included on the system, you see an alert and the font is substituted by one that is on the system. When you choose this option, Photoshop automatically selects an appropriate font if you enter text that results in incorrect or unreadable characters.

- **Show Font Names in English.** When you select this option, the font names appear in English, even if the font is for another language such as Chinese or Japanese. This is useful if you need to add characters from another language font but do not actually read the language.

- **Font Preview Size.** When you select this option, sample text in the actual font style is displayed next to the font name when you are selecting fonts from the lists in the Type tools or the Character menu. You can specify that the sample text appear small, medium, large, extra large, or huge. Enabling this option costs some additional processing time, so you may not want to enable it, and even if you do, you should keep the preview size as small as possible for your needs.

- **Choose Text Options.** You have the ability to specify one of three options that will define what options are available on the Text panel and Paragraph panel. These options are:

  - **Show Default User Interface.** When you select this option, these standard options are available in the Character and Paragraph panels.

  - **Show East Asian Text User Interface.** When you select this option, additional options for the Chinese, Japanese, and Korean text symbols are visible in the Character and Paragraph panels. If you are not working with these language sets, you should leave this option unselected.

  - **Show Complex Scripts User Interface.** When you select this option, additional options for the Middle Eastern and North African MENA languages such as Arabic, Farsi, and Hebrew will be available in the Character and Paragraph panels. Also when you select this option, Photoshop uses the MENA text composer to correctly compose right-to-left and complex scripts in the type layer.

FIGURE 18.1

Setting the preferences for text in Photoshop

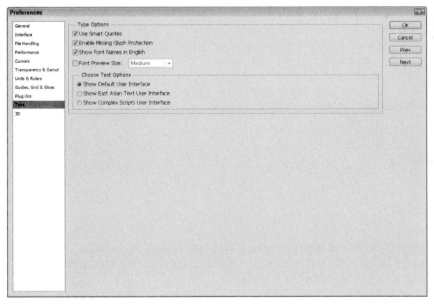

Using the text tools to add text

Photoshop provides four Toolbox tools that allow you to add text to your document. There are two Type tools and two Type Mask tools.

The two Type tools, shown in the Toolbox in Figure 18.2, add text as a vector text layer either horizontally or vertically. The great part about adding text as a layer is that you can go back at any time and edit or apply effects to the layer.

The two Type Mask tools, shown in the Toolbox in Figure 18.2, use the text you type to create a selection mask that can be converted to a vector or pixel mask or used as a simple selection.

> **NOTE**
>
> If you add text to a document that does not support layers, such as bitmap, the text is applied initially as a layer, but when the document is saved in the format that doesn't support vector layers, the text layer will be converted to raster pixels.

FIGURE 18.2

The Type tools allow you to add text to your documents as a vector text layer and to create selections from the text you type.

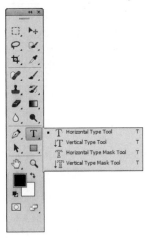

When you select one of the Type tools, a Type tool options bar becomes available, similar to the one in Figure 18.3. The options are applied to any text that is currently selected or to new text that you type into the document.

FIGURE 18.3

The Type tool options bar allows you to set options for selected text or text you are typing into the document.

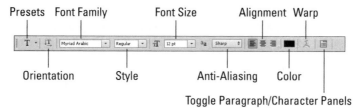

From the Type tool options bar, you can set the following options:

- **Orientation.** This option allows you to toggle the text between vertical and horizontal orientation.

- **Font Family.** This drop-down menu allows you to select the font family.

- **Style.** This drop-down menu allows you to select a typeface style such as italic, bold, hard, light, strong, and so on. The available options depend on the font that you have selected.

- **Font Size.** This drop-down menu allows you to set the size of the font used when displaying the text.

- **Anti-Aliasing.** This drop-down menu allows you to set the anti-aliasing method that Photoshop uses to render the edges of the font onscreen. Anti-aliasing tries to smooth the square edge effect by filling in the sharp edges and blending the text with the background. The more anti-aliasing you apply, the smoother the transition, although anti-aliasing that is too aggressive can produce artifacts around the edges of the text. You can select the following anti-aliasing options:

  - **None.** This applies no anti-aliasing.

  - **Sharp.** This displays type in the sharpest fashion.

  - **Crisp.** This displays type that is somewhat sharp.

  - **Strong.** This displays type with a heavier appearance.

  - **Smooth.** This adds the greatest amount of smoothing around the edges.

> **TIP**
>
> Too much anti-aliasing can result in some color artifacts around the edges of the font and may produce inconsistent results when producing low-resolution images such as those used on the Web. To reduce the inconsistency, deselect the Fractal Width option in the Character panel menu.

- **Alignment.** You can choose to set the alignment of the text to left, center, or right for horizontal text, and top, center, or bottom for vertical text.

- **Color.** Clicking this box launches the Select Text Color dialog box, which allows you to set the color used to fill in the text.

- **Warp.** Clicking this button allows you to apply Warp effects to distort the text.

- **Toggle Paragraph/Character Panels.** Clicking this button allows you to quickly open and close the Character and Paragraph panels. You use these panels frequently when working with text, so this is a great option.

You can add new text by using the Type tools either as point type or as paragraph type. Each of these options provides different advantages that are discussed in the following sections.

Adding text as a point type

When you add text as a point type, the text flows from a point that you place on the screen. The text flows from the point based on the alignment setting in the Type tool options bar. For example, if the text is aligned left, the text flows to the right; if the text is centered, the text flows in both directions away from the point. This option is useful if you want to create unbounded text in the image, but it does not provide as many features as a paragraph type.

To add text to an image as a point type, simply select either the Horizontal Type or Vertical Type tool from the Toolbox and click the document. A point is displayed, and you can type text from that point, as shown in Figure 18.4. Notice that a new vector text layer has been added to the Layers panel.

FIGURE 18.4

Adding text as a point type

Point Type

After you have added text as a point type, you can use the Move tool to select and change the position of the text in the newly created layer.

Adding text as a paragraph type

When you add text as a paragraph type, the text is placed inside a bounding box. The bounding box limits the flow of text, which offers the advantage of forcing the text to fit into a specified area. As text hits the side of the bounding box, it is wrapped down to the next line.

However, you do need to be careful. If the flow of the text exceeds the bounding box dimensions, some of the characters are hidden below the bottom of the box. This can result in missing text in the image if you do not increase the size of the bounding box or decrease the font size. When text is hidden below the bottom of the bounding box, the bottom-right control handle displays a plus sign.

To add text to an image as a paragraph type, select either the Horizontal Type or Vertical Type tool from the Toolbox and drag the mouse diagonally to create a bounding box, as shown in Figure 18.5. A bounding box is created, and you can type text into the box, as shown in Figure 18.5. Notice that a new vector type layer has been added to the Layers panel.

TIP

If you press and hold down the Alt/Option key while dragging to create the paragraph type bounding box, a dialog box appears, allowing you to set the height and width of the box. The values in the box are in pixel/point units denoted by *pt*. However, you can also specify the size in inches by using *inches* as the unit — for example, "3 inches."

You can change the size of the bounding box using the mouse to drag the control handles at the corners and sides. The bounding box provides another useful feature when working with text in that you can use the rotation controls in the corners to rotate the text, as shown in Figure 18.5.

18

FIGURE 18.5

Adding text as a paragraph type creates a bounding box that limits the flow of the text. You can use the rotation controls on the bounding box to rotate the text.

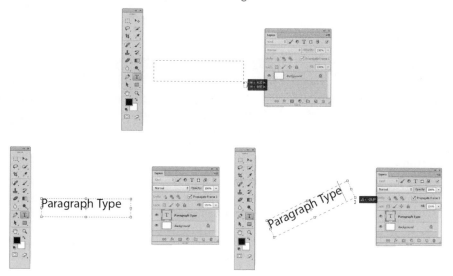

Editing vector text layers

After adding text to your document as a vector text layer, you can edit it at any time by selecting one of the Type tools and clicking the text in the document window. With the text object selected, you can use the mouse to select a portion of the text by dragging over it just as you would in any text editor.

> **NOTE**
>
> If you have vector text layers that overlap each other, clicking them selects the top layer. You may need to double-click the text thumbnail in the Layers panel to select text in a vector text layer that is underneath another one.

It is important to keep in mind that while you are editing text, some of the changes, such as font size and color, apply only to the selected text, while other changes, such as alignment and kerning, apply to the entire paragraph, regardless of what text is selected. Each time you press Enter/Return in a paragraph type text box, a new paragraph is started. That means you can make different format changes for each paragraph in the same paragraph type bounding box.

> **TIP**
>
> When you are in Edit mode, Photoshop displays selection guidelines and other editing aids. This can make it difficult to follow the text. While you are in Edit mode, you can press the Ctrl+H/⌘+H hotkeys to toggle displaying the guidelines and editing aids, and even turn the selection highlight on and off. This makes it easier to read the text and see the effect of making edits.

Photoshop provides a number of options to format and edit the text and to format and affect vector text layers. Some of these options are located in the Type tool options bar that we discussed earlier. Some of them are found in the Character and Paragraph panels, which we discuss later in this chapter.

Several options become available when you use one of the Type tools to right-click the text to open the Text Edit menu, shown in Figure 18.6. If the text is already selected when you right-click the mouse, a slightly different menu is displayed with options for the selected text. The following sections cover the options available in this menu.

> **NOTE**
>
> You should be aware that when in Edit mode, not all of these options are available. For example, you cannot rasterize the text or convert between point type and paragraph type. Also, many of these options are available from the Layers panel menu when you select the vector text layer.

Edit Type

The Edit Type option puts Photoshop in Text Edit mode in the vector text layer that you clicked. While in Text Edit mode, you can adjust the settings in the Type tool options bar or in the Character and Paragraph panels to edit and format the text.

FIGURE 18.6

Right-clicking text using a Type tool displays a menu that gives you several options to edit the vector text layer.

Check Spelling

The Check Spelling option launches a Check Spelling dialog box similar to the one in Figure 18.7 if there are any words in the text that do not exist in Photoshop's dictionary. The Check Spelling dialog box displays misspelled words, offers suggestions, and allows you to apply changes, ignore the misspelling, or add the word to the Photoshop dictionary. If you select the Check All Layers option, all vector text layers are spell-checked.

FIGURE 18.7

Photoshop provides a built-in spell checker that allows you to quickly find and fix misspelled words in your text.

Find and Replace Text

The Find and Replace Text option can be useful if you need to quickly find text in your document or if you have been misspelling a word and need to change the spelling in several different places. For the most part, you are not likely to add a lot of text to your images, so you may never need this feature. However, if you ever do, it can save a lot of time.

Rasterize Type

The Rasterize Type option converts the vector data in the vector text layer into pixel data. You can no longer edit it as text; instead, the layer is treated as a raster layer just as if you had used the paint tools to create the text. Converting the text to a raster image can be useful if you want to apply effects to the text as a pixel image — for example, applying a filter to soften edges.

Create Work Path

The Create Work Path option uses the vector anchor and line data from the selected text to generate the working vector path. The new working path is displayed around the text and is available in the Paths panel, as shown in Figure 18.8. The vector text layer remains unchanged, and you can still edit and use it as you normally would.

FIGURE 18.8

You can use the vector text layer to create a working path from the vector data in the text.

 For more information about how to edit and use vector paths, see Chapter 17.

Convert to Shape

The Convert to Shape option converts the selected vector text layer into a vector shape layer. The new vector shape layer replaces the vector text layer in the Layers panel, as shown in Figure 18.9. The vector text layer is no longer available for text editing; instead, you need to treat the layer as a vector shape layer.

Converting text to a vector shape opens a variety of possibilities for editing. For example, Figure 18.9 shows how we used the Direct Selection tool to drag some of the anchors and adjust the direction lines to completely alter the look of the character.

FIGURE 18.9

You can convert a vector text layer into a vector shape layer and then use the vector tools to edit and use the shape.

Horizontal/Vertical options

The Horizontal and Vertical options allow you to toggle the text arrangement from a horizontal flow to a vertical flow.

Anti-Alias adjustment

The Anti-Alias options allow you to quickly set the type of anti-alias adjustment to apply to the selected vector text layer.

Faux formatting

The Faux Bold and Faux Italics options allow you to apply a fake bold or italic style to the selected text. If you have selected a portion of the text, this option applies only to the selected text and not to the entire paragraph. If you have not selected any text, this applies to the entire paragraph. Typically, you should avoid using the Faux text options because they don't look nearly as good as if the font family has a supported bold or italics font.

Convert to Point Text/Paragraph Text

The Convert to Point Text and Convert to Paragraph Text options allow you to toggle the text between the point type and paragraph type styles. This can be useful if you want to add a bounding box to a point type text layer or if you want to remove the restrictions of the bounding box from a paragraph type text layer.

Warp Text

The Warp Text option allows you to apply a warp effect to the selected text. A dialog box similar to the one in Figure 18.10 is displayed that allows you to apply one of a number of warps, such as arcs, shells, and waves.

18

FIGURE 18.10

The Warp Text option allows you to apply several warping effects to text. You can control the amount of warp, direction, and distribution of the distortion that is applied.

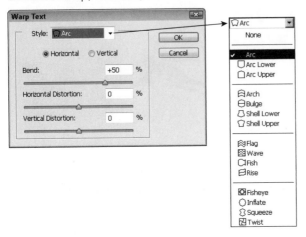

The Warp Text dialog box allows you to set the following options:

- **Style.** This drop-down menu allows you to select from one of the available warping options. The options are arranged in groups for arc, shell, wave, and radial distortions.

- **Horizontal.** This option applies the warp in a horizontal fashion from top to bottom.

- **Vertical.** This option applies the warp in a vertical fashion from left to right.

- **Bend.** This slider specifies the percentage of bend from −100% to +100%. The amount of bend determines the extent of the distortion applied to the text.

- **Horizontal Distortion.** This slider defines how the warp is distributed horizontally across the text. Using negative horizontal distortion has the effect of increasing the height of the text on the left side, making the text look as though it is getting farther away from right to left. Using positive horizontal distortion has the effect of increasing the height of the text on the right side and decreasing its height on the left side, making the text look as though it is getting closer from left to right.

- **Vertical Distortion.** This slider defines how the warp is distributed vertically across the text. Using negative vertical distortion has the effect of increasing the width of the top of the text while decreasing the width of the bottom, making the text look as though it is tipping forward. Using positive vertical distortion has the effect of decreasing the width of the top of the text while increasing the width of the bottom, making the text look as though it is tipping backward.

Using the available options in the Warp Text dialog box, you can create an amazing number of warping effects. Figure 18.11 shows a few of the different effects that warping can have on the text.

FIGURE 18.11

Using different combinations of the settings in the Warp Text dialog box results in an infinite number of warping effects on the text.

Arc Vertical
50% Bend

Shell Lower Vertical
30% Bend
25% Vertical Distortion

Flag Horizontal
80% Bend
-10% Horizontal

Squeeze Horizontal
30% Bend
30% Vertical Distortion

Layer Style

One of the great features of applying text as a layer is that you can apply layer styles to create some great effects that completely change its appearance. Because the effect is applied as a layer style to a vector text layer, you can still edit the text as you normally would and the layer style is applied to the edited text.

When you select the Layer Style option, the Layer Style dialog box appears. You can then make the layer style adjustments and apply them to the vector text layer. After you have applied the layer style, the applied effects are added to the vector text layer in the Layers panel, where you can edit them. For example, Figure 18.12 shows the Inner Shadow, Inner Glow, Bevel and Emboss, Gradient Overlay, and Stroke effects being applied to a vector text layer.

 You can do many different things when applying layer styles to vector text layers. For more information about layer styles and how to apply them, see Chapter 10.

FIGURE 18.12

Because vector text is applied as a layer, you can use the Layer Style option to apply a variety of layer styles to your text.

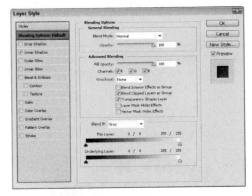

Using the Character panel

Most text settings can be applied from the Character panel. The Character panel is useful for viewing attributes that are applied to the selected text, and it allows you to quickly change text attributes.

Shown in Figure 18.13, the Character panel provides most of the options found in the Type tool options bar, as well as several additional options that help you define the behavior and appearance of the text.

FIGURE 18.13

The Character panel provides most of the necessary options to format text.

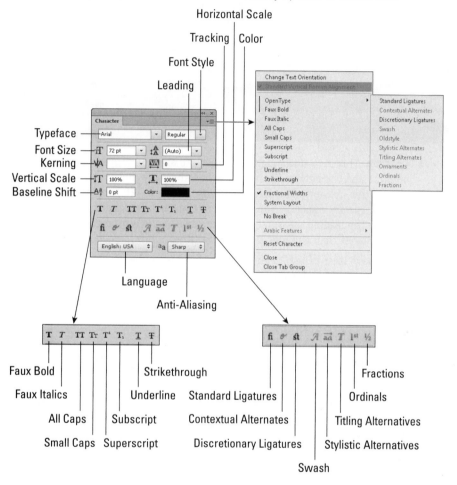

From the Character panel, you can set the following attributes of the text:

- **Font Family.** This drop-down menu allows you to select the font family. You can use the Type preferences settings discussed earlier in this chapter to have Photoshop display a sample of the font next to the font name; this makes it easier for you to select an appropriate font because you can see how it looks in the sample.

- **Font Style.** This drop-down menu allows you to select a typeface font style such as italic, bold, hard, light, strong, and so on. The available options depend on the fonts contained in the typeface that you have selected.

- **Font Size.** This drop-down menu allows you to set the size of the font used when displaying the text. You can select the font size from the drop-down menu, type the size into the text field, or hover the mouse over the Font Size option until the icon changes to a bidirectional arrow, which you then drag left or right to decrease or increase the value. By default, font size is specified in point units; however, you can change that by adjusting the Type setting in the Units and Rulers settings of the General Preferences panel in Photoshop.

> **TIP**
>
> The actual size varies between different fonts. You should first select the font family and font style before deciding on a font size.

- **Leading.** This drop-down menu specifies the amount of space between the bottom of one line and the bottom of the next when there are multiple lines in the text. You can set this option to the default of Auto, which is 120 percent of the font size, or you can specify a specific value to provide more or less space between the lines. Because the leading measures distance between the bottoms of the lines, if the leading is smaller than the font size, the two lines run into each other.

  If you have lines of text selected when you adjust the leading value, only those lines are changed. If you have no text selected when adjusting the leading, all the lines in the text are adjusted. Figure 18.14 shows an example of different leading values.

FIGURE 18.14

Adjusting the Leading setting alters the amount of space between the bottoms of two lines.

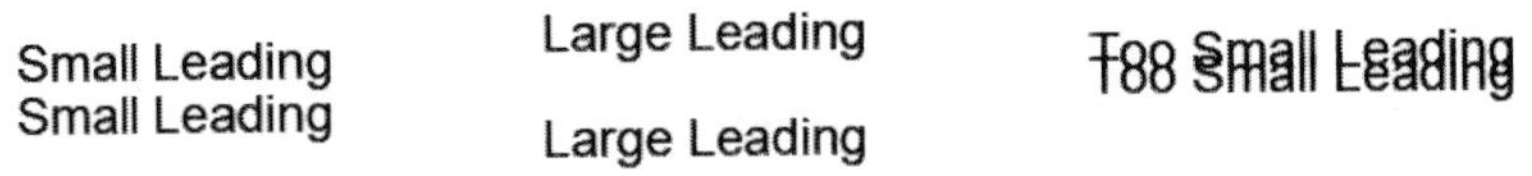

Small Leading
Small Leading

Large Leading

Large Leading

Too Small Leading

- **Kerning.** This drop-down menu specifies the amount of space between the individual characters in a word. The purpose of kerning is to solve the problem that occurs when two letters — for example, WA — look awkward when they are positioned next to each other, as shown in Figure 18.15. Using the Kerning option, you can set the kerning using one of three methods:

  - **Metrics.** This option uses metric information directly from the font to apply kerning to letters that require it when they are placed next to each other. This is by far the best option to use because the metric information is put into the font by the designer and usually is the most accurate. To apply metric kerning to text, select the vector text layer and then select Metrics from the Kerning drop-down menu.

- **Optical.** This option uses a Photoshop algorithm that scans the text, calculates the space between letters, and adjusts the spacing accordingly. This is the next best algorithm to use because Photoshop is usually pretty accurate at gauging the amount of kerning necessary. To apply optical kerning to a word, select the word and then select Optical from the Kerning drop-down menu. To apply optical kerning to the entire vector text layer, select the layer and then select Optical from the Kerning drop-down menu.

- **Manual.** If neither of these methods works for you, you can always manually adjust the kerning. To set the kerning value manually, position the cursor between the two letters in Text Edit mode and set a specific value in the Kerning field. You can also use the Alt/Option+ left or right arrow keys on the keyboard to adjust the kerning between the two letters in increments of 20.

FIGURE 18.15

Adjusting the kerning in words makes letter sequences that look awkward, such as WA, appear more aesthetically pleasing.

No Kerning = WATCH
Metrics Kerning = WATCH
Optical Kerning = WATCH

18

- **Tracking.** This drop-down menu specifies the amount of space between the leading edge of one character and the leading edge of the next character. Tracking is measured in positive and negative values. Adjusting the tracking negatively, called *tight tracking,* brings letters close together. Adjusting the tracking positively, called *loose tracking,* spreads the letters out. To adjust the amount of tracking in a vector text layer, select the vector text layer and set the value in the Tracking drop-down menu. To adjust the tracking of a specific word or set of words, select the text you want to adjust the tracking for and then adjust the value in the Tracking drop-down menu.

NOTE

Both the Tracking and Kerning options are measured in 1/1000 em, where *em* refers to the width of the lowercase *m* in the current font and font size. The reason em units are used is that if you change the font or font size later, Photoshop needs to adjust the tracking and kerning accordingly.

- **Vertical Scale.** This field adjusts the vertical height of characters in relation to the current font size setting. The scaling is based on percentages, so 100 percent uses the normal font height, but 200 percent uses double the normal font height. The width is not changed by this setting. You can use this setting to adjust the entire vector text layer or just the selected text.

- **Horizontal Scale.** This field adjusts the horizontal width of characters in relation to the current font size setting. The scaling is based on percentages, so 100 percent uses the normal font width, but 200 percent uses double the normal font width. The height is not changed by this setting. You can use this setting to adjust the entire vector text layer or just the selected text.

- **Baseline Shift.** This field specifies the position of the bottom of the selected text in relation to the baseline. This option is measured in the same units that font size is measured in, which is points by default. This option accepts both positive and negative values. Positive values raise the characters above the baseline, while negative values lower the characters below the baseline. The baseline shift gives you much more control than simply applying a subscript or superscript format to the text.

- **Color.** Click this field to launch the Select Text Color dialog box, which allows you to set the color used to fill in the text. You can use this setting to adjust the color for the entire vector text layer by selecting the vector text layer in the Layers panel, or just the selected text.

- **Text Format.** The following text formatting options allow you to apply the standard text style options to the selected text while you are in Text Edit mode or to the entire vector text layer if you have selected only the vector text layer in the Layers panel: Faux Bold, Faux Italics, All Caps, Small Caps, Superscript, Subscript, Underline, and Strikethrough.

- **Language.** This drop-down menu specifies the language option to use for the text when applying hyphenation, spell checking, and other language-specific text options.

- **Anti-Aliasing.** This drop-down menu allows you to set the anti-aliasing method that Photoshop uses to render the edges of the font on the screen. Anti-aliasing tries to smooth the square edge effect by filling in the sharp edges and blending the text with the background. The more anti-aliasing you apply, the smoother the transition, although being too aggressive with anti-aliasing can produce artifacts around the edges of the text. You can select the following anti-aliasing options:

  - **None.** This option applies no anti-aliasing to the text.
  - **Sharp.** Text appears sharpest.
  - **Crisp.** Text appears somewhat sharp.
  - **Strong.** Text appears heavier.
  - **Smooth.** This option adds the most amount of smoothing around the edges.

> **TIP**
>
> Too much anti-aliasing can result in some color artifacts around the edges of the font and may produce inconsistent results when producing low-resolution images such as those used on the Web. To reduce the inconsistency, deselect the Fractal Width option in the Character panel drop-down menu.

The Character panel drop-down menu allows you to set the following additional options:

- **Change Text Orientation.** This option allows you to toggle the text between vertical and horizontal orientation. This option applies to all the text in the vector text layer.

- **OpenType.** The OpenType options submenu allows you to toggle on and off the OpenType features that are available for the selected font. You can use this setting to adjust the features for an entire vector text layer by selecting the vector text layer in the Layers panel or just the selected text. Figure 18.16 shows some examples of the changes in text when you apply some of the OpenType features. The following is a list of the features that Photoshop supports:

  - **Standard Ligatures.** These are typographic replacements for certain pairs of characters, such as fi, fl, ff, ffi, and ffl.

  - **Contextual Alternates.** These are alternative characters that are included in some typefaces to provide better joining behavior.

  - **Discretionary Ligatures.** These are typographic replacement characters for additional character pairs, such as ct, st, and ft.

  - **Swash.** This option substitutes *swash glyphs* for certain characters. Swash glyphs are stylized letterforms with extended strokes or exaggerated flourishes.

  - **Old style.** This option replaces numerals with numerals that are shorter than regular numerals. Some old-style numerals are placed with their bottoms below the type baseline.

  - **Stylistic Alternates.** This option replaces certain characters with stylized forms for a more pleasing aesthetic effect.

  - **Titling Alternatives.** This option formats characters, typically in all capitals, for use in large type settings, such as titles.

  - **Ornaments.** This option adds a personal signature to the type family. These special characters can be used as title page decoration, paragraph markers, dividers for blocks of text, or as repeated bands and borders.

  - **Ordinals.** This option automatically formats ordinal numbers such as 1st and 2nd with superscript characters.

  - **Fractions.** This option automatically converts fractions separated by a slash to a shilling fraction (fraction using the "/" character).

FIGURE 18.16

Applying the OpenType options can add some nice features to the way text appears in the image.

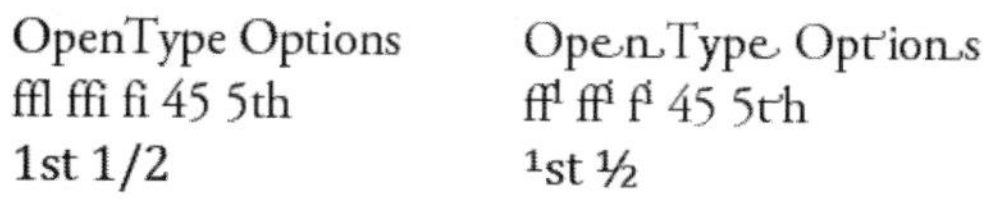

OpenType Options   Open Type Options
ffl ffi fi 45 5th   ff ff f 45 5th
1st 1/2   1st ½

- **Fractional Widths.** When you select this option, the tracking applied to the text can use values that do not exactly conform to the pixel width on the screen. Enabling fractional widths allows the text to be very clear and readable. You should leave this option enabled most of the time. The only time that you may need to disable it is when you are using very small fonts in images that will be displayed on a computer screen — for example, web graphics.

- **System Layout.** When you select this option, Fractional Widths is turned off and Anti-Aliasing is set to None. This option is typically used only when you are preparing images to be used on a small computer screen — for example, a cell phone or PDA (personal digital assistant).

- **No Break.** When you select this option, Photoshop does not hyphenate the selected words.

- **Reset Character.** This option resets the selected text to the Photoshop defaults. This is useful if you end up making so many changes to the text that you can't figure out why it doesn't look right.

Applying Paragraph panel settings

When you need to change how text flows within a paragraph or on a line, you will typically use the Paragraph panel. Many of the settings that you apply to text are found in the Paragraph panel.

Shown in Figure 18.17, the Paragraph panel provides the same alignment options found in the Type tool options bar, along with several additional options that help you define the layout of the text paragraphs.

From the Paragraph panel, you can set the following attributes of the text:

- **Align Left.** This option aligns the text to the left margin, with no justification.

- **Align Center.** This option aligns the text to the center, with no justification.

- **Align Right.** This option aligns the text to the right margin, with no justification.

- **Justify Left.** This option aligns the last line to the left margin, with justification in the rest.

- **Justify Center.** This option aligns the last line to the center, with justification in the rest.

- **Justify Right.** This option aligns the last line to the right margin, with justification in the rest.

- **Justify All.** This option fully justifies the paragraph including the last line.

- **Indent Left Margin.** This option specifies the amount to indent the paragraph relative to the left margin. Only the selected paragraph is affected by this setting.

- **Indent Right Margin.** This option specifies the amount to indent the paragraph relative to the right margin. Only the selected paragraph is affected by this setting.

- **Indent First Line.** This option specifies the amount to indent the first line of each paragraph.

- **Add Space Before Paragraph.** This option specifies the amount of space to add before the paragraph. This setting is in addition to the leading setting that you can set in the Character panel.

- **Add Space After Paragraph.** This option specifies the amount of space to add after the paragraph. This setting is in addition to the leading setting that you can set in the Character panel.

- **Hyphenate.** When you select this option, Photoshop tries to hyphenate words that fall beyond the right edge of the bounding box.

FIGURE 18.17

The Paragraph panel provides most of the necessary options to format paragraphs.

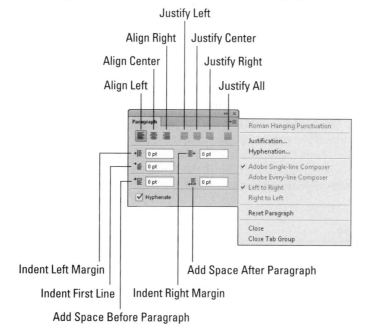

18

667

The Paragraph panel drop-down menu allows you to set the following additional options:

- **Roman Hanging Punctuation.** When you select this option, punctuation such as single quotes, double quotes, apostrophes, commas, periods, hyphens, em dashes, colons, and semicolons appear outside of the margin. This allows justified text to flow evenly down the right margin with the punctuation hanging over the edge.

- **Justification.** Selecting this option loads the Justification dialog box, shown in Figure 18.18, where you can set options to control how Photoshop applies justification to the paragraph. From this dialog box, you can set the ranges that Photoshop uses for the word, letter, and glyph, and the amount of leading to automatically apply to the paragraph when performing justification.

FIGURE 18.18

The Justification dialog box allows you to customize how Photoshop justifies text in the paragraph.

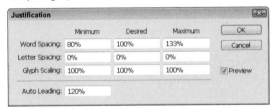

- **Hyphenation.** Selecting this option loads the Hyphenation dialog box, shown in Figure 18.19, where you can set options to control how Photoshop hyphenates words in the paragraph. From this dialog box, you can set the minimum word size, the minimum characters required on both sides of the hyphen, the maximum hyphen limit, and whether to hyphenate capitalized words.

FIGURE 18.19

The Hyphenation dialog box allows you to customize how Photoshop hyphenates words in the paragraph.

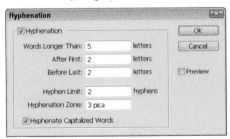

- **Adobe Single-line Composer.** This is the default option for paragraphs. When you select it, Photoshop composes type one line at a time, which is useful if you want to manually control how lines break. The Single-line Composer uses the following rules: longer lines are favored over shorter ones; compressed or expanded word spacing is preferred in justified text; hyphenation is preferred in non-justified text; compression is better than expansion.

- **Adobe Every-line Composer.** When you select this option, Photoshop considers a network of line break points for a range of lines, allowing it to optimize earlier lines in a paragraph in favor of reducing poor line breaks later. The Every-line Composer uses the following rules: lines falling closer to the right are favored and given a lower penalty for left-, right-, or center-aligned text; highest priority is given to the evenness of letter and word spacing for justified text; hyphenation is avoided when possible.

- **Left to Right.** Selecting this option sets text to roll left to right.

- **Right to Left.** Selecting this option sets text to roll right to left for languages such as Arabic, Farsi, and Hebrew.

- **Reset Paragraph.** Selecting this option resets the paragraph options to the Adobe default values. This is useful if you make too many changes and simply want to start over.

Using the Character and Paragraph Styles panels

The Character and Paragraph Styles panels available in the Window menu of Photoshop allow you to create character and paragraph presets that you can save, load, and quickly select during your editing workflow. Using presets allows you to organize text formatting and quickly format text.

> **NOTE**
> The Character and Paragraph Styles presets apply to the selected text in a text box when in Text Edit mode or all text in the box when not in Text Edit mode.

Creating and managing character styles

The Character Styles Panel allows you to create and manage the character style presets using the following options from the buttons on the bottom and panel menu:

- **Clear Override/Clear Modification.** If you make any adjustments to the text using the Type tool options or the Character panel, those changes revert to the values defined for the preset.

- **Redefine Style.** Any adjustments you make to the text using the Type tool options or the Type panel are applied to the preset and the preset is saved.

- **New Character Style.** Selecting this option creates a new character style preset.

- **Delete Style.** Selecting this option deletes the currently selected character style preset.

- **Style Options.** Selecting this option launches a dialog box, shown in Figure 18.20, that allows you to define the values used in the preset that are applied to the text when you select the character style. The Character Style Options dialog box contains the following three panels that allow you to define the character settings discussed earlier in this chapter:

  - **Basic Character Formats.** This panel specifies the style name, font family, style, size, color, and other basic text features.

  - **Advanced Character Formats.** This panel specifies the vertical and horizontal scale, as well as the baseline shift and language settings.

  - **OpenType Features.** This panel allows you to enable or disable OpenType features such as fractions, ligatures, and ordinals.

FIGURE 18.20

The Character Styles panel and Character Style Options dialog box allow you to create character style presets that improve your workflow when you add text to images.

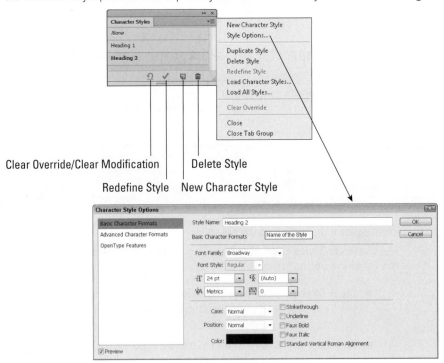

Creating and managing paragraph styles

The Paragraph Styles panel allows you to create and manage the paragraph style presets using the following options from the buttons on the bottom and panel menu:

- **Clear Override/Clear Modification.** If you make any adjustments to the paragraph using the Paragraph tool options or the Paragraph panel, those changes revert to the values defined for the preset.

- **Redefine Style.** Any adjustments you make to the paragraph using the Paragraph panel are applied to the preset and the preset is saved.

- **New Paragraph Style.** Selecting this option creates a new paragraph style preset.

- **Delete Style.** Selecting this option deletes the currently selected paragraph style preset.

- **Style Options.** Selecting this option launches a dialog box that allows you to define the values used in the preset that are applied to the paragraph when you select the paragraph style, as shown in Figure 18.21. The Paragraph Style Options dialog box contains the same three panels as described in the previous section, as well as the following four panels that allow you to define the paragraph settings discussed earlier in this chapter:

FIGURE 18.21

The Paragraph Styles panel and Paragraph Style Options dialog box allow you to create paragraph style presets.

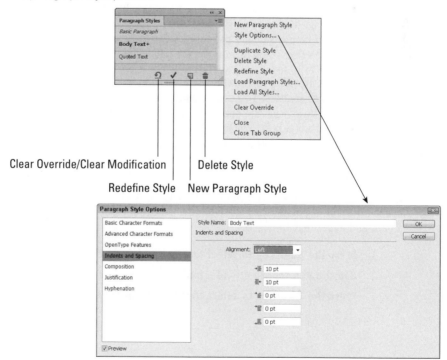

- **Indents and Spacing.** This panel specifies the paragraph alignment as well as the left and right indents.

- **Composition.** This panel specifies the composer as well as allowing you to enable or disable roman hanging punctuation.

- **Justification.** This panel specifies the word spacing, letter spacing, glyph scaling, and auto leading percentages.

- **Hyphenation.** This panel allows you to enable or disable auto-hyphenation in the paragraph and configure the settings used to define where hyphens occur.

Applying Text to Images

Text can be applied to images in a variety of ways. You can add text using a path to specifically control the flow. You can create your own textual effects using the vector tools allowing you to create some spectacular textual elements. Text can also be added to a specific area of an image by constraining it using a vector shape. The following sections take you through some examples that help illustrate some of the techniques that you can use to apply text as visual elements to images.

Adding text on a path

A great feature of Photoshop is the ability to attach text directly to a vector path. The text flows along the line segments of the path. When you attach text to a path, two new anchors are added to the path to support the text: the begin text anchor and the end text anchor. The begin text anchor controls where the text begins to flow on the path. The end text anchor controls where the text stops flowing on the path, similar to the edge of a bounding box.

The text anchors provide some useful features: They are controlled by the Direct Selection tool just like other anchors. You can reposition both begin and end text anchors as needed on the path. If text flows past the end anchor, the end anchor displays a plus sign to indicate that there is additional text. You can flow text in either direction on the path by dragging the begin anchor across to the other side of the path line.

Applying text to a path

In this example, we add text to an image by tying it to a curved path. Using this technique opens a variety of possibilities when adding text to images. Use the following steps to create a path and apply text to it:

1. **Press the P hotkey to select the Pen tool from the Toolbox.**
2. **Use the Pen tool to create a path, as shown in Figure 18.22.**
3. **Press the T hotkey to select the Horizontal Type tool from the Toolbox.**

4. **Use the Type tool to click the path you created in Step 2.**

   This adds a begin text anchor to the path, and Photoshop goes into Text Edit mode with the cursor attached to the path.

5. **Type the text you want to apply to the line.**

   The text flows with the path, as shown in Figure 18.22. Notice the circle at the end of the path. That is the end anchor for the text. Also notice that the text cursor moves as you type in the text.

6. **Press Ctrl+Enter/⌘+Enter to commit the text changes.**

FIGURE 18.22

Using the Type tool, you can click a path and add text that is bound to the flow of the line segments.

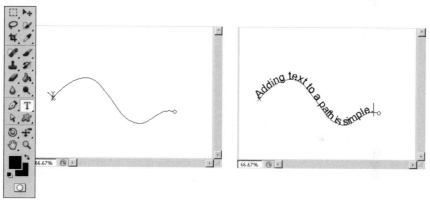

Editing text on a path

In this next example, we use the text applied in the previous example, but we move the starting point to illustrate some of the features that are available when working with text on a path. Follow these steps:

1. **Select the Direct Selection tool from the Toolbox.**

2. **Hover the Direct Selection tool over the first character in the text until the cursor changes to an I-beam with an arrow pointing to the right.**

   This is the begin text anchor.

3. **Drag the text to the right.**

   Notice that the text moves with the mouse, as shown in Figure 18.23. You can position the text to begin at any location on the path. Notice that the circle at the end of the line now contains a plus sign, indicating that there is additional text that is not visible.

4. **Drag the mouse down across the path line to move the text to the bottom of the line, as shown in Figure 18.23.**

   Dragging the mouse below the line forces the text to the bottom side of the path. Notice that the begin text anchor is now at the end of the path and the end text anchor is at the beginning.

5. **Hover the mouse over the line until the cursor changes back to the open arrow, and click the line to reveal the normal path anchor points.**

6. **Use the Direct Selection tool to adjust the position of the anchors as well as the direction points to adjust the path.**

   Notice that the text still flows with the path, as shown in Figure 18.23.

FIGURE 18.23

Dragging the begin text cursor downward across the line flips the text to the other side.

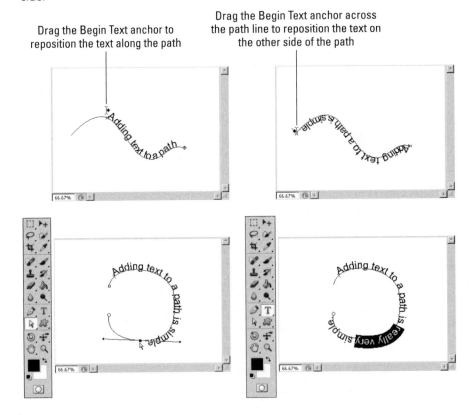

7. **Press the T hotkey to select the Type tool from the Toolbox.**

8. **Click the text with the Type tool.**

   Photoshop enters Text Edit mode.

9. **Add more text.**

   Notice that you can edit the text just as you normally do.

Constraining text using a vector shape

A great way to add a textual element to an image is to have the text flow inside an object containing the image. This allows the text to become a part of the image rather than just sitting on top of it.

In this example, we create a vector shape from a sunset in the image and then use that vector shape to constrain the text to flow within the clouds. Follow these steps:

1. **Open the image in Photoshop.**

2. **Use the Quick Selection tool to select an object in the image.**

   In this case, we selected the silhouette.

3. **Right-click the selection, and select Make Work Path from the pop-up menu. Set the tolerance to the necessary level.**

   In this case, we kept the tolerance at 2.0. A new path was added to the image, as shown in Figure 18.24.

4. **Double-click the path in the Path panel and give the path a name.**

5. **Press T to select the Type tool from the Toolbox.**

6. **Use the Type tool to pick a point inside the newly created shape.**

   As you move the cursor into the newly created shape, the I-beam cursor displays a circle around it, indicating that it will use the shape as a bounding box. A new vector text layer is added to the Layers panel, and another path to support the bounding box for the vector text layer is added to the Paths panel, as shown in Figure 18.24.

7. **Add the text to the image.**

   The text flows inside the newly created shape, shown in Figure 18.24, and you can edit it as you normally would.

 For more information about creating vector shapes, see Chapter 17.

NOTE

In case you are wondering, the text placed inside the image is *Lorem Ipsum,* which is just dummy text that is frequently used by graphic designers as filler text when demonstrating their work. Using the dummy text keeps viewers from being distracted by the content of the text and not focusing on the overall design elements.

FIGURE 18.24

Using custom shapes, you can constrain text to flow within the boundaries of an object in an image.

Select object   Create path from selection

Adding text in a Smart Object

Working with vector layers can be a big problem when you're adding text to images. Several layer options are not available for vector layers, including vector text layers. The solution to this problem is to convert the vector text layer to a Smart Layer. Because the content of a Smart Object is rasterized before applying it to the image, you can use all the raster editing functionality associated with layers.

> **TIP**
>
> Remember that the content of the Smart Object is rasterized when applied to the image. If you create your text larger than it is used in the actual document, Photoshop doesn't need to increase the size of the rasterized text, which reduces the amount of pixelation that occurs. There is still pixelation, but it is minimized.

In this example, we convert a text layer to a Smart Object so we can use the Warp effect to apply the text to a surface in the image. Follow these steps:

1. **Open the image in Photoshop.**

2. **Add text to the image, as shown in Figure 18.25.**

   Notice that the text sits flat on the surface of the image and really sticks out. We are about to change that.

FIGURE 18.25

The text in the image appears flat and intrusive to the photograph.

677

3. **Right-click the vector text layer in the Layers panel, and select Convert to Smart Object from the pop-up menu.**

   This converts the vector text layer to a Smart Object layer.

4. **Select the new Smart Object layer in the Layers panel if it is not already selected.**

5. **Press Ctrl+T/⌘+T to activate the Free Transform tool.**

6. **Use the Free Transform tool to position the text, now encased in a Smart Object layer, on the hood of the Jeep.**

7. **Ctrl-drag the corner handles of the Free Transform tool to match the general shape of the hood.**

8. **Right-click the text and select Warp from the pop-up menu to open the Warp tool.**

   Then use the Warp tool to warp the text to the surface of the Jeep, as shown in Figure 18.26.

FIGURE 18.26

Warping the Smart Object layer allows the text to appear as though it is part of the Jeep hood.

9. **Press Ctrl+Enter/⌘+Enter to accept the changes.**

   The results are shown in Figure 18.27. Notice that the text is much less intrusive to the picture and almost appears as though it was originally part of the image.

10. **Double-click the new Smart Object layer in the Layers panel to open the document for the Smart Object.**

    Notice in Figure 18.28 that the Layers panel for the Smart Object document contains the vector text layer, and you can still edit it just as you would any other vector text layer. Saving the document applies the changes to the original image.

FIGURE 18.27

With the text warped, it is much less intrusive to the picture.

FIGURE 18.28

You can still edit the vector text layer by double-clicking the Smart Object layer to load the Smart Object document.

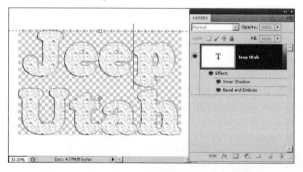

ON THE WEB

You can find the project used in this example on the book's website as Figure 18-28.psd. You can open the file in Photoshop and play around with the Smart Object layer.

Applying text as a mask

You can use the Type Mask tools to create a selection that looks exactly like text. The selection you create can be used just like any other selection to create as many different effects as you can think of.

There are two Type Mask tools: the Horizontal Type Mask tool and the Vertical Type Mask tool. These tools work in exactly the same way that the Type tools work: after you have created text on your screen, you can change the font, resize it, warp it, change the direction, or apply any one of the other options that are available to you with the regular Text tool — as long as it is selected. After you accept the type by clicking the check mark in the Options bar or choosing any other layer or tool, the text becomes a selection and can be altered at that point only by the selection tools and menus.

Here is an example of how it works. Create a selection mask with the Type Mask tools by following these steps:

1. **Click the Type Mask tool, which is nested with the other Type tools in the Toolbox, or press T repeatedly until the tool you want is activated.**

2. **Click your image (preferably on a second, duplicated layer) in the area where you want to begin typing.**

3. **Type your text.**

4. **Highlight your text, and adjust the font, size, text warp, and so on until you are satisfied with the results.**

   You can move the text by grabbing outside of the selection highlight and dragging, as shown in Figure 18.29.

FIGURE 18.29

As long as the text you type with the Type Mask tools is selected, you can use the Character panel and Type tool options bar to edit it.

5. **Press Ctrl+Enter/⌘+Enter to accept the changes.**

   Your text transforms into a selection, as shown in Figure 18.30.

FIGURE 18.30

After you accept the text, it becomes a selection.

From here you have several options: You can invert the selection so that everything but the text is selected; you can apply a fill or adjustment layer or a filter; or you can turn the selection into a layer mask by clicking the Add Vector Mask button in the Layers panel. In short, you can do anything to this selection that you can do with any other selection you make. Figure 18.31 shows the result of the selection after clicking the Add Vector Mask button.

FIGURE 18.31

The selection created with your text can be edited just like any other selection. In this case, we created a mask with it.

 You can create a clipping mask with text that achieves the exact same results demonstrated in Figure 18.31. Review masks in Chapter 10.

Summary

This chapter discussed using the Type tools to add text to images, the Character panel to format the text, and the Paragraph panel to control the flow of paragraphs. We also discussed some of the advanced features available in Photoshop that allow you to make text a visual element as well as just a textual element.

In this chapter, you learned these concepts:

- Adding text in a bounding box
- Constraining text to fit inside a vector shape
- Applying layer styles to text
- Putting a vector text layer inside a Smart Object in order to use raster tools such as the Warp tool
- Applying text to a vector path, where the text flow follows the path even if you edit the anchor points
- Using the Warp option to create some interesting textual elements
- Using text as a mask to apply it as a visual element

Part VI

Creating Artistic Effects

Distorting Images

IN THIS CHAPTER

Making transformations

Playing with Puppet Warp

Using Vanishing Point

Using Wide Angle Lens Correction

Distorting images sounds so dramatic that at first when you hear it, it's hard to think of anything but special effects. On the contrary, most image distortions are simple functions, such as resizing an image or adjusting its perspective to make up for lens distortions. Many of the distortions and transformations available in Photoshop are helpful when creating image composites. Using skew, warp, or vanishing point effects can change the way you perceive an image and make it blend better with other images.

This is especially true of layers that are not composed of images. Text and other vector layers can be transformed and distorted for the same reasons. You can use Vanishing Point to place text in perspective on any surface in an image. You can warp and distort shapes to give them the appearance of motion or just to make them look three-dimensional.

Using Transformations

Transforming an image can involve anything from rotating it or changing its size to making it completely unrecognizable by warping or skewing the pixels until nothing is where it belongs. Some of these changes are basic fixes — rotating an image that's been captured in portrait mode, scaling a placed image so it fits with the original document, or fixing perspective problems caused by camera mechanics. Other transformations are all about creating artistic effects — tugging and pulling objects and anatomy so they no longer look like the original captured image.

> **NOTE**
> Most transformations can't be performed on a background layer because it's locked. Double-click the background layer to change it into a standard layer.

Understanding the importance of the reference point

When you choose any of the transformations, a bounding box is created around the image or selection. Notice that in the center of most of the transformation bounding boxes, you see a crosshair, as shown in Figure 19.1. This crosshair is called the reference point, and it indicates the area of your image that is stable. When you rotate an image, it rotates around the reference point. For example, if the reference point is in the center of your image, it rotates in place. If it is placed on a corner of the image, the image rotates around that corner. The same is true of the Skew, Distort, and Perspective transformations. If you want the center of the image to be stationary while you perform these transformations, center the reference point. If not, you need to move the reference point.

You can move the reference point in two ways. One way is to use the reference point location (as shown in Figure 19.1) and click any of the squares shown, moving the reference point to that location. The other way is to simply drag the reference point into any other position on your image.

FIGURE 19.1

The reference point makes a difference in how the transformations affect your image.

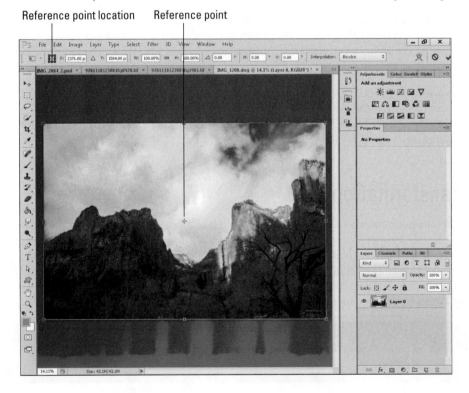

Scaling images

The Scale option simply changes the size of whatever you have selected, whether it is a layer or an active selection. You'll probably find yourself scaling frequently. Whenever you are combining more than one file, you often need to scale one of them so they are a good match. Elements such as text or shape layers can also be scaled. To apply the Scale option, choose Edit ⇨ Transform ⇨ Scale to create a bounding box around the selected layer and then drag any one of the handles in any direction to make the selection bigger or smaller, as shown in Figure 19.2. To scale proportionally, hold down the Shift key while dragging one of the corner handles or click the Maintain aspect ratio icon in the Options bar before you drag. This constrains the height and width to the same percentage. If you know what percentage you want your selection to be, you can type a width and height percentage in the appropriate boxes in the Options bar.

FIGURE 19.2

You can scale a selection using the handles on the bounding box or by typing a percentage.

Width and height percentages

Maintain aspect ratio

Handles to scale the image

> **CAUTION**
>
> If you have an active selection in your image when you activate a transformation, the area of your image that is selected is targeted for the transformation instead of the entire image.

Rotating images

You can use the Rotate option to straighten a photo, tilt a photo in a collage, and angle text or other elements to create the look you want. You probably don't want to use this option to turn a photo that is lying on its side because it was taken by turning your camera or scanning in the photo sideways. The other Rotate options (180°, 90° CCW, 90° CW) farther down the Transform submenu offer a much faster way to do this.

To rotate a selected layer, choose Edit ⇨ Transform ⇨ Rotate. A bounding box is placed around the image, and whenever you hover over a handle, you see a double-headed arrow, as shown in Figure 19.3. Click and drag your mouse to the left or right to freely rotate the image. To constrain the rotation to 15-degree increments, hold down the Shift key while you rotate. You can also type a specific degree in the Options bar to rotate the selection.

FIGURE 19.3

The Rotate transformation in action

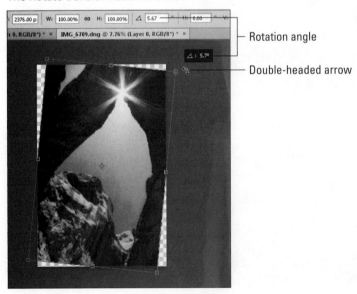

Rotation angle

Double-headed arrow

Skewing images

The Skew transformation allows you to move the corner handles independently of one another to pull or push the pixels in that corner closer toward or away from the reference point. This transformation actually morphs the pixels in the area that is being pushed or pulled by merging them or doubling them so it looks as if the image is still contained in its entirety in the skewed shape.

Skewing text is more constrained. Rather than moving each corner independently, the sides move together to create a shearing effect, as shown in Figure 19.4. To skew a selection, choose Edit ⇨ Transform ⇨ Skew. A bounding box is created, and you can pull on the corners to transform them. You can also type a degree of skew in the Options bar. This constrains your image to being skewed as a whole, moving two corners simultaneously rather than one corner at a time.

FIGURE 19.4

Pull on the corners or type a value in the Options bar to skew an object.

Distorting images

Distorting an image works much like taking a printed photograph and bending it this way and that to make it look different. Distorting in Photoshop works better because you can make distortions that are more dramatic without creating any wrinkles. The Distort option can make your selection look angled, bubbled, or squished. Choose Edit ⇨ Transform ⇨ Distort to create a bounding box around your selection. Use the handles to distort freely, as shown in Figure 19.5.

> **NOTE**
>
> If you have just created a path, such as the shape that is being used in Figure 19.5, you find that the Edit menu contains the Transform Path option, rather than Transform.

FIGURE 19.5

Using the Distort transformation can really change the look of your object.

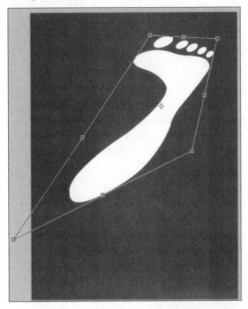

Changing the perspective of images

The Perspective transformation widens either the top or the base (or both) of your image to correct perspectives that can be warped by fish-eye lenses or simply by the focal length of the lens. The need for a perspective fix is most obvious in photos of tall buildings taken from the ground. Because of the perspective created by the lens, the buildings actually look as if they are leaning toward one another, as you can see in Figure 19.6. With a simple Perspective transformation, the tilt of the building is corrected. Pulling on the side handles when using the Perspective transformation skews it.

> **NOTE**
>
> As you change the perspective of an image, the center of the image becomes fatter. After you have restored the correct perspective, you can scale your image to be taller, taking out the width distortion that the perspective fix introduced.

Using the Warp transformation

The Warp transformation is great for giving a three-dimensional look to flat photos or objects. Because it uses a grid to create multiple points that you can adjust, it allows you to create more dynamic change than the transformation options that only provide you with a bounding box.

FIGURE 19.6

Fixing the perspective can reduce or eliminate leaning objects in an image.

When you select the Warp transformation, a grid is created across your selection that allows you to distort specific areas within that selection. You can pull and adjust each conjunction point to make changes that radiate from that point. Each corner of the grid also has two control point handles that control the curve of the grid and, therefore, the warp.

Choose Edit ⇨ Transform ⇨ Warp to create the grid around your selection. Figure 19.7 shows how an image of a fish was changed to look as if the fish were swimming through a three-dimensional space, rather than the two dimensions created by a flat screen. You can use any one of several preset warps by using the drop-down list in the Options bar shown in Figure 19.8.

FIGURE 19.7

Adding a three-dimensional look to this fish just took a little tweaking with the Warp tool.

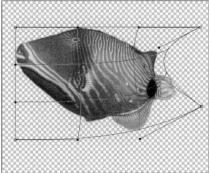

19

FIGURE 19.8

Using any one of these options creates a preset warp.

Using free transform

Using a few memorized hotkeys and a bit of ingenuity, you can perform any one of the previous transformations with the Free Transform option. The best thing about this option is that it already has a hotkey assigned to it, so rather than choosing Edit ⇨ Free Transform, you can simply press Ctrl+T/⌘+T to open a transformation bounding box. You can use each of the following transformation tools in this way:

- **Scale.** To scale your selection, just drag any of the handles like you would if you were using the Scale transformation alone.

- **Rotate.** To rotate your selection, hover just outside any of the handles on the bounding box to display the curved double-headed arrow that indicates you can rotate the box. Drag and rotate freely.

- **Skew.** To skew your selection, press and hold the Ctrl/⌘ and Shift keys simultaneously while dragging the handles.

- **Distort.** To distort your selection, press and hold the Ctrl/⌘ key while moving the handles. This allows you to distort freely without regard to the reference point. To distort using the reference point, use the Alt/Option key.

- **Perspective.** To change the perspective, press and hold the Ctrl+Shift/⌘+Shift or Ctrl+Alt/⌘+Option keys while dragging the handles.

- **Warp.** To warp a selection from any of the other transform tools, click the Switch between Free Transform and Warp Modes button shown in Figure 19.9. This toggles between the standard bounding box and the grid you see when performing a Warp transformation.

FIGURE 19.9

Click the Toggle between Free Transform and Warp Modes button from any transformation Options bar to warp your selection.

Toggle between Free Transform and Warp Modes

Using the Content-Aware Scale feature

The Content-Aware Scale feature allows you to make an image larger or smaller without shrinking or distorting the subject of the image. This is great for making photos smaller without actually cropping out any content or making photos larger to expand a background to get a more dramatic effect or in order to add features to the image.

Content-Aware Scale can work automatically by letting Photoshop guess what the main subject of the image is or by locking any pixels that are skin tones. However, these methods are hit-and-miss and leave you little control. The best way to use Content-Aware Scale is to create an alpha channel that protects the areas you want to stay constant.

Figure 19.10 is a photo of Brad in front of an Indian palace. Using Content-Aware Scale, we can change the perspective of the palace in the background. This is a great photo to use, because you can see how far you can push the hard lines in the image before they become broken up or warped. Keep an eye on the columns of the palace and the fence as you make changes.

19

ON THE WEB
You can download Figure 19-10 from this book's website and use it to experiment with the Content-Aware Scale feature.

We are going to show you the results of four different ways to use the Content-Aware Scale feature: first, without any protection at all; second, protecting skin tones; third, protecting an alpha channel and skin tones; and last, protecting just the alpha channel. For this example, we created two layers, one with the image and the second with a transparent background, which is larger than the image so we can scale larger.

FIGURE 19.10

We can scale the palace and leave Brad intact.

Try different methods of using Content-Aware Scale by following these steps:

1. **Create a selection around the area you want to preserve.**

   We created a selection around Brad. It doesn't have to be extremely precise, but a good outline is best.

2. **In the Channels panel, click Save Selection as Channel to create an alpha channel.**

   This channel will protect Brad from being squished.

3. **Turn on the visibility of the image, and disable the visibility of the alpha channel; then return to the Layers panel.**

4. **Choose Edit⇨Content-Aware Scale to create a bounding box around the image.**

5. **In the Options bar, make sure the Protect option is set to None and the Protect Skin Tones button (the silhouette of a man) is not highlighted.**

6. **Squeeze or stretch the image at will, keeping an eye on Brad and the straight lines of the palace.**

   You actually have quite a bit of latitude, especially side to side. Eventually, as you squeeze the photo down, you lose Brad's face. Figure 19.11 is just smaller than we could make the picture and retain a realistic version of Brad. The lines of the palace are starting to warp, as shown in the left photo. This image is significantly smaller than the original, so the Content-Aware Scale feature worked very well.

7. **Click the Protect Skin Tones button.**

    This shows you a real-time change, as shown in Figure 19.11 on the right. Brad's face is less distorted and his arms look right, but the rest of his body is hopelessly puckered and out of shape, along with most of the surrounding palace. This isn't the right option for this photo!

FIGURE 19.11

With no protection on the left, the Content-Aware Scale feature provides quite a squeeze before collapsing Brad's face. On the right, protecting the skin tones does nothing to protect the white of Brad's shirt.

8. **Click the Protect menu and select Alpha 1.**

    The pixels protected by the alpha channel revert to their original state. On the left of Figure 19.12, Brad looks great, but the palace is sadly out of shape. It turns out that Photoshop is interpreting the putty-colors of the palace as skin tones. Maybe protecting the skin tones is not the best option.

9. **Click the Protect Skin Tones button to turn it off.**

   On the right of Figure 19.12, we see that protecting the alpha channel and not the skin tones is the best option. By stretching this image just a little bit, we get a satisfactory result.

FIGURE 19.12

Even though the subject looks great on the left, the palace is puckered and misaligned. On the right, the subject is protected, and the palace has very few lines that are out of shape.

Using the Puppet Warp tool

The Puppet Warp tool gives you a lot of control when it comes to changing the way a previously flat, two-dimensional image looks. It works by placing a mesh over the selected area in your image, giving you the ability to warp and move individual areas, almost as if it were a piece of fabric. Using some pins to hold areas in place and others to move your image, you can choose which areas to move, how they'll move, and how far. Figure 19.13 shows a spider on its own layer. Using Puppet Warp, you can move each of her legs independently.

FIGURE 19.13

The independent nature of each one of these spider's legs makes her ideal for playing with the Puppet Warp tool.

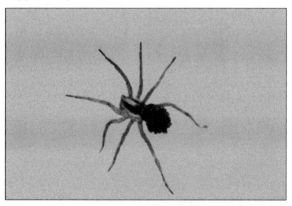

Follow these steps to use Puppet Warp on the spider:

ON THE WEB
Find the PSD of the spider saved as Figure 19-13 on this book's website.

1. **Select the layer containing the cutout of the spider.**

2. **Choose Edit ➪ Puppet Warp.**

   This changes the Options bar and places a grid over the spider, as shown in Figure 19.14. You can change the density of the mesh in the Options bar. Increasing the density gives you control over more specific areas, and decreasing the density allows you to move larger areas.

3. **Set the expansion by typing an amount in the Expansion field in the Options bar.**

   The expansion determines how many pixels outside the selected object the mesh will extend. A larger expansion makes movements larger and less precise. The default expansion of 2 pixels works well for this exercise.

4. **Click different areas of the spider to place pins in different locations.**

   Every time you place a pin, that spot on the spider is locked down and doesn't move unless you drag the pin. When you do move a pin, it uses the closest pin as a pivot point to rotate the selected area. For instance, if you place just one pin on the center of the spider and then move a second pin placed on the spider's leg, the entire spider rotates around the pin placed on her body. In order to move a leg by itself, you need at least four pins: two on the body to hold it firm, one on the knee of the leg that you want to move, and one on the end of the leg, as shown in Figure 19.15.

19

FIGURE 19.14

Puppet Warp places a moveable mesh over the selected layer.

FIGURE 19.15

Pin placement is an essential part of getting the adjustment you want with the Puppet Warp tool.

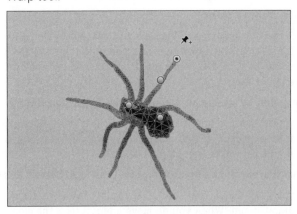

5. **From the Options bar, click the Mode down-arrow and select a mode that determines how the mesh responds to movement by the pin.**

   Rigid keeps the distances in the mesh more stable, making it harder to stretch the mesh and therefore the pixels. It is the best choice for limbs or other rigid objects.

Normal makes the mesh loose, more like a fabric, as it's moved, similar to moving a rag puppet. Distort not only moves the pinned area but also changes its perspective, making it larger or smaller, depending on the direction you are moving it. You want the spider's legs to stay straight, so choose Rigid.

6. **Click the pin at the end of each leg and move the leg to change the perspective of where the ground is underneath the spider.**

   You can move it freely, rotating it on the knee pin, even bending it toward the spider's body. We want to change the apparent plane that the spider is walking on to a horizontal one rather than vertical by bending the legs, thereby supporting the spider from underneath, as shown in Figure 19.16.

TIP

You can select and move more than one pin by pressing and holding the Shift key as you click each pin.

7. **Change the rotation of the mesh around the selected pin.**

   You can do this from the Options bar by choosing Auto or Fixed from the Rotate menu. Auto rotates the selection automatically based on how you move the pin. Fixed allows you to set your own rotation. You can type a rotation degree into the appropriate box, or you can hold down the Alt/Option key while you hover to the *outside* of the pin until a Rotation tool appears, as shown in Figure 19.16, and allows you to rotate the mesh around your selected pin. In the case of the spider, you can add feet or reduce unnatural bends caused by the initial pin movement.

FIGURE 19.16

Using the Auto Rotate option doesn't always give you the best results. You can hold down the Alt/Option key to freely rotate the mesh and take out any kinks.

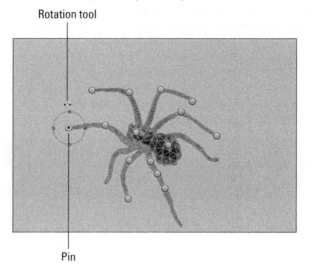

Rotation tool

Pin

8. **(Optional) If you've warped too far and aren't sure how to get back to where you started, you can delete your pins.**

   You can delete any of the pins you placed by holding down the Alt/Option key and clicking directly on the pin (scissors should appear) or by pressing the Delete button to delete any selected pins. Removing a pin also removes all the effects that are associated with that pin. If it held an area in place while another pin was moved, that area moves as if the pin had never been placed. If the pin was used to move the mesh, the mesh returns to the starting point.

Playing with the legs of a spider is a fun way to learn the basics behind the Puppet Warp tool, but although moving individual elements can be entertaining, the Puppet Warp tool is more useful in making adjustments and corrections in your everyday images. For instance, you could use it to correct crooked lines created by using the Content-Aware Scale feature or to tweak the perspective of images that have more complicated lens aberrations than you can fix by just widening the top.

Having Fun with the Liquify Filter

The Liquify Filter uses several tools to pinch and warp the pixels of your image in many different ways. You can use it for creating textures, giving tummy tucks, or creating realistic special effects. The Liquify filter is so versatile that it almost qualifies as an application on its own. It's certainly more than just a tool.

When you select the Liquify filter by choosing Filter ⇨ Liquify, your image opens inside the Liquify utility, as shown in Figure 19.17. Right away, you see how much you can do here. The Liquify utility works in a very similar way to Puppet Warp. A mesh overlay is placed over your image, creating a grid that you can pull and warp to change your image as if it were made of fabric. Each tool uses the mesh in a different way to create a different effect. The Reconstruct tools are also based on the mesh.

Identifying the Liquify tools

The Liquify tools are stacked neatly in their own Toolbox on the left of the Liquify utility. Some tools will be familiar to you, such as the Hand tool and the Zoom tool. Other tools are unique to the Liquify utility.

> **NOTE**
> While you are in the Liquify workspace, you can access each of these tools by pressing a hotkey. Hover over each tool to see its name and hotkey.

FIGURE 19.17

The Liquify utility in Photoshop has several tools and options.

Liquify tools

- Mesh Settings
- Tool Options
- Reconstruct Options Mode
- Mask Options
- View Options

You can find the following Liquify tools in the Toolbox:

- **Forward Warp.** This tool drags the pixels starting at the center of your cursor forward, following the direction you drag. The effect looks just like the wake of a boat. This is a very basic way to push pixels around and create very specific results, as shown in Figure 19.18.

- **Reconstruct.** This tool offers a simple way to restore specific areas of your image. Brush over areas that you've already distorted, and they are restored to their original pixel composition.

TIP

Holding down the Alt/Option key while either the Forward Warp tool or the Reconstruct tool is activated temporarily changes it to the other tool.

- **Twirl Clockwise.** This tool is like a curling iron for your pixels. To create twirls, press and hold your mouse button to twirl them around your cursor. Be sure to hold your mouse in one spot to do this; the longer you hold, the tighter the twirl is. If you want the twirl to go counter-clockwise, press and hold the Alt/Option key while you twirl.

19

FIGURE 19.18

The effects of the Liquify tools on a subject

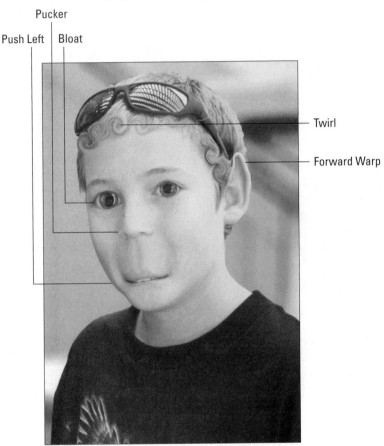

- **Pucker.** This tool is like having a miniature black hole in the center of your cursor; the longer you press and hold your mouse button, the more pixels are sucked into the center of your cursor. It creates a pinched or puckered look, great for hips and thighs.

- **Bloat.** This tool has the opposite effect of the Pucker tool, pushing pixels out from the center of your cursor. This makes it a great tool for lips and cheeks. Pressing and holding the Alt/Option key with the Pucker and Bloat tools changes one tool into the other.

- **Push Left.** This is another great tool for getting rid of bulges. Dragging this tool upward literally pushes the pixels the width of the brush to the left, blending the pixels to the right into the space left behind. This has a dramatic effect on hard lines. Despite its name, the tool is not limited in its direction: you can push pixels right by dragging downward, push them up by dragging to the right, and push them down by dragging left. In reality, the pixels are always pushed left of the drag direction. Pressing and holding the Alt/Option key reverses any one of these effects.

- **Freeze Mask.** This tool enables you to freeze areas of a preview image, thereby protecting those areas from modification or change. You can mask areas before or after you've used an effect on them without the Freeze Mask tool changing the effect; it just protects those areas from further changes. Click the Freeze Mask tool, and use the brush to paint over areas you want protected.

- **Thaw Mask.** This tool thaws frozen areas of a preview image, thereby enabling you to make changes to the previously frozen area.

Looking at Tool Options

The Tool Options enable you to modify the behavior of the brush used to apply the Liquify effects. They are basic brush settings and should be familiar to you if you've used Photoshop:

- **Brush Size.** This option changes the size of your brush and, therefore, the size of the effect that is being applied. The brush used to twirl curls in Figure 19.18 was much smaller than the brush used to make the broad mirror strokes in Figure 19.19.

- **Brush Density.** This option sets the amount of distortion that takes place the farther the pixels are from the cursor. If you set your brush to a density of 100, the effects are the same at the edges of the cursor as they are in the center.

- **Brush Pressure.** This option determines how fast the distortions are applied. If you want to apply settings slowly and carefully, lower the brush pressure.

- **Brush Rate.** This option works with the tools that are applied over time as you hold the mouse in place with the button pressed, such as the Twirl and Turbulence tools. You can specify the speed at which these effects are applied in this way.

- **Turbulent Jitter.** This option scrambles your pixels, and you can change the setting to determine how widely they are scrambled. A lower jitter scrambles pixels in a smaller area, avoiding the burnt look, but not creating a dramatic effect. A larger jitter scrambles pixels in many directions inside your cursor.

Saving a mesh

The *mesh* is a grid that is placed over the pixels of the photo in the Liquify filter. As you use the Liquify filter, the mesh changes and the correlating pixels change as well. Saving a mesh allows you to recreate your Liquify settings, giving you the option to change those settings at any time or to save multiple Liquify transformations for the same image.

To save your current Liquify status, click Save Mesh at the top of the options panel. You can browse and save the document independently of the image, just as if you were saving a new document in Photoshop. Make sure you choose a location where you can easily find the mesh file later. To load a saved mesh, click the Load Mesh button and browse to the location of the

19

mesh file. It is loaded into the Liquify utility and takes effect on the current image immediately, replacing the mesh that was previously there.

Restoring your image with Reconstruct and Restore All

When you are having fun with Liquify, it's easy to go overboard. The Reconstruct and Restore all buttons (refer to Figure 19.17) enable you to restore your image to its original state or restore the image partially, applying the filters only a fraction of the amount they were applied originally.

When you click the Reconstruct button, a fly-out menu appears with a slider that lets you set the percentage to reconstruct your image. As you move the slider, you can preview the changes to your image. At 100 percent, your image will display all the liquify changes you have made to it. As you move the slider to the left, the changes you have made to your image will be gradually reduced until you reach 0 percent, where your image will be completely restored. Set the slider to the percentage you like and click OK.

Simply click the Restore All button to restore your image to the one that you opened. The Reconstruct Options work using the mesh and the results you get are affected by any Freeze Masks you place over your image.

Modifying the Mask Options selections

The Mask Options section in the Liquify utility changes the way masks interact with one another by allowing you to add to them, subtract from them, or intersect them. Using the drop-down list that appears when you click any mask option, you can create or modify an existing Freeze Mask with any selections, transparencies, layer masks, or alpha channels already present in your image.

> **NOTE**
>
> In order to use a selection from the menu, you need to create a selection in the original document, save the selection using the Select menu, and then deselect the image before opening it in Liquify. If your image contains an active selection when you open it in Liquify, you can alter only the selected area.

The three buttons at the bottom of the Mask Options setting (refer to Figure 19.17) are straightforward:

- **None.** This removes any freeze mask placed over the image.
- **Mask All.** This creates a mask that covers the entire image.
- **Invert All.** This changes masked areas into unmasked areas, and vice versa.

Using the View Options

The View Options section lets you change the way you view an image in the Liquify utility. You can view helpful tools such as the mesh and any masks you've placed. Viewing the mesh gives you an insider's look at what is happening to your image as you use the Liquify tools.

Here are the View Options:

- **Show Image.** Toggle the visibility of the image on and off with this option. If the mesh, mask, or backdrop is visible, you see those elements, but if not, the document window is white.

- **Show Mesh.** Toggle the visibility of the mesh overlay that allows Liquify to work its magic. You can change the size of the mesh to small, medium, or large, which affects the detail of the Liquify effects. You can also change the color of the mesh.

- **Show Mask.** Toggle the visibility of the mask on and off with this option. You can also change the color of the mask.

- **Show Backdrop.** Toggle the visibility of other layers in your image with this option. These layers are not changed in the Liquify utility, but they may affect the way you want to make changes to the selected layer. You have several different viewing options that give you versatility in viewing other layers.

Changing Perspective with Vanishing Point

When you talk about the vanishing point in an image, you are suggesting as objects get farther away from the camera, they become smaller, eventually vanishing against the horizon. The rate at which this happens affects the perspective of the image. Because every image is different, the vanishing point is also different. Some images that contain hard corners, such as photos of buildings, can have more than one vanishing point.

Different perspectives and multiple vanishing points can make it difficult to fix an image by cloning or to create composites that look realistic, because it isn't always easy to get the perspective just right, even using the Transformation tools.

The Vanishing Point filter allows you to match the perspective of the target image when you clone or combine images so the new elements look realistic. Compared to trying to free-transform or tweak an element until the perspective is just right, the Vanishing Point filter is easy to use.

NOTE

Vanishing Point changes the perspective of two-dimensional images, which usually makes them look even more two-dimensional because there will be missing elements, such as compensating shadows on more than one side. Vanishing Point is ideal for creating banners, posters, car art, or other two-dimensional elements.

Figure 19.19 shows a photo with at least two vanishing points: the plane of the rock surface is one perspective, and the boys are a different perspective. You can use the Vanishing Point filter to place another image in the correct perspective on the face of the rock.

FIGURE 19.19

You can use Vanishing Point to change the perspective of elements in the image to match the perspective of the rock plane.

Follow these steps to learn how to use the Vanishing Point filter:

ON THE WEB
Download Figure 19-19 from the book's website to follow along with this exercise.

1. **Duplicate the layer you are going to open in Vanishing Point.**

   The Vanishing Point filter makes changes directly to the layer, so you want to keep your changes non-destructive to the original layer.

2. **With the duplicate layer selected, choose Filter ⇨ Vanishing Point.**

   The Vanishing Point utility opens, with the Create Plane tool automatically selected. Vanishing Point uses planes drawn by the user to determine perspective.

3. **Use the Create Plane tool to draw a four-sided plane that exhibits the perspective you want to emulate.**

   In Figure 19.20, we drew a grid that matched the plane of the rock face.

FIGURE 19.20

This grid follows the perspective of the rock.

4. **Edit the plane if needed.**

   After you draw the grid, the Edit Plane tool is automatically selected. You can move the grid as a whole or change it by selecting one of the handles. If the grid is blue, you've done a great job — it's in perspective. If it's yellow or red, you need to readjust it.

5. **Draw a second plane.**

   Click the Create Plane tool, and draw a plane. In our example, the second plane is in perspective with the children, as shown in Figure 19.21.

FIGURE 19.21

Two different planes are involved in this image.

6. **Choose one of the following options:**

   - **Clone one plane into the other.** Using the Stamp tool, you can Alt-click/Option-click in one plane and drag to clone it into the other plane, as shown in Figure 19.22.

   - **Create a selection in either plane.** Use the Marquee tool to create a selection in one plane and hold down the Alt/Option key while you drag it to another plane. The results are square and lack the softness that can be created with the Stamp tool, but the perspective changes and the image appears in the second plane.

FIGURE 19.22

The perspective of the boys has changed from one plane to the next.

- **Use the Transform tool to resize and rotate a newly moved selection.**
- **Use the Brush tool to paint.** The color, size, and other features of the brush are set before Vanishing Point is opened. You can also use the Eyedropper tool to change the paint color.
- **Copy a selection from another document into the Vanishing Point utility.** By using Ctrl+V/⌘+V, you can paste a previously copied document into Vanishing Point and place it on a plane.

7. **Click OK to exit Vanishing Point and apply the changes to your image.**

TIP

As you select each tool, the Options bar at the top of the Vanishing Point utility changes to reflect that tool. Watch for options that make the tools easier to use and more versatile.

Correcting Wide-Angle Lens Distortions

The Adaptive Wide Angle filter allows you to correct the distortions that inevitably result when you use a wide-angle lens to capture large buildings or expansive landscapes. It works by taking the warp out of the image that the lens introduced to it by bending the light. This feature will inevitably crop some of your image, and you may lose areas that you used your wide-angle lens to capture in the first place; therefore, you should use the Adaptive Wide Angle filter only when you don't mind losing some of the outside edges of your photo.

Figure 19.23 shows a photo taken with a wide-angle lens at a very small focal length of 10mm. You can see obvious distortions in the cliffs, which look stretched and bent.

FIGURE 19.23

Many photos taken with a wide-angle lens exhibit some distortion.

You can use the Adaptive Wide Angle filter to correct these distortions. Choose Filter⇨Adaptive Wide Angle to open the Adaptive Wide Angle filter, as shown in Figure 19.24. It is
a simple utility with the Toolbox on the left and the correction options on the right.

If the photo you open in the Adaptive Wide Angle filter is digital, chances are that Photoshop will recognize the lens used to create the photograph and adjust your photo accordingly. In this case, the projection model is set to Auto and theoretically, there is nothing more for you to do.

FIGURE 19.24

The Adaptive Wide Angle filter gives you the ability to adjust your images for wide-angle distortions.

Polygon Constraint tool

Constraint tool

If the Auto option is not available, you can choose from three other projection models. Click the Correction menu and select Fisheye, Perspective, or Full Spherical, depending on the lens that you used to capture the photo. With any one of these three options selected, you can customize the following settings:

- **Scale.** This option shrinks or grows your image inside the canvas. As you use the Adaptive Wide Angle filter to bend the edges of your image, you can use this slider to increase the size of your image, effectively cropping the uneven edges.

- **Focal Length.** This option allows you to set the focal length at which your image was taken.

- **Crop Factor.** This option allows you to adjust the warp placed on your image by the other settings, distorting it more or less.

All of these settings adjust your image as a whole. After you have changed them, you can customize areas of your image by using the tools on the left of the Adaptive Wide Angle utility (refer to Figure 19.25) to make custom changes. These are the tools available to you:

- **Constraint tool.** This tool allows you to specify straight lines in your image and have the perspective adjusted accordingly.
- **Polygon Constraint tool.** This tool allows you to draw an area composed of straight lines to indicate a flat plane.
- **Move tool.** This tool moves the photo around inside the canvas.

Even though the image shown in Figure 19.23 was auto-adjusted when we brought it in, we used the Constraint tool to make additional changes, as shown in Figure 19.25. A horizon line usually makes a big difference, as do long lines running along the side of the image. As you use the Constraint tool, you can maximize its effectiveness by choosing the orientation of each line that you draw. Use the handles that appear on the selected constraint line to change its orientation.

FIGURE 19.25

The Constraint tool allows you to customize the filter.

The Polygon Constraint tool is best for subjects with obvious planes, such as a building. Using an entire plane to adjust an image can create more efficient results. When you are finished making adjustments to your photo, click OK to exit the Adaptive Wide Angle filter. As you can see in Figure 19.26, the distortion in our photo has greatly improved; however, we have also lost much of the image as the altered edges have been cropped square.

FIGURE 19.26

The end result of using the Adaptive Wide Angle filter

Summary

In this chapter, we showed you several ways to distort or otherwise transform your images and several different reasons to do so. Whether you are resizing, tweaking images so they fit better into composites, or simply having fun creating artistic effects, you should have the skills to do so. You learned how to do the following:

- Perform several transformations
- Use the Content-Aware Scale feature
- Use the Puppet Warp tool
- Work in the Liquify utility
- Use Vanishing Point to change perspective
- Use the Adaptive Wide Angle filter to correct lens distortions

19

Applying Filters

IN THIS CHAPTER

Enhancing an image using Artistic filters

Transforming images using the Filter Gallery

Making non-destructive filter adjustments

Defining the behavior of the Photoshop filter algorithms

You can add many of these filters to an image using the Filter Gallery, a tool that allows you to preview the filter effect, change the filter settings, and add multiple filters in a viewable and changeable stack. Other filters must be added using the Filter menu.

You can add most of the filters as Smart Filters that are non-destructive and editable. Understanding Smart Filters and how they work gives you the flexibility to add multiple filters, change the order in which they are applied, edit their settings, create a blending option for each filter (an option you don't otherwise have), disable their effects, or delete them.

In this chapter, we focus on the fun, artistic filters as we show you how to apply these powerful tools to an image and modify their effects. With dozens of creative filters that you can combine, modify, and customize, the possibilities are seemingly endless.

> **NOTE**
>
> There are several examples of filters in the color insert in the center of this book.

Looking at Artistic Effects Filters

Most of the Photoshop filters create artistic effects by changing your image in a way that enhances its artistic value, at least for the project you are working on. These filters can make a photograph look like anything from a painting to a rubber stamp. They are divided into categories based on their relative properties and are found in the Filter menu. Following is a comprehensive list of the artistic effects filters and what they do.

This list doesn't include the corrective filters — namely the Sharpen, Blur, Noise, and Lens Correction filters, which are covered in Chapter 14. Liquify, Vanishing Point, and Adaptive Wide Angle Correction are covered in Chapter 19. The Video filters are covered in Chapter 25.

Exploring Artistic filters

The Artistic filters replicate effects that are usually achieved by hand rather than digitally. Although they don't always do a realistic job of this, they can give freehand-challenged artists options for creating drawing effects. All these options are available in the Filter Gallery:

- **Colored Pencil.** (Filter Gallery) This filter makes your image look as if the hard edges have been sketched using a colored pencil. This effect uses your background color as the color of the paper, so if your background is the default, you may get an image that is more gray than colorful. Change it to white or any other color to alter the look.

- **Cutout.** (Filter Gallery) Similar to a mosaic, this effect makes your image look as if it has been constructed of roughly cut paper.

- **Dry Brush.** (Filter Gallery) This filter makes your image look as if it was painted using a dry brush technique. This filter is subtle, although it reduces the colors in your image.

- **Film Grain.** (Filter Gallery) This filter adds a grainy look to your image by blending the shadows and midtones.

- **Fresco.** (Filter Gallery) This filter creates a rough image that mimics coarsely applied paint.

- **Neon Glow.** (Filter Gallery) This filter uses your foreground color and mixes it with a specified glow color to create a glow and soften your image.

- **Oil Paint.** This filter creates texture and specularity to mimic the look of an oil painting. You can change the look based on brush size and style. The end result will probably never be worth millions, but it is a fun, artistic effect.

- **Paint Daubs.** (Filter Gallery) This filter lets you choose from several brushes to create a painting from your image. The brush used and the settings applied can make your image range from a slightly softer look to an impressionistic look.

- **Palette Knife.** (Filter Gallery) This filter smoothes your image and introduces texture that simulates the canvas underneath. You can see an example of the Palette Knife effect in Figure 20.1.

FIGURE 20.1

The Palette Knife filter softens this image and gives it an impressionistic feel.

- **Plastic Wrap.** (Filter Gallery) This filter makes your image look as if it's been embossed and shrink-wrapped.

- **Poster Edges.** (Filter Gallery) This filter introduces banding in your image by significantly reducing the colors, and creates black strokes along the harder edges of your image.

- **Rough Pastels.** (Filter Gallery) This filter simulates a drawing made with pastel chalk. You have a lot of control over the texture applied to your image in this filter, with several textures to choose from and settings that increase the dimension and light of the chosen texture.

- **Smudge Stick.** (Filter Gallery) This filter softens an image by reducing the colors and smudging them.

- **Sponge.** (Filter Gallery) This filter introduces regular patches of missing color, as if the painting had been sponged while it was still wet.

- **Under painting.** (Filter Gallery) This is another filter primarily for adding texture, although you can make a significant difference to the look by adjusting the brush strokes as well. It simulates painting your image over a textured background (the under painting) and then reapplying the image over the top.

- **Watercolor.** (Filter Gallery) This filter simulates your image being painted with watercolors, giving it a soft, muted look. You can add contrast by increasing the shadow intensity.

Discovering Brush Stroke filters

The Brush Stroke filters make your image look different by changing the way the brush strokes are applied to it. Just like the Artistic effects, these effects are meant to mimic fine art:

- **Accented Edges.** (Filter Gallery) This filter adds highlights or shadows to the edges of your image, accentuating them and giving your image ultra-sharp edges while smoothing out the other areas.

- **Angled Strokes.** (Filter Gallery) This filter creates the impression that your image is painted using diagonal strokes. The lighter strokes are painted in a different direction than the darker strokes, creating a crosshatched appearance in areas of high contrast.

20

717

- **Crosshatch.** (Filter Gallery) This filter adds a crosshatch texture to your image. This effect creates a cleaner look than the angled strokes because the crosshatches are kept within the bounds of the colors contained in your image.

- **Dark Strokes.** (Filter Gallery) This effect creates more detail and darkness in the dark areas of your image because it creates short, tight strokes in those areas. It also softens the lighter areas in your image by using long, white strokes.

- **Ink Outlines.** (Filter Gallery) This filter simulates a picture drawn with ink, giving your image a contrasty, textured look. You can see an image before and after Ink Outlines has been applied to it in Figure 20.2.

FIGURE 20.2

Ink Outlines give this image a hard, contrasty look.

- **Spatter.** (Filter Gallery) This filter gives your image the look of a painting that was created using a spatter airbrush, including a lot of splotches and texture.

- **Sprayed Strokes.** (Filter Gallery) This effect is very subtle, especially if your image has a high resolution. It simulates the effect of painting your image by making strokes with a spray brush. You can determine which direction you want the strokes to run.

- **Sumi-e.** (Filter Gallery) In true Japanese style, the Sumi-e effect simulates a painting on rice paper using a heavily saturated brush. The end result is a rich painting with deep shadows.

Examining Distort filters

The Distort filters change the way your image looks by reshaping it in different ways. Most of these filters are not available in the Filter Gallery simply because the dialog boxes have more intensive settings than the other filters. You can find the Diffuse Glow, Glass, and Ocean Ripple filters in the Filter Gallery. Here's what the Distort filters do:

- **Diffuse Glow.** (Filter Gallery) This filter is great for creating the effect of an image taken with a soft diffusion filter, which is popular with portrait and wedding photography. The effect is a soft, ethereal look.

- **Displace.** For this filter, you need an image to specify as a displacement map. Any PSD file will do. The Displace filter uses the hard edges in the image that you specify to warp your original image around, as shown in Figure 20.3. Although we used a simple shape in this figure, you should try using another image just for fun. The results are interesting.

FIGURE 20.3

The river plus the footprint creates the image displacement shown here.

- **Glass.** (Filter Gallery) You can make your image look as if it's being viewed through glass with this filter. Several settings simulate all different types of glass.

- **Ocean Ripple.** (Filter Gallery) This filter gives your image the illusion that it is being viewed through water.

- **Pinch.** A mini-warp or liquify effect, this filter creates only one kind of distortion — a pinch to the center of your image that either pinches it in or bubbles it out.

- **Polar Coordinates.** The idea behind this very interesting-looking filter is that after it has been applied, you can place the resulting image in a mirrored cylinder to create a cylinder anamorphosis. When you look into the cylinder, the image appears not only undistorted but in 3D. If you happen to have a mirrored cylinder handy, you can see if it works with Figure 20.4.

NOTE

For some very interesting information on the cylinder anamorphosis art form, look up anamorphosis on Wikipedia.

20

- **Ripple.** Like disturbing water in the middle of a pond, you can create ripples in your image using this filter.

- **Shear.** This filter allows you to distort your image using a curve.

FIGURE 20.4

The Polar Coordinates distortion makes a flat image look very interesting.

- **Spherize.** This filter wraps an image around a sphere, giving it a 3D effect.

- **Twirl.** This filter twists an image around a point in the center of your image. You can choose how far to twist and in what direction.

- **Wave.** Just as if the surface of your image were the surface of a swimming pool, you can create waves in it with several controls that let you customize the look. The results are similar to the Ripple filter, but you have much more control over the results using the wave settings.

- **ZigZag.** This filter creates zigzag waves in an image, starting in the center and gradually decreasing as the effect moves outward.

Checking out the Pixelate filters

The Pixelate filters create different types of pixelation in your file. The dialog boxes are simple, focusing on the size of the pixelation. Some of the filters, such as the Fragment filter, don't have a dialog box at all. None of these filters are in the Filter Gallery. Here's what you can expect from the Pixelate filters:

- **Color Halftone.** This filter takes each color channel, divides it into rectangles, and changes the rectangles into circles. The effect is similar to watching an old television set where the colored pixels were easy to pick out, except the pixels are round in this case.

- **Crystallize.** This filter combines several adjoining pixels together to create hard-edge polygon shapes reminiscent of crystal formations.

- **Facet.** This filter combines pixels in the same area to soften the look of the image.

- **Fragment.** This filter adds texture to an image by averaging adjoining pixels and then offsetting them from one another. The Facet and Fragment filters don't have dialog boxes but work with a set number of pixels. This means that if your images are high resolution, you probably won't see a distinct difference when using either one of these filters.

- **Mezzotint.** This filter can create a very cool color effect by applying strokes that are randomly assigned to be black, white, or a fully saturated color. The result is an almost Art Deco effect that can really make your image pop. Although the resulting image is distinctly uninspiring in grayscale, you can see the dialog box in Figure 20.5.

FIGURE 20.5

The Mezzotint dialog box gives you several stroke options.

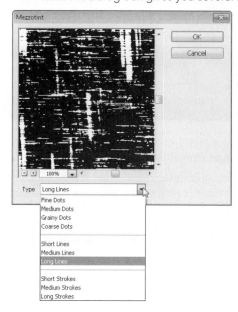

- **Mosaic.** This filter makes your image look as if it were created from square tiles of pixels. You can determine the number of pixels that are grouped into each tile, which makes it possible to create a visible effect with a high-resolution image.

- **Pointillize.** With this filter, you can turn your image into a painting that looks like it could have been created by Georges Seurat. This filter creates solid color points throughout your image.

Considering the Render filters

The Render filters range from the simple Clouds filter that creates clouds from the foreground and background colors without any input from the user, to creating a Lighting Effects filter that can require detailed input. These filters are not in the Filter Gallery.

- **Clouds.** This filter uses the foreground and background colors in a blend that resembles blotches more than clouds. You want to create a new layer on which to render the clouds, because the effect replaces anything that was on the layer before the clouds were rendered.

- **Difference Clouds.** This filter creates clouds using the foreground and background colors just like the Clouds filter and then blends them with the existing pixels using the Difference Blend mode. You can apply this filter multiple times for a different effect each time.

- **Fibers.** This filter creates streaks of color from the foreground and background colors that intermix to resemble fibers. This filter also replaces the pixels on the selected layer.

> **TIP**
> Not only can you add filters on top of one another to create unique effects, but filters such as clouds and fibers, which can be placed on their own layer, can also be used with the Blend modes to create unique effects on the layers beneath them.

- **Lens Flare.** This filter does a pretty good job of creating a realistic lens flare in your image. You can choose one of several flares and place it anywhere in your image.

- **Lighting Effects.** This filter adds unlimited lighting effects to your image to create dramatic results. You can create several lights, place them anywhere in your image, and change their properties so they resemble different types of light from spotlights to gel lights. Several presets are previewed for you in Figure 20.6. You can also create your own lighting effects and save them as additional presets.

Looking into the Sketch filters

The Sketch filters use the edges in an image to create texture, giving the image a rough, hand-drawn look in many instances. Many of these filters reduce your image to two or three colors, so simple images with a few distinct lines look better than images that have more detail. Keep an eye on your foreground and background colors (found in the Toolbox), because they are used to create most of the effects found in this menu. All of these filters are applied using the Filter Gallery:

- **Bas Relief.** (Filter Gallery) This filter creates a low-relief carving of your image using the foreground and background colors.

- **Chalk & Charcoal.** (Filter Gallery) This filter changes the background to a basic gray and roughly draws the highlights and midtone areas of your image in chalk that is the same color as the background. Using the foreground color as charcoal, the shadows are filled in. The right foreground and background colors are vital to achieving an aesthetically pleasing result.

- **Charcoal.** (Filter Gallery) This filter is made up of basically two colors with very little variations between them; the foreground color becomes rough charcoal strokes that trace major edges and fill in the midtones. The background color becomes the color of the paper.

- **Chrome.** (Filter Gallery) This filter gives your image a liquid metal look, as if it had been embossed in chrome, but with very smooth edges. Figure 20.7 shows an image of a flower rendered in chrome.

FIGURE 20.6

You can use these presets, among others, to create light in your image.

Circle of light (modified) Soft omni Five lights up

FIGURE 20.7

The Chrome filter produces a liquid metal look, especially in images with simple lines like this photo of a flower.

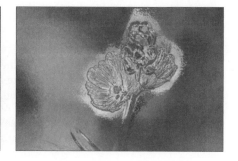

20

- **Conté Crayon.** (Filter Gallery) Conté crayons are made from a mix of clay and natural coloring agents such as iron oxide and charcoal; they are square and used to create rough, boldly lined sketches on textured paper. The Conté Crayon filter uses the foreground color to fill in the darker areas of your image and the background color for lighter areas. Because Conté crayons are usually black, sepia, or sanguine-colored, using these colors for your foreground and background creates a truer effect.

- **Graphic Pen.** (Filter Gallery) This filter reduces your image to two colors: the pen, which uses the foreground color to create fine, linear strokes to bring out the detail of an image, and the background color, which is used for the paper.

- **Halftone Pattern.** (Filter Gallery) This filter simulates the effect of using a halftone screen, adding a specified texture to your image, and again reducing it to a blend of your foreground and background colors. It can have a subtle texture or a very marked one, depending on the settings.

- **Note Paper.** (Filter Gallery) Similar to the Cutout filter, this filter creates an image that looks like it was constructed of handmade paper. Unlike the Cutout filter, it uses the foreground and background colors to determine the color of paper used, again creating an image from two colors.

- **Photocopy.** (Filter Gallery) This filter simulates a rough photocopy of your image, using the foreground and background colors as the paper color and toner.

- **Plaster.** (Filter Gallery) This filter simulates a plaster cast, smoothing the edges of your image and using the foreground and background color to give the image a 3D effect.

- **Reticulation.** This filter creates a grain over your image after reducing it to the foreground and background colors. This adds more texture and dimension.

- **Stamp.** (Filter Gallery) This filter gives the impression that your image has been applied with a rubber or wooden stamp, with the foreground color as the paper and the background color as the ink that the stamp has been dipped in. Images with simple lines make the best stamps.

- **Torn Edges.** (Filter Gallery) This filter is similar to the Note Paper filter, but it doesn't contain the texture that simulates the handmade paper in the Note Paper filter. Instead, the effect of this filter is very smooth.

- **Water Paper.** (Filter Gallery) This filter uses the colors in your image and "waters them down" to make your image look softer.

Using the Stylize filters

The Stylize filters work primarily by using the edges in your images to create interesting 3D effects from embossing to using the Extrude filter to make your image look like it was created with building blocks. Other Stylize filters mix up the pixels in your image to look like they've been diffused or hit by a high wind. Here's what you can expect:

- **Diffuse.** This filter softens the focus of your image by scattering pixels in a miniscule style. This effect is hardly noticeable on high-resolution photos, because no setting allows you to increase the amount of diffusion. Instead, you get a different kind of blurring filter.

- **Emboss.** This filter gives your image the look of having been pressed or embossed onto a gray sheet of paper. This filter uses the image colors for the raised outlines, giving this effect the look of a unique piece of art.

- **Extrude.** This filter makes your image look as if it were constructed of building blocks and you are looking down at it from the top. Using pyramids for your extrusion method gives your image a more impressionistic feel than using blocks, as you can see in Figure 20.8.

FIGURE 20.8

The first image uses blocks to create an extrusion from this image; the second uses pyramids.

- **Find Edges.** This simple filter doesn't use a dialog box; it simply finds the edges of your image and places them on a white background. It is not only useful for finding edges in your image, but because it uses the image colors for the edges, it also creates a beautiful effect all on its own.

- **Glowing Edges.** (Filter Gallery) This is the only Stylize filter found in the Filter Gallery. It finds the edges of your image and applies a neon glow to them on a black background. You can increase the effects of this filter by applying it more than once.

- **Solarize.** This filter blends a negative image and a positive image to create an interesting, dream-like image made up of the correct colors blended with the eerie negative colors.

- **Tiles.** This filter makes an image look like it was made of large, square tiles.

- **Trace Contour.** This filter creates a contour map effect by tracing a brightness transition in each of the color channels.

- **Wind.** This filter simulates your image being hit by wind while the paint was still wet. Several settings allow you to customize the wind-blown look.

20

Delving into Texture filters

The Texture filters create heavy, very obvious, texture effects. Most of these filters are self-explanatory. They can all be previewed in the Filter Gallery:

- **Craquelure.** (Filter Gallery) This filter simulates an image painted on cracking plaster.

- **Grain.** (Filter Gallery) You can add ten different types of grain to your image to create texture. Some of these grain types, such as Soft, create a muted look. Others, such as Vertical, change the look of your image dramatically.

- **Mosaic Tiles.** (Filter Gallery) This filter creates an image that looks as if it were created with irregular-shaped tiles with grout between them.

- **Patchwork.** (Filter Gallery) This filter simulates a patchwork quilt by creating squares that are solid colors and giving them the illusion of depth.

- **Stained Glass.** (Filter Gallery) This filter breaks an image into glass cells, with a lead border between them made up of the foreground color and a light source to give it the illusion that it is backlit. It can create a beautiful effect, as shown in Figure 20.9.

- **Texturizer.** (Filter Gallery) This filter applies one of four basic textures to your image: brick, burlap, canvas, or sandstone. You can choose several settings for each filter to customize the size and depth.

FIGURE 20.9

The Stained Glass filter divides your image into cells and adds an inner glow to simulate light.

 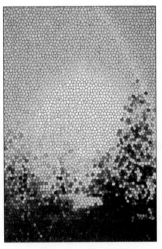

Defining the Other menu

The filters found in the Other menu option do all sorts of different things, from allowing you to create a Custom filter to moving a selection in your image a specified amount and filling in the areas left behind.

Here is a description of what each filter does:

- **Custom.** You can create your own Custom filter. We show you how to do this later in this chapter.

- **High Pass.** This filter removes low-frequency detail in an image, retaining the edges and smoothing the other areas into a medium-gray color. It is commonly used in conjunction with other filters or adjustments to apply sharpness to an image or to delineate the edges for a continuous-tone filter or image. For instance, many of the Sketch filters use only two colors. Figure 20.10 is an example of an image with the Note Paper filter applied to it both before and after applying the High Pass filter.

FIGURE 20.10

Using the High Pass filter first made the Note Paper filter more effective.

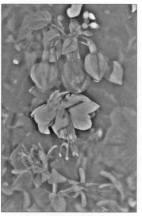  

| High Pass filter | Note Paper filter | High Pass + Note Paper filter |

- **Maximum and Minimum.** These filters affect black and white areas in your image. The Maximum filter spreads the white areas and reduces the black areas in an image; Minimum does the opposite. Although these filters are used mainly to modify masks, they can have a unique effect on images as well, giving them either a bright or dark impressionistic look.

- **Offset.** This filter is used with an image that has a selection created over it. It has the effect of moving the selection a specified amount within the image and replacing the moved pixels with transparent pixels, repeating edge pixels, or wraparound pixels. If no selection is created in the image, the entire image is offset.

20

Exploring the Filter Gallery

The Filter Gallery contains many of the artistic filters that are available in Photoshop. An incredibly useful tool, it allows you to preview the filters, change their settings, and add multiple filters to the same image before closing it.

To open the Filter Gallery, as shown in Figure 20.11, choose Filter⇨ Filter Gallery. The Filter Gallery contains three panes: the preview pane, the filter thumbnail pane, and the options pane.

FIGURE 20.11

The Filter Gallery is like the filter funhouse for images, containing many of the artistic filters available in Photoshop.

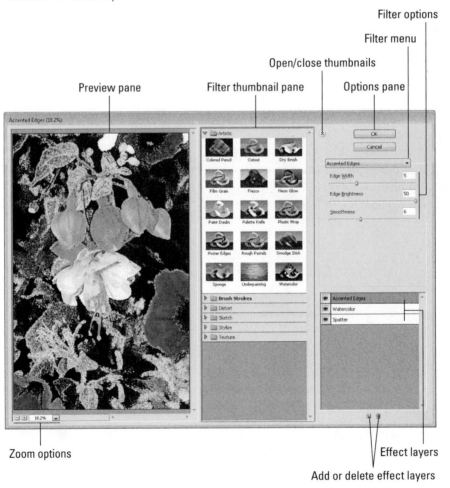

Looking at the preview pane

The left pane contains a preview of your image, showing you what it will look like after the filter or filters are applied to it. You can move your image around inside the preview pane by using the Hand tool (which displays whenever you hover your mouse over an image) to drag it around.

You can zoom in or out of your image using the + or – buttons at the bottom-left corner of the preview pane, or use the drop-down menu to choose a zoom percentage. If you choose Fit in View from the zoom options, your document is resized to fit into the preview pane. If you choose Fit on Screen, the Filter Gallery is resized to fit your entire screen and the image is then resized to fit into the preview pane, giving you the largest possible view of your entire image.

Checking out the filter thumbnail pane

The central window of the Filter Gallery contains the folders for the filter. Click the triangle next to each folder to display thumbnails of the effects contained in the Filter Gallery. These folders correspond with the Filter menu, but they are not comprehensive; they leave out the corrective filters as well as some of the Artistic filters that either require no input or require more specialized input than is available in the Filter Gallery.

Each of the thumbnails of the individual filters found in the filter thumbnail pane demonstrates a basic preview of what the filter does. As you click each thumbnail, the image in the preview pane also takes on the characteristics of the selected filter.

> **NOTE**
>
> Most of the filters in the Filter Gallery are memory-intensive and can take a few seconds to preview, especially if you have more than one applied.

You can close and reopen the filter thumbnail pane by clicking the double-arrow icon in the options pane. Closing the filter thumbnail pane makes your preview pane larger and gives you a better view of your image. You can still choose filters from the drop-down filter selection menu in the options pane.

Looking at the options pane

The last window in the Filter Gallery contains the settings for the selected filter. Beneath the OK and Cancel buttons is a drop-down menu that contains all the filters in the Filter Gallery. Whether you use this menu or click the filter thumbnails, the options for the selected filter will display. You can make changes to the way the filter is applied to your image, sometimes with dramatic results.

All three filters are applied to the image preview in Figure 20.11. Each is listed in the order it is applied, with the most recent filter on top. You can create a new filter effect layer by clicking the New effect layer icon at the bottom of the third window. When you have more than one filter, you can change the order in which they are applied by dragging and dropping them in a different order, as shown in Figure 20.12. To see what the preview would look like without one of the filters, just toggle the eye icon off, and the visibility of that filter is turned off.

> **NOTE**
> The Filter Gallery opens with the same filters applied using the same number of layers as the last time you opened it, no matter how long it's been or what document you opened last.

FIGURE 20.12

Moving the Accented Edges effect below the Spatter effect can change the end result in the image dramatically.

Using Smart Objects to Make Filter Adjustments

Applying filters directly to your images changes the actual pixel values and modifies the original data. Although you can use the History option to get back to the original state, after you save your file, those pixels become altered beyond recovery. Additionally, you may need to try several filter methods and sometimes combinations of filters to get the adjustment you are looking for, which is hard to do when you are trying to apply more than one filter, especially if some of your filters are not found in the Filter Gallery.

That is where Smart Objects can make a huge difference. When you apply a filter to a Smart Object, it is applied as a Smart Filter that you can turn on and off, adjust, reorder, and easily remove without destroying the underlying pixel data.

The best way to apply filters to images in a non-destructive way is to create a duplicate layer of the background and then turn that layer into a Smart Object. You can also simply turn the background layer into a Smart Object layer, but if you keep the background layer around, you can always create a new duplicate layer later to try another set of Smart Filters on.

Follow these steps to create a duplicate of the background layer and then apply Smart Filters to it:

1. **Open an image in Photoshop.**
2. **Right-click the background layer, and select Duplicate Layer from the pop-up menu.**

   The Duplicate Layer dialog box appears.
3. **Name the layer in the Duplicate Layer dialog box and then click OK to create the layer.**

   The new layer is added to the Layers panel.
4. **Right-click the new layer, and select Convert to Smart Object from the pop-up menu.**

   The layer is converted to a Smart Object, and a Smart Object icon appears on the layer thumbnail as shown in Figure 20.13.

FIGURE 20.13

A Smart Object has a Smart Object icon on the layer thumbnail.

5. **Apply a filter to the Smart Object.**

   In this example, we chose Filter ⇨ Filter Gallery from the menu and open the Artistic folder to apply a Watercolor filter to the Smart Object. When you have selected the Watercolor filter, you can make adjustments to the filter and click OK.

   The Watercolor filter was applied as a Smart Filter to the Smart Object, becoming a sublayer that was easily viewable and editable.

6. **Apply a second filter to the Smart Object.**

   In this example, we chose Filter ⇨ Filter Gallery and open the Brush Strokes folder to apply the Accented Edges filter to the Smart Object. When you have selected the Accented Edges filter, you can make adjustments to the filter and click OK.

   The Accented Edges filter was applied as a Smart Filter above the Watercolor filter, as shown in Figure 20.14.

FIGURE 20.14

Additional filters appear on the Layers panel, with the most recent one on top.

7. **Drag and drop the top filter below the second filter to change the look of your image.**

   In this example, we dragged and dropped Accented Edges below Watercolor, as shown in Figure 20.15.

   You may continue to make changes to your filters by right-clicking any Smart Filter to display the menu. From the menu, you can choose any of these menu options, or you can perform these functions by doing the following:

- Edit the filter settings by double-clicking the filter name.

- Double-click the Blending Options icon (to the right of the filter name) to change the Blend mode of that filter over your image.

- Disable the filter by clicking the eye icon, or delete the filter entirely by dragging the filter to the trash icon.

FIGURE 20.15

With a simple drag and drop, the order of the filters has been changed, altering the effect on the image.

Creating a Custom Filter

One of the most powerful filters Photoshop provides is the Custom filter. The Custom filter enables you to define most of the behavior of the filter algorithms in Photoshop. Most of these filtering algorithms work by focusing on one pixel at a time. Photoshop evaluates the color and brightness of the surrounding pixels and uses various algorithms to calculate what the new color and brightness of the current pixel should be. Then the algorithm moves to the other pixels until it has filtered every pixel in the image.

NOTE

Many of the filtering algorithms in Photoshop apply multiple filtering effects and even additional algorithms that are not available through the Custom filter. You can get some pretty good results with the Custom filter, but you cannot duplicate the results you can get in some of the other filters in Photoshop.

20

You can apply a Custom filter by choosing Filter⟹Other⟹Custom from the main menu bar in Photoshop to launch the Custom dialog box, shown in Figure 20.16. The Custom dialog box allows you to apply a weight to each of the neighboring pixels as well as the surrounding pixels when calculating the replacement pixel value.

FIGURE 20.16

Using the Custom dialog box in Photoshop allows you to define filters by setting weights for surrounding pixels, a scale value, and an offset value.

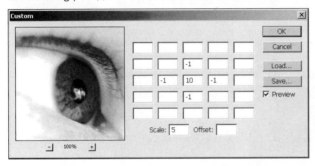

In addition to the weight for neighboring pixels, you can specify scale and offset values:

- **Scale.** The Scale value allows you to control the weight ratio between the center pixel and the surrounding pixels. Photoshop reduces the resulting pixel value by dividing it by the value of the scale. This allows you to apply filters that scale pixel values out of the 0–255 range by scaling them back in.

- **Offset.** The Offset value allows you to give an overall offset in brightness that is applied to the resulting pixel. Increasing the offset can compensate for filters that tend to make the image too dark; decreasing the offset can compensate for filters that make the image too light.

Here's how it all works. Photoshop selects a pixel, multiplies it by the center value in the Custom filter, takes the surrounding pixels defined in the Custom filter, and multiplies them by the corresponding values. Then it adds them all up, divides by the scale, and adds the offset to that number.

This might be a bit confusing at first, but look at the example filter shown in Figure 20.16; starting from a center pixel with a value of 100, one pixel up is 200, one pixel down is 200, one pixel left is 150, and one pixel right is 150. This equation is used to calculate the value that replaces the current pixel:

```
(100x10+200x-1+200x-1+150x-1+150x-1)/5 + 0 = 60
```

As you play around with the Custom filter tool, you start to realize the limitless possibilities of filters you can create with it. The following are some examples of different types of filters that you can create with the Custom filter tool shown in Figure 20.17:

FIGURE 20.17

Some examples of Custom filters

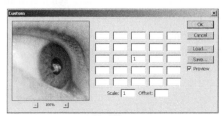

No Filter

Sharpen

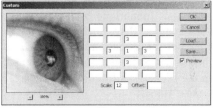

Blur

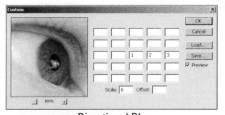

Directional Blur

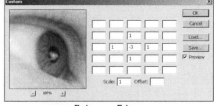

Enhance Edges

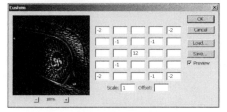

Highlight Edges

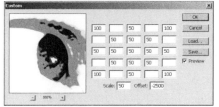

High Contrast

20

735

- **No Filter.** Applying a value of 1 for the current pixel applies no filter.
- **Sharpen.** Applying negative values symmetrically to the surrounding pixels and a positive value to the current pixel sharpens the image.
- **Blur.** Applying positive values symmetrically to the surrounding pixels and a positive value to the current pixel blurs the image and removes dust.
- **Directional Blur.** Applying positive values in only one direction to the surrounding pixels and a positive value to the current pixel blurs the image only in the direction of the pixel changes.
- **Enhance Edges.** Applying positive values symmetrically to the surrounding pixels and a negative value to the current pixel enhances edges in the image.
- **Highlight Edges.** Applying negative values symmetrically to corner pixels and a negative value to the current pixel highlights the edges in the image.
- **High Contrast.** Applying extremely high values for both the surrounding pixels and the current pixel results in a high-contrast effect.

Summary

This chapter presented a comprehensive listing of the Artistic filters and showed you how to apply them through the Filter menu and the Filter Gallery. You learned more about Smart Filters and how they work to create a non-destructive sublayer on your image that you can edit, move, or delete. And if being able to use more than a hundred filters, add them to each other, and change their settings and blending modes doesn't give you enough options, you can use the Custom filter settings to create just the look you want. You should know how to do these things:

- Find the right Artistic filter to get your desired results
- Use the Filter Gallery to apply a filter or multiple filters
- Create a Smart Object in order to add Smart Filters
- Create custom filters to achieve a unique result

Combining Images

When you begin to do more with Photoshop than just correcting photos, the first thing you might think of is image composites. An image composite is any image that has added elements, from a simple text caption to a complex photomontage.

Probably the most difficult part of creating a composite is producing a realistic image that doesn't look as if it's been made from more than one element. Even when the image itself is implausible, such as a shark silhouetted in the wave holding up a surfer, or a snowman in the desert, you want your viewers to look twice and wonder if it might just be true. We've lost count of the Internet photos that friends and relatives have forwarded and asked, "Photoshopped or not?"

In this chapter, you learn a few tricks of the trade for making your composites look great. We're sure that over time, you'll come up with a few tricks of your own. Every composite has its own unique problems. Having a thorough knowledge of the tools at your disposal in Photoshop is the best way to solve them.

Creating Seamless Composites

Creating a composite is much more than just combining two files and hoping they mesh well. Placement, perspective, lighting, and color all play key roles in whether a composite looks great or looks thrown together. Fortunately, there's a reason why a *Photoshopped* image is one that is considered too good to be real. We've shown you the tools you need to create great composites; now we show you how to use those tools to do just that.

Combining files

Photoshop can open well over 40 different types of file formats. You can combine most of these types ; for example, Photoshop has no problem combining a 3D file with a JPEG or TIFF image or layering it on top of an Illustrator file. More incredibly, Photoshop maintains the original aspects of each of these files so they can still be edited and manipulated inside a composite in the same way as they were edited and manipulated in a file by themselves. In fact, in many ways, it is easier to change a file after you have placed it. That way, you can be sure the changes are consistent with the result you are trying to achieve.

There are no magic tricks when combining files. It's easy, and you can do it in many ways. If you want to copy layers from one file to another, the easiest way, especially if you already have the files open, is to drag the object layer from the first file into the window of the second file. You can see how this is done in Figure 21.1.

FIGURE 21.1

Combining files can be as simple as dragging the object layer from the file you want to move into the window of the background file.

You can also combine files by copying and pasting a file, or a selection from a file, into a background image. As you paste a selection into your background file, a new layer is created containing that selection; this allows you to move and edit the selection.

If you want more control over where your placed file will be located in the background file and how large it will be, you can use the Place function by choosing File ⇨ Place from the main menu bar. When you use the Place function to import one file into another file, the imported file is placed inside a bounding box. You can drag and drop the bounding box wherever you want inside the background. You can also use the handles on the bounding box to resize or rotate the placed file as shown in Figure 21.2.

You can use the numeric values in the Options bar to set the position, size, and orientation of the placed file as well. When you have placed the file where you want it, you simply click the check box in the Options bar to accept the changes you made.

FIGURE 21.2

Using the Place command gives you more control over the file's size and position.

Another quick way to combine two complete files is to drag the file you want to place from Mini-Bridge into an open file. It is placed just as if you had used the Place command — as a new layer with a bounding box around it. If you are placing multiple files, using Mini-Bridge is the easiest way to place them.

Adjusting and transforming new layers

After you've placed a file as a new layer, you can edit and adjust it just as you would any other layer. You can move the contents of a layer by selecting it in the Layers panel and using the Move tool to drag and drop it where you want it to be.

You can change the size or rotate a file by choosing Edit ➪ Transform from the main menu bar. The Transform submenu has options such as Rotate, Scale, Skew, Warp, and Flip. You choose Rotate, Scale, and Skew to create a bounding box exactly like the one shown in Figure 21.2. You can then use the handles on the bounding box to make changes to the file. The Warp option places a grid over your file, allowing you to pull on strategic points to warp and bend it. You can flip your file horizontally or vertically by choosing the corresponding option. The flower in the background photo shown here needed to be flipped horizontally for the effect we had in mind, so we selected that layer and quickly flipped the photo, as shown in Figure 21.3.

CAUTION

Be sure the layer of the file you are attempting to change is highlighted in the Layers panel. If it's not, you may find yourself making changes to the wrong layer.

FIGURE 21.3

With the flower image flipped, we were able to place the girl as if she were seated on it.

If you need more leeway to move around or enlarge your files, you can change the canvas size by choosing Image ⇨ Canvas Size from the main menu bar. From this dialog box, you can expand the canvas without affecting the image it contains.

Blending composite files

When you have a 3D object placed within another file, you may find that they don't really seem to fit together. You can use the following quick tricks to make the files blend better.

Refining edges

When you create a selection of a file to place into a new file, you occasionally get rough, pixelated edges or an edge with a shadow around it. You can soften these edges as you make the selection or after you have placed it, as long as the area is still selected. Click Refine Edges in the Selection toolbar, or choose Select ⇨ Refine Edges from the main menu bar to open the Refine Edge dialog box.

 The Refine Edge dialog box and all its options are covered in Chapter 9.

Creating a drop shadow

Most objects in a lighted environment create a shadow somewhere in that environment. Creating a drop shadow is limited in mimicking an actual shadow, but in the right setting, a drop shadow works very well to create a shadow effect. You can also add a drop shadow to help blend the edges of an object or file you've placed.

You create a drop shadow by highlighting the desired layer and clicking the *fx* icon at the bottom of the Layers panel. You then select Drop Shadow from the option list and adjust the settings, previewing the file until you've created the effect you want.

The layer styles, including an example of creating a drop shadow, are covered in Chapter 10.

In this example, the drop shadow looks unrealistic, because it appears even throughout the background, despite the background being uneven. You can mimic the drop shadow in specific areas by using the Burn tool. By applying the Burn tool around the areas of the girl that are touching the flower, as shown in Figure 21.4, you can give the impression that she is casting a shadow over the flower.

FIGURE 21.4

Use the Burn tool to create shadow when the Drop Shadow option doesn't work.

ON THE WEB

You can try combining these two files by downloading Figure 21-4a and Figure 21-4b from the website.

Changing fill or opacity settings

Sometimes a selection placed in an image file looks hard, lacking the color subtleties and the light and shadow of the image. This is especially true of the fish as it was originally placed in Figure 21.5. The bright colors do not blend realistically with the earth tones of the mountain stream. Because none of the stream color appears on the fish, it looks just like what it is — a picture of a tropical fish sitting on top of the stream. You can blend the fish in by decreasing its fill and opacity settings. In many cases, decreasing these settings until just before you can really make out any details coming through gives your image a softer, more blended look. In this case, you definitely want the stream to come through very strongly, so decreasing the opacity of the fish down to around 50 percent would give you the best results, as you can see in Figure 21.5.

FIGURE 21.5

Reducing the opacity of the fish really helps it to blend into the natural setting.

Changing the Blending mode

If you want to change the way a placed file blends into its background, changing the Blending mode is a more dramatic way to do this than changing the Opacity or Fill setting. Blending modes are usually for creating artistic effects rather than realism in a composite. You can change the Blending mode by selecting the layer and using the Blending mode drop-down menu in the Layers panel to select a blending option. We used the Color Burn Blending mode to create the composite shown in Figure 21.6.

ON THE WEB

You can see how the final product was created by downloading the PSD file, Figure 21-6, from the website.

 You can learn the basics of Blending modes in Chapter 10.

FIGURE 21.6

Using the Blending modes creates an artistic effect with composite images.

Creating a Fill or Adjustment layer

If you have the top layer selected when you create a Fill or Adjustment layer, the new layer is placed over all the layers in your document. When you make the same changes to all the files in a composite, they have more in common and blend better. Even something as simple as placing a warming filter over both file layers can create depth and bond the files with a common look. Of course, the more dramatic fills and adjustments create an even more dramatic bond.

You can add a Fill or Adjustment layer by clicking the icon in the bottom of the Layers panel and choosing the fill or adjustment you want to apply.

 You can learn more about the Fill and Adjustment layers in Chapter 13.

Using masks to tuck in a composite file

The most effective method of blending files together is to use a mask to tuck one file behind components of another one. This method can make viewers look twice at even the most improbable photos. In Figure 21.7, the boy is distinctly out of place in this city, but he isn't out of place in this photo, because he is sitting correctly according to perspective. He's behind the foreground, including the largest building, but he's in front of the city in the background.

FIGURE 21.7

The boy overlooks a fantastic city.

This is accomplished using a mask to cut the shape of the building and foreground out of the boy so they appear to be in front of him from the perspective of the viewer. To follow along with this exercise, you'll need to choose a background that requires you to put your selection behind a portion of the background image.

You can use masks to tuck in a composite object by following these steps:

On the Web

You can download Figure 21-8 and Figure 21-10 from the website to follow along with this exercise.

1. **Create a selection around the object that you want to place in a new environment, taking the time to make the selection perfect for a seamless blend as shown in Figure 21.8.**

   In our example, as we selected the model, we did not select the hair that was sticking up on the top of his head; the resulting cutout was more realistic than fuzzy hair with a color fringe.

   FIGURE 21.8

   Select the boy out of his original photo

2. **Refine the edges of your selection.**

   You will want the edges as precise and smooth as possible in order to create a seamless blend in the composite image.

3. **Press Ctrl+C/⌘+C to copy the selection.**

4. **Open the photo you want to place your cutout in, and press Ctrl+V/⌘+V to paste the selection as a new layer in this document.**

5. **Choose Edit ⇨ Free Transform from the menu to resize and move the cutout into position.**

   You'll see that in our example, the model is sitting in front of the entire photo, as shown in Figure 21.9, so this is just a rough adjustment.

6. **Click the visibility button (the "eye" icon) next to the layer containing the cutout, to make it invisible.**

FIGURE 21.9

Use the Free Transform tool to correctly size and place your cutout in the background image.

7. **With the background layer selected, create a selection around the areas that should be placed in front of your cutout.**

    We took a little extra time in our example to cut out the balconies so that the boy would show through to create a sense of realism. In areas where they don't intersect, the selection doesn't have to be precise, as shown in Figure 21.10.

FIGURE 21.10

Select to create a mask that hides the areas of your cutout that should be behind your background photo.

8. **Choose Select ⇨ Inverse from the menu to reverse your selection in the background photo.**

   You want most of the image to be transparent. The areas that are not selected will form the mask.

9. **Refine the edges of the selection.**

   Don't feather the edges of this selection; you want the edges in these files to be sharp and clear. You can smooth the edges out a little, making sure to decontaminate any color fringes you may have around the edges.

10. **Output the selection to a layer mask, and click OK.**

    In our example, this masked the building and the foreground in the areas that weren't selected, so they disappeared from the image, as shown in Figure 21.11.

> **NOTE**
> You can click the Add Layer Mask button in the Layers panel to create a mask immediately from the selection.

FIGURE 21.11

The mask is created over the wrong layer.

11. **Turn the visibility of your cutout layer back on.**

12. **Click and drag the mask from the background layer to the cutout layer, as shown in Figure 21.12.**

    In our example, this masked out the areas of the boy that covered the foreground of the city.

13. **Click the link between the mask and the cutout to unlink them.**

This makes it possible for you to move or resize the selection without moving or resizing the mask, which should stay exactly where you've placed it.

14. **Resize or reposition the cutout as needed to make it fit into the image.**

FIGURE 21.12

Moving the mask cuts out areas of your initial selection instead of areas of the background.

The masks do most of the work when it comes to making the boy look as if he belongs in this image, but you can do other things as well. We cloned a building to place inside the boy's hand so that it would look like he was building the city, and placed a Levels adjustment over both photos that brightened them and helped the images blend.

 You can find another example of creating a mask to tuck in a second image in Chapter 10, which also includes more information on masks and how they work.

 You can find the finished image in color in the color insert in the middle of this book.

Using Multiple Images to Create a Photo Collage

You can create a photo collage by combining two or more photos in a single image to tell a bigger story than any single photo. Photo collages can be used for a number of purposes. For example, collages can display a photographer's work or tell a specific story for a magazine article. You can create photo collages in Photoshop in several ways. Figure 21.13 shows some examples of photo collages.

FIGURE 21.13

You can create collages to tell a bigger story in many ways.

Although all photo collages are different, they seem to have at least a few basic elements that should concern you, including the following:

- **Background.** Using multiple photos in the collage requires a common background on which to place the photos. The background can be either blank or one of the photos. If you want a photo to be the background, you need to crop or size that photo to the correct size of the finished collage. Which method you use is determined by the requirements of how the collage will be used.

- **Size.** Resizing the photos is usually necessary when working with multiple photos.

- **Layout.** Laying out each photo is important. The position and angle of each photo can make all the difference in the final appearance of a collage. Photoshop makes it easy to rotate and move images in a collage.

- **Layering.** Layering is different from layout and is specific to collages. A collage is really a 3D photo; layout provides the first two dimensions, and layering provides the third. Photoshop allows you to stack multiple photos on top of each other and quickly adjust which image is closest to the top by dragging and dropping layers to change their order in the Layers panel.

- **Shape.** Keeping the natural rectangular shape of a photo is common in many collages. Usually, a layout with square, crisp edges gives a collage a professional look and feel. However, sometimes, changing the shape of images in a collage is a better option. You can achieve a homey, scrapbook look by using selections and vector shapes to change the shape of the images in a collage.

- **Layer styles.** Adding layer styles such as borders, bevels, or drop shadows to the individual photos makes them pop, giving them a three-dimensional look and distinguishing them from one another.

Before you create a collage, make any color corrections or other image adjustments to the individual images you are planning to use in the collage. Making these changes is much easier in the original document with fewer layers.

Use the following steps to create a collage of multiple photos:

1. **Create the background.**

   If you want a specific photo to be the background, open the photo and crop or size it to the correct size of the finished collage. If you are creating a background, start with a new document and add any color, patterns, or other elements you want.

TIP

When building a collage on a created background, it is best to make the background as big as possible. This allows you to bring the images in full-size to keep as much detail in them as possible. You can always resize the image down after you create the collage. This won't work when you use a photo for the background, however, because you are limited to the size of the photo.

2. **Add photos to the background.**

   The easiest way to do this, especially if you have several files, is to create a collection of the files you are planning to use in Bridge and then use Mini-Bridge to drag them into the background document, as shown in Figure 21.14. The photos are added to the original document as layers, and you can move and resize them as they are placed.

FIGURE 21.14

You can drag multiple files from Mini-Bridge into one document, and they are placed as separate layers.

3. **Select the layer containing the photo you want to work with.**

   With multiple images on multiple layers, it is more important than ever that the Layers panel become an integral part of your workflow. Figure 21.15 shows a Layers panel with 19 layers representing different images placed in a collage.

   FIGURE 21.15

   Using several different images can result in a document with a lot of layers.

 Learn how to work with the Layers panel in Chapter 10.

4. **Tweak the size and placement of your images.**

   Although you were given the opportunity to resize images as you placed them in the document, seeing them all together and making other changes, such as the shape of the image, usually means you'll want to tweak size and placement. You can move the selected image using the Move tool, or resize or rotate it by using the Edit ⇨ Free Transform command.

5. **Adjust the order of the layers by using the Layers panel.**

   If your photos overlap each other, you may need to adjust which photo is on top. To change which photo appears on top in the image, drag the photo layer higher or lower in the Layers panel.

6. **Change the shape of each photo.**

If you want your photo to be a different shape than the (probably) rectangular image you brought in, change the shape by creating a selection inside the image and deleting the unselected pixels or creating a mask to hide them, as shown in Figure 21.16.

FIGURE 21.16

Changing the shape of an image is as easy as creating a selection and deleting extra pixels or creating a mask to hide them.

> **TIP**
> You can use a vector shape (either a preset or one you've drawn yourself) to create a path and use the Paths panel to create a selection. You can also use a vector shape to create a clipping mask. If your Layers panel is full of image layers, you can create a Smart Object from each image and change its shape in the original file.

7. **Click the layer styles icon in the Layers panel to add one or more layer styles and create borders, bevels, drop shadows, or other elements to your photo.**

These elements change as you change your photo. If you were to transform your photo, for instance, the effect would change with it. The changes add depth to individual photos, as you can see in Figure 21.17.

> **TIP**
> You can drag and copy the layer styles from one layer to another by pressing and holding the Alt/Opt key as you drag the layer styles. You can also do this by right-clicking the layer style, copying it, and then right-clicking each layer and using the menu option to paste the layer style. You can't use the hotkeys for this operation, because the hotkeys copy and paste the actual layers. However, you can assign hotkeys to this function.

FIGURE 21.17
Adding both bevel and stroke layer styles to this photo gives it depth.

Using Photomerge to Create a Panorama

Regardless of whether you have a wide-angle lens, you can use Photoshop to create a photo panorama that is much larger and of higher quality than you could capture in one shot. The Photomerge utility in Photoshop makes it relatively easy to create panoramas from multiple photos.

The most critical part of using software to create a panoramic photo from multiple shots is taking the appropriate photos in the first place. Being aware of how Photomerge works to create a panorama will give you the knowledge that you need to take appropriate photos. These aspects of taking multiple shots for a panorama will help you create the best results:

- **Rotational positioning.** Rotational positioning involves standing in the exact same place and rotating the camera around that single point to take the photos. The pictures should be taken with the most stability possible, so using a tripod or monopod is the ideal method.

> **Caution**
>
> A common mistake when capturing panoramic photos is to use parallel positioning. Parallel positioning involves taking a photo perpendicular to the scene and then moving the camera to a point that is parallel to the first point, still perpendicular to the scene and the same distance away from the scene. This type of positioning makes it very difficult for software to adjust the scene for the appropriate perspective.

- **Overlap.** To create the ideal conditions for blending the images into a seamless panorama, each image should overlap the next one by 40 to 70 percent. Less than this, and Photomerge may not be able to line up identical areas in the image. More than this, and it has a hard time appropriately blending the images.

- **Focal length.** Be sure to maintain the same focal length in all the images you want to use for a panorama; don't zoom into some of the shots and not others.

- **Lighting.** Maintain the same exposure for each photo. This can be trickier than it sounds. If the sun or other bright elements are present in some, but not all, of your images, and your camera is set for automatic exposure, then some of your images may be much darker than other images. If you have a camera where you can set the exposure manually, you may want to do that.

Use the following steps to create a single panoramic photo in Photoshop:

ON THE WEB

You can find the three photos that are used in the following exercise on the website saved as Figure 21-18a, Figure 21-18b, and Figure 21-18c.

1. **Open the photos you want to include in the panorama, and close any other photos that may be open in the editor.**

   The three photos used in this example are shown in Figure 21.18.

FIGURE 21.18

These three photos taken of a hotel in India are perfect for creating a panorama.

CAUTION

Do not adjust the photos, such as lighting and color, at this point. Photoshop has a harder time trying to merge the photos if there are even slight differences in these settings between photos.

2. **Choose File ⇨ Automate ⇨ Photomerge from the menu to open the Photomerge utility, as shown in Figure 21.19.**

FIGURE 21.19

The Photomerge utility is intuitive and easy to use.

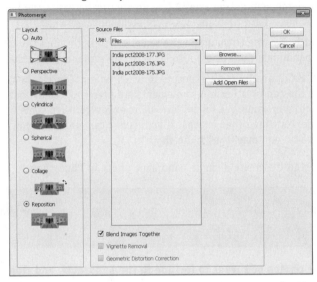

3. **Click the Add Open Files button to load the files that are currently open in Photoshop to the Use Files list.**

   You can also click the Browse button to browse to the files you want to merge if you don't have them open in Photoshop.

4. **Choose a layout option from the Layout menu.**

   You can choose from these layout options:

   - **Auto.** This option allows Photoshop to evaluate and determine which of the following settings works best for your photos. Just like any of the automated processes in Photoshop, this is a hit-and-miss setting.

   - **Perspective.** Using the center photo as a guide, the other photos are matched using the overlap areas and stretched or distorted to create continuance in the other photos.

   - **Cylindrical.** This option flattens out the bowtie effect that's created when taking several images in a circle.

   - **Spherical.** This option makes a panorama that is meant to be seen in a circle around the viewer.

   - **Collage.** This option resizes or rotates the images so that overlapping areas match, but it doesn't skew or otherwise warp the images.

   - **Reposition.** This option doesn't transform the images in any way; it just overlaps them in the best way possible.

For this example, choose Reposition because the images don't need to be transformed in any way to look good together.

NOTE

In Photoshop CS3, Photomerge had an interactive layout option that allowed you to make changes to the semi-finished panorama. In CS4, this option was removed because of significant improvements in Photomerge. If you would like to have more control over the Photomerge process, you can still add this option as a plug-in. PhotomergeUI is available in the optional downloads provided by Adobe on its website.

5. **Choose any of the following operations:**

   - **Blend Images Together.** This option finds the borders of the images and blends them together optimally for the best results.

   - **Vignette Removal.** If some or all of the images have lens vignettes, select this option to have them removed while the merge is taking place.

   - **Geometric Distortion Correction.** Use this option if any of the photos being used have distortions caused at the time of capture, such as barrel, pincushion, or fish-eye distortions.

   There are no vignettes or geometric distortions in the images of the hotel, so you only need to select the Blend Images Together option for this example.

6. **Click OK.**

   Photoshop needs several seconds to analyze and blend the photos together. When the merge is complete, it is displayed as a new document in Photoshop, as you can see in Figure 21.20. You'll notice that the result is not a perfect rectangle because the photos were adjusted to fit one another; when you use Photomerge, you'll have to crop the resulting document to fix these ragged edges.

FIGURE 21.20

With very little effort on our part, the merged photo was created.

Although the panorama is displayed as a single document in Photoshop, it is actually composed of as many layers as there were photographs to begin with, each with a mask that displays the areas that were cut from each photo to blend them, as you can see in Figure 21.21. This makes it possible for you to change the way the merge was created by adjusting each layer and each layer mask.

FIGURE 21.21

With each photo placed on its own layer in the panorama, you can easily change it.

Summary

This chapter demonstrated how the tools you have learned up to this point could be used to create the best composites. There were few examples in this chapter, but the possibilities are unlimited. You learned techniques that will help you create great composites, including the following:

- The best way to combine files
- Several ways to make a composite seamless
- Using masks to make an added element look like it belongs in an image
- Using Photomerge to create seamless panoramas

Part VII

Working with 3D Images

IN THIS PART

Creating and Manipulating 3D Objects

The 3D environment in Photoshop has been a part of the extended version since CS3, but it changed dramatically in CS4 with a new environment and expanded tools. With CS5, you could turn vector paths into 3D meshes with Repoussé, making it possible to open, maneuver, edit, and even create 3D objects in the extended version of Photoshop. In CS6, the tools have been simplified to make them more user friendly and several things have been added to make the workspace cleaner and easier to work with.

Although you can create basic 3D models and add textures to them in Photoshop, its main purpose is not to create, redesign, or even animate 3D objects or scenes. Instead, being able to work with a 3D object in Photoshop allows you to use the powerful Photoshop filters, styles, and other Paint tools to dramatically improve the way a 3D image looks and to create fantastic composites.

A 3D object is usually composed of at least two different files: the actual 3D object, which is a vector file; and the texture of the 3D object, or the file that defines what the 3D object will look like, which is a raster file. You need to understand how these files work together in the 3D environment in order to use the capabilities of Photoshop to change the look of a 3D object.

The Layers panel also looks different with a 3D object selected. A 3D object with a texture attached has at least one sublayer, often more than one. This chapter gives you a complete overview of how to work with 3D layers.

Understanding 3D File Formats

Whenever you work with a 3D model, you are working with a vector file. Vector files consist of geometric shapes that are defined by mathematical equations. When you change the size of a vector file, the image is simply recomputed and the file doesn't lose any quality.

A 3D object rendered in wireframe mode is a basic example of how vector images work. In the example in Figure 22.1, the outlines of the hat are stored in the computer numerically, with the length, width, and placement determined by mathematical equations describing each component.

FIGURE 22.1

No matter how large this hat becomes, the lines that make up its wireframe stay crisp.

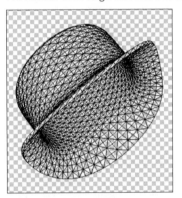

Because 3D images are vector files, editing them is very different than editing a raster image. You can't directly affect a 3D object with the raster tools, such as the Paint Brush or filters. These tools are designed to change pixels, and a vector file doesn't contain any pixels. Photoshop can rasterize any vector file, making it possible to use any of the tools or filters on that file, but rasterizing a 3D object flattens it, turning it into an image rather than a 3D model. Sometimes when you are creating a composite, you want to do just that, but most of the time, you want your 3D objects to maintain their 3D capabilities so that they can be manipulated and seen from any angle. Fortunately, Photoshop has provided several ways to adjust the appearance of a 3D object without affecting it directly.

By adding the 3D extensions, Photoshop added a new array of readable file formats to its already impressive repertoire. Photoshop supports six 3D file formats:

- **3DS.** This file format is used by 3ds Max, the most widely used 3D application. It has become the industry standard, and so most 3D modeling programs export their files in this format.

- **OBJ.** This file format uses data that translates into 3D geometry. OBJ is also a widely used industry standard.

- **DAE.** This file format, also known as COLLADA, is used by the video gaming industry. It was originally developed to facilitate transporting digital content from one creation tool to another. COLLADA is also a widely supported file format.

- **U3D.** This file format, short for Universal 3D, allows users to share 3D graphics with other users who don't have the 3D modeling program used to design the image. Like JPEG or TIFF files, U3D files are gradually becoming universally available to most image viewers.

- **FL3.** This file format is relatively new. FL3 stands for Flash 3D and is a native Adobe format.

- **KMZ.** This file format was created and is used by Google Earth. It is specific to the 3D geography that you see when you explore Google Earth.

When you are finished making changes to a 3D object, you have the option of exporting it as a 3D object rather than saving it as a PSD file. Choose 3D ⇨ Export 3D Layer to open the Save As dialog box. You can choose from several 3D formats to save your object. You can export 3D objects from Photoshop in all of the above formats except 3DS.

Looking at the 3D Workspace

Before you start creating and working with 3D objects in Photoshop, it is important to be familiar with the 3D workspace. Because working with 3D requires multiple tools, layers, and options, the Essentials workspace in Photoshop is inadequate for the job.

In order to work in 3D, it is vital that you change to the 3D workspace so that you have the 3D panel docked and ready to use. Click the Workspace Selector button on the right of the Tool Options bar to open the drop-down menu, and select 3D. This opens and docks your 3D panel and closes panels that are not as useful in this environment. The Properties panel remains along with the Layers panel.

The 3D panel and the Properties panel work together to efficiently provide you with the options you need to manipulate and edit different objects within your 3D scene. There are two different looks to the 3D panel; when you have a 3D layer selected, it looks completely different than when you have a different type of layer selected. In addition, the Properties panel changes depending on what you have selected in the 3D panel. It is very neatly laid out, and once you've become familiar with the basics, you should have no trouble using them to your best advantage.

NEW FEATURE

You're going to see a lot of changes to the look of the 3D workspace in CS6. The 3D panel is one of the bigger changes. It has fewer options than the 3D panel in CS5, but the capabilities have in many cases been enhanced. Instead of appearing in the 3D panel, many of the options have been moved to the Properties panel. When you are working in 3D, the Properties panel is an integral part of your workspace.

Other features of the 3D workspace that are important to understand are the 3D tools and the Picture in Picture window. The 3D tools allow you to manipulate your 3D objects, and the Picture in Picture window provides you with a secondary view of the changes you are making to your 3D scene.

Looking at the 3D panel

The 3D panel looks different depending on what type of layer you have selected in the Layers panel. If you have a non-3D layer selected, the panel lists the options for creating a 3D layer, as shown in the first image in Figure 22.2. If you have a 3D layer selected, the panel changes completely, listing the objects and materials contained in the 3D scene as shown in the second image in Figure 22.2.

FIGURE 22.2

The 3D panel can help you create or manipulate a 3D object.

Filter buttons

The filter buttons on the 3D panel are active when you have a 3D layer selected and allow you to filter your 3D layers so that only certain types are visible in the 3D panel. If you are working with the lights in your 3D scene, for example, you can click the Light Filter button, and only the lights are listed in your 3D layers.

The 3D layers are similar to layers in the Layers panel. Each 3D object has its own layer, and sublayers are added that include textures, materials, and lights. Just as you need to select a layer to work with it in the Layers panel, you need to select the 3D layer you want to work with in the 3D panel. This is true if you want to move it, transform it, or change the textures placed on it.

Learning about the Properties panel when 3D objects are selected

The Properties panel has different faces. This is especially true when you are working with 3D layers. The type of layer that is selected determines the options that are available, and there are many types of 3D layers with different options. You will learn more about these options over the next three chapters; for now, we want to show you how the Properties panel supports the 3D panel.

Figure 22.3 shows the configuration of the Properties panel when a basic 3D layer is selected in the 3D panel and when the material of that basic 3D layer is selected. The options are very different, even though the same 3D layer is selected in the Layers panel. The key to using the Properties panel successfully with 3D layers is to always remember that it portrays the properties of the 3D layer that is selected in the 3D panel.

FIGURE 22.3

The Properties panel displays the options available for the 3D layer that is selected in the 3D panel.

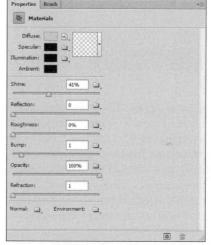

> **NOTE**
>
> In this chapter we are giving you a brief overview of the 3D and Properties panels so that you will understand how they work together in a 3D environment. They will be used consistently and explained in better detail throughout the next three chapters.

Looking at 3D objects in the Layers panel

The layers of a 3D object are more complicated than in most images. When you open a 3D object in Photoshop, if that object contains any textures at all, you have at least one sublayer listed under a textures heading. On top of that, every filter you can add or edit can be made into a 3D object that involves the Layers panel in one way or another. It doesn't take many changes to add several layers to a 3D file or composite. Don't panic yet: like a well-organized filing cabinet, the Layers panel is a clean and efficient way to organize your effects and filters.

Figure 22.4 shows the Layers panel after creating a ring by using the 3D shape from the layer option. The thumbnail of a 3D layer is distinctive. It includes the icon of a three-dimensional cube in the corner in addition to the thumbnail of the actual 3D object. This indicates that the 3D menu is active and that you can use the 3D tools on this layer.

FIGURE 22.4

A 3D layer in the Layers panel is distinctive.

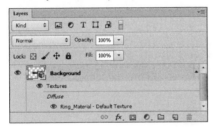

Notice the sublayers. The primary sublayer is named *Textures*. The Textures sublayer is a layer group containing one or more individual textures that are placed on the 3D object. Contained in the Textures layer group is a sublayer labeled *Ring_Material - Default Texture*. This layer is the texture that has been applied to the 3D mesh to give it surface area and color. This layer is actually an embedded file. Double-clicking it opens the default texture layer as a separate two-dimensional file that you can change and rename if you want. You can also add more textures to this object, which show up as additional layers under the Textures sublayer. Each of these textures can be opened and edited individually.

 Editing textures is a primary reason to bring a 3D object into Photoshop. We cover this aspect of 3D objects in greater detail in Chapter 24.

Finding the 3D tools

The 3D tools are used to rotate, roll, drag, slide, and scale a 3D object, whether that object is a camera, a light, or a mesh. Using these tools allows you to take full advantage of adding 3D objects to your scene or composite, because you can orient and place them anywhere you want.

These tools are found in the Tool Options bar when two criteria are met. First, you must select a 3D layer in the Layers panel. Second, you must select the Move tool in the Toolbox. When this is the case, the 3D tools appear in the Tool Options bar, as shown Figure 22.5. The tools work with the layer that you have selected in the 3D panel. You can select the entire scene, a mesh, materials, cameras, or lights. When you select any of these layers, the object contained in that layer moves with the tools. We will show you how to use these tools in detail later in this chapter.

FIGURE 22.5

The 3D tools allow you to manipulate the individual objects in your 3D scene.

3D tools

Using the Picture in Picture window

A useful feature of the 3D workspace is the Picture in Picture window. The Picture in Picture window shows a second, smaller view of your 3D scene using a different view from the main window so that you can more easily find your bearings, a necessary task whenever you are trying to manipulate a 3D scene on a 2D monitor.

When you select a 3D layer in the Layers panel as well as the Move tool, the Picture in Picture window is displayed, as shown in Figure 22.6. As you make changes to your scene, you see those changes reflected in the Picture in Picture window as well as the main view. The Picture in Picture window has two icons that allow you to change the view of the window or to swap the view with the main window.

FIGURE 22.6

The Picture in Picture window allows you to see two different views of your scene at the same time.

Change view

Swap main and secondary view

Opening and Placing 3D Files in Photoshop

If you often work with 3D models, you probably use a 3D modeling program that's built to create 3D objects and is much better at it than Photoshop was ever meant to be. When you bring these models into Photoshop, your goal is to do one or both of two things: to change the texture of your 3D file or to create an image composite using a blend of 3D objects, photos, text, and other Photoshop elements.

We've already shown you that a 3D model is a vector file, or a mesh, and it doesn't contain any color information. The texture of a 3D file is the raster file that is created to wrap the 3D object in, to give it color, texture, and definition. If you are bringing a 3D object into Photoshop to add a texture or edit the existing texture, you want to open it just like you open any supported file in Photoshop: Browse to the 3D file in Bridge or Mini-Bridge, and double-click to open it in Photoshop.

If you are creating a composite with more than one 3D object or other file, you want to place any secondary files into the first one as new layers. You can do this using the File ⇨ Place command, or you can place a 3D object by choosing 3D ⇨ New Layer from 3D File.

Creating 3D Files in Photoshop

You can create basic 3D meshes in Photoshop in several ways: You can use presets to create a quick and basic 3D object that doesn't have a texture applied and doesn't use an image as the texture; you can use the grayscale brightness values in an image to create a depth map; or you can use multiple two-dimensional cross-sections to create one 3D object. You can also create unique 3D objects from vector paths.

You have two options for choosing how to create a 3D object: you can use the 3D menu or the 3D panel, both shown in Figure 22.7. The 3D panel is more versatile and easier to access, so in most cases, you want to use it as your base of operations.

> **NOTE**
> If you have a 3D layer selected, these options in the 3D menu are grayed out and the panel options are different. Although you can merge 3D layers, you can't create more than one 3D object on a layer in Photoshop.

Selecting a source for a 3D object

When you use the 3D panel to create a new 3D object, you can use the Source menu to select a source for that object. This gives you the advantage of choosing what part of your file will be used to create the 3D object. You can choose from these sources:

- **Selected Layer(s).** This option uses only the content of the currently selected layer or layers to create a 3D object.

- **Work Path.** This option allows you to create a 3D object from a selected work path. Although you can create other 3D objects from layers containing paths (such as turning text into a 3D postcard, for instance), only a 3D extrusion can be created if you've selected this option.

- **Current Selection.** This option uses the current selection to create a 3D object, cutting the unselected areas from your image entirely. As with the work path option, this option only creates a 3D extrusion.

- **File.** This option uses the entire file to create a 3D object. You can use this option if you have an image composite that you want to wrap around a 3D preset or manipulate into a 3D scene.

FIGURE 22.7

You can use the 3D menu or the 3D panel to create new 3D objects.

Creating a 3D postcard

A 3D postcard is the simplest form of 3D object. It is essentially a two-dimensional image or object that has been converted to a 3D mesh so it can be manipulated with the 3D tools. It maintains its two-dimensional appearance, as you can see in Figure 22.8, but now you have the added versatility of being able to quickly manipulate it in 3D space, adjusting perspective or creating a unique look. You can also use many of the 3D tools to modify it, including editing its texture, adding lights, or combining it with other 3D objects to create a scene.

FIGURE 22.8

A 3D postcard is essentially a two-dimensional object that can be manipulated with the 3D tools.

Creating a 3D Extrusion

Creating a 3D extrusion gives you the capability to create a 3D object using an image or a vector path. The extrusion properties provide many different options for how your two dimensional file is interpreted into a 3D object.

NEW FEATURE

The 3D extrusion feature is not new to CS6, but it has a new name. In CS5 it was known as the Repoussé utility. Along with its new name, it got a new look. Now, instead of using a dialog box, you can use the Properties panel at any time to define the attributes of a 3D object that you have created.

The vector layer can be anything: text, a shape, some clip art, or your own custom drawing. You can also use an image layer. The thing to remember is that extruding a drawing of a complicated object does not look like a 3D model of that object. A vector image of a car, for example, is not going to look like a die-cast model after creating a 3D extrusion of it. Instead, it looks more like a mold of a car, with depth, but not much extra shape to the depth.

Of course, the result depends on the settings you choose, so you might decide to make a 3D swirl from the shape of the car rather than a mold, but the important thing is that you still are limited when it comes to creating technical 3D objects. That being said, creating 3D extrusions can bring your Photoshop creations to life and give them new depth.

Follow these steps to see how you can create a new 3D object by creating an extrusion from a 2D vector file:

1. **Create a new blank document of any size.**
2. **Create a vector path in the new document.**

We suggest you do something simple to start. We typed a name. You could also create a simple shape using the Shape tool.

3. **With the new vector layer selected, choose 3D Extrusion from the 3D panel and click Create.**

   You are warned that the vector layer must be rasterized in order to create a 3D object. Click Yes. This turns your vector layer into a 3D layer and displays the extrusion properties in the Properties panel, as shown in Figure 22.9.

FIGURE 22.9

The Properties panel displays many options for editing a 3D extrusion.

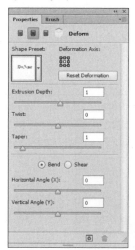

You can see that the Properties panel has three different menus for editing your extrusion. The Mesh menu allows you to determine the initial properties of your 3D object such as the shape and depth of the extrusion. The Deform menu allows you to twist, warp, and deform your 3D object, much like the transformation tools in Photoshop. The Cap tools change the surfaces of the 3D mesh, adding a bevel or inflating the front or back surface of your object.

> **NOTE**
> The final icon resembling a cube in the Properties panel is the Coordinates menu. This menu is available with any 3D object and allows you to enter coordinates for your object. The Coordinates menu is discussed later in this chapter.

Defining an extrusion using the Mesh properties

The Mesh properties are selected in the Properties panel by default when you create a 3D extrusion. Changing the mesh options allow you to define the basic parameters of the extrusion such as shadows and shape. There are three areas in the Properties panel when the Mesh properties are selected:

- **Setting Shadows and Opacity.** When you create a 3D object, you generally create a 3D scene complete with lights. The presence of lights in your scene gives you the option to have your object cast shadows within the scene or catch shadows from other objects placed in the same scene. You can click the check box next to each option to enable or disable these shadows; and you can disable the view of your 3D object or reduce the transparency using these options.

- **Choosing and Modifying a Shape Preset.** The next section of the Mesh menu is defined by a Shape Preset menu that gives you the capability to create several extrusions, from the mundane option of simply adding depth to the much fancier option of creating a twist. Click the Shape Preset drop-down menu to display these options, as shown in Figure 22.10. Once you've chosen an extrusion shape, you can choose a texture mapping option and use the slider to set the depth of the extrusion.

FIGURE 22.10

The Shape Preset drop-down menu has different varieties of extrusions.

■ **Changing the source file to modify a 3D extrusion.** Finally, you have the option to change the parameters of the original vector file, such as changing the color or attributes of text. The Edit Source button returns you to the original file to make changes that will immediately be reflected in the 3D file.

Transforming a 3D extrusion using the Deform properties

Deform is the second option in the Properties panel when a 3D extrusion is selected.. The modifications that you can make to your 3D extrusion are similar to using transformation options in Photoshop. You can twist, taper, bend, or shear your 3D extrusion until it is hardly recognizable. You can do this using the Extrusion Depth, Twist, and Taper sliders (refer to Figure 22.9) or you can use the Deformation Widget that appears over your 3D extrusion, as shown in Figure 22.11. Hovering over different areas of this widget highlights them and displays the property that has been highlighted. Then all you need to do is click and drag to apply the deformation to your 3D extrusion.

22

FIGURE 22.11

The Deformation Widget allows you to transform your 3D extrusion in several ways by clicking and dragging.

Changing the surfaces of a 3D extrusion using the Cap properties

The Cap properties in the Properties panel allow you to change just the surfaces of the 3D extrusion, adding a bevel or inflation to them. Like the Deform properties, you can use the sliders and settings on the Properties panel, or you can use the Cap Widget to make these changes by clicking and dragging the correct part of the widget, as shown in Figure 22.12. By using the Sides drop-down list, you can choose to apply these changes to just the front of your object, just the back, or to both front and back.

> **NOTE**
>
> Once you have created a 3D extrusion, you'll notice that the 3D panel is filled with objects, materials, lights, and cameras. This is similar to any 3D object that is open in Photoshop. These components of the 3D environment play a vital role in manipulating and changing the texture of a 3D object. We will be covering these topics in Chapters 23 and 24.

FIGURE 22.12

The Cap Widget allows you to make changes to the surface area of your 3D extrusion.

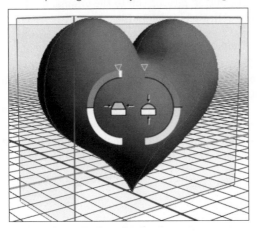

Making a 3D shape from a preset

Photoshop ships with 12 presets that create 3D shapes ranging from basic shapes, such as a cube, to more complex shapes, such as a wine bottle or a hat. These presets provide commonly used shapes that can be modified or combined to use in many different applications. These shapes use the selected layer as a texture. If you have a white background layer selected, the object is white. If you fill the background with a color or pattern, the object has that color or pattern. If you open or import an image and select that layer when you create the object, the image is wrapped around the 3D object and becomes the texture, as shown in Figure 22.13.

> **NOTE**
>
> You can easily edit textures in Photoshop, so if you're not yet sure how you want to wrap your object, don't let it stop you from creating it. You can change the texture later.

FIGURE 22.13

Creating a 3D shape from an image layer wraps the image around the new 3D object.

Just as with any presets in Photoshop, you can create and save your own objects as presets. This isn't done as easily as clicking a save preset button, however. The 3D object must be exported as a DAE (COLLADA) file and placed in Program Files ⇨ Adobe ⇨ Adobe Photoshop CS6 (64 bit) ⇨ Presets ⇨ Meshes (in Mac OS, Applications ⇨ Adobe Photoshop CS6 ⇨ Presets ⇨ Meshes). It then appears in the presets menu with the other shapes, ready to be created at any time, as shown in Figure 22.14.

FIGURE 22.14

When you place a new DAE file in the Meshes folder, it shows up in the presets list.

Creating a 3D mesh from a depth map

Creating a 3D mesh from a depth map creates a depth map based on the brightness levels of the image that you are using and turns that depth map into a 3D object. Areas of your image that have brightness values that are brighter than midtone are pushed out, and areas that are darker than midtone are pushed in. Midtone areas stay on the original plane. You can see a basic representation of this in Figure 22.15. We used a simple radial gradient, which created a smooth depth map.

When you create a depth map, you have four options:

- **Plane.** Creates a depth map centered on the original plane.
- **Two-sided plane.** Creates a mirror image of the original depth map.
- **Cylinder.** Creates a depth map and then wraps it into a cylindrical shape.
- **Sphere.** Creates a depth map and then wraps it into a ball.

FIGURE 22.15

A simple radial gradient makes it easy to see how Photoshop creates a mesh from a depth map.

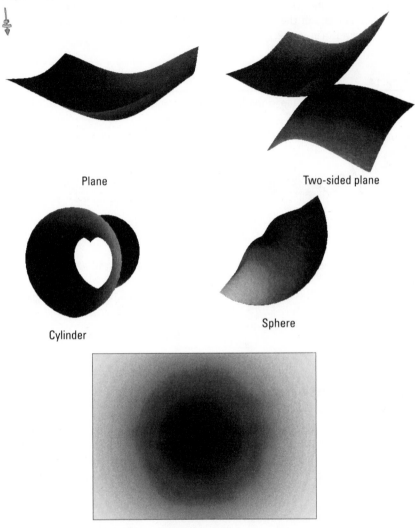

Plane

Two-sided plane

Cylinder

Sphere

Radial gradient

> **NOTE**
>
> Your image doesn't have to be in grayscale mode for this to work. Photoshop uses the green channel to create a depth map.

This type of 3D object is great for creating textures or another unique look for an image file. You can also use it to create planes from elevation maps or to save and re-create planes from one 3D modeling file to another. A simple image file can quickly become a mountain range, as shown in Figure 22.16.

FIGURE 22.16

Using an image to create a depth map can quickly create interesting planes.

Creating a 3D volume

The 3D volume option is used to create 3D objects from several image files that are slices of 3D objects, such as DICOM files. Using this option allows you to create a 3D object from the image layers that can be moved, manipulated, and viewed from all angles, giving you a versatile way to view these medical images.

Manipulating 3D Objects

Imagine that you are standing in a room. As you move in a straight line from left to right, you are moving along the X-axis. If you were to jump up and down in place, you would be traveling along the Y-axis. This is a two-dimensional plane, in which coordinates can be given with two numbers: an X location and a Y location. When you work with a two-dimensional file in Photoshop, you are working with an XY plane. To add the third dimension, the Z-axis is added, creating depth to the XY plane. To move along the Z-axis, you would walk from front to back within the room.

The 3D tools in Photoshop allow you to move 3D models within all three of these planes. If you have already used any 3D modeling software, you will be familiar with these tools. Photoshop has designed its manipulation tools to a standard look and feel. If you have never used 3D tools, you will find that they are fun and easy to use. Jumping in and working with them as we introduce them to you in this chapter is the best way to quickly familiarize yourself with them.

As you work with your 3D model, keep in mind that your final product in Photoshop will be a two-dimensional view, not a 3D scene or animation. This helps you keep in perspective what you can accomplish in Photoshop and how to do it.

Using the 3D tools

Using the 3D tools allows you to manipulate and orient a 3D object in many different ways so that you can achieve the view in which you want to display it, look at it as you add textures, or place it in a composite.

When you select a 3D layer and the Move tool, the 3D tools appear in the Options bar, as shown in Figure 22.17. These tools are used to move your object through 3D space. They operate on the 3D layer that you have selected in your 3D panel, allowing you to modify your scenes and composites quickly and easily.

FIGURE 22.17

The 3D tools allow you to rotate, roll, drag, slide, or scale your 3D objects.

> **TIP**
>
> It is incredibly difficult to explain moving an object through 3D space in a book with still shots. The quickest way for you to understand what we are trying to teach you is for you to use the tools in conjunction with this book. Create a quick 3D object by opening a new document, choosing 3D ⇨ New Shape from Layer, and choosing a shape from the menu. An irregular shape, such as the hat, is the best option for seeing the difference that moving it makes.

Turning 3D objects around a central point

Rotating or rolling an object around a central point gives you the latitude of looking at all sides of an object without actually changing its position in the 3D scene. You'll use these tools to look at the way texture has been placed on your object or to display a different side of your object to view.

Changing an object's orientation is the most obvious reason to use the Rotate and Roll tools. But you can also change the lighting on your mesh by rotating the object rather than moving the light. As you move your object, notice that if you have a light placed in your scene, the lighting changes on your object.

Another use for the Rotate and Roll tools is checking the texture of your object and making sure it is the way you want it, especially if you made any changes to it in Photoshop. To do this without changing the orientation of your object, select the scene layer from the 3D panel and rotate the entire scene as a unit.

You can turn a 3D object around a central point by using tools to rotate or roll the object. Rotating or rolling an object turns and skews it around the X-axis, Y-axis, or Z-axis. While using the Rotate and Roll tools, your object moves around a center point, which never changes position.

Rotating a 3D object

Using the Rotate tool rotates a 3D object around the X-axis and Y-axis. The X-axis is a line running side to side through the center of the object. Like a hot dog turning on a roasting stick, if you rotate your object only on the X-axis, the top of the object rotates toward you or away from you. The Y-axis runs up and down through the center of your object. As you rotate your object around the Y-axis, the sides of the object move toward you or away from you.

With the Rotate tool selected, click and drag back and forth across your 3D object to rotate it along the Y-axis, or drag up and down to rotate it along the X-axis, as shown in Figure 22.18. You can constrain the rotation to either the Y-axis or the X-axis by pressing and holding down the Shift key as you drag in the appropriate direction.

FIGURE 22.18

Rotating an object around both the X-axis and Y-axis

Rolling a 3D object

Rolling your object around the Z-axis is a similar concept to rotating your object around the X-axis or Y-axis. Visualize a line running from front to back through the center of your object, allowing it to roll left to right and back again. You can roll your object around the Z-axis by clicking and dragging back and forth with the Roll tool, as shown in Figure 22.19.

FIGURE 22.19

Rolling an object around the Z-axis

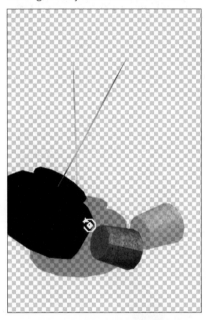

> **TIP**
>
> Although you can quickly skip through the 3D object tools by repeatedly pressing the K key, you can also press the Alt/ Option key to temporarily change the Rotation tool to the Roll tool, and vice versa.

Moving a 3D object through 3D space

Dragging or sliding a 3D object moves it to a different location in your 3D workspace. Moving your object allows you to place it in the desired position so you can create composites by adding a photo background or other 3D objects. Moving an object also enables you to adjust the lighting or change the perspective.

Dragging a 3D object

Dragging moves the object around the XY plane and is visually similar to using the Move tool to move a selection in a regular image file. You can drag your object by selecting the Drag tool in the Options bar or the Toolbox, as shown in Figure 22.20.

FIGURE 22.20

Using the Drag tool moves your object to a different position in the 3D space.

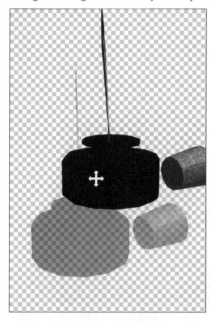

Sliding a 3D object

Sliding moves the object along the XZ plane, so you can move it side to side, just as you can with the Drag tool, or in and out along the Z plane. As you move your object toward you or away from you along the Z plane, it looks very similar to scaling, or resizing, your object, as shown in Figure 22.21. Although it looks the same, when working with 3D, sliding an object is a very different effect from actually making the object bigger or smaller, just as walking away from an object in real life doesn't change its actual size, just your perspective of it.

When you have the Drag or Slide tool selected, you can change the position of your 3D object numerically by entering values in the X, Y, or Z indicators in the Options bar.

FIGURE 22.21

Using the Slide tool looks similar to using the scale tool, but it doesn't change the size of your 3D object, just your perspective

Scaling a 3D object

You can use the Scale tool to change the size of a 3D object so that it will blend better with other elements in your document whether those elements are other 3D objects or other types of layers. Changing the size of your object will actually change the dimensions of it (unlike sliding it, which just changes your perspective of it). A 3D file is a vector file, so scaling it doesn't detract from its quality. The textures placed on a 3D file are raster files, however, so be careful not to reduce the quality of these textures by scaling a 3D file too large.

Scaling a 3D object in Photoshop is similar to using the Transform tools to scale an image or selection. By selecting the Scale tool, you can click and drag across your object to make it bigger or smaller, as shown in Figure 22.22. As you change the size of your 3D object by using the Scale tool, the proportions of the object are automatically maintained. By pressing and holding down the Alt/Option key while you click and drag, you can adjust the object non-proportionally by making it taller or shorter. If you press and hold down the Shift key, you can make your object wider or more narrow.

When you have the Scale tool selected, you can change the size numerically by entering values in the X, Y, or Z indicators in the Options bar. This is a better way to scale your object disproportionately. You can also change these values by scrubbing across the letter that applies to the value you want to change.

FIGURE 22.22

Use the Scale tool to make 3D objects larger or smaller.

Using the 3D Axis Widget

The 3D axis widget is used to perform all the manipulation techniques of the 3D tools. Using the widget, you can rotate, roll, drag, slide, or scale your object using the different arms and handles. Once you get the hang of it, it is faster and more efficient than continually switching between the standard 3D tools. Manipulating your 3D objects becomes fast and easy.

The widget has three different-colored arms extending in different directions as seen in Figure 22.23. Each arm represents a different axis or plane:

- Red = X
- Green = Y
- Blue = Z

The end of each arrow has a handle. The handles rotate or roll your 3D object, and each arm allows you to drag and slide each object. As you hover over the handles, you'll see that your cursor changes to the Rotate or Roll tool and an arc in the widget represents the direction your object is moving, as shown in Figure 22.24. As you hover the arms of the widget, the Slide tool appears. Click and drag to use each tool.

FIGURE 22.23

The 3D Axis Widget has three arms that are color coordinated to represent the three axes.

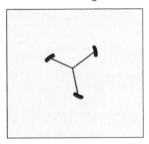

FIGURE 22.24

Use the handles at the end of the widget to rotate or roll your 3D object.

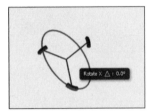

The 3D Axis Widget isn't always the easiest tool to use, especially if you want to make small, controlled movements, but it is certainly the most convenient. With a little practice, you can make quick, controlled manipulations without the need to toggle through the 3D object tools.

Typing in coordinates for your 3D object

You can also change the attributes of a 3D object by typing specific coordinates that change its position, its angle, and its size. This is a much easier way to manipulate your object, but only if you know the coordinates that you want to use.

To change a 3D object's position by typing coordinates, select the object layer in the 3D panel. In the Properties panel, select the Coordinates menu icon. This displays the coordinate settings, as shown in Figure 22.25. Type the coordinates in the appropriate boxes to place your 3D object in the correct position.

FIGURE 22.25

The Coordinates menu in the Properties panel allows you to specifically place a 3D object.

Summary

In this chapter, we introduced you to creating and using 3D objects in Photoshop. You learned about the following:

- Working with 3D file formats
- Understanding the 3D Workspace
- Creating 3D objects
- Changing the position of 3D objects

Editing 3D Scenes and Settings

W hen you are working with 3D scenes and objects in Photoshop, it is very important that you use the 3D workspace so that you can maneuver and edit scenes and settings from the 3D and properties panel docked right in your work area. The most important part of the work area is the 3D panel, which is similar to the Layers panel because it subdivides each 3D object into sublayers that include the meshes, textures, lights, and cameras that make up the 3D scene. You will learn how to recognize and use these layers to change the look of your 3D objects and scenes.

As you work with the 3D panel, you will also be using the Properties panel extensively to make changes to the layer that you have selected in the 3D panel. The Properties panel is incredibly versatile when it comes to 3D objects. It can look completely different depending on what type of layer you have selected. You will learn how to make the best use of these options so that you can use the powerful Photoshop tools to create a fantastic 3D object or scene.

Looking at the 3D Panel

The 3D panel contains the layers that make up a single 3D layer in the Layers panel. A 3D object generally consists of at least one mesh with several materials applied and at least one light to illuminate it. The 3D panel allows you to view, sort, and edit these components of a selected 3D layer.

The 3D panel has two basic components: a main area containing layers and a small header containing buttons, which enable you to sort layers. Three types of layers are found in the 3D panel — the mesh layers, material layers, and light layers — and they correspond to the filter buttons shown in Figure 23.1. You can see that each layer has a distinctive icon so that you can distinguish the layer types when looking at the 3D panel.

FIGURE 23.1

The 3D panel contains the layers that make up a single 3D layer in the Layers panel.

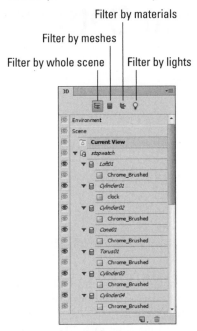

Working with a Whole 3D Scene

When you click the Filter by whole scene icon at the top of the 3D panel, you display every option available in your scene: the meshes, the materials applied to those meshes, and the lights placed in the scene. This gives you a good overview of the elements that make up your 3D object and how they fit together.

At the top of the layers, you find the Environment layer, the Scene layer, and the Current View layer. When highlighted, these three layers allow you to change properties that affect the entire 3D layer and your view of it.

Changing the properties of a 3D environment

The Environment layer in the 3D panel represents the lighting and background in your 3D scene. You can use the Environment layer to look at and edit the settings of these properties. To change the settings of the environment, click the Environment layer to highlight it. The Properties panel displays the Environment settings, as shown in Figure 23.2. The four areas in the Properties panel that you can edit and adjust are Global Ambient, IBL (Image Based

Lighting), Ground Plane, and Background. Each of these areas allows you to change specific settings that can add natural light or create special lighting effects.

FIGURE 23.2

When you select the Environment layer in the 3D panel, the Properties panel displays the properties of the lighting and background of the 3D environment.

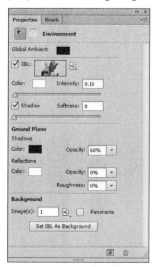

Changing the Global Ambient light

The Global Ambient light is the light that naturally exists in the scene. Double-click the Global Ambient Color swatch to change the color of the reflective surfaces in your 3D scene. This light doesn't cast any direct light or shadows, but it can add a cool or warm tone to your scene.

Using Image Based Lighting

Image based lighting, or IBL, allows you to add a gel lighting effect to your scene. You can create and load images to create an effect similar to placing a transparency over a light to change its color and effect. Double-click the folder icon next to the IBL image thumbnail to create or load a texture. The texture can be a color, a pattern, or even a photo.

NOTE

The icon next to the IBL image thumbnail is a folder icon before an image has been loaded and an image icon after, as you can see in figure 23.3.

The settings in the IBL area also allow you to control the intensity and the shadows cast by the IBL that you are using. Figure 23.3 demonstrates the effect that using a pattern for the IBL has on a rendered stopwatch.

FIGURE 23.3

Using a pattern to create a lighting texture over this stopwatch gives it an interesting texture and shadows.

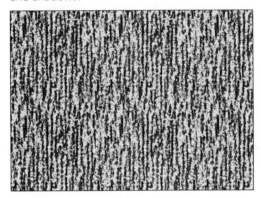 

Adjusting the Ground Plane properties

You can adjust the Ground Plane properties to change the way that the ground plane in your scene catches shadows and returns reflections. Just as in real life, different materials on the ground create different lighting effects. For example, the ground on a dark, wet night catches fewer shadows but has very reflective surfaces.

You can change the color of shadows and reflections. Setting the opacity determines how well they show up in the rendered image. You can also change the roughness of the reflection to add texture to it as if it is being cast on a rough surface.

Changing the Background settings

The Background settings allow you to place an image in the background of the 3D scene. This is one way to create a composite with images and 3D objects. Double-click the image icon to create or browse to an image to place behind your 3D object. The image is placed so that it fits — not fills — the canvas of your 3D scene. For this reason, it is easier to create composites by placing a 3D object in an image file rather than using this option.

Setting the properties of a 3D scene

The Scene layer in the 3D panel allows you to create a cross-section of your 3D object. This can come in handy when you want to look inside a 3D object or intersect that object with something else, or if you need only part of an object in a scene. The other properties of the Scene layer represent the way the 3D objects are rendered while you work with them. The simpler the 3D scene is displayed, the faster you can work with it in Photoshop. You can see the Properties panel with the Scene layer selected in Figure 23.4. We have selected the Cross Section check box so that you can also see the options for creating a cross-section that only appear when this option is selected.

FIGURE 23.4

The properties of a Scene layer allow you to control the way you view your 3D scene.

Creating cross-sections

A cross-section is created by cutting into a 3D object and looking into it. Cross-sections have several uses, allowing you to look inside 3D models or to use just a portion of a model in a composite. Cross-sections are great for use with architectural renderings, for example, allowing you to see inside the models of 3D buildings. In Figure 23.5, we cut the roof off a simple room to show you the interior. You can see that this could be a very valuable application for looking at or editing more complex buildings or furnished rooms.

You can also use cross-sections to cut down any 3D model for use in a composite. You can intersect a cross-sectioned object with another object or image, or you can just use the cut-down version of an object. By using two instances of the same 3D model, you can open a previously solid object, such as a box, by creating matching cross-sections.

FIGURE 23.5

This room had a roof before a cross-section was created.

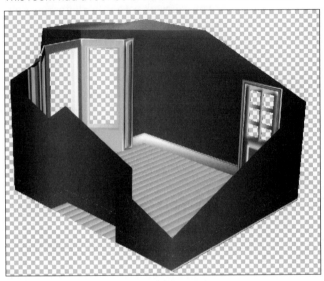

To begin, click the Cross Section check box in the Properties panel with a Scene layer selected. Additional cross-section options appear in the Properties panel. Your 3D object is cut exactly in half along the X-axis, as shown in Figure 23.6. Using the settings, you can create a cross-section on any plane, position it anywhere on your object, and tilt it from side to side or back to front.

When you create a cross-section, you can set the following options:

- **Slice.** Use this menu to select one of the listed axes to change the cross-section to that axis. The room in Figure 23.5 is cut along the Z-axis, while the balloon in Figure 23.6 is cut along the X-axis.

- **Offset.** Use this menu to enable a cross-section to cut your 3D object in half. By changing the offset, you can move that dividing line to cut off more or less of your object.

- **Tilt.** Use these settings to change the angle of the cross-section. By default, the angle of the cut is parallel with the base of your object. Tilt Y changes the angle of the cross-section front to back, and Tilt Z changes the angle side to side.

- **Plane.** Select this check box to create a plane that is a visual aid showing you exactly how the cross-section is cutting your object in two. You probably want to keep the plane visible while you are adjusting the settings for your cross-section in order to have a guide for what you are doing. You can also change the color or opacity of the plane.

- **Intersection.** Select this check box to outline the areas of the object that have been affected by the cross-section. You can change the color of the outline by clicking the color box and selecting a new color.

- **Side A/Side B.** Click these icons to view either side of your cross-section.

- **Flip.** Click this icon to determine which half of the object to show. If we had checked this option when we created the cross-section for Figure 23.5, we would have seen the roof of the house instead of the floor.

FIGURE 23.6

Clicking the Cross Section check box starts you out by cutting your object exactly in half.

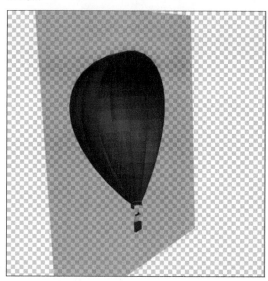

Changing the render properties

When you select the Filter by whole scene icon, the layers in the 3D panel are headed by a layer labeled *Scene*. With this layer selected, the render settings are active in the Properties panel (refer to Figure 23.4). You can adjust these settings to view your 3D scene at varying qualities and speed up your processing time. As with all the best options in Photoshop, a preset menu contains several options as well as the ability to customize the settings just the way you want them.

Using the render presets

Whenever you bring a 3D object into Photoshop or even create a new 3D object from the Photoshop presets, the render settings are already customized based on the settings that were specified previously for that object. Most of the time, these are higher-quality settings, giving you the best preview of the object but using a lot of computer resources. While you are positioning objects and creating scenes, you may not want to wait a long time to preview the finished object. Choosing a less-complicated render saves you time.

We wish we could tell you that the render presets were in order from the least to the most complicated, but the list is in alphabetical order, as shown in Figure 23.7. Most of the render settings are self-explanatory, and clicking each one gives you a preview. The simplest setting, Bounding Box, creates a bounding box framing your 3D object and turns off the visibility of the actual object. This is the fastest and easiest render, giving you maximum capability when it comes to movement. Other settings fall in the middle, rendering your object as a wireframe or shaded object. Figure 23.8 shows an example of three render settings.

> **NOTE**
>
> It goes without saying that the more powerful your computer is, the better you can work with 3D objects that have been rendered at higher settings. The render setting you use is based on your computer power as well as your personal preference for viewing your objects.

FIGURE 23.7

The render setting presets give you many options from simplistic to realistic.

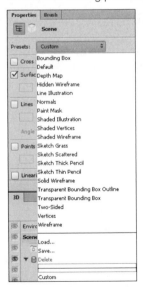

Editing the render settings

You can customize any of the render presets by using the other settings provided in the Properties panel. These options allow you to customize how your 3D objects are rendered so you can create the perfect balance between processing speed and best view.

FIGURE 23.8

The more complicated the render, the more time it takes to manipulate and edit it.

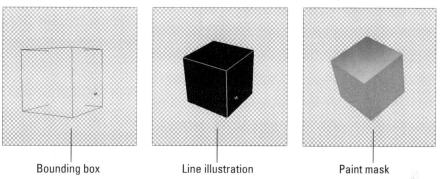

Bounding box   Line illustration   Paint mask

These options can be selected in conjunction with one another, depending on the settings you choose. For instance, you can choose an unlit texture for the surface and create a wireframe over it by selecting the Lines option. These are the main options available in the 3D Render Settings dialog box:

- **Surface.** These settings determine how the surfaces on your 3D model appear. You can choose from several face styles that include everything from the texture that has been placed on the model to a simple paint mask. If you choose Unlit Texture, you can use the texture option to change the way the texture looks. Other options are available with other face styles.

- **Lines.** These settings allow you to adjust the look of your object's edges. You can make them bolder or add more edges by increasing the crease threshold. A basic wireframe is one of the best options for viewing your object efficiently while manipulating it.

- **Points.** These options allow you to view and make changes to the way the vertices appear on your object. Vertices are the points made by the junctions of the polygons that make up the frame of the 3D model.

Changing the Current View

The last layer to appear exclusively in the Whole Scene view of the 3D panel is the Current View layer. This layer allows you to change the camera settings of your 3D scene, adjusting the angle at which you view your 3D scene and setting lens properties such as depth of field. You can also create a finished image that can be viewed in 3D with 3D glasses by changing the Stereo settings. To change your settings, click the Current View layer in the 3D panel to highlight it and then change the Properties panel to the Current View settings, as shown in Figure 23.9.

FIGURE 23.9

The properties of the Current View layer allow you to make changes to the camera settings.

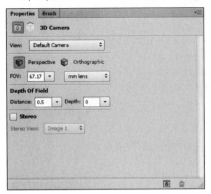

Setting the view

You can change the view of your 3D scene by changing the position of the 3D camera. To change the position of the camera in the 3D scene, click the View drop-down menu. You can choose to position the camera in one of several places such as the top or the back of the 3D scene. This immediately changes your view of the scene, and if a final render is made in this view, it renders in this view.

Changing the perspective

The next area of the Custom View properties allows you to change the perspective of the 3D object. Changing the perspective of your 3D object helps you to create composites by matching the perspective of your 3D object with either an image or the surrounding 3D scene. There are two types of perspective settings:

- **Perspective.** These settings allow you to change the perspective of the view so that it matches an image or other objects that you are using to make a composite. FOV stands for Field of View. You can change the field of view by degrees horizontal, degrees vertical, or by changing the size of the lens on your 3D camera. This allows you to change the view to match a photographic background that was shot with a specific lens.

- **Orthographic.** This view is just a fancy way of setting the scale of the 3D object in proportion to the surrounding 3D space. You can scale the view so that the object is larger or smaller within the scene.

Adjusting the depth of field

The Depth of Field options allow you to create blurriness in your 3D image based on the depth of field of the lens of your 3D camera. This setting allows you to blend a 3D object better with a photographic image taken at a particular depth of field.

Creating a stereo image

If you want to render your 3D object so it can be viewed with 3D glasses, choose the Stereo option and select a Stereo View setting. The options you have to choose from are Anaglyph, Lenticular, and Side by Side. The Anaglyph setting creates a 3D image that can be seen using the dual lens glasses, with red and green lenses, or red and blue lenses. The Lenticular setting creates an image that is composed of strips. Every other strip should be seen by the right eye, while the in-between strips should be viewed by the left eye. Glasses are not used for Lenticular 3D, the image or video is displayed on a corrugated screen. Side by Side 3D uses two images to create the illusion of 3D. Two images are displayed side by side, and an anamorphic viewer is used.

Working with Mesh Layers

The 3D mesh is the actual object — no textures, no lights, just the edges and vertices that make up the shape and form of the object. To make changes to the properties of a mesh, you must select the mesh layer in the 3D panel. Some objects have more than one mesh. If your 3D object has several meshes along with other layers, click the Filter by meshes icon at the top of the 3D panel to display only the mesh layers. This makes it easier to see and select the meshes you need to edit.

By selecting an individual mesh, you can manipulate it and edit its properties. When you select a mesh layer, the Properties panel displays the properties that you can adjust for the mesh, as shown in Figure 23.10.

FIGURE 23.10

You can change the properties of a mesh when you select the mesh layer in the 3D panel.

The sword shown in Figure 23.11 contains five meshes. These meshes include the blade, the grip, the guard, the ricasso, and the pommel.

FIGURE 23.11

This 3D sword contains five different meshes.

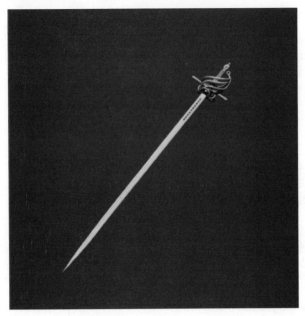

Each individual mesh has properties that can be changed. These properties have to do with the visibility of the mesh itself and the shadows it casts. To change these properties, select any one of these meshes from the 3D layers and change these settings:

- **Catch Shadows.** This option allows your object to catch shadows that are cast by other objects in your scene. In order for your object to catch shadows, you must place at least one light in your scene.

- **Cast Shadows.** This option allows your object to cast shadows. In order for your object to cast shadows, you must place at least one light in your scene.

- **Invisible.** This option turns off the visibility of the selected mesh, but leaves the shadows cast on the surface of the mesh behind.

- **Opacity.** This setting allows you to set the shadow opacity higher or lower to cast harder or softer shadows.

> **NOTE**
> You can rename a mesh, or any other 3D layer, by double-clicking its name.

You can move and manipulate individual meshes using the 3D tools that appear in the Options bar when you select both the mesh layer and the Move tool in the toolbox. To use these tools, hover over the mesh that you want to manipulate with the selected tool. A bounding box appears around the mesh, as shown in Figure 23.12. Click and drag to make changes to the mesh.

FIGURE 23.12

You can manipulate the sword's guard by hovering over it with the Rotate tool until the bounding box appears.

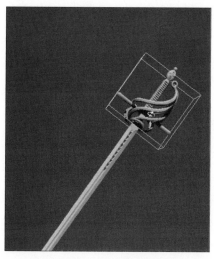

NOTE

When you select the Move tool, you can use the widget to manipulate meshes as well. You can also click the Coordinates button in the Properties panel to open the coordinates interface and type in precise coordinates for the mesh.

Editing the Textures and Materials of a 3D Object

You can apply several texture maps to each mesh associated with your object. These texture maps control the color, texture, and highlights of your object. Taken together, these textures constitute the material associated with a particular mesh. When you have several meshes in a 3D scene, you also have several materials associated with that scene. When you have a materials layer selected in the 3D panel, you work closely with the Layers panel to change the appearance of your object.

Figure 23.13 shows the 3D panel along with the Layers panel associated with the wine bottle that can be created from the 3D presets. You can see that three textures and three materials are associated with the bottle. This is deceptive, because you might think that having the same names, they are the same thing; however, we will take you through a couple of exercises to not only demonstrate the difference between them, but also show you how you can make changes to them.

FIGURE 23.13

The 3D panel lists the materials associated with your 3D object, and the Layers panel lists the textures.

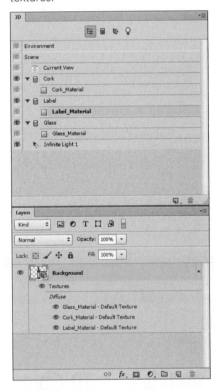

Editing textures

Textures are embedded layers in your 3D object. You can edit a texture by double-clicking the layer in the Layers panel. This opens the image file used to create the texture. You can then make changes to the image file and save it, and the changes are immediately reflected on your 3D object.

The label on the wine bottle created using the Wine Bottle preset is empty. You can make a custom label by following these steps:

1. **Create a new document in Photoshop.**

   We created an 11 x 8.5, landscape paper-sized document with a white background.

2. **Double-click the background layer to change it to a regular layer, and change the name of the layer to Label.**

> **NOTE**
>
> It isn't necessary to change the layer from a background layer to create a 3D object, but you want to change the name of this layer, so it must be changed to a regular layer.

3. **Use the 3D panel to create a new shape from a preset.**

   Choose Wine Bottle, and then click Create. The wine bottle shape appears, using the white background color for the label and leaving a transparent background, as shown in Figure 23.14. The white background used to create the label is now a sublayer in the 3D object named "Label."

FIGURE 23.14

Starting with a white background, we created a blank label on the wine bottle.

4. **Double-click the Label sublayer.**

   A new document opens in Photoshop. It looks just like the document you started with in Step 1.

5. **Place an image file, add text, create shapes, and paint to your heart's content.**

   Use all the tools in Photoshop to create a fabulous label. You can see ours in Figure 23.15.

FIGURE 23.15

You can create a label by double-clicking the Label texture layer and editing it.

6. **Press Ctrl+S/⌘+S to save your changes to the label and update your 3D file.**

   You can close the label file, or just click the tab of your 3D file to return to it. You see your new label wrapped around the bottle, as shown in Figure 23.16.

FIGURE 23.16

After you save your label, it is updated in your 3D document.

> **TIP**
>
> You probably want to leave the label file open long enough to make sure it looks the way you want it to. After all, it looks different on the bottle than it does as a flat document.

You can continue to make changes to the bottle and cork textures. When you open these files, you might be surprised to see that they are completely transparent; there is no color information at all. That's because their color and texture are being created in the Properties panel. We show you how in the next section.

Editing materials

Even with a nice label applied, the wine bottle is still a little flat and in need of work. Editing the materials to add color, texture, and dimension will make it look more realistic. The cork and bottle both get their color from the Material settings in the Properties panel. If you select the cork layer, the Properties panel displays the Material settings for that layer. You can see that Material settings are already applied to it. We could open the texture layer to apply a cork texture, but let's see if we can't make it look good by just using the Material settings.

Change the Material settings by following these steps:

1. **Select the Cork_Material layer from the 3D panel.**

   You see the Properties panel change to reflect the cork's Material settings, as shown in Figure 23.17.

FIGURE 23.17

You can edit the cork Material settings in the Properties panel.

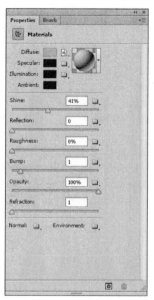

2. **Click the material picker to open it, as shown in Figure 23.18, and find thumbnails of available material presets.**

   Choose Wood Cork, and then click anywhere else in the screen to close the material picker. The settings all change to reflect the wood cork presets. The cork already looks 100-percent better!

FIGURE 23.18

A quick switch to the Wood Cork material makes a big difference in the way the cork looks.

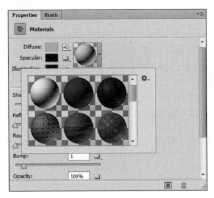

3. **Select the Glass_Material layer.**

   Again, the settings change. There is no preset in the material picker that meets your requirements here, so you have to create your own.

4. **Change the settings of the glass material.**

   You can change the following settings:

   - **Diffuse.** This is the heading that all the textures are placed under in the Layers panel. The diffuse texture is the primary color or texture of the selected material. The diffuse texture of the bottle is green, but the diffuse texture of the label is the one you created. You can click the Edit the Diffuse Texture icon next to the diffuse color and choose Open Texture to open the texture file, just as you did from the Layers panel, and edit it. In this case, you want to change the color of your bottle to a deeper green.

   - **Specular.** This setting determines the color of the specular highlights on your object. The specular highlights are the areas that are so reflective that they don't contain color information. These highlights are shown only in the color that you choose, not in any of the other colors placed in the materials of your object.

- **Illumination.** This setting allows you to create an inner glow. Click the color to change the color of the light. Black creates no illumination whatsoever, and white makes your object glow so brightly that it's transparent.

- **Ambient.** This setting sets the color of the ambient light. This isn't a dramatic change, but it can give your object a warmer or cooler look or slightly change the color.

- **Shine.** This setting determines how sharp the highlights are on the object. A shininess of 100 percent creates the sharp, clean highlights characteristic of glass. The shine can also be applied to specified areas using a grayscale map.

- **Reflection.** This setting determines the reflectivity of your object. The glass is highly reflective, so it is set by default to 100. You can also apply reflection maps to your object to make some areas more reflective than other areas.

- **Roughness.** This setting allows you to add roughness to your object to give it texture and to reduce the reflectivity. You can add a roughness map with this setting.

- **Bump.** This setting allows you to use grayscale values to create a bump map that simulates texture on your object. You don't want to add one of these to the glass material, but if you select the Cork_Material layer again and open the bump texture, you see the texture shown in Figure 23.19.

FIGURE 23.19

A bump map is also created by using a grayscale image.

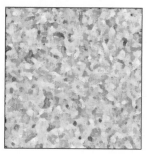

- **Opacity.** This setting changes the opacity of the material. You can set a universal opacity by using the slider, or you can load or create an opacity map. An opacity map uses grayscale values to determine the opacity of the materials. White creates 100-percent opacity and black is completely translucent, with different shades of gray being everything in between. By creating the opacity map shown in Figure 23.20, we changed the opacity of the top of the bottle, making it look a little more like translucent glass while giving it the appearance of only being partially full of liquid.

FIGURE 23.20

You can change the relative translucency of your object using an opacity map.

- **Refraction.** This setting changes the way light refracts through your scene. A setting of 1 approximates the refraction you get when light passes through air. You see a difference in this setting only in a final render.
- **Normal.** This setting uses a Normal map, which is a texture map that simulates texture just like the bump map, but it is much more versatile because it is based on the RGB values rather than just grayscale values.

- **Environment.** This setting uses an Environment map as a spherical panorama of the environment around the object. You don't actually see the Environment map around the object. Instead, you see a reflection of the environment in areas of your image that are reflective.

Creating and Modifying 3D Lights

The bottom filter in the 3D panel displays the light layers. When you select a light layer, the Properties panel displays the light settings, as shown in Figure 23.21. Whether you create a model in Photoshop or import a model from another source, Photoshop places a default infinite light in your scene. Without these lights, you can't see the details of your object; it appears very dark.

FIGURE 23.21

The Properties panel displays the properties of the selected light layer.

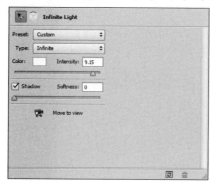

Besides the infinite lights, you can add two other types of light to your scene: point lights and spotlights. Each type of light is contained in its own group in the light layers. As you add additional lights, they appear under their particular light group. You can select a light to make changes to it or double-click it to change its name.

When you select a light layer, you can see that light in the document window placed in your 3D scene, as shown in Figure 23.22. Using the 3D tools, you can move and scale your light just as you can any 3D object contained in your scene.

FIGURE 23.22

When you have a light layer selected, the light is visible in your 3D scene.

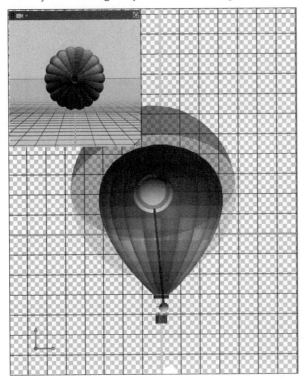

Adding new lights

Adding a new light is as simple as clicking the Add New Light to Scene icon at the bottom of the 3D panel. A drop-down menu opens, and you can choose the type of light you want to add. You can choose from the following types of light:

- **Point light.** This type radiates light in all directions from the light placement, creating the same effect, as a light bulb would have on the scene. Objects and surfaces that are closer to the light are brighter than those that are farther away. You can move a point light anywhere in your scene using the Light tools, but because it is useless to rotate it, that option is not available.

- **Spotlight.** This type of light can be pointed in a specific direction. The light emanates in a conical shape from the source, so the closer the object is to the light, the tighter and more concentrated the light is.

- **Infinite light.** This type radiates light uniformly from a single plane toward your 3D scene. They simulate the sun shining from a specific direction. Like the sun, infinite lights have a consistent intensity, so any surface that is hit directly by this light is lit with the same intensity, even if the surfaces are different distances from the light source. You can rotate infinite lights around your 3D scene.

Positioning lights

After you have created lights, you can manipulate and move them around your scene so you can create the lighting effects you want. You can position the lights using the 3D tools found in the Options bar when you select the Move tool in the Toolbox.

TIP

It is extremely important that you position your object the way you want it to look before you take too much time positioning your lights. When you move your object, your lights stay where they were placed, changing the light settings on the object. If you do want to view your object from a different angle without changing the light settings, use the Camera tool to change your view of the object. This creates the illusion of changing the position of the object as well as the lights.

You can also use the Properties panel to change the position of lights using the following settings:

- **Point Light at Origin.** Use this button to rotate the light in place so it is pointed directly at the center of your 3D scene.

- **Move to Current View.** Use this button to move the light to the exact position of the camera you are using to look at the scene, showing the source of the light and illuminating the face closest to you.

Changing the properties of a 3D light

With a light layer selected in the 3D panel, you can change the light setting in the Properties panel. These settings are available to you:

- **Preset.** This menu allows you to choose a lighting preset that imitates everything from the soft lights of dawn to the exciting, colored lights of Mardi Gras. You can also create your own light settings and add them to the presets using the Save Lights Preset option in the 3D panel menu.

- **Light type.** This option allows you to change a selected light from its current type to any other type of light. For instance, if you have an infinite light selected, you can change it to a spotlight using this option.

- **Color.** This option opens the Select Light Color dialog box when you click the color box. You can then choose any color you like for the color of your light. Obviously, changing the color of your light greatly affects the color of the materials applied to your object.

- **Intensity.** This option increases the intensity or brightness of the selected light. The default settings for newly created lights are fairly low. If you want to get a strong lighting effect, you can increase the intensity.

23

- **Shadow.** This option allows you to select a light that causes your objects to cast shadows in your 3D scene. If you have multiple lights applied to a scene, you may want only one or two to actually cast shadows so your scene is not busy with them.
- **Softness.** This option lets you choose how diffuse the shadow of a selected light is.

The following properties are available when using a spotlight only:

- **Hotspot.** This setting determines how intense the light of the spotlight is in the center.
- **Cone.** This setting determines the size of the light cone, creating a small, hot spotlight or a larger, more diffuse light.
- **Falloff.** This setting determines how fast the center of the spotlight fades to no light at all.
- **Inner and Outer.** These settings determine how much the intensity changes with distance.

Summary

This chapter covered most of the changes you can make to the look of your 3D object with the 3D settings. The 3D panel, combined with the Properties panel, is an incredibly versatile tool that allows you to make different kinds of changes to several aspects of your 3D scene, giving you a lot of creative potential in changing the look of your 3D scene. You learned about the following:

- Exploring the 3D panel
- Rendering 3D scenes
- Changing the meshes on 3D objects
- Editing and adding new materials to 3D objects
- Adding and changing the lights in a 3D scene

Using Photoshop Tools with 3D Layers

I n the last two chapters, you learned how the 3D workspace in Photoshop functions to allow you to create, manipulate, and change the look of 3D objects by changing their color, texture, and lighting. In this chapter, we show you how to integrate 3D objects into the Photoshop workspace, using the tools you are probably more familiar with to paint over your 3D objects and create adjustments, styles, and filters.

The last section of this chapter walks you through some very complex exercises that demonstrate some of the tools and techniques that you can use to create a successful composite with 3D objects and images. At this point, you should be familiar with all the techniques used to create these composites, but completing these exercises gives you practice using these tools and shows you how they can work together.

Using 3D Paint Mode

You can grab a paintbrush in Photoshop and start painting a 3D object. The paint conforms to the 3D object because even though you are looking at the 3D object, you are changing the texture file, which is wrapped around the 3D object. This gives you the distinct advantage of being able to change areas of the texture as it is mapped to your object, instead of trying to guess where to paint in a flat, rectangular texture file.

In addition to color, you can also paint texture, shine, opacity, and reflection onto a 3D object. This makes the 3D Paint tool a versatile way to change the materials of the 3D object.

Before we show you how to use the 3D Paint tools, we show you options for selecting areas of your object to paint on and hiding areas of your object that you want to protect. These options in Photoshop are definitely a little rough around the edges (literally as well as figuratively); still, they can be useful.

Hiding areas on a 3D object

You can create selections on a 3D object using the Selection tools just as you can with a two-dimensional image. The problem is that the selections you create are two-dimensional, and they won't conform to the 3D object. You can see in Figure 24.1 that, after creating a selection around the hat, we moved the hat, but the selection didn't move with it. You can use the Selection tools to make changes to a 3D object, but be sure that your object is placed just how you want it to be viewed, because the changes don't extend to unseen areas of your object.

FIGURE 24.1

The Selection tools are two-dimensional, and so rotating the object does not adjust the selection.

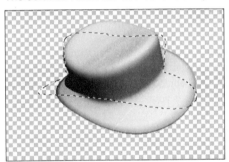

However, you can use the Selection tools to select paintable areas of your object or to hide areas that you want to protect. These tools are also affected by the fact that selections are two-dimensional. You can't simply select an area of your 3D object and hide it or paint onto it; you are limited by the way the two-dimensional selection interacts with the 3D object. This becomes apparent as you use the following tools to hide areas of your 3D object.

Use the Selection tools to select the area of your model that you want to hide, and select any one of these options from the 3D ⇨ Show/Hide Polygons menu bar:

- **Within Selection.** This option hides all the polygons that are enclosed within the selected area. Notice in Figure 24.2 that not all of the selected area disappears, only the complete polygons within the selected area.

- **Invert Visible Surfaces.** This option swaps the currently visible polygon areas with the areas that are hidden, so you can make changes to the opposite areas.

- **Reveal All Surfaces.** This option displays any areas that are hidden.

FIGURE 24.2

Within Selection protects hidden areas as well as revealing new ones inside the selection, whereas Invert Visible Surfaces reverses visibility to the opposite, outside of the selection.

Within Selection   Invert Visible   Reveal All

Painting on a 3D object

One of the most versatile tools in Photoshop is the paintbrush, which you can use to add color, erase pixels, and apply effects to images. Using the Brush tool, you can directly paint onto 3D object textures. So, are you ready to paint on your 3D object? Then grab a brush and let's start painting.

There are several additional options that you can choose from when using the Brush tool. These options allow you to use all of the functionality of the different brush tips to apply diffusion, specular color, roughness, reflectiveness, and many more aspects of the 3D textures. You can control and adjust each of these behaviors in the Materials section of the Properties panel when you select a 3D object in the 3D panel.

To select the 3D paint behavior, choose 3D ➪ Paint on Target Texture in the main menu bar and choose one of the following options:

NOTE

Photoshop requires a separate texture for each different effect that you want to paint on an object. For example, Photoshop requires a diffusion texture to paint diffusion on the object. If a texture of the type you are trying to paint does not exist in the 3D object, then Photoshop prompts you to add the texture.

24

- **Diffuse.** This option allows you to paint color onto the 3D object.
- **Specular.** This option allows you to paint on the color that is displayed as part of the specular textures, such as shine and reflectiveness. This can be especially useful if you are trying to add shadow effects to a highly reflective 3D object.
- **Illumination.** This option allows you to paint on lighting that doesn't require the background light object in the 3D scene.
- **Ambient.** This option allows you to paint on the color that is used for ambient light visible on reflective surfaces of the object. This color will interact with whatever global ambient color that is set for the entire scene.

- **Shine.** This option allows you to use the paintbrush to apply shine to the 3D object. This is a great feature for adding effects such as surfaces that are half painted or polished.

- **Reflection.** This option allows you to paint a reflectivity texture on the object. This is great for adding effects such as cars that are partially dirty, or dust on a mirror.

- **Roughness.** This option allows you to add roughness to the texture of a 3D object. The darker the paint color, the rougher the area. The airbrush tips work great with this option to add irregular texture to skin or rocks.

- **Bump.** This option allows you to add depressions and bumps to your 3D object. You can adjust the intensity of the bump painting in the Properties panel. The darker the paint on the bump texture, the deeper the depression in the 3D object surface.

- **Opacity.** This option allows you to use the paintbrush tools to apply opacity to the texture of the 3D object. If you think about all the things you can do with a paintbrush, you can get some really cool effects, especially if you are working with objects that have ambiguous surfaces such as clouds, smoke, or fire.

- **Refraction.** This option allows you to set the refractive index that is used when rendering the object. The refractive index defines the change in light direction as it moves between two different objects. For example when moving from air to water. The default value of 1.0 approximates air.

Painting color on a 3D object

In this example, we will take you through the process of painting on a 3D object to make it more realistic. The cello in Figure 24.3 has blank textures, so we want to liven it up by adding some color. You can use the following steps to add color to the body of the cello:

1. **Open the 3D panel to the material section and make sure the cello body is selected, as shown in Figure 24.3.**

2. **Choose 3D ⇨ Paint on Target Texture ⇨ Diffuse to paint on color.**

3. **Select a dark-brown color and a hard, round brush.**

4. **Drag the Brush tool over the cello to add color to it, as shown in Figure 24.4.**

   As you drag your brush, the color is restricted to the cello body because that is the material you have selected in the 3D panel. That gives you the freedom to make big, bold strokes that completely fill the cello with paint. You could just as easily use the Paint Bucket tool to drop the color onto the body of the cello.

> **NOTE**
>
> Three-dimensional objects created in Photoshop often tile the texture. You can see this when you paint on a section; the paint appears in several areas of the object. Hiding those areas doesn't stop the paint from being applied to them, because the paint is actually applied to the image file that is being used as the object's texture.

FIGURE 24.3

With the cello body selected in the Materials section of the Properties panel, it is the material affected by our painting.

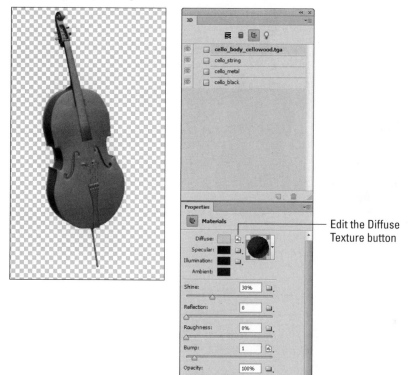

Edit the Diffuse Texture button

24

The brown is much better than the white, but it still doesn't look much like the texture of the wood that you would see on a real cello. You can add wood grain to the surface to make it more realistic using the following steps:

1. **Choose a bristly, angled brush to create some wood grain on the surface of the cello.**

2. **Select a darker brown color to create a deeper wood grain.**

3. **Paint strokes down the vertical axis of the cello body.**

   This time, you have to be much more careful with your paintbrush, creating straight, clean strokes that don't overlap. The finished effect looks more like wood, as you can see in Figure 24.5.

FIGURE 24.4

You can paint color onto the cello using the paintbrush in Photoshop.

FIGURE 24.5

Adding a second layer of paint makes the cello look more realistic.

You can open the texture file by clicking the cello body layer in the Layers panel or by selecting the Edit the Diffuse Texture button in the Materials section of the Properties panel (refer to Figure 24.3) and choosing Edit Texture. You can see in Figure 24.6 what the new texture looks like after our paint job. Oops! Forgot to paint the back!

FIGURE 24.6

Whoops! We missed some of the surfaces of the cello.

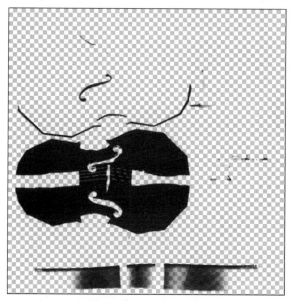

Painting textures on a 3D object

Now we show you how to take painting a 3D object beyond color. From the 3D menu, you can choose any one of the different textures to paint on. Follow these steps to see how it's done:

1. **Create a 3D shape from a layer in Photoshop.**

   The sphere is a good shape for this exercise because the texture isn't tiled, and the changes you make to it are not duplicated in other areas of the sphere. Figure 24.7 shows the basic sphere.

2. **Choose 3D ➪ Paint on Target Texture ➪ Bump.**

   Now as you paint directly onto your object, you make changes to a bump map.

 To learn more about the different types of texture you can apply to your 3D object and how to edit the texture files, see Chapter 23.

FIGURE 24.7

The sphere uses the texture map only once around it, so your changes appear only in the area that you make them.

3. **Open the material section of the 3D panel and select the sphere material.**

4. **Open the Materials section of the Properties panel, and click the Edit the Bump Texture icon next to the bump setting.**

   From the drop-down menu, select New Texture, as shown in Figure 24.8.

5. **Choose the brush that suits your needs, and drag over your 3D object.**

   The paint is applied to the bump map, which adds depth rather than color to your object, as you can see in Figure 24.9.

You can quickly see the merits of being able to paint directly on your object in this manner. Placing your brush strokes exactly where they need to be on the texture to get the effect you want is incredibly easy. You can continue to make changes to the different textures of your object in this manner, simply by choosing the texture you want to change in the 3D menu.

> **NOTE**
>
> If the texture you choose to paint on (glossiness, opacity, and so on) has not already been applied to your object, you can either create a new texture in the material section of the 3D panel as we had you do with the bump texture, or simply drag your brush over your object. After you've tried to paint into a texture that doesn't exist, Photoshop creates that texture for you.

FIGURE 24.8

Create a new bump texture to paint to.

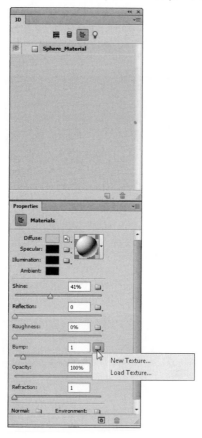

FIGURE 24.9

Painting on the bump map changes the extrusion of the object.

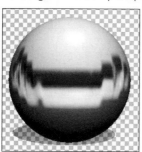

Adjustments, Layer Styles, and Filters

You can also change the look of a 3D object the same way you can change the look of any image — using adjustments, layer styles, and filters over the entire object. Especially when you use 3D objects in composites, you'll want to use these tools to create just the right look. This isn't as straightforward as working with an image file, so we show you how it works.

NOTE

You should not confuse using adjustments, layer styles, and filters on a 3D file with using these tools on a texture map. The texture maps attached to a 3D file are image files and can be adjusted in the time-honored method that is always used to adjust image files in Photoshop. This section focuses on applying these tools to a 3D layer.

Applying an adjustment to a 3D layer

You can apply an adjustment to a 3D layer in much the same way as you would apply it to an image file and for much the same reason. Often, as you adjust the light and color of the diffuse texture, you find that after it has been applied to a 3D object, it looks much different than it did as an image. It's much darker, for one thing. Applying an adjustment that changes the look of the light or color directly to the 3D object is often the solution to getting just the look you want without having to go back and forth between the 3D file and the texture file, trying to adjust the light and color.

TIP

If you are making adjustments to just your 3D object layer, be sure to clip the adjustment layer to your 3D object layer using the Clip to layer icon at the bottom of the Properties panel. This ensures that the adjustments are applied only to your 3D layer and not any other layers in your document.

 Learn more about adjustments and adjustment layers in Chapters 10 and 13.

Of course, these changes are made unilaterally to your 3D object, unlike the more subtle changes that you can make by adding and changing lights or making changes to individual texture maps. Another caveat to adding adjustments to a 3D layer is that you must add the adjustments through an adjustment layer. The adjustments in the Image menu are not available for a 3D object. If you want to add these adjustments, you must do one of two things:

- Rasterize your 3D layer by choosing either Layer ➪ Rasterize ➪ 3D or Layer ➪ Flatten Image from the Photoshop main menu bar.
- Turn your 3D layer into a Smart Object layer by choosing Convert to Smart Object from the Layers panel menu. We discuss 3D layers as Smart Objects later in this chapter.

Adding a layer style to a 3D layer

Applying a layer style to a 3D object is a wonderful way to add an effect that can't be achieved using the 3D textures. It is easy to add elements such as an inner glow, drop shadow, and stroke outline to your 3D object and spice up the way it looks. The best thing about using layer styles on a 3D object is that the style is reapplied each time you move your object, so creating a stroke around the cone in Figure 24.10 didn't leave behind a cone-shaped outline when we changed the angle of the cone. This is true for all the layer styles.

FIGURE 24.10

Layer styles are instantly reapplied every time you manipulate your 3D object.

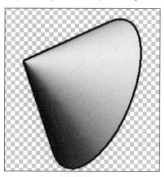

The layer styles are added as effects sublayers right along with the textures, as shown in Figure 24.11. You can change the settings of the styles that are applied by double-clicking any of the Effects layers to open the Layer Styles dialog box.

FIGURE 24.11

Layer styles appear as sublayers of your 3D object layer.

24

 The layer styles are covered in Chapter 10.

Applying a filter to a 3D layer

Applying a filter to a 3D layer is a trickier than adding an adjustment or layer style. You might want to add a filter directly to a 3D layer instead of adding it to the texture for the same reason that you would apply an adjustment directly to the 3D layer. The effects of a filter look different after the texture has been wrapped around your 3D object, and you can preview the filter in real time if you add it directly to your 3D object.

Furthermore, if your texture is tiled onto your 3D object, adding a filter to the texture makes the tiling apparent. When you add the filter directly to your object, it doesn't matter how you apply the texture; the filter is applied uniformly to the entire object.

You can add a filter directly to a 3D object, but it affects only the visible surfaces. If you move your 3D object after applying a filter, you see the filter's effects end, as shown in Figure 24.12.

FIGURE 24.12

We applied the Watercolor filter to the sphere and then rotated it a little. You can see the watercolor effect come to an abrupt stop.

Rotated to the left

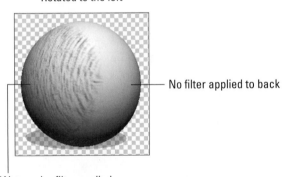

No filter applied to back

Watercolor filter applied

The best way to add a filter to a 3D object is to change it to a Smart Object. That shouldn't surprise you, because turning your layers into Smart Objects is the best way to add filters to them, no matter what type of layers they are. After you've turned your 3D layer into a Smart Object layer, you can add filters to it just as you would a Smart Object layer created from an image or any other kind of layer. These filters still affect only the visible surface, but when you open a Smart 3D Object and move it, the filter is reapplied to the new visible surfaces.

You can learn all about filters and Smart Filters in Chapter 20.

Using 3D layers as Smart Objects

To create a Smart Object from a 3D layer, right-click it and choose Convert to Smart Object from the menu. This converts the 3D layer into a Smart Object and changes the icon on the thumbnail from the 3D layer icon to a Smart Object icon, as shown in Figure 24.13. Now you have texture and effect files embedded inside a 3D object layer, which is embedded inside a Smart Object! It sounds complicated, but it allows you versatility in the changes that can be made (and then changed) to your 3D object.

FIGURE 24.13

When you create a Smart Object from a 3D layer, the icon on the thumbnail changes.

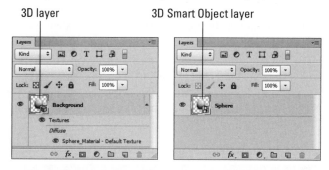

After you've turned your 3D layer into a Smart Object layer, you can apply Smart Filters that show up as (yes, another set of) sublayers. You can also add adjustments directly to your object and use the transformations found in the Edit menu, including the Puppet Warp.

A Smart Object layer gives you the best of both worlds. You can still make changes to your 3D scene by using the 3D Transformation tools to manipulate it, adding lights and textures, and doing anything else you want to do. Simply double-click the Smart Object layer, and your 3D layer opens as a separate file that you can change. These changes are immediately updated to the main file, even before you save your 3D layer file (save it before you close it, of course).

You can also open the texture files from the 3D layer file, just as you always could. The changes you make to these files are also updated in both the 3D layer file and the Smart Object file.

Now that you understand how to work with 3D objects as 3D layers and as Smart Objects, you are ready to use these versatile files to create fantastic composites.

24

Creating Composites

Now that you've gone over the basics, you can get started with the fun stuff! You are familiar with the tools that help you create fantastic images in Photoshop. Until now, we have showed you the basics of working with 3D objects. Now we take you through some exercises that put several of these techniques together to create composites using images and 3D objects. This gives you a chance to walk through a few examples before you venture out on your own. These examples are step-intensive, but they include several different techniques so you can see how those techniques work together. When you're finished, you'll have a better understanding of the fantastic things that you can do with a 3D model in Photoshop.

Flying a carpet over a lake

The following example shows you how to create a flying carpet over a lake. Because several different exercises go into creating this composite, we take you through them one at a time, with each exercise building on the last one so you can do them in more manageable parts. These exercise will help you understand how to use 3D objects and tools to add visual effects to a 2D image.

Creating a 3D rug

The first exercise is to create a 3D rug. You do this using the 3D extrusion feature. The following steps take you through the process of creating a 3D rug from the extrusion of a simple vector rectangle path:

1. **Create a new blank document in Photoshop.**

> **TIP**
>
> You'll find out quickly that working with 3D objects in Photoshop is a memory-intensive process. Because these objects are vector files and can be resized without losing quality, it's best to start with a small file. Smaller files save you time and ultimately frustration. Remember, however, that the textures applied to these files are raster files. You may want to create larger textures, even when the actual 3D file is small.

2. **Use the Pen tool to draw a rectangle in your document, as shown in Figure 24.14.**

   Press and hold down the Shift key while you are drawing so the lines are perfectly straight. After closing the rectangle, use the Direct Selection tool to make the last line of your rectangle straight, if needed.

3. **Choose 3D ➪ 3D Extrusion from Selected Path to convert the rectangle to a 3D object.**

4. **Select the Shape layer in the 3D panel.**

5. **Click the Mesh button in the Properties panel and change the depth to 0, as shown in Figure 24.15.**

FIGURE 24.14

Draw a rectangle to create a 3D rug using 3D extrusion.

6. **Click the Cap button in the Properties panel and create a bevel that gives the rug a nice edge, as shown in Figure 24.15.**

The numbers you use to create this edge will vary, depending on the size of your rug.

FIGURE 24.15

The 3D extrusion option gives depth and adds a bevel to your rectangle.

24

7. **Double-click the texture diffusion layer.**

   Because you created a bevel, you have two layers; choose the one that is *not* labeled "Extrusion." This opens the rug's texture for you to edit.

8. **Use the Paint Bucket tool to fill the texture with color.**

   We used a deep maroon, but it's your rug, so be creative!

9. **Click the Layer Styles icon (*fx*) at the bottom of the Layers panel.**

10. **From the Layer Styles menu, choose Pattern Overlay.**

    This opens the Layer Styles dialog box.

11. **Click the down arrow next to the pattern thumbnail to open the pattern selector.**

    Choose a pattern for your rug. We used the metal landscape. Don't forget to click the little black arrow in the pattern selector to open the pattern menu, where you can find additional pattern presets. The metal landscape pattern is found in the pattern presets.

12. **Change the opacity and scale of the pattern so your rug looks good.**

    These settings depend on the size and color of your rug.

13. **Try different blend modes until you find one that you like.**

    We chose Multiply. Click OK to close the Layer Style dialog box, shown in Figure 24.16.

14. **Save the texture document and return to the 3D model of the rug using the tab in the document window in Photoshop.**

    Leaving the texture document open enables you to quickly return to it to make changes if you find that you don't like the way the 3D object looks.

FIGURE 24.16

Adding color and a pattern makes the texture look more like a rug.

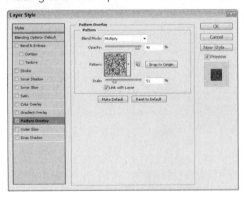

15. **Rotate and roll your rug until it sits at an angle as if it's coming in for a landing, as shown in Figure 24.17.**

16. **Save your rug file and close it.**

FIGURE 24.17

The rug is stiff as a board, but it is angled for a landing.

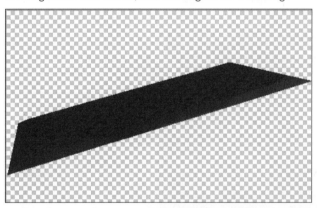

Placing the flying carpet into an image

Now that you are able to create 3D objects using the extrusion functionality in Photoshop, you are ready to start placing them into other images to enhance scenes. Follow these steps to create a flying carpet that any kid would want to ride on:

1. **Open Figure 24-18 from the website, as shown in Figure 24.18.**

   This photo works great for what you want to do because it has a large surface to work in.

2. **Choose File ⇨ Place.**

FIGURE 24.18

This tranquil scene is about to be livened up.

3. **Browse to the rug file you created in the last exercise, and click OK.**

4. **Place the rug in your image file, and scale it to fit the image.**

5. **Click the check mark in the Options bar to accept the placement.**

6. **If you need to make adjustments to the 3D file, such as changing the angle of the rug, double-click the Smart Object thumbnail in the Rug layer to open the 3D file and make those changes.**

Save the changes, and return to the image document. We changed the angle of the rug, as shown in Figure 24.19.

7. **With the Rug layer highlighted, choose Edit⇨Puppet Warp.**

FIGURE 24.19

It would be great if every 3D object that you placed looked just right, but it's easy to change it by opening the original file.

8. **Placing pins and using the mesh, change the rug to look more like a soft fabric, as shown in Figure 24.20.**

Give it wrinkles, and make it look like it's traveling through the air. This is a fun step, so play around and give your rug personality!

9. **Click the check mark in the Options bar to accept the changes.**

> **NOTE**
> Notice that the Puppet Warp is added as a Smart Filter? That means that you can return and edit it whenever you want.

24

FIGURE 24.20

The Puppet Warp tool is a great way to give your rug the illusion of motion as well as personality.

Adding details to complete the flying carpet composite

It's all about the details, isn't it? Especially in Photoshop, the details can make an okay image look like a great composite. You can add details to the image to give it that final touch. The following steps take you through the process of adding lights and shadows to enhance the realism of 3D objects:

1. **Double-click the Smart Object thumbnail in the rug layer to open the 3D object.**

2. **From the Lights section of the 3D panel, click the Add New Light icon and select Spot Light to add a spotlight to the rug scene.**

   Angle it so that it lights the rug from the same direction where the sun is shining in the photo.

3. **Save the changes, and exit the 3D file.**

4. **With the Rug layer highlighted, click the Layer Styles icon in the bottom of the Layers panel and choose Drop Shadow.**

5. **Set the spread and size depending on the brightness of your background image.**

   The bright image used in this exercise creates hard shadows, so set the spread and size to a smaller value. Hard sunlight makes hard shadows.

6. **Click OK to exit the Layer Styles dialog box.**

7. **Right-click the Drop Shadow sublayer, and choose Create Layer.**

   Click OK when you see the following warning: "Some aspects of the Effects cannot be reproduced with Layers!"

8. **Highlight the Drop Shadow layer.**

9. **Inside the image, use the Move tool to drag the shadow below the rug to rest on the lake.**

10. **Reduce the opacity of the shadow layer to match the opacity of other shadows in the image.**

    Your final result should be similar to Figure 24.21.

TIP

Depending on the angle of sunlight in your image, you may want to rotate, scale, or even warp the shadow to make it look more realistic. With the Drop Shadow layer selected, choose Edit ⇨ Transform.

11. **With the Rug layer highlighted, click the Layer Styles icon in the bottom of the Layers panel and choose Stroke.**

12. **Set the size, position, blending mode, and opacity to create a solid border that outlines the rug.**

13. **Click OK to exit the Layer Style dialog box.**

FIGURE 24.21

Light and shadow give the rug a realistic dimension in this image.

The steps you took to create a flying carpet follow a precise order. It's important to transform the rug by turning and warping it before creating the drop shadow. After the drop shadow has been separated into its own layer, it no longer mimics the changes made to the rug. In fact, you can make changes to the Drop Shadow layer separately.

These effects are just a sampling of several things that you can do. Play around with your file, and see if you can add even more realism to it. As with anything else you do, balancing the amount of time you spend with the effect you create is the key to being efficient.

Look at the Layers panel shown in Figure 24.22. You've created quite an array of layers. They are well organized and easy to understand, especially after you create them yourself. Take a moment to edit them or reorganize them if you are still not fully familiar with how they work.

FIGURE 24.22

The Layers panel shows a neat array of effects.

Giving the moon away

Now let us show you an example that uses different techniques. In this exercise, you create cross-sections and place more than one instance of an object in a file. You also place a second 3D object in the same file. You can make a present of the moon by following the steps in the following sections.

Creating a gift box

A great feature of Photoshop is its ability to modify and manipulate 3D objects. A great way to do this is by creating a cross-section and dividing the object. The following steps take you through the process of starting with a simple 3D box, cutting it in half to make a separate lid, and then adding an image texture to give the box a wrapped effect:

1. **Open Figure 24-23 from the website.**

   This is a PSD file of a 3D box with a lid, as shown in Figure 24.23.

FIGURE 24.23

Start with a 3D image of a box with a lid.

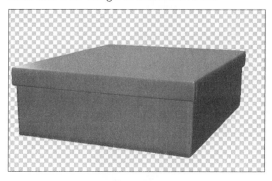

2. **Open the 3D panel to the Scene section, and select the Scene.**

3. **Change the following settings in the Properties panel: check Cross Section, click Flip Cross Section, uncheck Intersection, set the offset to +12, and click Z-axis.**

   You are left with the lid of the box.

4. **Rename the layer *Lid* by right-clicking the layer and selecting Layer Properties.**

5. **Choose File ⇨ Place, browse to Figure 24.23, and click Place.**

6. **Click the check mark to accept placement.**

7. **Double-click the thumbnail in the Figure 24-23 layer.**

   When you are reminded to save, click OK.

8. **Open the 3D panel to the Scene section.**

9. **Change the following settings: check Cross Section, uncheck Intersections, click Z-axis, and set the offset to 11.**

   You are left with the bottom of the box, minus the lid.

10. **Use the 3D Manipulation tools to place the bottom of the box so you can see into it.**

11. **Save the changes, and exit the file.**

12. **Rename the Figure 24-23 layer *Box* by right-clicking the layer and choosing Layer Properties.**

24

13. **Use the 3D Manipulation tools to tilt the lid so it looks like it is being opened, as shown in Figure 24.24.**

FIGURE 24.24

You can open the box by creating cross-sections of both halves.

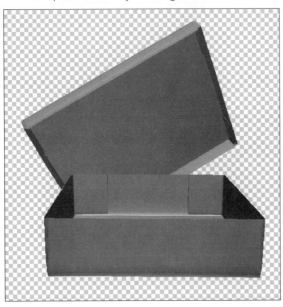

14. **Double-click Diffuse in the lid texture in the Layers panel of the Lid layer to open the texture.**

15. **Choose File ⇨ Place, browse to Figure 24-25 (downloaded from the website), and click OK.**

    This file is a pattern created from an image of a nebula, as shown in Figure 24.25.

16. **Stretch the pattern to fill the texture of the box.**

17. **Click the check mark in the Options bar to accept the placement of the pattern.**

18. **Save the changes to the texture, and close the texture file.**

    The lid of the box now has a new texture.

19. **Double-click the thumbnail in the Box layer.**

    When you are reminded to save, click OK.

20. **Double-click Diffuse in the box texture of the Box layer in the Layers panel to open the texture.**

FIGURE 24.25

This image was created using the Pattern Maker, a plug-in filter available from Adobe.

21. **Repeat Steps 16 to 20 to add the texture to the main part of the box.**

22. **Save this file, and close it.**

In these steps, you used the Cross Section tool to create and place the same 3D object in a file twice, and you added texture to both parts of that object. Your result should be similar to Figure 24.26. Now you are ready to create the moon.

FIGURE 24.26

The box is complete.

24

Creating the moon

In this section we take you through the process of applying a mapped image to a sphere to create a 3D moon object. Then we take you through the process of adding lighting to give it a realistic effect. Use the following steps to create a 3D sphere object that closely resembles the moon:

1. **Browse to Figure 24-27, and open it.**
2. **Double-click the Figure 24-27 layer, and rename the layer _Moon_.**

   This converts the background layer to a regular layer and gives it a descriptive name.
3. **Use the 3D Shape Preset in the 3D panel to create a sphere from the layer.**

   You see a representation of the moon, as shown in Figure 24.27.

FIGURE 24.27

Creating a sphere from the texture map of the moon

4. **Open the 3D panel to the Lights section.**
5. **From the Light Preset drop-down menu in the Properties panel, select Blue Lights.**
6. **Click the Layer Styles icon (_fx_) in the Layers panel, and choose Inner Glow.**
7. **Adjust the settings to give the moon a nice glow.**

   You can see our settings in Figure 24.28.

FIGURE 24.28

The moon isn't the moon without a glow. Use the layer styles to create one.

8. **In the Layer Styles dialog box, select Outer Glow.**

9. **Adjust the settings to give the moon a nice outer glow.**

10. **Click OK to exit the Layer Styles dialog box.**

11. **Save your file.**

Making a present of the moon

Now that you've created two 3D object files, let's add them to an image file to make a complete composite. Follow these steps to create a composite that gives the moon away as a gift:

ON THE WEB

Find the image used in this composite saved on the book's website as Figure 24-29.

1. **Browse to Figure 24-29, and open it.**

2. **Choose File ⇨ Place, browse to the 3D file of the box you created earlier, and click OK.**

3. **Position and size the box in the file however you'd like, and click the check mark to accept placement.**

Our results looked like Figure 24.29.

FIGURE 24.29

The box needs a mask to make it work inside this photo.

4. **Note the areas that need to be masked, and then hide the box by clicking the eye icon.**

5. **Using the Selection tool of your choice, select the areas that need to be masked, as shown in Figure 24.30.**

6. **Choose Select ➪ Inverse.**

FIGURE 24.30

Creating a selection of the areas that need to be masked

> **TIP**
>
> We created a jagged selection along the edge of the box as well as a selection around the face to take away the sharp edge that should have been sunk slightly into the carpet.

> **NOTE**
>
> You can, of course, select the areas that you want to be shown rather than the areas to be masked. Then there is no need to invert the selection.

7. **Click Refine Edge in the Options bar.**

8. **Adjust the settings to refine the edge of your selection.**

9. **Choose Output to Layer Mask and click OK to close the Refine Edge dialog box.**

10. **Drag the mask from the Image layer to the Box layer.**

11. **Click the eye icon to restore the Box layer to view.**

    Your box is masked into the photo.

12. **Choose File ⇨ Place, browse to the file of the moon, and click OK.**

13. **Size the moon to fit in the box, and click the check mark to accept placement.**

14. **Drag the Moon layer to the top of the Layers panel, placing it on top of the box.**

15. **Set the moon inside the box.**

16. **With the Moon layer highlighted, click the Rectangular Marquee Selection tool and create a selection that includes everything in the Moon layer that is above the box, as shown in Figure 24.31.**

FIGURE 24.31

Create a selection to mask the moon into the box

24

17. **Click the Mask icon in the Layers panel to create a mask from the selection.**

    The moon is placed into the box. Your finished product should look like Figure 24.32.

FIGURE 24.32

A realistic composite created with an image, 3D objects, and cool Photoshop tools

You can see that even the most rudimentary 3D objects can become very interesting by using Photoshop tools to enhance them. Just imagine what you can do with more elaborate 3D models.

ON THE WEB

If you would like to see the final PSD file used to create Figure 24.32, you can find it on the book's website as Figure 24-32.

Summary

In this chapter, you learned some of the advanced techniques for working with 3D objects, how to use the Photoshop tools to change them, and how to successfully add them to composite images. You learned how to do the following:

- Use the 3D paint tools to paint textures directly onto a 3D object
- Use adjustment layers, layer styles, and filters on a 3D object
- Create composites using images and 3D objects

Part VIII

Working with Video and Animation

Understanding Video Editing Basics

W hen working with video, Photoshop enables you to bring in pieces of video that need the special Photoshop touch and clean them up a bit. Photoshop does not enable you to create an extensive video project like Adobe Premiere Pro. With Photoshop, you can create fantastic composites with video files that you may not be able to accomplish in fine Photoshop style anywhere else. The Timeline panel gives you just enough capability to make working with video files an efficient and relatively uncomplicated process.

The first step in being able to edit your video files in Photoshop is to understand the video workspace. The Timeline panel is practically an application all by itself, giving you the ability to add, edit, and move video clips not only as layers but also through time. You can also add other layers, such as image files, text, and 3D objects. In this chapter, we show you how you can open, add, and maneuver these files within a video timeline so you are prepared to correct lighting and color and create artistic effects with video files and image files.

Working with Video Files

To work with video successfully, you need to know the basics of video file formats, why they are different, and how they work. Some file formats are of higher quality and, consequently, larger than those of lower quality. You must also understand aspect ratios. Photoshop has more possibilities for changing the aspect ratio than you might think. Using the right aspect ratio and understanding the settings are important to creating successful video files within Photoshop.

 Review the basics of video file formats in Chapter 3.

Setting aspect ratios

An aspect ratio is the relative width to height of a video or image. The frame aspect ratio indicates the ratio of the video or image frame. You are probably familiar with the 4:3 and 16:9 aspect ratios that are industry-standard television sizes. The next step in getting to know all about pixels is understanding the pixel aspect ratio.

Correcting the pixel aspect ratio

Individual pixels also have aspect ratios. Depending on the video standard, pixels have either a square aspect ratio or a rectangular aspect ratio. A computer monitor, for instance, is usually set up for square pixels. For example, a 4:3 monitor typically has a setting of 640 pixels wide and 480 pixels tall, which results in square pixels.

Televisions do not have square pixels. Their pixels match the aspect ratio of standard video, which is rectangular. That means that when you play a movie on your computer that is a standard video format, the video is distorted unless the pixel aspect ratio is taken into account and adjusted.

When you import a video file into Photoshop, it automatically performs a pixel aspect ratio correction on the document, so it appears just as it would on a television screen. This reduces the preview quality of the document, but it is only for preview purposes and doesn't change the document materially in any way, as shown in Figure 25.1.

You can turn off Pixel Aspect Ratio Correction and preview the video with all the pixels intact. The image looks distorted, but it actually contains the correct number of pixels. Simply choose View ⇨ Pixel Aspect Ratio Correction to toggle the correction on or off. Figure 25.2 shows an image with this feature turned off.

> **NOTE**
> You can view both pixel settings at once by choosing Window ⇨ Arrange ⇨ New Window for *(document name)*. This opens a second window containing your document. You can correct the pixel aspect ratio in one and leave the correction off in the other.

FIGURE 25.1

When Pixel Aspect Ratio Correction is turned on, the image looks normal.

FIGURE 25.2

This is like watching regular 4:3 television on a 16:9 television.

Changing video aspect ratios

Aspect ratios such as 4:3 and 16:9 are industry standard. You are probably less familiar with pixel aspect ratios, which is what Photoshop uses. The Photoshop preset aspect ratios enable you to translate pixel aspect ratios into more familiar terms. The number listed in parentheses

25

is the relative height of the pixel to a width of 1. For example, D1/DV NTSC (0.9) has a pixel aspect ratio of 1 pixel wide and .9 pixels high, making it slightly wider than it is high.

Here's a list of the pixel aspect ratios:

- **Square.** Most computer monitors have square pixels. Some video made for a 4:3 screen ratio is also captured at 640 x 480, making the pixels square.
- **D1/DV NTSC (0.91).** This is a standard capture ratio for pixels, with a pixel ratio of 720 x 480. Standard 4:3 televisions and video cameras both probably have this setting. Figure 25.3 shows an example of this aspect ratio.

FIGURE 25.3

A pixel ratio of 1:0.9 creates nearly square pixels and is just right for a 4:3 frame.

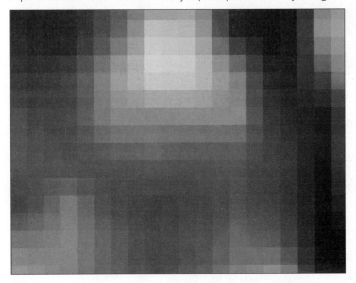

- **D1/DV PAL (1.09).** The PAL pixel ratios create a pixel that is taller than it is wide. This is the standard pixel aspect ratio used for 4:3 screens. PAL is the video format used in most countries outside North America.
- **D1/DV NTSC Widescreen (1.21).** This is the common pixel aspect ratio for an NTSC 16:9 screen. Most video cameras also shoot in this aspect ratio.
- **HDV 1080/DVCPRO HD 720 (1.33).** This is the standard pixel aspect ratio for big-screen movies and is becoming more popular with higher-quality video cameras. The frame size is 1440 x 1080 pixels for the highest-quality setting. The screen size used for this pixel aspect ratio is 16:9.

- **D1/DV PAL Widescreen (1.46).** This is the common pixel aspect ratio for PAL 16:9 screen.

- **Anamorphic 2.1 (2).** This pixel ratio — obviously more rectangular than the others — should be used only if your footage was shot with an anamorphic lens. An anamorphic lens creates wide pixels that condense to be shown at 4:3 or 16:9 aspect ratios.

- **DVCPRO HD 1080 (1.5).** This pixel ratio is used in a video ratio of 16:9. It has a high-quality pixel level with a 1280 x 1080-frame size. Figure 25.4 shows an example of this aspect ratio.

FIGURE 25.4

A pixel ratio of 1:1.5 creates rectangular pixels.

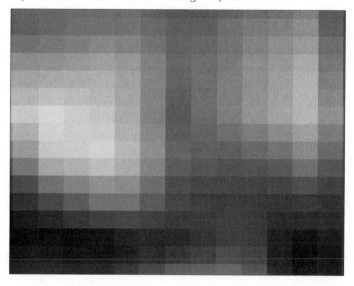

You can create a custom pixel aspect ratio by choosing View ➪ Pixel Aspect Ratio ➪ Custom Pixel Aspect Ratio. This opens a dialog box that allows you to name your custom ratio and set the height of the pixel (with the width equal to 1). Remember that you are setting only the preview ratio, however, so no matter what you see, your video plays back on a television at its normal aspect ratio. Figure 25.5 shows an example of an unusual aspect ratio.

It is important to understand pixel aspect ratio, but if you are wondering whether you are in over your head, don't worry too much. When you open a video file, the pixel aspect ratio is automatically set to the aspect ratio at which the video footage was shot. As long as you are editing just one aspect ratio, you should be okay. When it comes to adding an image to your video footage, however, you may want to correct its aspect ratio to match that of the video.

25

FIGURE 25.5

Although this video looks compressed in Photoshop, this is just a preview setting, so it plays back normally on a 4:3 television.

Correcting the aspect ratio of an image

You can add as many images to a video file as you want. The video file can even be set to the correct aspect ratio. When you place an image that doesn't fit the aspect ratio, any part of the image that doesn't fill the frame of the video is transparent, as shown in Figure 25.6.

FIGURE 25.6

A tall image set in a 4:3 aspect ratio shows transparency in the areas that the image doesn't cover.

You can solve this problem in one of two ways: you can create a background for all the images that are placed in the video, or you can create a background for each image. Either way, you need to create an image document that is the right pixel aspect ratio.

You can create a document in Photoshop with the correct pixel aspect ratio for your video file by following these steps:

1. **Choose File ⇨ New to open the New dialog box.**

2. **From the Preset drop-down menu, choose Film & Video.**

   This creates several presets for your document and gives you several more menu options, as shown in Figure 25.7.

FIGURE 25.7

The Film & Video preset in the New dialog box allows you to set the aspect ratio and resolution of your video file.

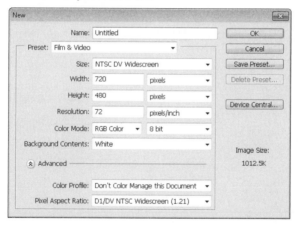

3. **Choose the size of your video footage from the Size drop-down menu.**

4. **From the Pixel Aspect Ratio drop-down menu, choose the pixel aspect ratio you want for your footage.**

5. **Click OK.**

The default settings created by the Film & Video preset are standard for most video files. If you want to create an HD video, you can change the number of pixels and the resolution to a higher quality, of course. You can also change the color settings and background contents, among other things. The important thing is to create a document that's the same size and pixel resolution as the video you are trying to create.

25

After you click OK to create the new document, you are reminded that Photoshop has just turned on the Pixel Aspect Ratio Correction for this document because it assumes that the document will eventually be part of a rendered video file.

The document created with the Film & Video presets looks different from the usual Photoshop document. Notice in Figure 25.8 that guidelines are added to the blank canvas. These guides don't print or show up on your video; they indicate the safe zones in the video file. As long as your action is contained within the outside bounding box and your text is contained within the inside bounding box, you won't lose any of the important pieces of your video to a television that cuts out the edges of the video and enlarges the center.

> **NOTE**
>
> The safe zones indicated by the guidelines are only relevant when you are creating an analog video. When you are creating or viewing digital video, the full image is displayed.

FIGURE 25.8

The Film & Video presets give you guides for placing and editing your video.

—— Action safe area

—— Title safe area

> **NOTE**
>
> If you are creating a video for the web, you probably chose the square pixel settings, which means the Pixel Aspect Ratio Correction doesn't have to be turned on. You can disregard the guides as well, because computer monitors play the entire video without cropping the edges.

You can now place an image in this document. You can also create a neutral background that you can place in the video file as a separate layer behind any photos that are placed in the video file.

Using video filters

Video filters reduce noise in a video file by removing static (lines) in moving video and preventing oversaturation and bleeding of colors. You can use video filters on video or image files that will be placed into video files. To access the video filter options, choose Filter⇨Video from the main menu bar.

De-Interlace

Interlaced video is created by generating every other line of video in one pass and then filling in the missing lines in the second pass. De-interlacing can clean up the appearance of video by removing either the odd or even lines and filling those lines in by either duplicating or interpolating the existing lines. The difference can be dramatic, especially on a computer monitor that has a high enough quality output to catch the variable scans. Figure 25.9 shows the same frame before and after de-interlacing.

FIGURE 25.9

The first image is fuzzy, and you can see the image echo. The second image has been de-interlaced and is much clearer.

Choose Filter⇨Video⇨De-Interlace to open the De-Interlace dialog box shown in Figure 25.10. You can select whether to use the odd or even lines of the video file and whether to use duplication or interpolation for filling in the gaps.

FIGURE 25.10

The De-Interlace dialog box gives you options for de-interlacing your video to clarify playback.

NTSC Colors

When you apply the NTSC Colors filter to an image or video file, you are restricting the colors used in that file to those used in analog television production. This keeps your video clean by preventing oversaturation and bleeding of colors. You can change the colors to NTSC colors by choosing Filter➪Video➪NTSC Colors.

Understanding the Features of the Timeline Panel

The Timeline panel consists of a timeline for creating animations or editing video through time. It has features such as a playhead that allows you to move through time in your file and lists the clips that are placed in your file. You can access clip properties that allow you to animate any clip in your file in different ways, depending on the clip type you select.

> **NEW FEATURE**
>
> The Timeline panel has a very new look in CS6. Although the functionality is virtually identical, the panel and the menu look very different and are much more user-friendly.

The Timeline panel has so many features that we break them into three categories for you: time adjustment, work area, and icons.

Adjusting time in the Timeline panel

Time is an important feature in any video-editing project. Because a video includes the fourth dimension of time, there needs to be a way of representing that dimension when you are looking at a video layer. A timeline is a standard way of doing just that. When a layer is placed inside the Timeline indicating duration, it is called a clip. The Timeline panel includes many time indicators and time features, as shown in Figure 25.11. These features give you a representation of how much time is involved in your video clip and let you move through that time to explore the entire video.

FIGURE 25.11

You can use the many time features of the Timeline panel to move quickly through your video.

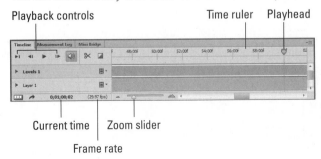

Here's what these features do and how to use them:

- **Playback controls.** The playback controls allow you to rewind, play, pause, and fast-forward your animation or video as well as move the playhead to the beginning of the video clip.

TIP
You can press the spacebar to play and pause your video.

- **Time ruler.** The time ruler indicates the time relative to the video clips.

- **Playhead.** The playhead is a slider that allows you to preview your video, or select a particular time, or frame in your video by dragging the slider back and forth across the video clips.

- **Current time.** The current time is a numerical representation of where the playhead is placed on the time ruler. Notice that the time indicated in Figure 25.11 matches exactly with the position of the playhead.

- **Current frame rate.** This number indicates how many frames are in every second of an animation or video. The default setting, which is the NTSC standard rate shown in Figure 25.11, is 29.97 frames per second.

- **Zoom slider.** The zoom slider is a handy feature that allows you to expand or reduce the time ruler. By zooming in, the length of each second in the Timeline increases. If you zoom all the way in, each frame takes up the same amount of space as each second did at the lowest setting.

- **Current frame.** The current frame can be viewed in lieu of the current time if you choose Panel Options from the Panel menu and select Frame Number. You can see in Figure 25.12 how the Timeline panel changes.

- **Frame ruler.** The time ruler becomes a frame ruler, indicating the number of frames relative to the video clips, when the Timeline panel is set to the frame number display, as opposed to the number of seconds.

FIGURE 25.12

You can change the panel options to show the current frame number in the Timeline panel.

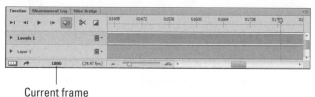

Current frame

25

Using the work area of the Timeline panel

The work area of the Timeline panel includes the video clips and other layers, as well as the tools that are used to view and manipulate them. The clips are represented by bars distributed through the Timeline to show duration. Each clip is labeled and has several tracks and properties that you can manipulate in your video-editing process, as shown in Figure 25.13.

FIGURE 25.13

The work area features of the Timeline panel include video clips and their properties.

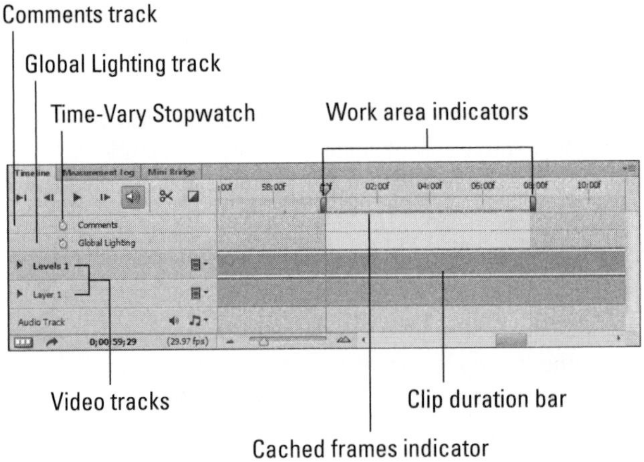

The work area of the Timeline panel includes the following features:

- **Comments track.** This track provides a space to enter comments in any area of the Timeline.

- **Global Lighting track.** This track allows you to animate global lighting throughout all of the clips at the same time.

> **NOTE**
>
> The Comments and Global Lighting tracks are no longer shown by default as they were in previous versions of Photoshop. You can view them by clicking the Timeline panel menu icon and choosing Show ⇨ Comments or Show ⇨ Global Lighting.

- **Time-Vary Stopwatch.** This feature can be turned on in any clip property that you can animate. It allows keyframe indicators to be placed inside the property clip.

- **Video tracks.** These layers correspond exactly to those in the Layers panel, and there is a video track for each clip layer placed in your video file. Notice in Figure 25.13 that the top clip is actually an adjustment layer. The video track menu, which you access by clicking the video icon, allows you to create groups from one or more tracks in the Timeline.

- **Work area indicators.** These indicators enable you to reduce your work area to the immediate area you are working on, by dragging them to different locations in your Timeline. When you start a playback, it is restricted to this area. You can also render and export just the segment of your video or animation contained inside the work area indicators. This feature is more useful as your file becomes longer in duration.

- **Audio track.** This track allows you to place an audio file along with the video files in your Timeline. The audio track menu, which you access by clicking the musical note icon in the audio track, allows you to make changes to your audio clip as well as add or delete audio tracks.

- **Cached frames indicator.** This indicator shows the frames that have been cached in the computer's memory and that can be easily previewed. When the line is solid, all the frames in that area have been cached. If the line looks jagged, only a few frames have been cached in that area. If the line is nonexistent, none of the frames has been cached yet. As you play back video, you'll notice that a limited number of frames can be cached. Consequently, past frames are discarded as new frames become cached.

- **Clip duration bar.** This bar indicates the duration of the clip inside the Timeline. Drag either end of the bar to lengthen or shorten it. You can edit the clip position and length in the Timeline in several ways, which we will cover when we discuss the Timeline panel menu later in this chapter.

Using the icons on the Timeline panel

The icons on the Timeline panel make certain actions, such as changing the look of the Timeline and deleting keyframes, quick to perform. Some actions perform their function with a quick click, and others require more input. The icons are labeled in Figure 25.14.

FIGURE 25.14

The icons on the Timeline panel allow you to quickly access different features.

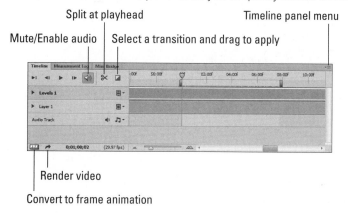

Split at playhead

Timeline panel menu

Mute/Enable audio

Select a transition and drag to apply

Render video

Convert to frame animation

The Timeline panel icons include the following:

- **Mute/Enable audio.** Clicking this icon allows you to quickly mute the audio during your video playback, or re-enable it.
- **Split at playhead.** Clicking this icon makes a break in your video clip at the playhead, creating a new video clip in the process.
- **Select a transition and drag to apply.** Clicking this icon opens a transition menu that allows you to choose from a few basic transitions, set the duration, and then drop it into place at either end of a video clip.
- **Convert to frame animation.** Clicking this icon changes the Timeline panel to frame animation. Your file is also converted to a frame-based animation. This option is viable only if you are working on an animation rather than a video file, because video files do not play in a frame animation.
- **Render Video.** Clicking this icon will start the video rendering process, opening a dialog box for you to establish settings and choose where you want your new video file saved.
- **Timeline panel menu.** Clicking this icon opens the Timeline panel flyout menu. This is a hefty menu, so we describe it in the following section.

Exploring the options in the Timeline panel menu

When you know the options that are available to you in the Timeline panel menu, you will find that your workflow will be more efficient and productive. The Timeline panel menu has many features, as shown in Figure 25.15. Some of them are intuitive, and some are covered in greater depth in this and the following chapters. We give you a quick rundown of the list so you'll have a comprehensive, at-a-glance resource.

FIGURE 25.15

The Timeline panel menu has all the options you need to use the Timeline effectively.

The Timeline panel menu includes the following options:

- **Go To.** This option allows you to move the playhead to any of the following places: a specified time, the next frame, the previous frame, the first frame, the last frame, the beginning of the work area, or the end of the work area.

- **Split at Playhead.** This option makes a break in your video clip at the playhead, creating a new video clip in the process.

- **Move & Trim.** This option allows you to move your video clips through time, or trim them shorter using the location of the playhead. You can see an example of a trimmed video in Figure 25.16.

FIGURE 25.16

The Levels track has been trimmed so that it only affects a part of the video track beneath it.

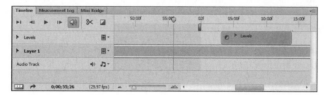

- **Convert Frames.** This option allows you to make one of the following conversions: take an image with several layers and create an individual frame from each layer; create a clip for every frame in your video or animation; or convert the Timeline to frame animation. See Chapter 28 for more information on frames and frame animation.

- **Work Area.** These options allow you to create a work area by setting the beginning or end of your work area to the playhead, as shown in Figure 25.17. You can also lift or extract your work area. If you lift the work area, all the clips in the work area are deleted, but a space the size of the work area is left in the Timeline. Extracting the work area deletes all the clips contained in the work area, closing the gap in the Timeline left by the deletion.

FIGURE 25.17

Changing the work area highlights a section of your animation or video so playback is restricted to that area.

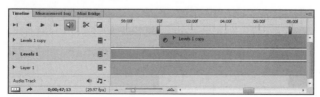

25

- **Keyframes.** These options allow you to create and make changes to keyframes in your Timeline. You will learn all about keyframes in Chapter 26.

- **Comments.** These options allow you to leave comments in the Comments track, view them, and edit them.

- **Loop Playback.** This option allows you to continuously play back your video.

- **Allow Frame Skipping.** This option allows you to skip frames as you preview an animation or video. This enables Photoshop to play the preview in real time, although the quality is not as good as the rendered version.

- **Show.** These options allow you to choose whether to show all clips, or just your favorite clips. You can choose to set up or edit your favorite clips. You can also choose to view the comments and global lighting tracks inside the Timeline.

- **Enable Timeline Shortcut Keys.** This option allows you to use the shortcut keys for the Timeline that are not available by default.

- **Enable Auto-Grouping of Clips.** This option automatically creates groups from clips in the Timeline. If you place a Levels adjustment over a video clip, for instance, it is automatically placed in a group with that video clip.

- **Enable Onion Skins.** This option allows you to view an overlay of the previous and next frame or frames. See Chapter 26 for more information.

- **Onion Skin Settings.** This option opens the Onion Skin Options dialog box, where you can set several options, including what frames become onion skins and their opacity. See Chapter 26 for more information.

- **Set Timeline Frame Rate.** This option allows you to change the frame rate of the Timeline, making your video a smaller file that is lower in quality or a larger file that is higher in quality.

- **Panel Options.** These options allow you to change the thumbnail size of the clips. You can also change the ruler on the Timeline from Timecode to Frame number.

- **Render Video.** This option renders your video with the changes you've made to it so that all the video frames are processed and cached, allowing you to watch your video in real time at full quality. Rendering can be a time-consuming process.

- **Close.** This option closes the Timeline panel.

- **Close Tab Group.** This option closes the entire tab group that includes the Timeline panel, the Measurement Log, and Mini-Bridge by default.

Accessing the Video Layers menu

The Video Layers menu is an important part of working with video and the Timeline panel. From this menu, you can create new video layers, copy and create new frames, and otherwise make changes to your video layers. Creating video layers is important when you want to make frame-by-frame changes, and as these changes are made, you'll find that being able to copy material from one frame to the next is very useful.

You can find the Video Layers menu by choosing Layer⇨Video Layers from the menu bar. As we start to show you more of the advanced techniques of animation and video, you will use the Video Layers menu more frequently. You can see this menu in Figure 25.18.

FIGURE 25.18

The Video Layers menu has advanced features that make video editing in Photoshop worthwhile.

The Video Layers menu includes the following options:

- **New Video Layer from File.** This option allows you to import a separate file as a layer in your existing file, similar to the Place command.

- **New Blank Video Layer.** This option adds a blank video layer to your document. A new blank video layer is handy for making changes to existing video, and it's imperative if you are animating an image or rasterized layer that doesn't already contain a video layer. In addition to the regular layer properties, a video layer contains an Altered Video track that allows you to make changes frame by frame. The new video layer is completely transparent until you add changes to it.

- **Insert Blank Frame.** This option creates a blank frame on the Altered Video track at the position of the playhead.

- **Duplicate Frame.** This option duplicates the current frame on the Altered Video track and places it directly after the selected frame.

- **Delete Frame.** This option deletes the current frame on the Altered Video track.

- **Replace Footage.** This option is useful when the file containing the original footage has changed locations and Photoshop can't find it. Click Replace Footage, and browse to the new location to correct the link between the original file and the Photoshop document you've created with it.

25

- **Interpret Footage.** This option is useful if you have video clips that contain alpha channels, as it allows you to determine how the alpha channels are interpreted. You can also change other options such as whether the video is interlaced, and you can modify the frame rate.

- **Hide Altered Video.** This option is the same as clicking the eye icon on a video clip you want to hide, except that it allows you to take the scenic route to do the same thing.

- **Restore Frame and Restore All Frames.** These options enable you to discard the edits you've made to any or all frames. All edits to video in Photoshop are non-destructive, meaning that they do not affect the original file.

- **Reload Frame.** This option allows you to reload the footage for the current frame in a video file you are working on. This is useful if the original footage of the video file has been changed and saved in a different application, because Photoshop eventually synchronizes the document and reflects those changes. Another technique is to use the playback controls to play the footage, which also allows Photoshop to reload the original file.

- **Rasterize.** This option rasterizes a video clip. A video clip is dynamic and can be modified frame by frame. When it is rasterized, it becomes a flat image, containing only the data in the frame that was selected when it was rasterized. That data plays continuously through the duration of the original video clip.

Setting clip favorites

As your project grows, the Timeline panel becomes unwieldy as you add more clips. You can hide clips that you are not working on to keep your work area neater and easier to work in. You do this by setting your clip favorites. You can set your clip favorites at any time during your project; in fact, you'll probably want to change your favorite clips often.

You can set up clip favorites by following these steps:

1. **Highlight the clips that you want to place among your favorites.**

   You can select multiple clips by pressing and holding the Ctrl/⌘ key as you click each clip. You can do this in either the Timeline panel or the Layers panel.

2. **Click the Timeline panel menu icon to open the flyout menu.**

3. **Choose Show ⇨ Set Favorite Clips.**

   The unselected clips no longer appear inside the Timeline, as shown in Figure 25.19. You can still view these clips in the Layers panel, and they still play when you pre-view your video.

4. **(Optional) You can change your clip favorites by choosing Show ⇨ All Clips and repeating Steps 1 to 3.**

FIGURE 25.19

Setting clip favorites cleans up the Timeline panel.

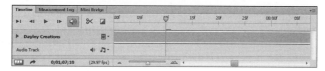

Creating video groups

Another way of organizing your Timeline panel is to create video groups. A video group contains one or more clips and appears as a single track in the Timeline panel. You can see which clips are contained in the video group by looking at the Layers panel, as shown in Figure 25.20. These clips can be any kind of layer, including video files, adjustment layers, or image files. It can be incredibly convenient, for instance, to place lighting and color adjustments where they are needed over a video clip and then to combine them all into a group. This not only makes the Timeline panel cleaner, but it also ensures that the adjustment clips stay where they need to be.

FIGURE 25.20

Creating a video group allows you to merge several tracks into one on the Timeline panel.

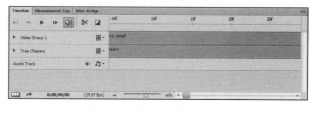

To create a video group, simply select the clips or tracks that you want to be included in the group, click the Video Track icon, as shown in Figure 25.21, and select New Video Group from Selection. This combines the selected clips into one track. As always, we encourage you to immediately rename the group so that you recognize it easily moving forward.

FIGURE 25.21

The Video Track icon allows you to create new groups.

Opening and Placing Video Files

Getting started with video editing in Photoshop is as easy as opening a video file. Once you have opened a video file, you can edit it by adjusting the light and color, rearranging the order of the video by splitting and moving areas of the clip, or adding special effects by painting or changing one frame at a time. You may even want to make changes to more than one clip at a time. After you have opened one video file, you can use the Place command to add more video files to the same document to create a composite.

Opening a video file

Opening a video file in Photoshop isn't any harder than opening any other kind of file. However, you need to import the smallest possible file for editing. Photoshop is not meant to create and manage extensive video projects, and a large video file can create a very unwieldy work area at best and bring your work in Photoshop to a grinding halt at worst.

You shouldn't be discouraged from bringing in as much video as you need to edit, but don't bring in any more than is necessary. You can trim larger video files down to an editable size in the video-editing program of your choice by creating a work area or trimming around the area you want to edit and rendering just that part to a separate video file that you can then import into Photoshop. Taking the time to trim a video file down to a manageable size saves you a lot of time and frustration later.

To open a video file in Photoshop, choose File ⇨ Open and browse to a video file with a supported extension. When the file opens, the Timeline panel is automatically selected from its tab group, and your newly imported video file appears as one uncomplicated clip in the Timeline. Figure 25.22 shows a video file that's been imported into Photoshop.

FIGURE 25.22

A newly imported video file contains one video track and the default audio track.

Adding additional video files

You can add video files to an open video document in several ways. For example, you can drag a video clip from another file into the window of the file it's being placed in, or you can choose Layer➪Video Layers➪New Video Layer From File. Either of these options places a new video clip on top of the selected clip in your file. Figure 25.23 shows two video clips placed together in the Timeline. Both videos are from the same wedding. Now we can combine clips from both videos to create one final video project.

Sometimes, you may want to add a new video file differently than just inserting it over the last one. For example, you may want to change the size of the file to create a picture-in-picture effect. In this case, you want to *place* the new video file. To do this, you choose File➪Place, and browse to the new video file. The new file is placed over the existing clips with a bounding box around it, allowing you to scale, rotate, and place it where you want, as shown in Figure 25.24.

25

FIGURE 25.23

Two video clips can be combined in the Timeline.

FIGURE 25.24

Create a picture-in-a-picture effect by placing and transforming the second file.

Of course, you can create the same effect after the fact by selecting the video clip and choosing Edit ⇨ Free Transform, but placing the video file saves the extra step.

NOTE

Whether you use the Place function or the Free Transform function, a transformed video layer becomes a Smart Object.

Importing image sequences

An image sequence is a series of image files that are saved in sequence for an animation or video. Usually, they are exported out of a video project. A video file is very memory-intensive to render, especially if it contains several layers, high-resolution images, or 3D objects. If you render a video project as an image sequence rather than a video, the rendered — and saved — images are preserved, even if your computer crashes, allowing you to start the rendering process where you left off. Photoshop allows you to import these rendered images together as one animation file.

You can import rendered images in two ways. The first way is to import the image sequence as a single layer, creating one video clip from the individual image files, just as if it had been a single video file. The second way is to import the image sequence into a stack, which gives each frame its own individual layer without any extra steps. We show you how to import using both methods.

NOTE

Before you import an image sequence, make sure it has been saved correctly. An image sequence should be a series of images saved with sequential filenames and placed in a folder that doesn't contain any other files.

Importing an image sequence into one layer

Opening an image sequence as one video layer is the fastest and preferred method of importing an image sequence.

You can open an image sequence as just one video layer by following these steps:

1. **Choose File ⇨ Open.**
2. **Browse to the folder containing the image sequence, and select the first file in the sequence.**
3. **In the Open dialog box, select the Image Sequence check box, as shown in Figure 25.25.**
4. **Click Open.**
5. **You are prompted to enter a frame rate for your image sequence.**

   If this is an exported video, select the original frame rate. If this is a series of still shots, select the frame rate that will work best, and click OK.

25

FIGURE 25.25

Be sure to select the check box labeled Image Sequence so all the files are opened.

You now have a simple file that looks just like you opened a video file, as shown in Figure 25.26. This file is generated quickly and is easy to work with.

Importing an image sequence into multiple layers

If you need your image sequence to be placed in separate layers, you can use a method that creates the layers, as the images are imported and opened. With this method, there is no waiting time to cache the frames after the file is created.

You can create an individual layer for every image in an image sequence by following these steps:

1. **Choose File ⇨ Scripts ⇨ Load Files into Stack.**

   This opens the Load Layers dialog box.

2. **Choose Folder from the Use menu.**

3. **Browse to the folder containing the image sequence you want to open, as shown in Figure 25.27.**

FIGURE 25.26

An image sequence can be opened to create a simple video clip that's easy to work with.

FIGURE 25.27

You can use the Load Layers dialog box to create individual layers for every image in a sequence.

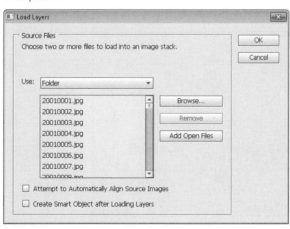

4. **Click OK.**

5. **Click the Timeline panel menu icon, and choose Convert Frames ⇨ Make Frames from Clips.**

   This creates one frame for each layer and places them in sequence to create a video. If your frame rate is set to 30 frames per second, for instance, each layer will be 1/30 second long and placed just after the layer below it in the Timeline.

> **CAUTION**
>
> As you make frames from layers, make sure your playhead is placed at the beginning of your Timeline. The first frame is placed at the location of the playhead.

Now your animation contains a separate layer for every image in your image sequence. This is handy if your image sequence is short, containing only a few images, but it's not great if you have several images. In Figure 25.28, you can see a view of our Timeline panel after importing a 5-second sequence. Of course, our frame rate is set to 30, so the file contains 150 images. That's 150 layers in the Timeline, 150 layers in the Layers panel . . . well, you get the idea.

FIGURE 25.28

This figure shows just some of the layers that are actually contained in this Timeline.

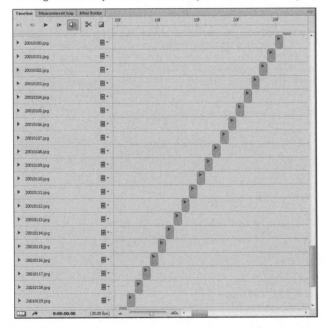

Trimming Video Clips

As you add new video clips to a project, you may find that you need to trim them. Trimming a video clip consists of cutting the unwanted ends off the clip, leaving the rest of the video intact. You can trim a clip in several ways — by manually dragging the clip duration bar, by using the Timeline menu options, or by splitting the clip, which is discussed later in this chapter.

Dragging the clip duration bar

The easiest way to trim a layer is to drag the ends of the layer to the point where you want the video to start or end. First, you need to place the playhead where you want to begin or end the clip. You can probably get to that spot just by your initial preview of your video clip. Then simply move the end of the layer duration bar by clicking and holding it as you drag it to the playhead. This isn't a precise method, but it works well for a preliminary trim. Figure 25.29 shows our attempt at lining up the layer duration bar and the playhead.

FIGURE 25.29

Dragging the end of the layer duration bar to trim it

When you drag the beginning of the clip to trim it, the clip doesn't automatically reposition itself at the beginning of the document. If you want your clip to start at the beginning of the document, you can do one of two things: drag and drop the already trimmed clip to reposition it or simply drag the untrimmed clip forward, moving it out of the beginning of the document. Place the playhead at the beginning of the document so you can preview the video as you are moving it out of the document.

Trimming clips using the Timeline menu option

If you want to trim your video more precisely, you can move the playhead to the proper area and click the Timeline panel menu. You then select Move & Trim ⇨ Trim Start/End at Playhead. This trims the clip to the current time. Again, this leaves the beginning of your clip at the playhead rather than at the beginning of your document, as shown in Figure 25.30.

TIP

You can move the playhead to the very frame you want to trim to by using the Select Next/Previous Frame icons located in the playback controls at the bottom of the Timeline panel.

25

FIGURE 25.30

Using the Timeline panel menu to trim the clip start or end to the current time leaves you with a gap at the front of your video document.

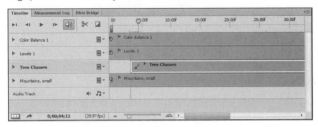

Moving Video Clips

Moving video clips is a straightforward process. You'll probably find yourself dragging clips around frequently without even thinking about it as you work on your video project. You can move clips around in more than one way, so we briefly cover each way so that you are aware of them.

Changing the clip hierarchy

Changing the clip hierarchy in a video project is done the same as in any other project. As you work in the Timeline, don't forget that the Layers panel is also v a part of your work area, as shown in Figure 25.31. Each clip is shown as a layer in the Layers panel. You can select, delete, and move layers in the Layers panel. To move a layer up or down in the hierarchy, you click it inside the Layers panel and drag it into position.

FIGURE 25.31

The Layers panel displays all the clips in the Timeline panel as separate layers.

As you can see in Figure 25.31, stacking many different types of clips can make the Timeline panel look busy. When you look at the Layers panel, you only have to understand how the layer hierarchy works to know which clips are visible. When you look at the Timeline panel, you need to understand the hierarchy, and how the clip duration bar works within the hierarchy.

In Figure 25.32, the clips are clearly marked so you can see which clips are visible and when. At the beginning of the Timeline, follow the clip layer hierarchy down to the first clip. As the Playhead moves along the Timeline, that clip is visible in playback until another clip, located above it in the hierarchy, takes precedence. After the top clip ends, the bottom clip in the hierarchy is the only one visible, so it is played until it is superseded by the second clip, which is located above it in the hierarchy. The concept is simple, but as you add more clips, it can look intimidating. Even if you understand exactly how it works, it takes practice and experience to understand what's happening with the clips at a glance.

> **TIP**
>
> You can set clip favorites to show only the clips that you are working with at any given time. Choose Set Favorite Clips from the Timeline panel menu.

FIGURE 25.32

To understand which clip is visible, look at the clip hierarchy, and then look for the first active clip.

Dragging clips inside the clip duration bar

To change the relative position of a video in your Timeline, you can simply click and drag its clip duration bar back and forth inside the Timeline, as shown in Figure 25.33. If your clip is visible, you can preview the movement in the document window. It looks like you are changing the position of the playhead manually, but of course, the clip is moving rather than the indicator. You can drag a clip right past the beginning or end of the document, effectively trimming the ends of the clip. This content remains available, because you can always drag it back into the document.

FIGURE 25.33

Simply click and drag a track inside the Timeline to move back and forth in time.

Moving the clip start and clip end points

The most precise way to move a clip is to use the panel menu to change the clip start or clip end point to the position of the playhead. Simply move the playhead to the position where you want the clip to begin or end, and choose Move & Trim ➪ Move Start/End to Playhead from the Timeline panel menu. This slides the indicated end of the clip to the playhead. If the clip has been previously trimmed, the Clip Start/End point is defined as the visible end of the clip. Figure 25.34 indicates this type of clip movement.

FIGURE 25.34

Using the Move Start to Playhead menu option snaps the beginning of this clip to the precise position of the playhead.

Splitting Clips

Splitting a Video clip cuts it cleanly into two pieces allowing you to add a transition, delete part of the video, or edit part of a clip independently from its other half. Once you have split a clip, it becomes two separate tracks, effectively creating two clips from one.

To split a video clip, you move the playhead to the location where you want the video split and click the Split at Playhead icon at the top of the Timeline panel. When a video clip is split, it is divided into two different layers, with the beginning of the split video segment on one layer and the end on another, as shown in Figure 25.35. If you watch a video right after you have split it, you won't see any difference in the video playback.

FIGURE 25.35

Splitting a clip creates two layers from one.

Even after a video clip has been split, the full content of the clip is on both layers. This means that you can drag either clip to duplicate the content of the other clip. In fact, this is a viable reason to split the clip in the first place. By dragging out the end of one of these clips and repositioning it, you can create a stutter effect in the video. That's great for kissing shots.

Another reason to split video clips is to insert something between the two clips — another video, a still shot, or a title. Figure 25.36 shows a title placed after the first segment of the split video.

25

FIGURE 25.36

Splitting a clip allows you to insert other clips between the two segments.

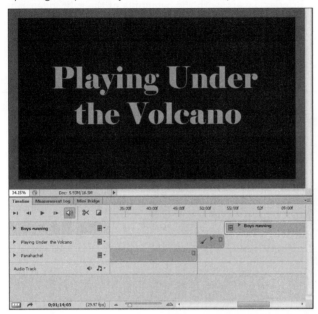

Lifting and Extracting Unwanted Sections of Video

You can clip your video and remove unwanted sections in just one-step by lifting or extracting them. You can lift or extract any portion of a video clip: beginning, middle, or end. Lifting a video creates a gap in the area where the video once occupied, and extracting the video takes the video out and closes the gap, so the video clip plays continuously.

Lifting a section of a video clip

Lifting a section of a video clip takes the work area out of the video, leaving a gap in the video the size of the video that has been removed.

To lift a section of your video, you select a video clip and set the work area around the section that you want to lift. Choose Work Area⇨Lift Work Area from the Timeline panel menu. The video clip is turned into two video clips, and a gap is created inside the work area. You can see in Figure 25.37 that the work area is empty. Now you can place another file to fill the gap.

FIGURE 25.37

Lifting the work area deletes the video clip inside the work area, but leaves a gap where the video used to be.

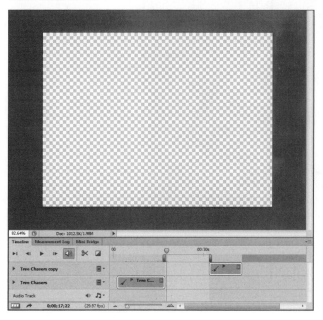

Extracting a section of a video clip

Extracting a section of video is a little different. Rather than deleting the video and leaving a gap, extracting it deletes the video and closes the gap. This is the easiest way to simply delete unwanted video from the middle of your video file.

You can extract a section of a video clip by selecting the video clip and setting the work area around the section you want to delete. Choose Work Area ➪ Extract Work Area from the Timeline panel menu. The video clip is turned into two video clips, and the second part of the video is moved into the work area to close the gap created by the extraction. Figure 25.38 shows that the extracted video has been replaced by the remaining video. This allows uninterrupted playback of your video file without having to fill the gap created by lifting a video file.

25

Extracting the work area deletes the video clip inside the work area and closes the gap.

Adding Still Shots or Other Elements to a Video Project

Adding still images or other elements, such as text layers or a 3D model, to your project is similar to adding video files. However, these kinds of files look different from a video file in both the Timeline and the Layers panel, so we will show you some of the things that distinguish these files.

You can add still image layers to your video project in several ways. When we say still image, we're lumping together all the different kinds of images that you can manipulate in Photoshop — photos, paint, vector images, and text. Therefore, it makes sense that you can add them in so many ways, from creating a new layer to placing a separate file.

Adding a blank layer

If you are building an image rather than importing it, you want to create a new layer for the image, especially if your other layers consist of video files. To add a blank layer, simply click the New Layer icon at the bottom of the Layers panel. You can also choose Layer⇨New⇨ Layer or press Shift+Ctrl+N/Shift+⌘+N.

A new layer is created in both the Layers panel and the Timeline, as shown in Figure 25.39. You should change the name of the layer immediately. You can move your layer up and down in the layer hierarchy by dragging and placing it in the right spot in the Layers panel.

A blank layer is an empty canvas waiting for you to create whatever you want. Once you have created a blank layer, it appears as a new track in the Timeline. As you add elements to this layer, it creates a clip, which you can then modify in the Timeline just as you would any video clip.

FIGURE 25.39

Adding a new layer is as easy as clicking the New Layer icon in the Layers panel.

Adding a text layer

Adding a text layer is as simple as choosing the Text tool from the Toolbox, clicking your document, and typing text. A separate text layer is automatically created, which allows you to move and edit the text separately from the rest of the file.

Creating a title for a video project is the perfect example of optimizing the Photoshop tools to create the best results for your video project. You can create a title for a video file in Photoshop, or you can create a title separately to import into a video project being created in a different application. Either way, the tools in Photoshop make it easy to create a custom, classy title.

Placing an image file

If you have a photo or an image that is a separate file, you need to add it to your video file for it to be part of your project. You can easily do this by choosing File ⇨ Place and browsing to the file you want to add. The file is added to the video file in a bounding box that you can scale and rotate to place the file just how you want it inside your video project.

You can drag a new file in by clicking the layer containing the still image and dragging it into the window of your video file. You can also copy and paste all or part of an image file.

25

Placing or dragging an image into your video file creates a new clip in your video containing the new image file. If you copy and paste an image, be sure to create a blank layer to paste it into. However, you bring an image in, make sure the layer is labeled well and placed in the hierarchy where it needs to be.

Adding or placing a 3D model

You can add or place a 3D model in the same way you add a still image: simply choose File ⇨ Place, or drag the object into your file. You can also choose 3D ⇨ New Layer From 3D File. This option adds the object as if it has been dragged in, and so you do not have a bounding box to change your placement options.

When a 3D object is brought into a video file, it is brought in as a 3D layer. You can transform the 3D object directly from the file it has been placed in. A 3D object is distinguished in the Layers panel by the 3D icon in the corner of the layer thumbnail, as you can see in Figure 25.40.

FIGURE 25.40

Three-dimensional objects have a distinct 3D icon in the corner of their thumbnail.

Summary

This chapter covered the basics of working with video in Photoshop. The Timeline panel has several features and menus, and you should now be familiar with what they are and how they work. You should also know how to do these things in Photoshop:

- Open and place video files
- Trim video footage
- Move video clips
- Split video clips
- Lift and extract unwanted video clips
- Add images and 3D files to a video project

25

Animating in the Timeline Panel

IN THIS CHAPTER

A nimation and keyframes are a big part of how the Timeline panel works and the effects you can create with your video files. Before we show you how to perform basic color correcting and image effects on your video files, we show you how to use the keyframes in the Timeline panel to change your effects over time.

Just as you've known since you were a kid, video and animation are produced by creating a series of images and showing them at such a high speed that it fools our brains into thinking that we are watching true motion. A standard frame rate to create realistic motion is 30 frames per second. When we were kids, we always wondered who had to draw and color the millions of pictures it took to make a full-length animation. Now we've watched enough special features titled "The Making of..." to have a good notion that animators even in the days before computers had many tips and tricks up their sleeves to make the animating process smooth and efficient

Animating in Photoshop not only employs many of the tips and tricks of efficient animating, but it can also automate some of the most tedious tasks. We've all seen clay animation productions — the animations created by moving clay figures a miniscule amount and taking a picture and then repeating the process until all the pictures put together create a movie. We'll tell you up front that some of the animation in Photoshop is going to be just like that, frame-by-frame animation. Not all of it will be, though, and that's where keyframes come into play.

A keyframe is one of the essential components of animating in Photoshop. A keyframe allows you to skip many of the tedious steps between "key" points in your animation. In this chapter, we show you what a keyframe is, what it does, and how you can create and edit it.

Creating and Editing Keyframes

When you are creating sequential images for an animation, a keyframe is any frame that defines a turning point in that animation. For example, if you want to animate a bouncing ball, the keyframes are the frames where the ball meets the ground and changes direction, and where the ball experiences the inevitable pull of gravity and begins its return to earth. All the frames in between are just continuations of the up or down movement.

The in-between frames are sometimes referred to as "in-betweens" or "tweens" for short. Creating these frames is called *tweening* or, in Photoshop terms, interpolating. When you create keyframes in the Photoshop Timeline panel, Photoshop is able to interpolate the frames between keyframes. This provides you as the user with an animation experience that is fun and easy, rather than tedious.

A keyframe is indicated in the Timeline by a little diamond or square, depending on the interpolation setting applied to it. The diamond or square is yellow if it is selected, or gray if it's not. You can create different keyframes in your animation to help you control position, opacity, style, and global lighting.

Creating keyframes

Create a keyframe in areas of your timeline where you want to make a change in the property you are animating. This will allow Photoshop to interpolate the frames in between each keyframe to create a smooth animation.

Creating a keyframe in the Timeline is a simple process. In the following example, we began a bouncing ball animation by creating a layer containing a circle over a blank canvas background.

You can create a keyframe by following these simple steps:

1. **Create a new file in Photoshop.**

   Use the default Photoshop size or larger.

2. **Use the Ellipse tool found in the Toolbox to draw a circle.**

   Press and hold the Shift key while you are drawing to constrain the ellipse to a perfectly circular shape. You can jazz it up by adding a color or layer style.

3. **Right-click your newly created shape layer to open the pop-up menu, and select Rasterize Layer.**

4. **Choose Window ⇨ Timeline to open the Timeline panel.**

   If the Timeline is in frame mode, click the Timeline panel menu and choose Convert to Video Timeline.

5. **Click the Timeline panel menu icon and choose Set Timeline Frame Rate.**

   This opens the Document Timeline Settings dialog box. Set the duration of the video to 20 seconds and click OK.

6. **Click the triangle next to the clip name in the Timeline panel to show the layer properties.**

7. **Click the Time-Vary Stopwatch icon next to the word Position to activate it.**

8. **Make sure the playhead is at the beginning of the Timeline.**

9. **Move your object, or selection, through the canvas to the position you want to use as the start of your animation, as shown in Figure 26.1.**

FIGURE 26.1

The ball is ready to drop.

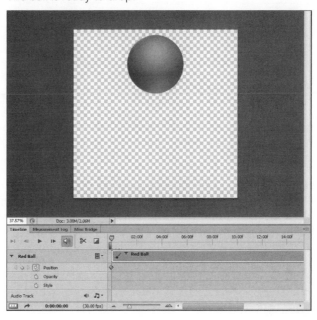

10. **Drag the playhead forward to 1 second.**

11. **Move your object again.**

    A keyframe is automatically created, as shown in Figure 26.2.

12. **Slide the playhead between the keyframes or play back this simple animation to watch how tweening works.**

FIGURE 26.2

We created a keyframe at the bounce.

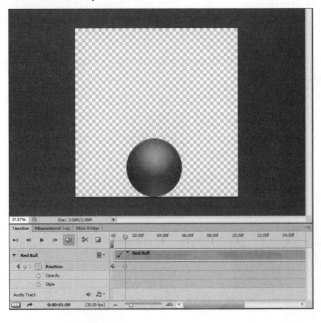

Now, throwing you into this exercise was like throwing you into the deep end of a pool. Don't worry, we won't let you sink; we just wanted you to get used to the water. We covered a few areas that you aren't familiar with yet, so let's go over them right now.

In Figures 26.3 and 26.4, note the differences in the layer properties listed in the Layers panel as opposed to the Timeline panel. The Layers panel shows the ball layer just as it would look without the Timeline panel open. The Timeline panel, on the other hand, shows you all new aspects of this layer.

FIGURE 26.3

The Layers panel is a familiar sight, containing the layers and properties you expect.

FIGURE 26.4

The Timeline panel shows a new array of clip properties.

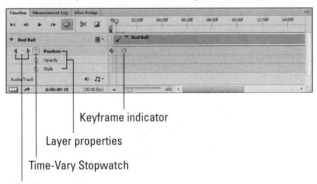

Keyframe indicator

Layer properties

Time-Vary Stopwatch

Keyframe navigators

When you click the triangle next to the clip name, you open a new world of possibilities. The layer properties that open are different areas where you can create keyframes. Anywhere you can create a keyframe, you can also create animation. In essence, you can animate in any of the listed layer properties. The properties listed in Figure 26.4 allow you to animate in any of the following ways: by changing the position of the layer, by changing the opacity of the layer, or by changing the layer style. Other layer properties exist, including animating transformations, global lighting, masks, and 3D properties, and we will cover these properties later in this chapter.

The stopwatch next to each of these sublayers is more correctly called the Time-Vary Stopwatch. By default, the Time-Vary Stopwatch is disabled, and you cannot create keyframes. Clicking the Time-Vary Stopwatch icon in each of these layers enables keyframing for that layer.

CAUTION

Disabling the Time-Vary Stopwatch after you have created keyframes deletes them. Be very careful that you do not accidentally disable the Time-Vary Stopwatch and lose all the work you put into creating keyframes.

When you enable the Time-Vary Stopwatch, the keyframe navigators come into view. These navigators enable you to jump from one keyframe to the next. Of course, the direction you jump depends on the arrow you click. You can edit the layer properties at an existing keyframe as long as the playhead is placed directly over the keyframe.

If the playhead is not placed directly over the keyframe, instead of that keyframe being edited, a new keyframe is created. This is an excellent reason to use the keyframe navigators. For instance, in Figure 26.5, we tried to change the drop position of the ball. The playhead wasn't placed correctly over the keyframe indicator, so we created a new keyframe. When we played this animation back, we were left with a jump in the ball's position at the end. If we had used the keyframe navigator, the playhead would be correctly placed to make the edit.

FIGURE 26.5

Changing the position of the ball with the playhead in the wrong position created a new keyframe.

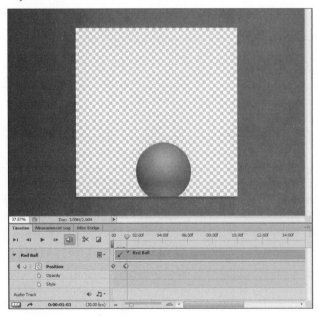

If you click between the two arrows of the keyframe navigator, you create a new keyframe. This isn't the most efficient method, because after you have created it, you need to change the layer property. If you change the layer property first, a keyframe is automatically created.

Editing keyframes

You can copy, paste, and delete keyframes inside the Timeline. This is an incredibly useful way to create many keyframes in a relatively short amount of time. Follow these steps:

1. **Select a keyframe by using the keyframe navigator or by placing the playhead over it.**

   A selected keyframe is highlighted in yellow. You can also select more than one keyframe by dragging a selection marquee around the keyframes you want to select or by clicking the Timeline panel menu and choosing Select All Keyframes.

2. **After you've selected one or more keyframes, right-click one of them to open the menu options for the selected keyframes.**

   You can also find these options in the panel menu.

3. **Choose Copy Keyframe, and close the menu.**

4. **Move the playhead to the location in the Timeline where you want to place the first keyframe.**

5. **Open the Timeline panel menu, and choose Keyframes ⇨ Paste.**

As you can see in Figure 26.6, we created a second bounce for the ball. We can go on copying and pasting keyframes to continue the bouncing motion.

You can delete a keyframe in the same way, by right-clicking it and choosing Delete Keyframes or by choosing Delete from the panel menu.

> **CAUTION**
>
> The hotkeys (Ctrl+C/⌘+C, Ctrl+V/⌘+V, and Ctrl+X/⌘+X) for copying, pasting, and deleting don't work the way you think they might when working with keyframes. That's because in addition to selected keyframes, you also have the clip layer selected in the Layers panel. If you use the hotkeys, you are copying and pasting in the Layers panel. If you are not careful, you could delete the layer you are working on.

You can drag selected keyframes around in the Timeline, placing them wherever you want. For example, one second is a very slow and ponderous bounce. Rather than creating a new keyframe closer to the beginning of the Timeline, you can just drag the second keyframe closer to the first one.

FIGURE 26.6

We copied and pasted the bouncing keyframes to create a second bounce.

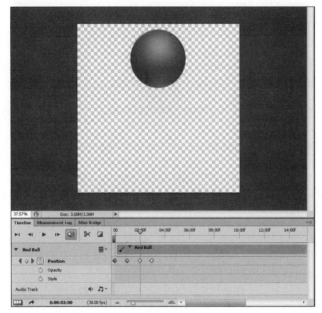

Setting interpolation

For our purposes, *Interpolation* is defined as the way that Photoshop determines what happens between the keyframes. The type of interpolation that we have demonstrated so far has been linear interpolation. It is called *linear interpolation* because the interpolation creates a path between keyframes. That path might be a continuous change of position, or it might be a shadow being gradually created through time. This is commonly called tweening. A second interpolation setting doesn't create a steady change. This interpolation setting is called *hold interpolation*. When you create a keyframe with a hold interpolation, Photoshop holds the current status of the layer until the next keyframe, which defines a new status.

Linear interpolation

Linear interpolation is the default setting in Photoshop, and you've seen how it works. After you've created keyframes, Photoshop figures out the difference between them and fills in the missing images at the frame rate specified in your file.

The shortest distance between two points is a straight line, and Photoshop doesn't take any other route. No matter what you do with the file before creating a second keyframe, Photoshop creates a smooth, mathematically exact transition between the two frames.

We emphasize *mathematically exact* because when you first try out this method of animation, you find more keyframes in a movement than you expected. We don't think we've ever seen a ball that bounced at a perfectly uniform speed. They usually go faster right after hitting the ground, hang in the air a little and then come down, speeding up as they do. That adds at least four keyframes to your bounce.

Hold interpolation

Changing keyframes to a hold interpolation is as easy as right-clicking them and choosing Hold Interpolation from the menu. The keyframes selected change to squares rather than diamonds, indicating that the interpolation is set to Hold. In Figure 26.7, we changed the keyframes in the position Timeline to hold interpolations. Now instead of steadily bouncing, the ball disappears and instantly reappears in a new position at each keyframe.

You can also see in Figure 26.7 that not all of the keyframe indicators are diamonds or squares. The last keyframe indicator looks like it can't decide which one it wants to be. The diamond on the left side of the keyframe indicator shows that the transition coming in is a linear interpolation. The square on the right half indicates that the interpolation going out is set to Hold.

FIGURE 26.7

When the position of the ball is set with a hold interpolation, the ball disappears and reappears in a new location immediately, rather than moving through space to get there.

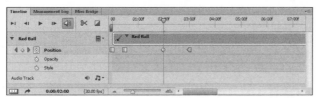

Creating comments

You can create keyframes to indicate comments that you want to make on your project. The Comment track is accessed by clicking the Timeline panel menu icon and choosing Show ⇨ Comments Track from the menu. This displays the Comments track in the Timeline, as shown in Figure 26.8. In this track, you can place comments on your project.

Comments are created just like keyframes. First, click the Time-Vary Stopwatch icon in the comment track. This creates your first comment box. Type your comment and click OK, as shown in Figure 26.9. An indicator is placed inside the comment track, as shown in Figure 26.8. To create subsequent comments, click between the keyframe navigators. You can also open the Timeline panel menu and select Edit Timeline Comment to create a new comment. *Do not* click the Time-Vary Stopwatch icon again; this deletes all your comments.

To read a comment, hover over the comment indicator until a window pops up, displaying the comment. To edit a comment, right-click the indicator and select Edit Comment.

FIGURE 26.8

A comment indicator looks and acts like a keyframe indicator in the Timeline.

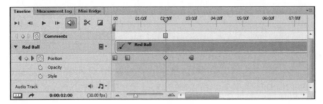

FIGURE 26.9

The Edit Timeline Comment dialog box allows you to place a comment anywhere in the Timeline.

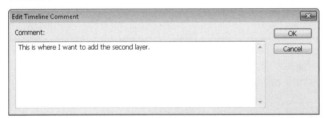

Animating the Position of a Layer

Creating a keyframe is a relatively simple process. Creating the right keyframe, however, can be tricky — even more so while animating position. The timing of a movement is vital. If you are attempting to create a realistic movement, such as a bouncing ball, you must time it so it looks like it's truly bouncing. Too slow and you get a floating quality; too fast and you get a spastic ball.

Choosing how many keyframes to place in a movement is key to creating a successful animation. Most true-to-life movements are not mechanical and precise. Placing several keyframes throughout a movement, even if it is in the same direction, can add variations in movement and speed that make it seem more realistic.

In this section, we will show you how you can animate positions across multiple layers, animating objects together so that they move in unison, as well as animating them individually. These are difficult concepts to demonstrate using still shots in a book, so follow along with the exercises and try them out for yourself so you can see the results on your own computer screen.

Getting keyframe placement right

Getting keyframe placement right is vital in creating realistic movements in your animation. The best place to start is by watching the movement you are trying to create happen in real life, or by imagining it in your head as you work. The simple movement of a bouncing ball needs several keyframes to create an animation that looks realistic. Think of how a ball slows as it reaches its apex and almost seems to hover for a moment before returning to the ground, building up speed as it goes.

You can create a realistic bouncing ball by adding several keyframes to the Timeline. Follow these steps:

1. **Create a new file in Photoshop.**

   Use the default Photoshop size or larger.

2. **Select the Ellipse tool in the Toolbox and draw a circle.**

   Press and hold the Shift key while you are drawing to constrain the ellipse to a perfectly circular shape. You can jazz it up by adding a color or layer style.

3. **Right-click your newly created shape layer to open the pop-up menu, and select Rasterize Layer.**

4. **Choose Window ⇨ Timeline to open the Timeline panel.**

5. **Click the triangle next to the clip name in the Timeline panel to show the layer properties, and click the Time-Vary Stopwatch icon next to the word Position to activate it.**

6. **Set the playhead to the beginning of the Timeline, and move the ball to the top of the canvas.**

7. **Move the Zoom slider to the right to expand the Timeline enough to show half-second increments.**

   The Zoom slider is found at the bottom of your Timeline panel. As you increase the size of the Timeline, 15f icons appear in the time ruler to indicate the half-second marks. The 15f indicates that 15 frames have gone by.

8. **Set the playhead to one-half second, and move the ball down to the bottom of the canvas.**

9. **Move the playhead about one-third of the way between the two keyframes, and move the ball up slightly to create a new keyframe.**

   This makes the first part of the ball animation drop slower than the second part.

10. **Select all three keyframes, and copy them by right-clicking one of them and selecting Copy Keyframe from the menu.**

> **TIP**
> You can select all the keyframes in any given layer property by clicking the name of the layer property.

11. **Move the time indicator to one second, and paste the keyframes.**

12. **Move the time indicator about a third of the way between one-half second and one second, when the ball is on its way back up, and create a new keyframe by moving the ball farther up along the path.**

    This makes the ball move faster through the first part of the bounce.

> **TIP**
>
> You can adjust the position of a keyframe by clicking and dragging it in the Timeline.

13. **Copy and paste all the keyframes several times at each new half second until the ball bounces several times in succession.**

    Your Timeline should look similar to the one in Figure 26.10.

FIGURE 26.10

Adding a few extra keyframes can make the ball's bounce more realistic.

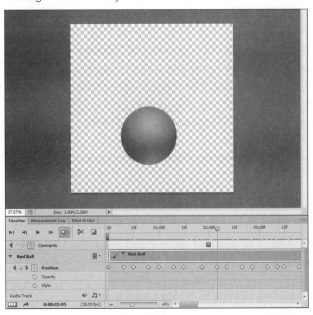

As you play this animation back, you see that adding a few additional keyframes improves the animation. You can add more keyframes that give the ball a brief pause at the apex of each bounce, or you can edit the position of the ball with each subsequent bounce so it doesn't bounce as high each time. You could even have it bouncing all over the walls like a trapped super ball. Trial and error will help you find the spots where a keyframe would be beneficial.

Animating positions in multiple layers

There may come a time when you want to animate the position of objects in different layers at the same time. For instance, if you added text to the bouncing ball, you would want the text to move along with the ball as it bounced around your screen.

> **NOTE**
>
> When animating Smart Object layers or text layers, the Position property layer is replaced by the Transform property layer. The Transform property allows for changes of position as well as the other transformations, as we'll discuss in the next section.

To animate both layers at once, you simply need to select the Position layer property in both layers by pressing and holding the Ctrl/⌘ key while you click each layer in turn. As you can see in Figure 26.11, the Position property layer is highlighted in the ball layer, and the Transform layer is highlighted in the text layer. Meanwhile, in the Layers panel, both object layers are highlighted as well. This allows you to move both objects simultaneously, creating keyframes in both Position layers. You can see how well this worked for the ball in Figure 26.12.

FIGURE 26.11

You can animate the position of two layers at once by selecting the Position properties in both layers in the Timeline panel.

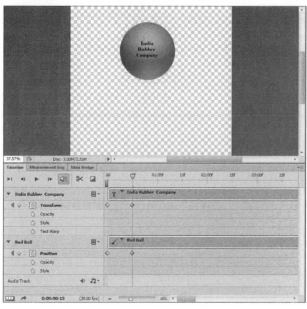

FIGURE 26.12

Now you can move the ball and the text together without losing the editing capability of either layer.

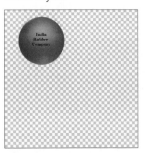 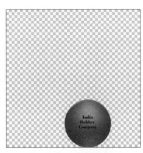 

CAUTION

As long as the Time-Vary Stopwatch is active, you don't even have to display the layer properties to set a keyframe. Any change in any of the layer properties sets a new keyframe, even if you can't see it. This means you can wreak havoc on your animation without even thinking by moving your layers around the document. Lock the position of your layer (using the Lock icons at the top of the Layers panel) whenever you are not actually creating keyframes.

Using Smart Objects to Animate Transformations

When you have a text layer or a Smart Object layer, you can animate transformations. This means you can scale, rotate, pan, or zoom your layer over time as well as change the position. You can do this with any layer, because any layer can be turned into a Smart Object layer.

Managing Multiple Layers

The more clips you have, the more unwieldy the Timeline panel can become, especially when you are displaying layer properties. Remember that you can change the settings to show only those clips you are working on.

The keyframes you have set operate whether the layer properties are being displayed or not, so reduce the view of the layer properties whenever you are not placing keyframes. This is a great way to avoid accidentally clicking the Time-Vary Stopwatch icon and deleting all those hard-placed keyframes.

A Smart Object layer is a layer composed of an embedded file. The embedded file is protected from changes made in the main file. Filters placed on a Smart Object change the appearance of the layer in the main file, for example, but the embedded file is protected in its original state and is easily accessed. In order to animate transformations on any layer that is not a text layer, that layer must be converted to a Smart Object layer.

 Smart Objects are covered in Chapter 10.

You can change a layer into a Smart Object layer and animate a transformation by following these steps:

1. **Open a file with which you would like to animate a transformation.**

   We used the file shown in Figure 26.13, animating the bubbles so that they drifted and changed size and shape.

FIGURE 26.13

There are several layers in this file that we can convert to Smart Objects so that we can their size, position, and shape.

2. **Select the layer that you would like to animate and choose Filter ⇨ Convert for Smart Filters.**

   Unless the layer you are using is already a Smart Object or a text layer, you need to convert it in order to animate a transformation.

3. **Choose Window ⇨ Timeline to open the Timeline panel.**

4. **Click the triangle next to the clip name in the Timeline panel to show the layer properties, and click the Time-Vary Stopwatch icon next to the word Transform to activate it.**

5. **Set the playhead to the beginning of the Timeline and place your object in the position from which you want it to start.**

   In this example, we wanted the bubbles to start right where they were in the image.

6. **Move the playhead to the next position.**

   We wanted our bubbles to drift slowly, so we decided to place our playhead at 3 seconds.

7. **Transform your Smart Object to create a new keyframe.**

   You can move your object just by dragging it. To transform it, press Ctrl+T/⌘+T to create a bounding box and then scale and rotate your object. We moved a bubble forward, and then enlarged and rotated it, as you can see in Figure 26.14.

FIGURE 26.14

By moving this bubble forward and changing its size, we've animated a transformation.

8. **Continue making changes until your animation is just how you want it.**

   We wanted to add a few keyframes to our bubble, giving it a little bit of bounce and changing its shape frequently so that it took on the characteristics of a floating bubble. Then we changed all the bubbles in this file.

Animating the Opacity Setting

The principles of animating opacity are essentially the same as animating position. You can create some cool effects by changing the opacity of layers over time; the Opacity setting lets you create ghosts, change the level of special effects, or simply create a fade transition. This feature can be particularly useful in creating video special effects. Keep in mind that as you learn the basics of creating keyframes, the applications of using keyframes can become very advanced.

Changing the opacity of a layer is as simple as adjusting the Opacity setting in the Layers panel. If the Time-Vary Stopwatch is activated in the Opacity layer property, simply adjusting the opacity at different locations in the Timeline creates keyframes.

With opacity, setting the keyframes isn't nearly as tricky as it is with changing position. It's as easy as deciding what opacity you want where in your animation and setting keyframes at those points. It required only two keyframes to reveal our secrets, as shown in Figure 26.15. You'd think they'd expect it from us by now, but our very gullible family was very relieved to see that the first image was not real.

The important thing here is not how hard it is to animate opacity; it's the flexibility that the tools in Photoshop give to this feature. You can animate the opacity of any layer in your project, including a fill and adjustment layer or a layer style that has been converted to its own layer. You can't animate the actual creation of a paint job or text, but as long as it's on its own layer, you can animate its opacity, fading it in or out over time. Of course, you can set the keyframes to hold interpolations as well, allowing your images or special effects to pop in and out of sight.

FIGURE 26.15

Animating the opacity of the background image with just two keyframes revealed the true risk involved in this feat.

In Figure 26.16, we created a Black & White Adjustment layer over the image of a lion, tinted it green, and applied the Darken Blend mode. These adjustments simulated this photo being taken with an infrared camera. By fading the opacity of the Black & White Adjustment layer over time, we can show you the daytime image that we started with.

FIGURE 26.16

Fading out the adjustment layer is the difference between night and day.

Using Keyframes to Animate Layer Styles

Animating layer styles is the most diverse of the animation capabilities in Photoshop. Animating position or opacity changes just one setting of the selected layer, but there are ten different layer styles. Every time you change the setting of any one of these styles, you can create a keyframe. Use the styles one at a time or together, or bring styles in and out at will. Adjusting layer styles allows you to animate a mind-boggling number of special effects.

Layer styles can be added to a layer by clicking the Layer Styles icon (*fx*) at the bottom of the Layers panel and choosing a style from the list. When you select a layer style, the Layer Styles dialog box opens. From the dialog box, you can edit the properties of the layer style you selected and select additional layer styles.

 The individual layer styles and their settings are covered in detail in Chapter 21.

After you add a layer style, click the Time-Vary Stopwatch icon next to the Style property. Adjust the playhead, and double-click the layer style in the Layers panel to open the Layer Styles dialog box again. Making any change in the Layer Style dialog box — such as adjusting the settings, adding a style, or deleting the style — creates a new keyframe. If you are over an existing keyframe, the changes you make to the layer style change the settings for that keyframe.

In Figure 26.16, we created an adjustment layer over the lion and animated it by fading the opacity. You can fade the opacity of a layer style, but not using the opacity setting in the Layers panel. You need to set the opacity of the style in the Layer Style dialog box.

Most of the time, animating layer styles is just plain fun. By animating a bouncing ball in conjunction with animating an inner glow, you can create the illusion of breaking a light bulb in a lamp, as shown in Figure 26.17.

FIGURE 26.17

A lighted lamp minding its own business

You can break the light bulb in a lamp by bouncing the ball in the house. Follow these steps:

ON THE WEB

For this exercise, you can find a PSD file of the lamp saved as Figure 26-16 on this book's website.

1. **Open Figure 26-16.**

   This is a PSD file that contains the lamp with an inner glow effect applied to it and the ball as separate layers that are ready to animate.

2. **Choose Window ⇨ Timeline to open the Timeline panel.**

3. **Click the triangle next to the Ball clip in the Timeline panel to open the layer properties.**

4. **Click the Time-Vary Stopwatch icon next to the Position property.**

5. **Create several keyframes throughout the Position property to animate the ball bouncing around the canvas.**

   At some point, have the ball go under the lampshade. From there, the ball drops straight down, bouncing once or twice before coming to rest.

26

6. **Click the triangle next to the Ball clip to close the layer properties.**

7. **Click the triangle next to the Lamp Copy clip to open the layer properties.**

8. **Move the Current Time Indicator to the beginning of the Timeline.**

   When you animate the layer style of the lampshade, you want the glow to be on in the beginning of the animation.

9. **Click the Time-Vary Stopwatch icon in the Styles property to activate keyframes.**

10. **Drag the playhead to the moment when the ball goes under the lampshade and hits the light bulb.**

11. **In the Layers panel, click the eye icon next to Effects on the Lamp Copy layer.**

    This turns off the light and creates a keyframe in the Style property.

12. **Select both keyframes in the Style property by clicking the property name or by dragging a selection marquee around both.**

13. **Right-click one keyframe, and choose Hold Interpolation.**

    This causes the light of the lamp to go out instantaneously instead of over time.

14. **Rewind and play back your animation, making any necessary adjustments, as shown in Figure 26.18.**

TIP

As you create animation files with several layers and styles, you'll find that the playback goes slower and slower. To get a better feel for the speed of your project, choose Allow Frame Skipping from the Timeline panel menu. This allows Photoshop to skip frames in playback mode. This helps playback go much faster, if a bit choppy. The final rendered product contains all the frames specified in the document settings.

FIGURE 26.18

Bounce the ball under the lampshade, and turn off the visibility of the lamp's inner glow to create the effect of the ball breaking the light bulb.

Animating the Global Lighting

Global Lighting is a property that is constant throughout a project. It animates the lighting effects of all the layers simultaneously so that shadows are consistent throughout your project. You can view the Global Light track by clicking the Timeline panel menu icon and choosing Show ➪ Global Light Track. This makes the track visible on the Timeline panel, as you can see in Figure 26.19.

FIGURE 26.19

You can view the Global Lighting track in the Timeline panel.

You can change lighting effects in the Layer Style dialog box in any layer style that requires an angle of light, such as the drop shadow or bevel and emboss. In any of the settings for these features, you can select Global Lighting, indicating that you would like the light settings to stay consistent throughout all the styles applied to that particular layer. Once you've selected this option, you can change the setting of the light in any of the layer styles and the light will also change in all other applicable styles.

Global Lighting on the Timeline panel affects the entire project, changing the light settings for all applicable styles throughout the layers. You animate Global Lighting just as you would any layer property, by clicking the Time-Vary Stopwatch icon and setting keyframes, changing the lighting position at each one.

In Figure 26.20, we animated the Global Lighting of the boy's shadow. It moves gradually from one side to the other, giving the illusion that in true teenage style, this boy is just hanging out all day. By animating the Global Lighting, we ensured that any other special effects we might add to this file would be lighted in the same way.

FIGURE 26.20

Animating the Global Lighting moves the shadow in the animation from one side of the boy to the other.

Using Keyframes to Animate Text

Text is just like any other layer in the Timeline panel; you can edit it by transforming it or changing its opacity or style. This is a fun and easy way to create playful captions or credits for animations, videos, or slide shows. Text has one more property that can be animated: the Text Warp property. Creating keyframes in the Text Warp property lets your text morph all over the screen.

You animate the Text Warp by creating a text layer and opening its properties in the Timeline panel. Of course, the layer properties that you want to animate must be activated, so click the Time-Vary Stopwatch icon in the Text Warp layer as well as any other layer you want to animate.

Now all you have to do is make the changes. To warp your text, simply choose the Warp Text option from the Options bar that appears at the top of the Photoshop work area whenever you have the Text tool highlighted. This opens a Warp Text dialog box where you can set the kind of text warp you want, as shown in Figure 26.21. From the drop-down menu, you can select several warp types, such as Arc, Wave, Flag, and so on. Then you can adjust the look of the warp you have chosen by moving the Bend, Horizontal Distortion, and Vertical Distortion sliders. When you are finished, click OK. The warp is created, and so is a keyframe, as shown in Figure 26.22.

FIGURE 26.21

The Warp Text dialog box allows you to distort the look of your text.

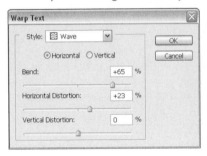

FIGURE 26.22

To begin animating text, add the text and choose a starting position for it

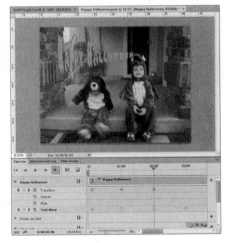

Now you can move on, creating a keyframe whenever you want to change the warp of the text or any of the other text properties, and really give your video some punch!

Animating Masks

When you add a mask to a layer in your image, you add two more properties of your layer that can be animated: the Mask Position property and the Mask Enable property. Animating the mask position allows you to change the position of the mask along with the position of the actual layer. If you have a mask created over a layer and you change only the position of that layer, the layer actually moves through the mask, changing which areas of the layer are visible. In order to keep the mask in place, you must animate the position of the mask as well.

Of course, you can also animate the mask without animating the layer position to create a unique effect. In some cases, you must animate the mask to create the illusion of movement in your layer. If you create a shape, for example, notice that a layer mask is created over a fill over the entire document. You can't really animate the position of a color fill with any noticeable results, which is why we had you rasterize the shape layer in the first example in this chapter, but you can animate the position of the mask to create the illusion that the shape is moving around the document.

You can also use the Mask Enable property to turn masks on or off in an animation. This property works only with a hold interpolation. In other words, the mask is enabled or disabled, never halfway in between.

> **TIP**
>
> Because the Mask Enable property cannot contain linear interpolation, you can't dissolve a mask in or out. You can create the same effect, however, by creating two layers. The first layer contains the unmasked area and the second layer contains the previously masked area (no mask would be needed in this case). Then you could animate the opacity of the second layer.

Building 3D Animations

When you open or create a 3D file in Photoshop, several new properties can be animated in the Timeline. Of course, you can animate the usual properties such as position and opacity, but added to that is the ability to animate the 3D scene position, 3D camera position, 3D render settings, and 3D cross-sections. You can also animate the lights, the materials, and the meshes. This gives you the ability to create 3D animations from scratch with 3D files. Because 3D files are three dimensional, you have greater latitude for creating a realistic animation than you do with simple two-dimensional images.

Figure 26.23 shows the Timeline with a 3D model of a Jeep Wrangler open in Photoshop. You can see that there are many possibilities for animating aspects of a 3D object. In this particular example, we couldn't toggle the 3D materials properties open to show in Figure 26.23 because there are over 30 materials that can be individually animated and the Timeline would no longer fit in the document window of Photoshop.

 In order to animate 3D properties, you need a basic understanding of how to manipulate 3D objects, which are covered in Chapter 22. You also need to understand how to change the properties of individual aspects of the 3D scene, which you can learn about in Chapter 23.

FIGURE 26.23

A 3D model has many properties that you can animate.

To demonstrate how quickly these properties can be animated, we sank the model of the Jeep into the rock. Follow these steps to learn how to animate 3D properties:

1. **Open an image file that can be used as a background for animating your 3D file.**

2. **Choose 3D ➪ New 3D Layer from File to open a 3D model as a new layer over your image file.**

3. **Open the Timeline panel.**

   The Timeline panel is generally docked with Mini-Bridge. Click the tab to display it. You can also choose Window ➪ Timeline.

4. **With the playhead set at the beginning of the Timeline, click the stopwatch icons in the 3D Scene Position property and in the 3D Cross Section property.**

   This activates the keyframes for those two properties.

5. **With the Scene layer selected in the 3D panel, set the start position of your 3D scene using the 3D tools found in the Options bar.**

> **TIP**
>
> Remember that the 3D tools are only visible when the Move tool is selected in the Toolbox.

6. **Click the Cross Section check box in the Properties panel to activate a cross-section of your 3D scene and set the cross-section properties.**

   In our scene, we wanted the Jeep to sink into the rock, so we set the cross-section to the z-axis, flipped it so that the upper section of the Jeep was visible, and offset it so that the starting position was below the tires of the Jeep, leaving the Jeep intact for now.

7. **Move the playhead forward in the Timeline to the desired time of the end result.**

   We wanted our animation to take four seconds, so we moved the playhead to the four-second mark.

8. **Change the properties of your cross-section to reflect the desired final result.**

   We simply changed the offset so that only the very top of the roof was showing.

9. **Change your scene position to the desired end result.**

   We moved our Jeep down so that the edge of the cropped roof rested on the rock.

10. **Play your animation to preview it.**

    We like to select another tool in the Toolbox, such as the Hand tool, as we watch the final result so that the ground plane and widgets disappear. You can see the results of our simple animation in Figure 26.24.

FIGURE 26.24

With the placement of just four keyframes, this Jeep appears to sink into the rock.

Learning the Basics of Rotoscoping

Keyframes are limiting, as you can't animate filters or even paint over time with them. However, you can animate just about anything by employing the technique of rotoscoping. Rotoscoping has been around almost as long as movies. It entails tracing animated characters or scenes over live-action film. It's a useful tool in aiding animators to create more realistic movement because they are copying that movement from life. It's also used to create special effects, such as the light sabers in the *Star Wars* films.

Today, with the use of computers, rotoscoping has taken on a broader definition. Now when you hear the term, it can mean any painting or editing of a video frame, whether or not that frame is over a live-action scene. With its powerful painting capabilities and filters, Photoshop is the champion rotoscoping tool. Although rotoscoping involves making time-consuming changes to video frame by frame, the effects that are possible are well worth the effort.

Creating a new video layer

The first thing you want to do to start animating frame by frame in the Timeline panel is to create a new video layer. Only video layers contain the Altered Video layer that can be changed frame by frame, so if your document doesn't already contain a video file, you need to create a new video layer in order to animate changes at all. Even if you already have video clips in your document, you want to create a new video layer in which to store changes. In fact, it's a good idea to create a new layer for each major element in your animation. Creating a new video layer is as simple as choosing Layer ➪ Video Layers ➪ New Blank Video Layer. A new video layer is added to your project.

> **TIP**
> The first thing you want to do with a blank video layer is give it a unique name that describes the element on that layer.

A video layer has one more property than other types of layers in the Timeline panel. That property, as you can see in Figure 26.25, is an Altered Video sublayer. Within that sublayer, frames can be altered one at a time to create an animation.

Creating modified frames

Now that you have a new blank video clip, you are ready to animate. You can animate frame by frame in the Timeline by creating modified frames inside of the blank video layer. By creating modified frames, you will be able to change your video in many ways to add elements and create special effects. We'll show you how this is done.

FIGURE 26.25

You can create an animation on a new blank video clip with the Altered Video property.

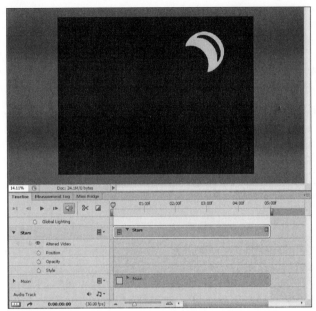

You can create individual frames inside any video layer by following these steps:

1. **With the blank video layer highlighted, move the playhead in the Timeline to the position where you want to make the first change.**

2. **Paint or otherwise make changes to the layer.**

3. **Click the triangle next to the name of your blank video layer.**

   This shows you the properties of that layer, including the Altered Video sublayer. Within the Altered Video sublayer, a small segment has appeared, indicating an altered frame, as shown in Figure 26.26.

4. **To build onto the changes you have already made, choose Layer ⇨ Video Layers ⇨ Duplicate Frame to move to the next frame and duplicate the frame you just created.**

5. **Make further changes to your animation.**

6. **Continue duplicating frames and making changes to your animation until you have completed it.**

   We animated stars appearing in the night sky, as shown in Figure 26.27.

FIGURE 26.26

The purple segment in the Altered Video layer indicates one altered frame.

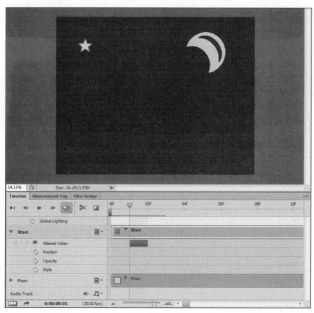

FIGURE 26.27

By animating these stars frame by frame, they appeared a little at a time in the night sky.

You may not want to build on the animation created in a previous frame. That's okay; just navigate to an unaltered frame and make new changes. You can move to the next frame by using the frame advance in the playback controls or by selecting Go to Next Frame in the Timeline panel menu. You can also choose Layer ➪ Video Layers ➪ Insert Blank Frame.

Using onion skins

An onion skin, a real onion skin right off an onion, is semitransparent and very thin; onion-skin paper is also semitransparent and thin — that's how it got its name. This quality has made it ideal for use in animation to make the transitions smoother from one frame to the next. The idea is that the previous frame can be traced onto the next frame, making the small changes necessary to create the illusion of movement.

Computer animation has made using onion skins an incredibly simple process. By temporarily making your animation frames semitransparent, you can create the next step in your animation by referring to the last one.

That's the basic idea. Photoshop allows you to set parameters for the Onion Skins feature that go far beyond just being able to see the last frame from the present frame such as seeing multiple frames at once in different stages of opacity. Besides having multiple settings for the Onion Skins themselves, there are other benefits of using Photoshop. You can create Onion Skins in any clip and make modifications in a different clip. For example, you might want to animate a motion trail for something that is moving in a video layer, such as a space ship. You could create Onion Skins in the live-action video layer and paint over the motion in a blank video layer.

To access the Onion Skin settings, select Onion Skin Settings from the Timeline panel menu. The Onion Skin Options dialog box opens, and you can set any number of ways for your Onion Skins to work. As you make changes in the dialog box, you can see how they affect the view of the current frame in the Timeline in real time, as shown in Figure 26.28.

FIGURE 26.28

The Onion Skin Options dialog box offers a much greater range of options than a piece of tracing paper.

You can use the following settings to modify the Onion Skins feature:

- **Onion Skin Count.** This section allows you to set the number of frames that you want to show through to the current frame, both before and after the current frame. You can show up to eight frames before and eight frames after.

- **Frame Spacing.** This field determines whether the frames being shown are consecutive or appear with gaps in between. A setting of 1 means the frames are shown in consecutive order. A setting of 2 means that only every other frame is shown.

- **Max and Min Opacity %.** These fields specify the maximum and minimum opacity of frames. If you have more than one Onion Skin Count, you probably want to see the closer frames at a higher opacity than those that are farther out from the current frame. These two settings allow you to set the maximum opacity for the closer frames and the minimum opacity for the farthest frames. The frames in the middle are a setting somewhere in between the two opacities.

- **Blend Mode.** This drop-down menu allows you to change the way the opacity setting is applied to the Onion Skins. Different files are easier to work with in different blend modes. You can choose from four blend modes: Normal, Multiply, Screen, and Difference.

When you have made the changes to the Onion Skin options, click OK to close the dialog box. The Onion Skins are automatically enabled with the settings you specified. You can toggle the Onion Skins on by choosing Enable Onion Skins from the Timeline panel menu.

As you move along in your animation, the Onion Skins move with you, helping you to create any frame along the Timeline. You can change the settings at any time as your needs change.

Restoring frames

As you make changes to various frames, you might come to a point where you want to discard the edits to one frame or all of them. This is as easy as selecting the frame that you want to restore to its original appearance and choosing Layer ⇨ Video Layers ⇨ Restore Frame. If you want to discard all the altered frames, choose Layer ⇨ Video Layers ⇨ Restore All Frames. Unfortunately, this process is not as easy as using the hotkey for deletion or dropping the altered layers into the trash, but hopefully you won't need to use it often.

Animating DICOM Files

A DICOM file is a medical image or series of images created when you have a sonogram, a CT scan, an MRI, or any number of procedures that take an image of the inside of your body. Photoshop has the capability to view these files as well as animate them. Animating a DICOM file is very similar to importing an image sequence. Of course, to create an animation, you must have a series of DICOM images.

To open a series of DICOM files and animate them, follow these steps:

1. **Choose File ⇨ Open.**

2. **Browse to a DICOM file that is a series of images.**

   DICOM files have the capability of saving an image sequence as one file. Select the file, and click OK. A dialog box opens, allowing you to set the parameters for opening the DICOM file, as shown in Figure 26.29.

3. **Select the frames you want to animate by pressing and holding the Ctrl/⌘ key as you select them one by one, or click Select All.**

4. **Click the Import frames as layers radio button in the options on the right side of the dialog box to create a layer for each frame that is imported.**

5. **Select Anonymize if you want to scrub out the headers contained in the DICOM images.**

6. **Click Open.**

7. **From the Timeline panel menu, select Make Frames from Layers.**

You can see in Figure 26.30 that a frame has been created for each image contained in the DICOM file. Now you can view the file as an animation or export it in a video file format.

FIGURE 26.29

You can open a DICOM file in several ways, or you can simply export it to a JPEG. In this example, you want to animate it, so you need to create a layer for each image in the DICOM file.

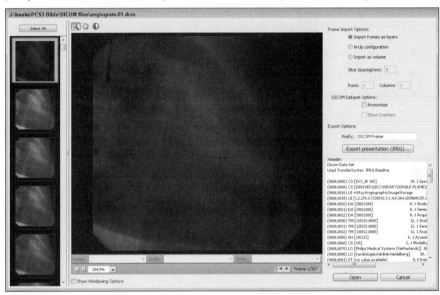

FIGURE 26.30

The Timeline (Frames) panel shows more clearly how each image has become a frame in this new DICOM animation.

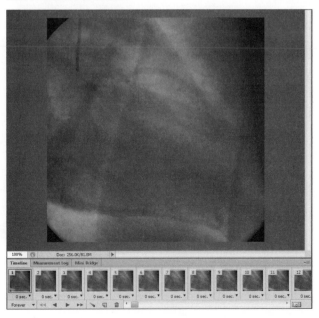

Summary

In this chapter, you learned how keyframes play an important part in making animation easy and fun. With the powerful Photoshop tools at your disposal in creating animations, what you can create is limited only by your imagination. You learned how to do the following:

- Create and edit a keyframe
- Animate the different properties of a layer
- Animate a text warp
- Animate one frame at a time
- Animate DICOM files

Correcting Video Files and Adding Artistic Effects

IN THIS CHAPTER

Changing the color and tone of a video

Using videos as Smart Objects

Correcting a video layer using filters

Cloning and healing within a video file

The basics of improving your video files by correcting lighting and color, adding artistic effects, or cloning and healing inside of them are not much different than making these changes to an image file. The tools are the same, and the effects they have on video files are identical to the effects they have on image files. The difference lies in how you want the effects applied to your video. Effects can be applied to the entire file, to a portion of the file, or to an individual frame. This chapter demonstrates different methods of application and gives examples of where you would use each one.

Enhancing Layers with Color Corrections

Color correction can enhance almost any photo, particularly when the photo was taken in bad lighting. Videos are even more susceptible to environmental lighting problems that need correction. When it comes to color correcting a video layer, you can use the Image menu to change the video frame by frame, or you can create a fill or adjustment layer that affects the entire video layer. Unless you are creating a special effect or animating a color correction, you want to skip the tedious process of color correcting frame by frame.

 This chapter assumes you know how and why to apply adjustment layers in Photoshop. In Chapter 10, you can learn about the individual fill and adjustment layers and what they can do to correct not only photos but also videos.

On the other hand, color corrections apply specifically to the image you are working with. They are different from filters in this respect. You can sharpen (to some degree) a video file arbitrarily over the entire file and probably not be disappointed with the results, but if you adjust the levels of a video file that contains a combination of lighter and darker images, you will find that the overall results are horrible. As you color correct, you want to carefully split the video layer into sections that consist of similar areas in color and tone.

Adding an adjustment layer to a video clip is as simple as selecting the video clip you would like to adjust and choosing an adjustment layer from the Layers panel, just as you would with an image file. The adjustment layer you choose is added to the Layers panel and is automatically grouped with the selected video clip. It is also linked with the video clip so that the adjustment only affects the selected video clip, and not any other layers that are below it, as shown in Figure 27.1.

FIGURE 27.1

An adjustment layer appears in a grouping with the video layer that it affects.

In addition, every fill or adjustment layer is created with a layer mask. If you have an area of your video file selected, the mask automatically reflects that selection. If you don't have anything selected in the file, the mask is white, indicating that the entire file is selected. You can delete or change the layer mask at any time, keeping in mind that it also affects the entire duration of the video clip.

When newly placed, an adjustment layer continues through the duration of the video clip that it is linked to. For instance, you can see in Figure 27.2 that we have added a Levels adjustment to the Wedding Exit clip and a Hue/Saturation adjustment to the Bride & Family clip. Because these adjustments are linked to their respective layers, the adjustments last for the duration of the clip only. You can change the way the adjustment affects your document by unclipping it from the video layer or changing its duration.

> **NOTE**
>
> In order for you to see the adjustment layers in Figure 27.2, we ungrouped the adjustments from the video layers. When these adjustments are placed in a group, they are not visible on the Timeline.

FIGURE 27.2

Because the adjustment layers are automatically clipped to the video clip that was selected when they were applied, they last for the duration of that clip only.

Unclipping an adjustment layer

Using the Properties panel, you can unclip the adjustment you created from the video clip it's attached to so that it affects all the layers. You may want to do this in order to create a Levels adjustment over several clips that were shot in similar lighting, or if you are adding a color effect to an entire video project. To unclip a fill or adjustment layer from the layer below it, select it in the Layers panel and click the New adjustments affect all layers below icon in the Properties panel. Once you've done that, the fill or adjustment layer expands to fill the entire duration of the video, as you can see in Figure 27.3.

917

FIGURE 27.3

When you unclip a fill or adjustment layer from the video layer below it, it affects the entire video file.

> **NOTE**
>
> A fill layer appears in the Layers panel and in the Timeline panel as its own layer. You can't clip a fill layer to the layer below it, only the adjustments that can be applied and changed using the Properties panel. You can use any of the other methods of restricting layers mentioned in this section on a fill layer.

Changing the duration of an adjustment layer

When you add an adjustment layer to your video, the duration is automatically set from the position of the playhead to the end of the video clip that is selected. To change the duration of the adjustment, you need to ungroup it from the video group in which it has been placed.

Follow these steps to change the duration of an adjustment layer:

1. **Right-click the group layer in the Layers panel.**

   This opens a shortcut menu specific to the group layer.

2. **Click Ungroup Layers.**

   This deletes the group layer, and each of the layers previously contained in this group become separate from the others. Your adjustment layer appears in the Timeline panel.

3. **Drag the beginning or end of the duration bar for the adjustment layer so it is exactly as long as you need it to be, as shown in Figure 27.4.**

 You can adjust the duration of any layer using several methods outlined in Chapter 26.

FIGURE 27.4

Changing the duration of an adjustment layer means ungrouping it, which allows you to access it in the Timeline.

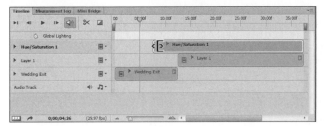

Applying Smart Filters to Video Files

You can add filters to a video clip in two ways: by adding them directly to a regular clip or by changing the clip into a Smart Object and adding Smart Filters. This has special implications for a video clip, because adding a filter directly to it changes only one frame of video, causing your filter to blip in and out of existence too fast for the eye to see. To avoid having to add a filter one frame at a time, you need to change your video layer into a Smart Object.

When you change a layer into a Smart Object, the thumbnail in the Layers panel changes to show that the layer is treated differently. After you've converted a video layer to a Smart Object, you can see a difference in the Timeline panel as well. Figure 27.5 shows the Timeline panel after the video layer has been changed to a Smart Object. There is no Altered Video property for a Smart Object. Now this layer is just like an image or 3D layer; any changes made to it affect the entire layer.

Adding a Smart Filter to a Smart Object that is an embedded video clip is no different than adding a Smart Filter to any other Smart Object. Choose a filter from the Filter menu, change the settings if necessary, and add it to your file. You can use corrective filters, such as the sharpening or blurring filters, or you can create artistic effects by applying other filters.

When you add a filter to a video clip that has been turned into a Smart Object, it affects the entire layer, and the filter is applied as a sublayer in the Layers panel, as shown in Figure 27.6. Now, as you play back your video, you see the filter's effects all the way through.

FIGURE 27.5

There is no Altered Video property in a Smart Object, even if it was once a video layer.

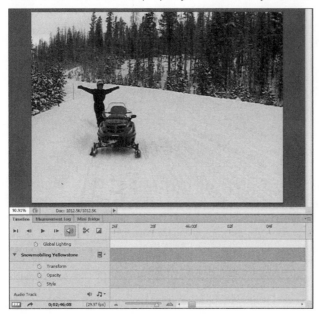

FIGURE 27.6

A Smart Filter is applied to the entire layer.

After you've converted a video layer to a Smart Object, you can use the embedded video clip to make changes to the Altered Video property. You can do this by double-clicking the Smart Object layer thumbnail. Photoshop opens the original document containing your video layer, as shown in Figure 27.7. When you finish making changes to the original file, save it and the changes are reflected in the new file containing the Smart Object. Turning your file into a Smart Object adds a few steps to the editing process, but if you want to apply a filter across the entire video layer, it's the only way to go.

FIGURE 27.7

Double-clicking the thumbnail of a Smart Object gives you two files to work with: one a video layer that can be changed frame by frame and the other a Smart Object file.

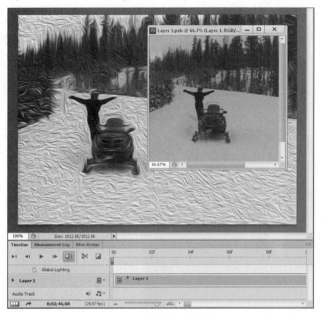

In essence, having the option to turn a video layer into a Smart Object gives you full editing capability. You can apply a filter frame by frame or you can apply the filter to the entire video clip. The method you use depends on the effect you are trying to create, of course. Using a filter to correct a video layer usually incorporates the entire file. If you are creating special effects, however, you may want to change your filter frame by frame or add it to a small segment of your video.

 The filters, including Smart Objects and Smart Filters, are covered thoroughly in Chapter 20.

Cloning and Healing Over an Entire Video Layer

As a general rule, cloning and healing in video layers is done on a frame-by-frame basis, simply because a video involves movement, and movement makes cloning or healing a specific area difficult and still achieve desirable results. There are instances, however, where you may be able to create a fix that lasts at least several frames, saving you from the tedious process of cloning frames one at a time.

In order to do this, the video must be stable, probably taken with the camera on a tripod, and the object or flaw that you want to remove must be stationary over several frames. The 3D video pictured in Figure 27.8 is a perfect example. The fern in the background is stationary through several frames. By creating a new blank layer over the video file and sampling all layers, we were able to create one clone fix that took the fern out over several frames, as shown in Figure 27.9. The fix worked until the shadow of the ball intersected with the cloned area, as shown in Figure 27.10. At this point, we ended the duration of the clone layer and used the Altered Video property to clone each frame separately, as demonstrated later in this chapter.

FIGURE 27.8

This video is stable and the fern is stationary, so we could clone it out of several frames with just one fix.

FIGURE 27.9

A blank layer placed over our video layer contained the fix, so the default duration lasted the entire video.

ON THE WEB
You can try this clone fix by downloading Figure 27-8 from the book's website.

FIGURE 27.10

The clone no longer worked at this point in the video, so we changed the duration of the clone layer and made frame-by-frame fixes.

 You can learn all about the cloning and healing tools and how to use them in Chapter 15. You will also find this video file used in another cloning example in that chapter.

NOTE
Cloning or healing to a blank layer is necessary if you want your fix to last more than one frame. This is because creating a cloning or healing fix on a video layer creates an altered frame in the Altered Video property and consequently changes only the frame you have currently selected.

Modifying Video Clips Frame by Frame

In Chapter 26, we introduced you to the basics of rotoscoping, and now we show you how you can use the rotoscoping techniques to apply corrections to your video on a frame-by-frame basis. Modifying video clips frame by frame enables you to make corrections and add artistic effects. For example, you can remove unwanted elements from video clips frame by frame by using the cloning and healing tools. You can animate transformations, such as skew, distort, and warp, frame by frame. You can also animate adjustments and filters by changing them frame by frame. In Figure 27.11, we animated a color adjustment over a still photo to give it more life.

FIGURE 27.11

To animate a color change, you need to apply the Color Balance adjustment frame by frame.

Adding an adjustment to a single frame

Throughout this book, whenever we have talked about adding adjustments to a file, we have shown you how to create an adjustment layer using either the Layers panel icon or the Adjustment panel. The versatility of having adjustments that you can move and edit has greatly outweighed the inconvenience of adding one more layer to the Layers panel. If you want to add adjustments to a video frame by frame, however, that all changes.

You can create an adjustment layer that affects only one frame of video, but you need to reduce its duration in the Timeline to one frame, and then create a new adjustment layer for the next frame. You can see that unless you are planning to change only a handful of frames — less than in the blink of an eye in a standard video file — creating a new adjustment layer for each frame of video quickly becomes unwieldy.

So, for the first time in this book, we are going to suggest that you use the Image ➪ Adjustments menu to apply the adjustments directly to a video layer, creating an adjusted frame in the Altered Video property of that layer. Although the adjustments made in the Altered Video property are hard to change, this is ultimately the better option.

With the video layer selected, choose Image ➪ Adjustments and select the adjustment you want to apply. The adjustment is added to the currently selected frame. You can then move to the next frame of video and add a new adjustment. Most of the adjustments have hotkeys, and an action is very useful if you are planning to make extensive adjustment changes.

Adding a filter to a single frame

The filters are simpler to add to a single frame of video than an adjustment. As we mentioned earlier in this chapter, you can't add a filter to an entire video file unless it is a Smart Object. Simply adding any filter to a video file creates a new segment in the Altered Video property. There are several reasons for adding a filter frame by frame. You can animate it by applying or reducing the filter effects over time, or you may want to apply a mask so the filter is applied only to selected areas of a video file. As the video changes, the mask needs to change as well, requiring work in each frame.

Cloning and healing video files

Most of the cloning and healing you do to a video file needs to be done frame by frame. The ability to use alternate clone sources is vital because you can clone one frame into another. For example, Figure 27.12 shows an image of a happy couple on their wedding day. They are preparing for a romantic kiss. The video effect is in slow motion, there's a great love song playing in the background, and love is in the air. Jump ahead several frames to Figure 27.13. The kiss is still very romantic, the music is still playing, but some unromantic company has joined the shot.

To fix this problem, activate the Clone Stamp tool and open the Clone Source panel. Rewind to the first frame, and Alt-click/Option-click to use it as a source. Using the overlay, place it over each of the next few frames to clone out the company with a few quick swipes of the mouse. Although the couple is moving, it's easy to use the architecture of the building as well as the light in the flowerbed to line up the overlay exactly, as shown in Figure 27.14. After the overlay is lined up, you can simply click and drag the Clone Stamp tool over the areas you want to hide, and the illusion is perfect, as shown in Figure 27.15.

FIGURE 27.12

This shot of the happy couple is unmarred.

FIGURE 27.13

Unexpected company distracts from the mood of the video.

FIGURE 27.14

Lining up the clone source is easy using stable objects in the video.

FIGURE 27.15

Cloning out the extras restores the romance.

Of course, you can see in Figure 27.16 that only one frame of your video has been changed so far. You're in for a long frame-by-frame fix. However, using the Clone Stamp is so much fun that it might even be enjoyable. To really use the five clone sources available to you in the Clone Source panel, you probably want to choose five different frames to clone so that as the camera moves even a miniscule amount, you have a clone source that easily matches the angle and size.

FIGURE 27.16

The Clone Stamp tool changes a video layer frame by frame.

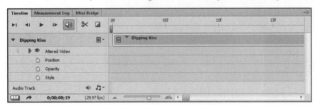

Locking the source frame

As you use the Cloning tool to change a video file frame by frame, one option in the Clone Source panel is going to be critical to your success. When you choose a clone source from a video file, you have the option to lock the source to the frame that you originally sampled or to move the source the same number of frames you move from the first target in the Timeline. In other words, after fixing the frame in Figure 27.16, we plan to move onto the next frame of video to fix that frame as well.

If the Lock Frame check box is selected in the Clone Source panel, as shown in the first panel in Figure 27.17, the clone source remains the same frame that we used to change the previous frame of video. In this case, frame 837 continues to be our source. If the Lock Frame check box is not selected, the clone source moves ahead one frame in our video. The second Clone Source panel in Figure 27.17 shows that the frame offset remains at –3 frames, no matter what frame we target.

If your video is stable, you may find that it's easier to use a locked source that you know is clear and free of defects. If your video is unsteady, it might be easier to use a frame offset that is only one or two frames away from the frame you are changing. In most cases, this helps to keep the source and sample frames similar.

FIGURE 27.17

Lock the target frame if you want it to be consistent throughout your edits with the Cloning tool.

27

Summary

In this chapter, you learned that applying fixes to a video file can be a tricky process involving both the Layers panel and the Timeline panel. Mastering the properties of each one has given you the capability to make corrections to your video as a whole or to make them frame by frame. You learned how to do the following:

- Add adjustments to video files
- Use filters to create fun artistic effects
- Clone and heal video layers

Animating Using Frames

N ow that you are familiar with how the Timeline works, we introduce you to the frame animation version of the Timeline panel. The frame animation version of the Timeline panel is very different from the Timeline; it has a different look and feel and different features to go along with it.

The video Timeline panel is made primarily for you to import video files and color correct, enhance, or create artistic effects with them. The frame animation version of the Timeline panel is meant primarily to be used with the painting and drawing tools to create cartoon animations, primarily animated GIF files for the web.

> **NOTE**
>
> Animated GIFs are small, animated images or icons that you see almost everywhere on the web. They are usually simple, such as animated smiley faces, and operate at an extremely slow frame rate, giving their motion a jerky appearance.

You'll find that the panels and menus of these two types of animation are completely different from one another. In this chapter, we introduce you to the frame animation version of the Timeline panel and show you different methods of animating using this panel.

Using the Timeline Panel's Frame Animation Interface

Although frame animation has most of the capability of the Timeline, you'll find that its strength lies in creating short, crude animations, such as animated GIFs. Being able to see each frame without dragging the playhead around is very handy. Frame animation can become unwieldy in a few frames, however, as you'll see when you begin to create animations in this chapter.

Some of the other advantages of frame animation are the ability to reverse frames or set the frame rate of each frame individually without much effort. If you change a Timeline to a frame animation, however, you permanently lose some of the properties of the keyframes set in your Timeline. You must determine which animation method you want to use before you begin a project. Before we show you how to create animations using the frame animation version of the Timeline panel, let's look at the features that distinguish frames from the Timeline.

Using the panel features

Just as the name implies, frames are represented by thumbnails of each individual frame in your animation. This gives it an entirely different look than the Timeline, as shown in Figure 28.1. The look of the animation is not the only thing that's changed; the actual panel has completely different options. Let's look at what the differences are and why they are different.

FIGURE 28.1

The frame animation version of the Timeline panel offers a unique set of options.

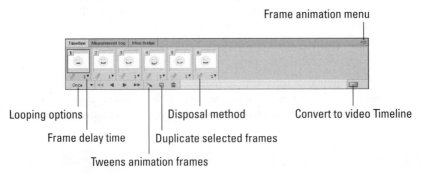

Frame animation menu

Looping options

Frame delay time

Tweens animation frames

Duplicate selected frames

Disposal method

Convert to video Timeline

Setting the frame delay time

The frame delay time allows you to quickly set the time you want each frame to last. Click the arrow next to the frame time below the thumbnail, and select the number of seconds or fractions of seconds you want your frame to last. Click Other if you would like to set a time that is not specified. You can select one frame at a time and set different rates, or you can select all the frames to change the rates in all of them at the same time. When you add a new frame to the animation, it automatically retains the delay rate of the frame immediately before it.

Changing the disposal method

The Disposal method icon doesn't appear by default on the frame icons, but if you right-click one or more selected thumbnails, you are asked to choose a disposal method. Choosing either Do Not Dispose or Dispose creates a different icon for each method of animation.

A disposal method simply determines whether the current frame is disposed of as the next frame is displayed. There are three disposal options:

- **Automatic.** This is the default option. It allows Photoshop to determine the disposal method for each frame automatically. The current frame is disposed of if the next frame contains layer transparency. When you select this option, no icon appears in the frame thumbnail.

- **Do Not Dispose.** This option preserves the current frame as the next frame is brought into view. If any part of the frame is transparent, the preceding frames show through.

- **Dispose.** This option disposes of the current frame as the next frame is displayed, preserving the transparency of the current frame.

Choosing your looping options

Setting the looping option simply determines how many times your animation plays without stopping. Click the Looping options icon to open a menu, and select Once, 3 times, Forever, or Other. If you select Other, a dialog box opens, allowing you to specify the number of times you want the animation to loop.

Tweening using frames

Keyframes are not in the frame animation version of the Timeline panel, but you can still take advantage of tweening. *Tweening* is the process of creating frames between two frames with different properties, making the change gradual over several frames. When you have enough frames, you give the change the illusion of true motion. Although the frame animation version of the Timeline panel has no layer properties, the properties that can be animated in the Timeline are the same properties that can be tweened using frames. These properties are position, opacity, and style.

To create tweening frames, select one or two frames in the panel and click the Tweens animation frames icon, shown in Figure 28.2. The Tween dialog box opens, as shown in Figure 28.3, allowing you to set options for the tweening.

FIGURE 28.2

Select one or two frames to tween.

FIGURE 28.3

You can set the tweening operation, number of frames to add as well as the layer, position opacity and effects options in the Tween dialog box.

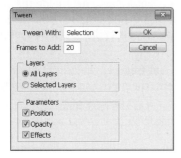

Tween with

The first option available in the Tween dialog box is the Tween With menu that allows you to set which frames you are going to tween, as follows:

- **Selection.** This is the default option if you've selected the two frames that you want to tween. If you don't have two frames selected, this option isn't highlighted.

- **First Frame.** This option can be chosen only if you have selected the last frame in the animation. If you select the First Frame option, Photoshop tweens between the last frame and the first frame of the animation, creating a seamless loop.

- **Last Frame.** This option is available only if you have the first frame of the animation selected. Just like the First Frame option, this creates tweening from the last frame to the first frame.

- **Previous Frame.** This option creates tweening between the selected frame and the preceding frame.

- **Next Frame.** This option creates tweening between the selected frame and the next frame.

Frames to add

The next option in the Tween dialog box is simply how many frames you want to have created between the frames you are tweening. You should take into account how long your frame rate is and the complexity of the difference in the frames you want to tween.

Layers

Next in the Tween dialog box, you can set the layers that will be affected by the tween. Choose All Layers if you would like to animate all the layers within the file, or choose Selected Layers to confine the tweening to layers you have selected. In Figure 28.2, we were animating the sun as well as the drop shadow of the boy, so we chose All Layers.

Parameters

The Parameters setting is reminiscent of the animation properties in the Timeline panel, where you can decide whether to tween all changes in position, opacity, and style or to tween only one or two of these parameters. Choosing a parameter is the equivalent of using linear keyframes in an interpolation, whereas deselecting a parameter is like creating a hold keyframe.

After you set the tweening options, click OK. The frames you have specified are created, as shown in Figure 28.4.

FIGURE 28.4

Just like setting keyframes, tweening creates a smooth transition from one frame to another by applying the change over a series of frames.

Duplicating selected frames

Click the Duplicate selected frames icon on the bottom of the frame animation version of the Timeline panel, and all the frames you have selected at the time are copied and pasted directly behind the last frame selected. This is a quick and easy way to duplicate the last frame and then make changes to it.

Converting to the video Timeline

To convert the frame animation version of the Timeline back to the video Timeline, click the icon labeled Convert to video Timeline. You should do this before you start working with your animation. Moving from the video Timeline causes some of the properties — keyframes in particular — to be lost. Toggling back to the video Timeline does not restore the lost properties. It's best to decide which version of the Timeline panel you want to work in before opening or creating a new document, and stick to that decision.

Activating the frame animation version of the Timeline panel menu

Click the menu icon to activate the flyout menu for the frame animation version of the Timeline panel. It is very different from the Timeline menu, so we introduce you to the different options in the next section.

Looking at the frame animation Timeline panel menu

Just in case you hadn't yet noticed, the frame animation panel menu lets you know that you are not working with the same tools as the video Timeline panel menu. As shown in Figure 28.5, the menus have completely different options.

FIGURE 28.5

Comparing the frame animation version of the Timeline panel menu with the video Timeline panel menu

These differences highlight the features of each panel and the reasons why each panel can perform equally important but different functions. We define the features found on the frame animation menu here. Many of these options are self-explanatory, but a few may be unfamiliar. If you find that a short definition isn't enough, don't worry. You'll see more on these features later in this chapter.

Here is a brief overview of the features:

- **New Frame.** This option creates a frame at the end of the animation. This frame is a duplicate of the last frame in the animation.

- **Delete Frame.** This option deletes any selected frames.

- **Delete Animation.** This option deletes all frames except the first one, leaving an image rather than an animation.

- **Copy Frame.** This option copies selected frames.

- **Paste Frame.** This option pastes copied frames. You can choose four options for pasting a frame:

  - **Replace Frames.** This option replaces all selected frames and their accompanying layers with the copied frames.

  - **Paste Over Selection.** This option pastes the copied frames over the selected frames, creating two levels of layers: the layers in view, belonging to the copied frames, and the layers that are hidden, belonging to the selected frames.

- **Paste Before Selection.** This option pastes the copied frames before the first selected frame.

- **Paste After Selection.** This option pastes the copied frames after the last selected frame.

- **Link Added Layers.** This option works in conjunction with the previous four options to automatically link layers in the pasted frame. It is a good idea to link the layers of frames in the animation so that you can more easily make adjustments while editing your animation.

- **Select All Frames.** This option selects all frames within the animation.

- **Go To.** This option selects the frame that you specify — next, previous, first, or last.

- **Tween.** This option performs the same function as the Tween icon in the panel. It creates a specified number of frames in between two selected frames to bridge the gap in their differences.

- **Reverse Frames.** This option reverses the order of any selected frames. If only one frame is selected, the order of the entire animation is reversed.

- **Optimize Animation.** This option allows you to reduce the file size of an animation by optimizing the frames to include only areas or pixels that change from frame to frame. You have two options for optimization: Bounding Box crops each frame to an area around the changing pixel, and Redundant Pixel Removal makes any unchanged pixels transparent. You can enable both of these options when optimizing the animation.

- **Make Frames From Layers.** This option is available when the animation contains only one frame or image. When you select Make Frames From Layers, all the layers contained in the image become an individual frame.

- **Flatten Frames Into Layers.** This option allows you to create an individual layer for each selected frame in the Layers panel.

- **Match Layer Across Frames.** This option allows you to align layers according to the parameters of position, visibility, and style.

- **Create New Layer for Each New Frame.** This option creates a new layer in the Layers panel for every frame created in the frame animation version of the Timeline panel.

- **New Layers Visible in All Frames.** This option makes the new layers that you create on any frame visible in all the frames. Deselect this option if you want to add a layer to a selected number of frames.

- **Convert to Timeline.** This option converts your frame animation version of the Timeline panel to the video Timeline panel.

- **Panel Options.** This option allows you to set a thumbnail size for the frames in your animation.

28

Using the animation features in the Layers panel

When you are using the frame animation version of the Timeline panel, you not only see differences in the Animation panel and the Panel menu, but in the Layers panel as well. The Layers panel includes an array of tools that allow you to unify changes made to the layers displayed in this panel. The properties that you can unify are the same properties that you can animate. By default, making changes to these properties takes place only on the selected frame. By unifying these properties, you can make changes to all the frames at once, similar to changing an entire layer across the Timeline. Figure 28.6 shows the icons that are used for this purpose.

FIGURE 28.6

The Unify icons are located in the Layers panel.

Unify layer visibility

Unify layer position | Unify layer style

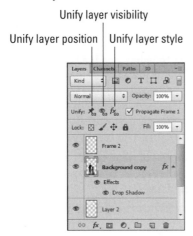

- **Unify layer position.** When you click this icon, you can change the position of a layer throughout the animation. Deselecting this option allows you to change the position of the selected image only, leaving the rest as they were.

- **Unify layer visibility.** When you select this option, changing the visibility of a layer changes the visibility in all frames; otherwise, only the selected frames are changed.

- **Unify layer style.** When you select this option, Photoshop creates a layer style across all the frames in the animation.

- **Propagate Frame 1.** When you select this option, all the changes made in the first frame of the animation are also made to subsequent frames in the animation. This is an easy way to make the changes that can be animated in other frames and still be able to change the position, opacity, and style of all the frames at once.

Creating Tweened Frame Animations

Creating tweened frame animation is the process of animating by generating new frames that transition step by step between two frames. This is similar to using keyframes in the video Timeline panel. Using tween frame animation you can quickly build an animation by just creating a few main frames and then animating between them.

Opening an image to animate

The first step is to open or create a file in which you want to animate at least one of three properties: position, opacity, or effects. An image that is composed of several layers and styles can be much more interesting and fun to animate than a simple image. Figure 28.7 shows an image created by using a composite of a photo, a 3D object, and several layer styles to show a gateway to another world. We used this image to animate the gateway opening.

FIGURE 28.7

A mysterious gateway

After opening a file, choose Window➪Animation if you don't already have the Animation panel open. The Animation panel opens by default to the video Timeline panel. Use the Convert to frame animation icon at the bottom-right corner of the panel to convert the panel to the frame animation version of the Timeline panel. You can also choose Convert to frame animation from the Panel menu.

Your image becomes the first frame in your new frame animation. For simple animations, you may want to take a moment to change the frame rate to a slower speed, such as 15 frames per second, by clicking the arrow at the bottom of the frame thumbnail. This makes the file smaller, but less smooth in transitions. Remember that you can also change the size of the thumbnails by opening the Panel menu and choosing Panel Options.

Creating keyframes

Now that you've opened a document and the animation panel, you need to create keyframes. The video Timeline panel allowed you to create keyframe icons that let you visualize where the changes were being made. It's also true that a keyframe is defined as a frame that determines a change in the animation process. In frame animation mode, you can actually visualize your keyframes, because they each have a frame thumbnail in the panel. The downside is that after you've tweened those keyframes, nothing distinguishes them from any other frame in the panel.

To create a keyframe, you need to determine what you plan to animate and how you want that animation to proceed. Is the image you opened the first, middle, or last of your animation? Before you create a new frame, change anything you need to in the first image to make it look like you want your first frame to look.

We wanted to make two new keyframes for our gateway to another world. First, we wanted the gateway to appear, and then to activate. Because we started with a view of just the photo, we changed the opacity of the layer containing the arch and the layer style to zero, as shown in Figure 28.8.

FIGURE 28.8

The first keyframe is a photo of a simple desert landscape.

Now you are ready to create a new frame. Click the Duplicate selected frames icon at the bottom of the frame animation panel. A new frame is created that has the exact same features of the first frame — the same frame rate and image. You need to make changes to this second frame to make it your second keyframe.

In our example, we turned the opacity of the gate up to 100 percent to create our second keyframe. The gate was in Dissolve Blend mode. After tweening these two frames, our gate came into view over several frames, as shown in Figure 28.9. We wanted our gate to dissolve in more slowly than we wanted it to activate, so we changed the frame rate of our second keyframe to one-half second, which was half the rate of the first keyframe.

FIGURE 28.9

We added an arch that was going to dissolve in slowly for the second keyframe.

You can continue to create keyframes just like this — create a new frame and make changes to it to create one more step in your animation. We had one more keyframe to create in our animation, so we created another frame and turned the opacity of the layer style up to 100 percent in that layer. Now we had the same image that we brought in, creating three distinct keyframes, as shown in Figure 28.10.

FIGURE 28.10

We created three distinct keyframes.

Tweening keyframes

Now that you've created the keyframes, it's time to create an animation by tweening them. Select the first keyframe, and click the Tween icon at the bottom of the animation panel. The Tween dialog box opens, allowing you to specify the tween settings. Tween to the next frame, and enter the number of frames to add to the animation. If you made changes to more than one layer, choose All Layers; if not, choose Selected Layers. Deselect any properties that are not being tweened.

With our first frame selected, we added five frames to tween it to the next frame. The only parameter we changed between the first frame and the second frame was the opacity of the gateway, so we chose Selected Layers and Opacity, as shown in Figure 28.11. After we added the frames between the first and second frame, we selected the second keyframe and repeated the process. The result was 13 frames, creating the animation of the gateway appearing, as shown in Figure 28.12.

FIGURE 28.11

You can customize the Tween dialog box to reflect your animation properties.

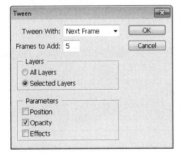

FIGURE 28.12

By tweening three keyframes, we created a complete animation.

As you create more frames, you start to see the limitations of frame animation. If you created an animation at the video standard, it would be 30 frames per second of animation. Our gateway animation was 9.5 seconds long; it was very jerky, and with the relatively miniscule number of 13 frames, it was already unwieldy and hard to manage. You can imagine what it would be like if we had tweened it out to 150 frames to create a smooth animation!

So even though the frame animation version of the Timeline panel can animate almost anything that the video Timeline panel can, its feasibility is limited to small, animated GIFs.

> **ON THE WEB**
>
> The project file used in Figures 28.7 through 28.12 is available as Figure 28-12, a PSD file, on the book's website. You can play the animation and try adding your own background and adjusting the animation.

Creating a Frame-by-Frame Animation

When you want to create an animation using the Paint tools in Photoshop, you need to animate it frame by frame, using a new layer for every frame. This enables you to add whatever paint or effects you want to each frame without affecting any of the other frames.

In this section, we show you how to use the Photoshop Paint tools to build an animation frame by frame. You can do this in two different ways: you can create a layered image, containing all the elements needed for an animation and then turn it into an animation, or you can simply start building the animation right in the frame animation version of the Timeline panel. We show you how to create an animation using both ways.

Creating an animation from a layered image

When you create an animation from a layered image, you need to first create an image with several layers that eventually become frames in your animation. You can create an image in Photoshop that contains all the layers needed to turn it into an animation in just a few simple steps:

> **ON THE WEB**
>
> You should try to do this activity with your own animation, just to get the hang of it. If you want to look at our final project, it is available as Figure 28-16, a PSD file, on the book's website.

1. **Open a new document in Photoshop.**
2. **Fill the background layer however you want, or leave it blank.**
3. **Click the Create A New Layer icon in the Layers panel to create a new layer.**
4. **In the new layer, create any part of the animation that will be present in every frame, as shown in Figure 28.13.**
5. **Create another layer.**

   In this layer, you create what is going to be the first real frame of your animation. This layer, combined with the first two layers, should make a complete image.

FIGURE 28.13

To animate a flower opening, we created a stem that was consistent throughout the animation.

6. **Continue creating new layers, changing each layer to create movement from the last layer.**

   Toggle your views of previous layers on and off when necessary. When you are finished, you should have a file that contains several layers, as shown in Figure 28.14.

7. **Save your file.**

FIGURE 28.14

Our animated flower contains six individual layers. When all the layers are visible, it looks very jumbled.

8. **Choose Window ⇨ Timeline to open the Timeline panel.**

9. **Click the Convert to frame animation icon at the bottom-right of the Timeline panel.**

   This converts it to the frame animation version of the Timeline panel.

10. **From the frame animation panel menu, choose Make Frames from Layers.**

    Each layer of your project becomes a separate frame inside the animation, as shown in Figure 28.15.

FIGURE 28.15

Before and after making frames from layers

11. **With the first frame selected (the background layer) and the Propagate Frame 1 option selected in the Layers panel, turn the visibility of the second frame on.**

    This should make the second layer visible in all other layers, as shown in Figure 28.16.

FIGURE 28.16

After turning the visibility of the second layer on by selecting the Propagate Frame 1 option, the stem is now visible throughout all the layers.

12. **With the first frame selected, choose Match Layer Across Frames from the frame animation panel menu.**

    This opens a dialog box that asks you which properties you want to match. Choose one or all of the properties, and click OK. Now you should have a solid background in each frame.

28

13. **Now that each frame is exactly how it should look, you can discard frames 1 and 2.**

   Click the Delete icon twice to accomplish this. You should be left with the full frames shown in Figure 28.17. You need to click the Yes button after clicking the Delete icon.

FIGURE 28.17

With the background and stem frames discarded, you now have your animation.

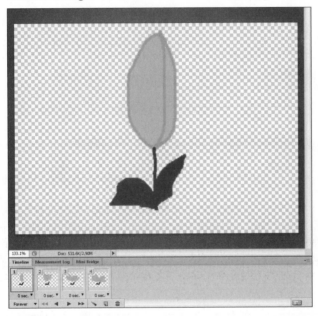

14. **From the frame animation panel menu, choose Select All Frames.**

15. **Click the arrow in the bottom-right corner of the first frame, and change the frame delay time to 1 frame per second.**

   Now your animation is ready to preview.

Creating a small, animated GIF with this method has several advantages. Although the Layers panel can eventually become unwieldy, it really is a neater alternative to trying to work with frames and layers at the same time, as you do in building an animation in the animation version of the Timeline panel. The disadvantage to this method is that any frame that includes changes in position, opacity, or effects must be re-created in a new layer.

Building an animation in the animation version of the Timeline panel

When building an image from scratch, you use the frame animation version of the Timeline panel to create new frames as you create new layers, or vice versa. Each new frame contains a change from the last frame, and over several frames, they turn into an animation.

You can build an animation by creating a new frame each time you make a change to your image.

ON THE WEB

You can find the final version of this animation saved as Figure 28-18 on the book's website.

1. **Open a new document in Photoshop.**
2. **Open the Animation panel by choosing Windows ⇨ Animation.**
3. **Click the Convert To Frame Animation icon at the base of the video Timeline panel to convert it to the frame animation version of the Timeline panel.**
4. **In the panel menu, select Create New Layer for Each New Frame.**
5. **In the panel menu, deselect New Layers Visible in All Frames.**
6. **Create a background for your animation on the existing frame, or leave it blank and create a new frame on which to create a background.**

TIP

To change the background layer into a regular layer that you can paint on, right-click it in the Layers panel and choose Layer From Background.

NOTE

As you create new frames, leave the visibility of the background on. This saves the extra step of matching the layer across frames.

7. **Click the Duplicate selected frames icon at the base of the frame animation version of the Timeline panel.**

   A new frame is created, as well as a new layer in the Layers panel. This frame initially has the same properties as your preceding frame.

NOTE

Because you are working in a new layer, you can change anything you want about your image and the changes are not reflected in any other frames. If you do want your changes to be consistent across frames, select New Layers Visible in All Frames from the frame animation panel menu.

28

8. Use the Photoshop tools to create the next frame for your animation.

9. Repeat Steps 7 and 8 until you have completed your animation, as shown in Figure 28.18.

10. Discard any background frames that aren't part of the animation.

FIGURE 28.18

Build an animation by drawing on one frame at a time.

When you build an animation using frames and layers, you can animate position, opacity, and effects instead of creating a new layer. For example, in the animation of our crayon family, each member of the family only had three poses: two walking poses and a face front pose. In frame 2, we showed Dad entering the picture; in frame 3, he walked farther into it with a different stride; in frame 4, we discarded the new layer and turned on the visibility of frame 2, moving Dad forward again. Figure 28.19 shows frames 2, 3, and 4 of our animation. We did the same with each figure in our animation.

FIGURE 28.19

As you build frames, you can reuse layers to animate position.

Looking at the Layers panel in Figure 28.20, you see that the frames are not in order. That's because the last few frames of our animation show a dog running in and joining the family. We wanted the dog to run behind the family, so after creating the layers that animated the dog, we dragged them under the layers that contained the family.

We also created a Hue/Saturation adjustment layer and changed the hue of the entire image every other frame by simply clicking the visibility of this layer on and off. You may be able to see the difference in Figure 28.19. We added this element so the whole picture would seem to change slightly between frames, not unlike storyboard animations that can be seen in commercials or children's television. You can add any filters or adjustment layers as you change each of your frames. Unlike the tweening process, you can animate anything as long as you are creating new layers.

FIGURE 28.20

Your frames don't have to be in order on your Layers panel.

Rendering Video

Once you are finished editing an animation or video project, you can render the project to a video file. Rendering a video is the process of combining all of the audio and video tracks into a single video file that contains all elements in final form. The video file can then be played on the computer, or distributed to others via the web, DVD, or other medium. To render the animation or video to a video file, choose File ➪ Export ➪ Render Video from the main menu bar to launch the dialog shown in Figure 28.21.

In the Render Video dialog box, set the following options and click the Render button to create the rendered video file:

 Chapter 30 discusses outputting animations to web file formats that can be incorporated into web pages.

- **Name.** This option specifies the name of the video file that will be rendered.
- **Select Folder.** This option allows you to specify the location to store the rendered video file.

949

FIGURE 28.21

The Render Video dialog box allows you to define the options used when rendering video and animation projects to video files.

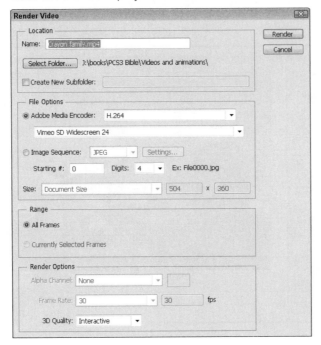

- **Create New Subfolder.** This option creates a new subfolder in the location specified by the Select Folder option.

- **Adobe Media Encoder.** This option renders the animation or video as a video file. It allows you to specify the file format to use when rendering the video file. The file options are DPX (Digital Picture Exchange), H.264, and MPEG-4. The second menu allows you to adjust the audio and video settings used to render the final video file.

- **Image Sequence.** This option renders the animation or video as a sequence of images of the type specified by the menu. Clicking the Settings button allows you to adjust the settings, such as compression, used to generate the image files.

- **Size.** This option specifies the document size used to generate the image files. You can select a standard format, such as NTSC, PAL, HDTV, and so on, from the menu.

- **Range.** This option allows you to specify whether to use all frames or only the currently selected frames when rendering the video.

- **Alpha Channel.** This option allows you to specify how to matte alpha channels into the video. Matting makes the partial transparency in the alpha channel blend better. The options are:

- **None.** This option does not apply alpha channels to the rendered video.
- **Straight Unmatted.** This option does not matte the alpha channel when rendering.
- **Premultiplied with Black.** This option uses a black background matte to render the semi-transparency in the alpha channel. This option is often the best for video that will be displayed on TVs.
- **Premultiplied with White.** This option uses a white background matte to render the semi-transparency in the alpha channel.
- **Premultiplied with Color.** This option allows you to specify a custom color to use for the background matte to render the semitransparency in the alpha channel. You select the color by clicking the color box to the right.
- **Frame Rate.** This option specifies the number of frames per second that will be rendered in the video.
- **3D Quality.** This option allows you to set the quality level at which 3D objects will be rendered: Interactive, Ray Traced Draft, or Ray Traced Final. Ray Traced Final is the highest quality, but is the slowest rendering option.

Summary

In this chapter, we showed you everything you need to know about the animation version of the Timeline panel and how to use it, by covering these topics:

- Working in the frame animation version of the Timeline panel
- Using tweening in frame animation
- Using the animation version of the Timeline panel to create a frame-by-frame animation

28

Part IX

Using Advanced Output Techniques

IN THIS PART

Printing and Color Management

C olor is one of the most important aspects in digital images. In fact, the look of most images completely depends upon their color composition. Unfortunately, color is not consistent as you move from device to device, so it is difficult to guarantee that the color corrections you make on one computer will match what you see on another or when the image is printed.

Color management solves these problems by assigning color profiles that describe the colors in a device, and then using those profiles to convert the image data as it is transferred from device to device. This chapter discusses color management and how Photoshop uses it to ensure the colors in your images are consistent as they are transferred to other devices and printed.

Understanding the Importance of Color Accuracy and Consistency

Few things are more frustrating than spending hours editing an image only to find that the finished product looks terrible when you print it. Differences in monitor quality and even the age difference between two monitors can result in severe variations in the color of an image. Additionally, differences in printers, ink, and paper also result in a high variance of color output. A good color management workflow helps you overcome these problems and gives you the best chance of matching the edited color with the final results when the image is outputted.

The following list describes a good color management workflow that helps you ensure accuracy when editing, distributing, and outputting images:

1. **Calibrate your monitor using either a software application or a hardware calibration device.**

   Because the pixels in your monitor fade with age, you may need to calibrate your monitor monthly or at least at the start of any big projects.

2. **Add color profiles that describe how color will appear on the output devices you are using.**

   Output devices can be specific monitors, portable devices, or printers.

3. **Set up color management in the Adobe software.**

   Photoshop provides proofing options to preview the way that images will appear when they are outputted.

4. **Save the color management data with the edited document.**

   This ensures that the edited document will contain the information you expect to use to output the image.

Understanding ICC color profiles

Color profiles mathematically define the way that a device interprets the level values that determine color in an image. International Color Consortium (ICC) color profiles must define the gamut (range) of colors that a device is capable of reproducing, because not all devices can produce the same color ranges.

Color Management Modules (CMMs), also called Color Matching Modules, such as Apple ColorSync and the Microsoft Windows Color System (WCS), use the ICC color profiles to match or convert the color levels between input sources and output devices. CMMs work by using the source ICC color profile provided along with the original file and the destination ICC color profile for the output device to convert the colors in the original file to the appropriate values that will give the most consistent color result in the output.

ICC profiles are typically provided by the manufacturers of monitors, printers, and other devices. Although these files are typically good enough for most needs, you may also want to develop your own profiles that take into account factors such as ambient lighting in your workspace, age of the monitor, and other variable conditions. Many high-end printing facilities provide profiles that allow you to accurately preview the final output from Photoshop before delivering the finished documents.

Embedding color profiles in image files

ICC profiles can be embedded into most of the common image file types, such as PSD, JPEG, EPS, TIFF, and PSB. Embedding the color profiles inside the actual document ensures that the images are displayed correctly when they are transferred between different devices.

To embed a color profile in an image, simply select the ICC Profile option, shown in Figure 29.1, when you use the File ⇨ Save As command from the main menu bar in Photoshop. The ICC Profile option displays only if you have added a color profile to the image and if the image file type supports color profiles.

FIGURE 29.1

You can embed a color profile in an image by selecting the ICC Profile option in the Save As dialog box.

You can also embed a color profile in an image when you are using the File ⇨ Save for Web & Devices command. When you select a file type that supports color profiles in the Save for Web & Devices dialog box, the embed color profile option becomes available.

> **NOTE**
>
> Most images automatically use the sRGB color profile because the web is the most common destination of images, and sRGB is the profile used for web production.

29

Using device-independent color profiles

A problem can occur with CMMs using the ICC color profiles: the RGB and CMYK colors can vary between different devices. This means that you can get inaccurate translation between the two-color modes.

To solve this problem, the Commission Internationale de l'Éclairage (CIE) developed a set of device-independent color models; the CIE XYZ and CIE LAB color spaces are two examples. These color spaces are used as interim spaces when converting between the different color models.

Calibrating Color for Monitors and Printers

The most important step in color management is to calibrate the monitor on the computer where you are editing images. If the monitor is not calibrated, you could spend hours getting the perfect color tones in the image only to find that your monitor was inaccurate and the colors don't really look that good.

There are two methods you can use for calibrating a monitor. The simplest, although least accurate, is to use software to manually adjust the gamma, brightness, contrast, and color that the system uses for the display. On Windows 7 systems, you can calibrate the monitor by selecting Start ⇨ Control Panel ⇨ Hardware and Sound ⇨ Display ⇨ Calibrate Color to bring up the calibration utility shown in Figure 29.2. On Mac OS systems, you can calibrate the monitor by using the Display Calibrator Assistant found in the Displays pane of System Preferences.

The most accurate method of calibrating a monitor is to attach a device called a calorimeter flat to the display surface. The calorimeter and display must be shielded from all ambient light. Then calibration software that comes with the calorimeter sends a series of color signals to the display and compares the values seen by the calorimeter with known expected values. This establishes the current offsets in the color display, and ICC profiles can be created and the display's brightness, contrast, and RGB settings adjusted.

Because ink and paper quality affect printer output so much, you cannot adjust the settings on a printer to calibrate color output. Instead, printers use ICC profiles that are created by printing a test sample with known output gamma, brightness, contrast, and color outputs. The sample test print is then analyzed by a photometer (sometimes called a spectrophotometer) to determine the actual output with known CMYK colors. Software that comes with the photometer then uses the difference between the two printouts to create the ICC profile. Although the photometer and software are expensive, you can typically find an ICC profile for your printer/ink combination on the Internet for a reasonable price (usually about $20 to $30).

FIGURE 29.2

Calibrating color on the display in Windows is a process that involves adjusting the gamma, brightness, contrast, and colors.

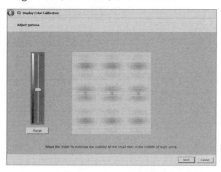
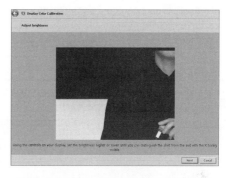

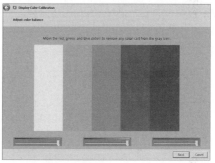

Using Color Management in Photoshop

Photoshop provides several different tools that allow you to define a specific set of colors that apply to an image, control the display and print color of images, as well as convert images to other color profiles. These tools help you to ensure that the same colors you see in Photoshop are the colors others see in the printed and distributed digital versions. If you plan to send your images to a printer or output them for others to view, you should become familiar with color management in Photoshop. The following sections discuss how to configure the color management settings in Photoshop, assign color profiles to images, and proof images using different color profiles.

Configuring color settings in Photoshop

Configuring color settings in Photoshop allows you to make sure that the same color ranges you are seeing on the screen can be transferred to other output devices such as printers. Photoshop provides a Color Settings utility, shown in Figure 29.3, to allow you to easily configure the color settings.

You launch the Color Settings dialog box by pressing Ctrl+Shift+K/⌘+Shift+K on the keyboard or by choosing Edit⇨Color Settings from the main menu bar. At first appearance, the dialog box may seem a bit unfamiliar and daunting. The next few sections discuss each of the options available in the Color Settings dialog box and will hopefully dispel any apprehension you have of using them.

FIGURE 29.3

The Color Settings dialog box allows you to configure the color workspaces and the color management policies.

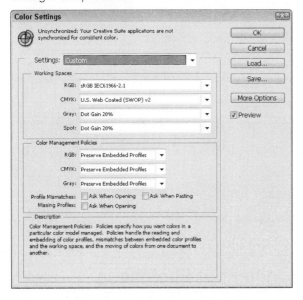

TIP

If you save your color settings as a preset file, you can use that preset in the Adobe Bridge Suite Color Settings dialog box (launched by pressing Ctrl+Shift+K/⌘+Shift+K in Bridge). The Suite Color Settings utility allows you to synchronize the color management profiles between Creative Suite applications.

Setting color options

The Settings menu option offers a list of preset color configurations that set the color options for the workspace and management policies for general purposes. If you really don't want to take the time to set up your own custom color configuration, you can use one of these presets. The list contains presets for North America, Europe, and Japan that fall into the following categories:

- **Monitor Color.** Choose this setting if you plan to use the images in a video or onscreen presentation. This setting uses the Monitor RGB option, which uses the current monitor's color space and in effect acts as if color management is turned off in Photoshop.

- **General Purpose.** Choose this setting if you need to use the image for both print and onscreen viewing. This setting uses the sRGB color profile that best supports most monitors as well as the U.S. Web Coated (SWOP) v2 color profile for CMYK that works well for printing.

- **Newspaper.** Choose this setting for images that are intended for output to newsprint. The CMYK workspace is set to U.S. Newsprint, and the Gray and Spot colors are set to use a 25-percent dot gain that works well for printing to newspaper-type material.

- **Prepress.** Choose this setting for images that are intended for output to a printer. The RGB workspace is set to Adobe RGB, which provides a good range of colors that map well to the CMYK color model used for printing; the CMYK workspace is set to U.S. Web Coated (SWOP) v2, which generally works well for printing.

- **Web/Internet.** Choose this setting for images that you intend to display on the web. This option sets the RGB workspace to sRGB, which is the best one for supporting a variety of computer monitors; the Gray workspace is set to Gray Gamma 2.2, which works best for displaying grayscale images on a variety of monitors.

You can also save any custom configuration that you define using the Save button and then load it later, even on another computer, by clicking the Load button.

Configuring color profiles

The Working Spaces settings allow you to configure the ICC color profiles that the RGB, CMYK, Grayscale, and Duotone models use to display the images on your monitor while you are editing them. Using the appropriate color model helps you edit and adjust your images so they look as good as possible when they are viewed on the output medium.

The following list describes some of the profiles that are available in each of the workspaces:

29

- **RGB.** Although there are many RGB color profiles, you will likely work with only two or three. The most common ones are Adobe RGB and sRGB IEC61966-2.1 (sRGB). The difference between the two is that the sRGB profile has reduced the gamut of colors it allows around the outer edges. This reduces the number of colors that can exist in the image so that the colors are supported on the widest range of computer displays possible. That way, the image looks exactly the same on all displays.

  Another RGB color profile that you might end up using is Monitor RGB. This profile sets the RGB working space to the current monitor space, which causes Photoshop to behave as if color management was turned off. This is actually handy if you are outputting the images to a medium that doesn't support color management, such as a video or a presentation application.

- **CMYK.** The CMYK color model is typically used for printed images. Therefore, each of the available CMYK color profiles actually corresponds to a specific ink-and-paper combination. When you convert an image from RGB to CMYK using the Image ⇨ Mode ⇨ CMYK color option, the CMYK color profile is used as a basis for the conversion between the two color models.

  The most common profile you will use is U.S. Web Coated (SWOP) v2. Other color profiles may be provided by your printing press or by a printer manufacturer.

- **Gray.** The Gray color profiles define the dot gain used to display images converted into grayscale when you choose the Image ⇨ Mode ⇨ Grayscale command. There are two basic options: one is to set the percent of dot gain, and the other is to select a gamma option that uses the gamma setting of your monitor to define the brightness of the midtones in the grayscale image. The most commonly used gamma option is Gray Gamma 2.2 because it supports most of the current monitors.

- **Spot.** This profile specifies the dot gain to use when displaying spot color channels and duotones.

Controlling the color profile in open images

The Color Management Policies section of the Color Settings dialog box provides control over how Photoshop manages the RGB, CMYK, and grayscale images that are opened. Many images already have ICC color profiles embedded in them, and the settings in this panel allow you to define how Photoshop uses those files in relation to the color profiles defined in the Working Spaces section.

For each of the three color modes, you can set the following options:

- **Off.** When you select Off, color management is disabled in images that you open or create. If you open an image with an embedded color profile, the color profile is ignored. You should be careful if you use this option while copying and pasting from one image to another, because although the color data is preserved, the colors may look different.

- **Preserve Embedded Profiles.** This is the default option and is the best option to ensure the most consistent colors between images that are edited on different computers. When you select this option, Photoshop maintains the embedded color profile information.

- **Convert to Working Profile.** When you select this option, Photoshop uses the color profile in the image to convert the data in the image to use the working color profile. The working color profile is then embedded in the image when you save it.

The Color Management Policies section also contains check boxes that allow you to activate dialog boxes that pop up if you open or paste data into an image that has an embedded color profile that mismatches the working profile or is missing. The dialog box warns you and allows you to determine at that time how to handle color management for that image, as shown in Figure 29.4.

FIGURE 29.4

Enabling the Ask When Opening and Ask When Pasting options in the Color Settings dialog box presents notifications that allow you to handle images that either do not have an embedded color profile or have a color profile that does not match the current working color space.

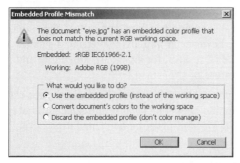

Controlling conversion between color profiles

When you click the More Options button in the Color Settings dialog box, the dialog box expands and displays a section that provides control over conversion between color profiles. Figure 29.5 shows the Conversion Options and the Advanced Controls settings.

In the Conversion Options section, you can configure the following options:

- **Engine.** This option allows you to specify the CMM that will be used to manage conversion between color profiles. Typically, you have two options: Adobe ACE is provided by Adobe and is available on both Windows and Mac OS; the other option is the default CMM that is provided with your operating system — for example, Microsoft ICM on Windows or Apple CMM on Mac OS.

- **Intent.** This option allows you to select one of the following settings that determine how the CMM interprets colors between color spaces:

  - **Perceptual.** When you select this option, all colors in the source color profile are compressed to fit in the destination color profile's gamut. Neighboring pixels are taken into consideration so the colors are adjusted proportionally. This provides a better perceptual translation because the relationship between the pixel and its neighbors is more important than finding the closest matching color.

  - **Saturation.** When you select this option, colors in the source color profile that do not exist in the destination color profile's gamut are changed to the closest color

29

value in the destination color profile without considering neighboring pixel values. This can result in a color shift that increases saturation in the image. Typically, this option is used only for images with many solid colors, and not for photographs.

- **Relative Colorimetric.** When you select this option, colors are translated between profiles by mapping white in the source color profile with white in the destination color profile and then using that mapping to adjust the rest of the colors. This option usually works very well; however, if you are converting a smaller color space to a larger color space (CMYK to RGB, for example), a banding and dithering effect can result in the darker areas of the image.

- **Absolute Colorimetric.** When you select this option, Photoshop maps the colors between the two spaces by mapping between the absolute lab coordinates in each color profile. This option is used for hard proofing and simulating output on a specific printer.

FIGURE 29.5

The More Options button extends the Color Settings dialog box and allows you to configure conversion and advanced controls for color management.

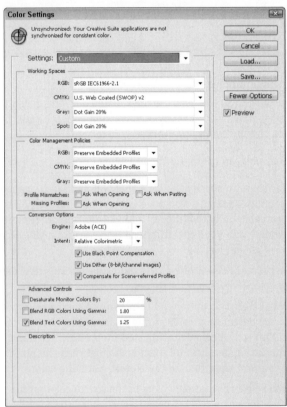

- **Use Black Point Compensation.** This option simulates the entire dynamic range of the printer to ensure that the shadow details in the image are preserved. You should select it if you plan to use black point compensation when printing the image.

- **Use Dither.** When you select this option, Photoshop mixes colors in the destination color profile to simulate colors in the source color profile. This helps reduce blocky and banding artifacts that can otherwise occur.

- **Compensate for Scene-referred Profiles.** This option compares the video contrast when converting from scene to output color profiles, similar to color management in After Effects. This option is specific to working with video files in Photoshop.

Configuring the Advanced Controls options

In addition to the Conversion Options described in the previous section, Photoshop provides more Advanced Controls options when you click the More Options button. In the Advanced Controls section, you can configure the following options:

- **Desaturate Monitor Colors By.** This option specifies a percentage to desaturate colors when they are displayed on the monitor. Selecting this option helps you visualize the full range of color spaces with a similar gamut of the monitor. However, this can result in color mismatches between monitor display and output. Deselecting this option can result in two distinct colors appearing as the same color on the monitor.

- **Blend RGB Colors Using Gamma.** This option controls how RGB colors in the image are blended together to produce composite data, such as blending layers or painting. Selecting this option blends the RGB colors in the color space based on the specified gamma setting. A gamma of 1.00 is considered "colorimetrically correct" and likely produces the fewest edge artifacts.

- **Blend Text Colors Using Gamma.** This option controls how text colors in the image are blended together to produce composite data, such as blending layers or painting. Selecting this option blends the text colors in the color space based on the specified gamma setting. A gamma of 1.00 is considered "colorimetrically correct" and likely produces the fewest edge artifacts.

29

> **NOTE**
> When you select the Blend RGB Colors Using Gamma option, layered documents look different when viewed in other applications than they appear in Photoshop.

Assigning color profiles to images

Photoshop allows you to assign color profiles to images. If the image already contains an embedded color profile, that color profile is replaced with the newly assigned color profile, but the level values in the image do not change.

To assign a color profile to an image, open the image in Photoshop and choose Edit ➪ Assign Profile from the main menu bar. A dialog box similar to the one shown in Figure 29.6 appears allowing you to set the following options:

> **CAUTION**
>
> Because layer adjustments, filters, and Blending modes are based on the original colors, assigning a color profile to the image may alter the appearance of the layers. You should always assign a color profile to the image before you begin editing it, if possible.

- **Don't Color Manage This Document.** This option removes any existing color profiles from the document, and Photoshop displays the image according to the current working color space.

- **Working [Color Model]: [Color Profile].** This option adds the current working color profile to the image and uses that profile to display it while editing.

- **Profile.** This option allows you to select a color profile from a drop-down menu that is embedded in the image. Which color profile is used to display the image depends on the color management settings described earlier.

FIGURE 29.6

Using the Edit ➪ Assign Profile option, you can add a color profile to an image or replace the currently embedded color profile.

Converting images to other color profiles

Photoshop allows you to convert images from one color profile to another. If the image already contains an embedded color profile, you likely want to keep the colors intact when moving from one profile to the next. Converting color profiles uses the color profile in the image to convert the color levels to match a new color profile and then embeds the new color profile in the image.

To convert an image from one color profile to another, open the image in Photoshop and choose Edit ⇨ Convert to Profile from the main menu bar. A dialog box similar to the one shown in Figure 29.7 appears. Clicking the Advanced option button expands the dialog box, and you can set the following options:

FIGURE 29.7

Using the Edit ⇨ Convert to Profile option, you can use the currently embedded color profile in an image to convert the image to another color profile and embed that color profile.

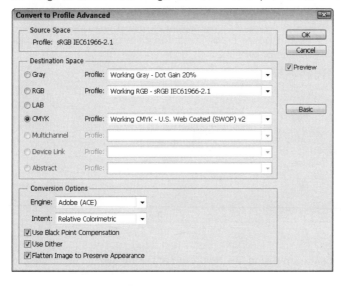

- **Source Space.** This option displays the source color space that was already embedded in the image.
- **Destination Space.** In the basic dialog box, this option allows you to select the ICC profile to convert the image. In the Advanced dialog box, this option allows you to select the color mode and color profile to use when converting the image. This option is often a better method to change the color mode because it gives you direct control over both the color mode and color profile.

- **Conversion Options.** The Engine, Intent, Use Black Point Compensation, and Use Dither options were discussed earlier in this chapter. The Flatten Image to Preserve Appearance option is provided to overcome the problem of blending layers. The problem with blending layers is that converting the layers individually and then flattening them results in a different pixel color than flattening first and then converting. This can be a tough choice if you need to use the layers later.

Proofing images using color management

In addition to embedding color profiles in images and setting the working color management settings, Photoshop provides quick proofing of images to see how they will appear in some of the common color profiles. This process is known as *soft proofing*.

To set up the proofing color space, choose View⇨Proof Setup and then select the color space. Photoshop uses the color space you selected when proofing. Choosing View⇨Proof Setup⇨Custom displays the Customize Proof Condition dialog box, shown in Figure 29.8.

FIGURE 29.8

Configuring the options in the Customize Proof Condition dialog box allows you to proof images in some of the common color profiles.

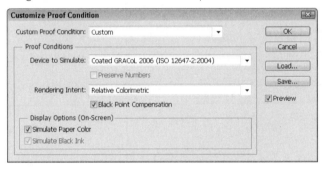

In the Customize Proof Condition dialog box, you can set the following customized color proofing options:

- **Device to Simulate.** This option allows you to select the color or device profile to use when proofing the colors in the image.
- **Preserve Numbers.** When you select this option, the colors appear without being converted to the color space of the specified output device.

- **Rendering Intent.** This option specifies how Photoshop converts colors from the document's gamut to the proofing gamut. When proofing photos, you likely want to use Perceptual or Relative Colorimetric.

- **Black Point Compensation.** This option simulates the entire dynamic range of the printer to ensure that the shadow details in the image are preserved when proofing. You should select it when proofing if you plan to use black point compensation when printing the image.

- **Simulate Paper Color.** If you select a CMYK-based device profile, this option simulates the slightly off-white property of actual paper according to the settings in the color profile.

- **Simulate Black Ink.** If you select a CMYK-based device profile, this option simulates the dark gray that the color profile specifies represents solid black.

- **Load/Save.** The Load and Save buttons allow you to load and save the custom proof settings.

After you have set up the proofing profile, you can proof the current image by choosing View⊏>Proof Colors from the main menu bar. The setting specified in the Proof Settings menu is used to display the image in the colors that match the output device. This is a great way to work in one color space but still see the results in another.

A useful aspect of the Photoshop proofing option is the ability to preview items using the Color Blindness options from the View⊏>Proof Settings menu. Many governments and other institutions now require common websites to use these profiles when displaying images. Even if you are not embedding one of these profiles in the image, you can use the proofing option to view what the image will look like if these profiles are used.

Printing Images from Photoshop

Printing images that you adjust from Photoshop provides a means to distribute your hard work to others. Printing images from Photoshop can be as simple as pressing Ctrl+Alt+Shift+P/ ⌘+Option+Shift+P to print a single copy using the configured print settings. Photoshop also provides much more control over printing of images when you press Ctrl+P/⌘+P to display the Print dialog box. The Print dialog box, shown in Figure 29.9, allows you to set up printing options, implement color management, access the printer settings, and add additional output to the printed image. Each of these settings allow for additional flexibility and enhanced quality in the printed version of the image.

29

FIGURE 29.9

When printing in Photoshop using the Print dialog box, you can set print size and orientation and use color management to ensure that the colors printed match those you saw when editing the image.

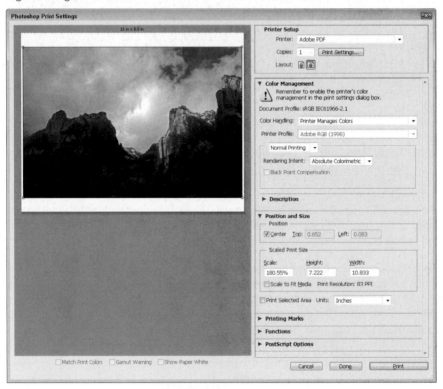

Configuring general printing options

The Print dialog box offers the following general printing options that allow you to control the orientation, size, and location of the printed image, as well as the printer settings:

- **Preview.** The preview window displays the image and its general location on the printed sheet of paper. The size of the paper is also displayed above the preview. The size of the paper is controlled by the Photoshop Print Settings dialog box.

- **Printer.** This menu allows you to select the printer from the list of installed system printers. This option also displays a notification that the printer needs calibration if it has not already been calibrated. You should calibrate the printer before printing from Photoshop so the output provides the best results.

- **Copies.** This field sets the number of copies to print.

- **Print Settings.** Pressing this button launches the settings dialog box for the print driver. The settings dialog box for the printer likely gives you even more control over options such as paper size, paper type, print quality, and so on.

- **Layout.** The orientation buttons allow you to switch between landscape and portrait layout when printing the image.

- **Position.** Using the Center option centers the image in the printable area on the printer. If the Center option is not selected, the Top and Left fields specify the relative position of the top-left corner of the image to the top-left corner of the printable area of the paper.

- **Scaled Print Size.** This option allows you to scale the size of the image so that it fits on the printed area perfectly. The scale field specifies the size percentage, where 100% is the original size. The Height and Width fields specify the height and width of the printed image. Selecting the Scale to Fit option disables the Scale, Height, and Width options, and the image is sized automatically to the same size as the printable area.

- **Units.** This setting sets the units used for the Position and Scaled Print Size options.

Using color management to print accurate colors

The most important aspect of color management is the ability to keep the output colors consistent with the colors that you see when editing the image. Therefore, printing with color management is an extremely important part of Photoshop. Two options are available to use color management when printing from Photoshop: you can either let Photoshop manage the colors, or let the printer manage the colors.

> **CAUTION**
>
> When you use Photoshop for color management, you need to disable color management in the printer driver. This varies from driver to driver, so you need to look in the printer manual to find out how to do this. Conversely, if you are using the printer to manage color profiles, you must enable color management in the printer driver. If either of these steps is ignored, the printer will print the wrong set of colors.

Using Photoshop to manage the colors means that Photoshop sends the color data to the printer already converted to the appropriate color profile gamut for that device. For accurate results, this requires the appropriate ICC profile that defines the color space for the printer.

Using the printer to manage colors means that Photoshop sends the printer the necessary color profile information for the current values in the image, and the printer converts the image data to the appropriate gamut.

To print an image using color management, make sure the color management settings have been configured properly and press Ctrl+P/⌘+P to open the Print dialog box. Expand the Color Management heading, and configure the following settings:

29

- **Color Handling.** This menu allows you to select the Printer Manages Colors option to use the printer for color management; the Photoshop Manages Colors option to use Photoshop for color management; or the Color Separations option (if the color model of the image is CMYK) to print a set of color separations or spot plates using the actual color values.

- **Printer Profile.** This option specifies the ICC color profile to use for the destination device. When you select the Photoshop Manages Colors option, this setting defines the color profile that Photoshop uses as the destination color profile when preparing the image to print.

- **Normal Printing.** This option uses the embedded color profile in the document or the working color profile configured in the Color Settings dialog box if no profile is present.

- **Hard Proofing.** If you select this option instead of the Document option, Photoshop emulates output from a different device than the current printer. This is known as a *hard proof*. Hard proofs are useful to test the output on less-expensive devices before sending the output to a high-quality printer. You need to set up proofing using View ➪ Proof Setup ➪ Custom to configure the device you want to emulate.

- **Rendering Intent.** This option, available when Normal Printing is selected, allows you to specify how Photoshop converts colors from the document's gamut to the printer's gamut. When printing photos, you likely want to use Perceptual or Relative Colorimetric. See the conversion options section earlier in this chapter for more details on the available options.

- **Black Point Compensation.** This option, available when Normal Printing is selected, allows you to enable black point compensation that will adjust for the differences between what the image and the output device consider to be black. This option is most useful if the gamut of the image and the gamut of the output device are similar but one is darker than the other is.

- **Proof Setup.** This option, available when Hard Proofing is selected, allows you to select either the current working color profile or the custom profile that you defined by choosing View ➪ Proof Setup ➪ Custom.

- **Simulate Paper Color.** This option, available when Hard Proofing is selected, allows you to select a CMYK-based device profile, and simulates the slightly off-white property of actual paper according to the settings in the color profile.

- **Simulate Black Ink.** This option, available when Hard Proofing is selected, allows you to select a CMYK-based device profile, and simulates the dark gray that the color profile specifies represents solid black.

- **Match Print Colors.** This option causes the print preview to show the colors as they will actually print. This is available only if Photoshop is used for color management.

- **Gamut Warning.** When you enable the Match Print Colors option, colors that are out of gamut in the image are highlighted in the preview option. This is extremely useful for determining the amount of color translation that must take place to print the image using the printer color profile. This is available only if Photoshop is used for color management and you have selected Match Print Colors.

- **Show Paper White.** This option displays the paper portion of the print preview to the color of white specified by the printer color profile. This gives you the most realistic preview of the printed area because paper is really off-white and can change the color cast of the image. This option is available only if Photoshop is used for color management.

Adding crop marks and additional output to printed images

An important part of the printing process is adding additional information to the photo to be used when processing. Photoshop allows you to quickly add and print additional information with your images, such as calibration bars, crop marks, and registration marks.

To control the additional output options when printing the image, expand the Printing Marks and Function headings, shown in Figure 29.10, and then configure the following settings:

- **Registration Marks.** This option adds registration marks on the corners of the image. Registration marks are used to align color separations.

- **Corner Crop Marks.** This option adds corner crop marks to the printed image so you can easily trim the printed document.

- **Center Crop Marks.** This option adds center crop marks to the printed image to aid in trimming the edges from the paper.

- **Description.** This option prints the description contained in the file. You can add a description by choosing File ⇨ File Info from the main menu bar.

- **Labels.** This option prints the filename above the image. When printing color separations, the separation name is printed as part of the label.

- **Emulsion Down.** This option prints the image backward so text is readable when the emulsion is down — in other words, when the printed side of the paper is facing away from you. Typically, this is used for printing images on film.

- **Negative.** This option prints a color negative of the image, including all masks and background colors. This is a bit different from using Image ⇨ Adjustments ⇨ Invert to create a negative because it converts the output and not the onscreen image.

- **Background.** This option launches a dialog box that allows you to specify the background color to be printed in the printable area outside of the image. For most images, the background color should be white or possibly black.

- **Border.** This option launches a dialog box that allows you to set the size of a black border that is printed around the image. The default size is 0, which means no border.

- **Bleed.** This option launches a dialog box that allows you to set the position of the crop marks in relation to the actual edge of the printed image. This has the effect of allowing space for ink to bleed into the paper without losing full quality around the edges.

29

FIGURE 29.10

When printing in Photoshop, you can use the Print dialog box to add crop marks, registration marks, calibration bars, and additional output to the printed image. You can also control the output form of the image by printing negative, emulsion down, and vector data.

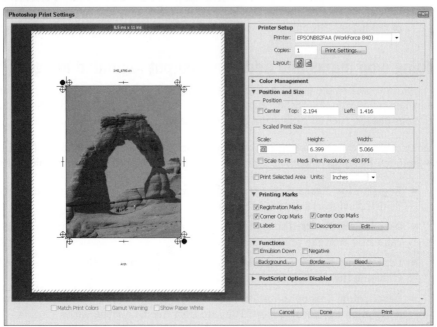

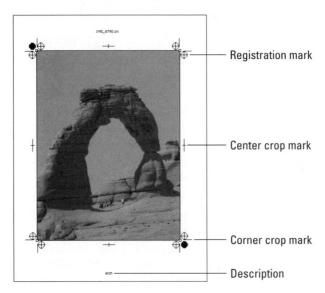

Registration mark

Center crop mark

Corner crop mark

Description

Summary

This chapter discussed using color management to keep colors consistent in your images from device to device. Color is one of the most important aspects in digital images and one of the most difficult things to get right when transferring images between systems or printing them.

Color management provides a means to keep colors consistent between devices by using profiles that define the color gamut in each device. These color profiles are then used to convert the color values in an image as it is transferred from device to device.

In this chapter, you learned the following:

- How ICC color profiles define the color gamut of a device, to accurately convert color data in images between devices.
- How color profiles are embedded in images when you save them in Photoshop.
- How to calibrate your monitor to ensure that the colors you see in Photoshop are consistent.
- How to configure color management in Photoshop.
- How to convert an image from one color profile to another without losing color consistency.
- How to proof images for different devices in Photoshop.
- How to easily include output options such as crop marks and calibration bars in your images.
- How to send vector data to the printer, resulting in crisper printouts of vector shapes and text.
- How to use color management when printing images from Photoshop to ensure consistency of color in the printed image.

29

Creating Images for the Web

IN THIS CHAPTER

Getting images ready for the web

Converting images to web formats

Enabling zooming and panning in web images

A lthough Photoshop is not typically thought of as a tool used for creating web pages, it does have some powerful features that can aid graphic designers in preparing images for web applications. One of the biggest obstacles to overcome when preparing images for the web is adjusting the size and file format to support the limited capabilities when viewing images on the web. That's where Photoshop comes in.

This chapter discusses some of the basics of how and why images are prepared for viewing on the web, such as color settings, slicing images, and adding transparency and animation. We also discuss the Save for Web utility that you use to prepare and output images in formats that are supported on the web with the necessary HTML data.

Preparing Images for the Web

You can prepare images for use on the web in many ways. Only a limited number of file formats are supported when viewing images on the web, so images must be converted to one of these formats. You may also need to reduce images to reasonable sizes that can be supported by limited network bandwidth. The following sections cover the basic web formats, using color management to ensure consistency between browsers, adding animation to images, and adding transparency to make images flow better with web page backgrounds.

Understanding web image formats

One of the most basic decisions that you face when preparing an image for the web is the file format of the image. You should decide on the file format before you make too many changes to the image, because these formats vary in color and transparency support. The following list describes the most common file formats used for the web:

 For more information about different file types, see Chapter 3.

- **GIF.** Graphic Interchange Format (GIF) images were the standard format for web images for a long time because the file size is very small relative to the image size. GIFs support only 256 colors, which is good for web icons, logos, and text but not so good for photographs. GIF images also support embedded animation that is triggered when the file is loaded. Another advantage of GIF files is that they support transparency, which allows the background color and patterns on the web page to show through parts of the image.

> **TIP**
>
> If you are planning on creating GIF or PNG-8 images, you should change the color mode to Indexed color, because that's the basic format of these file types. This keeps the colors in the image limited to the 256 colors of the indexed color table that are supported when you save the file, so you won't be editing colors that won't exist in the final image.

- **JPEG.** Joint Photographic Experts Group (JPEG) images support 16.7 million colors, so they are much better for displaying photographs or colorful images. They are supported by most web browsers, so they can easily be embedded in web pages or viewed as standalone files.

  JPEG images do not support animation or transparency, so they aren't commonly used for buttons, logos, and icons. Another downside to using the JPEG format is that unless you specify a lossless JPEG compression algorithm, JPEG compression can result in artifacts in the images.

- **PNG-8 and PNG-24.** Portable Network Graphic (PNG) images were created to replace GIF and, to an extent, JPEG images. PNG-8 images are similar to GIFs in that they use an 8-bit format and so support only 256 colors. PNG-8 files also support transparency and animation just like GIFs.

  PNG-24 is similar to JPEG in that it supports the same number of colors. However, because PNG-24 files use a lossless compression, file sizes are larger than JPEGs, although they do not exhibit the same types of artifacts. A big advantage of PNG-24 is that they support transparency in the image using an alpha channel.

- **WBMP.** Wireless Bitmap (WBMP) files use a 1-bit format that is widely supported by mobile devices that can display only black and white pixels. Most current devices support color images, such as JPEG and PNG, but if you are creating an image that needs to be displayed on all devices, you may want to create a WBMP copy along with the color copy.

Selecting the right color profile

When working with images that are intended for the web, you want to use the RGB color mode by choosing Image ➪ Mode ➪ RGB Color from the main menu bar. This is because RGB is the color mode that computer screens use to display images in web browsers.

You should use the sRGB color profile when editing images for the web. The colors in the sRGB profile are supported on most displays, so your images will look the same no matter what computer is accessing them.

> **TIP**
>
> You can proof the way that images will look on the web by choosing View ⇨ Proof Setup ⇨ Internet Standard RGB and then using the View ⇨ Proof Colors menu option to toggle proofing on and off. For more information about proofing and color profiles, see Chapter 29.

Slicing images for web use

Another task you may need to perform when preparing images for the web is to slice them up. Slicing an image involves assigning areas of the image as hot points that have meaning in the web page. These hot points can be assigned descriptions that pop up when the mouse hovers over that area of the image, and even links that allow users to navigate to different web pages or locations on the same web page by clicking different areas in the image. The following sections discuss the different types of slices that you can create and the tools that you can use to create and define the slices in the image.

Understanding slices

Photoshop provides four types of slices that vary in their behavior and how you create them. Slices are designated by a bounding box with an icon in the upper-left corner. The icon and color of the bounding box designate the type of slice. Figure 30.1 shows the icons used for each type:

FIGURE 30.1

The user, layer-based, and no image slices are designated by different icons in the upper-left corner. The auto slices are designated by a gray bounding box and icon. The following list describes the types of slices:

- ▣ User slice
- ▣ Auto slice
- ▣ Layer based slice
- ▣ No image slice

   - **User slice.** User slices are the basic slices that you draw yourself. They are designated by a blue bounding box and the icon shown in Figure 30.1.
   - **Layer-based slice.** Layer-based slices are created by selecting a layer in the Layers panel and then choosing Layer ⇨ New Layer Based Slice from the main menu bar. This creates a rectangular slice the size of the content of the layer. A great feature of layer-based slices is that the slice boundary is automatically adjusted if you change the size of the content in the layer or add a drop shadow.

30

- **No image slice.** A no image slice instructs Photoshop to treat that region in the image as HTML-encoded text. The text that is displayed in the web page is configured using the Slice Options dialog box, discussed later in this chapter.

  Using HTML-encoded text areas in the image keeps the text crisp even if the display size in the browser is changed. Another important benefit is that the encoded text is readable by search engines, making the content available for web searches.

- **Auto slice.** Auto slices are slices that Photoshop automatically generates and assigns to the areas of the image that are not defined as user, layer-based, or no image slices. Auto slices are designated by the same icon as user slices but have a gray bounding box instead of blue.

Creating slices

The Slice tool, shown in Figure 30.2, is used to quickly carve up an image into slices. Using the Slice tool, you can create slices in one of three ways:

FIGURE 30.2

The Slice tool allows you to quickly carve up an image into slices either manually or by using guidelines.

- **Manually.** You can create slices manually by dragging the Slice tool across an image to create a bounding box. The Style setting in the Slice tool options menu allows you to control how slices are created. The Normal style allows you to create a simple rectangle by dragging the cursor. Holding down the Shift key while dragging creates a square box. The Fixed Aspect Ratio style forces the rectangle to match the ratio specified by the Width and Height settings. The Fixed Size style creates a bounding box that is the exact size specified by the Width and Height settings.

  Figure 30.3 shows how you create the slices by dragging the Slice tool. Notice that the area selected is defined as a user slice and the rest of the area is automatically sliced up into auto slices.

- **Using guidelines.** A great way to create slices is to define guidelines in the document by choosing View ➪ New Guide from the main menu bar. After all guidelines are created, you can click Slices From Guides to create a set of slices based on the guidelines. Figure 30.3 shows how the slices are created from guidelines. Notice that all the slices created are user slices.

- **From layers.** As mentioned earlier, you can create a slice by selecting a layer from the Layers panel and then choosing Layer ➪ New Layer Based Slice. Figure 30.3 shows how a layer-based slice is created from a layer that contains an image. Notice that a layer-based slice is created around the image, and the rest of the document is carved up into auto slices.

FIGURE 30.3

You can create slices manually by dragging the Slice tool, automatically based on guidelines, or from a layer.

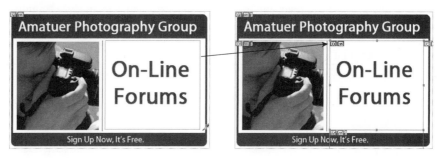

Manually creating slices

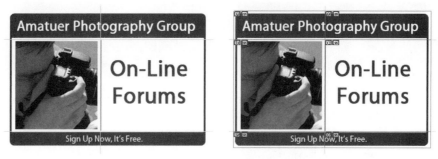

Slices from guidelines

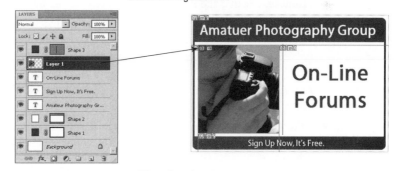

Slices from layers

30

TIP

You should use the fewest slices you can to keep the HTML code as simple as possible. Avoid having slices overlap each other, and try not to leave gaps between the slices because this forces Photoshop to create auto slices to fill those areas. It might help to choose View ➪ Snap To ➪ Slices to have the slices snap to each other to avoid gaps as you draw them.

Configuring slices

The Slice Select tool, shown in Figure 30.4, is used to select, manipulate, and configure the slices after they have been created. Using the Slice Select tool, you can change the size of the slices by selecting them and dragging the control handles on their bounding boxes.

FIGURE 30.4

The Slice Select tool allows you to quickly manipulate and configure slices.

> **NOTE**
>
> You can access most of the slice configuration options by right-clicking the icon in the upper-left corner of the slice to display the Slice pop-up menu. From this menu, you can change the order of the slice as well as promote, delete, and divide it.

You can select one or more slices and use the following options in the Slice Select tool options bar to organize and configure the selected slices:

- **Order.** These options adjust the order of the selected slices to the top, up one, down one, or to the bottom.

- **Promote.** Clicking the Promote button promotes an auto or layer slice to a user slice.

- **Divide.** Clicking the Divide button launches the Divide Slice dialog box, shown in Figure 30.5. From the Divide Slice dialog box, you can specify either evenly spaced or fixed slice divisions to be added to the current slice. The result is that the current slice is divided into the specified set of slices, as shown in Figure 30.5.

- **Align.** The Align options allow you to quickly align the selected slices with each other. Only the selected slices are affected.

- **Hide Auto Slices.** Clicking the Hide Auto Slices button hides the auto slices from the document display window. This allows you to more easily see the interaction with the other slices.

- **Slice Options.** The Slice Options button launches the Slice Options dialog box shown in Figure 30.6. From the Slice Options dialog box, you can set the type of the slice to Image, No Image, and Table. When you set the slice to Image, you can configure the HTML tag information for the image slice, as shown in Figure 30.6. When you select No Image, you can set the text that is converted to HTML-encoded text.

  You can set the dimensions of the slice in the Dimensions settings. The X and Y fields specify the coordinates of the top-left corner of the slice box. The W and H fields set the width and height in pixels.

FIGURE 30.5

Using the Divide Slice dialog box, you can divide a slice horizontally and/or vertically into a set of equally spaced slices.

FIGURE 30.6

The Slice Options dialog box allows you to configure the HTML settings, dimensions, and background options for the slice.

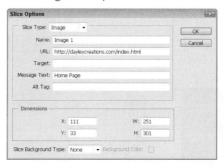

The Slice Background Type option allows you to set the background type to black, white, or a custom color. You can also set the background to matte. The Matte setting is used for the partially transparent areas in images. PNG and GIF files support only fully opaque or fully transparent pixels, so the matte color is used to blend in the partially transparent pixels to fully opaque pixels. Typically, you would set the matte color to the same color as the background of the web page.

Adding transparency to images

An important aspect of some web images is the ability to use transparency to help an image blend better into a web page. Image files are always rectangular with a height and width dimension. When you place a rectangular image in a web page, it stands out from the background.

The way to solve that problem is to add transparency to the image and save it as a GIF or PNG file. The transparent areas of the image allow the background of the web page to show through it, making the image blend with the background.

The simplest way to create transparency is to add a layer mask alpha channel to the image that masks the area of the image you want to be opaque. You can do this by following these steps:

1. **Open the image in Photoshop.**

2. **Select the area of the image that you want to remain opaque in the web page.**

   Figure 30.7 shows that the moon is selected in the image.

FIGURE 30.7

To add transparency in an image, simply select the areas that you want to remain opaque and select Add a Layer Mask in the Layers panel.

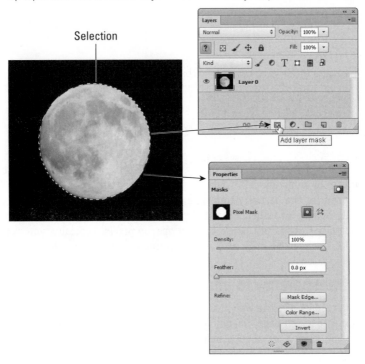

3. **Click the Add a Layer Mask option in the Layers panel shown in Figure 30.7.**

   A new layer mask is created using the current selection with a corresponding layer mask alpha channel. The area outside the selection becomes transparent.

Figure 30.8 shows the layer mask and alpha channel that result from adding the pixel mask. Notice the transparency in the image that results from the layer mask alpha channel. Because the alpha channel is embedded in a GIF or PNG file, the transparency is also embedded.

 You can easily tweak the mask used for transparency by using the techniques discussed in the alpha channel section of Chapter 11 and the layer masks section of Chapter 10. This allows you to fine-tune which areas of the image are transparent.

FIGURE 30.8

Adding a layer mask alpha channel to an image results in transparency that can be embedded in the alpha channel of the image.

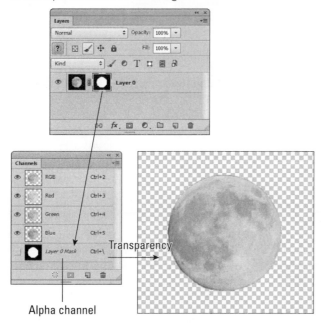

Alpha channel

Animating images

Another important aspect of web page images is animation. Animation can be used in a variety of ways, from dancing icons to web ads. Animation in web ads is particularly important because you can get much more information to the viewer by changing the text and images displayed in the image. For example, Figure 30.9 shows a simple animated web ad that updates the text over a period of time to display features of the website.

30

FIGURE 30.9

Using transparency helps the image fit better with the background of the web page.

 To learn how to animate the image using the Photoshop timeline, see Chapter 28.

Outputting Images to the Web

The most powerful tool that Photoshop provides to output images to the web is the Save for Web utility. This interface has three basic purposes. One is to preview how the resulting image will look and behave. The second is to convert the image to a size, format, and set of colors that are supported in web browsers. The third is to save the image to the appropriate format with the needed supporting HTML code to render the image in a browser.

To launch the Save for Web utility, shown in Figure 30.10, choose File ➪ Save for Web or press Ctrl+Alt+Shift+S/⌘+Option+Shift+S. The Save for Web utility has a lot going on in it, but don't be intimidated. After you get the hang of using it, you'll appreciate how well it is laid out. The following sections discuss the various parts of the interface to familiarize you with the workflow of outputting images to the web.

FIGURE 30.10

The Save for Web utility allows you to make the necessary adjustments to the file format, size, colors, and other items to prepare images for the web.

Toolbar   Preview layout   File output settings

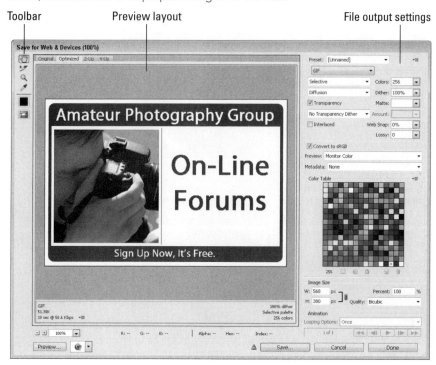

Using the preview layout and toolbar

The preview layout is designed to give you a sense of what the final image will look like as you prepare it for the web. The preview layout offers four tabs that define what version or versions of the image are displayed in the preview pane. The options are Original, Optimized, 2-Up, and 4-Up.

The optimized preview shows what the image will look like based on the values in the file output settings to the right of the preview. The 2-Up and 4-Up tabs display either two or four versions of the image, respectively. You can select a version by clicking in the preview pane and using the control settings on the right to adjust the values of that version. Using the 2-Up and 4-Up options is a great way of previewing different versions of the image, as shown in Figure 30.11. In the example, we use three file formats, but you could just use the 4-Up view to compare four optimization settings for the same file type.

30

FIGURE 30.11

Using the 4-Up preview, you can compare four versions of the image to see which file output settings are best.

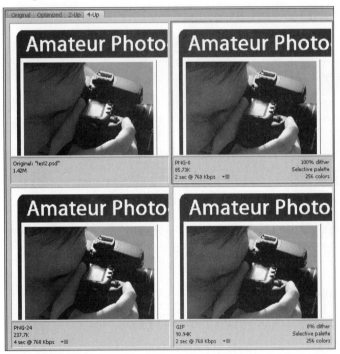

Notice in each of the preview panes that the file format is listed along with the size and download time. The image size can be very important if you need your web image to conform to a standard that limits the maximum image size, such as for advertisements. You can adjust the download rate using the pop-up menu.

Below the preview panes you can see the RGB levels as you pass the cursor over pixels in the image. Also displayed on that line are the Alpha, Hex, and Index values of the pixel currently under the mouse. Here's what those settings mean:

- **Alpha.** The Alpha value displays the value of the alpha channel, with 255 being completely opaque and 0 being completely transparent.
- **Hex.** The Hex value shows the hexadecimal value of the pixel. The hexadecimal value is very useful if you are trying to match colors in the HTML code with colors in the image.
- **Index.** The Index value is the index in the color lookup table for the pixel directly under the cursor.

The following tools are used to control and manipulate the image in the preview shown in Figure 30.12:

FIGURE 30.12

The image in the preview pane can be controlled and manipulated using the tools in the toolbar.

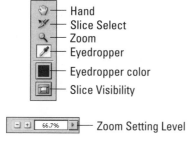

Zoom Setting Level

- **Hand.** The Hand tool moves the image inside the preview pane. This is especially useful if you are zoomed in on an image and want to check out different locations. Using the Hand tool moves the images in all preview panes.

- **Slice Select.** The Slice Select tool works just like the one in the Photoshop Toolbox described earlier in this chapter. You can manipulate the slices using the control handles, right-click to display the slice options, and double-click a slice to set the HTML options.

- **Zoom.** This tool allows you to zoom in on a specific area of the slice by dragging a rectangle around that portion.

- **Eyedropper.** The Eyedropper tool is used to select colors in the image. The color is selected in the color table, discussed later in this section.

- **Eyedropper color.** This icon displays the currently selected color. Clicking this icon displays the color chooser.

- **Slice Visibility.** This tool toggles the visibility of slices on and off. You typically want slices to be visible only when you are editing them.

- **Zoom Level.** This tool gives you the ability to quickly set a specific zoom level for the preview pane.

Setting File output options

The most important aspect of the Save for Web utility is the ability to convert images from the editing format to a format that is suitable to be displayed on a web page. The file output settings pane in the Save for Web utility allows you to define the web file format and parameters used to convert the image to that format.

Each file format provides different output options used in conversion. Figure 30.13 show the options for GIF, JPEG, and PNG-24. (PNG-8 is not shown because the options are identical to GIF with the exception that the Lossy option is omitted.)

30

FIGURE 30.13

The file output settings pane allows you to control options used when converting the image from the editing format to the web file format.

The following list describes each of the output options:

- **Preset.** This menu provides a list of predefined settings for general purposes such as JPEG High Quality or PNG-8 128 Dithered.

- **File Format.** This menu allows you to specify the output file format. These file formats were discussed earlier in this chapter.

- **Color Reduction Algorithm.** This menu allows you to specify the conversion method used to convert the image from the current format to the web format. When converting color images to another format, especially one supporting fewer colors, Photoshop must decide what colors to use in the destination file for source pixels that don't match up. The following list describes how each conversion option maps colors:

  - **Perceptual.** This option gives priority to colors for which the human eye has greater sensitivity. This is often the best choice because most web images are intended for viewing only.

  - **Adaptive.** This option creates a palette from the colors that appear most commonly in the image. This typically keeps the most detail in the image because there is a wider range of pixels in that area to support detail.

  - **Selective.** This option is similar to the perceptual option, but it favors broad areas of color while preserving the web colors. This usually produces images with the highest color integrity, if not the best perceptual integrity.

  - **Restrictive.** This option uses a standard 216-color color table common to both Windows and Mac OS, ensuring that no browser dither is applied to colors when the image is displayed using 8-bit color. Because this option creates larger files, you should use it only if browser dithering is of high priority.

  - **Custom.** This option allows you to create your own custom color palette when converting the image. The color palette is customized in the Color Table pane in the Save for Web utility.

  - **Black-White.** This option uses only black and white colors in the output image.

- **Grayscale.** This option uses a grayscale color palette to convert the image to grayscale.

- **Mac OS.** This option uses the Mac OS color palette to convert the image. You should only use this option for images that will be viewed from Mac OS browsers.

- **Windows.** This option uses the Windows color palette to convert the image. You should only use this option for images that will be viewed from Windows browsers.

- **Color.** This field specifies the number of colors in the color palette that is used by the conversion algorithm to convert the image. A smaller number here usually results in a smaller file size.

- **Dither.** This field allows you to select the method Photoshop uses to dither the image during conversion. Dithering simulates colors not available in the color display system of the computer. Often when you convert an image with continuous color tones to a smaller number of colors, banding is the result. One downside of dithering is that it increases the size of the image.

Figure 30.14 shows an example of the banding that occurs in an image when you convert it to 64 colors, as well as the effects that dithering has to simulate more colors by diffusing the pixels on the boundaries. Notice the banding in the non-dithered image and how using diffused dithering results in the appearance of more skin tones than exist in the actual image.

FIGURE 30.14

Using dithering when reducing the number of colors in an image can resolve banding effects and give the appearance of more colors in the image than actually exist.

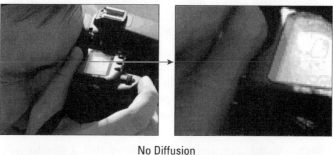

No Diffusion

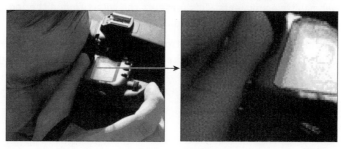

Diffusion

You can specify the following methods for applying dithering to the image during conversion:

- **No Dither.** This option applies no dithering to the images. This results in a smaller file size but may also result in banding, as shown in Figure 30.14.

- **Diffusion.** This option attempts to smooth transitions by scattering the colors of the two neighboring pixels along the edges. When you select this option, you can control the amount of dithering by adjusting the percentage value in the Dither field to the right. The more you increase the Dither setting, the larger the file size that results.

- **Pattern.** This option applies dithering by using a predefined pattern of pixels to attempt to produce the intermediate colors between the bands.

- **Noise.** This option applies dithering by introducing random pixels in the image. This option usually results in the least appealing results.

- **Dither.** This field specifies the percentage of dithering to apply to the image. A larger amount of dithering softens edges and removes pixelation but results in some blurring of the overall image.

- **Transparency.** GIF and PNG-8 files support transparency, but only in the fully transparent pixels. If you enable the Transparency option, Photoshop tries to preserve the semitransparent information, such as drop shadows, by applying a matte to the semitransparent pixels to create a fully opaque pixel.

  The color of the matte used is determined by the Matte setting. If the matte color matches the background color of the web page, the image looks much better when it is viewed on the web page.

  If you enable transparency, you can also specify a dithering option in the drop-down menu below Transparency. The dithering options are the same as for the image conversion, but they apply only when adding the matte to semitransparent pixels.

- **Interlaced.** This option sends a version of your image that contains information for every other line of pixels to the browser first so the browser can render a low-resolution copy to the user while the rest of the image is downloaded. This can improve the speed with which web pages are loaded, but it also results in a larger image file. This option is not used very much anymore because Internet connections are much faster now.

- **Web Snap.** This field specifies a tolerance level that is used to shift colors to the closest web palette equivalents. This prevents the colors from dithering in the browser. The higher the value, the more colors are being shifted.

- **Lossy.** This field allows you to control how aggressive the GIF compression algorithm is when compressing the images. The higher the number, the more aggressive the algorithm is, thus reducing the file size. However, this also results in more data being lost during compression. Typically, you can get away with a value of 5 to 10 for most GIF images without sacrificing too much quality.

- **Quality.** This field specifies the JPEG image quality setting from Low to Maximum. This setting is a tradeoff; the higher the quality, the better the image but the larger the file size. You can also control this option by setting a value between 0 and 100, where 100 is the maximum quality.

- **Progressive.** This option displays the image progressively in the web browser. Progressive means that the image is displayed as a series of overlays, allowing the browser to display a low-resolution image that progressively gains quality as more of the image is downloaded. Using this option results in a larger file size.

- **Blur.** This field specifies an amount of blur that is added to the image. Adding blur applies a Gaussian Blur filter to the image and allows JPEG images to be compressed more, resulting in a smaller file size.

- **Optimized.** This option creates an enhanced JPEG file with a slightly smaller file size. This is great for reducing the file size, but some older browsers do not support enhanced JPEG images.

- **Embed Color Profile.** This option embeds the color profile in the image.

 Color management is an important aspect of web images because the images will be viewed on a variety of displays and you want the images to appear the same on all of them. See Chapter 29 for more information about the sRGB color profile and color profiles in general.

- **Convert to sRGB.** This option converts the image to the sRGB color profile, which is the default color model for displaying images in web browsers on many different displays.

- **Preview.** This menu allows you to specify the color profile used to render the images in the preview pane of the Save for Web utility. Basically, this option controls the gamma used to display the image in the preview pane. Because Mac OS prior to Mac OS X 10.6 used a different gamma than Windows, images display differently and are sometimes washed out on one system when they look fine on another. Take a minute to use the different preview options to verify how the image will look on the different platforms.

- **Metadata.** This menu allows you to set the metadata information to include with the converted file. Metadata is a great way to keep track of information in the file. The problem is that sometimes the metadata contains information you do not want to distribute to anyone downloading the file from the web — for example, camera settings or personal information.

The Metadata menu allows you to control what metadata is included in the web image. The options are None, Copyright, Copyright and Contact Info, All Except Camera Info, and All. The excess metadata items are stripped out of the converted file.

30

In addition to the settings in the file output pane, you can also use the following options from the side menu that help when configuring the file output settings:

- **Optimize to File Size.** This option launches the Optimize to File Size dialog box, shown in Figure 30.15, which allows you to specify a file size and then use that size to automatically configure the options to match the desired output settings. The Start With options allow you to use the currently selected file format or allow the dialog box to choose either JPEG or GIF. The Use options allow you to control how the output is applied to slices in the image.

FIGURE 30.15

The Optimize to File Size menu option in the file output settings pane allows you to specify a desired output size for the image, and Photoshop automatically sets the output options necessary to result in the specified file size.

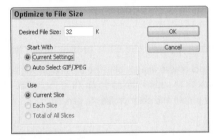

- **Edit Output Settings.** This option launches the Output Settings dialog box, which controls how the image is actually finalized for the web. The Output Settings dialog box is really four different dialog boxes, shown in Figure 30.16, which allow you to set the following output options:

  - **HTML.** This section allows you to configure the HTML settings such as using XHTML, tag casing, line encodings, and how to encode the HTML tags.

  - **Slices.** This section allows you to specify whether slices are encoded as an HTML table or CSS, as well as the default naming scheme used for slices. The naming options should be familiar to you by now.

  - **Background.** This section allows you to control whether the image is to be viewed as the background for the web page or just an image. You can also specify the color to use as the background for the web page.

  - **Saving Files.** This section allows you to configure the file naming, compatibility, and location to output images to. When Photoshop saves the image, it generates several supporting HTML, CSS, and other files.

FIGURE 30.16

The Output Settings dialog box allows you to configure how the image is actually finalized for the web, including HTML, CSS, slice, background, and other settings.

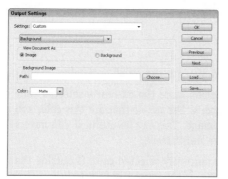

Manipulating the Color Table

The Color Table pane in the Save for Web utility allows you to control and manipulate the color palette used for GIF and PNG file conversion. Only colors in the color palette will exist in the outputted image, so manipulating the colors in the Color Table pane lets you control the colors in the outputted image.

You can select colors in the table by clicking the table with the mouse or by clicking in the image using the Eyedropper tool. You can select multiple colors in the table by holding down the Shift key while you click them. After you have colors selected in the table, you can use the following options, shown in Figure 30.17, to control the color palette:

FIGURE 30.17

The Color Table pane allows you to use the color palette to manipulate the colors and transparency that will be included in the outputted image.

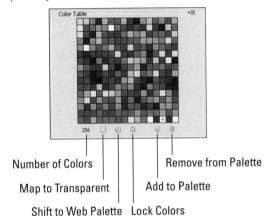

Number of Colors

Map to Transparent

Shift to Web Palette   Lock Colors

Remove from Palette

Add to Palette

- **Number of Colors.** This field displays the number of colors in the color table.

- **Map to Transparent.** This option maps the currently selected color or colors in the Color Table to transparent pixels. The pixels that are this color will be transparent in the outputted GIF or PNG-8 image. This can be useful if you have solid colors in the image that you want to make transparent.

- **Shift to Web Palette.** If the currently selected color is outside the web palette, it will be shifted into the web palette. If the currently selected color is already shifted into the web palette, it is "un-shifted" back out.

- **Lock Colors.** This option locks the currently selected color so it isn't dropped from the outputted image. This option is especially useful if you have a specific one-color item — such as a logo or symbol — that you want to ensure remains in the original color in the outputted image.

- **Add to Palette.** This option adds the color from the Color tool in the preview area to the color palette. This allows you to define specific colors that you want included in the color palette.

- **Remove from Palette.** This option removes the selected color or colors from the color palette, allowing you to add additional colors.

Setting the image size

The Image Size pane in the Save for Web utility, shown in Figure 30.18, allows you to control the size of the outputted file without affecting the size of the original. The Image Size pane allows you to set a specific height and width for the image using the H and W settings. If you select the lock icon, height and width changes are proportional. You can also set the size of the output image using the Percent field when 100% is the original size.

When changing the size of the image, Photoshop must interpolate the values of pixels that either didn't exist in the original image because the size is growing, or are the result of multiple pixels if the size is decreasing. The Quality option allows you to specify which of the Photoshop interpolation algorithms to use. The options are Nearest Neighbor, Bilinear, Bicubic, Bicubic Smoother, and Bicubic Sharper.

FIGURE 30.18

The Image Size pane allows you to control the size of the outputted image without affecting the size of the original image.

 Image resizing, including the various algorithms used in the Quality setting, is discussed in more detail in Chapter 3. See the resizing section of that chapter when deciding which algorithm to use.

Previewing animation controls

The Animation pane in the Save for Web utility provides two features. The first is to set the Looping Options that will be embedded with the animated image. You can set the Looping Options to Once, Forever, and Other. If you select Other, a dialog box appears that allows you to set the number of times to loop the animation. How many loops you choose is purely subjective. Playing the animation too many times can be annoying with some images but is necessary in others.

The Other setting of the Animation pane, shown in Figure 30.19, allows you to preview the animation in the preview pane. The Play, Rewind, and Fast Forward options allow you to see each of the frames in the animation and preview the behavior.

FIGURE 30.19

The Animation pane allows you to preview the animation as well as control the number of times the animation is played when the image is viewed.

30

Previewing output in a browser

A great feature of the Save for Web utility is the ability to quickly preview the image in a web browser by clicking the Preview button. When you click the Preview button, the image is displayed in the web browser based on the output settings.

All the supporting web code is displayed below in the image, as shown in Figure 30.20. The HTML files are also created in the output directory so you can actually test the images in the web browser.

> **NOTE**
>
> The list to the right of the Preview button in the Save for Web utility, allows you to configure a list of web browsers to test and to select the web browser used by the Preview button. This allows you to quickly test web images against a series of browsers.

FIGURE 30.20

The Preview button in the Save for Web utility launches a web browser that allows you to quickly preview the look and behavior of the image before saving it.

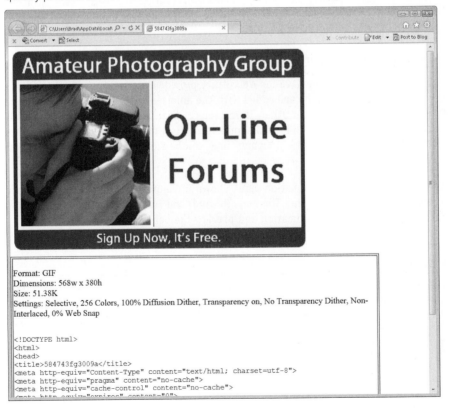

Adding Zoomable Images to Websites

Photoshop provides the Zoomify plug-in as an additional feature to output images to the web. Zoomify carves an image up into a series of JPEG tiles that can be used by a Flash browser utility to quickly zoom in and out, as well as pan images in a web page. By breaking the image up into a series of tiles, less data needs to be sent to the web browser, so the performance in viewing images is very good.

To launch the Zoomify tool, shown in Figure 30.21, choose File ⇨ Export ⇨ Zoomify from Photoshop's main menu bar. The Zoomify utility allows you to specify the output location and a base name to use for the output files. You can also specify the JPEG quality using the Image Tile Options settings. The Browser Options allow you to set the width and height, in pixels, that the Zoom utility takes up in the browser.

FIGURE 30.21

The Zoomify utility is used to carve up a high-definition image into a series of smaller JPEG tiles so the image can be easily zoomed in and out and panned using a Flash Player in a web browser.

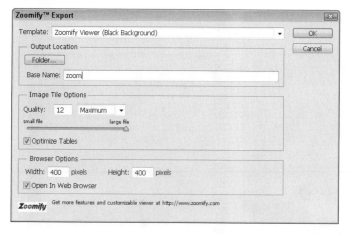

The following is a list of the files and folders that are generated by the Zoomify tool in the Output Location. You can transfer these files and folders to your web browser to be included in your website:

- **<Base Name>.html.** This is the HTML file based on the Base Name setting that is used to display the Zoomify Flash Player utility. The appropriate code in this file can be cut and pasted into your web page code to include the image on your website.

- **<Base Name>.** This is a folder based on the Base Name setting that contains the following items:

30

- **ImageProperties.xml.** This specifies data necessary for the Zoomify Flash Player.

- **zoomifyViewer.swf.** This is the Zoomify Flash Player utility that renders the images and provides the controls in the browser to zoom in and out on the image.

- **TileGroup#.** This is a series of folders that contain the JPEG tiles of the image. Each tile is named using the #-#-#.jpg filename format. Each number represents a location in the image and zoom scale, and the numbers are used to display the zoomed portions of the image.

Figure 30.22 shows how a Zoomified image appears in a web browser. Using the utility, you can easily zoom in and pan to an individual balloon.

> **NOTE**
> When you click the OK button in the Zoomify Export dialog box, a web browser launches to display the Zoomified image. You may need to enable the Zoomify ActiveX application when the browser launches.

FIGURE 30.22

You can easily zoom in on and pan around a high-resolution image that has been Zoomified.

Summary

Photoshop provides several powerful features that can aid graphic designers in creating and preparing images for web applications. Photoshop provides the tools necessary to convert image formats to formats supported by web browsers, set the size of images to reduce the bandwidth they require for download, and apply color profiles to ensure that the image colors are consistent across multiple web browsers.

Photoshop also provides features that allow you to quickly add animation and transparency to give your images a much better look and feel. This chapter discussed the Save for Web utility, which allows you to quickly configure image file formats, preview output, convert images, and generate the HTML output necessary to support them.

In this chapter, you learned the following:

- How to convert images to file formats that are supported by web browsers.
- How to use color profiles to ensure that image colors remain consistent between web browsers.
- How to add transparency to web images so they blend in better with the web page.
- How to use Zoomify to add high-resolution images than can be zoomed and panned to web pages.
- How the Save for Web utility allows you to control what image metadata is included in web images so you can show copyright information but hide camera settings.
- How to preview images in web browsers before outputting them to the new file format.

30

Automating and Scripting Workflow in Photoshop

IN THIS CHAPTER

Using scripts to simplify workflow tasks

Assigning actions and scripts to Photoshop events to automate tasks

Photoshop is a powerful application with many tools and utilities that provide limitless ways to create and edit images. The power of Photoshop comes with one big drawback: it has so many tools, menu options, and panels that navigating through them can be difficult, especially if you need to perform repetitive tasks on several files.

To solve that problem, Photoshop has provided several tools that make it possible to automate much of your workflow by using batch processing and scripting. Batch processing involves performing the same set of commands on a group of files. Scripting involves applying a script as either a one-time command or each time a workflow event occurs. The following sections discuss using the Photoshop automation and scripting tools to make your image editing easier and faster.

Automating Workflow in Photoshop

When editing images, one of the best ways to save time and increase your productivity is to automate repetitive tasks that need to be done on a series of photos. For example, a set of photos taken with the same lens at a wedding dinner may all need a lens correction filter applied as well as a color correction to adjust for the lighting at the event. If you were to make those adjustments to each image individually, it would take a lot of time.

Photoshop has a couple of great utilities that help you automate the workflow necessary to make the same adjustments to a series of photos with one simple command. The Batch and Droplet utilities allow you to quickly apply custom actions to files to save time when editing.

 Creating custom actions is covered in Chapter 5. You can refer to that chapter to find out how to build the actions and action sets that can be used by the Batch and Droplet utilities.

Batching multiple images

The Batch processing utility allows you to apply a customizable action to a set of images and control how the images are processed.

The way batch processing works is that you define a location for a set of files, select one of the customized actions defined in the Actions panel, and then define how you want the processed photos to be outputted. When the batch of images is processed, Photoshop opens each image, performs the steps in the selected action on the image, and saves the adjusted image to disk where you can then perform custom adjustments later.

You can start batch processes in a couple of different ways: by selecting the files in Bridge and then choosing Tools ⇨ Photoshop ⇨ Batch from the main menu bar or by choosing File ⇨ Automate ⇨ Batch from the Photoshop menu bar. Whichever way you choose, Photoshop opens the dialog box shown in Figure 31.1.

FIGURE 31.1

Using the Batch dialog box, you can define a custom action that is applied to a set of source files, and define a location and file-naming format to use when saving the edited images.

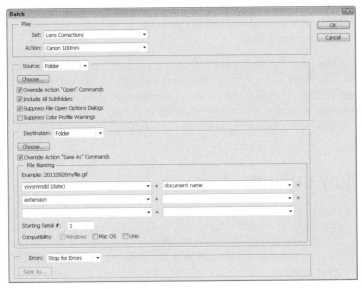

 Bridge is a great application for organizing and managing your images, and is discussed in Chapter 6. Using the Photoshop Batch utility is usually the best way to perform batch editing on images.

The following options are available in the Batch processing utility:

- **Play.** This section allows you to define what action to perform on each of the files specified by the Source settings. You can choose from the following options:

  - **Set.** This menu displays a list of the defined sets in Photoshop. The default set provides some standard actions such as Vignette and Custom RGB to Grayscale. However, you will likely be creating your own action sets with customizable actions. For example, you may want to create an action set with lens-correction filter actions for each of your lenses.

  - **Action.** This menu allows you to specify the action to be performed on each image when the files are processed. Actions can perform anything from a simple one-step edit to a series of complex edits. The options available from the Action menu represent the list of actions that are contained in the selected set in the Actions panel.

- **Source.** This menu allows you to define where Photoshop gets the source images to be edited. You can select files from four different sources: Folder, Import, Opened Files, and Bridge.

  When you select Folder, you can click the Choose button to launch a dialog box that allows you to select a folder that contains files to be included in the batch edit.

  Selecting Import allows you to process images from a digital camera, scanner, or PDF. The Import option is available only if you specify that you want to batch process folders when you are importing them into Photoshop or Bridge.

  Selecting Opened Files batch processes all images currently open in Photoshop.

  Selecting the Bridge option batch processes the files currently selected in Bridge. The Bridge option is available only when you are using the Bridge interface to launch the Batch processing utility.

  The Source option also allows you to use the following settings to control how Photoshop handles image files from the source location:

  - **Override Action "Open" Commands.** When you select this option, batch processing overrides the choice of files specified for an "Open" command in the action. This does not override the settings in the Open command, just the choice of files.

    This option is necessary for actions that include Open commands for the most recent or current files because the most recent file is always the first image in the set of source files. You should not enable this option for actions that do not contain an Open command.

    You can leave this option disabled if the action does not include an Open command or if the Open command is on another file that is required for the action but not the actual file that is being edited.

  - **Include All Subfolders.** When you select this option, images in all subfolders in the selected folder are also batch processed. This allows you to process images in multiple folders so you can keep your files well organized.

- **Suppress File Open Options Dialogs.** When selected, this option hides the File Open dialog boxes. Instead of requiring you to specify the open options, Photoshop uses the default values. This option is especially useful if you are batch processing camera RAW images, because you can preset how to treat the images and bypass the dialog box when batch editing.

- **Suppress Color Profile Warnings.** When you select this option, the color policy messages, such as color mismatch or missing color profiles, are not displayed.

- **Destination.** This menu allows you to control how and where the edited images are saved to disk. You can specify one of three different destinations: None, Save and Close, and Folder.

  If you select None, the images are edited but left open in Photoshop unless the action includes a Save or Save As command. If you select Save and Close, the original image is overwritten by the edited image on disk.

  If you select Folder, you can use the Choose button to select a destination folder to save the edited images. The edited images are saved in that location using the name formatting specified in the File Naming setting.

  The following options allow you to override the Save As command and define the file naming convention:

> **CAUTION**
>
> You should select the Save and Close option only if you are confident that the action will give you the best results. After the original file is overwritten, you cannot go back and undo the edits.

- **Override Action "Save As" Commands.** When you select this option, batch processing overrides the destination folder and the file names specified by a Save or Save As command in the action. This does not override the settings in the Save commands, just the destination and name of the files.

  You do not need to enable this option for actions that do not contain a Save or Save As command.

> **NOTE**
>
> A lot of options are available in the Save As dialog box in Photoshop that are not available in the Batch dialog box — for example, compression, saving layers, and so on. Typically, you want to record a Save As command into the editing that sets these options. In addition, you can use a Save As command in the action to change the file type of the images during the batch process.

- **File Naming.** The file-naming section allows you to set the naming convention that is used to save the edited file. You define the file convention by selecting the appropriate components from the menus shown in Figure 31.2. You can also type into one of the field components static text that is included in the filename.

  When the edited file is saved, these components are used in the order specified to create the filename. When you use the components, you can include the document name and extension in different casing formats, serial letters, multi-digit numbers, and different date formats.

> **NOTE**
>
> When using Digit Serial Numbers, the numbers start with the number specified in the Starting serial# field and are pre-fixed by enough zeros to force them to the number of specified digits. When using serial letters, the first image starts with a/A.

FIGURE 31.2

The File Naming options in the Batch dialog box allow you to select filename components based on date, document name, extension, and serialized letters or numbers.

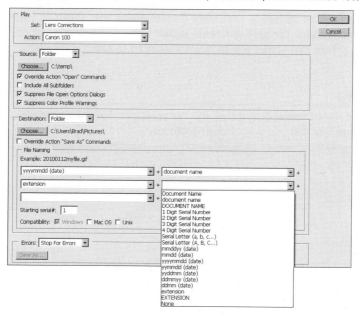

- **Compatibility.** The Windows, Mac OS, and Unix options allow you to limit the naming conventions to support Windows, Mac OS, and Linux/Unix systems. This is useful if you plan to share your images with others who may be using different systems.

- **Errors.** This menu allows you to control how errors in the batch processing are handled. You have two options:

    - **Stop For Errors.** When you select this option and an error occurs when editing one of the files in the batch, an error message is displayed and the processing stops there. No additional files are processed.

- **Log Errors To File.** When you select this option and an error occurs when editing one of the files in the batch, the error message is logged to a file and the processing continues. You can set the location of the log file by clicking the Save As button. The log file is in text format and you can read it with any text editor to determine which files failed and why.

Creating droplets to process images

Droplets are very similar to batch operations with the exception that instead of selecting a source for files, you specify a location where you want to save the processing information in the file system. The processing data is converted to an executable file that processes any files or folders that are dragged and dropped onto it.

You can create a droplet by choosing File ⇨ Automate ⇨ Create Droplet from Photoshop's menu bar. Notice that the options in the Create Droplet dialog box, shown in Figure 31.3, are similar to the Batch options. The only difference is that instead of a Source option, you have a Save Droplet In option that allows you to select a location to save the droplet.

FIGURE 31.3

Using the Create Droplet dialog box, you can create an executable file that applies an action to any image files that you drag and drop onto it.

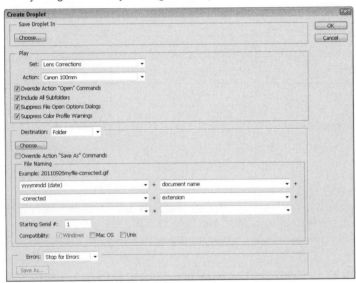

To create the droplet, fill in the Save Droplet In, Play, Destination, and Errors settings and click OK. An executable file is created in the location you specified. To use a droplet, simply use the file system interface to drag and drop files or folders onto the droplet. The droplet uses Photoshop to perform the specified action and save the adjusted files.

> **TIP**
>
> You can move a droplet between Windows and Mac OS systems. When moving a droplet from Windows to Mac OS, or vice versa, drag and drop it onto the Photoshop application icon on the new system. Photoshop converts the droplet so that it can be used on that system. If you are planning to move a droplet from Mac OS to Windows, make sure to name it with the ".exe" extension once it is on the Windows system so it can be executed on the Windows system.
>
> You should be aware, however, that file references in actions do not work across Windows and Mac OS systems. If an action refers to a file, such as in an "Open" or "Save As" command, the droplet prompts for the location of the file if it is used on a different system.

Using Scripting to Speed Up Workflow

Another great way to save time and increase your productivity when editing images is to use the scripting capabilities in Photoshop. Two main types of scripts are available in Photoshop: predefined scripts and event-driven scripts. Predefined scripts are run once when you select them from the File⇨Scripts menu shown in Figure 31.4. Event-driven scripts are triggered and executed by events in your normal editing workflow. The following sections discuss how to use of each of these types of scripts.

FIGURE 31.4

The File⇨Scripts menu in Photoshop provides several predefined scripts that perform tasks that speed up your workflow.

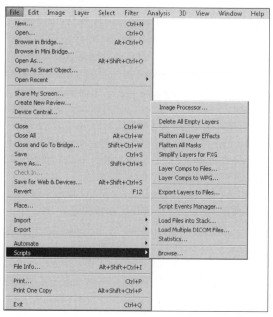

Using the Photoshop scripts

Predefined scripts are similar to other commands in Photoshop with the exception that they typically perform more than just one task on a single item. The predefined scripts are JavaScript or AppleScript scripts that perform a series of Photoshop tasks to reduce the number of keystrokes and mouse clicks you need to make. While the JavaScript scripts are cross-platform, the AppleScript scripts only work on Macs. The following is a list that describes the predefined scripts available from the File ➪ Scripts menu:

- **Image Processor.** This option launches a dialog box that allows you to process a set of files, for example, by converting format, changing names, running actions, and so on.

 The best place to use the Image Processor is from Bridge while you are managing your files. To find out how to use the Image Processor utility to convert and process images from Bridge, see Chapter 6.

- **Delete All Empty Layers.** This option removes empty layers from the image. This can be a useful tool to clean up an image when you have used a lot of layers when editing.

- **Flatten All Layer Effects.** This option flattens all the effects that apply to the currently selected layer in the Layers panel. This rasterizes all of the layer effects so you can apply additional filters or other tools that require the layer to be flattened.

- **Flatten All Masks.** This option applies the layer masks in all layers. The layer masks affect only the layer to which they are linked.

- **Simplify Layers for FXG.** This option simplifies layer settings so that they are compatible with the Adobe FXG file format. FXG is an XML-based file format that is used in graphics for web applications that are created by applications such as Adobe Flash or Flex 4.

- **Layer Comps to Files.** This option opens a dialog box, similar to the one in Figure 31.5, which allows you to specify a file type and location using the following options:
  - **Destination.** This field specifies the location on disk where you want to create the files.
  - **File Name Prefix.** This field specifies the name prefix that is applied to the saved files. The rest of the filename includes a numerical index and the file extension that you specify in the File Type drop-down menu.
  - **Selected Layer Comps Only.** This option allows only the currently selected Layer Comps in the image to be saved as individual image files in the specified location. Otherwise, all Layer Comps are saved as individual files.
  - **File Type.** This menu specifies the file format to use when saving the image. You can select BMP, JPEG, PDF, PSD, Targa, TIFF, PNG-8, or PNG-24.
  - **Include ICC Profile.** This option specifies whether to include the current ICC color profile with the saved images. It is always a good idea to include a color profile when saving images.
  - **PSD Options.** If the file type has additional options, then you can set those options here.

FIGURE 31.5

You can use the Layer Comps To Files script utility to convert the Layer Comps in the current document into individual files.

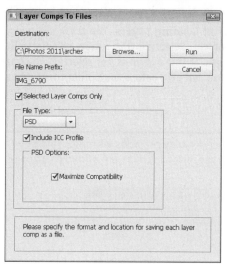

- **Layer Comps to WPG.** This option converts the Layer Comps in the image into individual WPG (Web Photo Gallery) files.

- **Export Layers to Files.** This option opens a dialog box, similar to the one in Figure 31.5, except that instead of only saving Layer Comps, all layers are saved to files.

- **Script Events Manager.** This option allows you to attach specific actions to workflow events in Photoshop. The Script Events Manager is discussed in more detail in the next section.

- **Load Files into Stack.** This option opens the Load Layers dialog box, shown in Figure 31.6, which allows you to combine a set of files into a stack. A stack is a set of image files taken of the same subject from the same camera position. Image stacks loaded as layers can be converted to a smart object and then processed using the options located in the Layers ➪ Smart Objects ➪ Stack Mode options discussed later in this section.

From the Load Layers dialog box, you can configure the following options:

- **Use.** This menu allows you to specify whether to use files or a folder as the source for the set of files. The Browse, Remove, and Add Open Files buttons allow you to add files and remove files and folders from the Use list.

- **Attempt to Automatically Align Source Images.** When you select this option, Photoshop tries to find common edges in the images and automatically adjusts the rotation and position so the images are as closely aligned as possible. Aligning the images is important for the stack mode algorithms to work well.

- **Create Smart Object after Loading Layers.** The stack mode algorithms are based on processing a smart object. Selecting this option automatically creates a smart object from all the images. If this option is not selected, the images are loaded as individual layers that you can edit before combining them into a smart object.

FIGURE 31.6

The Load Files into Stack script utility provides a simple dialog box that allows you to select files and define how the individual files are added to a newly created stacked document.

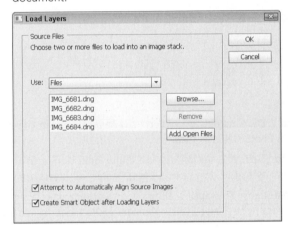

 Another great place to create image stacks is from Bridge while you are managing your files. Using the Bridge application to stack and unstack images is covered in Chapter 6.

- **Load Multiple DICOM Files.** This option opens a dialog box that allows you to select a folder containing a set of DICOM image files. The DICOM files in the folder are added as individual layers to a new document in Photoshop.

- **Statistics.** This option opens the Image Statistics dialog box, shown in Figure 31.7. This is similar to the Load Files into Stack option, except that it automatically converts the images into a single smart object and then applies the stack mode that you specified in the Choose Stack Mode drop-down menu. Statistics is a better option than Load Files into Stack if you do not want to align the images manually, or if you don't want to edit any of the layers before applying the stack mode to the set.

FIGURE 31.7

The Image Statistics dialog box allows you to set the stack mode that is applied after some files are automatically converted into a single smart object.

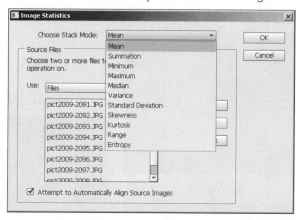

Using stack modes to analyze multiple images and reduce noise

Photoshop provides several options for processing images that have been stacked into a smart object using the Load Files into Stack script described in the previous section. These stack mode options can analyze the differences between images and combine the images to reduce noise. The following stack mode options can be found in the Layers ➪ Smart Objects ➪ Stack Mode menu:

- **Entropy.** This is calculated based on the number of bits that would be necessary to encode the data from all images in a set. Areas of the image that are different show up white in the resulting image and areas with little difference show up as black. This is a great option for locating missing items between one image and another or embedding hidden copyright notices.

  Figure 31.8 shows an example of using the Entropy stack mode to analyze two digital images. Notice that they both look the same, but when the Entropy mode is used, a clear copyright notice is shown. The copyright notice was added by creating a text selection mask, as discussed in Chapter 18, copying it to a new layer, and then slightly adjusting the position. You can't see the change because it is in a busy area of the image.

TIP

For the best results, images that you intend to edit using the stack mode options should be taken from a fixed position such as a tripod with a stationary subject. At the very least, the images must be similar enough that you can align them in the set.

FIGURE 31.8

Using the Entropy mode, you can quickly compare a digital image with the original to reveal an embedded copyright message.

Original

Entropy Stack mode

Copyrighted

Dayley Creations
Copyright © 2010

- **Mean.** This option averages the pixels for all images in the stack and uses the average value for the stacked image. This is usually the best option for noise reduction if the images are very similar.

- **Summation.** This option calculates the pixel values in the stacked image by adding values from all images in the stack. This increases the resolution in the more faint areas of the images, but the brighter areas just become white.

- **Minimum.** This option uses the minimum channel value for all non-transparent pixels in the stacked image. This is good for stacks of images where you want to darken the overall image.

- **Maximum.** This option uses the maximum channel value for all non-transparent pixels in the stacked image. This is good for stacks of images where you want to lighten the overall image.

- **Median.** This option takes the middle value for all images in the stack and uses that value for the stacked image. This option works better than the Mean mode for noise reduction if there is a lot of variance in the lighting and color of the images, such as scratches or dark areas.

Figure 31.9 shows an example of how you can use the Median mode to remove unwanted items. Notice that the three images of the moon have a silhouette of a bird in front, so none of them is a clean shot. You can remove the bird by stacking the three images and applying the Median mode as shown in the results.

FIGURE 31.9

Using the Median mode, three images of the moon with a silhouette in front can be processed into a single clean image.

- **Variance.** This option is similar to the Standard Deviation option. Areas that match are black, and areas that do not match are gray to white, based on the variance in the stacked image.

- **Standard Deviation.** This option calculates the stacked image values based on the standard deviation from the square root of the variance. This can help you analyze areas of the images that are different; the different areas show up as a lighter value based on the amount of variance while areas that are the same across all stacked images are black.

- **Skewness.** This option calculates the pixel value based on the variance of the pixels away from the average. This shows how close the pixel values are to each other.

- **Kurtosis.** This option calculates the stacked image based on peakedness or flatness of the levels in the image. Areas that match a normal distribution of levels appear lighter while areas that are flat or overpeaked appear darker.

- **Range.** This option calculates the pixel value in the stacked image based on the maximum pixel value minus the minimum pixel value. This shows the range of variance in the stacked images.

Use the following steps to apply a stack mode to a series of photographs:

1. **Choose File ⇨ Scripts ⇨ Load Files into Stack from the main menu bar.**

2. **Add the files you want to apply to the stack as described earlier.**

3. **Select the Attempt to Automatically Align Source Images option.**

   This option tries to align the images so that they match up correctly.

> **NOTE**
>
> You may need to manually align the images in the smart object if the Attempt to Automatically Align Source Images option fails to align them completely. To align the images manually, double-click the smart object layer to open the smart object. The images are in separate layers, and you can use the Move tool to move the images in each layer until they are aligned.

4. **Select the Create Smart Object after Loading Layers option.**

   This converts the image layers into a single smart object.

5. **Click the OK button.**

   The images are processed into a single document in Photoshop with a smart object layer.

6. **Select the newly created smart object layer.**

7. **Open the Layers ⇨ Smart Objects ⇨ Stack Mode menu and select the stack mode that you want to apply to the image.**

   The resulting image in the document window is changed to the results of the stack mode.

Scripting workflow events

Photoshop provides the Script Events Manager, shown in Figure 31.10, that gives you access to certain program events that occur during normal editing workflow. The Script Events Manager lets you attach scripts or actions to these events so that the script or action is run each time an event occurs during your editing workflow.

Scripting workflow events can be a big timesaver because they automatically perform actions you want to happen without needing to remember them. For example, you can configure the open file event to automatically save a JPEG copy, so that each time you start editing a file, you have a JPEG backup.

You can load the Script Events Manager utility by choosing File ⇨ Script ⇨ Script Events Manager from the Photoshop menu bar. The Script Events Manager allows you to use the following options to assign scripts and actions to workflow events:

- **Enable Events to Run Scripts/Actions.** When you select this option, the associations in the scripted events list are active when you are working in Photoshop. When this option is deselected, the events are ignored and no action or script is run.

- **Scripted Events List.** This field lists the current associations between events and actions/scripts. The Add button allows you to add the association defined by the

Photoshop Event, Script, and Action settings to this list. The Remove and Remove All buttons allow you to remove associations from the list.

- **Photoshop Event.** This menu displays a set of Photoshop events that you will encounter during the normal workflow, including Start Application, New Document, Open Document, Save Document, Close Document, Print Document, Export Document, and Everything (all available events).

- **Script.** This menu specifies a script that should be associated with an event and should be run each time the event occurs. The menu displays the available scripts. The default script options are limited; however, the menu also provides a browse option so you can select a JavaScript or AppleScript from the file system.

- **Action.** This option specifies an action that should be associated with an event and that should be run each time the event occurs. The first drop-down menu allows you to select the action set from the available action sets defined in the Actions panel. The second drop-down menu allows you to select the action from the available actions defined in the Actions panel. Because you can easily create custom actions using the Actions panel, you have a lot of options when associating actions with events.

 Creating custom actions is covered in Chapter 5. You can refer to that chapter for the information necessary to build the actions and action sets that can be associated with workflow events.

FIGURE 31.10

The Script Events Manager allows you to associate an action or a script with normal workflow events so that each time an event occurs, the action is performed, or the script is run.

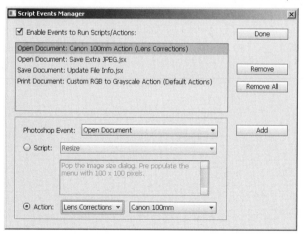

Summary

This chapter discussed using the Photoshop automation and scripting tools to speed up your image-editing workflow. Photoshop provides the Batch and Droplet tools, which allow you to perform the same set of commands on a set of files without opening each file individually.

Photoshop also provides several scripts that perform a set of repetitive operations, such as flattening layer masks using a single menu option. In addition to the scripts, Photoshop provides the Script Events Manager, which allows you to associate actions and scripts with normal workflow events. Each time an event occurs during your workflow, the associated action is performed.

In this chapter, you learned the following:

- How to use custom actions to process a set of image files all at once.
- How to save a predefined action as a droplet, and how to drag and drop a file onto that droplet in order to apply the action.
- How to use Photoshop scripts that allow you to perform repetitive actions.
- How to use the Statistics scripts to load a series of photos into a stack and then automatically process the set of files to clean up noise in a way that is not possible with a single file.
- How normal workflow events such as opening or saving a file can be tied to actions such that the action is automatically applied when the event occurs.

Part X

Appendixes

IN THIS PART

Timesaving Keyboard Shortcuts

IN THIS APPENDIX

Getting familiar with standard toolbar shortcuts

Using common menu command shortcuts

Working with extended toolbar shortcuts

Learning keyboard shortcuts is one of the best ways to improve your performance and experience with Photoshop. With hundreds of tools and menus, navigating with the mouse can take time. Knowing the keyboard shortcuts for actions that you frequently perform can make editing faster and less cumbersome.

The purpose of this appendix is to give you a sample of the most common shortcuts you will encounter in Photoshop. Both the Mac and PC keyboard shortcuts are listed in the tables.

Using Toolbox Shortcuts

The Toolbox shortcuts in Photoshop provide quick access to common Toolbox options such as selecting the Brush tool or cycling through the Brush, Pencil, Color Replacement, and Mixer Brush tools. When you press the shortcut keys, the tool is selected and ready to use. When you press a cycle shortcut key sequence, Photoshop cycles through each of the different tools located in the toolset of the Toolbox.

Table A.1 provides a list of most of the standard Toolbox shortcuts.

TABLE A.1   Standard Toolbox Shortcuts

Photoshop CS6 Standard Toolbar	PC Shortcut	Mac Shortcut
Move tool	V	V
Rectangular Marquee tool	M	M
Cycle Marquee tools	Shift+M	Shift+M
Lasso tool	L	L
Cycle Lasso tools	Shift+L	Shift+L
Cycle Quick Selection, Magic Wand tools	Shift+W	Shift+W
Crop tool	C	C
Cycle Crop, Slice tools	Shift+C	Shift+C
Eyedropper tool	I	I
Cycle Eyedropper, Color Sampler, Ruler, Note, and Count tools	Shift+I	Shift+I
Spot Healing Brush	J	J
Cycle Spot Healing Brush, Healing Brush, Patch, and Red Eye tools	Shift+J	Shift+J
Brush tool	B	B
Cycle Brush, Pencil, Color Replacement, and Mixer Brush tools	Shift+B	Shift+B
Clone Stamp tool	S	S
Cycle Clone Stamp, Pattern Stamp tools	Shift+S	Shift+S
History Brush tool	Y	Y
Cycle History Brush, Art History Brush tools	Shift+Y	Shift+Y
Eraser tool	E	E
Cycle Eraser, Background Eraser, and Magic Eraser tools	Shift+E	Shift+E
Gradient tool	G	G
Cycle Gradient, Paint Bucket tools	Shift+G	Shift+G
Blur, Smudge, Sharpen tools	None	None
Dodge tool	O	O
Cycle Dodge, Burn, Sponge tools	Shift+O	Shift+O
Pen tool	P	P
Cycle Pen, Freeform Pen tools	Shift+P	Shift+P
Add, Delete, Convert Anchor Point tools	None	None
Horizontal Type tool	T	T

Photoshop CS6 Standard Toolbar	PC Shortcut	Mac Shortcut
Cycle Horizontal Type, Vertical Type, Horizontal Type Mask, and Vertical Type Mask tools	Shift+T	Shift+T
Path Selection tool	A	A
Cycle Path Selection, Direct Selection tools	Shift+A	Shift+A
Rectangle tool	U	U
Cycle Rectangle, Rounded Rectangle, Ellipse, Polygon, Line, and Custom Shape tools	Shift +U	Shift +U
Hand tool	H	H
Rotate View tool	R	R
Zoom tool	Z	Z
Swap Foreground, Background Color	X	X
Default Foreground and Background Colors	D	D
Edit in Quick Mask Mode	Q	Q

Accessing Menu Options Quickly

The menu command shortcuts in Photoshop provide quick access to common menu options. Rather than using the mouse to cycle through the menu, you can simply press the keyboard shortcut.

Table A.2 provides a list of most of the common menu shortcuts.

> **NOTE**
> On Macs, shortcuts requiring F-keys, such as Shift+F5, may also require the Fn key to be pressed depending on the physical keyboard and the settings in the Keyboard System Preferences.

TABLE A.2 Common Menu Command Shortcuts

Popular Menu Commands	PC Shortcut	Mac Shortcut
New Document	Ctrl+N	⌘+N
Open Document	Ctrl+O	⌘+O
Browse in Bridge	Ctrl+Alt+O	⌘+Option+O
Close Document	Ctrl+W	⌘+W
Print Document	Ctrl+P	⌘+P
Undo	Ctrl+Z	⌘+Z
History Step Forward	Ctrl+Shift+Z	⌘+Shift+Z

(continued)

TABLE A.2 *(continued)*

Photoshop CS6 Standard Toolbar	PC Shortcut	Mac Shortcut
History Step Backward	Ctrl+Alt+Z	⌘+Option+F
Fade	Ctrl+Shift+F	⌘+Shift+F
Fill	Shift+F5	Shift+F5
Free Transform	Ctrl+T	⌘+T
Color Settings	Ctrl+Shift+K	⌘+Shift+K
Image Size	Ctrl+Alt+I	⌘+Option+I
Canvas Size	Ctrl+Alt+C	⌘+Option+C
Levels	Ctrl+L	⌘+L
Curves	Ctrl+M	⌘+M
Hue/Saturation	Ctrl+U	⌘+U
Color Balance	Ctrl+B	⌘+B
New Layer	Ctrl+Shift+N	⌘+Shift+N
New Layer via Copy	Ctrl+J	⌘+J
Group Layers	Ctrl+G	⌘+G
Select All	Ctrl+A	⌘+A
Deselect All	Ctrl+D	⌘+D
Inverse Selection	Ctrl+Shift+I	⌘+Shift+I
Refine Edge	Ctrl+Alt+R	⌘+Option+R
Proof Colors	Ctrl+Y	⌘+Y
Gamut Warning	Ctrl+Shift+Y	⌘+Shift+Y
Zoom In	Ctrl+plus(+)	⌘+plus(+)
Zoom Out	Ctrl+minus(−)	⌘+minus(−)
Fit on Screen	Ctrl+0	⌘+0
Show Actual Pixels	Ctrl+1	⌘+1
Show/Hide Extras	Ctrl+H	⌘+H
Rulers	Ctrl+R	⌘+R
Brush panel	F5	F5
Layers panel	F7	F7
Info panel	F8	F8
Photoshop Help	F1	⌘+/
Increase Brush Diameter	]	]
Decrease Brush Diameter	[	[
Increase Brush Hardness	Shift+[	Shift+[
Decrease Brush Hardness	Shift+]	Shift+]

Working with Extended Toolbox Shortcuts

The extended Toolbox shortcuts in Photoshop provide quick access to the CS6 extended Toolbox options, such as selecting the 3D Rotate tool or cycling through the 3D Object Rotate, 3D Object Roll, 3D Object Pan, 3D Object Slide, and 3D Object Scale tools. When you press the shortcut key, the tool is selected and ready to use. When you press a cycle shortcut key sequence, Photoshop cycles through each of the different tools located in the toolset of the Toolbox.

Table A.3 provides a list of most of the extended Toolbox shortcuts.

TABLE A.3 Extended Toolbox Shortcuts

Photoshop CS6 Extended Tools	PC Shortcut	Mac Shortcut
3D Object Rotate tool	K	K
Cycle 3D Object Rotate, 3D Object Roll, 3D Object Pan, 3D Object Slide, and 3D Object Scale tools	Shift+K	Shift+K
3D Rotate Camera tool	N	N
Cycle 3D Rotate Camera, 3D Roll Camera View, 3D Pan Camera View, 3D Walk Camera View, and 3D Zoom Camera tools	Shift+N	Shift+N

Extending the Capabilities of Photoshop with Plug-Ins

IN THIS APPENDIX

Installing plug-ins to extend Photoshop

Downloading optional plug-ins from the Adobe website

Photoshop is a powerful image-editing application. However, one of the best features of Photoshop is that you can add features and functionality that don't already exist by installing plug-ins. A lot of plug-ins are available from Adobe as well as other sources that provide specialized functionality for a variety of purposes.

Installing Optional Photoshop Plug-Ins

You can install Photoshop plug-ins using two methods. The simplest way is to copy the plug-in file into the Adobe Photoshop CS6/Plug-ins folder where Photoshop is installed. The second way to install plug-ins is to create another folder for the added plug-ins. This allows you to keep third-party plug-ins in a separate location out of the Adobe application folder where they might be removed if you uninstall Photoshop.

NOTE

You need to restart Photoshop after installing a plug-in. Some plug-ins require additional steps, so make sure you check out the readme file that comes with the plug-in. You can disable a plug-in from being loaded by putting a tilde (~) character in front of the filename or the name of the folder that contains the plug-in file. If you put a tilde in front of a folder name, all plug-ins in that folder and any subfolders are ignored.

To add another plug-in folder, press Ctrl+K/⌘+K to open the Preferences dialog box and select the Plug-Ins option, as shown in Figure B.1.

FIGURE B.1

You can add a plug-in folder using the Photoshop Preferences dialog box.

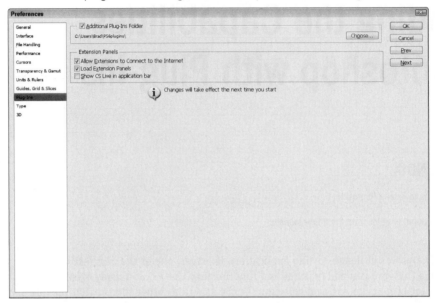

From the Plug-In Preferences panel, you can control the following features of plug-ins:

- **Allow Extensions to Connect to the Internet.** When you select this option, the optional plug-ins are allowed to access the Internet from your computer when Photoshop is running. This allows them to update or provide functionality from web services. However, you should be sure that you trust the plug-in provider before enabling this option.

- **Load Extension Panels.** When you select this option, the extension panels are loaded in addition to the normal Photoshop panels. These panels typically provide important functionality for using the plug-in.

CAUTION

Do not move plug-ins from previous versions of Photoshop, or third-party plug-ins that have not been updated, into the Photoshop CS6 Plug-Ins folder. Do not add a plug-ins folder from a previous version of Photoshop as an additional plug-ins folder in the Photoshop preferences. In addition, if you are running the 64-bit edition of your operating system, all third-party plug-ins must be updated for 64-bit operating systems before you install them into the 64-bit version of Photoshop.

You can get plug-ins from the following locations:

- **Adobe download site/CS6 installation disk.** Provides optional plug-ins that can be downloaded and installed at no cost.

- **Adobe Marketplace for Photoshop.** Provides a lot of great plug-ins that are available for purchase. The plug-ins here are from Adobe approved publishers, meaning that Adobe has reviewed and accepted the publisher. Plug-ins from the marketplace are more likely to work well than those from other locations. You can find the Adobe Marketplace at www.adobe.com/cfusion/marketplace/index.cfm?event=marketplace. home&marketplaceid=2.

- **Third-party websites.** Provides information on Photoshop CS6 websites that offer to sell you plug-ins. Keep in mind that these plug-ins may not be Adobe certified like the ones on the Adobe Marketplace website.

Using Optional Plug-ins from Adobe

Adobe provides several optional plug-ins on their website for downloading. These plug-ins provide some great additional features to Photoshop that are very useful and can be fun to use. Some of the optional plug-ins available for download are as follows:

> **TIP**
>
> You can view information about an installed plug-in by choosing Help ⇨ About Plug-in from the main menu in Photoshop and then selecting the installed plug-in from the list.

- **SGIRGB.** The SGIRGB format plug-in allows you to read and write files in the SGI image format. This format is commonly used by software on the Silicon Graphics platform. The SGI image format plug-in recognizes the file extensions .sgi, .rgb, .rgba, and .bw.

- **Softimage.** The Softimage format plug-in allows you to read and write files in the Softimage picture format. This format is commonly used by 3D rendering software from Softimage.

- **Pattern Maker.** The Pattern Maker plug-in provides a user interface in Photoshop that allows you to create patterns by slicing up an image and reassembling it. The pattern can be made of one large tile or multiple duplicate tiles. You can then save the patterns and use them in other images.

- **PhotomergeUI.** The PhotomergeUI plug-in provides a step-by-step user interface that operates in conjunction with the Photoshop Photomerge utility. This gives you greater control and provides better results when combining two or more images into a panorama.

- **Digimarc.** The Digimarc plug-in provides a panel and tools that allow you to quickly define and embed watermarks in your photos to protect them from unauthorized use.

- **Web Photo Gallery.** The Web Photo Gallery is a popular plug-in that allows you to output images to a web gallery. The ability to create a Web Photo Gallery is now available in the Adobe Bridge CS6 Output workspace. We highly recommend creating your Web Photo Galleries using Bridge, as described in Chapter 6.

Finding Resources

Although this book covers most of the information you need to create fantastic and professional results in Photoshop, you should check out what other resources are available to increase your Photoshop skill set. This appendix provides some starting points to find additional resources, such as where to find help, get general information about Photoshop, download resources from the web, find professional organizations, and get professional training.

Getting Started

An important part of learning to use Photoshop is recognizing when you need help and ideas. Another important part is being able to find the information you need. Help comes in many different forms. These websites provide the information, tutorials, and tips as well as downloads such as brushes and patterns to help you get started:

- www.adobe.com/support/photoshop

  This is the official Adobe help site, offering the latest information on Photoshop.

- www.adobe.com/designcenter/video_workshop

  This site contains several video tutorials on Adobe products including Photoshop.

- www.dayleycreations.com

  This is the authors' website. We publish some tips and tutorials and other items related to Photoshop here. This is also a place where you can go to leave feedback about the book.

- www.photoshoptips.net

  This site publishes articles, tutorials, and tips.

- www.smashingmagazine.com

  This site is mostly dedicated to web development. However, they provide some great Photoshop tutorials as well as general image creation techniques.

- www.photoshopessentials.com

  This has several well-done tutorials and tips as well as some brush downloads.

- www.layersmagazine.com

  This site provides a number of tutorials for most of Adobe's CS products. They also provide some useful reviews of Photoshop plugins.

- www.photoshopuser.com

  This site is run by the National Association of Photoshop Professionals (NAPP) and contains video tutorials, articles, and a help desk.

- www.brushes.obsidiandawn.com

  This site allows you to download free brushes, images, patterns, and shapes.

Finding General Information

Photoshop is by far the most popular photo-editing application on the market. Consequently, many websites provide good information on Photoshop. The following websites are great places for general information about using Photoshop and learning about digital image editing:

- www.photoshopnews.com

  This site publishes the latest news and rumors about Photoshop and contains a great list of links to sites that provide resources on Photoshop.

- www.creativepro.com

  This site publishes articles on Photoshop and provides community blogs and forums.

- www.retouchpro.com

  This membership community provides blogs and chats about digital retouching.

- www.digitaldog.net

  This site publishes articles, tutorials, and tips on Photoshop and digital editing.

Acquiring Professional Resources

If you're serious about working with Photoshop and you want to mingle with other Photoshop professionals, these websites can help you find the best information available:

- www.photoshopuser.com

    This site is operated by NAPP, the largest organization for Photoshop professionals. It offers tons of information, articles, tutorials, downloads, and a professional help desk.

- www.istockphoto.com

    This site provides a service to buy and sell stock photos.

Benefitting from Training and Conferences

Adobe offers some great training opportunities and the Photoshop community at large offers even more training. Taking advantage of these opportunities can increase your skill set and help you connect with other professionals:

- www.adobe.com/training

    This site provides information about Adobe Certified instructors and training centers in your area.

- www.photoshopworld.com

    This site provides all the information you need about the largest Photoshop conference, which is held twice a year.

- www.lynda.com

    This site provides online training resources for several products, including Photoshop.

- www.photoshopcafe.com

    This site provides several tutorials on Photoshop.

Getting Certified on Adobe Products

Being certified on Adobe products can improve your productivity, increase your employment options, and greatly enhance your career. You'll find no better place than the official Adobe website:

- www.adobe.com/support/certification

    This website contains information about how to become an Adobe Certified Associate, Expert, or Instructor.

Index

Index

Index